# ANTIQUE & CONTEMPORARY
# Advertising
## MEMORABILIA

### Identification & Value Guide
### SECOND EDITION

B. J. Summers

**COLLECTOR BOOKS**
*A Division of Schroeder Publishing Co., Inc.*

## Dedication:

This book is dedicated with sympathy to Elizabeth and Laura, a couple of ladies I've come to know, love, and respect, and the Earl Whitte family who lost a loving husband and father in a tragic plane accident recently.

Also to Dr. Clive Cussler, Ralph Wilbanks, and Steve Howard. Words alone seem shallow, but thank you for your genuine kindness and respect for your fellow man.

And last, but certainly not least, to three very special people, Amy, Terry, and Benjamin.

COLLECTOR BOOKS
P.O. Box 3009
Paducah, Kentucky 42002-3009
www.collectorbooks.com

Copyright © 2005 B.J. Summers

The current values in this book should be used only as a guide. They are not intended to set prices, which vary from one section of the country to another. Auction prices as well as dealer prices vary greatly and are affected by condition as well as demand. Neither the author nor the publisher assumes responsibility for any losses that might be incurred as a result of consulting this guide.

### Searching For A Publisher?

We are always looking for people knowledgeable within their fields. If you feel that there is a real need for a book on your collectible subject and have a large comprehensive collection, contact Collector Books.

# Acknowledgments

Many thanks to the following for their valuable contributions, either by supplying photographs or allowing their collectibles to be photographed:

**Past Tyme Pleasures**
2491 San Ramon Valley Blvd., #1
925-484-6442
e-mail: pasttyme@excite.com
Steve and Donna Howard produce several yearly advertising absentee auctions with a great colorful catalog and complete item descriptions. Call for a catalog or check them out at www.pasttyme.com.

**Farmer's Daughter Antiques**
6330 Cairo Rd.
Paducah, KY 42001
270-444-7619
Bill and Jane Miller have one of the neatest shops you'll ever find. The mix of advertising (Bill's specialty), and primitives (Jane's specialty) is a winning combination in everyone's book. Their shop is easily located just a mile off 1-24 at Exit 3. You can't miss the big barn — stop by and talk to one of the friendliest couples in the antique world.

**Richard Opfer Auctioneering, Inc.**
1919 Greenspring Drive
Timonium, MD 21093
410-252-5035
Richard Opfer Auctioneering, Inc. provides a great variety of antiques and collectibles auctions. Give his friendly staff a call for his next auction catalog.

**Charlie's Antique Mall**
303 Main St., P.O. Box 196
Hazel, KY 42049
270-492-8175
Located in the historic community of Hazel, Kentucky, on Main St., this place has it all. The manager, Ray Gough, has some great dealers with a wide variety of antiques and collectibles and some of the friendliest help you'll find. This border town mall can keep even the pickiest collector busy for the better part of a day.

**Wm. Morford**
RD #2
Cazenovia, NY 13035
315-662-7625
Wm. Morford has been operating one of the country's better cataloged phone auction businesses for several years. He doesn't list reproductions or repairs that are deceptive in nature. In each catalog is usually a section with items that are for immediate sale. Try out this site and tell him how you got his name and address.

**Rare Bird Antique Mall**
212 South Main St.
Goodlettsville, TN 37072
615-851-2635
If you find yourself in the greater Nashville, Tennessee, area, stop by this collectors' paradise. Jon and Joan Wright have assembled a great cast of dealers who run the gamut of collectible merchandise. Step back to an era when the general store was the place to be, and be prepared to invest some well-spent time.

**Buffalo Bay Auction Co.**
5244 Quam Circle
Rogers, MN 55374
612-428-8879
A great catalog auction with a good variety of advertising fare. If advertising is your cup of tea, you'll enjoy browsing their catalog with its excellent quality photographs and descriptions.

**Twin Lakes Antique Mall**
Hwy. 641 North
Gilbertsville, KY 42044
270-362-2218
Located conveniently in the heartland beside beautiful Kentucky Lake, this new mall is great. Ed and Dee Hanes run a super clean mall in this vacation land with a good selection of general line antiques and collectibles. You'll find a better than average selection of gas collectibles (Ed's hobby).

**Antiques, Cards and Collectibles**
203 Broadway
Paducah, KY 42001
270-443-9797
Right on the river in the historic Michael Hardware building, Ray Pelley has three floors filled with antiques and collectibles. Easy to find just off the loop in downtown Paducah. If you need help, Ray, Donna, and Emma are always ready with information and a smile.

**Creatures of Habit**
406 Broadway
Paducah, KY 42001
270-442-2923

A touch of the unusual is the first thing you'll notice when you walk into Natalya's and Jack's shop. With an ample supply of out-of-the-ordinary advertising, this is a "must stop" when in the area. Good merchandise and plenty of friendly help are a winning combination.

**The Illinois Antique Center**
308 S.W. Commercial
Peoria, IL 61602
309-673-3354

Overlooking the river in downtown Peoria, this huge warehouse has been remodeled by Dan and Kim and now has a wonderful selection of antiques and collectibles. It is always a great source of advertising signs, statues, and memorabilia. You'll find an ample supply of smiling faces and help here. Plan on spending the better part of a day.

**Gary Metz's Muddy River Trading Company**
P.O. Box 18185
Roanoke, VA 24014
540-982-3886

Gary probably produces one of the best advertising auctions in this country. While his emphasis is primarily on Coca-Cola and other soda products, he certainly isn't limited to those fields. Gary is probably one of the nicest people you'll ever meet. Give him a call and send for his next catalog to open up a whole new level of collecting.

**Pleasant Hill Antique Mall and Tea Room**
315 South Pleasant Hill Rd.
East Peoria, IL 61611
309-694-4040

Bob Johnson and all the friendly staff at this mall welcome you for a day of shopping. And it'll take that long to work your way through all the quality antiques and collectibles at this mall. When you get tired, stop and enjoy a rest at the tea room where you can get some of the best home-cooked food found anywhere. All in all, a great place to shop for your favorite antiques.

**Michael and Deborah Summers**
Paducah, KY 42001

My brother and sister-in-law are avid collectors and have been invaluable in helping compile information for this book. Mike and I have spent many days chasing down treasures at auctions.

**Bill and Helen Mitchell**
226 Arendall St.
Henderson, TN 38340
731-989-9302

Bill and Helen have assembled a great variety of advertising with special emphasis on Coca-Cola, and they are always searching for new finds. So if you have anything that fits the bill, give them a call or drop them a letter.

**Patrick's Collectibles**
612 Roxanne Dr.
Antioch, TN 37013
615-833-4621

If you happen to be around Nashville, Tennessee, during the monthly flea market at the state fairgrounds, be certain to look for Mike and Julie Patrick. They have some of the sharpest advertising pieces you'll ever hope to find. And if Coca-Cola is your field, you won't be able to walk away from the great restored drink machines. Make sure to look them up, you certainly won't be sorry.

**John and Vicki Mahan**
1407 N. 4th St.
Murray, KY 42071
270-753-4330

John's specialty is porcelain signs, but like most collectors, he's certainly not limited to signs. He's always looking to buy, sell, or trade, so give him a call.

**Autopia Advertising Auctions**
19937 N.E. 154th St., Bldg. C2
Woodinville, WA 98072
425-883-7653

Autopia produces great mail, phone, and fax auctions. The catalogs are second to none, with great clear photos and very detailed product descriptions. Their auctions contain a complete line of advertising collectibles, so call them for a catalog

4

# Introduction

What would you be willing to give to return to a slower, simpler time of life — before the scenes of 9/11 were forever etched in your mind, when you could sit on your porch swing and enjoy an ice cold bottle of Coke with peanuts? Most of us would, and some do, give almost any amount of money to be able to recapture that peaceful place. Our key to that world is through advertising. Coca-Cola Santa, soda fountain ads with the gang enjoying a cool Coke, pancakes by Aunt Jemima, colorful light-up gasoline globes — all this and more play a part in our desire for a simpler way of life. I hope this book helps the beginner as well as the advanced collector in their search for the ideal collectible piece of advertising.

Entries are listed alphabetically, using either the company name or recognizable product name. A brief description of the advertising piece is next. The condition is noted as follows: NOS-New Old Stock; M-Mint;

NM-Near Mint; Exc-Excellent; VG-Very Good; G-Good; F-Fair; P-Poor. Also in parentheses after the price is a code that will tell you how I arrived at the listed price. If you see a (B), then you know that the price quoted is an actual paid price at auction (please remember that some auction prices can be artificially high due to two determined bidders, and likewise low due to a lack of interest at that particular sale); (D) denotes a retail price placed on an object by a dealer, which may or may not have sold. (C) refers to a value placed by a collector. With many photos you will see a photo credit that indicates the origin of the item. The listed price may or may not have originated from that source.

It is my purpose to report market values, not to set prices. A well-educated collector is always one step ahead of the collecting crowd.

Enjoy.

| Year | Patent # | Year | Patent # | Year | Patent # | Year | Patent # | Year | Patent # |
|---|---|---|---|---|---|---|---|---|---|
| 1836 | 1 | 1866 | 51,784 | 1896 | 552,502 | 1926 | 1,568,040 | 1956 | 2,728,913 |
| 1837 | 110 | 1867 | 60,658 | 1897 | 574,369 | 1927 | 1,612,700 | 1957 | 2,775,762 |
| 1838 | 546 | 1868 | 72,959 | 1898 | 596,467 | 1928 | 1,654,521 | 1958 | 2,818,567 |
| 1839 | 1,061 | 1869 | 85,503 | 1899 | 616,871 | 1929 | 1,696,897 | 1959 | 2,866,973 |
| 1840 | 1,465 | 1870 | 98,460 | 1900 | 640,167 | 1930 | 1,742,181 | 1960 | 2,919,443 |
| 1841 | 1,923 | 1871 | 110,617 | 1901 | 664,827 | 1931 | 1,787,424 | 1961 | 2,966,681 |
| 1842 | 2,413 | 1872 | 122,304 | 1902 | 690,385 | 1932 | 1,839,190 | 1962 | 3,015,103 |
| 1843 | 2,901 | 1873 | 134,504 | 1903 | 71 7,521 | 1933 | 1,892,663 | 1963 | 3,070,801 |
| 1844 | 3,395 | 1874 | 146,120 | 1904 | 748,567 | 1934 | 1,941,449 | 1964 | 3,116,487 |
| 1845 | 3,873 | 1875 | 158,350 | 1905 | 778,834 | 1935 | 1,985,878 | 1965 | 3,163,865 |
| 1846 | 4,348 | 1876 | 171,641 | 1906 | 808,618 | 1936 | 2,026,516 | 1966 | 3,226,729 |
| 1847 | 4,914 | 1877 | 185,813 | 1907 | 839,799 | 1937 | 2,066,309 | 1967 | 3,295,143 |
| 1848 | 5,409 | 1878 | 198,733 | 1908 | 875,679 | 1938 | 2,104,004 | 1968 | 3,360,800 |
| 1849 | 5,993 | 1879 | 211,078 | 1909 | 908,436 | 1939 | 2,142,080 | 1969 | 3,419,907 |
| 1850 | 6,981 | 1880 | 223,211 | 1910 | 945,010 | 1940 | 2,185,170 | 1970 | 3,487,470 |
| 1851 | 7,865 | 1881 | 236,137 | 1911 | 980,178 | 1941 | 2,227,418 | 1971 | 3,551,909 |
| 1852 | 8,622 | 1882 | 251,685 | 1912 | 1,013,095 | 1942 | 2,268,540 | 1972 | 3,631,539 |
| 1853 | 9,512 | 1883 | 269,820 | 1913 | 1,049,326 | 1943 | 2,307,007 | 1973 | 3,707,729 |
| 1854 | 10,358 | 1884 | 291,016 | 1914 | 1,083,267 | 1944 | 2,338,081 | 1974 | 3,781,914 |
| 1855 | 12,117 | 1885 | 310,163 | 1915 | 1,123,212 | 1945 | 2,366,154 | 1975 | 3,858,241 |
| 1856 | 14,009 | 1886 | 333,494 | 1916 | 1,166,419 | 1946 | 2,391,856 | 1976 | 3,930,271 |
| 1857 | 16,324 | 1887 | 355,291 | 1917 | 1,210,389 | 1947 | 2,413,675 | 1977 | 4,000,520 |
| 1858 | 19,010 | 1888 | 375,720 | 1918 | 1,251,458 | 1948 | 2,433,824 | 1978 | 4,065,812 |
| 1859 | 22,477 | 1889 | 395,305 | 1919 | 1,290,027 | 1949 | 2,457,797 | 1979 | 4,131,952 |
| 1860 | 26,642 | 1890 | 418,665 | 1920 | 1,326,899 | 1950 | 2,492,944 | 1980 | 4,180,867 |
| 1861 | 31,005 | 1891 | 443,987 | 1921 | 1,364,063 | 1951 | 2,536,016 | 1981 | 4,242,757 |
| 1862 | 34,045 | 1892 | 466,315 | 1922 | 1,401,948 | 1952 | 2,580,379 | | |
| 1863 | 37,266 | 1893 | 488,976 | 1923 | 1,440,362 | 1953 | 2,624,046 | | |
| 1864 | 41,047 | 1894 | 511,744 | 1924 | 1,478,996 | 1954 | 2,664,562 | | |
| 1865 | 45,685 | 1895 | 531,619 | 1925 | 1,521,590 | 1955 | 2,698,434 | | |

A.A. Godkin Chemist, sign, brass, for drug store, 72" x 9", EX, $275.00 B. *Courtesy of Riverview Antique Mall.*

AC Aircraft Products, sign, metal, "Recognized Servicenter," 17¾" x 24¼", VG, $215.00 C. *Courtesy of Collectors Auction Services.*

Ace of Drinks, sign, cardboard, die cut, framed and matted, 8" x 11⅞", EX, $75.00 C.

Acme Cowboy Boots, sign, neon on painted metal, 20¼" x 12½", NM, $750.00 B.

AC Oil Filter, sign, metal, one-sided 10" x 30", EX, $300.00 C. *Courtesy of Collectors Auction Services.*

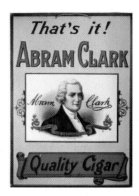

Abram Clark, sign, cardboard, countertop, easel back, "That's it!, Quality Cigar," 9" x 12¼", VG, $95.00 C. *Courtesy of Collectors Auction Services.*

A & P calendar, paper, showing shopkeeper and customers, full pad, 1903, 15" x 19", EX.....................................................$195.00 C

A & P, sign, cardboard, die cut, double-sided, kids in a wheelbarrow being pushed by a man, "going to the Great Atlantic and Pacific Tea Company," 5½", x 8½", 1884, EX ................. $95.00 C

A & P, tea bin, wooden, slanted lid, and A & P logo in front and on lid in old red paint, EX ..................................................... $295.00 B

A & W Root Beer, dispenser, for counter use, hinged top, company logo on front, 1910s, 19" x 18" x 30", VG ..................$325.00 C

A & W Root Beer, mug, glass, applied color label, 4" tall, EX. $8.00 C

A Sur-Shot, vet tin, large capsules for "Bot and Worm remover," 3½" x 5" x 2½", EX.............................................................. $75.00 B

A-B-C Bohemian Beer, sign, celluloid, eagle logo of American Brewing Co., located in St. Louis, G ....................................................$125.00 C

A-B-C Bohemian Beer, sign, celluloid, from the American Brewing Company, St. Louis, MO, 9" x 6½", EX ......................... $425.00 D

A. Hussey & Co., match holder, tin, litho, die cut, "while others think, we work," 7" H, EX ............................ $1,550.00 B

A.A. Godkin Chemist, sign, for drug store, brass, 72" x 9", G $135.00 C

A.B.C. Chewing Gum, poster, cardboard, framed, girl at beach in early bathing attire, Canadian, 13" x 28", G............ $135.00 C

A.B.C. Chewing Gum, sign, A.B.C. bathing girl on the beach, product message at bottom, 13" x 28", EX ....................$250.00 C

A.C. Huff Music Store, tip tray, metal, "High Grade Pianos," pretty woman in center, 4⅛" dia., EX............................................ $95.00 B

Adams' Tutti-Frutti, sign, paperboard, young girl, 8¼" x 12½", 1910, EX, $295.00 C.
*Courtesy of Buffalo Bay Auction Co.*

Adkins & Cochran Fine Footwear, sign, cardboard, die cut, little girl with basket, easel back for counter use, her right hand originally held an item that is now missing, 1900s, 14" x 7", VG, $45.00 C. *Courtesy of B.J. Summers.*

Admiral Cigarettes, sign, paper litho, scantily clad woman on board ship at look-out, 16" x 22½", EX, $175.00 C. *Courtesy of Buffalo Bay Auction Co.*

Admiration Cigars, sign, "Mild and Mellow To The Last Inch," 11" x 15", 1930s, VG, $475.00 B. *Courtesy of Muddy River Trading Co./Gary Metz.*

Aeroshell Lubricating Oil, sign, porcelain, one-sided, die cut, "Stocked Here," 38" x 19¾", VG, $3,000.00 B. *Courtesy of Collectors Auction Services.*

Aetna Insurance, sign, metal, double-sided flange, "Coast-to-Coast Insurance Service Aetna-ize," 15" x 20", VG, $60.00 C.

**A.F. Movitt Prescription Druggist,** calendar, cardboard, die cut, from Chicago, IL, young girl with flowers, 11½" x 17", EX ..........$185.00 B

**A.W. Kerr,** calendar, paper and cardboard, with paper tear sheet at bottom, from Hurricane, WI, small girl carrying a woven basket, 6" x 9½", 1907, EX.................... $75.00 D

**Aaron Burr Cigars,** box, cardboard, inside label has Aaron Burr in moonlight silhouette, 9" x 6", EX ...........................$45.00 C

**Abbott's Bitters,** thermometer, wood, painted message, 5⅛" x 21", G .................................................. $175.00 D

**ABC Oil Burners,** sign, metal, die cast, 11" x 8", EX .........$150.00 B

**ABC Oil Burners,** sign, metal, die cast, 11" x 8", NM.................$195.00 C

**AC Oil Filter Service,** sign, tin, double-sided, flange, 13½" x 11¾", 1940s, EX ................................................. $435.00 C

**AC Spark Plugs,** sign, metal, AC method of cleaning, with donkey in bath tub, cost 5¢, vertical rectangle, black and yellow, VG ..$145.00 B

**AC Spark Plugs,** sign, metal, name in white on blue base, 1940s, 18" x 9", EX ....................................................... $95.00 C

**AC Spark Plugs,** sign, tin, self-framing, with spark plug, NOS, 8¾" x 17⅞", 1941, NM.............................................. $235.00 C

**Ace High Motor Oil,** can, tin, touring car scene, 1930s, 6" x 4", dia., EX............................................................................ $225.00 C

**Acme Brand Coffee,** can, tin, litho, embossed slip lid, American Stores Co., polka dot banner around bottom, 1-lb., EX...... $90.00 C

**Acme Cowboy Boots,** sign, neon on painted metal, 20¼" x 12½", VG ............................................................. $325.00 C

A. Hussey & Co., match holder, tin, litho, die cut, good graphics, "while others think, we work," 7" H, VG, $1,500.00 C. *Courtesy of Richard Opfer Auctioneering, Inc.*

Alliance Coffee, sign, cardboard, die cut, "For Coffee Contentment Serve Alliance Coffee," man in chef's wear tipping a cup of coffee, 1910, 12½" x 16⅛", NM, $350.00 C.

Allyn & Blanchard Co., match holder, tin litho, 7" H, EX, $325.00 B.

American Airlines, clock, metal body, glass face, light-up cover, trademark AA in center, 15" dia., VG, $225.00 C.

American Eagle Fire Insurance Company, New York, sign, painted tin with wood frame, 20½" x 26½", NM, $895.00 D.

American Clean Cutter, tobacco cutter, cast iron, rare design, difficult to find, G, $295.00 D.

---

**Acme Cowboy Boots,** sign, neon, 20¼" x 12½", EX ......... **$550.00 C**

**Acme Cycle Co.,** pocket catalog, 1894, 6¾" x 4⅝", EX.......**$20.00 C**

**Acme Paint,** sign, tin, dealer courtesy line and the product name at the top, EX .......................................................................... **$85.00 C**

**Acme Quality Paints,** sign, porcelain, double-sided, image of paint can, 14⅝" x 20", NM........................................................... **$275.00 C**

**Acme Quality Paints,** sign, porcelain, double-sided, paint can in center, 14½" x 20", VG...................................................... **$95.00 D**

**Acme Quality Paints,** sign, porcelain, paint can on front, 14½" x 20", G................................................................................ **$75.00 C**

**Acorn Stove,** match holder, metal, "Over 1,000,000 in use," 5" x 6", VG .................................................................................**$145.00 C**

**Action Advertising Clock Co.,** salesman's sample, metal and glass, with flip cards to left of neon clock, 24" x 7" x 12½", 1950s, EX ...............................................................................**$325.00 C**

**Adam Forepaugh & Sells Bros.,** poster, cardboard, Big United Shows, circus activity on front, 17½" x 13", G.................. **$275.00 C**

**Adam Forepaugh & Sells Circus,** poster, carboard, circus scene, 17½" x 13", VG................................................................. **$160.00 D**

**Adam Forepaugh,** cigar, box, cardboard, inner label depicting circus scene, 9" x 6", VG .......................................................**$325.00 C**

**Adams' California Fruit Chewing Gum,** display, counter, by H.D. Beach Co., gum packs, 6¾" x 4¾" x 6", 1917, EX .................**$595.00 C**

**Adams' Chewing Gum,** box, cardboard, photos in center of both sides, 7½" x 1" x 9", EX .................................................... **$115.00 C**

**Adams' Honey Chewing Gum,** tin, 9" x 5⅝" x 1", VG ....................**$100.00 B**

**Adams' Pepsin Gum,** display case, wood and glass, designed to sit flat on counter and show products, change tray, 1910s, 16" x 12" x 3", VG.............................................................................**$300.00 C**

American Express Co.
Agency, sign, porcelain,
raised lettering, heavy,
18½" x 16½", EX,
$1,550.00 B. *Courtesy of
Wm. Morford Investment Grade
Collectibles.*

American Express, sign,
porcelain, flange, "Money
Orders Sold Here," white lettering on blue background,
16" x 13", EX, $250.00 B.
*Courtesy of Riverview Antique Mall*

American Fence, thermometer,
porcelain, scale reading posts
and fence with three way protection against rust, 19" tall,
VG, $200.00 B.

American Hat Works Co.
Inc., sign, porcelain,
40¼" L, VG, $355.00 C.

American Insurance Company,
Newark, N.J., sign, porcelain, one
sided, 20" x 14", VG, $175.00 C.

American Negro Exposition,
screened print, framed,
seven-color, "Chicago Coliseum, July 4 to Sept. 2," 1940,
EX, $195.00 D. *Courtesy of Crea-
tures of Habit.*

**Adams' Pepsin Gum,** display, cardboard, counter top, die cut, young girl with advertising on her back, 2¼" x 5", NM....$200.00 C

**Adams' Pepsin Gum,** store bin, tin, with hinge top, product messages on all sides and lid, 7" x 6" x 5", EX ...................$340.00 B

**Adams' Pepsin Tutti-Frutti Gum,** store display, counter, 6⅜" x 5¼" x 4¼", EX.............................. $150.00 C

**Adams' Pure Chewing Gum,** jar, glass, counter top, decorated lid and front label, 1910s, 5" x 5" x 12", EX............. $225.00 C

**Adams' Red Rose Pure Chewing Gum,** sign, paper, single-sided, 12¾" x 6¼", G ............................... $325.00 B

**Adams' Spearmint,** display, countertop, 6½" x 4¾" x 6", EX.. $245.00 B

**Adams' Sweet Fern Chewing Gum,** box, cardboard, two-piece, with small girl, 4¾" x 8⅝" x 1⅜", EX ......................... $135.00 B

**Adams' Sweet Rubber Tolo Chewing Gum,** tin with lift-off lid, made to hold 200 pieces of gum, colors still strong on cover, stork in lower right, 4½" x 4⅝" x 1", EX.................... $1,100.00 B

**Adams' Tutti-Frutti Chewing Gum,** box, Lillian Russell on front, EX ...................................................................... $225.00 B

**Adams' Tutti-Frutti Gum,** sign, paper board, with young girl, 8¼" x 12½", 1910, VG .................................................$275.00 C

**Admiral Cigarettes,** sign, paper, litho, scantily clad woman on board ship at look-out, 16" x 22½", VG..............$75.00 D

**Admiration Cigars,** sign, "Mild and Mellow To The Last Inch," 11" x 15", 1930s, G................................................................. $550.00 C

**Admiration Cigars,** sign, plaster, three-dimensional, moon-faced cigar smoker, EX.......................................................... $1,500.00 B

American Red Cross, poster, cardboard, 3-d, in shadow box frame, a nurse and bugler, 1930 – 40s, 12½" x 21", EX, $450.00 B.

American Stores Co., sign, entitled "The Younger Generation," 14¼" x 18¼", NM, $135.00 C.

American Tel. & Tel. Co., rain gauge, metal and glass, never used, original instruction papers still in rain tube, 1950s, 4½" x 4½", NM, $45.00 C. Courtesy of B.J. Summers.

Amoco Battery Cable Service, sign, tin, embossed die cut, 17" x 10", NOS, EX, $195.00 C. Courtesy of Autopia Advertising Auctions.

Amoco, poster, cardboard, single-sided, 61" x 28", VG, $125.00 C.

---

**Admiration Ice Tea**, cooler, stoneware set with lid and pedestal, VG ....................................................................$450.00 C

**Admiration Miniatures**, sign, tin, litho, easel back, 5¾" x 7½", EX ................................................................ $295.00 C

**Advance-Rumely Power Farming Machinery**, sign, cardboard, farming scenes and machinery, 15" x 21", EX ............................ $225.00 C

**Advo Peanut Butter**, container, tin, litho, pry lid, to be used as a measuring cup when empty, 12 oz., EX ............ $125.00 B

**Aeco Coffee**, can, metal, key wind top, 1 lb, EX ....................$85.00 C

**Aetna Automobile Insurance**, sign, tin, painted black lettering on orange, 24" x 12", VG ........................................ $115.00 C

**Aetna Insurance Co.**, calendar, paper, sleeping night watchman, all months displayed on same page, 1890, 19" x 26", VG .......$400.00 C

**Aetna**, gas globe, glass, wide body with two lens, 13½", EX .. $2,785.00 B

**After Dinner Cigars** box, cardboard, outer label shows three men at a table being served dinner, 5" x 5", VG..............................$55.00 C

**Agent Quaker Tea**, sign, porcelain, flange, foreign item, 18" x 9½", VG............................................................... $395.00 B

**Aircraft Oats**, container, metal, litho, birds and circling airplane, 1 lb. 4 oz., VG........................................................ $183.00 B

**Airline Flexible Flyer**, sled, wood and metal, salesman's sample, 23" x 9", EX................................................................$750.00 B

**AJJA Tobacco**, sign, porcelain, older gent and younger man enjoying a smoke, self-framing, "T.P. Bruxeles 359-254-1951," 21½" x 25½", EX................................................................ $295.00 C

**Akron Brewing Co., Akron, Ohio**, decal, factory scene on wood, 1930s, 36" x 24", NM ...................................................... $210.00 B

**Akron Brewing Co., Akron, Ohio**, sign, tin, litho, White Rock Beer, 33" x 24¾", VG ................................................................ $560.00 B

Anderson Tire Service, playing cards, plastic coated, company information on each card, full deck in original box, 1940 – 1950s, 2½" x 3½", VG, $30.00 C. *Courtesy of B.J. Summers.*

Andes Stoves & Ranges, match safe and strikes, 4⅝" x 6¼", G, $175.00 D.

Apache Trail, cigar tin, rare, litho, Indian on horseback, good strong colors, 5¾" H, EX, $875.00 B. *Courtesy of Richard Opfer Auctioneering, Inc.*

Anheuser-Busch, poster, paper, framed, "The Father of Waters," 19" x 13¼", EX, $80.00 B.

Arco Motor Club, paperweight, metal, 5", VG, $100.00 B.

Arbuckles' Ground Coffee, sign, tin, embossed, man with paper and girl with cup of coffee, "It smells good Daddy," 27" x 11", EX, $475.00 B. *Courtesy of Muddy River Trading Co./Gary Metz.*

---

Al G. Barnes Wild Animal, poster, paper, circus tiger riding a horse, reprint, 13½" x 19", VG .........................................$20.00 B

Alabama Brewing Co., serving tray, metal, woman dressed in red, EX................................................................................. $450.00 C

Alabama National AA Motor Club, sign, porcelain, die cut, double-sided, 23⅝" x 16¼", NM ...................................... $245.00 C

Aladdin, can, tin, litho, "The Wonderful Coffee," with Aladdin lamp in center of product message, 3-lb., EX ........................... $170.00 B

Alaska Fur Co., sign, wood, carved, with seal over company lettering, 51" x 76", EX ......................................... $18,000.00 C

Albert Pick Co. Chicago Cigar, trade stimulator, oak case, 14" x 22" x 5½", 1895, EX................................................ $650.00 C

Alberta Government Telephones, sign, porcelain, flange, "Use Long Distance," old candlestick phone in center, 19" x 18½", G. $425.00 B

Alemite Gas-Co-Lator, display, counter top unit, shows how your gas is filtered as you drive, 16¾" x 19½" x 4¼", EX.......... $450.00 C

Alexander Humbolt Cigar, sign, paper, embossed, heavy, image of Humbolt, 24" x 18", VG ........................................... $400.00 C

Alexander, poster, litho, "The man who knows," 28¼" x 42", red, black and white, EX......................................., $105.00 D

Alexander, poster, litho, "The man who knows," red, black, and white, 28¼" x 42", VG ...................................... $65.00 C

Algonquin Hotel Cigars, box, cardboard, inner label with street scene, 9" x 6", EX ............................................... $185.00 C

Arm & Hammer Soda, sign, cardboard, litho, framed, copyright 1908 by Church & Dwight Co., signed by Robin Snipe, 14½" x 11½", EX, $110.00 C.

Armour & Co., sign, tin, embossed, woman at meat counter, 27" tall, EX, $275.00 B.

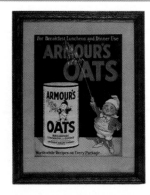

Armour's Oats, sign, paper, "Worth-while Recipes on Every Package," young boy holding oats and a package of product on front, 21" x 26¾", VG, $85.00 B. *Courtesy of Collectors Auction Services.*

Arrow Beer, sign, cardboard, matchless body, framed, 22" x 34", EX, $250.00 B. *Courtesy of Muddy River Trading Co./Gary Metz.*

Arrow Coffee, container, metal, from Atwood Co., Minneapolis, Mn., Indian with bow drawn, 1-lb., EX, $1,125.00 B. *Courtesy of Buffalo Bay Auction Co.*

A-S-K Supply Inc., lighter, metal, by Brown & Bigelow, advertising on one side only, never used, 1¼" x 2¼" x ⅜", NM, $30.00 C. *Courtesy of B.J. Summers.*

---

Alice Foote Coffee, container, tin, lithographed screw-on lid, silhouette of lady on front, 4" x 6", EX .................................... $55.00 B

Alka Seltzer, display box, counter top, advertising on all sides, 25¼" x 6¼" x 6¼", F .............................................. $35.00 D

Alka Seltzer, display, metal, painted, counter top, litho, boxes on front cover, 12" x 9½", EX .............................................. $145.00 C

Alka Seltzer, sign, cardboard, die cut, Speedy, easel back for counter display, 21¾" x 39¾", VG .................................... $235.00 C

Alka-Seltzer, box, paper, linen, "effervescent analgesic alkalizing tablets," 25¼" x 6¼" x 6¼", EX ............................................ $30.00 C

Alka-Seltzer, store display, metal, 12" x 9½", VG ............. $100.00 C

Alka-Seltzer, store display, tin, litho, 7" x 12" x 9¾", EX .. $135.00 C

Alka-Seltzer, thermometer, metal, dial-type with Speedy, "Headache Upset Stomach," 12" dia., EX ........................... $375.00 B

All American Motor Oil, container, North America and vehicles, 1920s, 2 gal, EX ................................................................ $95.00 C

All Jersey Milk, license plate attachment, aluminum, die cut, painted cow, 9⅞" x 5⅝", NM .................................................... $135.00 C

Allcock's Plasters, sign, paper, two girls sitting on dock with feet dangling near the water, one with a plaster on her back, 11¼" x 28", 1884, EX ................................................................ $200.00 C

Allens Red Tame Cherry, figure, chalkware, girl with apron, 26", VG ..................................................................... $775.00 C

Allens Red Tame Cherry, sign, tin, couple at table and boy in tree, 18" x 28", VG ................................................................ $3,500.00 C

Alliance Coffee, sign, cardboard, die cut, "For Coffee Contentment Serve Alliance Coffee," man in chef's wear tipping a cup of coffee, 1910, 12½" x 16⅛", G ..................................................... $95.00 C

Alliance Coffee, sign, cardboard, die cut, elderly man in chef's hat and coat holding a cup of coffee, 12½" x 16⅛", 1910, EX . $265.00 D

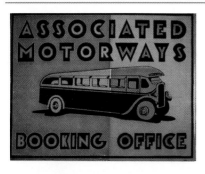

Associated Motorways Booking Office, sign, porcelain, double-sided, 23¼" x 18", VG, $1,600.00 B. *Courtesy of Collectors Auction Services.*

Athlete Smoking Mixture, tin, rounded corners, name to right of man, 6" x 4", EX, $550.00 C.

Ath-Lo-Pho-Ros Rheumatism and Neuralgia Remedy, window display, three-piece, tri-fold, 20¼" x 18¾", NM, $275.00 B.

Atlantic Aviation Motor Oil, banner, canvas, "Zero Cold Test," 26" x 36", VG, $80.00 B.

Atlantic Beer, sign, cardboard, fold-out airplane, 1940s, 27" x 22", VG, $325.00 B.

Atlantic Gasoline, gas globe, metal and glass, logo in center of lense, 21½", VG, $425.00 B.

**Allied Mills Inc.,** sign, porcelain, die cut, flour sack with horse and rider in center, 21" x 34", EX ................................. $500.00 C

**Allied Mutual Casualty Company,** license plate attachment, tin, embossed, convex, "Protected Car," NOS, 4⅛", EX .......... $195.00 C

**Allied Van Lines,** toy truck, metal, Buddy L, "Nation Wide Movers," 30" long, VG ...................................................... $375.00 C

**Alligator Rainwear,** sign, cardboard, counter top, pictures alligator, 1950s, 5" x 10", EX ..................................... $25.00 C

**Allis Chalmers,** sign, porcelain, A-C lettered on the diagonal, 11" x 11", EX ....................................................... $125.00 C

**Allstate Battery Check,** thermometer, metal, dial-type, with battery at top of face, 16" dia., EX.................................... $195.00 C

**Allstate,** fire extinguisher, unused condition, 2¾" x 4¾", EX. $55.00 C

**Allyn & Blanchard Co.,** match holder, tin, litho, 7", G.... $100.00 C

**Alonso Rejas,** tray, metal, "Clear Havana, Made at Key West, Fla.," with early Vienna-type woman in center, 10" dia., EX... $400.00 B

**Alta Crest Certified Milk,** sign, tin over cardboard, embossed, designed to be either string hung or used on counter with easel back, 11⅜" x 6⅜", EX........................................................$150.00 C

**Alta Crest Farms,** bottle, glass, blue applied color label, 1920s, 1 qt., VG .................................................................$85.00 C

**Amalie,** clock, light-up, metal body with glass face, "Pennsylvania Motor Oil," 15" dia., EX................................................. $250.00 C

**Amalie,** thermometer, metal body with glass front, dial-type scale, "Pennsylvania Motor Oil," 9" dia., EX ................................. $85.00 C

**Amber Soap,** sign, tin, P & G man in the moon, 19" x 13", EX .$90.00 C

Atlantic Motor Oil, banner, cloth, howling wolf and "Don't Be Afraid Of The Big Bad Wolf," 36" x 58", G, $210.00 B.

Atlantic, oil can, metal, name and company logo on side, 1 gal., VG, $95.00 B.

Aunt Jemima, display, cardboard, die cut, string-climbing, 1905s, EX, $1,995.00 C. *Courtesy of Wm. Morford Investment Grade Collectibles.*

Aunt Jemima, sign, porcelain, curved, hard-to-find piece, "Flour," manufactured by Burdick in Chicago, G, $6,000.00 B. *Courtesy of Muddy River Trading Co./Gary Metz.*

Aunt Jemima, pancake grill, metal with plastic knobs, Aunt Jemima decal, "The Quaker Oats Company, Chicago, ILL," 24½" x 16" x 26", VG, $2,800.00 B. *Courtesy of Collectors Auction Services.*

Ambrosia Tobacco, cutter, cast iron, counter top, 16" x 9", VG .................$190.00 B

America Ace Coffee, tin , key-wind lid, front has aviator with a coffee cup, 1 lb., EX ................. $175.00 C

America's Pride Cigars, box, cardboard, inner label of Washington crossing the Delware, 9" x 6", EX ........ $15.00 C

American Ace Tea, can, cardboard, pry lid, pilot on one side and airplane on other side, 4-oz., EX ........ $140.00 B

American Airline, clock, light-up, metal body and glass face and cover, trademark AA in center of clock, 15" dia., NM........$495.00 C

American Airlines, playing cards, vinyl, with blue and red A's on white background ...... $10.00 C

American Amoco Gas, sign, porcelain, "credit card accepted," 1940s, 15" x 24", EX........ $175.00 C

American Bakeries Company, building plate, bronze, 26" x 15", EX........ $95.00 B

American Beauty Coffee, grinder, original tin cup and cast iron bottom, 4¼" x 3¼" x 12", EX........$435.00 C

American Beauty Coffee, grinder, original tin cup and cast iron bottom, 4¼" x 3¼" x 12", G........ $275.00 C

American Blend, pocket container, tin, litho, 3⅛" x 4⅜" x ⅞", EX $1,450.00 B

American Brakeblok, clock, glass, painted, reverse light-up advertising, 15" dia., EX........ $375.00 D

American Brewing Co., serving tray, metal, "Liberty Beer in Bottles Only," 12" dia., EX........ $200.00 C

American Can Company, paperweight thermometer, tin, litho shaped like canning tin, "gift to 1907 National Canner's Convention," NM........ $350.00 B

American Clean Cutter, tobacco cutter, cast iron, rare design, difficult to find, EX........ $350.00 C

American Eagle Fire Insurance Company, New York, sign, tin, painted, wood frame, 20½" x 26½", G........ $325.00 C

Auto Hotel, globe, glass, light-up, rare item, 16" dia., G, $350.00 B.

Automatic Cone Co., Icy Pi sign, paper, framed, "The Snappy Pal for Ice Cream," 12" x 19", VG, $75.00 C.

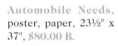

Automobile Needs, poster, paper, 23½" x 37", $80.00 B.

Avon, sign, tin, single-sided, "Brilliant Polish for Boots and Leggings," product can in center, 3" x 8", G, $75.00 C.

---

**American Eagle,** shot shell box, cardboard, one-piece, 2½" x 2½" x 2½", EX ................................................................$55.00 C

**American Eagle,** shot shells box, cardboard, one-piece, eagle logo on front, EX ........................................................ $35.00 B

**American Entertainment Co.,** poster, paper, litho, "Marvelous Moving Pictures and Illustrated Songs," 20½" x 30½", VG...... $135.00 C

**American Entertainment,** poster, paper, litho, by Hennegan & Co., Cincinnati, 30" x 30½", EX.................................. $25.00 B

**American Express Co.,** sign, tin with embossing, Established 1841, "Money Orders, Foreign Drafts," 1913, 27" x 20", EX....... $900.00 C

**American Express,** sign, cardboard, money order, "To send money...anywhere at anytime...for any purpose," 13" x 17", 1921, EX .................................................................... $75.00 B

**American Express,** sign, metal, painted, double-sided, flange, trademark logo in center, promoting their credit cards, 18¾" x 23¾", G ....$65.00 B

**American Express,** sign, porcelain, flange, "Money Orders Sold Here," 16" x 13", white lettering on blue background, NM. $275.00 D

**American Express,** sign, porcelain, one-sided, "Travelers Cheques accepted here," 10" x 4½", VG........................................... $90.00 B

**American Family Soap,** sign, tin, die cut, eagle on top, 19" x 20", EX....................................................................$7,500.00 C

**American Fence,** sign, tin, outdoor scene including fence, EX..$95.00 C

**American Gems Cigars,** box, wooden, pretty ladies on inner label, 1890s, EX ........................................................................ $35.00 C

**American Girl Cigars,** box, cardboard, inner lid with pretty woman, 1896, 9" x 6", EX ............................................................. $35.00 C

**American Hat Works Co. Inc.,** sign, porcelain, 40¼" L, EX ..$385.00 C

**American Ingot Iron Road Culverts,** sign, metal, embossed painted, white lettering on blue, 20" x 5½", NM ...........$110.00 D

**American Ingot Iron Road Culverts,** sign, metal, embossed, painted, white lettering on blue, 20" x 5½", EX ........................................ **$90.00 D**

**American Lady Coffee,** tin, litho, pretty young lady on front and back, 5½" x 9½", G .........................................................**$140.00 B**

**American Line,** pocket mirror, "Philadelphia, Liverpool, Queenstown," advertising with steamship, 1¾" dia., NM .........**$45.00 C**

**American Motor Hotel Association/Member,** sign, porcelain, sunburst in center containing AMHA initials, 1951, 20" x 25", EX .............. **$235.00 C**

**American Motors Co.,** playing cards, vinyl, celebrating the Pacer wide body small car, unopened and sealed in plastic, M .... **$25.00 C**

**American Navy Plug Tobacco,** sign, tin, litho, framed, American Navy tin tobacco tag, "For delicious lasting taste," 16" x 3¼", VG .........................................................................**$145.00 B**

**American Negro Exposition/Chicago Coliseum,** print, framed, 7-color screened, 1940, NM.......................................... **$350.00 C**

**American Pale Beer,** labels, uncut, full sheet, framed, 8¼" x 12", EX....................................................................... **$95.00 C**

**American Pencil Co.,** sign, cardboard, in shape of roadster, three deminisonal, EX .................................................. **$110.00 C**

**American Powder Mills,** tin, one-pound powder container, goose scene, 4" x 1¼" x 5¾", EX ........................................ **$95.00 C**

**American President Lines,** playing cards, vinyl, stars in center of card, full deck, EX .................................................. **$15.00 C**

**American Railway Express,** sign, wood, original gold lettering, 1910s, 72" x 11", EX ............................................... **$475.00 C**

**American Seal Paint,** calendar, paper, Uncle Sam and Spanish-American War heroes, 1899, 13" x 21", NM ...................... **$334.00 B**

**American Standard Lager Brew Co.,** sign, glass, reverse painted eagle on branches, 56¼" x 36½", VG ................................ **$850.00 B**

**American Standard,** clock, plastic, light-up, "Heating-Air Conditioning," 15" dia., EX ............................................. **$135.00 C**

**American Steel Farm Fences,** match holder, wire and fences, 4" x 5" x 1", EX ................................................................ **$85.00 C**

**American Stores Co.,** sign, "The Younger Generation," 14¼" x 18¼", EX...................................................................... **$95.00 C**

**American Sunrise Lard,** tin, litho, village and Indians, 8-lb., EX ............................................................................**$430.00 B**

**American Sunrise Pure Lard,** tin, litho, container from the American Packing Company, Indian scene, 12½" x 14¼", G ...................**$30.00 C**

**American Telephone and Telegraph and Associated Companies,** sign, porcelain, flange, Bell System bell in center, "Public Telephone," 20" x 20", EX .......................................................**$255.00 C**

**American Tobacco Co.,** sign, paper, litho, framed, Omar Turkish Blend Cigarettes with father and son enjoying a smoke together, 18¼" x 25", VG ........................................ **$405.00 B**

**American Tobacco Co.,** sign, paper, Uncle Sam looking character, 1899, 18" x 26", EX ........................................ **$575.00 C**

**American Wringer Co.,** sign, tin, embossing, "No 514 Royal, Warrented For 5 Years," EX .................................................... **$185.00 C**

**Ammen's Baby Powder,** tin, baby's face on front, 1960s, EX...**$15.00 C**

**Amoco,** banner, cloth, winter lubricants, service station with car driving up hill in winter weather, 37½" x 35", G ............. **$135.00 C**

**Amos & Andy Longfellow,** cigar box, wood, paper litho inside lid, embossed lettering on sides, 9" x 7" x 2½", EX.............. **$150.00 B**

**Amos and Andy,** cigar box, wood, 50 count, F .................. **$40.00 B**

**Amos N Andy,** candy box, cardboard, litho, 8½" x 11¾", VG.. **$100.00 B**

**Amos N Andy,** compact, metal and plastic, Amos N Andy on lid, 2" x 2", EX............................................................................ **$425.00 B**

**Amrhein's Bread,** door push, metal, painted, "Ask for...It's fresher," red, white on blue, 26" x 3", EX ........................................ **$75.00 D**

**Amstel Light,** sign, neon, "on tap," three colors, NM ........**$135.00 C**

**Amstel,** light, neon, on tap, three colors, EX...................**$125.00 D**

**Anastasia,** movie poster, paper, Yul Brynner and Ingrid Bergman, 26½" x 41", VG ..................................................... **$35.00 B**

**Anchor Buggy Co.,** advertisment, cloth of buggy, 38" x 64", G ...**$675.00 B**

**Andrew D. White,** cigar tip tray, "Mild and Satisfying," 4¼" dia., F .............................................................................**$35.00 B**

**Andrew Johnson Cigars,** box, cardboard, inner label portrait of Andrew Johnson 1900s, EX............................................... **$55.00 C**

**Andrews Shoe Repair,** globe, light-up, 15" dia., G ...................**$225.00 B**

**Andy Gump Biscuits,** display, paper, die cut, Loose-Wiles Biscuit Co., Sunshine Bakery, 11" x 12", EX............................... **$350.00 C**

**Andy Gump Cigars**, box, cardboard, Andy smoking a cigar, 5" x 5", EX.......... **$250.00 C**

**Angelus Marshmallons**, pocket mirror, glass and metal, cherubs, 1¾" x 2¼", EX.......... **$125.00 C**

**Angelus Marshmallow**, pocket mirror, cherubs, 1¾" x 3½", G ..**$75.00 B**

**Angelus Marshmallow**, tape measure, celluloid, product box on side, 1½" dia., EX.......... **$75.00 B**

**Angelus Marshmallows**, sign, cardboard, easel back, die cut, small angel holding box of product, 5½" x 11¾", EX.......... **$875.00 B**

**Anheuser-Busch Brewing Association Faust Beer**, sign, tin, litho, pretty girl holding drum, 21½" x 36", VG.......... **$1,650.00 B**

**Anheuser-Busch Brewing Association**, serving tray, metal, with factory and activity, eagle and hops around border, 1900s, 19" x 16", EX..........**$2,250.00 C**

**Anheuser-Busch Budweiser**, sign, cardboard, embossed, 16" x 11", EX.......... **$95.00 B**

**Anheuser-Busch Budweiser**, sign, tin, self-framing, litho, pretty young girl holding a bottle and glass of the product, 25½" x 37½", VG.......... **$1,650.00 B**

**Anheuser-Busch Ginger Ale**, pocket mirror, celluloid front, A-B logo, EX.......... **$95.00 B**

**Anheuser-Busch**, dispenser, stoneware, by Cardley & Hayes, NY, "5¢," good strong lettering and color, 1919, NM. **$125.00 B**

**Anheuser-Busch**, ice scraper, metal, rare, "Have you made the Budweiser Beer test?," 3¾" x 3", 1930s, EX.... **$100.00 C**

**Anheuser-Busch**, lighter, pewter, shaped like a finger candle, 6½" x 5½", NM..........**$45.00 B**

**Anheuser-Busch**, poster, paper, litho, pretty woman in risque dress holding an eagle in one hand and a bowl of roses in the other hand, 26½" x 36½", VG.......... **$1,025.00 B**

**Anheuser-Busch**, print of Custer's Last Fight, in wood frame, 46" x 36", 1896, EX.......... **$395.00 C**

**Anheuser-Busch**, sign, paper, litho, Attack on an Emigrant Train, 15" x 7½", EX.......... **$95.00 B**

**Anheuser-Busch**, sign, paper, litho, The Father of the Waters, from an original by Oscar Berninghaus, 16" x 7½", NM ..**$95.00 B**

**Anheuser-Busch**, sign, tin over cardboard, doctor with medical bag walking toward house, 12⅝" x 7⅝", EX.......... **$45.00 C**

**Anheuser-Busch**, sign, tin, self-framing, litho, St. Louis World's Fair with train dining car scene, 22¼" x 28¼", 1904, EX.......... **$475.00 B**

**Animal Crackers**, container, tin, still sealed, 1989, 8" x 6" x 2½" NM..........**$15.00 C**

**Anker-Holth**, sign, porcelain, cream separator, "We use the...," 14" x 10", EX.......... **$115.00 C**

**Anteek Beer**, backbar statue, composition, bartender with product name on apron, 22" T, VG.......... **$275.00 D**

**Anteek Beer**, backbar statue, serving man, 22½" T, EX....**$400.00 D**

**Antikamnia Tablets**, tip tray, metal, "two every three hours...insomnia & nervousness," woman seated in chair in tray center, 4¾", EX..........**$100.00 B**

**Antisepticon Gum**, sign, cardboard, litho, woman on cover, 6⅜" x 10⅝", EX.......... **$1,150.00 B**

**Apache Trail Cigars**, tin, Indian on horseback, NM...**$2,065.00 B**

**Apache Trail Cigars**, tin, oval, Indian on horseback, hard-to-find item, EX.......... **$1,500.00 C**

**Apache Trail Cigars**, tin, rare, litho, Indian on horseback, good strong colors, 5¾" H, G.......... **$500.00 C**

**Apollinaris**, sign, paper, in frame and mat, "The Queen of Table Waters," "Pretty Polly...The Queen of the Turf," horse and handler, 22½" x 27½", G.......... **$40.00 B**

**Apollinaris**, tip tray, metal, rectangular, "The Queen of Table Waters," woman with glass of product, 6" tall, EX.......... **$65.00 B**

**Apple a Day**, crate label, paper, Washington Apples, 11" x 9", EX.**$8.00 C**

**Aqua Velva**, sign, cardboard, counter use, Mammie Van Doren, 1950s, 24" x 16", EX..........**$30.00 C**

**Aratex Semi-Soft Colors**, sign, cardboard, for trolley car use, "3 for $1," 21" x 11", EX.......... **$85.00 C**

**Archer Lubricants**, can, metal, Indian shooting an arrow, 1950s, 1 qt., VG..........**$85.00 C**

**Arden Dairy Golden Valley Cheese**, sign, masonite, die cut, product package, 26½" x 12", EX..........**$225.00 C**

**Arden Dairy**, hat badge, 4¼" x 1½", EX.......... **$225.00 C**

**Arden Dairy**, sign, porcelain, delivery boy carrying a rack with various products and holding a bottle of milk, 14" x 24", NM .**$1,900.00 B**

**Arden Ice Cream**, sign, masonite, bevel edge, 12" x 7¼", EX.**$200.00 C**

**Arden Ice Cream**, sign, porcelain, oval, 48" x 36", 1959, NM.**$425.00 C**

**Argo**, display box, cardboard, oversized, counter top, consumer size package, 9½" x 5⅜" x 18", EX.......... **$135.00 C**

**Argood Cigar**, tin, liberty, "handmade 5¢ cigar," 5½" x 5", EX. **$95.00 C**

**Arm & Hammer Soda**, sign, cardboard, framed, litho, copyright 1908 by Church & Dwight Co., signed by Robin Snipe, 14½" x 11½", G..........**$75.00 D**

**Arm & Hammer Soda**, trading card display, crow on limb, 11¾" x 14¾", VG.......... **$95.00 B**

**Arm & Hammer**, sign, paperboard, promoting Arm & Hammer Soda, 14¼" x 11", 1910s, EX.......... **$225.00 C**

**Armory & Sharps Rifle Co.,** letterhead, paper, factory scene, 1877, 8½" x 11", EX.................................................. $45.00 C

**Armour Franks,** sign, tin, embossed, young boy eating a hot dog, 15" x 12", EX ........................................ $235.00 B

**Armour Franks,** sign, tin, embossed, young man and a hot dog, 15¼" x 11½", VG ...................................... $180.00 B

**Armour Star,** sign, tin, self-framed litho, The Ham What Am and Bacon Too, 13" x 37½", VG .............................. $500.00 B

**Armour's Oats,** sign, "Worthwhile Recipes on Every Package," young boy holding oats and a package of product on front, 21" x 26¾", G................................................ $55.00 C

**Armour's Old Black Joe Fertilizer,** sign, tin, embossed, self-framing, man playing a banjo, 36" x 17½", VG .................. $210.00 B

**Armour's Star Ham,** sign, tin on cardboard, ham and eggs on plate beside freshly cut ham, 19" x 13¼", VG.................. $65.00 B

**Armour's Star Ham,** sign, tin over cardboard, ham and eggs, 19" x 13", NM.................................................. $500.00 C

**Armour's Star Hams and Bacon,** sign, tin, early, embossed, lady purchasing a ham from a young boy in a meat shop, litho by Meek and Beach Co., 21½" x 27½", 1901, VG....................... $475.00 B

**Armour's Star Products,** mirror, butcher with bacon and ham, 18" x 33", G........................................... $175.00 C

**Armour's,** dispenser, milk glass, "Drink, Veribest Root Beer," NM................................................ $1,210.00 B

**Armstrong's Quaker Rugs,** puzzle, cardboard, small boy and girl playing on a rug, 1930s 9" x 6", EX ..................... $55.00 C

**Aromints,** pennant, felt, "for the breath," roll of the products, 28" long, 1912, EX ............................... $175.00 C

**Aromints,** pennant, felt, "for the breath," roll of the products, 28" long, 1912, G...............................$115.00 C

**Around the World Motor Oil,** can, tin, world circled by cars, 1920s, 2 gal., EX ............................... $175.00 C

**Arrow Beer,** sign, cardboard, matchless body, framed, 22" x 34", VG ......................................... $135.00 B

**Arrow Coffee,** container, Atwood Co., Minneapolis, Mn., Indian with bow drawn, 1lb., VG ...................... $1,000.00 C

**Arrow Coffee,** container, metal, slip lid, by the American Can Co., Indian on front with bow drawn, 1lb., NM...........$750.00 B

**Arrow Collars,** sign, cardboard, young man, EX ...................... $350.00 C

**Arrow Loaded Paper Shells,** box, cardboard, two-piece, EX. $95.00 B

**Arrow Shirts,** sign, cardboard, couple in rowboat, 29" x 23", EX .................................................. $95.00 C

**Arrowhead Hosiery,** box, cardboard, Indian lady on horse, 4½" x 15" x 1½", EX............................................ $55.00 C

**Artie Cigar,** display, tin, designed for counter top use, Artie sitting atop a building enjoying his product, 6¼" x 9½", EX ..........$475.00 C

**Artificial Portland,** sign, cement, porcelain, single-sided, cannon, 13¾", VG ...................................... $65.00 B

**Asbach Uralt Brandy,** bottle, glass, display, 20" tall, EX. $25.00 C

**Ashland Flying Octanes,** globe, glass, ethyl logo, 1930s, 16" dia., EX.................................................$475.00 C

**Ashland Kerosene,** globe, glass, wide lens, hull body, two speed lettering on Ashland, 13½" dia., EX............................. $575.00 C

**Ask Alexander,** poster, paper, litho, 30½" x 44½", 1920s, EX.$325.00 B

**Astor Wine Co.,** sign, mail order house, San Francisco & Hornbrook, Calif, NM ...................................... $45.00 C

**Ath-Lo-Pho-Ros Rheumatism and Neuralgia Remedy,** window display, cardboard, three-piece, 20¼" x 18¾", VG..........$175.00 C

**Atkinson Cordial,** sign, paper, "Wormwood Cordial...Farwell" print, 13" x 11", EX .......................................... $325.00 C

**Atlanta Cigars,** box, cardboard, pretty girl beside drapped flag, 1870s, EX ............................................ $450.00 C

**Atlantic Ammunition Co.,** box, cardboard, Chamberlin Cartridge, 20 gauge shell, EX ...................................... $185.00 C

**Atlantic Bulk Plant,** sign, porcelain, double-sided, dealer, 35" x 27", F...............................................$35.00 B

**Atlantic Stove Co.,** furnace, metal, salesman sample, 7", EX.$550.00 C

**Atlas Assurance Co. Limited of London,** sign, porcelain, one-sided, "Established 1808," man holding the world, 17¾" x 11¾", G..$180.00 B

**Atlas Underwear Co.,** paperweight mirror, glass, man in underwear, for Richmond Union Suits, 4" dia., .......................................$155.00 C

**Atlas Van lines,** doll, cloth, Atlas Annie, in original bag, 1970s, 16", EX ............................................ $25.00 C

**ATSC Transmission Conditioner,** thermometer, dial-type, 12" dia., EX ................................................ $135.00 C

**Atwater Kent Radio,** illustrated booklet, paper, 1927, 47 pages, EX .................................................$32.00 C

**Atwater Sweet Potatoes,** can, metal, paper label, sweet potatoes N0. 3, EX ................................................ $9.00 C

**Augustiner Beer,** sign, tin, painted, 19⅞" x 13¾", EX. $65.00 C

**Augustiner Beer,** sign, tin, properly aged, painted, 20" x 13¾", G ................................................ $45.00 C

**Aultman & Taylor Farm Machinery,** sign, paper, farm scene including the products sold, 36" x 15", EX...................... $400.00 C

**Aultman Miller,** calendar, farm machinery, 6" x 8½", 1881, EX..................................................................... $325.00 B

**Aunt Jemima Buckwheat Pancakes,** clock, cardboard face, plastic body, electric, Aunt Jemima, 7½" x 7", VG ........................... $500.00 B

**Aunt Jemima Cooking and Salad Oil,** paper panel from 5-gal. tin, framed, Quaker Oats Co., 8" x 13", EX .................................. $58.00 B

**Aunt Jemima Flour,** sign, porcelain, curved, hard-to-find piece, manufactured by Burdick, Chicago, NM ............................................. $7,500.00 D

**Aunt Jemima Pancakes,** banner, cloth, Aunt Jemima and a plate of pancakes, 58" x 34", EX ......................................................... $500.00 B

**Aunt Jemima,** bell, wood and metal, souvenir in original box, "Memphis Tenn" on apron, "Made by Hollander Novelty Co., Baton Rouge, La.," 4" H, 1941, VG.................................................. $125.00 D

**Aunt Jemima,** Breakfast Club scale, "Old Kentucky Home, Belknap Hdw. & Mfg. Co., Louisville, Ky.," cardboard face of Aunt Jemima, 6¼" x 8¼" x 8", VG ........................................................... $350.00 B

**Aunt Jemima,** display, cardboard, die cut stand-up, Aunt Jemima holding a hot plate of pancakes, "self rising and ready mixed," 12½" x 20", G............................................................................ $375.00 B

**Aunt Jemima,** display, cardboard, die cut, string climber, premium toy with the product box and Aunt Jemima on a string, marked Germany, 6" x 13¼" Jemima, 2¼" x 4" box, 1905, NM .............................. $3,050.00 B

**Aunt Jemima,** display, cardboard, die cut, string-climbing piece, 1905s, VG ......................................................... $1,300.00 C

**Aunt Jemima,** doll, uncut, double-sided, Uncle Moses, 10" x 33", 1915, EX ...............................................................$80.00 B

**Aunt Jemima,** flour sack, Aunt Jemima on front, 25-lb., EX ..$85.00 C

**Aunt Jemima,** pancake box, cardboard, Aunt Jemima on front, will hold 24 packages of product, 13" x 9" x 13¾", VG... $100.00 B

**Aunt Jemima,** pancake grill, metal, plastic knobs, Aunt Jemima decal, "The Quaker Oats Company, Chicago, ILL," 24½" x 16" x 26", G ....................................................................$1,100.00 C

**Aunt Nellie's Coffee,** tin, litho, key-wound, 1-lb., EX................. $266.00 B

**Aurora cigars,** box, cardboard, inner lid depicting woman in clouds, 5" x 5", VG...........................................................$15.00 C

**Austie's Brown Beauty Tobacco,** tin, litho, mammy, 8½" x 5¾" x 5½", VG .................................................................$620.00 B

**Austin Healy,** sign, paper, Austin Healy MK111 sports convertible, 1960s, 25" x 35", EX.................................................$135.00 C

**Austins Gun Powder,** sign, paper, Champion Duckling Powder, in original frame, 24" x 11", EX..............................................$1,500.00 C

**Auto-Lite Spark Plugs,** display, cardboard, die cut, Rita Hayward in a grass skirt, 11¼" x 14" x 5¾", VG ......................................... $170.00 B

**Auto-Lite Spark Plugs,** sign, cardboard, easel back, "Don't Miss," billboard, NOS in original envelope, spark plug, 21⅝" x 14", EX...................................................................... $235.00 D

**Auto-Lite Spark Plugs,** sign, metal, two-sided, painted, flange, "Ignition Engineered," 19" x 12", VG ............................... $145.00 C

**Auto-Lite Spark Plugs,** sign, tin, double-sided, flange, Cleaning Service Motor Tune Up, 11" x 11", EX...................................................$185.00 C

**Auto-Lite,** sign, porcelain, authorized electric motometer owen dyneto service, 35¾" x 25½", EX ..................................... $200.00 C

**Autocrat Whiskey,** serving tray, metal, card players, 17" x 14", EX.........................................................................$250.00 C

**Autolite Batteries,** sign, tin, self-framing, 18" x 60", VG .. $125.00 B

**Automatic Electric Washer Co., Newton, IA,** paperweight, pretty girl inside, EX ...........................................................$65.00 B

**Avalon Cigarettes,** sign, paper on cardboard, woman in hat in center and message at bottom, "You'd Never Guess They Cost Less," 20" x 30", EX........................................................ $65.00 D

**Avis,** playing cards, vinyl, showing their GM rentals, sealed, never opened, EX .........................................................$15.00 C

**Avon,** decanter, glass, in shape of spark plug for cologne, EX.....$12.00 C

**Avon,** talc tin, California Perfume Co., Trailing Arbutus 1977, 5½" tall, EX ...................................................................... $20.00 C

**Ayer's Cathartic Pills,** sign, cardboard, die cut, litho, older black man with a black girl on his knee and a boy kneeling beside him, 7½" x 12½", VG .........................................................................$500.00 B

**Ayers Cathartic,** sign, cardboard, old doctor treating young child, 7¼" x 12½", EX ..................................................... $325.00 D

**Ayers Sarsaparilla,** figures, cardboard, die cut, holding a bottle of the product, easel back, 12" T, EX ................................... $65.00 C

**Azalea,** crate label, paper, citrus, W.H. Clark Fruit Co., Jacksonville, FL, 1940s, 9" x 9", EX................................................$95.00 C

B-1 Lemon-Lime Soda, poster, cardboard, original wood frame, B-1 logo at top center, EX, $240.00 B. *Courtesy of Muddy River Trading Co./Gary Metz.*

Babbitt's Soap Powder, trade card, cardboard, litho, Uncle Sam and gold miners, 5½" x 4", EX, $110.00 B. *Courtesy of Past Tyme Pleasures.*

Babb Motors, thermometer, wood and glass, likeness of ships wheel with sailing scene in center of face, 1940 – 50s, 7¾" dia., EX, $55.00 C.

Baco-Curo, sign, cardboard, embossed, die cut, cures the tobacco habit, 9½" dia., NM, $425.00 B. *Courtesy of Past Tyme Pleasures.*

Baker Oldsmobile Co., lighter, metal, car emblem on side, never used, 1950 – 60s, 1½" x 2¼" x ¼", NM, $45.00 C. *Courtesy of B.J. Summers.*

Baker's Breakfast Cocoa, tip tray, metal, "Walter Baker & Co. Ltd., Dorchester, Mass.," farm house and woman with tray of product, 6" dia., EX, $190.00 B.

Banquet Ice Cream, sign, cardboard, 30½" x 18¾", VG, $325.00 C.

---

B & B Overalls, thermometer, porcelain, man in overalls, EX .................................................$1,800.00 C

B-1 Lemon-Lime Soda, poster, cardboard, original wood frame with B-1 logo at top center, G ......................................$75.00 D

B-1 Lemon-Lime Soda, sign, tin, single-sided, die cut, in shape of bottle, 1940s, VG ..............................................$95.00 D

B-B Dairy Feeds, Poultry Feeds, sign, metal, Buffalo, N.Y., 24" x 12", EX.......................................................$50.00 B

B.B. French Corsets, sign, cardboard, product in use on mannequin, 15" x 10", 1875s, NM .....................................$195.00 C

B.F. Goodrich, sign, cardboard, with rubber footwear, "Litentufs, Lite in weight, tuf to wear out," 14" x 19½", NM ..................$65.00 D

B.F. Goodrich, sign, metal, large company name painted over the top of a tire, 35" x 23", EX ......................................$75.00 C

B.F. Gravely's Plug Cut Tobacco, tin, litho, turban-wearing person, 6½" x 3¼", EX.................................................$75.00 C

B.H. Voskamp's Sons, sign, paper, litho, importers and wholesale grocers, a couple of kids on dock, 21" x 26", EX.............$1,500.00 B

BHL Black Indian, Cigar Store Indian, carved wood, with message at bottom, 20" x 20" x 73", G.................................$13,000.00 B

B.P.O. Elks, tip tray, metal, large moose in tray center, "45th Annual Reunion Grand Lodge, July 1909, Los Angeles, California," 4⅛" dia., G.............$25.00 B

Babbitt's Soap Powder, trade card, cardboard, litho, Uncle Sam and gold miners, 5½" x 4", F.......................................$45.00 C

Babe Ruth Gum, change receiver, glass, store counter top, 4¼" x 2" x 6¼", EX........................................................$80.00 B

Baby Ruth, candy box, cardboard, movie stars from "Gypsy," 1950s, 6" x 12", EX.....................................................$35.00 C

Barber Pole, sign, porcelain, red, white, and blue, 6" x 29", VG, $265.00 C.

Barber Pole, wooden, carved face at top, 8" x 8" x 55", VG, $950.00 B. *Courtesy of Collectors Auction Services.*

Barber Shop, sign, cast iron, milk glass, three-piece, 11½" x 31", NM, $1,100.00 B. *Courtesy of Wm. Morford Investment Grade Collectibles.*

Barber Shop, pole, porcelain, light-up, with glass cylinder and top globe, 13" x 87", EX, $3,000.00 B. *Courtesy of Collectors Aution Services.*

Barksdale Bros. Co., Inc., bowl, china, premium, flowers painted on front side, message on the back side reads "Furniture and picture framing, No. 131 So. Third St, Paducah, KY," 1920s, 9¾" x 3", VG, $55.00 C. *Courtesy of B.J. Summers.*

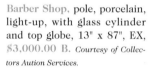

Bauer Pottery, sample jug, stoneware, miniature, "Compliments J.A. Bauer Pottery Paducah, KY," two tone, rare item, 1900s, 3⅛" tall, VG, $175.00 C. *Courtesy of B.J. Summers.*

Baugh's Fertilizers, thermometer, wood, cow at top of scale, 12" tall, VG, $85.00 B.

---

**Baby Ruth,** jar, glass, barrel shaped counter item with tin lid, EX...**$25.00 C**

**Baby Ruth,** tape dispenser, porcelain, paper product label, 10½" x 2", G...**$30.00 C**

**Baby Ruth,** tape dispenser, porcelain, with paper labels, "Curtiss...Candy and Gum,"10½" x 2", EX...**$50.00 D**

**Bachanan & Lyall's Tobacco,** sign, promoting Neptune tobacco, 11½" x 15½", VG...**$55.00 C**

**Bachlor Cigars,** display case, tin, slant front glass top, 12" x 11", EX...**$275.00 C**

**Baco-Curo,** sign, cardboard, embossed, die cut, cures the tobacco habit, 9½" dia., P...**$75.00 C**

**Bacon & Stickney Eagle Brand Coffee,** can, tin, blue eagle and key wind lid, 1 lb, EX...**$85.00 C**

**Badger Mutual Fire Insurance,** paperweight, cast iron, in the shape of a badger, 1937, EX...**$65.00 C**

**Badger Pure Barley Malt Extract,** sign, tin, company logo and name, "The National Beverage Distributing Co.," 18" x 12", EX...**$75.00 C**

**Bagdad Coffee,** pail, metal, 5 lb., EX...**$135.00 C**

Bay State Liquid Paints and Varnishes, sign, tin, litho, chain hung with panel for color chart, 1908, 20¼" x 19¾", EX, $700.00 B.

Barney Oldfield, blotter, heavy paper, "Boedeker Brothers, Higginsville, MO," 6" x 3¼", $100.00 B.

Barnsdall Dependable Products, sign, porcelain, double-sided, 47½" x 47½", VG, $250.00 B.

Barq's Root Beer, sign, tin, embossed, by Donaldson Art Sign Co., Covington, KY, bottle in spotlight, 35½" x 19½", EX, $110.00 B. *Courtesy of Buffalo Bay Auction Co.*

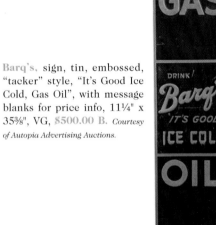

Barq's, sign, tin, embossed, "tacker" style, "It's Good Ice Cold, Gas Oil", with message blanks for price info, 11¼" x 35⅜", VG, $500.00 B. *Courtesy of Autopia Advertising Auctions.*

Bartels Beer, sign, metal, painted, 18" dia., EX, $150.00 C.

Bartels Brewing Co., ashtray, cone-shaped, 4⅝" x 4", G, $600.00 B.

---

**Bagdad Coffee,** pail, metal, bail handle, good strong colors, 7½" x 9", EX ............................................................$250.00 C

**Bagdad Short Cut Smoking,** sign, paper on cardboard, man holding vertical pocket tin, 1909, 20" x 30", EX ....... $233.00 B

**Bagdad Smoking Tobacco,** sign, metal, man with pipe, 1909, 24" x 33¼", EX.................................................................$450.00 C

**Bagdad Tobacco,** humidor, ceramic, with Bagdad on front, 5" x 6½", EX......................................................................$120.00 B

**Bagdad Tobacco,** jar, ceramic, trademark, man in center, small lid, EX .............................................................................$195.00 C

**Bagley & Co.'s Fast Mail,** can, tobacco, paper label of train, large slip lid, 5" x 5½", 1910s, EX......................................$395.00 D

**Bagley's Clam Bake,** sign, cardboard, tobacco, string hung, die cut, old clammer holding tobacco package, 8" x 6¼", EX.........$145.00 C

**Bagley's Compass Cut Plug Tobacco,** container, tin, round with pry lid, VG .............................................................................$85.00 C

**Bagley's Old Colony Mixture,** pocket tin, litho, vertical, woman wearing bonnet, John J. Bagley Co., Detroit, Mich., 2" x 3" x ¾", EX..... $575.00 B

**Bagley's Old Colony Smoking Tobacco,** pocket tin, vertical, colonial girl in cameo, G.........................................................$255.00 C

**Bagley's Sun Cured tobacco,** sign, papier mache of sun face, 25" dia, EX ............................................................................$850.00 C

**Bagley's Sweet Tips Smoking,** tin, litho, vertical pocket container, G ..................................................................................$65.00 B

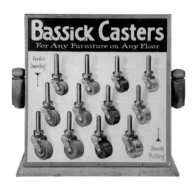

Bassick Casters, display, wooden, metal, and wood, casters on front, 13" x 12¾" x 4¾", NM, $55.00 C.

Bayer Aspirin, sign, cardboard, trifold, litho, "Does Not Depress The Heart," 42⅝" x 33¾", G, $175.00 B.

Beacon Shoes, display, composition, lighthouse on rock, with product name beaming out from light source, 6¼" x 10½", NM, $95.00 C. *Courtesy of Creatures of Habit.*

Beasley Marble & Granite Co., sign, paper, company information and photos of the founders, scenes of the business at work, framed, matted, under glass, 19" x 19½", EX, $175.00 C. *Courtesy of B.J. Summers.*

Beech-Nut Fruit Drops, original artwork, matted and framed, "Refreshing as fresh fruit," 1940s, 20" x 12", EX, $450.00 B.

Beech Nut Gum, display, cardboard, die cut stand up of young woman with a drum container of gum, 14½" x 38", VG, $140.00 B.

Belar Cigars, sign, tin, self-framing, 9⅞", VG, $45.00 B.

---

Bailey's Pure Rye, tip tray, metal, round with product bottle and shot glass on tray center, "Used medicinally & socially," 4¼" dia., VG ...................................................................................$140.00 B

Baker Guns catalog, paper, displaying their various products, 1928, 8 pages, EX......................................................................$100.00 C

Baker's Breakfast Cocoa, tip tray, metal, round, "Walter Baker & Co. Ltd., Dorchester, Mass.," farm house and woman with tray of product, 6" dia., G............................................................$115.00 C

Baker's Chocolate Cocoa, tin, EX ....................................$125.00 C

Baker's Chocolate, poster, paper, girl with tray, 26" x 36", EX..$350.00 C

Baker's Chocolate, sign, tin, partial message reads "Pure Delicious Nutritious," 17" x 23", G ..................................................$750.00 C

Baker's Coconut, tin, litho, give-away item, coconut cake on front, 2½" x 6¼", VG ................................................. $95.00 D

Baker's Delight Baking Powder, barrel, wood, paper label with trademark mammy with large pan of biscuits, 12½" x 16¾", VG . $275.00 C

Baker's Delight Baking Powder, barrel, wooden, handle on lid and paper label, 12½" x 16¾", EX...........................................$150.00 B

Baker's Delight Baking Powder, pail, tin, litho, mammy with rolls in pan, 12¼" dia. x 14½", VG ...................... $330.00 B

Belle of Monroe Whiskey, mini jug, stoneware, a label of LoeBloom & Co., jug was made by Bauer, 1890 – 1900s, 3" tall, EX, $175.00 C. *Courtesy of B.J. Summers.*

Ben Bey Superfine Cigar, tin, VG, $55.00 C.

Bendix Sales and Service, sign, metal, double-sided, flange, 18" x 18", VG, $245.00 B.

Bennett's Metal Polish, match holder, tin, litho, metal polish can on front, 5"H, VG, $355.00 C. *Courtesy of Richard Opfer Auctioneering Inc.*

Ben S. Wood, ashtray, milkglass, "Stolen From..." on all three sides, 4" x 4" x 4", NM, $55.00 C. *Courtesy of B.J. Summers.*

Betsy Ross 5¢ Cigar, sign, tin, advertisement, self-framed, 20" x 24", EX, $725.00 C.

B.F. Goodrich Shoes, sign, cardboard, "Litentufs, Lite in weight, tuf to wear out," 14" x 19½", EX, $35.00 D. *Courtesy of Pleasant Hill Antique Mall & Tea Room/Bob Johnson.*

Baker's Delight Baking Powder, sign, cardboard, black cook, 12" x 14", G ................................................$175.00 C

Bakers Nursery Talcum Powder, tin, litho, stork and babies, 2¼" x 6" x 1¼", EX.............................................$85.00 C

Bald Eagle Whiskey, pocket mirror, glass and metal, colorful eagle perched atop a mountain with sunburst showing behind him, 2¼" long, EX ................................................$85.00 C

Bald Eagle Whiskey, tray, tin, serving, litho, woman and cherub, 13⅝" x 16⅝", 1890s, EX.....................................$235.00 C

Balkan Cigarette, box, women in Turkish dress, 6¼" x 2⅞" x 1⅛", VG .............................................................$45.00 C

Balkan Sobranie Turkish Cigarettes, cigarette box, "Handmade of the finest Yenidje Tobacco," tobacco on animal-drawn wagons, 6¼" x 7⅞" x 1⅛", EX.....................................$35.00 D

Ball Brand Shoes, sign, cardboard, easel back, young boy and shoe with message, 1949, 29" x 20", EX .....................$50.00 B

Ballantine Ale & Beer, sign, cardboard, woman with a glass of beer, partial message "America's Finest," VG.............................$55.00 C

Ballantine Beer, clock, light-up, "ask the man for," 15" x 15", G.$95.00 D

Ballantine Beer, clock, metal and glass, light-up, "ask the man for," 15" x 15", EX ................................................. $135.00 D

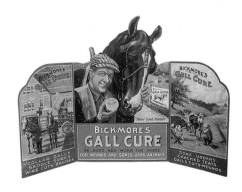

Bickmore Easy-Shave Cream, sign, cardboard, die cut, man applying product to shaving brush, 13" x 21", NM, $55.00 C.

Bickmore's Gall Cure, sign, cardboard, die cut, three-panel, horses and people and other period scenes, 41" x 33¼", NM, $375.00 C. *Courtesy of Autopia Advertising Auctions.*

Big Ben, tobacco tin, horse on front of tin, Brown Williamson Tobacco Co., rare piece, 1-lb., VG, $95.00 C.

Big Ben, pocket, tin, vertical, Big Ben clock tower on front, "Roll Cut," marked, unusual, EX, $1,100.00 B. *Courtesy of Buffalo Bay Auction Co.*

Big Boy, sign, cardboard, single-sided, 14" x 22", G, $40.00 B.

Binder's Beverages, sign, metal, painted, "they're better," bottle in center of message, orange and black on white, 20" x 28", F, $60.00 C. *Courtesy of Patrick's Antiques.*

Big Giant Cola, sign, tin, embossed, 23½" x 11½", G, $50.00 B.

---

**Ballantine XXX Ale,** sign, tin, 70" x 22", VG.....................$125.00 B

**Ballard Ice Cream,** serving tray, metal, young woman enjoying ice cream at a table, 13" dia., EX.....................$155.00 C

**Ballentine's Canadian Malt Ale,** bottle, glass, pre-prohibition paper label, 1 qt, VG .....................$55.00 C

**Baltimore American Ale & Beer,** sign, tin, painted, 10¢, 35¾" x 18", G..$85.00 C

**Baltimore American Beer,** sign, painted, 35¾" x 18", EX .$105.00 D

**Bambino Smoking Tobacco,** pocket tin, vertical, ball player and bat, EX.....................$725.00 C

**Bancroft Tennis Racquets,** sign, celluloid over cardboard, tennis racquet, from Whitehead & Hoag, 6" x 9", EX .....................$400.00 B

**Bandage Increvable "Baudou,"** sign, tire, single-sided, foreign, mermaid holding a tire, G .....................$1,500.00 C

**Banjo Tobacco,** sign, paper label from David Dunlop, Petersburg, Va., U.S.A., older black gentleman playing a banjo, 12½" x 2" x 6¼", 1880s, EX .....................$125.00 B

**Banjo Tobacco,** sign, stone litho by A. Moen Co., David Dunlop Tobacco Co., Petersburg, Va., black man playing the banjo while a couple of black women dance, 12¾" x 6½", 1880s, EX .....$375.00 D

Birchola, dispenser, ceramic, decorated with cascading leaves, metal pump at top, 14" tall, 1910, EX, $1,850.00 B. *Courtesy of Buffalo Bay Auction Co.*

Bit-O-Honey, sign, tin, embossed, 20" x 9", EX, $650.00 B. *Courtesy of Muddy River Trading Co./Gary Metz.*

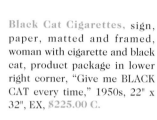

Black Cat Cigarettes, sign, paper, matted and framed, woman with cigarette and black cat, product package in lower right corner, "Give me BLACK CAT every time," 1950s, 22" x 32", EX, $225.00 C.

Black Cat Shoe Dressing, clock, tin, wind-up, with black cat, 17½" x 23½", G, $900.00 B.

Blanke's Coffee, store bin, tin, litho, horseback rider on front, 24¾" H, EX, $600.00 B. *Courtesy of Richard Opfer Auctioneering Inc.*

Blatz, backbar display, "at Local Prices," skater, EX, $135.00 C. *Courtesy of B.J. Summers.*

Blatz Beer, backbar display, light-up, when lit, bars behind man appear to move, VG, $145.00 D. *Courtesy of Pleasant Hill Antique Mall & Tea Room/Bob Johnson.*

---

**Bank Note Cigars,** box, cardboard, designed to resemble American currency, 9" x 6", VG.............................................................$15.00 C

**Banner Buggies,** sign, paper, stone litho, pretty young woman with buggy info on sash button, 1900s, EX ...............................$335.00 B

**Banner Milk,** sign, porcelain, one-sided, "It Tastes Better," 24" x 14", VG......................................................................... $70.00 B

**Banquet Ice Cream,** sign, glass, reverse painted, soda and sundae, 23" x 37", EX .............................................................$1,300.00 C

**Banquet Tea,** teapot, stoneware, "A Wonderful Flavor, Iced Hot," VG .......................................................................................$155.00 C

**Bar-B-Q Rolled Oats,** can, paper on tin, with slip lid, 7-oz., EX..$225.00 C

**Barbarossa Premium Beer,** sign, paper, embossed, hanging, tavern, Merlin and elves in cameo, 10½" x 13½", NM .....................$65.00 B

**Barber Greene,** toy, metal grain loader, green, 6½" x 12", EX..$225.00 C

**Barber Pole,** porcelain, red, white, and blue, 6" x 29", EX .$275.00 B

**Barber Pole,** wooden, carved face at top, 8" x 8" x 55", EX.$1,100.00 C

**Barber Shop Milwaukee Sentinel News,** sign, porcelain, single-sided, 48" x 10", G ................................................................$225.00 B

Blatz Beer, backbar display, bottle and can man, Milwaukee's Finest Beer, VG, $135.00 D. *Courtesy of B.J. Summers.*

Blatz Beer, backbar display, man at keg, "We serve the finest people everyday, At Local Prices," light-up, VG, $130.00 C. *Courtesy of B.J. Summers.*

Bloodhound Chewing Tobacco, sign, tin, "A Dog-gone Good Chew," J.V. Reed & Co., Louisville, KY, 26" wide, VG, $100.00 B.

Blew's Red Gum Cough Syrup, box, cardboard, distributed by Lang Bros., a quick look at the contents reveals its healing power: 20% alcohol, an ounce of morphia, and chloroform, 7½" x 2½" x 1¾", EX, $35.00 C. *Courtesy of B.J. Summers.*

Blue Coral Treatment, sign, canvas, litho, 93" x 34½", VG, $110.00 C.

Blue Parrot Coffee, tin, great colors and parrot on limb, extremely rare piece, 6" H, EX, $5,000.00 B. *Courtesy of Richard Opfer Auctioneering Inc.*

Blue Mountain Chocolates, sign, tin, embossed lettering, "Agency...Pure As Nature," 10" x 6½", VG, $65.00 B.

---

Barber Shop, globe, milk glass, fired-on lettering, 9½" x 9½" x 12", VG ........................................................$750.00 B

Barber Shop, light-up pole, milk glass cylinder with red stripe, light green porcelain holder, 11" x 26", VG....................................$425.00 B

Barber Shop, sign, cast iron, milk glass globe, three-piece, heavy center bracket, bottom milk glass stripe pole, 11½" x 31", EX..$1,100.00 B

Barber Shop, sign, double-sided, flange, "Barber Shop," 20" x 24", EX ....................................................$240.00 B

Barber Shop, sign, porcelain, curved, single-sided, 15½" x 24", VG .........................................................$250.00 B

Barber Shop, sign, porcelain, two-sided, flange, red, white, and blue, 24" x 12", G ..........................................$115.00 C

Barber Shop, sign, porcelain, two-sided, flange, red, white, and blue, 24" x 12", NM.................................... $275.00 B

Barbey's Sunshine Beer, clock, metal and glass, light up, large sun, 22" dia, EX..................................................$425.00 C

Barclay's Ale, sign, man holding a large glass of ale, 14" x 21", EX ....................................................**$65.00 B**

Barclay's Lager, sign, tin, litho, man with glass of product, 1910, 14" x 21", EX .................................................**$75.00 B**

Bardahl Try It, sign, die cut, Bardahl man with a case of the product, 10" x 10", EX...........................................$175.00 C

Barefoot Boy Tomatoes, can, metal, paper label with small barefooted boy, NM ...............................................**$10.00 C**

Blue Plate Coffee, sign, celluloid over metal, 12" x 7", G, $85.00 B.

Blue Ridge Bus Lines, sign, glass, etched, 21½" x 18½", G, $160.00 B. *Courtesy of Collectors Auction Services.*

Bobolink Silk Hose, sign, vinyl layering on cardboard, original art work, 25¼" x 37¼", EX, $100.00 B. *Courtesy of Collectors Auction Services.*

Bock Beer, sign, paper, framed, copyright 1925, NM, $375.00 D.

Bockman's Charity Club Coffee, container, metal with pry lid, painted label, Bockman's Charity Club Dry Roast Coffee, The E.W. Bockman Coffee Co., Incorporated Paducah, KY," 1900s, 44 oz., G, $75.00 C. *Courtesy of B.J. Summers.*

Booker T. Motel, Colored, sign, single-sided, from Humboldt, Tenn., 24" x 15½", G, $900.00 B. *Courtesy of Collectors Auction Services.*

---

Barns-Dall, pump sign, porcelain, with "B square" logo in center and message around edges, "Be Square To Your Engine," 3" dia., EX ......$150.00 C

Barnsdall B Square Motor Oil, sign, porcelain, double-sided, dealer, 29⅜" dia., F ....................$275.00 B

Barnsdall Be Square, gas globe, glass, one-piece, etched with trademark logo in center, 16½" h, VG ....................$2,200.00 C

Barnsdall Monamotor Oil, sign, tin, original wood frame, 18" x 72", 1920s, NM ....................$450.00 C

Barnsdall Super Gas, sign, porcelain, double-sided, ethyl logo, 30" dia, G....................$175.00 C

Barnsdall Super-Gas, gas globe, milk glass, three-piece, 15½" x 16½", EX....................$550.00 B

Barnum & Bailey, poster, paper, litho, lion's head with bare teeth exposed promoting "greatest show on earth," 16¾" x 24½", EX................$125.00 C

Barnum and Bailey's Greatest Show on Earth, poster, clown bowing, 25" x 17", VG................................$25.00 D

Barq's Root Beer, sign, tin, embossed, by Donaldson Art Sign Co., Covington, KY, bottle in spotlight, 35½" x 19½", NM......$135.00 D

Barq's, menu board, metal, "Drink Barq's It's Good" in message space over menu space, 19" x 27", EX ................$75.00 D

Barq's, sign, tin over cardboard "Drink Barq's it's good," sandwich and bottle of Barq's, 11" x 14", EX .................................. $150.00 B

Barq's, sign, tin over cardboard, "Drink Barq's it's good," sandwich and bottle of Barq's, 11" x 14", VG....................$125.00 C

Barq's, sign, tin, double-sided, flange, "Drink Barq's it's good," 21½" x 14", NM....................$350.00 C

Barq's, sign, tin, embossed, "It's Good Ice Cold...Gas, Oil," "tacker" style, with message blanks for price info, 11¼" x 35⅜", G...$400.00 C

Booster Cigar, sign, paper, man smoking a cigar while his lady adjusts her stocking, "High Grade Cigar Manufacturers, "Stirton & Dyer, London, Canada," 1910, NM, $1,775.00 C. *Courtesy of Buffalo Bay Auction Co.*

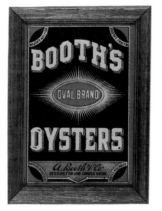

Booth's Oysters, sign, tin, embossed, wood frame, "A. Booth & Co. Oysters, Fish and Canned Goods," 30" x 22", EX, $325.00 B. *Courtesy of Collectors Auction Services.*

Borax Extract of Soap, sign, tin, single-sided, 24" x 7", VG, $95.00 B.

Borden's, sign, porcelain, neon, Elsie, VG, $1,700.00 B.

Borden's, salt and pepper shakers, ceramic, Elsie and Elmer, 2⅜" x 4", VG, $125.00 D.

Borden's, clock, light-up, "Fine Dairy Products," by Pam, 15" dia., G, $265.00 D.

Borden's Ice Cream, sign, tin, double-sided, embossed, "Tony's Mkt.," 51" x 56" x 9", VG, $675.00 B.

**Barrus Mustard,** display box, wood, paper litho label on lid with product information, 21" x 10½" x 5", VG............... $135.00 B

**Barteldes Seed Co.,** tin, unopened, with T-N-T popcorn, EX...$85.00 B

**Bartels Beer,** sign, canvas, professor holding a glass of beer, 56" x 26", EX .........................$425.00 C

**Bartels Beer,** sign, metal, painted, 18" dia., G.....................$125.00 D

**Bartels Beer,** sign, tin, self-framing, 18½" dia., F .....................$75.00 B

**Bartels Lager, Ale & Porter, Syracuse, NY,** tip tray, metal, man with large tankard, 4⅛" dia., EX........................$100.00 B

**Bartholomy Ale,** tip tray, metal, pretty young lady, 4¼" dia., VG .........................$140.00 B

**Bartholomy Brewing Co.,** sign, cardboard, pretty lady holding grain, 29" x 40", VG.........................$625.00 B

**Bartholomy Brewing,** tip tray, metal, "Beers, Ales & Porter, in Kegs & Bottles," woman on large bird, 4¼" dia., EX.................$110.00 B

Borden's Malted Milk Balls, jar, glass and metal, counter top, diamond shaped label on front, original lid, 9" tall, EX, $300.00 B.

Borden's, sign, with the Bordens' daughter Gail, Eagle Brand Condensed Milk, 13½" x 16", NM, $425.00 C. *Courtesy of Buffalo Bay Auction Co.*

Bordens, sign, tin, one-sided, "Trucks," 24" x 12", G, $160.00 B.

Boulevard Coffee, container, cardboard, Henry Horner & Co., Chicago, Ill., paper label with street scene, 1-lb., EX, $325.00 C. *Courtesy of Buffallo Bay Auction Co.*

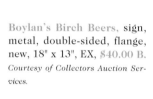

Boswell's, plate, china, restaurant name at top, by Syracuse China, 10½" x 7¼", VG, $65.00 C. *Courtesy of B.J. Summers.*

Boylan's Birch Beers, sign, metal, double-sided, flange, new, 18" x 13", EX, $40.00 B. *Courtesy of Collectors Auction Services.*

Boy Scouts, poster, paper, litho, "We, too have a job to do," 19¾" x 29½", VG, $325.00 C.

---

**Baseball Centennial,** license plate attachment, tin, painted, celebrating the 100th anniversary of baseball, 3½" x 4⅝", EX..........$275.00 C

**Bass Ale,** sign, celluloid over tin, for men, easel back, 7" x 9", EX .................................................................$55.00 C

**Bass Ale,** tap handle, fox hunt scene, EX......................................$30.00 D

**Bassick Casters,** display, metal and wood, with casters on front, 13" W x 12¾" x 4¾" D, EX.............................................$30.00 B

**Battle Creek Food Co.,** booklet, paper, with information on "Healthful Living," 65 pages, EX .........................................$25.00 C

**Baum's Polish,** display, cardboard, die cut, woman in touring car, 9" x 10", VG .................................................................$55.00 C

**Baum's Wonderful Polish,** sign, cardboard, die cut, vintage auto with top down being driven by a lady with scarf blowing in the wind, NOS, 9¼" x 10⅜", NM.......................................$195.00 C

**Bausch and Lomb Optical,** sign, cardboard, looks like canvas with vintage-dressed folks looking through a hand-held telescope, 17" x 21½", VG .................................................$85.00 C

**Bavarian Premium Beer,** sign, tin, hanger, man enjoying the product, 9" x 6", EX .................................................................$20.00 C

**Baxters 5¢ Cigar,** sign, tin, self-framing, embossed, drum in center, "beats all...how good they are," 9½" x 13¾", VG ................$80.00 B

**Bay State Paints,** sign, porcelain, double-sided flange, Pilgrim and product name, 15" x 15", EX.............................................$185.00 C

Brattleboro Steam Laundry, thermometer, wood, painted, 9¼" x 18", VG, $410.00 C. *Courtesy of Riverview Antique Mall.*

Briggs & Stratton, sign, light-up, with clock and illusion wheel for the "easy-spin starting," "Authorized Service – Parts," 38" x 10" x 4½", EX, $395.00 C. *Courtesy of Autopia Advertising Auctions*

Brook Hill, bottle, glass and silverplate, square bottle with square neck set at different angle, silver plate cover by Merry & Pelton, St. Louis, MO, there are several variations of this bottle, this is one of the more common variations, 1900 – 1910s, 9" x 4", EX, $100.00 C. *Courtesy of B.J. Summers.*

Brook Hill, domino, one of a complete set of premiums given by Friedman, Keiler & Co. distillers, Brook Hill was probably their best-selling label, 1890 – 1910s, 1⅝" x ⅞" x ¼", EX, $10.00 per piece C. *Courtesy of B.J. Summers.*

Brook Hill, drinking glass, reuseable, plastic and paper, "compliments of Friedman, Keiler & Co. Distillers, Paducah, KY," designed to be used as a sanitary drinking devise in a time of TB and other diseases, in its own carrying case, 1900 – 10s, 3" x 3½" closed, EX, $65.00 C. *Courtesy of B.J. Summers.*

Brook Hill Whiskey, mini jug, stoneware, front stencil, "Brook Hill Whiskey, Compliments The Rhodes Cafe," whiskey label by Friedman, Keiler & Co., jug by Bauer, 3" tall, EX, $275.00 C. *Courtesy of B.J. Summers.*

Brookfield Rye, sign, tin, self-framing, litho, scantily clad woman holding a bottle of the product, "made famous by public favor," 23" x 33", EX, $925.00 C. *Courtesy of Wm. Morford Investment Grade Collectibles.*

Bayer Asprin, sign, tin, with partial message "Safe For Aches and Pains," 18" x 15", EX ............................................$65.00 C

Bayerson Oil Works, calendar, two lions, at bottom on original frame is message, 1914, EX ...................................$85.00 D

Beacon Oil, sign, porcelain, double-sided, fan blade design, 30" dia., EX ............................................................$875.00 B

Beacon Shoes, display, composition, Lighthouse on Rock, with name beaming out from light source, 6¼" x 10½", EX ........$80.00 D

Beacon Shoes, sign, glass, reverse painted in wood frame, 14⅜" x 20½", G............................................................$75.00 C

Beacon Shoes, sign, glass, reverse painted product name, 15" x 21", VG ..................................................................$95.00 C

Beacon Shoes, sign, glass, reverse painted, lighthouse "There Are None Better," logo in center, 14½" x 20½", NM..............................$155.00 D

Beacon Tires, sign, metal, painted, double-sided, flange, with lighthouse inside tire, "low mileage cost," 17" x 24¼", VG....$3,250.00 B

Bear Wheel Alignment, Wheel Balancing, sign, metal, die cut, bear holding message board, 36" x 54½", VG ..............................$575.00 B

Beau Bryan Brummell, sign, cardboard, George Beau Brummell in top hat, 22½" x 29, EX ....................................................$175.00 C

Brooks Bros., bowl, china, with Little Boy Blue, front message reads, "Compliments Of Brooks Bros., The Only Cash Furniture Store in Town," early premium, 1930 – 40s, 5½" dia., EX, $75.00 C.

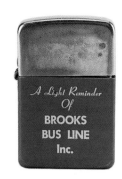

Brooks Bus Line, Inc., lighter, metal, made by Park Lighter, "A Light Reminder Of...," 1950 – 60s, 1½" x 2¼" x ¼", G, $30.00 C. *Courtesy of B.J. Summers.*

Brother Jonathan, tin, store, chewing tobacco, Brother Jonathan sitting in a tobacco patch, from F.F. Adams Tobacco Co., Milwaukee, 8¼" x 12", EX, $895.00 C. *Courtesy of Wm. Morford Investment Grade Collectibles.*

Brown Foreman Distillers, sign, tin, litho, by Schonk & Co., whiskey salesman with bartender sampling whiskey, "It's a credit to Old Kentucky, I told you so," 1900 – 10s, 27" x 18", F, $1,295.00 C.

Brown's-Oyl, sign, tin, single-sided, embossed, "for Fords," 13¼" x 20", G, $325.00 B.

Buchanan & Lyall's Planet Neptune Chewing Tobacco, sign, cloth scroll, pat. June 12, 1877, 11½" x 15½", F, $45.00 C.

Buckeye Root Beer, dispenser, ceramic, no pump, 12" high, G, $375.00 C.

---

**Beauty Shop,** globe, milk glass, light-up, one-piece, with etched lettering, 11" x 12½", VG.................................... $425.00 B

**Beaver Coal,** paperweight, composition, in shape of lump of coal, 3" x 5½" x 4¾", EX.................................$50.00 B

**Beck's Bottled Beer,** tip tray, metal, eagle on red, white, and blue shield in center of tray, 4⅛" dia., G .....................$140.00 B

**Bee Brand Playing Cards,** display, store counter boxes, regular decks of playing cards, 8¼" x 6" x 12", EX.............................$300.00 B

**Bee Hive Overalls,** pocket mirror, glass and metal, with pretty shirtless girl in overalls, partial message, "Bee Hive Overalls Best Maid," 1¾" x 2¾", EX .......................................$225.00 C

**Beech-Nut Brand Chewing Gum,** Valentine card, mechanical, 7" x 5", EX.................................................................$75.00 C

**Beech-Nut Brand Coffee,** container, tin, key-wound, litho, leaf in oval on front, 1-lb., EX ......................................$70.00 D

**Beech-Nut Chewing Tobacco,** counter canister, early vintage car on lid, and partial message "Our Visit To The Beech-Nut Plant Will Stand Out," super general store item, 10" x 7" x 16", EX.....$150.00 C

**Beech-Nut Chewing Tobacco,** sign, porcelain, packaging at left of sign, 22" x 10½", F .........................................................$65.00 D

**Beech-Nut Chewing Tobacco,** sign, porcelain, product at left, 22" x 10½", EX....................................................................$135.00 B

**Beech-Nut Chewing Tobacco,** sign, porcelain, product package and name, NM ..........................................................$195.00 C

**Beech-Nut Coffee,** tin, key wind lid, 1 lb., VG.........................$20.00 D

Budde, seltzer bottle, front etching reads "A. G. Budde Jr, Bottling Co., Paducah, KY.," 1900s, 12" x 3½" dia., EX, $150.00 C. *Courtesy of B.J. Summers.*

Budweiser, poster, cardboard, "Attack on the Overland Stage 1860," 41" x 28½", VG, $155.00 C.

Budweiser, clock, plastic, Clydesdales, 36" x 20" x 7", VG, $375.00 C. *Courtesy of B.J. Summers.*

Budweiser Draught Beer, sign, metal and glass, art deco styling with eagle logo holders for reverse painted glass message bar, 18½" x 3" x 9½", EX, $386.00 B. *Courtesy of Buffalo Bay Auction Co.*

Budweiser Draught, sign, plastic, light-up, team in front of a frosty mug of beer, 16½" dia., NM, $85.00 C. *Courtesy of B.J. Summers.*

Budweiser, print, framed, litho, Custer's last fight, Anheuser-Busch, St. Louis, Missouri, U.S.A., 44" x 34", NM, $375.00 C.

Buell's Brighton Blend Coffee, tin, litho, lady enjoying the product, 4½" x 6", G, $160.00 B.

Beech-Nut Coffee, tin, key-wound top, 1-lb., F................................$18.00 D

Beech-Nut Gum, sign, heavy paper, billboard showing man on pole and partial message "Any Time," 1950s, 19'6" x 8'6", EX......$75.00 D

Beech-Nut Spearmint Gum, display, cardboard, 3-D, in shape of gum container, 15" x 4¼" x 4¼", EX..................................$65.00 D

Beech-Nut, cigar tin, with beech nut on tree, 50 count, 1920s, EX..............................................................................$55.00 C

Beech-Nut, display, metal, counter top store bin with Beech Nut package on lift lid, "Quality made it famous," 9¾" x 8" x 9", EX..............................................................................$235.00 B

Beech-Nut, sign, cardboard, litho, gum package, "It costs you no more...to enjoy Beech-Nut...the Quality Gum," in original wood frame, 46½" x 22½", EX..................................................$135.00 B

Beechum's Pills, display, die cut, easel back, young boy, 2¼" x 5¼" NM..............................................................................$195.00 C

Beefeater Gin, backbar display, composition, 8½" x 17", EX.$115.00 D

Beefeater Gin, backbar statue, wood and composition, "The Imported One," 8½" x 17", VG......................................................$95.00 D

Beefeater Gin, display, composition and wood in shape of guard with spear, 1960s, 9" x 17", VG............................................$85.00 C

Beeman's Pepsin Chewing Gum, sign, cardboard, embossed, die cut, young woman in low-cut dress, 13½" x 17¾", NM .. $325.00 D

Beeman's Pepsin Chewing Gum, trade card, woman sitting on a product box, 3½" x 5½", EX.........................................$30.00 B

Beeman's Pepsin Gum, card, sleeping baby that wakes up when held to light, hard-to-find item, 3¼" x 5", EX..................................95.00 C

Beeman's Pepsin Gum, pocket mirror, EX......................$160.00 B

Beeman's Pepsin Gum, sign, tin strip, gum package, 17½" x 2½", EX..............................................................................$275.00 B

Buffalo Bill's Wild West Show, poster, paper, litho, Buffalo Bill on horse, 22½" x 35", EX, $1,600.00 B. *Courtesy of Collectors Auction Services.*

Buffalo Brand Tobacco, box, wood, from J.R. Smith & Co., Paducah, KY, 1900s, 16½" x 5¼" x 4¾", VG, $55.00 C. *Courtesy of B.J. Summers.*

Buffalo Brewing Co., sign, tin, litho, various bottles on table in home, 22½" x 28½", EX, $1,450.00 B.

Buffet, pocket match safe, metal, giveaway "Compliments of Gray & Detzel Buffet, 107 S. 4th St., Paducah, Ky," 1900s, 1½" x 2⅜" x ½", G, $35.00 C. *Courtesy of B.J. Summers.*

Bull Dog Cut Plug, match striker, tin, die cut, litho, "Deluxe Straight Leaf, Finest Bright Burley Tobacco, Dog Won't Bite," 6¾"H, EX, $1,800.00 B. *Courtesy of Richard Opfer Auctioneering Inc.*

Buick, sign, tin, embossed, dealer, Bangor, Mich., 1920s, 19½" x 13½", VG, $235.00 C. *Courtesy of Muddy River Trading Co./Gary Metz.*

Buick, 1915 pennant, felt, one-sided, 28½" x 11", VG, $275.00 C.

---

Beeman's Pepsin Gum, sign, tin, gum package and partial message "Aids Digestion," 18" x 3", EX............................................$400.00 D

Belar Cigars, sign, tin, self-framing, litho, advertising with easel back for counter display, graphics of product on sign, 10" x 7½", F ...................................................................................$20.00 D

Belar Cigars, sign, tin, self-framing, litho, product and message in center, 10" x 7½", NM ...........................................$150.00 C

Belding's Spool Silk, display case, wood and glass, three drawers, 32" tall, EX ..............................................................$1,100.00 D

Belfast Tobacco, counter tin, F...........................................$95.00 C

Belga Vander Elst, sign, porcelain, self-framing, foreign, 18½" x 27½", G.......................................................................$325.00 B

Bell Brand Chocolates & Bon Bons, sign, tin, litho, advertising with graphics of cherubs around a center bell, EX.....................$355.00 B

Bell Ethyl Gas Globe, plastic body with two glass lens, 13½" dia., VG.$475.00 B

Bell System, Public Telephone, sign, porcelain, double-sided, with arrow pointing to pay station, 12½" x 5½", EX ...................$210.00 B

Bell System, Public Telephone, sign, porcelain, flange, featuring the bell in the center, 18" x 18", EX .........................................$135.00 B

Bell System, Public Telephone, sign, porcelain, square, double-sided, advertising, 18" x 18", VG ......................................................$95.00 B

Bell System, sign, porcelain, die cut, flange, with message part of sign in die cut circle, 16¼" x 14", EX..........................................$175.00 C

Bell System, sign, porcelain, double-sided, advertising for Southwestern Bell Telephone with logo Bell System bell in center, these normally hung at pay phone locations, 11" x 11", 1950s, EX..........$180.00 B

Belle Plains Candy Kitchen, calendar, framed, embossed, die cut, 1916, VG ..............................................................................$90.00 C

Bull Durham, display box, cardboard, the bull has a cowboy up a tree, 11½" high, VG, $95.00 C.

Bull Durham, sign, tin, round, original wood frame, "Genuine Smoking Tobacco," rare item, 36" x 38", EX, $2,300.00 C.

Bull Durham, poster, original stamped frame from the American Tobacco Co., bull fighter in arena, 1909, EX, $1,600.00 B. *Courtesy of Buffalo Bay Auction Co.*

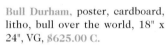

Bull Durham, poster, cardboard, litho, bull over the world, 18" x 24", VG, $625.00 C.

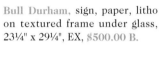

Bull Durham, sign, paper, litho on textured frame under glass, 23¼" x 29¼", EX, $500.00 B.

Bull Durham, statue, composition, "Standard Smoking Tobacco," bull, embossed lettering, 22"W x 17¾"H x 7½"D, EX, $1,800.00 C.

Bull Durham, sign, paper, youngster sitting on a porch railing smoking a pipe, 1890s, 10" x 13", VG, $70.00 B.

---

**Belzile Ice Cream,** sign, metal, double-sided, with graphics of ice cream cone, 22" x 28", VG........................................$100.00 B

**Bemgal Shirts,** sign, paper, litho, advertising of tiger, litho by Colortype, NY, 8¼" x 11", EX........................................$110.00 B

**Ben Hur Rye Whiskey,** sign, glass, reverse advertising for saloon with top hanging chain, 10" x 4⅛", EX........................................$225.00 C

**Ben-Hur Coffee,** tin, key-wound, litho of horse-drawn chariot on front, 10½" x 11½", EX........................................$240.00 B

**Bendix Radio,** clock, cardboard with glass face and cover , light-up, advertising body Telechron Inc., Ashland Mass., U.S.A., C.A.P., Product of Bendix Aviation Corporation, 15" dia., VG........................................$210.00 B

**Bennett Coffee,** Tin, litho with small lid, graphics of company headquarters , 7" x 7" x 11", EX........................................$100.00 B

**Bennett's Metal Polish,** match holder, tin, litho, of metal polish can on front, 5"H, G........................................$275.00 C

**Berghoff Beer,** sign, tin on cardboard, advertising of bird dogs in snowy field, 21" x 13", EX........................................$120.00 B

**Berghoff Beer,** sign, tin over cardboard, advertising with hunting dogs in the field, string hung, 21" x 13", VG........................................$95.00 C

**Berghoff Beer,** sign, tin over cardboard, hunting dogs in the field, string hung, 21" x 13", VG........................................$95.00 C

**Berma Coffee,** container, tin, coffee plantation scene, screw lid, 1 lb., EX........................................$125.00 D

**Bernheim Distilling Co.,** sign, paper, local preacher preforming a wedding ceremony for a black couple, 1897, 16½" x 12", EX........................................$75.00 C

**Berry Bros. Oil Finish,** trade card, cardboard, Uncle Sam, EX........................................$30.00 C

**Berry Brothers Toy Wagon,** pocket mirror, youngsters with wagon and dog, 2" dia., EX........................................$126.00 B

Bull Frog Shoe Polish, sign, tin, litho, frog, double-sided, 17¾" x 13", G, $4,000.00 B. *Courtesy of Richard Opfer Auctioneering Inc.*

Bunny Bread, sign, tin, self-framing, embossed, trademark, 27½" x 12", G, $325.00 B.

Burger Bohemian Beer, sign, tin, by Hy Hintermeister Burger Brewing Co.,Cinncinati, O., 20½" wide, G, $95.00 B.

Burger Chef, playing cards, plastic coated, full deck in original box with business name in oval in center of each card, Paducah, Kentucky, 1960 – 70s, 2½" x 3½", G, $15.00 C. *Courtesy of B.J. Summers.*

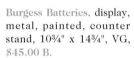

Burgess Batteries, display, metal, painted, counter stand, 10¾" x 14¾", VG, $45.00 B.

Burlington Pure Rye, glass, painted label and gold rim, 1900s, 4½" x 3¾", NM, $55.00 C. *Courtesy of B.J. Summers.*

Berry Brothers Varnishes, pocket mirror, celluloid, Whitehead & Hoag, young boy with wagon 2¾" x 1¾", EX......$140.00 C

Berry Brothers Varnishes, pocket mirror, young boy pulling wagon, 2¾" x 1¾", G ......$100.00 B

Berry Brothers Varnishes, sign, tin, painted with embossed lettering, "When You See Varnishes and Hard Oil Finish," The Tuscaro Adv. Co., Coshocton, Ohio, 27½" x 19½", G......$165.00 C

Berry Brothers Varnishes, sign, tin, painted with embossed lettering, "When You See Varnishes and Hard Oil Finish," The Tuscaro Adv. Co., Coshocton, Ohio, 27½" x 19½", VG......$200.00 D

Bertson, candy box, tin, hinged lid, company advertising on the sides, 14½" x 12", EX......$45.00 C

Berwind Briquets, sign, tin, single-sided, "Why go south? Burn Berwind Briquets," 20" x 14", VG......$75.00 B

Beta Beer, sign, round, light-up, 17" dia., VG......$150.00 B

Bethelem Extra Fancy Rio Coffee, store bin, Three Cow logo at top left inside star, John Bird Co., Maine, 1900s, 10" x 17", G......$155.00 B

Bethlehem Liquor, serving tray, metal, elk in center, 13¼" dia, EX......$145.00 C

Betsy Ross 5¢ Cigar, sign, tin, self-framed, 20" x 24", EX.$700.00 C

Betsy Ross Cigar, sign, tin, self-framing, oval, Betsy and the flag, 20" x 24", VG......$625.00 C

Betsy Ross Coffee, tin, litho, Akron Grocery Co., 4" dia. x 6", EX.$50.00 B

Betsy Ross Tea, tin, pry lid, Betsy Ross and the flag, VG......$55.00 C

Betsy's Best Flour, sign, cardboard, paper litho, "Bake and See Why," bag to left of message, 38½" x 21½", EX......$150.00 B

Bettendorf Steel Gear Wagon, tip tray, metal, wagon in center of tray, additional product info below wagon image, 4⅞", EX......$275.00 B

Betty Rose Coats and Suits, sign, wood, painted, with cut-out lettering, 24" x 5¼", EX......$75.00 D

Between the Acts Cigar, sign, paper, litho, Donaldson Bros., NY, young girl in early dress and bonnet, 12½" x 29", 1880s, VG......$1,800.00 C

Between The Acts, sign, paper, litho, "Trihos. Hall Tobacco Co., NY," young girl with bouquet of roses, 1910, 16" x 25", G.$165.00 B

Beverly Farms Milk, clock, glass and metal, Pam, light-up, 15" dia. VG......$65.00 C

Burr-Oak, tobacco cutter, cast iron, Harry Eeissinger Tobacco Co., Louisville, Ky., EX, $225.00 D.

Buss Clear Window Fuses, display, metal, great graphics, 1920s, 18¼" x 13¼" x 5", EX, $125.00 D.

Buster Brown and Tige, sign, silk-screened, cloth, mounted on die cut wood block, 24" x 20", EX, $375.00 C.

Buster Brown Bread, sign, metal, double-sided, die cut, hanging, featuring Buster and Tige, 18" x 13½", EX, $5,600.00 B. *Courtesy of Wm. Morford Investment Grade Collectibles.*

Buster Brown, sign, glass and wood, reverse decal and painting, 10" x 10", EX, $145.00 C.

Buster Brown, sign, plastic and metal, light-up, 14½" x 6¼", VG, $225.00 C.

Bevo Beert, sign, self-framing, fox sitting on bench, partial message "The All Year Round Soft Drink," EX...................$375.00 C

Bickmore Easy-Shave Cream, sign, cardboard, die cut, man applying product to shaving brush, 13" x 21", EX.......................$35.00 C

Bickmore Easy-Shave Cream, sign, die cut, litho, man spreading the product on his shaving brush, 13" x 21", VG.........................$20.00 C

Bickmore Gall Salve, box, counter display, originally held gall salve tins, 8" x 5½" x 2½", EX .....................................$95.00 C

Bickmore Gall Salve, poster, cardboard, horses crossing a mountain pass, "for all wounds and sores on animals," 32" x 20", EX....$60.00 B

Bickmore Gall Salve, sign, metal, gray horses on mountain path, "For All Wounds," 1940 – 50s, 34" x 22", VG.......................$75.00 C

Bickmore Gall Salve, sign, paper, "For all wounds and sores on animals," 34" x 21½", EX .............................................$95.00 C

Bickmore's Gall Cure, sign, cardboard, three-panel, die cut, horses and people and other period scenes, 41" x 33¼", EX ...........$300.00 C

Bidu, sign, tin, embossed, with caballero on donkey, "We Serve Ice Cold," 16" x 16", NM.........................................................$125.00 B

Big Ben Smoking Tobacco, pocket tin, the famous London tourist destination, 3" x 4½", VG.................................................$500.00 C

Big Ben, pocket tin, vertical, Big Ben clock tower on front, "Roll Cut" marked, unusual, P....................................................$125.00 B

Big Ben, pocket tin, vertical, tower of Big Ben on front and back, pipe and cigarette tobacco, VG.........................................$300.00 D

Big Ben, pocket tin, vertical, with the usual version "Pipe and Cigarette," EX..............................................................................$950.00 B

Big Ben, tin, horse on front of tin, Brown Williamson Tobacco Co., rare piece, 1-lb., G...............................................................$65.00 D

Big Boy, sign, tin, embossed, "Pale Dry in green bottles only 5¢," 19" x 9", EX.............................................................................$88.00 B

Big Chief Soda Water, sign, tin, heavy embossing, Indian Chief, EX..............................................................................................$975.00 C

Big Chief, cigar box, wooden, horses and Indians on inside lid, 50 ct., EX.......................................................................................$55.00 B

Big Giant Cola, sign, tin, label of bottle lifting weights, 24" x 12", EX ................................................................................$135.00 C

Butterfly Quality Bread, door push, porcelain on aluminum frame, 1930s, VG, $195.00 C.

Butter Krust Bread, sign, porcelain, die cut, 1930s, 14" x 18½", EX, $2,100.00 B. *Courtesy of Muddy River Trading Co./Gary Metz*

Butter-Krust, sign, paper, litho, framed, pretty young girl, 22" x 32½", EX, $800.00 B.

THE QUALITY MAKES YOU LIKE
# BUTTER-NUT BREAD
"Rich as Butter - Sweet as a Nut"

Butter-Nut Bread, sign, tin, embossed, 13¾" x 5⅞", G, $120.00 B.

Byer-Schmidt-Clark & Co., cigar box opener, metal, in shape of hatchet, small tip off bottom of blade, but a scarce item, Whol, Grocers, Paducah, KY, 6½" x 2½", G, $150.00 C. *Courtesy of B.J. Summers.*

---

Big Mac Coffee, tin, litho, key-wound lid, 1- lb., EX ..........$145.00 C

Big Red Soda, sign, composition board, bottle and product name, 15" x 36", 1960s, EX......................................$175.00 C

Big Smith Shirts, sign, cardboard, WW11 airplanes, 1940s, EX .$45.00 C

Big Smith Work Clothes, clock, metal and glass, light-up, for store use, 15" dia, EX .................................$145.00 C

Big Snap Cigar, box, wood, paper litho on inside lid showing a black man with a cigar, 5" x 4½" x 1½", VG......................$350.00 B

Big West Oil Co of Montana, pocket lighter, Zippo, NOS, 1¼" x 2¼", NM ..................................$125.00 C

Billings-Chapin, sign, cardboard, die cut, worker and customer that move with each other, 32" 29", VG ................................$475.00 C

Biltrite Shoes, sign, cardboard, litho, shoe cobbler working on a shoe, "Get Longer Wear by Shoe Repair," 21½" x 32½", EX ..........$30.00 B

Biltrite, door push, promoting rubber heels and non-slip soles, 32" x 3", VG ..................................$150.00 C

Binder's Beverages, sign, metal, painted, "they're better," with bottle in center of message, orange and black on white, 20" x 28", EX..................................$180.00 D

Bing Crosby Ice Cream, container, wax cardboard, Bing Crosby on front, NOS, pint, NM ......................................$35.00 D

Binghampton Oil Ointment, tin, oil rigs, 1880 – 90s, 5" x 5" x 7", EX.$235.00 D

Birchola, dispenser, ceramic, decorated with cascading leaves, metal pump at top, 14" tall, 1910, VG ..........................$1,650.00 C

Birchola, sign, tin, double-sided, flange, bottles, EX................$76.00 C

Bird Brand Steel Cut Coffee, tin, litho, small canister top, colorful bird on perch, G..................................$97.00 B

Bird's Eye Frozen Foods, button, metal pin back, patriotic red, white, and blue colors, EX..................................$10.00 C

Bire-ley's, sign, metal, bottles of their flavors, "Got a Minute ?...Enjoy Bire-ley's Real Fruit Taste," 1930s, 15" x 36", G..$135.00 C

Bireley's, lights, glass and metal, bottle shaped, orange lights with embossed names on the bottle part and silver painted circular brackets, superb deco styling on the brackets, 1920 – 30s, 12" tall, EX, for matching pair..................................$1,000.00 C

Bireley's, sign, metal, painted, "Drink Bireley's non-carbonated beverages," 28" x 10", 1950s, EX..................................$35.00 D

Bireley's, sign, tin, one-sided, with raised field showing fruit, "For real fruit taste, drink," 36" x 15", 1949, VG......................$175.00 B

**Bireley's,** thermometer, tin, tilted bottle, "Drink Bireley's non-carbonated beverages," 4½" x 15¾", 1950s, EX ................................$155.00 B

**Bishop's Move Tobacco,** tin, litho, chessboard and players, 3¼" x 2¼" x 1", EX................................................................................$45.00 D

**Bissell's Carpet Sweeper,** display, floor unit, 23" x 59", F ...$55.00 B

**Bit-O-Honey,** sign, tin, embossed, 20" x 9", VG ...............$495.00 D

**BL Tobacco,** sign, porcelain, circle in square, 15" sq., EX........$250.00 C

**Black Caps,** sign, tin, cure for Gonorrhoea Gleet in two to five days, the Safety Remedy Co., Canton, Ohio, 7" x 10", 1900, EX..$55.00 D

**Black Cat Cigarettes,** sign, cardboard, woman and cat, partial message "Give Me A Black Cat Everytime," 19" x 27", EX.......$135.00 C

**Black Cat Cigarettes,** sign, tin, die cut, cat's head with company lettering below, 48" x 51", EX ...................................................$625.00 C

**Black Cat Stove and Shoe Polish,** bill hook, celluloid and metal, celluloid button has black cat in center, 2¼" dia., NM ......$138.00 B

**Black Cat Whiskey,** display, chalkware, cat sitting on a lettered base, 19", EX.................................................................$2,900.00 D

**Black Diamond Whiskey,** sign, paper, two smart dressed black couples, partial message "Rich and Mellow," 15" x 20", EX...............$1,475.00 D

**Black Label Beer,** sign, cardboard, die cut, man carrying case of product, three-dimensional, 110" x 23", NM ....................$95.00 D

**Black Patti's Troubadours,** poster, paper, litho, "Lloyd G. Gibbs...The Black Jean DeReike," 21" x 31", 1954, VG ..$75.00 B

**Black Pete Toffee Tin,** 6½" x 4" x 9½", G ............................$55.00 C

**Black Rose Tea,** sign, cardboard, die cut, young girl wearing a bonnet holding a poster for the product, 7½" x 16", EX ..........$155.00 B

**Black Sheep 5¢ Cigar,** cigar container, tin, litho, "A Sanitary Package for 25¢," 3¼" x 5½" x ¾", EX .................................$275.00 B

**Black Spots Cigar,** box, wooden, paper litho inside and outside, three boys eyeballing a watermelon, 15" x 4½" x 5", VG ...$975.00 C

**Black Spots,** cigar box, wooden, inside label showing three black youngsters about to devour a watermelon, 250 ct., F ..........$230.00 B

**Black-Draught,** sign, metal, double-sided, flange, "a Good laxative," 12" x 6½", G .........................................................$115.00 E

**Black-Hawk Coffee,** tin, paper label, Indian bust on front, slip-lid, The Black Hawk Coffee and Spice Co., Waterloo, IA, 1- lb., EX ....$375.00 B

**Blackbird Red Pepper,** tin, paper on cardboard, red-winged blackbird on front label, 1½ -oz., VG ............................$85.00 D

**Blackwells Durham Tobacco Co.,** tin, litho, for cut plug product, Julie Carrs Tobacco, 1½" x 4½" x 3¼", EX.....................................$300.00 B

**Blanke's Coffee,** store bin, tin, litho, horseback rider on front, 24¾" H, VG .....................................................................$495.00 D

**Blanke's Grant's Cabin,** tin, litho, cabin on label, with hinge lid, 5" x 3¼" x 2¾", 1910, VG ................................................$155.00 C

**Blanke's Tea,** pot, stoneware, blue and white, pouring spout, Grant cabin, EX.............................................................$190.00 B

**Blanke's,** store bin, metal, curved front with lift slant lid, message on front and sides, 15½" x 18" x 25", VG.....................$500.00 C

**Blatz at Local Prices,** statue, skater, VG ..........................$120.00 C

**Blatz Beer,** display, backbar, light-up, when lit, bars behind man appear to move, G.....................................................$125.00 D

**Blatz Beer,** display, metal, built to resemble a Blatz man playing banjo beside bottle, 10" x 7" x 18", EX.................$145.00 C

**Blatz Pilsner Beer,** sign, cardboard, die cut, easel back, bottle, 1947, 7" x 27", NM .............................................. $45.00 D

**Blatz,** bottle and can man, backbar statue, "Milwaukee's Finest Beer," G ...........................................................$100.00 C

**Blatz,** display, backbar, light-up, man at keg, "We Serve The Finest People Everyday, At Local Prices," EX............$155.00 C

**Blatz,** display, backbar, metal and plastic, can barrel man holding mug of beer, 6½" x 10½", EX...............................$145.00 D

**Blatz,** display, backbar, plastic and glass, bottle, man holding mug of beer with one hand and pennant in other hand, 6¾" x 15½", EX..............................................................$135.00 D

**Blatz,** serving tray, metal, "Old Heidelberg, better because it's ester aged," 13¼" x 10½", G........................................$105.00 D

**Blatz,** sign, alto-plaster, F. Scott Fitzgerald in German pub, Blatz Old Heidelberg, 1933, 42¾" x 27¾", EX.............$175.00 B

**Blatz,** sign, tin over cardboard, with embossed figures, "Milwaukee's most exquisite beer," 10½" x 13¾", EX...............................$165.00 B

**Blend 150 Coffee,** tin, key-wound, 1-lb., EX......................$75.00 C

**Bliss Coffee,** tin, key-wound, 1-lb., F................................$20.00 D

**Blu-J Brooms,** sign, cardboard, double-sided, die cut, string-hanging, bird on broom, 4" x 10½", EX................................$95.00 C

**Blue and Scarlet,** lunch pail, tin, Booker Tobacco Co., Richmond, VA, with top wire handle, blue, scarlet, and gold, G.....................$135.00 C

**Blue Bonnet Cigars,** label, paper, blue bonnet and partial message "Cured Ripe Tobacco," 9" x 6", EX.....................................$10.00 D

**Blue Bonnet Coffee,** tin, litho, key-wound lid, red-haired woman wearing blue hat, 1-lb., EX.............................................$1,700.00 B

**Blue Bonnet Coffee,** tin, litho, key-wound, woman in blue hat on front, 1-lb., G ................................................................$300.00 D

**Blue Buckle Work Garments,** sign, porcelain, one-sided, "Strong for work, Overalls Pants Shirts," 13" x 4½", G....................$115.00 B

**Blue Coal,** sign, tin, embossed, burning piece of coal and partial message "Blue Coal Sold Here," 24" x 11½", EX................$125.00 D

**Blue Crown Spark Plugs,** display, has plug on top of electrical display that fires when button on box is pushed, never used, 9" x 8¾" x 5", NM................................$235.00 C

**Blue Flame Coffee,** tin, litho, 10-lb., VG.............................$55.00 B

**Blue Parrot Coffee,** tin, parrot on limb, extremely rare piece, 6" H, VG.........................................$4,000.00 C

**Blue Ribbon Bourbon,** oleograph, framed, cabin beside stream, 48" x 38", EX ........................................$550.00 D

**Blue Ribbon Bourbon,** oleograph, framed, cabin beside stream, 48" x 38", NM........................................$600.00 D

**Blue Ribbon Coffee,** sign, cardboard, caravan traveling down road to meet ship, 26" x 19", VG................................$650.00 C

**Blue Ribbon Coffee,** sign, silk screen on paperboard, natives carrying beans to the ships in the harbor, 26" x 19", 1906, EX .$950.00 D

**Blue Ribbon Malt Extract,** sign, cardboard, string hanger, "America's Biggest Seller," 10½" x 13½", EX...........................$150.00 C

**Blue Ribbon Spice,** tin, litho, tropical scene on label, Peoria, IL, 1-oz., EX .............................................$65.00 C

**Blue Twins Cigar,** box, wood, paper, litho, "Factory No. 815 9th District, State of Penna.," boys dancing with boxes of twin cigars, 9" x 5¼" x 2¾", VG .......................................$350.00 B

**Bluff City Beer,** sign, cardboard, easel back, "Swing To Bluff City Beer," 12" x 8," EX ......................................$18.00 D

**Boar's Head Tobacco,** sign, celluloid, boar's head and product name, 11" x 8", EX ......................................$65.00 D

**Board of Trade Tobacco,** display, wood box with paper labels and a glass window on front side, Power & Stuart Tobacco Co., 12½" x 12½" x 10½", EX ....................................$195.00 C

**Bob White Baking Powder,** tin, paper, litho over can, never opened, bobwhite quail on front, 2⅛" x 3¼", NM ......$200.00 B

**Bob White Tobacco,** tin, litho, quail on front and hunting scene on back, 4" L, G.........................................$160.00 B

**Bock Beer,** ad, paper, framed, copyright 1925, EX ..........$300.00 B

**Bock Beer,** sign, metal, hangers from Donaldson Litho Co., Newport, Ky., serving girl with tray of product, 18½" x 26½", NM........$330.00 B

**Bock Beer,** sign, paper hanger with metal strip, by Donaldson Litho Co., old gent wearing apron enjoying a glass of beer, 19" x 30", 1900s, EX .......................................$195.00 C

**Bold Cigars,** sign, paper, framed, battleships, "the National Smoke," 21" x 27", EX........................................$185.00 B

**Bond Bread,** sign, porcelain, large lettering of product name, 1930s, 48" x 18", EX .......................................$300.00 D

**Bond Street Pipe Tobacco,** tin, Philip Morris & Co, New York, London, EX........................................$35.00 D

**Bonnie Bro's Distillers,** sign, glass reverse painted, etching of factory, original frame, 45" x 34", EX.....................$1,300.00 D

**Booker T. Motel, Colored,** sign, single-sided, Humboldt, Tenn., 24" x 15½", F.........................................$125.00 C

**Booster Cigar,** sign, paper, man smoking a cigar while his lady adjusts her stocking, "High Grade Cigar Manufacturers...Stirton & Dyer...London Canada," 1910, VG ...............................$1,100.00 C

**Boot Jack Chewing Tobacco,** sign, glass, reverse painted with beveled edges and original chain, "Costliest Because Best," 1900s, 8" x 12", EX.............................. $550.00 B

**Boot Jack Chewing Tobacco,** sign, glass, reverse painted with beveled edges and original chain, "Costliest Because Best," 1900s, 8" x 12", VG .........................................$425.00 C

**Booth's Compound Derma Talcum,** container, cardboard, paper label containing frolicking cherubs, 2¼" x 4⅛" x 1¾", EX ...$400.00 B

**Booth's Oysters,** sign, tin, embossed, wood frame, A. Booth & Co. Oysters, Fish and Canned Goods, 30" x 22", VG...............$275.00 C

**Borax Extract of Soap,** sign, metal, for washing everything, painted, 24" x 7", EX........................................$145.00 D

**Borax,** sign, cardboard, die cut, mule team and people enjoying the product, 54" x 24" x 33", EX .........................................$1,400.00 D

**Borax,** sign, porcelain, early, "Welcome ask for Borax Soap," 36" x 6", EX .........................................$295.00 C

**Borden's Ice Cream,** calendar, paper, with Boy Scout promotion at top of tear sheet and Elsie on both sides of sheets, 16" x 33", 1945, EX .........................................$175.00 C

**Borden's Ice Cream,** sign, metal, flange, double-sided, painted, Elsie the Cow in the left side of the sign, 24" x 15", EX.............$350.00 C

**Borden's Ice Cream,** sign, tin, Elsie and product name, 28" x 20", VG .........................................$125.00 D

**Borden's Ice Cream,** sign, tin, Elsie, 24" x 12", NM ..$175.00 C

**Borden's Instant Coffee,** jar with screw top, paper label, 5-oz., EX .........................................$7.00 D

**Borden's Malted Milk,** sign, cardboard, die cut, maid holding a tray of products, partial message reads, "A Food For Everyone," EX.........................................$275.00 D

**Borden's Malted Milk,** tip tray, metal, maid holding a tray of the product, message on outside ring reads "The Malted Milk in the Square Box," 4½" dia, NM.........................................$475.00 D

**Borden's Milk,** sign, cardboard, double-sided, Elsie home for the holidays, 25" x 30", EX.........................................$55.00 D

**Borden's Richer Malted Milk,** can, metal, lid, 6" x 8½", EX ........$110.00 B

**Borden's,** clock, light-up, Elsie in center of clock, 20½" dia., G .................................................................$235.00 D

**Borden's,** clock, light-up, Elsie in the familiar flower collar, 17½" x 17½", VG.................................................$350.00 D

**Borden's,** cookie jar, Elsie figural head on lid, 12" T, 1940, EX....$250.00 D

**Borden's,** sign, metal, self-framed, embossed, Elsie in the famous daisy collar, 17½" x17½", EX ........................................$155.00 C

**Borden's,** sign, metal, the Bordens' daughter, Eagle Brand Condensed Milk, 13½" x 16," EX ...............................$350.00 C

**Borden's,** sign, tin, embossed, Elsie, NOS, 17½" x 17½", NM ...$250.00 C

**Borden's,** tip tray, metal, woman with product package, "The Malted Milk In The Square Package," 4½" dia., EX.......$230.00 B

**Boren Supreme Gasoline,** globe, glass lens on plastic guill body, 1940s, 14" dia., EX .................................................$275.00 C

**Born Steel Range,** match holder, tin, litho, early kitchen range, "Oven Heats In 10 Minutes," 5" H, G .............................$380.00 B

**Bossy Brand Cigar,** oil lamp, cow on globe, "Buy The Incomparable...Look for the star...on every cigar," with handle on oil holder, 4" x 5" x 7½", EX.................................................$800.00 B

**Boston Fish Co.,** tip tray, metal, young woman, from the Mpls. Grocer, 305 Hennepin Avenue, 4¼" dia., EX.........................$120.00 B

**Boston Garter,** display, wood, 9¾" x 14" x 5¾", VG...................$160.00 B

**Boston Tire & Rubber Co.,** tip tray, metal, pretty girl with bouquet of flowers, "Automobile, Bicycle, and Carriage Tires," 4¼" dia., G ...................................................................$200.00 B

**Boulevard Coffee,** container, cardboard, paper label, street scene Henry Horner & Co., Chicago, IL, 1-lb., VG.......................$250.00 C

**Bouquet Roasted Coffee,** tin, paper, litho, slip lid, Tracy & Co., Syracuse, NY, 1-lb., NM .......................................$60.00 B

**Bowers Windproof Lighter,** display card, cardboard, countertop, die cut, easel back, with lighters, G .................................. $25.00 C

**Bowey's, Hot Chocolate Powder,** tin, litho, small canister lid, hot chocolate being served, 7" x 10", NM .........................$70.00 B

**Bowl of Roses Pipe Mixture,** tin, vertical, litho, man smoking pipe in front of fireplace, 3" x 4⅜" x ⅞", EX ................$325.00 B

**Boyce Moto Meter,** sign, tin, die cut, pretty woman with "Authorized Service Station" message, 1910s, 22" x 19", EX .....$5,000.00 D

**Boyce Moto Meter,** sign, wood, litho, "Know the heat of your motor and prevent costly repairs," 19" x 13", VG .....................$850.00 B

**Brabo Coffee,** tin, litho, screw lid, Geo Rasmussen Co., Chicago, Ill., 1-lb., EX........................................$135.00 C

**Brach's Candy,** display, wood, stand-up rabbit with hat pegs, 48" H, EX.....................................................$25.00 C

**Brach's Candy,** display, wood, stand-up rabbit, with hat pegs, 48" H, NM...............................................$35.00 C

**Brach's,** box, two-part with majorette twirling baton, "Swing, Swing's the thing," 1930s, 9" x 9" x 1½", EX.........................$31.00 B

**Brandy Wine Soda,** sign, cardboard, woman riding on eagle, 22" dia., EX...............................................$195.00 C

**Brandy Wine,** sign, paper, woman riding on eagle, Seminole Flavor Co., Chattanooga, TN, 1939, 22" dia., NM ...........................$75.00 B

**Brattleboro Steam Laundry,** thermometer, wood, painted, 9¼" x 18", G ...............................................$350.00 D

**Braun's Town Talk Bread,** sign, tin, one-sided, self-framing, embossed, 35½" x 23½", G.................................$75.00 D

**Breakfast Call Coffee,** tin, litho, Independence Coffee Co., Denver, Colo., 4⅛" x 5⅞", EX .............................$60.00 B

**Breakfast Call Coffee,** tin, small lid, 6" x 9", EX...................$75.00 C

**Breck,** clock, plastic and metal, light-up, Breck girl in the message space above the clock, 13" x 25" x 3¾", VG .........$125.00 C

**Breyers Ice Cream,** sign, porcelain, double-sided, top hanging, "Sodas," 36" x 27", VG ...............................$600.00 B

**Bridgeman Ice Cream,** sign, porcelain, double-sided, 36" x 24", VG ...............................................$295.00 C

**Briggs & Stratton Authorized Service-Parts,** sign, light-up, clock and illusion wheel for the "easy-spin starting," 38" x 10" x 4½", VG ...............................................$310.00 C

**Bright Globe Range,** tip tray, metal, round with product on tray center, 4⅛" dia., EX...............................$160.00 B

**Brilliant,** tin, paper, tobacco mixture, Weisert Bros. Tobacco, St. Louis, MO, 4½" x 2¾" x 1¾", EX.........................$85.00 C

**Bristol Fishing Rods,** calendar, couple fishing from a canoe, with metal bands on top and bottom, 16" x 31", 1918, EX......$275.00 C

**British Navy Chewing Tobacco,** sign, cardboard, "Strictly Union Made," swimming sailors, Canadian product, 9" x 18", EX ..$69.00 B

**Bromo-Seltzer for Headaches,** sign, tin, embossed, 20" x 9", NM..$65.00 B

**Brooke Bond,** sign, porcelain, dividend tea, 30" x 20", NM .$100.00 B

**Brookfield Rye,** sign, tin, self-framing, litho, scantily clad woman holding a bottle of the product, "made famous by public favor," 23" x 33", F ...............................................$275.00 C

**Brookside Quick Cook Oats,** container, winding brook, 3-lb., EX ...............................................$175.00 C

**Brother Jonathan Chewing Tobacco,** counter tin, Brother Jonathan sitting in a tobacco patch, from F.F. Adams Tobacco Co., Milwaukee, 8¼" x 12", G...............................$500.00 C

**Brotherhood Tobacco,** lunch tin, EX ...............................$225.00 C

**Brown Betty Coffee,** container, pry-lid, woman with flower in hair, 3-lb., EX........................................................$195.00 B

**Brown Collegian Cut,** pocket mirror, clothing, 1¾" dia., EX .$425.00 B

**Brown's Worm Lozenges,** sign, cardboard, standing advertising for medicine, 10⅞" x 13⅞", EX................................................$400.00 B

**Browning,** sign, cardboard, laminated, crossed long guns, 9¼" x 9½", EX .....................................................................$50.00 D

**Brucks Beer-Ale,** sign, tin, embossed, countertop, "over 85 years continous brewing," in shape of horse shoe, 11½" x 11¼", EX ..$115.00 B

**Brunswick Cocoanut,** tin, small lip, woman on front, 3¼" x 3¼" x 6¼", VG ...............................................................$45.00 C

**Bubble Up Drink,** sign, tin, double-sided, disc, 14" dia., 1940s, EX ..........................................................................$175.00 C

**Bubble Up,** menu board, metal, with message over black board area, self-framing with rolled edge, 19" x 30", NM........$85.00 D

**Bubble Up,** sign, tin, one-sided, "Drink...," 27¼" x 12⅜", 1920s, F ..$50.00 B

**Buck Cigar,** sign, metal, die cut, in shape of deer head, "King of the Range," with embossed lettering, 10¼" x 12¼", EX ..$750.00 B

**Buckeye Beer,** sign, tin, self-framing, embossed, "on draught here," 13½" x 2¾", EX ..................................................$75.00 B

**Buckeye Cultivators,** sign, metal, double-sided, flange, "We Sell Buckeye Cultivators," 18½" x 9", VG .............................$95.00 B

**Buckingham Cut Plug Smoking Tobacco,** tin, trial-size, with recessed lid, EX .........................................................$155.00 B

**Buckingham Cut Plug Tobacco,** container, tin, lithographed, 5" x 5", EX ...................................................................$40.00 B

**Buckingham Cut Plug Tobacco,** pocket package, John J. Bagley Co., EX .........................................................................$95.00 B

**Buckingham,** pocket tin, tobacco, EX ...............$150.00 C

**Buckingham,** pocket tin, vertical, "Bright Cut Plug," full tax stamp, VG .............................................................................$65.00 B

**Buckingham,** tobacco container, paper, unopened with tax stamp, EX .................................................................................$125.00 C

**Bud's Union 76,** salt & pepper set, ceramic, 3½" tall, EX .$250.00 C

**Buddha Talcum,** tin, litho, container, "Lingering Oriental Fragrance," Buddha image on front, 16-oz., NM .....................$30.00 B

**Budweiser Beer Tray,** metal, litho, St. Louis in the '70s, 17½" x 12¾", 1914, VG .........................................................$90.00 B

**Budweiser Beer,** sign, light-up, cash register light, 10¼" x 8¼", EX .$45.00 D

**Budweiser Draught Beer,** sign, glass, art deco styling with eagle logo holders for reverse painted message bar, 18½" x 3" x 9½", VG .............................................................................$295.00 C

**Budweiser Draught Beer,** sign, light-up, pair of hunting dogs, EX ..$145.00 C

**Budweiser Draught,** sign, light-up, team in front of a frosty mug of beer, 16½" dia., EX ....................................................$75.00 C

**Budweiser Girl,** sign, cardboard, a pretty girl holding a bottle of the product, 20½" x 35", G ...........................................$600.00 B

**Budweiser,** clock, metal, back with glass front light-up, "Enjoy DuBois...DuBois Brewing Co., DuBois, PA," 15" dia., EX ..$225.00 D

**Budweiser,** door push, metal, take home, painted, in bad shape, but they aren't very common, P...........................................$35.00 D

**Budweiser,** globe, light-up, fired-on lettering, "on draught," from the Solar Electric Co., Chicago, 12" dia. x 12½" H, VG.$675.00 C

**Budweiser,** pitcher, nickel silver, from Wallace Bros. with script "The Budweiser" on the side, 9¼" H, NM .....................$85.00 C

**Budweiser,** print, framed lithograph of Custer's last fight, Anheuser Busch, St. Louis, Missouri, U.S.A., 44" x 34", EX..............$325.00 D

**Budweiser,** serving tray, metal, steamboat and wharf scene, 17½" x 13", 1914, EX .....................................................$100.00 B

**Budweiser,** sign, light-up, with hitch at bottom, "King of Beers," 9½" x 14¾", EX ........................................................$35.00 C

**Budweiser,** sign, paper, litho, mounted on cardboard, "The New..You've waited 7 years for this...served everywhere," mug in hand, 1920s, 21" x 11", G .........................................$41.00 B

**Budweiser,** sign, plastic convex cover, light-up, "King of Beers," 15" x 20", EX ........................................................$95.00 C

**Budweiser,** watch, plastic, electric, grandfather for indoor use only, Mfg. Everbrite Electric Signs, Milwaukee, WI, 15½" dia., VG.$50.00 B

**Buffalo Bill Saddle Soap,** sign, Buffalo Bill sitting on his horse, 1½" x 5", EX ...........................................................$725.00 B

**Buffalo Bill's Wild West Show,** book, by McLaughlin Bros, with stone litho graphics on front and back covers, 1887, EX...$126.00 B

**Buffalo Bill's Wild West Show,** poster, paper, litho, Buffalo Bill on horse, 22½" x 35", VG...............................................$1,200.00 C

**Buffalo Brand Peanut Butter,** pail, tin, litho, 1-lb., EX .....$175.00 B

**Buffalo Club Rye Whiskey,** sign, tin, litho, from Chas W. Shonk Co., with buffalo head in center cameo, 23½" x 34", VG.$475.00 B

**Buick Motor Cars,** thermometer, porcelain, vertical, dealer address at bottom, 1915, 7¼" x 27", white on blue, EX.................$350.00 C

**Buick, Bangor, Mich.,** sign, tin, embossed, dealer, 1920s, 19½" x 13½", G ..............................................................$150.00 C

**Buick,** clock, die cut, cloisonne award in image of radiator, 4" x 5½", EX ...........................................................$550.00 C

**Buick,** sign, porcelain, "Authorized Service," dealer, single-sided, 42" dia., EX ........................................................$600.00 B

**Bull Durham Smoking Tobacco**, sign, cardboard, double-sided, litho, with sweethearts on fence with product pouch hanging off to side, 9" x 11¾", VG................................................$795.00 B

**Bull Durham**, display unit, cardboard, trademark bull, 8" x 5¼" x 12", EX..................................................$550.00 B

**Bull Durham**, poster, original stamped frame from the American Tobacco Co., bull fighter in arena, 1909, VG....$1,200.00 C

**Bull Durham**, sign, "Blackwell's Bull Durham smoking tobacco," man at window, 24" x 31", 1880s, EX............................$595.00 C

**Bull Durham**, sign, tin, embossed, litho, strong colors, "1 oz. bag 5¢," bull in center, 8½" x 12", EX ................................$1,400.00 B

**Bull Frog Shoe Polish**, sign, tin, litho, frog, double-sided, 17¾" x 13", NM...............................................$7,500.00 C

**Bull Frog Shoe Polish**, tin, 2¾" dia., EX .....................$98.00 B

**Bull's Eye Beer**, sign, porcelain, bull's eye target in center, 18" x 18", EX..................................................$320.00 B

**Bull's Eye Beer**, sign, porcelain, from Golden West Brewing Co., Oakland, California, 18" sq., EX................................$350.00 C

**BullBrand Feeds**, tip tray, metal, with bull on tray center, Maritime Milling Co., Inc., Buffalo, NY..., 6⅝" L, EX.....................$75.00 B

**Bulova**, clock, tin, litho, 15" x 15", NM........................... $155.00 C

**Bunker Hill Brewery**, pin back, "Oh Be Jolly," owl, Owl Musty, 1¼", EX ...............................................$75.00 CN

**Bunte Marshmallow**, tin, youngster in front of large tin of product, 12½" x 9½", EX ......................................$200.00 B

**Bunte Rabida Dark Caramels**, candy box, cardboard, two-piece, factory scenes on both sides, 7½" x 11" x 3½", EX .............$30.00 C

**Burger Beer**, clock, electric, tin litho face, 18½" x 3" x 14½", VG .$65.00 B

**Burger Beer**, sign, counter top light-up, 10" x 10" x 2½", NM..$135.00 C

**Burma Cola**, sign, tin, oval, embossed, string hung, "It's different...It's better," 13½" x 9½", NM ...................$125.00 B

**Bursley's Coffee**, container, tin, litho, key-wound, 1-lb., EX.$30.00 B

**Busch Beer**, clock, western scene, light-up, 15" x 15", G ....$55.00 C

**Busch**, bill hook, with message button, Busch Shoe Repair Co., Wichita, 2" x 7¾", EX.....................................$145.00 C

**Busch**, sign, paper, top and bottom metal strips, John B. Busch Brewing Co., vintage people eating at table, 15½" x 19½", 1910s, NM ...............................................$220.00 B

**Buscho**, sign, tin, litho, prohibition, "A non-intoxicating cereal beverage...serve cold," 10" x 7", EX .....................$95.00 B

**Buss Auto Fuses**, sign, tin, "Why Be Helpless," man in front of older period car in headlights of oncoming car, 8½" x 7½", EX..$100.00 C

**Buss Clear Window Fuses**, display, metal, with great graphics, 1920s, 18¼" x 13¼" x 5", VG ............................$110.00 B

**Buss**, fuse cabinet, "Why be helpless," 6½" x 3½" x 8", 1920s, EX ...............................................$85.00 B

**Buster Brown and Tige**, throw rug, round, shoe store with their image on the face, 54" dia., EX............................$315.00 B

**Buster Brown Bread**, sign, metal, hanging, double-sided, die cut, featuring Buster and Tige, 18" x 13½", G ................................$1,500.00 C

**Buster Brown Shoe Company**, calendar, paper, with Buster and Tige in center of monthly pages and underwater scene at top, 8½" x 19", NM........................................$40.00 B

**Buster Brown Shoes**, bandana, 1940s, EX .....................$75.00 C

**Buster Brown Shoes**, plate, 5½" dia., NM...............$150.00 C

**Buster Brown Shoes**, sign, neon, Buster and Tige, 54" x 55", EX.....................................................$1,400.00 B

**Buster Brown Shoes**, sign, plaster, bas-relief, Buster Brown and Tige, 1940s, 17" round, NM .................................$320.00 B

**Buster Brown**, air tank inflator, fits on the head of air or helium tank, 20" x 21" x 24", EX.....................................$125.00 B

**Buster Brown**, clock, metal body and glass face and cover, light-up, from the Pam Clock Co. 15" dia., F.....................$500.00 B

**Buster Brown**, clock, metal body with glass cover and face, light-up, Buster Brown and Tige, from the Pam Clock Co., has 15" dia., P ...............................................$375.00 C

**Buster Brown**, plaque, plaster, embossed, Buster and Tige, 12" x 12", EX...............................................$275.00 C

**Buster Brown**, plate, Buster and Tige, 7½", VG.................$35.00 D

**Buster Brown**, poster, cloth backed, featuring animal impersonator George Ali, 27" x 40⅞", EX...............................$75.00 C

**Buster Brown**, sign, paper, Buster and Tige, easel back, 14" x 14", EX ...............................................$95.00 D

**Buster Brown**, sign, tin, double-sided, litho, with Buster holding shoe, "Buster Brown shoes...Get them here," 15" x 23½", G.......$1,000.00 B

**Buster Brown**, sign, tin, two-piece, die cut, Buster and Tige, 19" x 21", Buster 22" x 32½", G.................................$950.00 B

**Butter Krust Bread**, sign, porcelain, die cut, 1930s, 14" x 18½", G...............................................$1,100.00 C

**Butter-Nut Bread**, door push, porcelain, G .....................$215.00 C

**Butter-Nut**, coffee can, "Specially mellowed, The Delicious Coffee," key-wound top, Paxton and Gallagher Co., Omaha, Nebraska, 1-lb., EX ...............................................$20.00 D

**Butterfly Quality Bread**, door push, porcelain on aluminum frame, 1930s, G...............................................$170.00 B

222 Cigar Stores, pocket match safe, celluloid and metal, "Compliments of ...Paducah, KY, 222 Broadway, Palmer Hotel," 1920s, 2⅜" x 1½" x ⅞", EX, $45.00 C. *Courtesy of B.J. Summers.*

Cabin Still, sign, alto-plaster, this is a hard to fine variation of this sign, made of plaster and horse hair, 16¾" x 12¾", NM, $120.00 B.

California Poppy Brand Oranges, box end label with litho by Dickman Jones, San Francisco, poppies in bloom, 10½" x 11", 1890s, EX, $525.00 B. *Courtesy of Past Tyme Pleasures.*

Calumet Baking Powder, regulator clock, wood, metal, and glass, 1900 – 1920s, 36½" tall, VG, $1,190.00 C

Campbell's Soup, trolley card, cardboard, litho, 20½" x 12", VG, $95.00 C.

Campbell's Soup, thermometer, porcelain, features facsimile of tomato soup can with dial-type thermometer in center of can, great graphics, 7"W x 12"H x 1¼"D, NM, $2,100.00 B. *Courtesy of Muddy River Trading Co./Gary Metz.*

Campbell's sign, porcelain, curved, pole-mounted, "Vegetable Soup," 13" x 22½", scarce item, VG, $4,450.00 B.

C & F Motor Sales, calendar, paper, scouts in church scene over tear sheets, "Dodge and Plymouth," 16" x 33", 1954, EX......$45.00 B

C. Person's Sons Importers and Distillers, Buffalo N.Y. sign, tin, embossed, litho, promoting Buffalo Club Rye Whiskey, 23½" x 34", VG ..................................................................$375.00 C

C. Pfeiffer Brewing Co, Detroit, Mich., tip tray, metal, bottle in tray center, 4" dia., EX.....................................................$100.00 B

C.D. Kenny Co. Coffee, pail, metal, with wire handle, containing Hanover Brand Fresh Roasted Coffee, 3-lb., EX ............$995.00 D

C.P.W. Motor Car Enamel, poster, cardboard, man with older model touring car, 17¾" x 21¾", EX .....................................$195.00 C

Cabin Still Bourbon, sign, hard rubber relief with product name above cabin scene, 17" x 13", EX ........................$75.00 C

Caddy Label Tobacco, sign, King Neptune riding on giant shell with naked mermaids, from David Dunlop, Virginia, 1880s, EX..$140.00 B

Cadillac Official Service, sign, porcelain, crown shields with lettering, double-sided, 40" x 30", EX.....................$625.00 D

Cadillac Service, clock, plastic, Cadillac logo in center, 12" dia., EX......................................................................$210.00 D

Cadillac, clock, metal and glass, light up, octagonal, 18" x 18", VG ......................................................................$675.00 D

Cafe Empire Blend Coffee, can, tin, litho, 4⅜"x 5½", EX....$70.00 B

Cal-Tex Soles, clock, metal and glass, light up, black cat in center, 14" dia, EX ......................................................$675.00 D

Cali-Orange Syrup, dispenser, glass, with frosted globe on reverse painted base with product decal on front and reverse side, EX......................................................................$290.00 B

California Dairy Industries Association, sign, porcelain, double-sided, cow and an award ribbon, 25" x 22", EX ..............$425.00 C

California Fruit Gum, sign, cardboard, raised finish, die cut, youngsters about to kiss, 10" x 13½", EX...................................$450.00 B

California Gold Label Beer, light, wood and cloth, in shape of covered wagon, 23" x 12", EX................................................$155.00 D

Canada Dry, sign, metal, hard to locate sign with all 5 flavors, 47" tall, F, $200.00 B.

Canada Dry Spur, sign, tin, one-sided, embossed, 26" x 22½", G, $135.00 B.

Canada Dry, display, cardboard, die cut, counter top with easel back, "The Best Drink of All," 15½" x 28", VG, $35.00 C. Courtesy of Collectors Auction Services.

Canadian National Telegraph and Cable Office, sign, porcelain, flange, NM, $395.00 D. Courtesy of Riverview Antique Mall.

Capital Gasoline Atlantic, gas globe, metal and glass, 20" high, VG, $425.00 B.

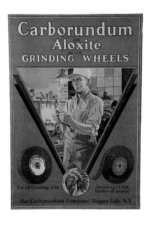

Carborundum/Aloxite Grinding Wheels, sign, canvas litho, workman holding a chisel in workshop, products at bottom, NOS, 28" x 40", NM, $165.00 D. Courtesy of Autopia Advertising Auctions.

Carter the Great, poster, cardboard, framed by the Otis Lithograph Co., Cleveland, Ohio, made in U.S.A/4630-M, 42" x 78", EX, $500.00 B.

Caskey Pontiac, playing cards, plastic coated with "redi-slip finish," by remembrance, full deck with original box, all cards feature company information and small child with a pajama problem in front of a television, 1940 – 50s, 2½" x 3½", VG, $25.00 C. Courtesy of B.J. Summers.

---

**California Nugget Chop Cut Pipe Tobacco,** tin, flat pocket, 2¾" x 4½" x ¾", EX......................................................$75.00 C

**California Peanut Co.,** pail, tin, litho, container with whimsical comic characters all around pail, 3¼" x 3¾", EX ............$175.00 C

**California Perfume Co.,** tin, baby talc, litho, container with youngsters playing, 1¾" x 4½", EX .........................$275.00 B

**California Poppy Brand Oranges,** label, paper, box end by Dickman Jones, San Francisco, poppies in bloom, 10½" x 11", 1890s, G................................................................................$175.00 C

**Calotabs for Biliousness,** thermometer, wood scale, promoting the cure for biliousness torpidity, 4" x 15⅛", VG......................$90.00 B

**Calso Gasoline,** sign, porcelain, white lettering for pump, 11" dia, EX ................................................................$175.00 C

**Calso Supreme Gasoline,** pump sign, porcelain, die cut, 11" x 13¾", NM .......................................................$550.00 B

**Calso Supreme Gasoline,** pump sign, porcelain, one-sided, with die cut chevrons at bottom, 11" x 13¾", VG ........................................$250.00 C

**Calumet Baking Powder,** clock, wooden case, Regulator with glass front, Roman numerals on face, 38" tall, EX..........................$825.00 D

**Calumet Baking Powder,** thermometer, wooden, product container at top of scale, 6" x 22", 1920s, VG....................$275.00 B

**Calumet,** calendar, give-away with "Weekly Kitchen Reminders" pocket with the Calumet Boy and product tin, 9½" x 15½", EX ......$45.00 D

**Calvert Whiskey,** clock, electric, light-up bubble, "Clear Heads Choose Calvert," owl in center, Telechron, NM .................$175.00 C

**Cambridge Coffee Whole Bean,** can, tin, litho, 3½" x 7¼", EX .......................................................................$210.00 B

**Camel Cigarettes,** poster, cardboard, die cut, man in tuxedo and woman enjoying a cigarette, 32" x 29½", VG....................$75.00 B

Cascade Uncle Sam Beer, tray, metal, by Bacharach & Co., San Francisco, high ranking dignitaries agreeing about the purity of Cascade, 17" x 12½", VG, $510.00 B.

Caskey Pontiac, sewing kit, celluloid container, "When You're Ready To Buy-See Us Last", 1940 – 50s, EX, $20.00 C. Courtesy of B.J. Summers.

Case, eagle, cast iron, 57½" tall, VG, $2,600.00 C.

Castle Gate Coal, sign, porcelain, one-sided, strong colors, "The Main Highway to Fuel Satisfaction," 30" x 12", EX, $375.00 C.

Cat-Tex Soles, clock, light-up, reverse painted, cat on cover, "We rebuild shoes, like new at less than ½ new cost," 14½" dia., EX, $620.00 B. Courtesy of Buffalo Bay Auction Co.

Celery Rye Whiskey, sign, tin, embossed lettering and images, "Contains All the Virtues of the Wonderful Celery Plant," 19" x 12," VG, $200.00 B.

Centlivre Brewing Co., poster, paper, framed, brewery in Fort Wayne, Ind., 42" x 29", G, $645.00 B.

Centlivre's Nickel Plate Beer, poster, litho, dining car scene, in period frame, 26¾" x 31", NM, $500.00 C. Courtesy of Autopia Advertising Auctions.

Central Union Cut Plug, lunchpail, metal with wire handle, 7½" long, G, $70.00 B.

Camel Cigarettes, sign, metal, painted, "smoke," product package in spotlight at bottom of sign, 12" x 18", yellow on red, G...$45.00 D

Camel Cigarettes, sign, porcelain, flange, "Sold Here," yellow on red, 12" x 18", G.................................................$145.00 D

Camels Cigarettes, sign, paper, die cut, young lady in swim suit, "Camels Cool Mild," 5¼" x 14¾", 1954, EX........................$35.00 B

Cameron & Cameron, tobacco tin, square corner, Louisiana Perique from Richmond, VA, 3½" x 2½" x 1½", EX...........$160.00 B

Campbell & Co.'s Ale, sign, paper, wood frame, 28½" x 22⅝", EX.................................................................$55.00 D

Campbell & Co.'s Edinburgh Ales, sign, framed, 28½" x 55½", EX.................................................................$35.00 C

Ceresota Flour, match safe, tin, die cut, 2½" x 5½", VG, $325.00 D.

C.F. & I. Coals, sign, porcelain, "Produced by the Colorado Fuel and Iron Company," 20" x 16", VG, $325.00 C.

Champions Spark Plug Service, sign, metal, for cleaning plugs back when 10,000 miles was just about it for plugs unless they were cleaned, 10" x 27", VG, $140.00 B.

Champion Spark Plugs, sign, cardboard, die cut, vintage race car driver with oversized spark plug, 14½" x 6", EX, $675.00 C. Courtesy of Autopia Advertising Auction.

Charles Denby Cigar, display, cardboard, die cut, stand-up, black boy drummer advertising the product, 17" x 29½", 1899, VG, $1,800.00 B. Courtesy of Collectors Auction Services.

Charlex Razor, display, celluloid and metal, 26½" closed, VG, $650.00 B. Courtesy of Collectors Auction Services.

Cheerio, sign, tin over cardboard, man holding bottles of Cheerio, "It's Lewie's Refreshing Beverages I Want," 11" x 8", G, $45.00 C. Courtesy of Muddy River Trading Co./Gary Metz.

Chero-Cola, sign, cardboard, single-sided, ballplayer, "Ice Cold Served Here,"12" x 18", VG, $300.00 C.

Cherry-Cheer, sign, cardboard, hanging, great graphics, "Drink...It's Good," 1920s, 7" x 11", EX, $210.00 B. Courtesy of Muddy River Trading Co./Gary Metz.

---

**Campbell Brand Coffee,** pail, tin, litho, with wire handles, camels on desert, 4-lb., EX ...................................................$75.00 B

**Campbell Kids,** bank, cast iron, 4¼" x 3¼" x 2", 1900s, EX...$175.00 C

**Campbell's Coffee,** tin, with bail type handle, desert scene with camels and men, from Bloomington, IL, 4-lb., EX ..............$75.00 B

**Campbell's Soup,** cookie jar, ceramic with the Campbell Kids, 1991, EX....................................................................$45.00 D

**Campbell's Soup,** pocket mirror, advertising of soup can on front, 1¾" x 2¾", EX .....................................................$225.00 C

**Campbell's Soup,** potholder, with Campbell's kids on surface, G.$15.00 D

**Campbell's Soup,** sign, tin, "Ready In a Jiffy," Campbell's kid, 17½" x 11½", EX .....................................................$175.00 C

**Campbell's Soup,** thermometer, porcelain, tomato soup can with dial-type thermometer in center of can, great graphics, 7"W x 12"H x 1¼"D, EX.....$1,500.00 C

**Campfire Marshmallows,** tin, campfire scene, 8" x 2¼", EX ....$95.00 C

**Campfire Marshmallows,** tin, round container with lid, "the original food," G ...................................................................$15.00 D

**Canada Dry Beverages,** sign, porcelain, with logo at left of message, 24" x 7", NM.......................................................$135.00 B

**Canada Dry Ginger Ale,** truck, tin, litho, friction, by Rasko, product on side of delivery style truck, 1950s, NM..................$225.00 C

**Canada Dry,** clock, light-up, Pam Clock Co., 15½" x 15½", VG..$95.00 B

**Canada Dry,** door push, with bottle in hand, embossed, "The best of them all," EX ................................................................$125.00 C

Cherry Smash, bottle topper, cardboard, "Our Nation's Beverage," 1920s, EX, $70.00 B.
*Courtesy of Muddy River Trading Co./Gary Metz.*

Chevrolet Trucks, poster, paper, "Advance Design," 50" x 38½", G, $150.00 C.

Chevrolet, poster, cardboard, Impala, 34½" x 20½", VG, $45.00 C.

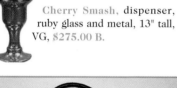

Cherry Smash, dispenser, ruby glass and metal, 13" tall, VG, $275.00 B.

Chevrolet, sign, masonite, die cut, chain-hung emblem, 21" x 9½", 1950s, EX, $350.00 C.

Chevrolet, clock, "Super Service," 15⅛" x 15⅛", VG, $310.00 B.

Chicago Kahn Bros., display, tin, clothing, 17" x 14" x 11", VG, $80.00 B.

Chew STAG Tobacco, cutter, EX, $150.00 C.

**Canada Dry**, sign, cardboard, ginger ale and club soda bottles, 28" x 34", VG ..................................................$35.00 D

**Canada Dry**, sign, porcelain, "Drink Canada Dry Beverages" message in both script and block, 1941, 35" x 12", EX ............$175.00 C

**Canada Dry**, sign, tin, double-sided, flange, shield logo, "Drink," 17½" x 14½", EX..............................................$160.00 B

**Canada Dry**, truck, toy, with Canada Dry cases on side, 8" x 3" x 5", EX ..................................................................$145.00 C

**Canadian Club 5¢ Cigar**, sign, cardboard, man with product, 21" x 13½", NM .................................................................$50.00 B

**Canadian National Telegraph and Cable Office**, sign, porcelain, flange, EX ....................................................................$365.00 D

**Canadian Northern Express**, sign, porcelain, double-sided, 26" x 14", G ..........................................................................$850.00 C

**Candee Brand Boots**, salesman sample of rubber high top boots, 5¼" x 3" x 1", NM..............................................................$125.00 C

**Candee Rubbers**, sign, cardboard, hanging, puppy being chased by young girl, 10½" x 12½", NM....................................$85.00 B

**Candee Shoes**, sign, cardboard, from McCord Rubber Co., Chicago, Ill., kids playing with kittens, 1910s, 10" x 12½", EX ..................................................................................$165.00 B

**Candy Bros., Fruit Juice Tablets**, serving tray, tin, litho, bottles of product, "Always Fresh," 13¾" x 16¾", EX.....................$925.00 B

Chicago Motor Club, courtesy car marquee, glass with reverse painted information, 14½" x 8" x 4", EX, $300.00 B.

Chico's Ice Cream, sign, porcelain, 36" wide, G, $80.00 B.

Chief Garden Tractors & Implements, sign, metal, double-sided, painted, flange, with Indian, 17⅝" x 13⅜", G, $115.00 B.

Chief Watta Pop, lollipop holder, molded plaster Indian head holds 17 lollipops, VG, $370.00 B.

Christo, dispenser, ceramic, barrel shape, 12" long, VG, $795.00 C.

Cities Service Koolmotor, sign, tin, double-sided, "The Perfect Pennsylvania Oil," both sides shown, 20¾" x 12", VG, $550.00 B.

Canoe Club, sign, cardboard, in metal frame, "Once You Try It-You'll Always Buy It," 30" x 14", VG ................................$65.00 B

Canuck 28 Gauge, shell box, black powder, 3¼" x 3¼" x 2½", EX .................................................................$95.00 C

Capital Brand Coffee, tin, with wooden knob bail handle, from the Atwood Co., 10-lb., EX ....................................$200.00 B

Carborundum Brand Sharpening Stones, banner, canvas, litho, three men sharpening different implements, NOS, 28" x 40", NM ................................................$150.00 C

Carborundum/Aloxite Grinding Wheels, sign, canva, litho, workman holding a chisel in workshop, products at bottom, NOS, 28" x 40", EX ........................................$135.00 C

Cardinal Beer, tip tray, metal, round, "The Beer with the Real Hop Flavor," red-haired woman with bouquet of flowers, 4⅛" dia., EX................................................$110.00 B

Cardui, fan, woman on couch on front side, product messages on reverse side, wooden handle, EX ........................$15.00 D

Careystone Asbestos Shingles, sign, metal, painted, embossed, 29" x 11½", EX.................................................$85.00 D

Careystone Asbestos Shingles, sign, metal, painted, embossed, 29" x 11½", VG.................................................$65.00 D

Carlsberg, sign, porcelain, foreign, "calling for," glass of beer with a full head of foam, G .........................................$75.00 C

Carmacks Barber Shop, combination wrench and screwdriver, premium, give-away, NM .........................................$35.00 C

Carmen Condom, tin, litho, pin-up girl with fan and shawl, good strong colors, 1⅝" x ⅝", EX................................$170.00 B

Carnation Cigars, tin, paper label with carnation flower, from League Cigar Co., 25 ct., EX................................$70.00 B

Citizens Bank and Trust Co., bank, metal, spring loaded lever allows coins to be placed in slot and then blasts them into the rocket, opens at bottom, 11½" tall, VG, $55.00 C. *Courtesy of B.J. Summers.*

City National Bank Bldg., souvenir, china, "Made In Germany" stamp on bottom and likeness of bank on front, gold trim, 1910s, 5" tall, EX, $75.00 C. *Courtesy of B.J. Summers.*

City National Bank, bank, metal, with round bail handle, front brass customer information label, key opens on bottom, 3½" x 2" x 1½", VG, $95.00 C. *Courtesy of B.J. Summers.*

Clark Bar, thermometer, wooden, "Clark Bar, join the millions," 1920s, 5½" x 21½", NM, $1,550.00 B. *Courtesy of Muddy River Trading Co./Gary Metz.*

Clark, razor, celluloid and metal, in original box, box shows Bob Clark Paducah, KY, Bob's High Test, razor is marked "Bob Clark Bar Sup, Paducah, KY" and "Bob's High Test," 6" long closed, EX, $65.00 C. *Courtesy of B.J. Summers.*

Clark, razor, celluloid and metal with brass ends, in the likeness of an Indian with full headress, no box, razor is marked, Bob Clark, Paducah, Ky, Made In Germany, and Chief Paduke, 6" long closed, EX, $55.00 C. *Courtesy of B.J. Summers.*

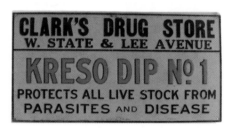

Clark's Drug Store, sign, metal, Kreso Dip No.1, 23" x 12", VG, $75.00 B.

---

**Carnation Fresh Milk,** sign, porcelain, die cut, milk bottle, 22" x 23", EX .................................................................$275.00 C

**Carnation Gum,** tip tray, tin, "Chew Dorne's," "Taste the Smell," litho, with carnations, 4⅜" dia., EX ...................................$475.00 B

**Carnation Gum,** tip tray, tin, litho, Carnation Chewing Gum with carnations, 4¼" dia., EX....................................................$210.00 B

**Carnation Ice Cream,** hat badge, die cut, painted, with ice cream sundae in center, 2" x 2", NM ..............................$775.00 B

**Carnation Ice Cream,** sign, porcelain, single-sided, die cut, 22" x 23", VG ................................................................$550.00 B

**Carnation Malted Milk,** container, metal, milk glass with lid and fired-on lettering, 6½" dia. x 8½", EX ................................$210.00 B

**Carnation Milk,** sign, cardboard, die cut, milk bottle in center, "Carnation Fresh Milk," 24" x 24", EX..............................$325.00 C

**Carnation Milk,** sign, paper, litho, Perry Triplets, 36¾" x 22½", VG ........................................................................$550.00 B

**Carter Carburetor,** globe, milk glass, light-up, iron construction with product name 13½" x 27½", red, EX ......................................$575.00 C

**Carter the Great,** poster, cardboard, framed by the Otis Lithograph Co., Cleveland, Ohio, made in U.S.A/4630-M, 42" x 78", NM .........$650.00 D

Clark's Teaberry Gum, sign, "That Mountain Tea Flavor," 11¾" x 8¾", EX, $350.00 B.

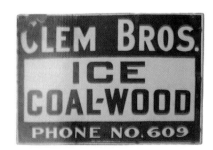

Clem Bros Ice, sign, porcelain, Coal-Wood, 20" x 14", F, $10.00 B.

Cleo Cola, sign, cardboard, cut-out, pretty girl with the product, art deco style, 25" x 26", 1939, G, $300.00 B.
*Courtesy of Muddy River Trading Co./Gary Metz.*

Cleveland and Buffalo, tip tray, metal, oval, "The Great Ship Seeand-bee...C&B Line," with ship at sea, 6¼"L, VG, $375.00 C.

Clicquot Club, clock, glass and metal, electric light up, Eskimo logo, "time to serve," 1960s, 15" sq., VG, $200.00 B.

Clicquot Club, clock, metal and glass, telechron electric light up, Eskimo holding a bottle, round, 1950s, VG, $150.00 B.

Clicquot Club Kola, sign, porcelain, "Enjoy," Eskimo with bottle, 1940 – 50s, 30" x 12", EX, $200.00 B.

**Carter's Alma Infants Underwear,** sign, cardboard, die cut, easel back, young child over message, 14" x 15½", EX ............$423.00 B

**Carter's Infants Underwear,** sign, cardboard, easel back, die cut, infant over message, 14" x 16", EX................................$220.00 B

**Carter's Infants Underwear,** sign, cardboard, easel back, young child playing with tin climbing monkey, 14½" x 18¾", EX ..........$400.00 B

**Carter's Ink,** sign, tin, self-framing, man writing, litho by Kaufmann & Strauss, 1900s, 25" x 19", VG......................................$500.00 D

**Carter's Inky Racer,** box, with original bottle and instructions, black runner on front, 3" x 3" x 1", EX ............................$55.00 C

**Carter's Overalls,** sign, porcelain, speeding train, 15" x 6", EX .$1,500.00 D

**Carter's Union Suits for Boys,** sign, cardboard, die cut, easel back, young boy with scooter, 14" x 15½", NM ..............................$341.00 B

**Carter's Union Suits for Girls,** sign, cardboard, die cut, easel back, young girl writing on blackboard, 1910, 15" x 14", NM......$645.00 B

**Carter's Wash & Wear Overalls,** sign, cardboard, standup, "Guaranteed A New Pair If You Are Not Satisfied," 20" x 14", EX.....$115.00 D

**Carter's White Lead Paint,** thermometer, porcelain, message panel at top of scale and paint bucket at bottom, 1910s, 7" x 28", EX.$275.00 D

**Casablanca Fan Co.,** sign, porcelain, company logo and message "Authorized Dealer," 20" x 16", EX ....................................$500.00 D

**Casarets,** sign, paper, litho, candy cathartic, "Best for the Bowels," 41" x 28", VG....................................................................$335.00 B

**Cascarets Candy Carthartis,** sign, cardboard, die cut, lady sleeping on cloud, 26" x 20", VG....................................................$85.00 D

**Case,** dislpay, cast iron, eagle, 57½" tall, G ...................$1,975.00 C

**Case,** sign, porcelain and neon, double-sided, eagle on globe, 72" x 40" x 12", EX ...............................................................$2,500.00 D

**Case,** sign, porcelain, light up, metal housing and neon letters, 12½" x 20" x 72", VG ................................................................$805.00 B

CLIX, display, barber shop barber pole, "Clix Always Clicks, Smooth Shaving," lights up, 17½" x 26", NM, $400.00 D. *Courtesy of Rare Bird Antique Mall/Jon & Joan Wright.*

Cloverbloom Butter, display, cardboard, die cut, store with usual dairy scenes, 31¼" x 16¼", EX, $210.00 B. *Courtesy of Autopia Advertising Auctions.*

Cloverdale Soft Drinks, thermometer, dial reading, 12" dia., VG, $275.00 B.

Cloverleaf Farm and Home Store, mirror, metal and glass, designed to fit on a car visor before they were standard equipment, 1930s, 3½" x 4¼", VG, $85.00 C. *Courtesy of B.J. Summers.*

Cobb Invincible, cigars, full box in original unopened packages, from the Paducah, KY, factory, featuring the McDonald image of Irvin S. Cobb, 1920 – 30s, 50 count, NM, $350.00 C. *Courtesy of B.J. Summers.*

Coca-Cola, ad, *National Geographic,* Edgar Bergen and Charlie McCarthy, 1950, G, $15.00 C. *Courtesy of B.J. Summers.*

Coca-Cola, ad, *National Geographic* back page, "Christmas together ... Have a Coca-Cola," 1945, 6¾" x 10", G, $8.00 C. *Courtesy of B.J. Summers.*

---

**Casewell's National Crest Coffee,** tin, key-wound, litho, 1-lb., EX ........................................................................$30.00 B

**Castle Hall Cigar, D.S. Erb & Co.,** sign, tin, self-framing, litho, 37½" x 13", EX..............................................................$220.00 B

**Castle Hall Cigar,** sign, tin, self-framing, 37½" x 13", VG .$185.00 B

**Castle Hall,** sign, cardboard, "The New Arrivals/Twin Cigars," 12" x 10", EX ...............................................................$85.00 D

**Castrol Motor Oil,** thermometer, porcelain, self-framing, scale type, 9" x 30", VG ....................................................$175.00 B

**Castrol,** sign, tin, "Authorized Dealer," 18" dia, EX...............$100.00 C

**Castrol,** sign, tin, die cut, 18" x 23½", VG .........................$75.00 B

**Castrol,** thermometer, woman with quart of product, 8¼" x 6", EX .........................................................................$60.00 B

**Caswell's Coffee,** tin, litho, woman in cameo center, 3-lb., EX..$135.00 C

**Cat-Tex Soles,** clock, light-up, black cat in center, 14" dia., F..$135.00 C

**Cat-Tex Soles,** clock, reverse painted, light-up, cat on cover, "We rebuild shoes, like new at less than ½ new cost," 14½" dia., G...............................................................$275.00 C

**Catarct Pilsener Beer,** tray, metal, serving size with deep sides, 12" dia, EX...................................................................$85.00 C

**Caterpillar,** watch fob, metal, dozer on one side and earth scraper on reverse, EX ................................................................$35.00 C

**Caterpiller,** clock, metal and glass light up, partial message reads "Time To Buy," 15" dia, VG.............................................$400.00 D

**Cattaraugus Knife,** sign, cardboard, die cut, by the Cattaraugus Cutlery Co., Little Valley, N.Y., 12" x 15", EX.........................................$90.00 B

Coca-Cola, poster, cardboard, single-sided, litho, woman and daughter at table, "and Coke too," 35½" x 55", VG, $125.00 C.

Coca-Cola, art, original, canvas, woman wearing summer hat and blouse with a sandwich and bottle of Coke, 46" x 21", VG, $275.00 B.

Coca-Cola, ashtray, bronze colored, depicting 50th Anniversary in center, 1950s, EX, $75.00 C. *Courtesy of Mitchell collection.*

Coca-Cola, ashtray, chrome, this is the chromed version of the Bakelite ashtray that most of us are familiar with, believed to have been produced for use in coke executives offices, 1930s, NM, $1,200.00 B.

Coca-Cola, ashtrays, set of four, ruby red, price should be doubled if set is in original box, 1950s, EX, $425.00 C. *Courtesy of Mitchell collection.*

Coca-Cola, bank, metal, truck, still in original box, "Advertising Dept" on side, new, NM, $35.00 C. *Courtesy of Sam and Vivian Merryman.*

Coca-Cola, axe, "For Sportsmen," "Drink Coca-Cola," 1930, EX, $950.00 C. *Courtesy of Mitchell collection.*

---

**Cattaraugus Knife**, sign, cardboard, die cut, woodworker sharpening his Cattaraugus knife, Niagara Litho Co., 12¼" x 15¼", G...**$110.00 B**

**Cedarhurst Whiskey**, sign, tin, bear's head, 12" x 8", EX..**$475.00 C**

**Cel-Ray**, sign, tin, door plate with partial message that reads "Vitamin D Added," 1930 – 40s, 10", EX......................................**$75.00 C**

**Celluloid Starch**, sign, cardboard, "Mail Trade Marks to Premium Dept. Philadelphia," young girl ironing, 14" x 12½", EX....**$100.00 B**

**Centlivre Tonic**, sign, cardboard, "Builds up the system, gives strength and enjoyment to life...for sale here," serving worker with hospital attire, from Fort Wayne, Ind. Brewing Co., 22" x 12", EX..........................................................................**$350.00 C**

**Centlivre's Nickel Plate Beer**, poster, litho, dining car scene, in period frame, 26¾" x 31", VG ..........................................**$400.00 C**

**Central Brewing Co.**, tip tray, metal, round, "Highest Grades of Pure Lager, Ales & Porter," horse in center of tray, 4½" dia., EX...........................................................................................**$150.00 B**

**Central Union Cut Plug**, lunch pail, metal, gold lettering on red background, message reads "Central Union Cut Plug," VG.........**$120.00 D**

**Central Union**, tobacco pail, metal, lunchbox-size with wire handle on lid, 7" x 4½" x 4¼", EX ................................................**$175.00 C**

**Cer-ola**, sign, cardboard, couple at beach, 17" x 11", G....**$45.00 D**

**Cer-ola**, sign, cardboard, hanging, Prohibition, "A Triumph in Soft Drinks...Made by Kolb at Bay City, Mich.," 11" x 17", EX .....**$75.00 C**

**Ceresota Flour**, bill holder, metal and cardboard, image of Ceresota Boy, 6" x 3", EX ...............................................................**$155.00 D**

Coca-Cola, bank, plastic, church, "You'll feel right at home drinking Coca-Cola," EX, $135.00 C. *Courtesy of Sam and Vivian Merryman.*

Coca-Cola, bank, truck delivery box van with dynamic wave on side, NM, $35.00 C. *Courtesy of Sam and Vivian Merryman.*

Coca-Cola, belt, web construction with metal slide buckle that has the dynamic wave, and "Enjoy Coke" on front, 1960s, NM, $20.00 C. *Courtesy of Sam and Vivian Merryman.*

Coca-Cola, blotter, paper, with man on bicycle, 7¾" x 3½", EX, $150.00 B.

Coca-Cola, blotter, "Friendliest drink on earth" with bottle in hand and world globe, 1956, 8" x 4", NM, $35.00 C. *Courtesy of Sam and Vivian Merryman.*

Coca-Cola, border, paper, corrugated, full unused roll, baseball batter and "Major League Baseball," 1960s, EX, $35.00 C. *Courtesy of Sam and Vivian Merryman.*

Coca-Cola, border, paper, corrugated, Santa in chair, full unused roll, EX, $30.00 C. *Courtesy of Sam and Vivian Merryman.*

---

**Ceresota Flour,** match holder, barrel-style, young boy on top of barrel, in original box, 3" x 6", NM .....................................$500.00 B

**Ceresota Flour,** match holder, bread box-style, young boy sitting on stool on top of product, 3" x 6", EX ...............$375.00 C

**Ceresota Flour,** pinback, 1½" dia., EX ..........................................$55.00 C

**Ceresota Flour,** pocket mirror, metal and glass, Ceresota Boy on back side, 1910s, EX .............................................................$95.00 C

**Ceresota Flour,** puzzle, cardboard, partial message reads "The Flower of Flours," 1900s, 9" x 7", EX ................................$145.00 C

**Ceresota,** match holder in likeness of Ceresota boy on barrel, "Prize Bread Flour of the World," 2¼" x 5½", M............................$725.00 C

**Ceresota,** match holder, tin, litho, "Prize Bread Flour," young boy cutting loaf of bread, 5" H, EX .........................................$375.00 C

**Chadwick's Spool Cotton,** cabinet, wood, with six lettered drawers, 32" x 15", EX ....................................................................$625.00 D

**Chalmers-Motor Car Co.,** sign, cardboard, Detroit, Mich, U.S.A., 20" x 21", VG..................................................................$155.00 C

**Champagne Velvet Beer,** sign, tin over cardboard, fisherman holding small fish behind his back while his buddies show off larger catches, 19" x 14", VG ......................................$135.00 D

**Champagne Velvet Beer,** sign, tin over cardboard, fisherman running from two skunks while carrying his lunch, 19" x 14", VG.........$90.00 C

Coca-Cola, border, paper, Christmas light-up Coke truck, 1996, EX, $50.00 C. *Courtesy of Sam and Vivian Merryman.*

Coca-Cola, bottle, gold, 50th Anniversary 1899 – 1949, Everett Pidgeon, in bottle cradle, 1949, EX, $200.00 C. *Courtesy of Mitchell collection.*

Coca-Cola, bottle lamp, with cap and original marked brass base, very rare and highly desirable, 1920s, 20", NM, $7,200.00 B. *Courtesy of Muddy River Trading Co./Gary Metz.*

Coca-Cola, bottle, premix, 1920s, green, EX, $65.00 C. *Courtesy of B.J. Summers.*

Coca-Cola, bottle, straight sided block print bottle with large S on body and starting up neck, "Coca-Cola Bottling Co. Decatur, 9 oz., VG, $35.00 C. *Courtesy of Sam and Vivian Merryman.*

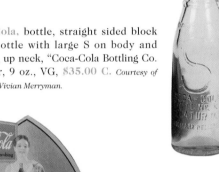

Coca-Cola, syrup can with paper label, red and white, 1940s, one gallon, EX, $300.00 D.

Coca-Cola, bottle topper, Bathing Girl, "Drink Coca-Cola Delicious and Refreshing," rare, 1929, VG, $1,800.00 B. *Courtesy of Gary Metz.*

---

**Champagne Velvet Beer,** sign, tin over cardboard, litho, man in stream fishing, 19½" x 14½", VG ......................................$160.00 B

**Champion Brewery,** serving tray, metal, pretty young lady, "Extra Brewed for Bottling," 14" x 17", EX ........................................$165.00 C

**Champion Implements,** calendar, paper, with products and tear sheets at bottom, 3½" x 6¼", 1902, NM..............................$195.00 B

**Champion Spark Plugs,** clock, steering wheel, 11½" dia., ..$375.00 D

**Champion Spark Plugs,** sign, cardboard, die cut, vintage race car driver with oversized spark plug, 14½" x 6", G............................$300.00 C

**Champion Spark Plugs,** sign, porcelain, single-sided, spark plug in center, 30" x 14", G.......................................................$135.00 B

**Champion Spark Plugs,** sign, reverse glass, spark plug, 10¼" x 13¼", EX ........................................................................$295.00 D

**Champion Spark Plugs,** sign, tin, embossed, "Cost Less, More Power," spark plug, 14¾" x 5⅜", NM ............................$595.00 C

**Champion,** sign, double-sided, flange, "dependable, Spark Plug Service," NOS, 18" x 12", '50s, NM .....................................$165.00 C

**Champlain Horse Nails,** calendar, paper board, litho, horse and rider, bottom tear sheets, 11" x 14", 1888, VG.................................$275.00 B

**Champlin Distributor Motor Oils,** sign, tin, single-sided, with wood frame, 59" x 29½", VG .........................................................$135.00 B

**Champlin Refining Co.,** sign, cardboard, with old man winter blowing cold wind on vintage touring car, 58½" x 28½", VG ..........$650.00 B

**Chappell's Ice Cream,** menu, celluloid, fountain and ice cream on front, 5" x 7¼", 1920s, NM......................................................$125.00 C

Coca-Cola, bottle topper, cardboard, die cut, girl with tray, three-dimensional, rare item, 1920s, 11½" x 14", NM, $2,600.00 B. *Courtesy of Muddy River Trading Co./Gary Metz.*

Coca-Cola, bottle topper, cardboard, six pack in food basket, 1950s, 8" x 7," EX, $550.00 C. *Courtesy of Bill Mitchell.*

Coca-Cola, bottle topper, plastic, "We let you see the bottle," 1950s, EX, $475.00 C. *Courtesy of Mitchell collection.*

Coca-Cola, bumper, sticker, Max Headroom pleading "Don't Say the 'P' Word," 1980s, EX, $10.00 C. *Courtesy of Sam and Vivian Merryman.*

Coca-Cola, sign, porcelain, button, "Drink Coca-Cola," 2' diameter, NM, $375.00 B. *Courtesy of Muddy River Trading Co./Gary Metz.*

Coca-Cola, calendar, 1963, reference edition with Santa Claus holding a bottle in middle of electric train display in front of Christmas tree with helicopter flying around his head, M, $50.00 C. *Courtesy of Mitchell collection.*

Coca-Cola, calendar top, bamboo, from the Coca-Cola Bottler in Herrin, Illinois, minus tear sheets, mountain scene and small village on water, difficult to locate good examples of this item, VG, $250.00 C. *Courtesy of Mitchell collection.*

---

**Chappell's Milk,** clock, metal and plastic, light-up, gold, red and yellow, 16" x 16", EX .......................................................$195.00 C

**Chariots,** condom tin, racing chariot on cover, 2⅛" x 1⅝" x ¼", EX .........................................................................$180.00 B

**Charles Denby Cigar,** display, cardboard, diecut, stand-up depicting a black boy drummer advertising the product, 17" x 29½", 1899, G .........................................................................$1,200.00 C

**Charles Denby Cigar,** sign, cardboard, die cut, black boy in bellman's uniform with a box of the product, "Dese Denby's sho tastes different from ordinary cigars," 12¼" H, VG.....................$250.00 B

**Charles Denby,** tip tray, metal, oval, "Where cigars are Made, Evansville, Ind.," factory in tray center, 6", EX ...........................$75.00 C

**Charles the Great Cigars,** sign, tin, litho, full box of the product, EX ...............................................................................$220.00 B

**Charles W. Cranshaw/Atlantic,** spoon, sterling and enamel, black man on handle, EX.........................................................$375.00 B

**Charter Oak Stoves,** trade card, cardboard, young courting couple, 3" x 4½", EX.......................................................................$9.00 C

**Chas A. Grove's Sons Whiskey,** serving tray, metal, two dogs at table smoking cigars, 14" sq, EX ......................................$525.00 C

**Chas A. Grove's Sons Whiskey,** tray, metal, Indian casing buffalo, 13¼" sq, VG .................................................................$700.00 D

Coca-Cola, calendar, perpetual, desk, showing day, month, and year, 1920, EX, $400.00 C.

Coca-Cola, calendar, fishtail top and replaceable bottom tear sheets, 1960s, EX, $475.00 B. *Courtesy of Muddy River Trading Co./Gary Metz.*

Coca-Cola, sign, porcelain, Canadian, "Fountain Service," 1935, 27" x 14", NM, $1,300.00 D. *Courtesy of Muddy River Trading Co./Gary Metz.*

Coca-Cola, can, waxed paper, a prototype can that was never put into production, dynamic wave contour, red, 12 oz., EX, $135.00 B. *Courtesy of Collectors Auction Services.*

Coca-Cola, card table, bottle in each corner, advertisement sheet under side of table boasts of the fact it's so strong it can hold a grownup standing on it, 1930, VG, $275.00 C. *Courtesy of Mitchell collection.*

Coca-Cola, carrier, metal, two bottle holder with sign on front "Enjoy Coca-Cola While You Shop, Place Bottles Here," 1950s, EX, $65.00 C. *Courtesy of Mitchell collection.*

Coca-Cola, carrier, metal, three case bottle rack with "Place Empties Here, Thank You" at top, red, G, $375.00 C. *Courtesy of Mike and Debbie Summers.*

---

**Chas. D. Kaier Co. Ltd, Mahanoy City, Pa.,** tip tray, metal, round, bottle in center of tray, 4⅛" dia., EX...................................$55.00 B

**Chas. P. Shipley Saddlery Co.,** clothes brush, premium in original box, 7" x 2" x 1½", EX....................................$35.00 C

**Chas. S. Higgins' Laundry Soap,** sign, cardboard, die cut, a black wash woman with a tub of clothes, 7" x 12", EX...............$300.00 C

**Chase & Sanborn Choice Quality Coffee,** tin, with small lid, 7¼" x 9¼", 4-lb., EX ................................................$175.00 C

**Chase & Sanborn Coffee,** poster, paper, older men discussing the world events in a rural grocery store, 1897, 20" x 23", EX...$175.00 C

**Chase & Sanborn Coffee,** tin, sample size with slip lid, "High Grade," NM.............................................................$45.00 D

**Chase & Sanborn Standard Java,** trade card, cardboard, cat being hugged by a little girl, EX .......................................$20.00 C

**Chase & Sanborn's Coffee,** tin, sample size, with original mailer box and letter from company, 2" T, EX............................$100.00 B

**Chase & Sanborn,** store bin, tin, with embossed lettering "Old Gov't Java" on front with litho birds, flowers, and stems, 1880s, 13" x 14" x 19", G...................................................$420.00 B

**Chase & Sanborn,** tin, litho, counter top store coffee bin promoting "Standard Java," 13" x 13" x 21", EX ....................................$295.00 D

**Chase and Sanborn Drip Grind Coffee,** tin, key-wound lid, 1-lb., F ..$15.00 D

**Chateau Quebec Tobacco,** tin, round, "a cool mellow pipe tobacco," F .........................................................$23.00 D

Coca-Cola, clock, counter, light-up, restored, 1950, $850.00 C. *Courtesy of Muddy River Trading Co./Gary Metz.*

Coca-Cola, clock, neon, counter, light-up, "Pause ... Drink Coca-Cola," showing bottle spotlighted, restored, rare and hard-to-find piece, 1930s, EX, $5,500.00 C. *Courtesy of Mitchell collection.*

Coca-Cola, clock, light-up, Pam Clock Co., Brooklyn 1 NY, U.S.A, green outside ring and red center, NOS, 15" dia., NM, $675.00 C.

Coca-Cola, clock, light-up, message board at bottom, 11" x 12", NM, $185.00 B. *Courtesy of Autopia Advertising Auctions.*

Coca-Cola, clock, metal, plastic message strip at top, light-up, 27" x 18½" x 4½", EX, $725.00 C.

Coca-Cola, clock, neon, rainbow panel from 9 to 3 o'clock, "Drink Coca-Cola, Sign of Good Taste," red and white, 1950s, 36" across, NM, $1,550.00 B. *Courtesy of Muddy River Trading Co./Gary Metz.*

Coca-Cola, clock, neon, spotlighted bottle at 6 o'clock, square, green wrinkle on outer case, 1930s, 16", EX, $825.00 B. *Courtesy of Muddy River Trading Co./Gary Metz.*

---

**Chattanooga & St. Louis**, spittoon, cast iron and porcelain, with raised lettering, EX.............................................$250.00 C

**Checker Taxi**, sign, cardboard, hanging, vintage car, 11" x 7", 1920s, EX .................................................$125.00 C

**Checkers Tobacco**, pocket tin, slip lid with checker board, 3" x 4½", EX.................................................$255.00 C

**Checkers**, match safe, tin, cough drops, litho, striker on base, 3" x 1½" x ¼", EX.............................................$55.00 C

**Cheer Up Beverages**, license plate attachment, tin, embossed, painted, 6" x 6¼", EX ..........................................$155.00 C

**Cheer Up Soda**, fan pull, cardboard, die cut, green bottle, EX..$22.00 D

**Cheer Up**, glass, "Drink," in spotlight, EX ...........................$35.00 B

**Cheerio Coffee**, can, tin, key-wound, litho, singing bird, 5" x 4", G.................................................................$190.00 B

**Cheerio**, sign, tin over cardboard, "It's Lewie's Refreshing Beverages I Want," man holding bottles of Cheerio, 11" x 8", F............$30.00 C

**Chef Baking Powder**, container, cardboard, paper label, pry lid, Montreal, 3" x 4½", EX .......................................$175.00 C

**Chef Coffee**, tin, litho, key-wound, chef on front, rare piece, Lee & Cady, Detroit, 1-lb., EX.......................................$500.00 B

**Chero-Cola**, blotter, cardboard, with partial message that reads "Drink Chero-Cola, There's None So Good," EX ...........$25.00 C

Coca-Cola, clock, glass, metal frame, "Drink Coca-Cola in bottles" in red center, original jumpstart motor, 1939 – 1942, EX, $550.00 B. *Courtesy of Muddy River Trading Co./Gary Metz.*

Coca-Cola, clock, telechron, red dot in hour positions with white background and white wings, 1948, 36" wing span, VG, $475.00 C. *Courtesy of Mitchell collection.*

Coca-Cola, coin purse, engraved gold lettering, "When thirsty try a bottle," "Coca-Cola Bottling Company" with a paper label bottle to the left of lettering, 1907, maroon, EX, $100.00 C. *Courtesy of Mitchell collection.*

Coca-Cola, cooler, glascock junior size, complete with cap catcher, 1929, EX, $1,800.00 C. *Courtesy of Mitchell collection.*

Coca-Cola, cooler, metal, glascock salesman's sample, complete with under cooler case storage, NM, $1,500.00 C. *Courtesy of Mitchell collection.*

Coca-Cola, cooler, counter dispenser, salesman's sample, original carrying case and complete presentation unit, light inside lights up glasses, very rare, 1960s, 4½"w x 6½"d x 6¾"h, EX, $2,500.00 B. *Courtesy of Muddy River Trading Co./Gary Metz.*

Coca-Cola, cooler, metal, salesman sample, these were used to carry into the general store, feed stores, and anywhere a Coke could be sold. The business owner could see the product without the need for the salesman to carry the full-sized item. Originally these items had a carrying case and informational booklets inside the cooler, but most were discarded when they were given to kids to use as toys. Highly sought after items, 12" wide, G, $1,250.00 – $3,800.00 B.

---

**Chero-Cola,** pencil, wooden, square shaped with full eraser, "Drink Chero-Cola in Bottles 5¢," NM ...............................................$5.00 C

**Chero-Cola,** sign, cardboard, "Drink Chero-Cola In The Twist Bottle," landscape scene, EX .....................................................$30.00 D

**Chero-Cola,** sign, metal, painted, "Drink, There's none so good," sunburst and bottle to left side of sign, G ...........................$75.00 D

**Chero-Cola,** sign, metal, painted, "Drink...There's none so good," sunburst and bottle to left side of sign, G ...........................$75.00 D

**Chero-Cola,** sign, paper, "In The Twist Bottle," 24" x 18½", VG ...........................................................................................$525.00 C

**Cherrio Coffee,** tin, bird in a top hat, 1 lb., EX...................$55.00 D

**Cherry BloDrink,** "Cherry Blossoms A Blooming Good Drink," 1920s, 8" x 3", EX.............................................................$25.00 D

**Cherry Blossom Shoe Polish,** sign, tin, three kittens in shoes, 17¾" x 27¾", NM ......................................................................$195.00 C

Coca-Cola, cooler, metal, embossed name and lettering, single lift top, good size for home use, 34" high, EX, $475.00 B.

Coca-Cola, sign, glass and metal, light up, counter, "Please Pay When Served," red and white, 20" x 12", 1948, VG, $2,000.00 B. *Courtesy of Muddy River Trading Co./Gary Metz.*

Coca-Cola, sign, metal and glass, light-up, counter, waterfall motion, "Pause and Refresh," 1950s, EX, $1,150.00 B. *Courtesy of Muddy River Trading Co./Gary Metz.*

Coca-Cola, sign, metal and cast iron, crossing guard, reverse side has image of bottle, reproductions of these with the MEXican iron bases seem to be everywhere, most of the reproductions seem to be priced in the $400.00 – 500.00 range. Due to the repros prices on the originals have a wide variation, detection of the repros can usually be found in the thickness of the metal and the size and lettering on the base. If you're buying one to use as a driveway ornament a repro will work fine, but always beware if you're looking for the real deal, 1950s, 63" tall, F, $850.00 B.

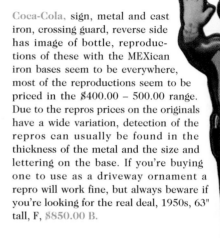

Coca-Cola, cuff links, gold finish, "Enjoy Coca-Cola," glass shaped, 1970s, EX, $65.00 C. *Courtesy of Mitchell collection.*

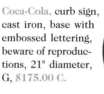

Coca-Cola, curb sign, cast iron, base with embossed lettering, beware of reproductions, 21" diameter, G, $175.00 C.

**Cherry Blossoms** sign, tin, children sitting on a balance supported by a real glass bottle, 1920s, 10" tall, EX .............**$1,425.00 C**

**Cherry Blossoms,** blotter, cardboard, oval, logo with flowers and bottles, 1920s, 8" x 3", EX....................................**$23.00 D**

**Cherry Blossoms,** bottle topper, tin, litho, die cut, youngsters on sides, 11½" x 6¼", 1920s, EX .......................................**$495.00 D**

**Cherry Blossoms,** serving tray, metal, bottle and wording "In Bottles Only," VG ....................................................**$95.00 C**

**Cherry Blush,** sign, tin, cherries on a branch, "Drink Cherry Blush...Cherries Only Rival," 1920s, 9" x 6", EX ........**$475.00 C**

**Cherry Brand,** pocket mirror, celluloid and metal, "Fine Chocolates and Bon Bons," ornate gold handle and frame, 2" x 4", VG..........................................................................**$90.00 B**

**Cherry Cheer,** sign, cardboard, "Cheer Up...1/2¢...It's Good," 1920s, 14" x 10", EX.....................................................**$295.00 C**

**Cherry Cheer,** sign, cardboard, hanging, "Drink...It's Good," 1920s, 7" x 11", G .........................................................**$175.00 C**

**Cherry Chic,** syrup dispenser, ceramic, in shape of ball with flared bottom, 10" tall, VG.....................................**$6,500.00 D**

**Cherry Smash,** bottle, cardboard, topper, "Our Nation's Beverage," 1920s, VG..........................................................**$50.00 C**

**Cherry Smash,** sign, cardboard string hanger, glass and a trail of Cherries, 11½" x 6", EX.............................................**$75.00 C**

**Cherry Smash,** sign, cardboard, reverse glass decals over the cardboard in oval frame, 10" x 12", NM....................**$345.00 C**

Coca-Cola, curb sign, metal, double-sided, fishtail sign over bottle, 22½" x 33" x 24", VG, $425.00 C.

Coca-Cola, sign, cardboard, embossed, die cut, "Delicious and Refreshing, at Soda Fountains," children being instructed by the rabbit, very rare item, 6½" x 7", 1890s, EX, $16,000.00 B.
*Courtesy of Muddy River Trading Co./Gary Metz.*

Coca-Cola, dispenser, counter-top, Dole, white and red, 14½" x 11½" x 25", G, $675.00 B. *Courtesy of Muddy River Trading Co./Gary Metz.*

Coca-Cola, dispenser, porcelain base, frosted glass body and lid, white lettering on red base, 1920s, 17" tall, NM, $6,200.00 B. *Courtesy of Muddy River Trading Co./Gary Metz.*

Coca-Cola, display, cardboard and metal, mechanical cowboy that's designed as a point of sale item, hands and eyes move, 1950s, 36" x 60", VG, $1,300.00 B.

Coca-Cola, display, cardboard, double-sided, mechanical cowboy for store point of sale use, 1950s, 72" tall, VG, $1,200.00 B

Coca-Cola, door pull plate, porcelain, "Pull ... Refresh Yourself," button facsimile at bottom, green, red, and white, 4" x 8", 1950s, EX, $450.00 B.

**Cherry Sparkle**, sign, tin, embossing of a man and his hat, 1930 – 40s, 13" x 6", EX..................$425.00 C

**Chest-O-Silver**, oats box, litho, treasure chest, from Keokok, LA, 2-lb. 10-oz., EX .................$60.00 B

**Chesterfield Cigarette**, sign, cardboard, die cut, college couple enjoying a smoke, "Chesterfield...Sound Off For...Much Milder," 1940 – 50s, 11½" x 16", EX.................$25.00 D

**Chesterfield Cigarette**, thermometer, with embossing and self-framing, 5¾" x 13½", VG.................$110.00 B

**Chesterfield Cigarette**, tin, flat, fifties, hinged, G .............$15.00 D

**Chesterfield Cigarettes**, ashtray, metal, in shape and likeness of a cigarette package, VG .................$22.00 D

**Chesterfield Cigarettes**, banner, paper, heavy with graphics of cigarette packages, 42" x 19", VG.................$165.00 D

**Chesterfield Cigarettes**, door push, porcelain, with pack of cigarettes in center, 1920 – 30s, 4" x 9", EX .................$175.00 D

**Chesterfield Cigarettes**, sign, cardboard, Betty Grable, 21" x 22", EX.................$125.00 C

**Chesterfield Cigarettes**, sign, cardboard, George Burns and Gracie Allen working around a radio microphone, 22" x 21", 1940s, EX.................$335.00 C

**Chesterfield Cigarettes**, sign, cardboard, heavy, band leaders Fred Waring and Henry James, 21" x 11", VG .................$85.00 D

Coca-Cola, door push, porcelain, "Refresh Yourself," button artwork, green, red, and white, 4" x 8", 1950s, NM, $525.00 B. *Courtesy of Muddy River Trading Co./Gary Metz.*

Coca-Cola, door pushes, identical, fishtail design, "Drink Coca-Cola Be Really Refreshed," 1960s, NM, $875.00 B. *Courtesy of Muddy River Trading Co./Gary Metz.*

Coca-Cola, door push, porcelain, "Ice Cold Coca-Cola In Bottles" on front with "Thank You, Call Again" on reverse side, white lettering on red background, 1930s, 25" x 3¼", NM, $475.00 B. *Courtesy of Muddy River Trading Co./Gary Metz.*

Coca-Cola, door push, porcelain and wrought iron, "Drink Coca-Cola," 1930s, EX, $425.00 C. *Courtesy of Mitchell collection.*

Coca-Cola, clock, leather, boudoir, bottle-shaped with clock face in center of body, "Drink Bottled...So Easily Served," 1910, 3" x 8", G, $1,500.00 B. *Courtesy of Muddy River Trading Co./Gary Metz*

Coca-Cola, sign, metal, button, with curved sides, "Drink," 12" dia., white lettering on red, NM, $350.00 C.

Coca-Cola, mirror with thermometer at upper left, with silhouette girl panel at bottom, "Drink Coca-Cola In Bottles," 1939, 10" x 14", VG, $450.00 B.

**Chesterfield Cigarettes,** sign, metal, die cut, flange, "Buy...Here," packages under message, 11¾" x 16½", VG.........................$45.00 D

**Chesterfield Cigarettes,** sign, metal, painted, double-sided, flange, cigarette packages, 11¾" x 16½", EX ..........................................$95.00 C

**Chesterfield Cigarettes,** sign, paper, woman opening a pack of cigarettes, 18" x 24", EX ....................................................................$85.00 C

**Chesterfield Cigarettes,** sign, porcelain, flange, double-sided, "Buy Chesterfield Here," 1950s, 17" x 11" x 1½", EX.....$145.00 B

**Chesterfield Cigarettes,** sign, tin, painted with tobacco leaves and cigarette pack, 19" x 29", EX...............................................$45.00 D

**Chesterfield Cigarettes,** thermometer, cigarette pack and tobacco leaves, 6" x 13½", G..............................................................$75.00 C

**Chesterfield Cigarettes,** tip tray, metal, "They Satisfy," with product in center of tray, 6½" L, G..................................................$65.00 B

**Chesterfield,** sign, metal, die cut, painted, flange, "Buy...Here," package at top of sign, 12" x 15", EX .................................$75.00 D

**Chevrolet Motor Cars,** calendar, early touring car in front of house with large porch, 1920, F .................................................$175.00 C

**Chevrolet Motor Cars,** calendar, paper, farm scene with family, 1920, 16" x 31", EX .........................................................$155.00 C

**Chevrolet,** bank, cardboard, Chevy logo and both a car and truck, EX...................................................................................$35.00 C

**Chevrolet,** coin, metal, commerative for the 1954 Corvette, EX .$20.00 C

**Chevrolet,** pen and pencil set by Parker, "The Heartbeat of America," EX ...................................................................................$25.00 D

**Chevrolet,** postcard, cardboard, standard size, divided back, unused postally, front side has real photo of a 1939 four door Chevrolet, 1939, 5½" x 3½", NM...............................................................$9.00 C

Coca-Cola, vending machine, "Drink, In Bottles," successor to the table-top 27, much sought after for home use because of their compact size, white on red, restored, 1950s, 25½" W x 52" H x 17½" D, NM, $2,300.00 C. *Courtesy of Patrick's Collectibles.*

Coca-Cola, sign, iron frame, "Drink," 24" dia. with a 16" metal button on one side and a 10" button on reverse side, VG, $675.00 B.

Coca-Cola, fountain dispenser, "Drink...ice cold," white on red, NM, $825.00 D. *Courtesy of Patrick's Collectibles.*

Coca-Cola, sign, masonite, "Drink," bottle in spotlight at bottom of diamond, made by Evans-Glenn Co., Marietta, GA, Made In USA, 12-46, 1946, 48" x 48", G, $695.00 D.

Coca-Cola, sign, metal, painted, self-framing, "Drink," couple at right of message, 1940s, 33½" x 12", NM, $650.00 C.

Coca-Cola, driver's cap with round "Drink" patch and hard bill, hats like this are becoming hard to locate, EX, $125.00 C. *Courtesy of Sam and Vivian Merryman.*

Coca-Cola, festoon, cardboard, Bathing Girls, total of 5 pieces, hard to find, 1946, 14' long, EX, $1,700.00 B.

---

**Chevrolet,** poster, paper, "Guardian Maintenance," 17" x 44", EX ..........................................................$105.00 B

**Chevrolet,** sign, cardboard, die cut, "Bow Tie," 30" x 10¾",...$80.00 B

**Chevrolet,** sign, masonite, die cut, chain-hung emblem, 21" x 9½", 1950s, VG.......................................................$275.00 C

**Chevrolet,** sign, metal, die cut, bow tie, 20½" x 7", VG.....$450.00 B

**Chevrolet,** sign, metal, die cut, owl, light up, "For Economical Transportation," 22" x 34", EX..........................................$775.00 C

**Chevrolet,** sign, porcelain, double-sided, "Sales & Service," 28" x 40", EX.....................................................................$225.00 C

**Chevrolet,** sign, tin, painted arrow pointing to the service area, 76" x 45", VG ...................................................................$225.00 C

**Chevron Supreme Gasoline,** patch, cloth, for sleeve, 2¾" dia., G ..........................................................................$10.00 C

**Chevron,** poster, paper, framed, 43" x 57", VG .................$125.00 C

**Chevron,** sign, tin, painted, 7¼" dia., EX..........................$100.00 C

**Chew STAG Tobacco,** cutter, G .........................................$95.00 D

**Chickencock Whiskey,** container, tin, key-wound, Distillers Corp. Limited with brewery on reverse, rooster on front panel, scarce item, 4¼" x 3" x 7½", 1931, EX.................................................................$350.00 C

**Chiclets,** container, tin, countertop, litho, "Help Yourself," featuring your favorite flavor, EX ....................................................$115.00 B

**Chiclets,** sign, tin, die cut, monkey, 1910s, EX.............$1,100.00 D

Coca-Cola, festoon, cardboard, Girl's Heads, 5 piece total, 1951, 7' long, EX, $1,600.00 B.

Coca-Cola, festoon, cardboard, lily pads, 5 piece, 1935, EX, $2,600.00 B. *Courtesy of Muddy River Trading Co./Gary Metz.*

Coca-Cola, festoon, cardboard, Locket, 5 pieces, woman in open locket, 1939, 11' long, VG, $800.00 B.

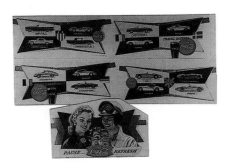

Coca-Cola, festoon, cardboard, Sports Car, 5 piece, 1958, 11" long, EX, $1,000.00 B.

Coca-Cola, festoon, cardboard, Square Dance, 5 pieces of dancers, 11" long, 1957, EX, $1,300.00 B.

Coca-Cola, festoon, cardboard, State Birds, in original envelope, 1956, 10' long, VG, $900.00 B.

Coca-Cola, festoon, cardboard, Travel, 6 pieces with various traveling signs, 1954, 10' long, EX, $750.00 B.

**Chief Beer,** label, paper, Indian in full headress, 1930s, EX ......................................................................$20.00 C

**Chief Oshkosh,** cigar box, wooden, with Indian on inside cover wearing top hat, 1916, 50-count, EX..................................$70.00 B

**Chief Watta Pop,** display, countertop, shaped like an Indian head in full war bonnet with locations for the pops immediately behind the bonnet, 8½" x 5" x 9½", EX......................................$500.00 C

**Chief Watta Pop,** lollipop holder, plaster, lollipop, Indian chief with headdress that holds 17 lollipops, VG..................$400.00 C

**Chocolate Honey Dairy Drink,** sign, paper, young black girl, 7" x 18", 1940s, EX..............................................................$65.00 C

**Chocolate Sundae,** sign, tin, die cut, embossed, sundae, 15" x 24", NM ................................................................$275.00 C

**Choctaw Rentals-Service,** sign, porcelain, Indian head in spotlight, 10" x 10", EX .....................................................$185.00 C

**Chore Boy Sponges and Scouring Pads,** toy, vinyl, in shape of Chore Boy standing on a sponge, 1991, 6" tall, EX.............$25.00 C

**Christian Feigenspan Brewing Co.,** serving tray, metal, woman with red ribbon in hair, 13¼" dia., EX ...............................$85.00 D

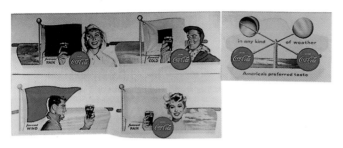

Coca-Cola, festoon, cardboard, Weather, 5 pieces, whirly wind item is center piece, 1956, 12' long, EX, $1,200.00 B.

Coca-Cola, festoons, wooden, three-piece set manufactured by Kay Displays, 1930s, 37" x 10" center, 9" x 11½" end pieces, NM, $2,800.00 B.
*Courtesy of Muddy River Trading Co./Gary Metz.*

Coca-Cola, sign, tin, flange fishtail, double-sided, red on white and green, 1960s, 18" x 15", VG, $325.00 C.

Coca-Cola, game, girl sitting in field, 1974, M, $20.00 D.

Coca-Cola, golf bag, vinyl, items such as this are usually made under license of Coke by another company strictly for the retail market. As a general rule serious collectors do not place much value on these items, 36" tall, VG, $15.00 B.

Coca-Cola, game box, contains two decks of 1943 cards unopened, plus marbles, dominos, chess, and checkers, 1940s, NM, $475.00 D. *Courtesy of Muddy River Trading Co./Gary Metz.*

Coca-Cola, shade, leaded glass, early reproduction item, 16" dia., EX, $200.00 B.

**Christmas Plum Pudding Sundae,** poster, paper, Santa Claus examining a sundae, 20¾" x 9", EX ............................................$140.00 B

**Christy Bros. Animal Show,** poster, heavy paper, animals and large crowds, 28" x 42", G............................................$500.00 D

**Chrysler,** sign, metal, painted, flange, "MoPar Parts," 23¾" x 16¾", black, orange on yellow, EX...............................................$225.00 D

**Chrysler-Plymouth Sales & Service License,** topper, metal, bot logos, VG ............................................................................$45.00 C

**Chum's,** tip tray, metal, round man in tux seated at table with product and large dog, "Scranton Distributing Co.," 4⅛" dia., EX .......$375.00 B

**CIL Ammunition,** sign, cardboard, large moose at water, 20" x 25", EX ...........................................................................$115.00 D

**Cinco Tobacco,** container, metal, lunch pail style, EX.................$95.00 D

**Cinderella Ice Cream,** sign, cardboard, Cinderella in background, 11" x 14", EX ....................................................................$225.00 C

**Cinderella Ice Cream,** sign, cardboard, Henderson Creamery Co. Inc., young child sitting on steps with bowl of product, "Tickles Your Tummy," 14" x 10½", G ......................................................$95.00 D

**Cinderella Ice Cream,** sign, cardboard, youngster sitting on steps eating ice cream, 13⅞" x 10⅝", VG...................................$175.00 C

**Circle A Soda Water,** art plate, china, company logos and the Texas Cotton Palace, G ............................................................$600.00 C

**Citgo,** patch, cloth, for sleeve, 2⅜" sq., EX........................$10.00 C

**Cities Service Kold Pruf,** sign, cardboard, double-sided, die cut, pigeon holding a thermometer, 11½" x 18", NM ...............$275.00 C

Coca-Cola, handbook, used for sales preparation in retail stores, white lettering on red, 1950s, EX, $30.00 C. *Courtesy of Muddy River Trading Co./Gary Metz.*

Coca-Cola, invitation to attend the opening of the Paducah, Kentucky, Coca-Cola plant, picture of the bottling plant at top of sheet, 1939, G, $35.00 C. *Courtesy of Mitchell collection.*

Coca-Cola, ice pick, squared wooden handle, "Coca-Cola in Bottles" and "Ice-Coal Phone 87," 1930 – 1940s, EX, $35.00 C. *Courtesy of Mitchell collection.*

Coca-Cola, ice pick, wooden handle, bottle opener in the handle end, 1930, EX, $40.00 C. *Courtesy of Mitchell collection.*

Coca-Cola, sign, Kay Displays, plywood and metal, "Pause Here," yellow, red, and black, 37" x 10", 1930s, G, $1,550.00 B.

Coca-Cola, menu board, Kay Displays, plywood, "Drink" logo at top, 1930 – 1940s, 20" x 37", G, $325.00 B. *Courtesy of Muddy River Trading Co./Gary Metz.*

Coca-Cola, sign, Kay Displays, wire and wood, bowling scene, 1940s, 16" diameter, EX, $425.00 B. *Courtesy of Muddy River Trading Co./Gary Metz.*

Cities Service Koolmotor Gas, globe, plastic and glass, in company shaped clover design, 1920 – 30s, 14" x 14", VG..$575.00 C

Cities Service Motor Oil, sign, metal, double-sided, flange, oil can and partial message "Cities Service Oil Sold Here...," 22" x 12", EX .................................................$225.00 C

Cities Service National Charge Cards Accepted Here, sign, metal, flange, double-sided, 20" x 12", EX....................................$175.00 C

Cities Service Oils, gas globe, metal body with glass lens, clover design, 1920s, 15" dia, VG ....................................$425.00 C

Cities Service Oils, Koolmotor Gas, globe, glass, hull body with glass lens, trademark cloverleaf design, 13½" dia., VG ................$800.00 B

Cities Service Oils, sign, porcelain, die cut, double-sided, 23¾" x 23¾", EX....................................................................$350.00 B

Cities Service, clock, light-up, Pam Clock Co., New Rochelle, NY, with the trademark 3-leaf clover in center, 15" dia., G...$375.00 D

Cities Service, clock, light-up, Pam Clock Co., New Rochelle, NY, with the trademark 3-leaf clover in center, 15" dia., VG $450.00 D

Cities Service, map holder, metal, 3 tiers for maps, 1930s, 12½" x 20", EX .........................................................................$125.00 C

Cities Service, sign, porcelain, die cut, clover shape of company logo, inside cast iron frame, 60" x 60", EX ....................................$775.00 C

Citizen's Coal Company, tip tray, metal, round, deer with large rack in center, "Our Modern Coal Pocket Insures Clean Coal," 4¼" dia., EX ..............................................................................$40.00 D

City National Cigar, tin, full slip lid, "Mild and pleasing...quality supreme," 50-count, EX .....................................................$75.00 C

City of Ardmore, sign, porcelain, one-sided, oil derrick and a large bull, 16" x 10½", VG.............................................................$295.00 D

Clabber Girl Baking Powder, order book, cardboard and paper, Clabber Girl, 1940s, 3¾" x 8", VG ......................................$15.00 D

Clabber Girl Baking Powder, sign, single-sided, embossed, 34" x 11¾", G...............................................................................$60.00 B

Clabber Girl Baking Powder, sign, tin, double-sided, "The Double-Acting Baking Powder," 34" x 11½", G.......................$50.00 C

Coca-Cola, menu board, Kay Displays, wood and masonite, 16" button at top center, manufactured to resemble leather, 17" x 29", EX, $525.00 B. *Courtesy of Muddy River Trading Co./Gary Metz.*

Coca-Cola, menu board, Kay Displays, wood and metal, rare and hard to find, 1940s, F, $550.00 C. *Courtesy of Muddy River Trading Co./Gary Metz.*

Coca-Cola, sign, Kay Displays, wood, "Lunch with us, a tasty sandwich with Coca-Cola," difficult to find, 1940s, 9" x 13", EX, $2,900.00 B. *Courtesy of Muddy River Trading Co./Gary Metz.*

Coca-Cola, menu board, Kay Displays, wood with metal trim, "Drink Coca-Cola," 1940s, EX, $675.00 C. *Courtesy of Mitchell collection.*

Coca-Cola, sign, Kay Displays, "Work Refreshed" with "Education" center medallion, 23" x 11½", 1940s, EX, $375.00 B. *Courtesy of Muddy River Trading Co./Gary Metz.*

Coca Cola, kerchief, "The Cola Clan," Silhouette Girl from Coca-Cola collectors' banquet, 1970s, white and red, EX, $35.00 C. *Courtesy of Mitchell collection.*

Coca-Cola, knife, one blade and one opener, "Coca-Cola Bottling Company," 1910s, EX, $300.00 C.

---

**Clabber Girl,** recipe book, paper, Clabber Girl, 1930s, 18 pages, EX............................................................$15.00 D

**Clark & Host,** tin, paper label, youngster in lap of older gentleman, "My Favorite Coffee," 5½" x 9½", EX..................................$115.00 C

**Clark Bar,** display, box, cardboard, designed to ship and then open for shelf display, EX............................................$26.00 B

**Clark Bar,** thermometer, wood, painted, bar clock figure at top, 19" H, G .............................................................$325.00 B

**Clark Bar,** thermometer, wooden, "join the millions," 1920s, 5½" x 21½", VG ..........................................................$700.00 C

**Clark Bar,** thermometer, wooden, product at top of scale, "4 p.m. Clark Bar," 1920s, 5¼" x 19", F .........................................$125.00 B

**Clark Bar,** toy, vinyl, Clark Boy holding a candy bar, 8½" tall, EX .................................................................$105.00 C

**Clark's Honest Square,** box, two-piece, with elves making candy, 110" x 11" x 2½", EX....................................................$28.00 B

**Clark's Mile-End Spool Cotton,** calendar, paper, pretty young lady with a parasol, full monthly tear sheets, 1886, 20" x 30", EX.$700.00 D

**Clark's ONT,** display, metal with slanted sliding glass panels for product access, 15" x 10" x 7", EX ...................................$300.00 C

Coca-Cola, lamp shade, leaded glass ball, extremely rare item, this one has correct history, and comes with all original hardware, 1917, 11½" dia., EX, $26,000.00 B.

Coca-Cola, license plate attachment, "Aloysius Purple Flashes...Drink Coca-Cola in Bottles," a great advertising item that was probably developed for a special local interest event, 11" x 4", NM, $295.00 C. *Courtesy of Buffalo Bay Auction Co.*

Coca-Cola, sign, cardboard, Lillian Nordica, 26" x 46", 1905, EX, $4,100.00 B.

Coca-Cola, light fixture, colored leaded glass, with bottom beaded fringe, "Coca-Cola 5¢," "Pittsburgh Mosaic Glass Co., Inc., Pittsburgh, Pa.," rectangular, 1910, 11" w x 22" x 7½" h, EX, $12,000.00 C.

Coca-Cola, Lionel train in original box, engine has dynamic wave logo at cab, the cars advertise Fanta, Tab, Sprite, and the caboose has a large wave logo, 1970s, EX, $425.00 C. *Courtesy of Sam and Vivian Merryman.*

Coca-Cola, sign, tin, self framed, both a bottle and a can with a fishtail "Coca-Cola," "Luncheonette," 59¼" x 23¼", EX, $375.00 C.

Coca-Cola, mask, paper, Max Headroom, rubber band to hold it onto the head, 1980s, EX, $25.00 C. *Courtesy of Sam and Vivian Merryman.*

---

**Clark's Super Motor Oil**, sign, porcelain, double-sided, oil pouring from an upturned can, 30" dia., EX.................$1,050.00 B

**Clark's Teaberry Gum**, sign, "That mountain tea flavor," 11¾" x 8¾", VG ......................................................$275.00 B

**Clark's Teaberry Gum**, sign, tin, partial message reads "...That Mountain Tea Flavor," 12" x 9", EX .................$335.00 D

**Clark's Thread**, box, wood, paper, litho, kids playing Blind Man's Bluff, 4¼" x 3¼" x 1½", 1920s, VG..........................$95.00 D

**Clark's Thread**, sign, cardboard, young girl with her dog promoting Clark's Spool Cotton thread, 12⅝" x 17⅝", EX ........$325.00 D

**Clark's Thread**, trade card, cardboard, "A Bare Chance" and a cartoon bear, 1879, EX ......................................$42.00 C

**Clark's Zagnut**, decal, display case, bar both wrapped and unwrapped, "A Real Treat," 9" x 5", EX...........................$30.00 B

**Clarks Mile End Spool Cotton**, sign, paper, litho, man in cotton field with bag around his neck and spool of the product in other hand, 18½" x 24", EX ......................................................$600.00 B

**Class Cigars**, tin, from the Cordove Cigar Co., peacock on both sides and most of the 1909 stamp left, 50-count, VG .................$40.00 C

**Clauss Shears**, sign, die cut, woman holding an enlarged pair of shears, "Clauss/Freemont, O" on shears, 20" x 51½", EX .$35.00 D

**Clemak Razor**, sign, porcelain, flange, man feeling his smooth shave, 12" x 12", EX ......................................................$800.00 B

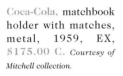

Coca-Cola, matchbook holder with matches, metal, 1959, EX, $175.00 C. *Courtesy of Mitchell collection.*

Coca-Cola, matchbook, mock-up of Westinghouse cooler, $85.00 C.

Coca-Cola, menu board, metal-lined with fishtail logo, 19½" x 28", G, $125.00 B.

Coca-Cola, menu board, plastic, with dynamic wave logo at top, 12½" x 16½", EX, $40.00 C. *Courtesy of Sam and Vivian Merryman.*

Coca-Cola, menu board, wood and masonite, slip menu blanks, 1930s, 26" tall, VG, $375.00 B.

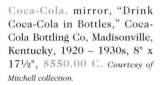

Coca-Cola, mirror, "Drink Coca-Cola in Bottles," Coca-Cola Bottling Co, Madisonville, Kentucky, 1920 – 1930s, 8" x 17½", $550.00 C. *Courtesy of Mitchell collection.*

Coca-Cola, mold made of solid iron, for 10 oz. no return bottle, very heavy, EX, $475.00 C.

---

**Cleo Cola,** sign, cardboard, cut-out, pretty girl with the product, art deco likeness, 25" x 26", 1939, EX ......................$450.00 C

**Cleo Cola,** sign, tin, embossed, Cleopatra, 27⅜" x 12½", EX .$275.00 C

**Cleveland and Buffalo,** tip tray, metal, oval, with ship at sea, "The Great Ship Seeandbee...C&B Line," 6¼" L, G....................$300.00 B

**Clicquot Beverages,** sign, tin, embossed, Eskimo in center spotlight, 30" x 12", NM ......................$100.00 C

**Clicquot Club Beverages.** sign, free-standing, Eskimo, "we recommend," 10" x 4¾" x 3", EX.....................................$75.00 C

**Clicquot Club Ginger Ale,** calendar, woman giving the Eskimo Clicquot Club boy a ride on her bicycle, 12" x 24", 1942, NM...............$100.00 B

**Clicquot Club Ginger Ale,** sign, tin, embossed, Eskimo image in center, 30" x 12", NM..........................................$150.00 B

**Clicquot Club Soda,** calendar, paper, metal strips on top and bottom, red-haired woman and child, full pad, 1942, NM.......$225.00 C

**Clicquot Club Telechron,** clock, light-up, Eskimo holding bottle, 15" dia., 1940s, NM....................................$525.00 C

**Climax Peanut Butter,** pail, metal with press lid and bail handle, 16 oz., EX ...........................................$125.00 C

**Climax The Black Shells,** box, paper litho over cardboard, shot shells 4⅛" x 4⅛" x 2½", G .................................$60.00 C

**Climax Thin Plug,** tobacco tin, P. Lorillard Co., G......................$40.00 D

**Climax-Plug Tobacco,** cutter, P. Lorillard Tobacco Co., EX..$140.00 D

**Climax-Plug,** tip tray, litho, with flowers, "Chew," EX ...............$75.00 D

**Clinton and Damascus Steel Safety Pins,** tip tray, hand holding product, "Oakville Company, Waterbury, Ct.," 4½" x 6", EX..........................................................$85.00 B

**Clinton Brewing Co.,** tray, metal, pretty girl with glass, "Drink Pointer Bottle Beer," 13¼" x 13¼", EX ......................$195.00 C

Coca-Cola, newspaper, Paducah Sun-Democrat, June 18, 1939, advertising the opening of a new bottling plant, F, $75.00 C. *Courtesy of Mitchell collection.*

Coca-Cola, note pad holder for candlestick phone, price includes phone which also has a courtesy coin box, 1920s, EX, $900.00 B. *Courtesy of Gary Metz.*

Coca-Cola, opener, saber-shaped "Drink Bottled Coca-Cola," 1920s, EX, $200.00 C.

Coca-Cola, opener, brass key, "Drink Coca-Cola in Bottles" 1910s, EX, $120.00 C.

Coca-Cola, opener, metal, gold plated, bottle-shaped, Nashville, Tennessee, celebrating 50th Anniversary, 1952, EX, $85.00 C.

Coca-Cola, sign, tin, pilaster, rare version with the message "Refresh Yourself," under button, 16" x 52", 1950, EX, $1,400.00 B. *Courtesy of Muddy River Trading Co./Gary Metz.*

Coca-Cola, plate, "Drink Coca-Cola Good with food," Wellsville China Co., 1940 – 1950s, 7½", VG, $750.00 B. *Courtesy of Muddy River Trading Co./Gary Metz.*

---

**Clinton's Violet Talc,** container, pretty young woman on front, 2½" x 4", VG ...................................................$100.00 B

**CLIX, Smooth Shaving,** display, barber shop three-dimensional razor blade display, barber pole lights up, "Clix Always Clicks," 17½" x 26", G .......................................................$100.00 D

**Clover Farm Coffee,** tin, litho, key-wound lid, from Cleveland, Ohio, 1-lb., EX...............................................................$35.00 C

**Clover Leaf Ice Cream,** sign, painted metal, with a wrought iron hanger, four leaf clover, 46" x 45", EX .........................$425.00 D

**Cloverbloom Butter Cottage,** display, cardboard, die cut, with usual dairy scenes, 31¼" x 16¼", NM ...............................$225.00 C

**Cloverdale Soft Drinks,** menu board, tin, courtesy panel at top in white, 18" x 24", EX................................................$365.00 C

**Cloverine Talc,** tin, litho, woman on front, EX .........................$300.00 B

**Cloverleaf Milk,** clock, metal frame with bubble glass front, "Famous for Purity," 16½" dia., EX......................................$65.00 B

**Clown Cigarettes,** pack, full, unopened, from Axton Fisher Tobacco Co., Louisville, KY, with clown head on cover, VG.......$25.00 B

**Clown Cigarettes,** sign, cast iron, in shape of embossed horseshoe, used to hold papers down at street corner news stands, 6" x 8½" x 2", NM ...........................................................................$102.00 B

**Clown Cigarettes,** thermometer, round, dial-type, "You'll never know how good Clown Cigarettes are till you touch a match to one," G.........................................................................$225.00 D

**Club 100 Count,** box, cardboard, hunting scene, 7¾" x 7¾", EX ........................................................................$575.00 B

**Club City Brewing Co.,** calendar, paper, with full pad and both top and bottom metal strips, 16" x 33¼", 1947, VG .........$45.00 C

Coca-Cola, playing cards, double deck in container similar to eight-pack holder, 1970s, EX, $65.00 C. *Courtesy of Mitchell collection.*

Coca-Cola, playing cards, friends and family, 1980, M, $55.00 C.

Coca-Cola, postcard, Coca-Cola Bottling Co., No. 1 at Paducah, Kentucky, with picture of bottling plant at Sixth and Jackson St., 1920s, $85.00 C. *Courtesy of Mitchell collection.*

Coca-Cola, poster, cardboard, "Accepted Home Refreshment," 1940s, 56" x 27", G, $120.00 B.

Coca-Cola, poster, cardboard, "Accepted home refreshment," young couple sitting in front of a fireplace enjoying popcorn and bottled Cokes, 1942, VG, $425.00 B. *Courtesy of Muddy River Trading Co./Gary Metz.*

Coca-Cola, poster, cardboard, "Have a Coke," with skater, 1955, F, $500.00 B. *Courtesy of Muddy River Trading Co./Gary Metz.*

Coca-Cola, poster, cardboard, horizontal, "All set at our house," with boy holding cardboard six pack carrier, 1943, EX, $650.00 B. *Courtesy of Muddy River Trading Co./Gary Metz.*

---

**Club Lake Coffee,** tin, paper, litho, lake and club house, 3-lb., G ............................................................................$75.00 D

**Clyde Beatty and Cole Bros. Circus,** poster, paper, litho, framed, growling lion and tiger, 28½" x 41½", G ..............................$100.00 B

**Clyde Beatty Cole Bros.,** poster, circus with lion tamer and lion with signature of Roland Butler, 21" x 36½", G................................$25.00 D

**Clyde Beatty Cole Bros.,** poster, paper, litho, circus advertising with clown face, 25" x 21", VG.................................................$35.00 B

**Clyde Beatty Cole Bros.,** poster, paper, litho, circus with signature by Roland Butler and image of large tiger on front, 28" x 21", G ........................................................................$35.00 B

**Clyde Beatty Cole Bros.,** poster, paper, litho, promoting the greatest show on earth, 14" x 25", VG.........................................$30.00 D

**Clyde Bros. Circus,** poster, paper, Johnstown on Friday June 3, with the world's largest chimpanzee, 28" x 50", VG.............$40.00 C

**Clysmic Table Waters,** tip tray, metal, deer and pretty long haired nymph at creek, 4" x 6", VG ..............................................$225.00 D

**Co-Ed Dresses Sold Here,** sign, tin, litho, young woman in graduation cap and gown, 12" x 13", VG ....................................$65.00 B

**Co-op Golden Tires,** ashtray, brass, embossing in center, 1950s, 4" x 2¾", EX.............................................................................$35.00 D

**Co-Op Oil Ass'n.,** license plate attachment, 10" x 4⅝", EX ..$135.00 C

**Cobbs Creek Whiskey,** thermometer, tin, whiskey bottle, "Select Your Drink According To The Temperature," 39" tall, EX ..$75.00 C

**Coca-Cola Sprite Boy,** sign, paper, window, "Take Some Home Today," NOS, 25" x 10", 1950, NM..........................................$335.00 C

**Coca-Cola,** 6-pack, miniature, red, EX ...............................$85.00 C

**Coca-Cola,** bicycle, manufactured by Huffy in 1986 to commemorate the 100th anniversary of Coca-Cola, 26", M ............$895.00 D

Coca-Cola, poster, cardboard, horizontal, "Coke knows no season," snow scene with a bottle in foreground and a couple of skiers in the background, framed, 1946, 62" x 33", G, $350.00 C.

Coca-Cola, poster, cardboard, horizontal, "Face your job refreshed," woman wearing visor beside a drill press, 59" x 30", VG, $800.00 C.

Coca-Cola, poster, cardboard, horizontal, "Got enough Coke on ice?," three girls on sofa, one with phone receiver, framed, Canadian, 1945, G, $350.00 C.

Coca-Cola, poster, cardboard, horizontal, "Hospitality Coca-Cola," girl lighting a candle with a bottle in foreground, 1950, 59" x 30", EX, $900.00 D.

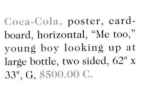

Coca-Cola, poster, cardboard, horizontal, "Me too," young boy looking up at large bottle, two sided, 62" x 33", G, $500.00 C.

Coca-Cola, poster, cardboard, horizontal, "The pause that refreshes," girl in yellow dress propped against table holding a bottle, in a reproduction frame, 36" x 20", EX, $925.00 B. Courtesy of Muddy River Trading Co./Gary Metz.

Coca-Cola, poster, cardboard, horizontal, "What I want is a Coke," girl on sandy beach in swimsuit reaching for a bottle, in original wooden frame, hard to find, 1952, VG, $1,100.00 D.

---

Coca-Cola, bicycle, manufactured by Huffy in 1986 to commemorate the 100th anniversary of Coca-Cola, 26", M ............$900.00 C

Coca-Cola, bottle carrier, aluminum, with embossed lettering on each side, holds 12 bottles, 1940s, EX..............................$225.00 D

Coca-Cola, bottle rack, wire with metal rack sign at top, "Take Some Home Today," G..........................................................$95.00 D

Coca-Cola, bottle thermometer, tin, die cut, 5¼" x 16¾", 1953, EX ...........................................................................................$95.00 C

Coca-Cola, bottle topper, paper, "Drink...Delicious and Refreshing," woman in yellow scarf with umbrella, 1927, EX.............$2,000.00 B

Coca-Cola, bowl, green, "Drink...Ice Cold," Vernonware, 1930s, VG........................................................................................$375.00 B

Coca-Cola, button, metal, "Drink," iron frame is 24" dia. with a 16" on one side and a 10" button on reverse side, EX..............$875.00 C

Coca-Cola, calendar page, framed, 12¾" x 21¼", VG .................$45.00 B

Coca-Cola, calendar, Army nurse holding a bottle of Coke, complete with all pads, 1943, EX.......................................................................$575.00 C

Coca-Cola, calendar, boy at well with dog, enjoying a bottle of Coke, partial pad, 1932, EX .............................................$750.00 C

Coca-Cola, calendar, Elaine seated with parasol holding glass of Coke, full pad, framed, 1915, EX......................................................$4,000.00 C

Coca-Cola, calendar, featuring June Caprice, early star, with glass of Coke, full pad, although this is an early piece, it is somewhat common, 1918, EX .................................................................$385.00 C

Coca-Cola, calendar, Flapper Girl, partial calendar pad, framed, this particular calendar shows both the bottle and glass, 1929, EX ......$925.00 C

Coca-Cola, calendar, girl in blue hat with glass of Coke, full calendar pad, framed, 1921, EX .............................................$1,275.00 C

Coca-Cola, calendar, girl with snow skis, 1947, EX.....................$325.00 C

Coca-Cola, calendar, Soda Fountain, 1901, G ......................$4,500.00 C

Coca-Cola, poster, cardboard, horizontal, "You taste its quality," woman with flowers and a bottle of Coke, framed under glass, 1942, 36" x 20", NM, $1,150.00 B. *Courtesy of Muddy River Trading Co./Gary Metz.*

Coca-Cola, poster, cardboard, horizontal, large, "America's Favorite Moment," a couple in a diner booth, each with a bottle, 1940s, 36" x 20", EX, $295.00 C. *Courtesy of Muddy River Trading Co./Gary Metz.*

Coca-Cola, poster, cardboard, original factory frame, three boxers, hard to find this item, 1960s, 35" x 19", F, $185.00 C.

Coca-Cola, poster, cardboard, "Play refreshed," young lady in tennis attire sitting on a Coke lift top floor cooler, enjoying a bottle of Coke, 1949, NM, $2,700.00 B. *Courtesy of Muddy River Trading Co./Gary Metz.*

Coca-Cola, poster, cardboard, pretty girl with bottle of Coke, "The Pause That Refreshes," not in the best of shape, but I decided to include it because it's seldom seen, 30" x 49, F, $375.00 C.

Coca-Cola, poster, cardboard, pretty lady enjoying a bottle of Coke and the message "Refreshing," in original gold frame, 1949, G, $375.00 B. *Courtesy of Muddy River Trading Co./Gary Metz.*

Coca-Cola, poster, cardboard, roller skating couple relaxing at soda fountain with bottled Coke, 29" x 50", VG, $160.00 B.

---

**Coca-Cola,** calendar, two women at beach, one with parasol and glass, other sitting with bottle of Coke, no month pad, 1918, EX ...............................................$1,250.00 C

**Coca-Cola,** calendar, Victorian girl at table with fern, 1898, G....$7,500.00 C

**Coca-Cola,** calendar, with Betty in bonnet, this is the version with her holding the product, but with message at upper right of picture, 1914, G...............................................$1,800.00 C

**Coca-Cola,** calendar, woman in evening wear with glass, full pad, framed, 1928, EX ...........................................$825.00 C

**Coca-Cola,** calendar, woman wearing broad-brimmed hat, partial calendar pads, 1944, G ...................................$300.00 C

**Coca-Cola,** carton case, waxed cardboard, red on yellow, EX .$75.00 D

**Coca-Cola,** carton case, waxed cardboard, red on yellow, VG .$50.00 D

**Coca-Cola,** carton rack, adjustable wire, "Drink..., take enough home,"with message sign at top, EX .................................$200.00 D

**Coca-Cola,** change receiver, glass, with reverse glass lettering, "Drink 5¢," 1904, 6" dia., VG ...........................................$750.00 B

73

C

Coca-Cola, poster, cardboard, single-sided, "The Pause That Refreshes," three women workers gathered around cooler for break, 1940s, G, $325.00 C.
*Courtesy of Collectors Auction Services.*

Coca-Cola, poster, cardboard, "Shop Refreshed," young girl in front of a fountain dispenser enjoying her Coke from a glass, 1948, 41" x 23½", NM, $2,000.00 B. *Courtesy of Muddy River Trading Co./Gary Metz.*

Coca-Cola, poster, cardboard, "The best is always the better buy," girl with grocery sack and six pack, framed under glass, 1943, EX, $975.00 B. *Courtesy of Muddy River Trading Co./Gary Metz.*

Coca-Cola, poster, cardboard, "The pause that refreshes," girl on beach in swim suit, add $250.00 if in original aluminum frame, 1950s, 36" x 20", F, $300.00 C. *Courtesy of Mitchell collection.*

Coca-Cola, poster, cardboard, three women, "Friendly pause," 1948, 16" x 27", NM, $1,500.00 B. *Courtesy of Muddy River Trading Co./Gary Metz.*

Coca-Cola, poster, cardboard, for truck, "Yield to the children," 67" x 32", 1960s, NM, $95.00 C. *Courtesy of Muddy River Trading Co./Gary Metz.*

---

Coca-Cola, cigarette case, frosted glass, anniversary, 1936, EX..$600.00 C

Coca-Cola, clock, aluminum body with glass front, electric light-up clock, "Drink Coca-Cola" in red dot center, with original box, Modern Adv. Co., 15" dia., EX .................................................$575.00 B

Coca-Cola, clock, leather, "Drink Bottled...So Easily Served," boudoir bottle-shaped with clock face in center of body, 1910, 3" x 8", VG.................................................................$1,800.00 B

Coca-Cola, clock, light-up, "things go better with Coke," with logo button in lower right corner, 16" sq., VG...........................$125.00 B

Coca-Cola, clock, light-up, girl drinking a Coca-Cola from a bottle in spotlight at bottom, 15" dia., VG...................................$725.00 B

Coca-Cola, clock, light-up, message board at bottom, 11" x 12", EX ...................................................................................$150.00 C

Coca-Cola, clock, light-up, message board for billards between product message and clock, 24" x 37½" x 3½", VG........$375.00 C

Coca-Cola, clock, light-up, neon, around outside of face with spotlight bottle in center above the number 6, 15½" sq., EX..$825.00 B

Cola-Cola, poster, cardboard, vertical, "Face the sun refreshed," pretty girl in white dress shielding her eyes from the sun with one hand while holding a bottle with the other, 1941, 30" x 53½", VG, $625.00 C.

Coca-Cola, poster, cardboard, vertical, framed, "Home Refreshment on the way," 24½" x 50", VG, $650.00 C. *Courtesy of Muddy River Trading Co./Gary Metz.*

Coca-Cola, poster, cardboard, vertical, "Coke Time," in original wooden frame, EX, $950.00 B. *Courtesy of Muddy River Trading Co./Gary Metz.*

Coca-Cola, poster, cardboard, vertical, "Have a Coke," girl with bottle in each hand in front of drink machine, 1940s, 16" x 27", EX, $350.00 C. *Courtesy of Muddy River Trading Co./Gary Metz.*

Coca-Cola, poster, cardboard, vertical, "Refresh your taste," girl in sailing scene, in original wooden frame, 16" x 27", 1950s, EX, $725.00 C. *Courtesy of Mitchell collection.*

Coca-Cola, poster, cardboard, vertical, "Right off the ice," girl at ice skating rink, 1946, 16" x 27", EX, $400.00 C. *Courtesy of Muddy River Trading Co./Gary Metz.*

Coca-Cola, poster, cardboard, vertical, "So easy to carry home," with woman in rain with umbrella, 1942, EX, $400.00 C. *Courtesy of Muddy River Trading Co./Gary Metz.*

Coca-Cola, clock, light-up, Pam Clock Co., Brooklyn 1 NY, U.S.A., with green outside ring and red center, NOS, 15" dia., EX ..$550.00 D

Coca-Cola, clock, light-up, reverse painted fishtail "Drink Coca-Cola" in center, 15" x 15", NM ....................................$325.00 C

Coca-Cola, clock, metal body with glass face and cover, light-up, with fishtail logo in center, 15¼" sq., EX..........................$400.00 B

Coca-Cola, clock, wood framed, "Drink in bottles," message spotlighted in center of face, 1940s, 16" x 16", G................$200.00 C

Coca-Cola, container, waxed cardboard, "Drink...in Bottles," used both as popcorn container and ice bucket, 5T3 Lily Nestrite tub, EX...............................................................................$25.00 D

Coca-Cola, cooler radio, "Drink...Have a Coke," 1950s, EX.$850.00 B

Coca-Cola, cooler, plastic, "Drink...in bottles," new molded in the shape of drink machine, 22½" x 35" x 12", red, EX.......$350.00 D

Coca-Cola, decal, Sprite Boy in bottle cap hat beside Coke bottle, 4½" x 8", EX ...........................................................$20.00 D

Coca-Cola, decal, Sprite Boy in bottle cap hat beside Coke bottle, 4½" x 8", NM....................................................................$25.00 C

Coca-Cola, dispenser, ceramic, with base, bowl, spigot and lid, marked The Wheeling Pottery Co., 1896, 18" tall, EX .$6,000.00 B

Coca-Cola, door handle, figural bottle found on newer coolers in stores, 2⅜" x 7⅞" x 1½", NM....................................................$100.00 C

Coca-Cola, door pull, plastic and metal, "Have a Coke," handle shaped like a bottle, 1950s, EX.........................................$200.00 D

Coca-Cola, drink dispenser, Vendo #23, restored, 1940s – 1950s, NM ............................................................$1,400.00 D

Coca-Cola, Drink, button, metal, with curved sides, 12" dia., white lettering on red, NM .......................................................$295.00 C

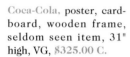

Coca-Cola, poster, card-board, vertical, "The drink they all expect," similar to horizontal poster of this year but show-ing full length artwork of cou-ple preparing for entertaining, 1942, EX, $700.00 B. *Courtesy of Muddy River Trading Co./Gary Mets.*

Coca-Cola, poster, cardboard, vertical, "Thirst knows no sea-son," couple building a snow-man, graphics are great, 1942, 30" x 50", NM, $725.00 C.

Coca-Cola, poster, cardboard, with enter-tainer singing in front of microphone with bottle, "Entertain your thirst," 1940s, 36" x 20", EX, $600.00 B. *Courtesy of Gene Harris Antique Auction Center, Inc.*

Coca-Cola, poster, card-board, wooden frame, seldom seen item, 31" high, VG, $325.00 C.

Coca-Cola, poster, card-board, "Work Refreshed," blacksmith scene, 30" x 50", VG, $200.00 B.

Coca-Cola, poster, cardboard, "Yes," girl on beach with bottle, if found in original frame add $400.00 to this price, 1946, 56" x 27", EX, $500.00 C. *Courtesy of Mitchell collection.*

Coca-Cola, poster, card-board, "Your Thirst Takes Wings," woman aviator with a bottle of Coke, 1940s, 36" x 20", G, $425.00 C.

Coca-Cola, dry box, Westinghouse, 10-case master with a hinged lid that opens side to side instead of front to back, embossed, "Drink... Ice Cold," restored, white on red, 1950s, 45⅛" x 36" H x 30½" D, EX .................................... **$1,850.00 D**

Coca-Cola, flare glass, clear, with etched syrup line, Coca-Cola in curve section of 5¢, EX ..................................................... **$750.00 C**

Coca-Cola, fountain dispenser, "Drink...Ice Cold," white on red, EX ................................................................................. **$725.00 D**

Coca-Cola, hat, cloth, soda fountain attendant with "Drink Coca-Cola" patch, NOS, NM ...................................................... **$160.00 C**

Coca-Cola, license plate attachment, metal, "Aloysus Purple Flashes...Drink Coca-Cola in Bottles," a great advertising item that was probably developed for a special local interest event, 11" x 4", EX.................................................................................. **$250.00 C**

Coca-Cola, lighter, embossed lettering, Coca-Cola logo on lid, bottle pulls apart in middle for lighter access, 2½" T, EX ............. **$55.00 D**

Coca-Cola, menu board, molded plastic, football graphics around menu selections, 31½" x 34½", VG ..................................... **$35.00 C**

Coca-Cola, mirror with thermometer at upper left, "Drink Coca-Cola In Bottles," silhouette girl panel at bottom, 1939, 10" x 14", EX...**$950.00 B**

Coca-Cola, music box, miniature shaped as a box cooler, "Drink...Ice Cold," plays "Let Me Call You Sweetheart," 1950s, EX........**$150.00 C**

Coca-Cola, picnic cooler, metal with side handles and metal latching top, "It's the real thing," with dynamic wave contour logo, 18" x 13" x 16½", white on red, G......................................................**$150.00 D**

Coca-Cola, plate, china, sandwich, "Drink," with bottle and glass in center, Knowles, EX ......................................................**$300.00 C**

Coca-Cola, poster, paper, educational, "Our America" chart four in the electricity series, distributed to schools for teaching aids, great graphics, but low in demand, 1940s, EX, $25.00 D. *Courtesy of Creatures of Habit.*

Coca-Cola, poster, paper, "Ritz Boy," first time Ritz Boy was used, framed under glass, 1920s, F, $700.00 C. *Courtesy of Mitchell collection.*

Coca-Cola, sign, porcelain, double-sided with metal hanger, "Prescriptions," "Made in U.S.A 1933, Tenn. Enamel Mfg. Co., Nash," designed to hang over sidewalk from building arm, white and yellow lettering on red and green, 60½" x 46½", 1933, EX, $1,200.00 B.

Coca-Cola, puzzle, in original box, young lovers in front of an old general store with an early Coke cooler, 1000 pieces, EX, $25.00 C. *Courtesy of Sam and Vivian Merryman.*

Coca-Cola, rack sign, cardboard, featuring Eddie Fisher on radio, 1954, 12" x 20", EX, $135.00 C. *Courtesy of Muddy River Trading Co./Gary Metz.*

Coca-Cola, clock, rocking bottle, made by Swihart Products, red and green on white background, 1930s, 20", G, $750.00 C. *Courtesy of Mitchell collection.*

Coca-Cola, route coupon, paper, from Paducah, Kentucky, EX, $25.00 C. *Courtesy of Mitchell collection.*

Coca-Cola, poster, 50th anniversary, "Drink," two girls sitting on product banner holding bottles of Coke, 1936, 27" x 47", EX......$1,850.00 C

Coca-Cola, poster, cardboard, "Drink in bottles, Quality you can trust," original frame, 1950s, VG...............................$160.00 B

Coca-Cola, poster, cardboard, "Drink, Refreshment right out of the bottle," 1940s, EX .........................................$850.00 D

Coca-Cola, poster, cardboard, "Drink, Refreshment right out of the bottle," 1940s, VG .........................................$700.00 D

Coca-Cola, poster, cardboard, "I'd Love It," 31¾" x 21¼", G..$175.00 C

Coca-Cola, poster, cardboard, horizontal, "Hospitality in your hands," woman with serving tray of bottled Coke, 1948, 36" x 20", EX.........................................$350.00 C

Coca-Cola, poster, cardboard, horizontal, "Join the friendly circle," friends swimming around float with cooler of Cokes, 1955, 36" x 20", EX.........................................$450.00 C

Coca-Cola, poster, cardboard, horizontal, "Join the friendly circle," friends swimming around float with cooler of Cokes, 1955, 36" x 20", VG.........................................$375.00 C

Coca-Cola, poster, cardboard, vertical, in original frame, "Take Some Home Today," girl with bottle of product at party, 16" x 27", EX.........................................$675.00 C

Coca-Cola, poster, paper on cardboard, young girl and mother, "...and Coke too," 26¾" x 16", 1946, G...............................$90.00 B

Coca-Cola, posters, educational, "Our America," set of four, 32" x 22", 1946, EX.........................................$120.00 B

Coca-Cola, radio, small in shape of radio cooler, "Drink...Ice Cold," 1950s, EX .........................................$250.00 C

Coca-Cola, school tablet, crossing guard, "Safety First...Compliments of the Atlanta Coca-Cola Bottling Company," 8½" x 11", EX..$12.00 C

Coca-Cola, seltzer bottle, green glass, acid etched EX......$225.00 C

Coca-Cola, salesman merchandise book, hardback 5-ring binder, 1942, EX, $400.00 D. *Courtesy of Chief Paduke Antiques Mall.*

Coca-Cola, plate, china by Knowles China Co., luncheon size, bottle and glass in center, 1930s, VG, $450.00 B.

Coca-Cola, sandwich plate, "Drink Coca-Cola Refresh Yourself," Knowles China Co., luncheon sizes, 1931, NM, $775.00 B. *Courtesy of Muddy River Trading Co./Gary Metz.*

Coca-Cola, Santa cut out, cardboard, showing small boy peering around a door at Santa who's opening a bottle, easelback, 3-dimensional, 1950s, VG, $230.00 C. *Courtesy of Mitchell collection.*

Coca-Cola, Santa figurine, porcelain, Royal Orleans, Santa seated holding a child and a bottle while a small boy kneels at a dog sitting up, one in a limited set of six, 1980s, $130.00 C. *Courtesy of Mitchell collection.*

Coca-Cola, Santa hanger, cardboard, "Add Zest to the Season," Canadian, 1949, 10½" x 18½", EX, $900.00 B. *Courtesy of Muddy River Trading Co./Gary Metz.*

Coca-Cola, Santa poster, cardboard, "A Merry Christmas calls for Coke," Santa seated in green easy chair while elves bring him food, 1960s, 16" x 24", VG, $65.00 C. *Courtesy of Mitchell collection.*

Coca-Cola, serving tray, metal, litho, topless woman, "Wherever Ginger Ale, Seltzer or Soda is Good...Coca-Cola is Better–Try It," 1908, EX ....................................................$4,800.00 C

Coca-Cola, sign, "Now! 12-oz. cans too!," rack with cans & bottles circling the globe, 10½" x 22", EX ...................................$50.00 D

Coca-Cola, sign, "Sold Here...Ice Cold," arrow with original hanging arm, red, green, and white, 30" x 21½", 1927, EX ....$850.00 C

Coca-Cola, sign, cardboard, "Drink...Delicious and Refreshing," cowboy in original wood frame, good graphics, EX ..$1,150.00 B

Coca-Cola, sign, cardboard, die cut, "So Refreshing," young waitress with serving tray of Coca-Cola in glasses, designed to be either string hung or used on counter with the easel back, 17" x 20", EX.........................................................................$550.00 C

Coca-Cola, sign, cardboard, double-sided, clown background, 16" x 27", EX.........................................................................$210.00 B

Coca-Cola, sign, cardboard, double-sided, clown background, 16" x 27", VG .........................................................................$175.00 C

Coca-Cola, sign, cardboard, embossed, die cut, "Delicious and Refreshing...at Soda Fountains," children being instructed by the rabbit, super rare item, 6½" x 7", 1890s, EX .........$16,000.00 B

Coca-Cola, sign, cardboard, Lillian Nordica, 26" x 46", 1905, EX ..$4,100.00 B

Coca-Cola, sign, double-sided, sidewalk on legs, fishtail sign over bottle, "Drink...Ice Cold," 22½" x 24" x 33", EX...............................$425.00 B

Coca-Cola, sign, grocery store aisle divider, 30" x 13", VG..$110.00 B

Coca-Cola, sign, masonite, "Drink," bottle in spotlight at bottom of diamond, made by Evans-Glenn Co., Marietta, GA, Made In USA, 12-46, 1946, 48" x 48", EX.........................................................................$900.00 C

Coca-Cola, sign, metal, hanging arrow, double-sided, with hanging arm, 30" x 21½", 1920s, EX ...............................................$925.00 C

Coca-Cola, Santa, stand up, cardboard, Santa Claus resting one arm on a post while holding a bottle with the other, a holly Christmas wreath is shown in the rear, 1960s, EX, $95.00 C. *Courtesy of Mitchell collection.*

Coca-Cola, score card, paper, St. Louis Cardinals souvenir, vendor on back with St. Louis products that make the game more enjoyable, EX, $30.00 C. *Courtesy of Mitchell collection.*

Coca-Cola, Santa poster, Santa trying to keep a small dog from waking a sleeping boy and girl, with message and price space at bottom, 30½" x 47", EX, $45.00 C. *Courtesy of Sam and Vivian Merryman.*

Coca-Cola, score keeper, cardboard, keeps score of runs, hits, and errors by both teams, by score wheels, 1900s, VG, $135.00 C. *Courtesy of Mitchell collection.*

Coca-Cola, shade, ceiling, milk glass with original hardware, 1930s, 10", EX, $1,500.00 D.

Coca-Cola, sheet music, paper, "Rock Me to Sleep Mother," with Juanita on cover drinking from a glass, 1906, EX, $875.00 C.

Coca-Cola, sign, tin, sidewalk, "French Wine Coca" in original condition in original sidewalk frame. This cola was the forerunner of Coca-Cola. This sign is extremely rare, NOS, 1880s, sign 20" x 28" with frame 37" tall, NM, $10,000.00 B. *Courtesy of Muddy River Trading Co./Gary Metz.*

---

Coca-Cola, sign, metal, painted, self- framing, "things go better with," message to left of bottle, red, white, and green, 35¼" sq., G ...............................................................................$275.00 D

Coca-Cola, sign, metal, painted, self-framing, "Drink," couple at right of message, 1940s, 33½" x 12", EX .........................................$550.00 D

Coca-Cola, sign, metal, self-framing, "Have a Coke," with spotlight bottle in center, white and yellow on red, 18" x 54", EX ...$350.00 C

Coca-Cola, sign, metal, self-framing, painted, "Enjoy big king size...ice cold here," fishtail in center and bottle at right, red, white, and green, 27¾" x 19¾", EX...................................$300.00 C

Coca-Cola, sign, metal, self-framing, painted, "Enjoy big king size...ice cold here," with fishtail in center and bottle at right, red, white, and green, 27¾" x 19¾", VG ..........................$295.00 C

Coca-Cola, sign, paper, "Your choice of sizes," 16" x 27", 1960s, EX.....................................................................................$25.00 B

Coca-Cola, sign, paper, double-sided, framed, "Serve...Taste treat for the year," 1956, EX...................................$125.00 D

Coca-Cola, sign, paper, double-sided, store framed, "Serve...Taste treat for the year,"1956, NM.................................................$135.00 D

Coca-Cola, sign, porcelain, die cut, "Drink," script with copyright in tail of first C, EX...............................................................$750.00 C

Coca-Cola, sign, porcelain, double-sided, "Drink," 52½" x 35½", G .......................................................................................$225.00 B

Coca-Cola, sign, porcelain, double-sided, die cut, "Arndt Groc," 42" x 50", EX................................................................................$675.00 C

Coca-Cola, sign, metal, sidewalk, "Drink Coca-Cola, Ice Cold," 32" tall, EX, $140.00 B.

Coca-Cola, sign, cardboard, 3-D, "Boy oh Boy," boy in front of cooler with a bottle in hand, 1937, 36" x 34", VG, $850.00 C. *Courtesy of Mitchell collection.*

Coca-Cola, sign & clock, metal and neon, strong art deco influence with spot light 6 pack, "It's time to take home a carton," difficult item to locate, 25" tall, VG, $1,800.00 B.

Coca-Cola, sign, cardboard, ballerinas, "Pause Refresh," 1953, 27" x 56", VG, $375.00 B.

Coca-Cola, sign, cardboard, sunbather in round blue background, framed and under glass, by Snyder & Black, rare, 1938, 22", NM, $2,700.00 C. *Courtesy of Mitchell collection.*

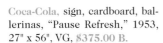

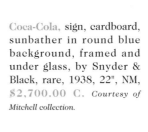

Coca-Cola, sign, cardboard, sunbather in diamond blue background pictured with a Coke button and a bottle, framed and under glass, 1940, 23" x 22", NM, $1,700.00 C. *Courtesy of Mitchell collection.*

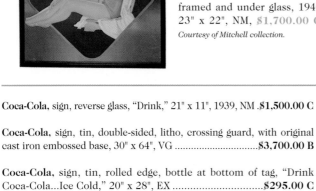

Coca-Cola, sign, cardboard, "Be Really Refreshed," in metal frame, scene of skiers, 36" x 20", 1955, EX, $325.00 C.

---

Coca-Cola, sign, reverse glass, "Drink," 21" x 11", 1939, NM .$1,500.00 C

Coca-Cola, sign, tin, double-sided, litho, crossing guard, with original cast iron embossed base, 30" x 64", VG ..............................$3,700.00 B

Coca-Cola, sign, tin, rolled edge, bottle at bottom of tag, "Drink Coca-Cola...Ice Cold," 20" x 28", EX ..............................$295.00 C

Coca-Cola, sign, tin, self-framed, fishtail under message with bottle and diamond can, "Luncheonette," 59¼" x 23¼", VG.......$360.00 B

Coca-Cola, sign, tin, self-framing, painted, with fishtail sign in center, 27" x 9¼", VG ...............................................................$175.00 C

Coca-Cola, sign, tin, single-sided, self-framing, painted, bottle on right of name tag, EX.........................................................$215.00 C

Coca-Cola, sign, whirly bird, eight-sided, spinning, NOS, 1950s, NM ...........................................................................$775.00 C

Coca-Cola, syrup bottle with metal lid, "Drink," 1920s, EX...$1,200.00 C

Coca-Cola, thermometer, metal, die cut, bottle, 1933, EX ...$300.00 B

Coca-Cola, thermometer, metal, die cut, bottle, of Dec. 25th, 1923 bottle, 1931, EX ................................................................$385.00 C

Coca-Cola, thermometer, tin, cigar-style, "Drink...Sign of Good Taste," 8½" x 30", 1950s, EX.............................................$400.00 B

Coca-Cola, thermometer, tin, double bottle, embossed 1941, 7" x 16", BEWARE: This thermometer has been reproduced, G ........$315.00 C

Coca-Cola, sign, cardboard, boys playing around bottle, Canadian, 1930s, 11½" x 11½", NM, $4,700.00 B. *Courtesy Muddy River Trading Co./Gary Metz.*

Coca-Cola, sign, cardboard, couple with snow skis, "Now! Have a Coke," 1950, 27" x 56", VG, $425.00 B.

Coca-Cola, sign, cardboard, cut out, "Drink Coca-Cola, The Pause that Refreshes," used as a window display by Niagara Litho Co., N.Y., 1940s, 32½" x 42½", VG, $975.00 C. *Courtesy of Mitchell collection.*

Coca-Cola, sign, stand ups, cardboard, cutout, Toonerville, 14 pieces, G, $1,900.00 B. *Courtesy of Muddy River Trading Co./Gary Metz.*

Coca-Cola, sign, Cardboard, die cut, "Drink Coca-Cola, Delicious and Refreshing, Ours is Ice Cold," 1900s, 9" x 19", F, $495.00 C. *Courtesy of Bill Mitchell.*

Coca-Cola, sign, cardboard, cut out, "The Pause That Refreshes Drink Coca-Cola," superb piece, not seen very often, 1937, 34" x 14", VG, $200.00 B. *Courtesy of Muddy River Trading Co./Gary Metz.*

Coca-Cola, thermometer, tin, embossed, bottle on background plate, 1938, EX.................................................$350.00 D

Coca-Cola, thermometer, wooden, "Delicious Refreshing," Coca-Cola 5¢, 1905, 4" x 15", EX ...............................$700.00 B

Coca-Cola, toy dispenser with original box, 12" x 6" x 9", 1950s, VG.................................................................$65.00 B

Coca-Cola, toy shopping cart, masonite, EX ....................$550.00 C

Coca-Cola, tray, metal, serving, "fishing boy with dog," 1931, EX ...............................................................................$900.00 C

Coca-Cola, tray, metal, serving, bobbed hair girl with bottle, 1927, EX .......................................................................$825.00 C

Coca-Cola, tray, metal, serving, foxskin fur girl with glass of Coke, 1921, EX .......................................................................$725.00 D

Coca-Cola, tray, metal, serving, girl in afternoon, 1938, EX.$350.00 C

Coca-Cola, sign, cardboard, die cut easel back, boy on bike, 29" x 20", 1950s, F, $260.00 B.

Coca-Cola, sign, cardboard, die cut, "Every Bottle Sterilized," 1930s, 14" x 12", EX, $1,100.00 C. *Courtesy of Bill Mitchell.*

Coca-Cola, sign, cardboard, die cut, lady with parasol and a straight-sided bottle of Coke, rare, 1900s, 24" x 27", G, $5,200.00 B. *Courtesy of Muddy River Trading Co./Gary Metz.*

Coca-Cola, sign, cardboard, die cut, service girl in uniform with bottle of Coke, 1944, 25" x 64", EX, $600.00 B. *Courtesy of Gene Harris Antique Auction Center, Inc.*

Coca-Cola, sign, cardboard, die cut six pack, 1954, EX, $750.00. *Courtesy of Gary Metz.*

Coca-Cola, sign, cardboard, die cut, Coke snowman that folds out from back to produce a three-dimensional effect, probably part of a larger sign, VG, $900.00 B. *Courtesy of Collectors Auction Services.*

Coca-Cola, sign, cardboard, die cut, woman sitting on bench with bottle, "Delicious and Refreshing, Coca-Cola in bottles," 1900s, 18" x 28½", G, $8,000.00 B. *Courtesy of Bill Mitchell.*

Coca-Cola, tray, metal, serving, Hilda Clark, 1903, 9¼" dia., NM ........................................................$3,600.00 C

Coca-Cola, tray, metal, serving, Johnny Weissmuller, BEWARE: This tray has been reproduced, 1934, EX.....................................................$975.00 B

Coca-Cola, tray, metal, serving, Madge Evans, 1935, EX .....$475.00 C

Coca-Cola, tray, metal, serving, menu girl, 1950s, EX ........$95.00 D

Coca-Cola, tray, metal, serving, oval, "Drink...Delicious and Refreshing," with the Hamilton King Coca-Cola Girl holding a glass of Coke, 1913, VG....................................................$375.00 C

Coca-Cola, tray, metal, serving, oval, "exposition girl," 1909, 13½" x 16½", EX ....................................................................$2,750.00 C

Coca-Cola, tray, metal, serving, oval, with "Garden Girl," 1920, 13¼" x 16½", EX ....................................................................$875.00 C

Coca-Cola, tray, metal, serving, painted, "Drink," "curb service" 1927, EX.........................................................................$1,100.00 C

Coca-Cola, tray, metal, serving, rectangular, Francis Dee, 1933, NM ..........................................................................................$950.00 B

Coca-Cola, tray, metal, serving, rectangular, girl in ice skates sitting on log, 1941, EX .......................................................$375.00 C

Coca-Cola, tray, metal, serving, red-haired girl with yellow scarf, with solid background, 1950 – 1952, EX .......................................$250.00 C

Coca-Cola, tray, metal, serving, Soda Jerk, 1928, EX .......................$825.00 C

Coca-Cola, sign, cardboard, "Enjoy Tab," 1960s, EX, $65.00 C.

Coca-Cola, sign, cardboard, girl at beach with bottle and "Drink..." in the sky, 1940, 30" x 50", EX, $1,500.00 B.

Coca-Cola, sign, cardboard, marching glasses, framed, 34" x 11", 1948, EX, $725.00 B. *Courtesy of Muddy River Trading Co./ Gary Metz.*

Coca-Cola, sign, cardboard, "Play Refreshed," sports scene, 1951, 36" x 20", VG, $1,100.00 B.

Coca-Cola, sign, cardboard, pretty woman in two piece swim suit on lifeguard stand being offered a bottle of Coke, "Yes," 1947, 30" x 50", EX, $1,900.00 B.

Coca-Cola, sign, cardboard, pretty woman with a carton of the product, "Take Home a Carton," 1939, $1,400.00 EX, $1,400.00 B.

Coca-Cola, sign, cardboard, "Refreshment Ahead," 1952, 20" x 36", VG, $650.00 B.

---

Coca-Cola, tray, metal, serving, swim suit girl with glass, fountain sales, 1929, EX .................................................. $450.00 C

Coca-Cola, tray, metal, serving, two girls at early model convertible, 1942, EX .................................................. $400.00 C

Coca-Cola, tray, serving, oval, "Drink...Delicious and Refreshing," Betty 1914, VG .................................................. $450.00 C

Coca-Cola, tray, serving, running girl on beach in yellow bathing suit, 1937, EX .................................................. $375.00 C

Coca-Cola, truck, metal, "Drink," cargo with working headlights and taillights, red, yellow, and white, 1950s, EX ........... $375.00 C

Coca-Cola, truck, metal, toy, Sprite Boy, "Take some home today," 1940s, red and yellow, EX .................................................. $450.00 C

Coca-Cola, tumbler, pewter glass, bell-shaped with Coca-Cola on shoulder, EX .................................................. $380.00 C

C

Coca-Cola, sign, cardboard, "Refreshment you go for," girl on bicycle, 1944, 36" x 20", VG, $400.00 B.

Coca-Cola, sign, cardboard, "So easy...So welcome," two women and a little girl, 1952, 56" x 27", EX, $475.00 B.

Coca-Cola, sign, cardboard, "So Refreshing," couple enjoying Coke at pool side, 1946, 30" x 50", VG, $1,400.00 B.

Coca-Cola, sign, cardboard, trolley car, "Relieves fatigue, Sold everywhere," good graphics, 1907, 20" x 10¼", F, $3,400.00 B. Courtesy of Muddy River Trading Co./Gary Metz.

Coca-Cola, sign, cardboard, trolley car, "Tired?, Coca-Cola relieves fatigue," 1907, 20½" x 10¼", F, $2,300.00 B. Courtesy of Muddy River Trading Co./Gary Metz.

Coca-Cola, sign, cardboard, "What you want is Coke," pretty girl fishing, 1953, 27" x 56", EX, $1,250.00 B.

Coca-Cola, window display, cardboard, cameo fold-out, 1913, VG, $5,200.00 B. Courtesy of Muddy River Trading Co./Gary Metz.

Coca-Cola, vending machine, small dual chute with four bottle stacks inside that alternately dispense the product, will only use 6½-oz. bottle, "Drink, In Bottles," white logo on red front, 1950s, 25" W x 58" H x 15" D, VG ............................................$1,500.00 D

Coca-Cola, vending machine, successor to the table-top 27, much sought after for home use because of their compact size, "Drink, In Bottles," restored, white on red, 1950s, 25½" W x 52" H x 17½" D, EX ..$2,000.00 C

Coca-Cola, vending machine, Vendo 39 with bottle drop at center of door, approx. 80,000 made, restored, "Drink," '40s – '50s, 27" W x 58" H x 16" W, white on red, NM ................................$2,995.00 D

Coca-Cola, visor, paper, adjustable, "Drink... Have a Coke," G...$5.00 D

Coca-Cola, wet box, Cavalier 6-case master, "Drink," red with white lettering, G .....................................................................$725.00 D

Cochran, sign, metal, painted, paint can man running & spilling paint with "Made better last longer," 36" x 24", VG..............$75.00 D

Cochran, sign, metal, two-sided, painted, "made better lasts longer," 36" x 24", EX..........................................................$55.00 C

Coleman's Self-Service Drug Store, playing cards, plastic finish, full unopened with cellopane still on box, big vase of red flowers on table and company information at bottom, 1940 – 50s, 2½" x 3½", NM .......................................................................................$30.00 C

Coles Pentrating Liniment, sign, porcelain, "Removes All Aches & Pains," 6⅛" x 16", EX..............................................................$575.00 C

Colgan's Orange Gum, display cabinet, wood and etched glass, 17½" T, G.............................................................................$1,000.00 C

Coca-Cola, sign, cardboard, window display of mother and daughter at fountain, "Refresh At Our Fountain," 1935, 41" x 44", EX, $4,000.00 B.

Coca-Cola, sign, cardboard, with celebrities Francis Dee and Gene Raymond at the beach, 1930s, G, $1,100.00 B.

Coca-Cola, sign, fashion girl, one of four fashion girls, framed and under glass, 1932, EX, $5,800.00 C. *Courtesy of Mitchell collection.*

Coca-Cola, sign, gloglas, "Pause," and diagonal bottle, 1937, 12" x 10", EX, $12,000.00 B.

Coca-Cola, sign, gloglas with the always popular bottle in hand, "We Serve...," 12" x 10", EX, $14,500.00 B.

Coca-Cola, sign, masonite and metal, "Beverage Department," Sprite Boy on the end of the wings and button in center, 1950s, 88" x 16", EX, $2,100.00 B.

Coca-Cola, sign, masonite and metal, unusual, 1960s, 64" high, G, $225.00 C.

---

**Colgate Shaving Cream,** sign, wood and paper, 42" x 35½", VG .................................................................**$325.00 D**

**Colgate's Baby Talc,** sample, tin, litho, young child on front, screw-on lid, NM .........................................................**$137.00 B**

**Colgate's Dactylis Talc Powder,** sample, tin, litho, young girl on front, NM .......................................................**$88.00 B**

**Colgate's Talc Powder,** sign, paperboard, container in center, 10" x 18", EX....................................................**$120.00 B**

**Colgate,** sample, box with soap and talc and die cut booklet on how to use product, 3" x 4" x 1", EX .........................**$225.00 C**

**Colgate,** sign, die cut, Colgate baby holding a tin of Cashmere Bouquet, 8½" x 13½", 1913s, EX..........................................**$275.00 C**

**Colgate,** sign, die cut, Colgate baby holding a tin of Cashmere Bouquet, 8½" x 13½", 1913s, EX............................................**$295.00 C**

**Collar Buttons,** display case, brass with glass cover, 1910s, 14" x 10", EX ...................................................**$2,000.00 C**

**College Girl Talc,** tin, litho, tennis girl on front, 1¾" x 1¾" x 6", EX....................................................**$350.00 B**

**Collins & Co. Axe,** sign, tin on cardboard, embossed, 20" H, G .**$35.00 C**

Coca-Cola, sign, masonite, horizontal, "Drink Coca-Cola Fountain Service," fountain heads on outside of lettering, 1930 – 40s, 27" x 14", EX, $1,200.00 B. Courtesy of Muddy River Trading Co./Gary Metz.

Coca-Cola, sign, metal, double-sided, "In any weather Drink Coca-Cola," thermometer on one side fits on outside of screen door, while the "Thanks Call Again" fits on the inside of the door, rare, 1930s, EX, $2,100.00 B. Courtesy of Muddy River Trading Co./Gary Metz.

Coca-Cola, sign, metal, double-sided, triangle, hung from overhead wrought iron holder with great filigree at top, 1937, EX, $4,000.00 B. Courtesy of Muddy River Trading Co./Gary Metz.

Coca-Cola, sign, metal, "Drink Coca-Cola in Bottles," original bent wire frame and stand, white lettering on red background, wire is painted white, 1950s, EX, $300.00 C. Courtesy of Gary Metz.

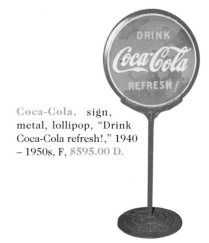

Coca-Cola, sign, metal, lollipop, "Drink Coca-Cola refresh!," 1940 – 1950s, F, $595.00 D.

Coca-Cola, sign, metal, painted message with courtesy panel at top of sign, 69" x 27", EX, $400.00 B.

Coca-Cola, sign, metal, rolled frame edge, "Pick up 12... Refreshment for All," with artwork of 12 pack carton, 1960s, 50" x 16", EX, $550.00 D. Courtesy of Rare Bird Antique Mall/Jon & Joan Wright.

---

**Collins Axe,** sign, cardboard, hanging axe and globe, "The Best is the Cheapest," 1915, 10" x 20", NM ..................**$65.00 C**

**Collins Baking Co.,** calendar in diamond configuration with tear sheets at bottom of picture, "Collins Celebrated Bread," 1909, 8" x 8", EX ..................**$55.00 D**

**Collins Baking Co.,** calendar, girl in bonnet, "Collins Celebrated Bread," 8" x 8", 1909, EX ..................**$35.00 C**

**Colman's Mustard,** display box, wooden, store, "Grand Prix Highest Award, Paris 1900," 1900s, 21"W x 4"H x 12¼"D, F ............**$30.00 B**

**Colonial Bread,** door push, metal, painted, adjustable, "is good," 36" x 3½", EX ..................**$135.00 D**

**Colonial Club 5¢ Cigar,** label, litho on canvas-type paper, woman in green dress with straw hat, EX ..................**$675.00 C**

Coca-Cola, sign, metal, whirly top with original base with four wings and eight sides for advertisement, NOS, 1950, NM, $750.00 C.

Coca-Cola, sign, neon, metal base, "Coca-Cola in bottles," great colors, 1950s, EX, $3,000.00 D. *Courtesy of Muddy River Trading Co./Gary Metz.*

Coca-Cola, sign, neon, original wrinkle paint, 1939, 17" x 13½", G, $1,700.00 B. *Courtesy of Muddy River Trading Co./Gary Metz.*

Coca-Cola, sign, paper, die cut, woman in heavy cold weather coat with hood, advertising Coke in a glass, framed and matted, "Round the world, 1944," litho in USA, 1944, EX, $295.00 D. *Courtesy of Riverside Antique Mall.*

Coca-Cola, sign, paper, Edgar Bergen and Charlie McCarthy, CBS Sunday Evenings, 1949, 22" x 11", EX, $200.00 C. *Courtesy of Mitchell collection.*

Coca-Cola, sign, paper, printer's proof of 1923 cardboard poster, found in the estate of Mrs. Diana Allen who posed for this in 1922, 15½" x 25", 1922, EX, $8,000.00 B. *Courtesy of Collectors Auction Services.*

Coca-Cola, sign, paper, two women drinking from bottles sitting in front of an ocean scene with clouds in the sky, 1912, 16" x 22", VG, $4,750.00 C.

**Colonial Club Cigars,** sign, metal, painted, double-sided, flange, promoting their 5¢ cigars, 18½" x 8¾", G......................$120.00 B

**Colonial Health Guard Ice,** sign, porcelain, single-sided, 21" x 11¾", EX................................................................$400.00 B

**Colonist,** label, cardboard, litho, Minute Man type image, "Up to the Minute...5¢ Cigar...Save The Bands," 1900s, 13¼" x 19¾", NM.$223.00 B

**Colt Arms,** ad, paper, Texas Ranger, 1920s, 20" x 32", EX.$2,200.00 C

**Colt Firearms,** catalog, paper, gun in hand on cover and some of the history of Colts inside along with current models, 10" x 7¼", 1950s, EX ................................................................$75.00 B

**Columbia Accredited Dealer,** sign, porcelain, record in center, 30" x 20", NM................................................................$575.00 C

**Columbia Beer,** tray, metal, Bavarian man with the product, 13½" x 16¾", EX................................................................$275.00 C

**Columbia Bicycles,** ad, paper, bicycle being carried across a creek, 7½" x 10", VG ................................................................$35.00 C

**Columbia Brewing Co.,** clothes brush, premium, "Columbia Brewing Co....Tacoma Wash.," 8" x 2" x 1½", 1900s, EX ..$65.00 D

**Columbia Dispatch Newspaper,** thermometer, porcelain, "Ohio's Greatest Home Daily," 7" x 27", EX ................................$250.00 C

Coca-Cola, sign, plastic, light-up, rotating, "Shop Refreshed Drink Coca-Cola," 1950s, 21" tall, G, $525.00 B. *Courtesy of Muddy River Trading Co./Gary Metz.*

Coca-Cola, sign, plywood, double-sided, "Slow School Zone Enjoy Coca-Cola, Drive Safely," 1950 – 1960s, EX, $950.00 C.

Coca-Cola, sign, porcelain, Canadian, "Coca-Cola Bottling Company," 1940s, 21" x 11½", VG, $650.00 B.

Coca-Cola, sign, porcelain, die cut, hanging, "Distributor over "Drink...," superb item, difficult to locate, Tenn. Enamel Co., 96" x 72", VG, $1,050.00 B.

Coca-Cola, sign, porcelain, double-sided, hanging, from the Harry Myers General Store, Hagerstown, MD, 60" x 42", VG, $825.00 B.

Coca-Cola, sign, porcelain, double-sided, "Fountain Service" drink Coca-Cola "Delicious and Refreshing"

Coca-Cola, sign, porcelain, double-sided, hanging style, four attached 12" bottles, "Baker Airport Office," 1942, 52" x 58", EX, $750.00 B.

Coca-Cola, sign, porcelain, one-sided, neon, "Drug Store... Fountain Service," 86" x 58" x 8", G, $3,500.00 B. *Courtesy of Collectors Auction Services.*

---

**Columbia Flour,** pocket mirror, metal and glass, "A Perfect Product," 2⅛" dia, EX ......................................................**$215.00 D**

**Columbia Match Holder,** sign, tin, embossed, die cut, wall-hung, promoting Columbia Flour, in the shape of Miss Liberty, 2¼" x 5½", G..............................................................................**$500.00 C**

**Columbia Mill,** match safe, wall mount, die cut, patroitic lady and flour sack, 2" x 5½", EX.......................................**$900.00 C**

**Columbia Motor Oil,** can, metal, pour spout and handle, 2 gal., EX ...................................................................................**$65.00 C**

**Columbia Pure Manila Rope,** sign, tin, man holding rope, 1900s, 11½" x 17", EX.......................................................................**$65.00 C**

**Columbia Records,** sign, porcelain, record with blue Columbia label, 24" dia., EX............................................................................**$525.00 C**

**Columbia Spice,** tin, litho, vintage woman in center cameo, Sutherland & McMillian Co., Pittston, Pa., 2-oz., VG ...................**$275.00 A**

**Columbus Shock Absorber,** sign, tin, authorized dealer, flange, double-sided, product beside message, 19" x 12½", VG.....**$185.00 C**

**Colvert's Milk,** sign, tin, one-sided, embossed, 29" x 15", G..**$15.00 B**

Coca-Cola, sign, porcelain, self-framing, single-sided, Tenn. Enamel Manufacturing Co. Nashville, "Fountain Service," yellow, red, white on green, 60" x 45½", EX, $2,200.00 B. *Courtesy of Collectors Auction Services.*

Coca-Cola, sign, tin, 50th Anniversary celebration, 1936, VG, $1,500.00 B.

Coca-Cola, sign, tin, "Drink Coca-Cola," 24" iron frame, one side has a 16" button while the opposite side as a 10" plastic button with a small light which creates a back light, VG, $1,050.00 C.

Coca-Cola, sign, tin, distributors, oval, from McRae Coca-Cola Bottling Co. in Helena, Georgia, featuring pretty long-haired girl, 1910, EX, $3,500.00 D.

Coca-Cola, sign, tin, "Drink Coca-Cola," marching bottles, note shadow on bottles, 1937, 54" x 18", NM, $800.00 B. *Courtesy of Muddy River Trading Co./Gary Metz.*

Coca-Cola, sign, tin, embossed, "Gas Today," spotlight blackboard in center, 1936, 18" x 54", G, $750.00 C. *Courtesy of Muddy River Trading Co./Gary Metz.*

Coca-Cola, sign, tin, "Drink Coca-Cola," spotlight bottle at right, 54" x 19", G, $75.00 B.

---

**Combat High Grade 5¢ Cigar,** sign, cardboard, embossed and stamped, pretty lady in center, 6" x 10", EX .............................$295.00 C

**Comfort Medicated Talc Powder,** tin, litho, baby face on one side and nurse on back side, 2" x 3⅜", EX .........................$775.00 B

**Comfort Powder,** tin, small happy child and a nursemaid, 2½" x 4", EX................................................................$125.00 C

**Comfort Talc Powder,** tin, litho, nurse in early uniform, 2" x 3⅜", VG ..................................................................$600.00 B

**Commerical Club,** sign, cardboard, maple syrup, embossed, 6" x 13", EX ..................................................................$75.00 D

**Commoner Cigars Box,** label, paper, Oliver Cromwell, 4" x 4", EX..................................................................$15.00 C

Coca-Cola, sign, tin, embossed, "Take Home a Carton," early 6 pack in center yellow spotlight, 1938, 54" x 18", EX, $950.00 B.

Coca-Cola, sign, tin, embossed, 1923 bottle, "Delicious – Refreshing," 54" x 30", 1934, EX, $525.00 B. *Courtesy of Muddy River Trading Co./Gary Metz.*

Coca-Cola, sign, tin, embossed, a place to list the gas price for the day, 1930s, 28" x 20", G, $825.00 B.

Coca-Cola, sign, tin, featuring Elaine holding a glass, 1916, 20" x 30", VG, $5,700.00 C.

Coca-Cola, sign, tin, featuring the famous Betty, self-framing, scarce item, has had some restoration, 31" x 41", VG, $1,600.00 B.

Coca-Cola, sign, tin, "Now! Enjoy Coca-Cola at home," hand carrying cardboard six pack, rare and hard to find, Canadian, 1930s, 18" x 54", F, $1,050.00 B. *Courtesy of Muddy River Trading Co./Gary Metz.*

Coca-Cola, sign, tin, rolled edge, bottle at bottom of tag, "Drink Coca-Cola, Ice Cold," 20" x 28", VG, $225.00 B.

---

**Commonwealth Brand Coffee,** tin, litho, "Warranted Pure," White House on front, slip lid, 1-lb., EX .........................................$80.00 B

**Commonwealth Title Insurance and Trust Co.,** thermometer, paper face with degree scale arched over the name., 9¼" dia, EX .............................................................................$25.00 D

**Community Brand Coffee,** pail, metal, large two-story southern mansion, from Baton Rouge, LA, 6¾" x 8", EX..................................$275.00 C

**Compeer Snuff,** trade card, EX.........................................$145.00 C

**Comrade Coffee,** tin, litho, J.A. Folger, Kansas City & S.F., CA, 1-lb., EX..............................................................................$125.00 C

**Condition,** box, cardboard, unopened, contains animal powder that claims to cure almost everything, ½" x 2¼" x 7", NM ..........$65.00 C

**Congress Beer,** match holder, metal, capital building, 5" x 5½", VG .....................................................................................$185.00 C

**Congress Security Tires,** sign, porcelain, double-sided, flange, Congress Rubber Co., East Palestine, Ohio, 14¼" x 17", NM........$325.00 C

**Conkey's Poultry Remedies,** thermometer, wooden, scale, 4" x 15⅛", G...............................................................................$110.00 B

**Connolly's Arch Grip Kangaroo Shoes,** sign, glass, reverse paint, kangaroo in upper right corner, 17¼" x 8¼", EX............................$95.00 C

Coca-Cola, sign, tin, "Take a case home Today," 1950s, 19" x 28", VG, $325.00 B.

Coca-Cola, sign, tin, "Things go better with Coke," Coke glass, 1960s, 20" x 28", EX, $950.00 B. *Courtesy of Muddy River Trading Co./Gary Metz.*

Coca-Cola, sign, wood and bent metal, "Drink Coca-Cola, Please pay when served." This is an unusual double-sided flange sign, 1940 – 50s, 15" x 12", EX, $1,250.00 B. *Courtesy of Muddy River Trading Co./Gary Metz.*

Coca-Cola, sign, wood finish with chrome accents, "Thirst asks nothing more," difficult piece to locate, 38" x 10", G, $775.00 B. *Courtesy of Muddy River Trading Co./Gary Metz.*

Coca-Cola, sign, wood and masonite, "Take Home the new Home Case," cardboard case in center spotlight, 1940s, 18" x 48", EX, $1,600.00 B. *Courtesy of Muddy River Trading Co./Gary Metz.*

Coca-Cola, Siphonmix marquee top for a coin operated machine that dispensed the drink in a cup, totally restored, EX, $2,000.00 B.

Coca-Cola, sign, cardboard, die cut, young waitress with serving tray of Coca-Cola in glasses, "So Refreshing," designed to be either string hung or used on counter with the easel back, 17" x 20", VG, $475.00 B. *Courtesy of Muddy River Trading Co./Gary Metz.*

---

**Conoco Super Motor Oil,** license plate sign, pilgrims, 13½" x 6⅜", EX..................................................$150.00 C

**Consolidated Biscuit Co.,** biscuit box, cardboard, shaped like two-story house, with message on chimney, 1932, 9" x 8½" x 5", EX.........$85.00 B

**Consolidated Ice Company,** dresser mirror, winter scene on back, EX..................................................$80.00 B

**Consolidated Ice Company,** dresser set with advertising on back of mirror, VG..................................................$110.00 C

**Constans Coffee,** tin, from Minneapolis, Minn., "Constantly Good," 5½" x 9½", VG..................................................$20.00 B

**Consumer's Beer,** sign, tin, "ask father," man with glass of beer, embossed, from Consumers Brewing Co., Hills Grove, RI, 1940s, 28" x 9¾", NM..................................................$275.00 D

**Consumer's Beer,** sign, tin, "Ask Father," man with white hair holding glass of product, 27¾" x 9¾", EX..................................................$175.00 C

Coca-Cola, Sprite Boy ball game with glass cover and metal back, VG, $150.00 C. *Courtesy of Mitchell collection.*

Coca-Cola, Sprite Boy blotter, paper, Sprite Boy and a bottle of Coke, 7¾" x 3½", EX, $25.00 C. *Courtesy of Sam and Vivian Merryman.*

Coca-Cola, Sprite Boy fan, cardboard with wooden handle, "A way to win a welcome wherever you go," Starr Bros. Coca-Cola Bottling Company, Mt. Vernon, Illinois, 1950s, $115.00 C. *Courtesy of Mitchell collection.*

Coca-Cola, Sprite Boy outdoor sign, tin on wood frame, joins together in center, Sprite Boy with bottle, "Have a Coke," 1949, 8' x 10', EX, $1,200.00 B.

Coca-Cola, Sprite Boy sign, Kay Displays, wood and masonite, "Sundaes" and "Malts" with 12" button in center and Sprite Boy on each end, 1950s, 6'6" x 1', NM, $1,050.00 B. *Courtesy of Muddy River Trading Co./Gary Metz.*

Coca-Cola, Sprite Boy sign, masonite, Sprite Boy in arrow through cooler, 1940s, EX, $850.00 C. *Courtesy of Mitchell collection.*

---

**Consumer's Beer,** sign, tin, embossed, "ask father," Consumers Brewing Co., Hills Grove, RI, 1940s, 28" x 9¾", EX ........**$225.00 B**

**Continental Brewing Co.,** sign, paper, colonist drinking a large stein of beer, 19½" x 15", VG..........................................**$225.00 D**

**Continental Cigar,** box, wooden, 50-ct., EX.....................**$125.00 C**

**Continental Cubes Cigars,** tin, rare piece, difficult to find, 7½" H, F .................................................................................**$200.00 B**

**Continental Cubes Tobacco,** pocket mirror, celluloid, vintage dressed lady resting on large container of Continental Cubes tobacco, 1¾" x 2¾", EX.............................................................**$400.00 B**

**Continental Cubes,** pocket mirror, celluloid back, 2¾" T, EX..**$125.00 C**

**Continental Life Insurance Company,** tip tray, metal, round, "Saint Louis," insurance building in tray center, 4¼" dia., EX ........**$45.00 B**

Coca-Cola, sugar bowl, complete with lid, "Drink Coca-Cola," 1930, M, $375.00 C; Creamer, "Drink Coca-Cola," 1930s, VG, $325.00 C. *Courtesy of Mitchell collection.*

Coca-Cola, bottle rack, wire with metal rack sign at top, "Take Some Home Today," VG, $145.00 C.

Coca-Cola, toy dispenser, original box, 12" x 6" x 9", 1950s, EX, $90.00 B.

Coca-Cola, tray, metal, serving, "Coca-Cola" with good litho by Western Coca-Cola Bottling Company of Chicago, Illinois, without the sanction of the Coca-Cola Company, 1908, EX, $5,500.00 D. *Courtesy of Muddy River Trading Co./Gary Metz.*

Coca-Cola, tray, metal, serving, featuring Elaine (modeled by film star Faye Tincher), manufactured by Stelad Signs Passaic Metal Ware Company, Passaic, New Jersey, rectangular, 1916, 8½" x 19", EX, $675.00 C. Beware of reproductions. *Courtesy of Mitchell collection.*

Coca-Cola, thermometer, round Pam front dial with the messages "things go better with Coke" at top and "Drink Coca-Cola" at bottom, 1960s, 12" diameter, NM, $250.00 B. *Courtesy of Muddy River Trading Co./ Gary Metz.*

**Continental Life Insurance Company,** tip tray, metal, skyscraper on face, EX ..................................................................$95.00 C

**Continental Trailways Bus Depot,** sign, porcelain, one-sided 36" x 18", white & black on red, EX ...........................................$135.00 C

**Cook's Beer,** sign, metal over cardboard, woman with long gloves, 1936, 18" x 29", F................................................................$195.00 D

**Cook's Beer,** sign, tin over cardboard, hanging, black waiter rushing a bottle of product to his master, "De Boss Sho' Likes His Cook's," 21" x 13", VG................................................................$1,200.00 B

**Cook's Beer,** sign, tin, litho, older gent enjoying a glass of the product, 19½" x 27", 1907, EX ...................................................$700.00 B

Coca-Cola, thermometer, tin, "Drink Coca-Cola in Bottles," Phone 612, Dyersburg, Tennessee, with minder notations for oil, grease, and battery, 1940s, VG, $50.00 C. *Courtesy of Mitchell collection.*

Coca-Cola, train, Express Limited, still in original box with all components present, box shows a little shelf wear but nothing that detracts from the display, 1960s, EX, $450.00 C. *Courtesy of Sam and Vivian Merryman.*

Coca-Cola, train tank car, HO gauge, "Enjoy Coca-Cola," 1980s, EX, $55.00 C. *Courtesy of Mitchell collection.*

Coca-Cola, truck, plastic, Marx, with original six Coca-Cola cases, Canadian, 1950s, red, EX, $525.00 B. *Courtesy of Muddy River Trading Co./Gary Metz.*

Coca-Cola, uniform, with round drink patch, 38 regular, VG, $125.00 C.

Coca-Cola, uniform coat, brown with square red dynamic wave logo patch, nicknamed the hunting coat, original Riverside manufacturer's tag, EX, $55.00 C. *Courtesy of Sam and Vivian Merryman.*

---

**Cook's Champagne,** sign, tin, litho, woodgrain look, product in center oval, 24" x 20½", EX................................$110.00 B

**Cook's Goldblume Beer,** sign, tin, self framed on cardboard, policeman and early model auto creating problems with a skittish horse, 21" x 13", EX ....................................................$115.00 C

**Cookie Jar DeLuxe Mellow Mild Modern Cigarettes,** package, cookie jar on front, rare, EX ...............................$15.00 D

**Coopers Sheep Dipping Powder,** sign, porcelain, single-sided, trump card, 20" x 30", EX .............................................$850.00 B

**Coors Malted Milk,** from Adolph Coors Company, Golden, Colorado, 25-lb., VG .................................................$56.00 B

**Copenhagen,** dispenser, tin, litho, store, 3" x 14½", VG..............$20.00 B

**Coppertone,** clock, Coppertone girl and her dog pulling down her swim suit to expose untanned areas, 36" x 36" x 8", VG...$1,000.00 C

**Corbin Lock,** sign, paper, litho, 24" x 20", 1890s, VG .$125.00 C

**Coreco Penn Motor Oil,** sign, tin, painted strip with oil can at left of message, 21" x 7", EX ....................................$500.00 B

**Coreco Petroleum Products,** sign, porcelain, one-sided, "Pennsylvania Motor Oils," "6 quarts of service for the price of 4," 20" x 14", VG ...................................................................$350.00 B

Coca-Cola, uniform pants and shirt, still in original wrapping, made by Riverside, dynamic wave patch, NM, $75.00 C. *Courtesy of Sam and Vivian Merryman.*

Coca-Cola, vending machine, Vendo model 44, restored, red and white, 1950s, 16" x 57½" x 15½", NM, $2,400.00 B. *Courtesy of Collectors Auction Services.*

Coca-Cola, vending machine, Vendo V-81, much sought after for home use due to its compact design and ability to dispense different size bottles, 1950s, 27" x 58" x 16", white on red, VG, $1,300.00 C. *Courtesy of Mike and Debbie Summers.*

Coca-Cola, vending machine, Westinghouse salesman's sample, standard box, metal, EX, $2,200.00 C. *Courtesy of Mitchell collection.*

Coca-Cola, wall pocket, pressed fiber board, three-dimensional, 9" x 13", EX, $650.00 C. *Courtesy of Mitchell collection.*

**Cork Distilleries Co. Ltd,** sign, tin, self framed, product bottle and a bottle of corks, 17" x 13", EX.........................................$225.00 C

**Corona,** sign, tin, painted, die cut, bottle, 5¼" x 20", EX....$65.00 D

**Cortez Cigars,** tip tray, metal, "For Men Of Brains…Made At Key West," 6⅛" L, G .................................................................$65.00 B

**Corticelli Silk Thread,** cabinet with pull-out drawer and lift top to show spool storage, silk worm and messages on front drawer, unusual item, 20½" x 14½" x 4", VG...................................$900.00 C

**Corvette,** sign, metal, sales and service, 1953, 18" x 12", VG..$125.00 C

**Corylopsis Talcum Powder Page,** tin, litho, geisha girl kneeling on front side of container, NM..................................................$193.00 B

**Cottolene,** tip tray, metal, black woman and child picking cotton, 4¼" dia., EX.................................................................$75.00 C

**Cotton State Exposition, Atlanta Ga,** match holder, two boys by a bale of cotton sharing a watermelon, 2½" h, VG .................$425.00 B

**Count Casper,** sign, cardboard, die cut, 8¾" x 13¼", 1900s, VG.$110.00 C

**Country Club Beer,** clock, glass and wood, horse and rider, 19" sq, VG ..............................................................................$135.00 C

**Country Club Cigars,** tin, country scenes on three sides, 50-ct., VG ..............................................................................$125.00 C

**Country Club Coffee,** tin, litho, key-wound container, 1-lb., EX.$35.00 C

Coca-Cola, window display, cardboard, three piece, "with good things to eat," 1941, 36" x 30", EX, $275.00 B.

Coca-Cola, window display, paper, die cut, glass shaped, "Drink Coca-Cola," rare, 12" x 20", EX, $1,800.00 B. *Courtesy of Muddy River Trading Co./Gary Mets.*

Coleman's Self-Service Drug Store, playing cards, plastic cel-u-tone finish by Congress, full double deck set in original box with company information on each card, 1940 – 50s, 2½" x 3½", VG, $55.00 C. *Courtesy of B.J. Summers.*

Collins & Co. Axe, sign, tin on cardboard, embossed, 20" H, NM, $50.00 B. *Courtesy of Richard Opfer Auctioneering, Inc.*

Colonial Club 5¢ Cigar, sign, litho on canvas type paper, woman in green dress with straw hat, NM, $800.00 B.

Columbia Chainless Bicycle, poster, paper, 1897, 37½" x 87", VG, $750.00 B. *Courtesy of Collectors Auction Services.*

**Country Club,** lunch pail, metal, with top-attached pail handle, "Smoking or Chewing Kentucky Long Cut, The Scotten Tobacco Co., Detroit, Mich.," 7" x 4¾" x 4½", EX..................................$325.00 B

**Country Life Tobacco & Cigarettes,** sign, paper, litho over cardboard, British piece, 23" x 14¼", G...........................$105.00 B

**Court House Turmeric,** spice tin, cardboard with paper label, 1½-oz., EX ...................................................................$45.00 C

**Covered Wagon Cigar,** box, cardboard, covered wagon scene on inside lid, 50-count, EX...........................................$40.00 B

**Covington Bros. Co. Wholesale Grocers, Paducah, Ky.,** tobacco cutter, VG..................................................................$145.00 C

**Cow Brand Baking Soda,** sign, paper, litho, Church and Dwight Co., 18" x 14½", EX .....................................................$160.00 B

**Cow Brand Baking Soda,** tin, sample size, unopened, 1¾" x 1" x 2½", EX.......................................................................$65.00 C

**Cow-Ease,** display, metal, litho, rack with example sprayer and man spraying livestock, 21" x 12" x 34", EX....................$750.00 B

**Cowan's Chocolate,** sign, paper, well-dressed young girl in original "Cowan's" frame, 18" x 25½", EX......................................$350.00 B

**Crack Shot Cigars,** box labels, inner lid with ladies head, EX...$75.00 C

**Cracker Jack,** fortune wheel, tin, litho, premium from box, 1930s, VG ...............................................................................$75.00 C

Columbia Flour, match holder, tin, embossed, die cut, wall-hung, Miss Liberty, 2¼" x 5½", EX, $1,050.00 B. *Courtesy of Wm. Morford Investment Grade Collectibles.*

Columbia Theater, meal ticket, inaugural performance, could be used and kept as a souvenir, 1927, 3½" x 1½", NM, $55.00 C. *Courtesy of B.J. Summers.*

Comfort, calendar, litho, embossed, promoting yearly subscriptions to Comfort, 5¾" x 11½", VG, $75.00 C.

Comfort Medicated Talc Powder, tin, litho, baby face on one side and nurse on other side, 2" x 3⅜", EX, $775.00 B. *Courtesy of Wm. Morford Investment Grade Collectibles.*

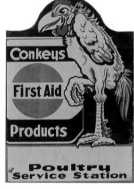

Conkeys First Aid Products, sign, metal, die cut, painted, old bird beside message, 14" x 20", VG, $165.00 C. *Courtesy of Collectors Auction Services.*

Co-op Motor Oil, sign, tin, single-sided, embossed, self-framing, 20" x 10", VG, $130.00 B.

---

Cracker Jack, handkerchief, cotton cloth, with multiple rows of Cracker Jack Boy and dog, 12" X 30", VG ............................$100.00 C

Crayola Crayons, display, cardboard standup, 1950s, 7½" x 12", VG ....................................................................$45.00 C

Crazy Cat, license plate attachment, tin, animated, die cut, tongue and eyes that move with the car's movement, 4¼" x 5⅛", EX.......$135.00 C

Crazy Water Crystals, sign, cardboard, easel back, "Just add it to your drinking water," 9¾" x 13½", EX.................................$55.00 D

Cream Buying Station, Swift & Company, sign, porcelain, double-sided, 41½" x 14½", white on blue, G.......................$195.00 D

Cream Buying Station, Swift & Company, sign, porcelain, double-sided, 41½" x 14½", white on blue, VG.............................$210.00 C

Cream Dove Shortening & Peanut Butter, pocket mirror, metal and glass, farm boy holding up a can of the product, 2¼" dia., EX..........................................................................$525.00 C

Cream of Wheat, box, cardboard, bowl of Cream of Wheat, 14¼" x 13½", VG....................................................................$50.00 B

Cream of Wheat, Rastus doll, framed, 33⅓" x 25", VG..$110.00 B

Cream Peanut Butter, pail, tin, wire bail handle, slip lid, EX...$95.00 C

Creamo Brand Coffee, tin with pry-lid, 1-lb., EX .....................$85.00 C

Cremo Cigars, store bin, metal with wood graining, lettering on front with cigar, 1930 – 40s, VG.....................................$135.00 C

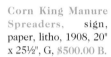

Coppertone, clock, Coppertone girl and her dog pulling down her swim suit to expose untanned areas, 36" x 36" x 8", EX, $1,600.00 B. *Courtesy of Collectors Auction Services.*

Cork Distilleries Co., sign, tin, framed, case of bottles and single paper label cylinder bottle, 19" x 15", EX, $225.00 C.

Corn King Manure Spreaders, sign, paper, litho, 1908, 20" x 25½", G, $500.00 B.

Corticelli Silk Thread, store cabinet, with pull-out drawer and lift top to show spool storage, silk worm and other messages on one drawer, unusual item, 20½" x 14½" x 4", EX, $1,300.00 B. *Courtesy of Wm. Morford Investment Grade Collection.*

Covington Bros & Co., tobacco cutter, metal, counter use for retailers usually given out by the wholesale grocer, 1930s, 15" x 8", VG, $225.00 C. *Courtesy of B.J. Summers.*

Covington Bros. Co. Wholesale Grocers, tobacco cutter, cast iron, Paducah, KY., G, $135.00 C. *Courtesy of B.J. Summers.*

**Crescent Flour,** door push, tin, embossed, with sack of flour in center, 3¾" x 9¾", EX ...........................................................$295.00 B

**Crescent Macaroni,** lunch pail, tin, with wire handles, G ...$75.00 D

**Crescent Peanuts,** tin, with top pry-lid, Crescent Nut & Chocolate Co., Philadelphia, PA, EX ...................................................................$250.00 B

**Crescent Salted Peanuts,** tin, pry-lid, crescent moon over star, 8½" x 9½", EX.........................................................................................$125.00 B

**Cresota Flour,** match holder, tin, die cut, litho, with unusual vertical match pocket, "Prize bread of the world," 5½" x 2⅜", NM ...$575.00 B

**Cresota Flour,** match holder, tin, die cut, litho, trademark boy slicing bread, 2½" x 5½", EX .........................................................................$400.00 B

**Cresthaven Ice Cream,** sign, reverse glass, light-up, 14" x 6" x 4", EX ..........................................................................................$200.00 B

**Crisco,** sign, porcelain, die cut of Crisco can, "For Cooking...Better than Butter," 14" x 20", EX.........................................................$4,500.00 B

**Crisco,** sign, porcelain, die cut, can with lettering above and below, 1900s, 14" x 10", VG....................................................................$1,800.00 D

**Crispo Lily Sodas, Lily Biscuit Co., Chicago,** cracker tin with lid, red and white striped, G .....................................................................$45.00 D

**Crosley Radio,** sign, glass, reverse painted, in shape of globe, 12" dia, VG .......................................................................................$575.00 C

**Crosley Radios and Home Appliances,** sign, metal, neon, back with glass front, G ......................................................................................$525.00 D

**Crown Beer,** calendar, paper, girl holding a rose, full monthly pad, 1915, 10" x 34", EX ...........................................................................$355.00 C

**Crown Brewing Co.,** sign, cardboard, embossed, die cut, man in driving goggles driving a vehicle made of beer barrels, 14" x 14", EX.................................................................................................$1,500.00 C

**Crown Gold Gasoline,** sign, metal, small boy, 20" x 11½", EX.$225.00 C

**Crown Quality Ice Cream,** sign, tin, embossed, 18" x 24", G.$165.00 C

C. Person's Sons Importers and Distillers, sign, tin, embossed, litho, promoting Buffalo Club Rye Whiskey, Buffalo N.Y., 23½" x 34", EX, $475.00 B. *Courtesy of Collectors Auction Services.*

Crazy Water Crystals, sign, cardboard, easel back, "Just add it to your drinking water," 9¾" x 13½", EX, $75.00 C. *Courtesy of Pleasant Hill Antique Mall & Tea Room/Bob Johnson.*

Cream Farina Cereal, sign, cardboard, die cut stand up of small girl with product box and mixing bowl, 1920s, 19" x 28", EX, $450.00 C.

Crounce Corporation, lighter, metal, company inital logo on side, made by Zippo, advertising on one side only, never used, 1¼" x 2¼" x ¼", NM, $35.00 C. *Courtesy of B.J. Summers.*

Crounce Corporation, playing cards, plastic, still sealed in plastic with seal intact, "Playing Cards...U.S. Int. Rev.," 2½" x 3½", NM, $35.00 C. *Courtesy of B.J. Summers.*

Crown Quality Ice Cream, sign, tin, embossed, in wood frame, Anderson and Patterson Mfgs., Worcester, Mass., 21" x 29", VG, $500.00 B. *Courtesy of Collectors Auction Services.*

---

Crown Quality Ice Cream, sign, tin, embossed, wood frame, Anderson and Patterson Mfgs., Worcester, Mass., 21" x 29", VG. $500.00 B

Crubro Apple Butter, sign, cardboard, litho, trolley car advertisement with young girl with several geese, 19½" x 12", EX ....$75.00 B

Crystal Club Pale Dry Ginger Ale, thermometer, metal, painted, dial-type located in neck of bottle, 7" x 27", VG................$85.00 C

Crystal Spring Brewing Co., match striker, stoneware with metal strike plate, EX...............................................................$325.00 C

Crystal Spring Brewing Co., tray, porcelain with brass rim, company name, 12" dia, EX.......................................................$450.00 C

Cuban Seal, cigar tin, "For Satisfaction," G.......................$35.00 D

Cudahy's Diamond "C" Hams, sign, tin, die cut, litho, double-sided, flange, young woman with a platter of product, hard-to-find item, EX.............................................................................$2,800.00 B

Culture Crush Cut Smoking Tobacco, pocket tin, upright with white lettering name, EX...................................................$225.00 C

Cunningham's Ice Cream, tray, metal, serving, "The Factory Behind The Products," manufacturing factory in center, oval-shaped, 1917, 18½" x 15", EX.........................................$110.00 B

Crystal Club Pale Dry Ginger Ale, sign, metal, painted, with dial-type thermometer located in neck of bottle, 7" x 27", EX, $100.00 C.

Crystal White Family Soap, sign, cardboard, trifold die cut display of mother and young child at bath time, 40½" x 33", VG, $200.00 B.

Cuesta Rey Habana Cigars, tray, metal, pretty girl with flowers in her hair, EX, $135.00 C.

Culley & Co., brush, wood and fiber, Roy L. Culley & Co., 415 to 417 Broadway, "Culley's Clothes Wear Best," 1910s, 7" x 2¼" x 1½", EX, $65.00 C. Courtesy of B.J. Summers.

Cunningham's Dairy, bottle, glass, front label, "Cunningham's Dairy, Grade A Raw Milk, Phone 3581-R," rear label has baby in bed, "Best for Baby, Best for You," 1950s, 1 pt., NM, $30.00 C. Courtesy of B.J. Summers.

Curlox Hair Nets, display box, wooden, decals, for counter top use, 15" wide, VG, $200.00 B.

---

Cupid Bouquet, pocket tin, little cigars, flat with cupid in lower right corner, 3½" x 3¼" x ⅜", EX .......................................$55.00 B

Cupid Coffee, tin, paper, litho, container from Excelsior Mills, E.B. Millar Co., Chicago, with Cupid grinding coffee, 1900s, 3¾" x 6¾", EX ....................................................$175.00 B

Cupids Best Cigars, box label, paper, cupid offering a box of cigars to a woman, 9" x 6", EX.......................................................$35.00 C

Cupples Co., tobacco cutter, arrow, EX...........................$135.00 D

Cushman Motor Vehicles, sign, porcelain, double-sided, flange, cushman logo, 20" x 14" x 1½", EX .............................................$595.00 D

CV Beer, sign, pressed board, black man drumming, 16½" x 10½", EX.....................................................................................$110.00 B

CV, sign, embossed, "Please Pay When Served," mother dogs and pups, Terre Haute Brewing Co., 16½" x 10½", EX..............$35.00 B

Cyclone Twister Cigar, sign, cardboard, cyclone above the product name, 1920s, 9" x 11", EX.................................................$115.00 C

Dad's Old Fashioned Root Beer, sign, tin, painted, "Drink, in Bottles," 26¾" x 19", VG, $245.00 C.

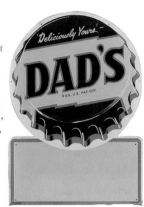

Dad's Root Beer, sign, tin, self-framing, embossed, bottle cap and message blank, 20" x 28", G, $160.00 B.

Dad's Root Beer, sign, tin, bottle cap, "unbelievable," 1950 – 60s, 60" x 32", VG, $425.00 B.

Daggett & Ramsdell's, display cabinet, tin, litho, with great colorful front, scarce, 10½" H, EX, $1,300.00 B. Courtesy of Richard Opfer Auctioneering, Inc.

Dairylea Ice Cream, fan, die cut, cow jumping over the moon, ice cream cone handle, NM, $155.00 B. Courtesy of Buffalo Bay Auction Co.

---

**D-X credit card**, sign, porcelain, double-sided, "Credit Cards Honored Here" with diamond logo, designed to be hung on swinging arm, 1960s, 18" x 12", VG .................................................$95.00 D

**D-X**, license plate attachment, metal, reflective, 5½" x 4", EX.$35.00 D

**D. Agostini**, calendar, paper with metal top and bottom strips, "Confectionery-Home Made-Ice Cream," images of American and Italian Lady Liberty, 15½" x 22", EX.....................................$55.00 B

**D. Geisberg Millinery Shop**, dish, Indian on horseback looking at an airplane, 6¼" dia., EX.....................................$75.00 C

**D.M Ferry & Co.**, seed box, wooden, great paper litho on inside lid, 11½" x 9¾" x 6¾", EX ............................................$350.00 D

**D.M. Ferry Flower Seeds**, display box, wood with paper litho label on inside lid, 12" x 7" x 4", NM............................$350.00 D

**DAB**, tapper handle, Imported German Beer, EX.................$30.00 D

**Dad's Cookie Jar**, store jar, glass, embossed, "Property of Dad's Cookies," clear pyrex, 10½" x 15", VG .........................$165.00 B

**Dad's Old Fashioned Root Beer**, sign, tin, painted, 26¾" x 19", G.............................................................................$225.00 C

**Dad's Root Beer** sign, metal, die cut, bottle cap, "The old fashioned Root Beer," 20" x 28", EX.....................................$250.00 C

**Dad's Root Beer**, sign, "Diet," bottle cap, 29" dia., EX.......$95.00 C

**Dad's Root Beer**, sign, cardboard, die cut, in likeness of 1/2 gal jug, 1950s, VG.............................................................$65.00 C

**Dad's Root Beer**, sign, tin, embossed, bottle cap, 1950s, 20" x 28", VG.............................................................................$155.00 D

**Dad's Root Beer**, sign, tin, litho, embossed, self-framing, "tastes like Root Beer should!," 31" x 12", EX.........................$195.00 D

**Dad's Root Beer**, teddy bear, cloth, 8½" tall, EX .............$20.00 D

**Daggett & Ramsdell's**, display cabinet, tin, litho, with great colorful front, scarce, 10½" H, VG .................................$900.00 C

Dairy Made Ice Cream, tray, serving, "you're sure it's pure," young girl eating ice cream, 10½" x 13½", EX, $325.00 B. *Courtesy of Muddy River Trading Co./Gary Metz.*

Dairy Made Ice Cream, sign, tin, embossed, "You're sure-It's Pure," 19" x 27", EX, $300.00 B.

Dairy Queen, clock, metal and glass, electric light up, ice cream cones in place of even numbers, 1950s, VG, $400.00 B.

Daisy Brand, sign, reverse painted glass, light-up, "One of America's Finest Dairies," small child on limb with birds singing the praises, 1950s, EX, $350.00 C. *Courtesy of Michael and Debbie Summers.*

Dauntless Coffee, Food Products, sign, cardboard, litho, 18¾" x 10¾", VG, $35.00 B. *Courtesy of Collectors Auction Services.*

Davis Carriage M'F'G Co., sign, metal, "Headquarter for Everything to Ride In or Work with," 20" wide, VG, $225.00 B.

Davis D-X Service Station, thermometer, glass and metal, with information for Leon Davis D-X Service Station at 13th and Broadway, restful scene at left of cabin in the woods, 1950s, 8" x 4", EX, $25.00 C. *Courtesy of B.J. Summers.*

Daily Double Cigars, tin, litho, horse racing scene, 4" x 5¼", EX .$65.00 C

Daily Habit Cigars, box label, paper, parrot on perch, 9" x 6", VG ..................................................................................$20.00 C

Dairy Brand Roasted Coffee pail, with wood knob wire bail handle, from Foley Bros. Grocery Co., St. Paul, Minn., farm scene on front cover, 5-lb., EX ....................................................$650.00 B

Dairy Brand, sign, metal, light-up back with reverse painted glass front, "Milk-Ice Cream," 1950s, 25¾" x 6¾", G .$275.00 C

Dairy Brand, tin, vanilla, half-gallon, round, "Ice Cream...New York," EX ........................................................................$35.00 C

Dairy Made Ice Cream, sign, tin, embossed, wood frame, "You're Sure-It's Pure," baby with cone, 26" x 35", G ................................$700.00 B

Dairy Made Ice Cream, sign, tin, litho, "You're Sure-It's Pure," young boy enjoying some ice cream, 19½" x 28", G........$580.00 B

Dairy Made Ice Cream, tray, serving, "you're sure it's pure," young girl eating ice cream, 10½" x 13½", VG ...........................$275.00 C

Dairylea Ice Cream, fan, cardboard, die cut, crescent moon man with cone for handle, "Dairylea Ice Cream," EX ..............$165.00 D

Dairylea Ice Cream, fan, die cut, cow jumping over the moon, ice cream cone handle, EX ....................................................$130.00 C

Dairymen's League Member, sign, porcelain, 14" x 7", NM.$95.00 C

Dairymen's League, sign, porcelain, one-sided, member, 14" x 7", G ..........................................................................................$40.00 B

Deering IHC, calendar, paper, litho, young woman with horse, initials carved into fence post, full calendar pad, 1912, 13¼" x 23¼", NM, $440.00 B. *Courtesy of Buffalo Bay Auction Co.*

Defense Bonds, poster, framed, "this year give a share in America," Santa Claus promoting bonds and stamps, 24" x 30", VG, $85.00 C.

De Laval Cream Separator, sign, porcelain, double-sided, flange, "Local Agency," 18" x 26½", VG, $775.00 B.

De Laval Cream Separator, match holder, tin, die cut, 4" x 6⅜", G, $350.00 B.

De Laval Cream Separators, sign, tin, die cut, cow with advertising on back side of cow, 5½" x 3¼", EX, $235.00 C.

De Laval Cream Separators, sign, tin, litho, strong colors, 29½" x 40½", NM, $2,700.00 B. *Courtesy of Richard Opfer Auctioneering, Inc.*

Daisy Brand, sign, reverse painted glass, light up, "One of America's Finest Dairies," small child on limb with birds singing the praises, 1950s, G..........................................$250.00 D

Daisy Fresh Coffee, can, metal, key-wind top, large white Daisy logo, 1 lb, EX .......................................$65.00 D

Daisy Hair Tonic, sign, tin, litho, "Look your best-it pays," 9" sq., 1915, VG ..........................................$135.00 C

Dale Bros. Coffee, sign, porcelain, friar ready to enjoy a cup of steaming hot coffee, 42" x 14", EX...................$675.00 C

Damascus Ice Cream, sign, porcelain, die cut, 1920s, 18" x 17", EX.........................................$1,400.00 B

Damascus Milk, sign, porcelain, die cut, double-sided, milk bottles in partiotic colors, 18" x 28", EX........................$135.00 C

Damascus Milk, sign, porcelain, die cut, double-sided, two bottles of pasteurized milk, complete with hanging arm, 17¾" x 28½", NM ......................................$1,950.00 C

Dan Patch Cut Plug, tin, with horse and sulky, Scotten, Dillon Co., Detroit, G..........................................$35.00 D

Dan Patch Perfectos Cigar, box, wood, inside lid has company logo, EX ..............................................$185.00 C

Dandro Solvent, display, tin over cardboard, hand holding bottle, can be string hung or mounted easelback, early tin litho, 13¼" x 9¼", EX...........................................$135.00 C

Dandro Solvent, sign, tin over cardboard, for dandruff and beautifying the hair, beveled edge easel back, bottle in hand at right of message, 13" x 9", NM....................$175.00 B

Dandy Cola, sign, tin, self-framed, embossed, "Enjoy Life," Dandy Cola bottle, EX .........................................$160.00 C

Daniel Scotten & Co, wood barrel, paper litho label, "Fine Cut Chewing Tobacco," farmyard dance and young girl with horse, 16" dia. x 21½", VG ..................................$875.00 D

Delco...Battery Service, sign, metal, painted, with battery in upper right corner, "United Service Motors," 30" x 22", NM, $250.00 C.

Dentyne-Beeman's Pepsin, display, countertop, die cut lady on each side of unit, 10" x 3¾" x 7½", 1920s, NM, $3,950.00 B. *Courtesy of Buffalo Bay Auction Co.*

Devoe Paints & Varnishes, sign, tin, double-sided, die cut, litho, kneeling Indian, painted face, beside Devoe Paints, 15" x 26", VG, $1,900.00 B. *Courtesy of Collectors Auction Services.*

Dewar's White Label Whisky, sign, metal, die cut, old English servant with a tray of the product bottle and glass, 9" x 20½", EX, $255.00 B.

Dexter's Dairy Milk, carton, wax cardboard, funnel shape, 9½" tall x 4" base, F, $25.00 C. *Courtesy of B.J. Summers.*

Diamond Dyes, cabinet, tin, litho, front featuring the Page in the People's Court, 27" H, VG, $700.00 C. *Courtesy of Richard Opfer Auctioneering, Inc.*

---

Daniel's Veterinary, sign, cardboard, promoting their medicines, with dogs playing cards at round table, 18" x 13½", 1915, EX.....$165.00 C

Dante Cigar box, inner label, paper, red devil, 9" x 6", EX...$145.00 D

Darmouth Chocolates, banner, canvas, "Demand," elves eating the product, 44" x 16", VG .........................$225.00 C

Dauntless Coffee, poster, canvas, painted, Roman soldier, Terre Haute, Ind., Mattoon, Ill., 60" x 36", EX .........................$375.00 D

David Bradley Mfg. Co., card, young child with a small dog, 9½" x 7½", EX.........................$45.00 C

David Bradley Plows and Cultivators, tape measure, wood, implements, 4' long, G .........................$115.00 D

David's Prize Soap, sign, paper, black family, "Dar's Money In It!," 36" x 26", framed size, EX.........................$275.00 C

Davidson's Bread, sign, porcelain, "Ask for...They're Different," heavy, 16" x 4", EX .........................$875.00 B

Davidson's Chocolates & Bon Bons, sign, tin on cardboard, young girl smelling a flower, 13" x 19", EX .........................$345.00 B

Davis Pain Killer, sign, cardboard, bottle surrounded by crowd of people, 24" x 18", F .........................$3,500.00 C

Dawn Typewriter Ribbon, can, tin, girl reaching for the stars, EX .........................$25.00 D

Dawson's Ale & Beer, clock, glass and metal, horse and "Time Out For Dawson's," EX .........................$95.00 C

Dawsonia Toffee, tin, two black performers on front, slip-on lid, 5¾" x 3¾" x 6½", G .........................$50.00 C

Dayton Cub Tires, sign, cardboard, die cut, easel back, bear cub, 10½" x 20½", G.........................$100.00 C

Dayton Tires, clock, metal body with glass face and cover, light-up, trademark triangle in center with horse head, 15" dia., VG.$265.00 B

Diamond Dyes, cabinet, tin, litho, little girl, 20" H, EX, $1,300.00 B. *Courtesy of Richard Opfer Auctioneering, Inc.*

Diamond Dyes, cabinet, wooden, embossed tin litho front, show woman dyeing fabric at table, 29½" H, EX, $2,400.00 B. *Courtesy of Richard Opfer Auctioneering, Inc.*

Diamond Dyes, cabinet, wooden, rare tin litho on front door, by Wells and Hope Co., 30½" H, EX, $2,300.00 B. *Courtesy of Richard Opfer Auctioneering, Inc.*

Diamond Dyes, cabinet, wooden, embossed tin sign on door, "It's easy to dye with…," 23" W x 30" H x 10" D, VG, $695.00 B.

Diamond Dyes, cabinet, wooden, embossed tin sign on door, "The Standard Package Dyes of the World," VG, $575.00 C.

Diamond Dyes, display case, tin, 18½" x 15⅝", VG, $125.00 C.

---

De Laval Cream Separator, calendar top, Jacob Bender, Sutton, Nebr., young boy with black dog in wagon, 1922, 12" x 19", EX .........$85.00 B

De Laval Cream Separator, calendar top, well-known classic lady and cow, EX .........................................................$185.00 C

De Laval Cream Separator, calendar, full monthly pad, young boy and girl, 11⅞" x 23¾", 1916, EX ...................................$650.00 B

De Laval Cream Separator, sign, tin, litho, gesso frame, "The De Laval Separator Co., 165 Broadway, New York and 42 Madison St., Chicago," 29½" x 41", VG ...........................................$1,150.00 B

De Laval Cream Separator, tin, die cut, cow and calf with paper about product, VG.................................................$175.00 B

De Laval Cream Separators, counter display, metal with embossed separator, "The world's Standard," 13½" x 19½", VG .......$575.00 D

De Laval Cream Separators, sign, metal, "Farm & Dairy Separator" separator, 1938, 20" x 14", EX .............................$225.00 C

De Laval Cream Separators, sign, tin, litho, strong colors, 29½" x 40½", EX................................................................$2,300.00 C

De Laval Cream Separators, sign, tin, self-framing, cream separator, "Earn Their Cost Yearly," 1900s, 14" x 10½", VG ......$295.00 C

De Laval Cream Separators, tip tray, metal, round, "The World's Standard," woman and child at product, 4¼" dia., EX .......$145.00 C

De Laval Milker, sign, decal on metal, lacquered, double-sided, 1940s, 4¼" x 20", EX .......................................$120.00 B

De Laval, calendar, salesman's sample with prices and info for 1921 on back, young boy with fish on front, 12" x 18½", 1919, EX ................................................................$350.00 D

De Laval, match holder, tin, die cut, litho, cream separator beside packaging box, 4" x 6¼", EX............................$575.00 B

De Laval, match holder, tin, die cut, separator in shape of product, 4" x 6½", EX ...........................................$575.00 D

Diamond Dyes, sign, double-sided, die cut, rare, EX, $1,600.00 B. *Courtesy of Wm. Morford Investment Grade Collectibles.*

Diamond Edge Tools, sign, tin, embossed, single-sided, "Hazel Lumber Co., Hazel, Ky.," 27½" x 9¾", VG, $75.00 D.

Diamond Matches, book dispenser, metal, one-cent, store counter top item, 10½" x 13½" x 5½", VG, $495.00 C.

Dibert Bros & Co. Cigars, sign, paper on tin, 14" x 10", VG, $450.00 B.

District of Columbia Motor Club, poster, paper, 17" x 22", G, $55.00 C.

Dixie Milk, sign, cardboard and paper, 14" x 22", G, $145.00 C.

De Laval, sign, metal, "Authorized Dealer," on arm, G ................$350.00 B

De Laval, sign, metal, painted, "We use...better farm living, better farm income," G................................................................$85.00 D

De Laval, sign, young farm boy and a couple of calves, 11½" x 16", EX ........................................................................$125.00 C

De Laval, tip tray, metal, cream separator in center by the Savage Manufacturing Co., NY, "Over 750,000 in use," 4¼" dia., VG ........$250.00 B

De Vilbiss Atomizers, display, cardboard tri fold, boy spraying dog, 42" x 31", EX ....................................................$275.00 C

De Witt's Cod Liver Oil, display, heavy paper, counter use, litho, message for product, 21" x 13½", VG ...............................$45.00 D

De-Luxe Blue-Ribbon, condom container, tin, litho, German shepherd on front cover, 1¾" x 2⅛" x ¼", EX .........................$725.00 B

Dead Shot Smokeless Powder, pinback, celluloid, goose, ⅞" dia., EX ........................................................................$60.00 B

Dead Shot Smokeless Powder, watch fob, celluloid and brass, company information on back side and duck in flight, EX...............$225.00 C

Dead Shot Tobacco, container, tin, paper transfer on front, hunting dog laying beside the hunter's gun, 4" tall, EX.....................$35.00 C

Decker Bros. Pianos, sign, heavy paper, young girl surrounded by a floral wreath, 1882, EX...........................................$96.00 B

Dee-Light, sign, tin, Drink, painted, bottle in center, 6" x 17¾", G ................................................................................$25.00 C

Dee-Lights, sign, metal, painted, bottle in center, 6" x 17¾", EX..$45.00 D

Deep Rock Gasoline & Motor Oil, sign, porcelain, double-sided, company product information, 24" x 32", EX ..............$200.00 C

Deep-Rock Gasoline Oils-Greases, globe, metal body with two glass lenses, high profile, 15" dia., G.........................................$270.00 B

Deep-Rock Gasoline, sign, porcelain, double-sided, "Motor Oil," 32" x 24", VG ................................................................$375.00 C

Dixie Queen Plug Cut Tobacco, canister, tin, pretty girl on front, 5" dia. x 6½", G, $120.00 B.

D.M. Ferry & Co. Standard Onion Seeds, poster, paper, litho, 1911, 18½" x 30½", G, $160.00 B.

Doan's Pills, thermometer, porcelain, 6½" x 24", EX, $210.00 D.

Dodge Dependable Service, sign, porcelain, double-sided, dealer, 42" dia., EX, $1,100.00 C. *Courtesy of Autopia Advertising Auctions.*

Dodger Beverage, sign, steel, die cut in shape of bottle, 16" x 65", EX, $475.00 C.

Domino, The Mild Cigarette, sign, cardboard, die cut, framed, unusual and hard to find, 28" x 44½", EX, $475.00 C.

---

**Deep-Rock Prize Oil,** sign, tin, self-framing, single-sided, embossed, 27" x 19⅛", G......................................................$65.00 B

**Deere Hay Loader,** sign, paper, tri-fold flyer, pasture scene and impliments, 14" x 11", EX ....................................$145.00 C

**Deerfoot Farm Sausages,** sign, cardboard, pig, 15¼" x 11", EX ..$93.00 B

**Deering Harvesting Machines,** calendar, paper, bird dogs and hunter, full monthly sheets, 1908, EX ..............................$195.00 C

**Deering IHC,** calendar, paper, litho, young woman with horse, initials carved into fence post, full calendar pad, 1912, 13¼" x 23¼", VG ............................................................................$355.00 C

**Defender Motor Oil,** can, metal, soldier with camp in background, 1940 – 50s, 2 gal., EX ....................................................$65.00 C

**Defense Bonds,** poster, framed, "this year give a share in America," Santa Claus promoting bonds and stamps, 24" x 30", EX.......$100.00 C

**DeKalb Hybrid Corn,** sign, tin, embossed, painted, St. Thomas Metal Signs, Ltd., St. Thomas, Ont., winged corn logo, 19¼" x 13¼", EX ..............................................................................$175.00 B

**DeKalb Hybrid Corn,** sign, tin, embossed, painted, St. Thomas Metal Signs, Ltd., St. Thomas, Ont., winged corn logo, 19¼" x 13¼", VG .............................................................................. $155.00 C

**DeKalb,** sign, bolted together to form a single double-sided sign with bolted-on wings, 31⅜" x 16", VG.................................$75.00 C

**Del Monte Coffee,** container, key-wound, natives and plantation around container, 2-lb., EX .........................................$80.00 B

**DeLaval Cream Separators,** calendar, paper, full monthly tear sheets, woman, 1938, G ...................................................$45.00 C

**Delaware Co. Fair,** license plate attachment, tin, Manchester, Aug. 8 – 11, die cut, embossed, 6" x 6¼", EX ..$115.00 C

**Delaware Punch,** clock, metal, "Delicious Anytime," 18" x 14", F...............................................................................$145.00 D

**Delco Batteries,** sign, metal, battery and information, 1940 – 50s, 70" x 19", EX ..................................................................$95.00 C

**Delco Battery Service,** sign, tin, diagonal lettering over battery, 30" x 22", EX........................................................................$195.00 C

Donald Duck Beverages, sign, Donald wearing a sailor cap, Canadian, 28" x 20", 1940 – 1950s, VG, $725.00 C.

Dorian Private School, thermometer, glass and metal, flower garden path scene, scale type, reading gauge on right, 1930s, 5" x 7", VG, $55.00 C. *Courtesy of B.J. Summers.*

Double Cola, door push, metal, "Drink, Double measure, Double pleasure," 34" x 4½", red on aluminum, EX, $135.00 D. *Courtesy of Patrick's Collectibles.*

Double Cola, menu board, "Drink," message at top center, 19¾" x 27½", green, white, yellow, and black, NM, $215.00 C.

Double Cola, sign, metal, painted, flange, "Drink," copyright 1947, The Double Cola Co., Chattanooga, Tenn., 18" x 15", NM, $325.00 C.

Double Cola, sign, tin, embossed, bottle pouring liquid into glass, "Drink Double Cola," 1940 – 50s, 28" x 20", EX, $475.00 B.

Delco, sign, metal, painted, "Battery Service, United Service Motors," battery in upper right corner, 30" x 22", EX ..........................$175.00 C

Delco, sign, two-sided, painted, "the original equipment battery," battery in spotlight at lower left corner, 22½" x 18", G ....$140.00 B

Denison's Coffee, pennant, felt, "Ask for," 25", NM....................$82.00 B

DeNobili Cigar Company, sign, tin, embossed, painted, "that different smoke," "3 for 5¢," 19" x 6", EX .....................$55.00 D

Dentyne Gum, sign, porcelain, horizontal lettering EX.....$145.00 C

Dentyne-Beeman's Pepsin display, countertop, die cut, lady on each side of unit, 10" x 3¾" x 7½", 1920s, NM..........$3,950.00 B

Denver Sandwich Candy 5¢, sign, tin, single-sided, embossed, 23¾" x 11¾", G.........................................................................$75.00 B

Derby Smoking Tobacco, sign, cardboard, embossing, horse and rider, 17½" x 22½", VG....................................................$2,500.00 C

Derby, gas globe, glass body with two glass lenses, wide Derby star, 13½" dia., VG................................................................$375.00 D

Derby, gasoline globe, glass body with two lenses, 13½" dia., EX ........................................................................................$450.00 C

Desert Brand Java and Mocha Coffee, container, key-wound, from Browning & Baines, Wash., D.C. desert scene on front, 1-lb., EX ................................................................................$130.00 B

Desert Gold Tobacco, tin, litho, horse head in cameo in center, 3-lb., EX.................................................................................$550.00 B

DeSoto Dealer Catalog, "America's Smartest Low-priced Car," 11½" x 9", 1938, EX.............................................................$50.00 B

DeSoto Hotel Bath House, sign, metal, reflective, applied lettering, "Fire Proof, Hot Springs, Ark.," 28" x 20", EX ....................................$225.00 C

DeSoto Hotel Bath House, sign, metal, reflective, applied lettering, "Fire Proof, Hot Springs, Ark.," 28" x 20", VG....................................$165.00 D

Double Cola, sign, tin, embossed, self-framing with wood backing, 45" x 45", G, $165.00 D.

Double-Orange, sign, cardboard, round, "Truly Delightful," artwork by Rolf Armstrong, 1920s, 18" dia., EX, $190.00 B. *Courtesy of Muddy River Trading Co./Gary Metz.*

Douglas Ethyl Gasoline, sign, tin, embossed, 14" x 10", G, $350.00 B.

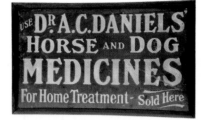

Dr. A.C. Daniels' Horse and Dog Medicines, sign, wooden with wood frame, 30½" x 18¼", VG, $525.00 C.

Dr. Bell's Pine Tar Honey Compound, bottle, glass with paper label, embossing on sides and back, full never opened bottle, although the box is not complete it does add to the value, 1900 – 1910s, 2¼" x 7¼" x 1¼", EX, $35.00 C. *Courtesy of B.J. Summers.*

Dr. Caldwell's Syrup Pepsin, sign, cardboard, die cut, stand-up, countertop, 27" x 37", VG, $135.00 C.

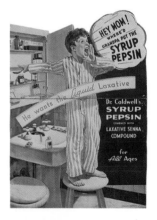

---

**DeSoto Plymouth Approved Service,** sign, porcelain, die cut, dealer, 42" dia., 1930s, VG ......................................................$875.00 B

**Detroit Brewing Co. Bottled Beer,** sign, tin on cardboard, beveled, young lady in cameo sipping the product, 13" x 19", 1911, EX..$225.00 C

**Devoe Paints & Varnishes,** sign, tin, double-sided, die cut, litho, kneeling Indian with painted face beside Devoe Paints, 15" x 26", EX ....................................................................................$2,500.00 C

**Devotion Coffee,** tin, key pry-lid, litho, couple ready for devotion, 1-lb., EX.................................................................................$109.00 B

**DeWitt's Tonic Pills,** sign, cardboard, easel back, fish and yellow-slickered fisherman, 13" x 21", G.......................................$235.00 B

**Dexter Cement,** sign, porcelain, hand in triangle, 12" x 28", EX.$175.00 D

**Dexter's Bread,** sign, porcelain, "Don't forget Dexter's Mother's bread," 18" x 24", EX .....................................$235.00 B

**Diamond Chewing Tobacco,** thermometer, tin, litho, manufactured by Allen & Ellis, Cincinnati, 5" x 10", EX...........................$400.00 B

**Diamond Crystal Salt,** sign, tin litho, advertising of champion cattle, with thermometer at left of message, 20" x 14½", VG ...$95.00 D

**Diamond D Coffee,** container, cardboard, Dwinell-Wright Company, New York, N.Y., 1-lb., EX .............................................$35.00 D

**Diamond Dyes,** cabinet, good strong graphics of washer woman, 22¼" x 29½" x 9¾", EX ...............................................$1,225.00 B

**Diamond Dyes,** cabinet, metal with wood graining, double doors with lettered diamonds, VG ...............................................$95.00 C

**Diamond Dyes,** cabinet, tin, litho, front featuring artwork of the Page in the People's Court, 27" H, EX...............................$800.00 C

**Diamond Dyes,** cabinet, tin, litho, front of little girl, 20" H, VG..$975.00 C

**Diamond Dyes,** cabinet, tin, litho, on all sides, 18½" x 16" x 6¼", G.............................................................................................$90.00 B

**Diamond Dyes,** cabinet, wood with tin embossed door that displays children playing jump rope, 15" x 24", EX.........$950.00 C

Dr. Daniel's veterinary, cabinet, wood and tin, door with litho of the doctor and some of his "cures," 29" high, VG, $695.00 C.

Dreikorn's Good Bread, sign, tin, single-sided, with rolled lip, 27½" x 16", EX, $90.00 B.

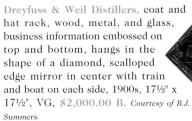

Dreyfuss & Weil Distillers, coat and hat rack, wood, metal, and glass, business information embossed on top and bottom, hangs in the shape of a diamond, scalloped edge mirror in center with train and boat on each side, 1900s, 17½" x 17½", VG, $2,000.00 B. *Courtesy of B.J. Summers.*

Dreyfuss, Weil & Co., Distillers, flask, canteen style, company message on one side and fox hunt scene on the opposite side, extremely rare, 1890 – 1900s, 6" wide x 7" tall x 2½" thick, EX, $750.00 C. *Courtesy of B.J. Summers.*

Dr. Morse's, sign, cardboard, die cut, easel back, promoting Indian Root pill, Indian in canoe, 19½" x 9½", EX, $250.00 D. *Courtesy of Buffalo Bay Auction Co.*

---

Diamond Dyes, cabinet, wood, embossed tin door with woman with ribbons, 22½" x 30", EX.................................$2,200.00 D

Diamond Dyes, cabinet, wood, Standard Package Dyes, 15" x 24½", EX ..............................................................$1,500.00 C

Diamond Dyes, cabinet, wooden, "Evolution," tin litho on door, "Fast Colors...Domestic & Fancy Dyeing," EX............$1,200.00 B

Diamond Dyes, cabinet, wooden, embossed tin door, "The Standard Package Dyes of the World," EX .........................$700.00 C

Diamond Dyes, cabinet, wooden, embossed tin litho front, woman dyeing fabric at table, 29½" H, VG................$1,800.00 D

Diamond Dyes, cabinet, wooden, embossed tin sign on door, "It's easy to dye with…," 23" W x 30" H x 10" D, NM .................$825.00 D

Diamond Dyes, cabinet, wooden, rare tin litho on front door, by Wells and Hope Co., 30½" H, VG .....................................$1,500.00 D

Diamond Dyes, cabinet, wooden, with the "Evolution" tin litho on door, 1900s, EX...................................................$975.00 C

Diamond Dyes, sign, cardboard, die cut, Gutman artwork of girl dyeing doll clothes, 1910s, 17" x 11", EX ..........$1,350.00 C

Diamond Dyes, sign, cardboard, die cut, parrot perched in center with logo and "Use Diamond Dyes," 14" dia., EX ...........$1,475.00 D

Diamond Dyes, sign, double-sided, die cut, rare, G ....................$700.00 C

Diamond Match, container, tin, litho, family watching father as he uses the new striker, 4½" x 1⅝" x 2¼", VG ...........$800.00 B

Diamond State Brewery, Wilmington, Delaware, tray, tin, serving, litho, deep dish with old man with stein and dog, 12" dia., EX ..$95.00 C

Diamond Tires, door push, porcelain, die cut, Squeegee Tread tires, with circle logo at top, 11" tall, EX ......................................$575.00 C

Dr. Nut, sign, gloglas, product bottle, "We Serve...," 1930s, 12" x10", EX, $2,500.00 B.

Drobish Bros., nickel drop cigar trade stimulator in oak cabinet, 14½" x 19½", 1897, EX, $2,000.00. *Courtesy of Past Tyme Pleasures.*

Dr. Pepper, sign, cardboard, double-sided, in original wood frame, "A lift for life," 10, 2, and 4 o'clock at top, 1950s, 31½" x 19", EX, $375.00 C. *Courtesy of Muddy River Trading Co./Gary Metz.*

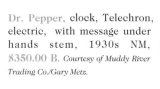

Dr. Pepper, clock, plastic and metal, light-up, die cut, 11½" dia., G, $175.00 C.

Dr. Pepper, clock, reverse painted glass front, electric, in the art deco style, rare, 1930s, 22" x 17", EX, $3,700.00 B. *Courtesy of Muddy River Trading Co./Gary Metz.*

Dr. Pepper, clock, Telechron, electric, with message under hands stem, 1930s NM, $350.00 B. *Courtesy of Muddy River Trading Co./Gary Metz.*

Dr. Pepper, sign, cardboard, hanging, clock face, hands at 10, 2 & 4, 13" x 13", circa 1920s, VG, $3,100.00 B. *Courtesy of Muddy River Trading Co./Gary Metz.*

**Dick Custer Cigars Box,** label, paper, cowboy and gun, "Holds You Up," 9" x 6", VG .....................................$12.00 D

**Dick Custer Cigars,** container, litho, Custer on front, "Holds You Up," EX...........................................................$741.00 B

**Dickinson's Ace Clover,** cup, porcelain, 1900s, VG ............$35.00 C

**Diehl Beer,** sign, cardboard, die cut, framed, waiter holding a tray with glasses and bottles of beer, 13" x 19½", VG.............$200.00 B

**Diehl's Bread,** sign, porcelain, "Sold Here," "It's Thoroughly Baked," 24" x 12", EX.........................................$200.00 C

**Diet Rite Cola,** sign, tin, embossed, bottle, "Sugar Free," 1960s, 54" x 18", VG .................................................$115.00 C

**Diet-Rite Cola,** sign, metal, self-framing, painted, "sugar free," bottle to left of message, 33" x 12", NM...........................$145.00 C

**Diet-Rite Cola,** sign, metal, self-framing, painted, "sugar free," bottle to left of message, 33" x 12", EX ..........................$125.00 D

**Dignity Cigar,** sign, paper, woman in fancy full length gown, partial message "Smoke The Great," 12" x 23", VG...$210.00 D

**Dill's Best Smoking Tobacco,** pocket container, tin, pretty young woman in fancy cameo in center, slip lid, EX ......................$15.00 C

**Dill's Foot Powder,** tin, litho, foot in cameo in center of container, 2½" x 4⅝" x 1⅜", EX .........................................$110.00 B

**Dilworth's Golden Urn Coffee,** tin, litho, screw-on lid, 1-lb., EX...................................................................$225.00 C

**Dimitrino,** tobacco tin, superb graphics, street scene on one side and carpet scene on other side, 5" x 5" x 1½", EX ..........$135.00 C

Dr. Pepper, poster, cardboard in wood frame, "I'd Give A Month's Pay For A," WWII era, 28½" x 18½", EX, $400.00 C.

Dr. Pepper, menu board, tin over cardboard, 17" x 23", EX, $195.00 D.

Dr. Pepper, sign, glass, glo glass brand, "Energy-up Drink Dr. Pepper, Good For Life, Ice Cold," 1930s, 14" x 11", EX, $2,500.00 B. *Courtesy of Muddy River Trading Co./Gary Metz.*

Dr. Pepper, sign, tin, double-sided flange, fountain, 1961, 22" x 15", EX, $900.00 B.

Dr. Pepper, sign, tin, embossed, "Take Home, A Carton" with a 6 pack in center spotlight, 1930s, 19" x 27", VG, $1,150.00 B.

Dr. Pepper, sign, metal case, Vibera-Lite, animated, Dr. Pepper Hot "devilishly different," 24" x 13" x ⅜", 1950 – 1960s, EX, $2,200.00 B.

**Dining Car Coffee,** tin, litho, key-wound lid, black waiter serving the product in railroad dining car, 1-lb., EX ...................$130.00 D

**Diplomat Whiskey,** sign, tin, litho, in early gesso frame, "Just Right," "Glasner Barzen Distilling and Importing Co., Kansas City, Mo." men seated around table, 50" x 37½", VG .................$550.00 B

**Dixie 1¢ Bubble Gum,** box, store display, 7" x 7" x 3", EX .$50.00 B

**Dixie Gasoline,** sign, oval, double-sided, original stand, "Oils, Power to Pass," 24" x 46", F .......................................................$450.00 D

**Dixie Kid Cut Plug,** pail, tin, lithographed, wire handle "He was bred in old Kentucky," 8" x 5½" x 4", VG...............................................$400.00 B

**Dixie Queen Pipe Cut Tobacco,** canister, small top, 4¾" x 6¼", EX .......................................................................................$385.00 B

**Dixie Salted Nuts Peanuts,** tin, young black boy holding peanuts in his mouth, #10 pry lid from Wilkes-Barre Can Co., EX.....$365.00 C

**Dixie Tailoring Co.** pocket mirror, Statue of Liberty, "made to measure clothes," 1¾" x 2¾", EX...............................$120.00 B

**Dixon's Stove Polish,** sign, group of men gathered around a stove, 6¼" x 5", EX ......................................................................$85.00 D

**Dixon's Stove Polish,** trade card, Lime Kiln Club, with sales pitch for product, 1886, 5" x 6¼", NM.......................$50.00 B

**DM Ferry & Co.,** sign, cardboard, girl with dog holding vegetables, 1900s, 19" x 29", EX...........................................$225.00 D

**Doan's Kidney Pills,** thermometer, wood, die cut, man with bad back, "Is Your Back Bad Today," 5" x 21", VG ...............$115.00 C

**Dobbs Hats,** display, composition, mechanical, man wearing a Dobbs hat and fishing clothing and moving a rod back and forth, 24" x 16" x 56", EX ...........................................................................$3,000.00 D

**Dode Meeks Company,** calendar, Livestock, pretty young woman in center, unusual diamond shape, 11" x 11", 1906, EX ........$140.00 B

Dr. Pierce's Favorite Prescription, sign, paper, litho, girlhood, womanhood, and motherhood, "For Sale Here," great colorful graphics, 11¼" x 48", G, $1,200.00 B. *Courtesy of Richard Opfer Auctioneering, Inc.*

Dr. Pierce's Prescription, decal on window glass, woman in a flared glass with a glass holder, 1890s, G, $2,400.00 B. *Courtesy of Muddy River Trading Co./Gary Metz.*

Dr. Schol's, sign, cardboard, die cut, woman being helped with one of their products by a young salesman, 45" x 38½", NM, $350.00 B.

Dr. Swett's, The Original Root Beer, sign, tin, embossed, 24" x 9", G, $425.00 B. *Courtesy of Muddy River Trading Co./Gary Metz.*

Drummond's Horse Shoe, sign, cardboard, die cut, in frame, 17" x 21", VG, $165.00 C.

Drummond Tobacco Co., Enterprise Mfg. Co., tobacco cutter, Philadelphia, Pat. April 13, 1875, EX, $190.00 C.

Dr. Wells, sign, tin, self-framing, embossed, "The Cooler Doctor," 31" x 11½", VG, $125.00 C.

---

**Dodge Dependable Service,** sign, porcelain, double-sided, dealer, 42" dia., EX ............................................................$1,100.00 C

**Dodge Plymouth Approved Service,** sign, porcelain, double-sided circle with rocket ship shaped direction pointer hanging under main message, 42" dia., EX .............................................$275.00 C

**Dodge Plymouth** Dependable Service...Dodge Trucks, sign, porcelain, round, die cut, dealer with arrow in center, 48" dia., 1930s, EX...............................................................................$1,600.00 B

**Dodge Plymouth,** sign, porcelain, neon, 60" x 28", VG....$1,850.00 C

**Dodger Beverage,** sign, steel, die cut, shape of bottle, 16" x 65", EX ........................................................................$450.00 C

**Doe-Wah-Jack Round Oak Stove,** calendar, full pad of monthly tear sheets, embossed Indian with peace pipe, 1924, 10½" x 21", EX ........................................................................$330.00 B

**Doe-Wah-Jack,** calendar, Indian in hunting scene, with full calendar pad, 10½" x 20¾", 1922, EX ......................................$360.00 B

**Dog 'n Suds,** sign, neon, dog with tray with frosty root beer and a hot dog, 8' x 7'6", EX..............................................$3,000.00 D

**Dom Dom Benedictine Liqueur,** sign, porcelain, single-sided, bottle, 49" x 39", G..............................................................$150.00 B

**Domestic Sew Machines,** sign, neon, light-up, on metal base, with domestic oil cans, EX......................................................$465.00 D

**Domestic Sew Machines,** sign, neon, light-up, on metal base, with domestic oil cans, NM ......................................................$495.00 C

**Domestic Sewing Machine,** sign, paper, graphics and story line tell how great married life is if you have their product, 14" x 20", EX .........................................................................$155.00 C

**Domestic Sewing Machine,** sign, paper, litho, "This is the machine that I'll have...," 1890s, 14" x 20", EX.............................$125.00 C

**Domestic,** tip tray, metal, litho, "it stands at the head," 4¼" dia., VG ........................................................................$205.00 B

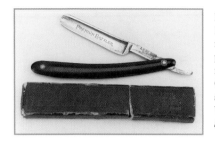

**DuBois Son & Co Premium Rattler**, razor, celluloid and metal, original box, originally priced at $2.50, razor is marked L.S. DuBois Son & Co., Paducah, KY, box shows some wear, 6" long closed, VG, $65.00 C. *Courtesy of B.J. Summers.*

**Dudley Dairy**, bottle, glass with painted label, rear label "Dudley's Safe Milk" with image of small child reaching for a bottle of milk at the front door, front painted label also has embossed company name, 1930s, ½ pt, EX, $45.00 C. *Courtesy of B.J. Summers.*

**Dudley Dairy Products**, pocket mirror, celluloid and glass, early premium, 1920 – 30s, 3" x 2", VG, $35.00 C. *Courtesy of B.J. Summers.*

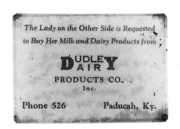

**Duke's Mixture Coupons**, sign, cardboard, with items that could be redeemed with the coupons, 19" x 28", G, $375.00 C.

**Duke's Mixture**, door push, porcelain, hard-to-find, "the roll of fame," with tobacco pouring from bag into man's hand, 5¼" x 8", EX, $425.00 B. *Courtesy of Buffalo Bay Auction Co.*

**Duke's Mixture**, sign, porcelain, tobacco being poured onto cigarette paper, "ready to roll," 1920 – 30s, 4¼" x 8¾", EX, $450.00 B.

**Dominion Ammunition Co.**, shell box, black powder for 28 gauge shotguns, 3¼" x 3¼" x 2½", EX ............................................$95.00 C

**Domino**, sign, cardboard, die cut, framed, heavy, "The Mild Cigarette," unusual and hard to find, 28" x 44½", EX........$475.00 C

**Domino, Smoke**, sign, cardboard, die cut, framed, "The Mild Cigarette, Let your taste be the judge," 34" x 42", EX................$450.00 C

**Don Remo**, change receiver, reverse glass image with cigar cutter on side, 9½" x 6", EX ........................................................$302.00 B

**Donald Duck Beverages**, sign, metal, self-framing, Donald Duck and product message, 28" x 20", EX.............................................$365.00 B

**Donald Duck Chocolate Syrup**, tin, Donald Duck on the front, from the Atlantic Syrup Co., marked Walt Disney Productions, 15-oz., 1950s, NM .....................................................................$120.00 B

**Donald Duck Coffee**, tin, litho, Donald Duck on front, from Goyer Coffee Co., Greenville, Miss., 1-lb., VG .........................................$250.00 C

**Donald Duck Cola**, sign, paper on cardboard, die cut, "Tops for Flavor," bottle cap to left of bottle sitting on ice, duck image on bottle, 22" x 26", EX ..........................................................................$85.00 D

**Donald Duck Florida Orange Juice**, can, paper label, Donald Duck looking around juice glass, 1-qt., EX ....................................$25.00 B

**Donald Duck High Grade Pure Coffee**, tin, litho, key-wound lid, Donald Duck on front, 1-lb., EX.......................................$797.00 B

**Donald Duck Oats**, box, paper label cardboard, Donald Duck, 3-lb., VG ...................................................................................$275.00 B

**Donald Duck Soft Drinks**, button, celluloid/tin, Donald Duck in center, 9" dia., EX.............................................................$275.00 C

**Donald Duck Straws**, box, Donald Duck, Mickey Mouse, and Pluto with clear window to view contents, 3¾" x 8¾", EX............$45.00 D

**Donaldson Litho Company**, salesman sample, fair at Newport, KY, Aug., 5, 6, 7, 8, 1913, great graphics, 1913, 20" x 30", EX.$275.00 B

Duke's Mixture, sign, blacks going down a hill in an out of control vehicle, 17" x 14", EX, $145.00 B.
*Courtesy of Buffalo Bay Auction Co.*

Dunlop Tire, clock, porcelain, 39" dia., VG, $235.00 C.

Dunn Drugs, large number finger wheel, plastic with self-stick backing, usually given to the elderly for phones in the days of rotary dials, 1960s, 4¼" dia., EX, $5.00 C. *Courtesy of B.J. Summers.*

Du Pont Auto Polishes, poster, cardboard, three-piece litho, young black boy seeing his reflection in auto trunk, 37½" x 46", VG, $2,100.00 B. *Courtesy of Collectors Auction Services.*

Du Pont Car Polish, window display, cardboard, young woman in shiny vintage convertible, 35" x 34½", EX, $675.00 B. *Courtesy of Wm. Morford Investment Grade Collectibles.*

**Donaldson Litho Company,** salesman sample, fair at Newport, KY, Aug., 5, 6, 7, 8, 1913, great graphics, 1913, 20" x 30", NM...**$290.00 B**

**Dortmunder Union,** tapper handle, wooden, EX.......................**$30.00 D**

**Dot Coffee,** can, tin, front cover pictures large dot with product name, VG.................................................................................**$85.00 C**

**Double Cola,** clock, electric, "Drink Double Cola" in center bull's eye, 12" dia., 1950s, EX.......................................................**$165.00 B**

**Double Cola,** door push, metal, "Drink, Double Measure, Double Pleasure," 34" x 4½", red on aluminum, G ......................**$95.00 D**

**Double Cola,** Ideal "slider," "Drink," a great box because of its large capacity and small room, this particular version is painted in the 1940s scheme, restored, 1950s, 37" W x 42" H x 19½" D, yellow and black on red, NM ...........................................................**$1,895.00 D**

**Double Cola,** menu board, "Drink," at top center, 19¾" x 27½", green, white, yellow, and black, EX ...........................**$175.00 D**

**Double Cola,** menu board, metal, self-framing, "Enjoy," at top center, with burst coming from behind oval logo, 19½" x 28", white lettering on red oval, black, EX .............................................**$155.00 D**

**Double Cola,** menu board, single-sided, self-framing, 20" x 28", VG...............................................................................................**$85.00 B**

**Double Cola,** sign, metal, painted, flange, "Drink," copyright 1947, The Double Cola Co., Chattanooga, Tenn., 18" x 15", EX .**$275.00 C**

**Double Cola,** sign, metal, painted, V-shaped, "Drink Double Cola," 32" x 20", VG ...........................................................................**$275.00 B**

**Double Cola,** sign, tin, die cut, flange, "Drink," NOS, 18" x 15", 1947, NM .......................................................................................**$575.00 C**

**Double Cola,** spare tire cover, "Swell Drink...We Think," with silkscreen the Double Cola twins, 27" dia., EX................**$50.00 B**

**Double Cola,** thermometer, metal, "Make it a Double...or nothing," painted, red & white, G...................................................**$95.00 C**

**Du Pont Generations,** sign, tin, self-framed, bird dogs in the field and different generations teaching and learning about hunting, by Edmund H. Osthaus, 23" x 33", EX, $1,700.00 B. *Courtesy of Past Tyme Pleasures.*

**Du Pont Smokeless Shotgun Powder,** sign, titled The End of a Good Day, hunting scene, framed, 1911, 18" x 27", EX, $650.00 B. *Courtesy of Muddy River Trading Co./Gary Metz.*

**Duskil Mop Company,** can, metal, directions call for mop to be oiled and placed in this can when not in use, 4" x 6¾" dia., EX, $45.00 C. *Courtesy of B.J. Summers.*

**Dutch Boy Paint,** sign, tin, single-sided, embossed, EX, $250.00 C.

**Dutch Boy,** sign, metal, double-sided, "Atlantic White Lead," with the boy in the swing, 14" x 26", 1925, EX, $5,200.00 B. *Courtesy of Buffalo Bay Auction Co.*

**Dutch Boy White Lead Paint,** sign, tin, litho, double-sided, Dutch Boy with the paint bucket string holder below him, 13¾" x 28", EX, $1,300.00 B.

**Duty Calls,** poster, paper, "doughboy" leaving home for war, 1917, G, $225.00 D.

---

**Double Tip,** condom tin, litho, Distributed By Department Sales, Co., New York, NY, woman sitting at water's edge, 2¼" x 1⅝", EX ..............................................................$750.00 B

**Double-Orange,** sign, cardboard, round, "Truly Delightful," artwork by Rolf Armstrong, 1920s, 18" dia., NM................................$235.00 D

**Douglas Aviation Tested Gasoline,** pump sign, porcelain, 12" x 12", NM ........................................................................$675.00 C

**Douglas Aviation Tested Regular Gasoline,** pump sign, aluminum, 12½" x 18", NM..............................................................$675.00 C

**Douglas Blend Gasoline,** pump sign, aluminum, embossed, 14" x 10", NM..............................................................................$450.00 C

**Douglas Premium Gasoline,** pump sign, aluminum, embossed, 10" x 10", G.............................................................................$125.00 C

**Dove Brand Meats,** sign, tin, litho, woman holding doves, for the Roth Meat Packing Co., Cincinnati, 19⅝" x 27¾", EX.....$775.00 C

**Dove Spice,** tin, litho, pair of doves on label, Cincinnati, O., 2-oz., EX ................................................................................$135.00 C

**Dow and Company,** ashtray with steam roller, 5" x 5½" x 3½", VG...........................................................................................$40.00 B

**Dr. A. C. Daniels',** tip tray, tin, litho, horse and cattle medicines, with images of horses in center, 4¼" dia., EX...................$145.00 D

**Dr. A.C. Daniels' Horse and Dog Medicines,** sign, wooden wood frame, 30½" x 18¼", G......................................................$475.00 D

**Dr. A.C. Daniels' Horse, Cat, and Dog Medicines,** sign, tin, embossed "Use...For Home Treatment," 28" x 17½", EX.....$135.00 D

**Dr. A.C. Daniels' Veterinary Medicine,** thermometer, wooden, 5⅝" x 24" x ¾", G........................................................................$300.00 B

**Dr. A.C. Daniels' Veterinary Medicines,** cabinet, wood with embossed tin front that pictures Dr. Daniels' products, 21½" x 28½" x 7½", EX......................................................................$1,600.00 C

116

**Dr. A.C. Daniels',** sign, cardboard, horses in center inset with the message surrounding the artwork, 13⅞" x 19⅝", EX .........$650.00 B

**Dr. Brown's Celery Syrup,** dispenser, glass bowl, milk glass, 7" sq base x 10½", EX ....................................................................$75.00 C

**Dr. Caldwell's Laxative Syrup Pepsin,** sign, cloth, "Cures Constipation Indigestion," 46" x 22", EX .............................$695.00 C

**Dr. Caldwell's Syrup Pepsin,** door push, porcelain, "You Can Depend On...The Family Laxative," 4" x 7", EX................$255.00 C

**Dr. Caldwell's Syrup Pepsin,** sign, metal, double-sided, porcelain, "The Perfect Laxative," 24" x 16", EX ..................................$3,500.00 D

**Dr. Clark's Life Balsam,** sign, paper, lady in yellow dress and crown promoting the healing powers of the product, 9" x 13", EX ......................................................................................$525.00 C

**Dr. Collis Brown's Chlorodyne,** sign, porcelain, medicine that is good for all sorts of ailments, 14" x 14", EX ...................................$175.00 C

**Dr. D Jayne's Expectorant & Tonic Vermifuge,** sign, paper, "For Coughs and Colds," 13½" x 29", EX .........................$575.00 C

**Dr. D. Jaynes Family Medicine,** sign, glass, wood frame, gold lettering, 21¾" x 21½", EX ..........................................$175.00 C

**Dr. Daniels',** cabinet, tin, dog and cat remedy, featuring woman and pets, 20" x 14" x 5", EX ....................................$2,100.00 C

**Dr. Daniels',** medicine cabinet, tin litho on front with images of Dr. Daniels and his cures, 21½" x 7¾" x 28½", EX .............$1,925.00 B

**Dr. Daniels',** store card, dog medicine, dogs playing baseball with dogs as spectators in the bleachers, 15" x 12", EX................$175.00 C

**Dr. Daniels',** store card, dog medicine, dogs playing football, 20" x 14", EX ............................................................$225.00 C

**Dr. Drake's Glesco Cough & Croup Remedy,** sign, metal, young couple looking into a crib, "For Young & Old," 11½" x 14¼", EX ............................................................$225.00 D

**Dr. Frost's Homeopathic Remedies,** cabinet, wood, tin door listing the ailments and remedies, EX .........................................$425.00 C

**Dr. Graves Tooth Powder,** sign, reverse foil on black glass, "Dr. E.L. Graves unequaled tooth powder," 12" x 22" x ¼", 1900s, NM..........................................................................$495.00 C

**Dr. Greene's Nervura,** thermometer, wood, painted, "Dr. Greene's Nervura For The Nerves," 14" tall, EX ................................$55.00 C

**Dr. Haile's Ole Injun System Tonic,** sign, paperboard, Indian Chief in full headress, "For The Kidneys, Liver & Stomach," 13½" x 20½", VG ...........................................................................$25.00 D

**Dr. Hess Medicated Powder,** container, tin, horse collar logo, 4 oz., EX.....................................................................$25.00 D

**Dr. Jayne's Family Medicines,** sign, glass with wood border, lettering in gold, "Dr. Jayne's Family Medicine," 21¾" x 11½", VG ...........$135.00 D

**Dr. Jayne's Family Medicines,** sign, stone, litho, Martha Washington with the original Dr. Jayne's stamped mat and in vintage frame, 16" x 20", 1900s, EX .....................................................$300.00 B

**Dr. Kellogg's Asthma Remedy,** container, tin, slip lid, EX..$20.00 C

**Dr. Kilmers Indian Cough Cure,** container, glass with paper label, Indian tribe on the move, 2½" x 5½", 1870s, EX .....................$95.00 C

**Dr. King's,** match holder, tin, litho, large brick building on front, by H.D Beach, 3½" x 5", VG ....................................................$135.00 C

**Dr. Lesure's Veterinary Medicines,** cabinet, wood with glass door, marquee at top with company lettering, 16" x 28" x 6", EX ...........................................................................$2,200.00 D

**Dr. Lions Celebrated Stomach Bitters,** calendar, paper, 3 ladies using the product, full monthly pad, 13" x 17", EX .........$25.00 C

**Dr. McMunn's Kinute of Quinine & Cinchonine,** sign, paper, sick woman inside and men outside, 14" x 10", EX ......................$1,200.00 C

**Dr. Melvins Vegetable Pills,** trade card, cardboard, black man, EX.............................................................................$15.00 D

**Dr. Miles Nervine,** sign, cardboard, die cut, young girl in early attire holding a bottle of the product, 9" x 21", 1902, EX..$225.00 C

**Dr. Miles Remedies,** calendar, child holding a rose, full monthly pad, 1908, G ..........................................................................$65.00 C

**Dr. Morse's Indian Root Pills,** ad, cardboard, die cut, easel back, Indian paddling a canoe, 19½" x 9½", G ...........................$135.00 C

**Dr. Morse's Indian Root Pills,** ad, cardboard, tri-fold, die cut, countertop, Indian preparing a meal, 41½" x 27", VG ..............$550.00 B

**Dr. Morse's Indian Root Pills,** display, cardboard, die cut, Indian and village scene, 40" x 27", EX ............................................$195.00 C

**Dr. Morse's Indian Root Pills,** trade card, cardboard, Indian on horseback fighting a bear, "Comstock's Dead Shot Worm Pellets," EX..............................................................................$25.00 D

**Dr. Morse's Root Pills,** sign, cardboard, has great graphics of Indian activities, easel back, countertop design, 24½" x 13", EX..$153.00 B

**Dr. Morse's,** sign, cardboard, die cut with easel back, promoting Indian Root pill, featuring Indian in canoe, 19½" x 9½", VG......$200.00 C

**Dr. O'Neill's Vegetable Remedy,** container, tin, Dr. O'Neill in center cameo, slip lid, 1910s, 2" x 1½", EX .............................$25.00 C

**Dr. P Hall's Catarrh Remedy,** sign, metal, Dr. Hall on product box, 1880s, 45" x 30½", VG.........................................................$75.00 C

**Dr. Palmers Almomeal Compound,** tin, litho, in original box with great art of pretty red-haired woman on front, NM.............$25.00 B

**Dr. Pepper,** ad, paper, in original aluminum frame with logo at top, "and Ice Cream," product in ice, 1950s, 22" x 17", EX........$95.00 C

**Dr. Pepper,** bottle carrier, wooden, "Good For Life!," "Loaned Not Sold Deposit Returnable" on handle, rare and hard to find, 12-package, 15¼" x 5¼" x 9¼", EX........................$275.00 D

**Dr. Pepper,** bottle carrier, wooden, "Good For Life!," "Loaned Not Sold Deposit Returnable" on handle, rare and hard to find, 12-package, 15¼" x 5¼" x 9¼", VG........................$255.00 C

**Dr. Pepper,** bottle, glass, embossed label and clock, 6½", VG........$8.00 D

**Dr. Pepper,** calendar, paper, 10-2-4 bottle cap logo, 1950s, EX .$55.00 C

**Dr. Pepper,** calendar, paper, girl in bowling alley holding a bottle of Dr. Pepper, 1961, 16" x 23½", EX........................$45.00 C

**Dr. Pepper,** calendar, paper, girl in raincoat at Niagara Falls, 1977, EX........................$25.00 C

**Dr. Pepper,** clock, electric, Telechron, with message under hands stem, 1930s, M........................$500.00 C

**Dr. Pepper,** clock, metal body and bubble glass cover, Telechron, name in center of face in plaid logo, 13½" dia., 1930s, EX........$295.00 D

**Dr. Pepper,** clock, metal body with glass cover and face, light-up, "Drink Dr. Pepper" banner at bottom, 15½" sq., EX........$150.00 C

**Dr. Pepper,** clock, metal, with glass face and front, neon, 6" x 21½", VG........................$850.00 B

**Dr. Pepper,** clock, neon, 10-2-4 logo on face, 14" dia., VG........$195.00 D

**Dr. Pepper,** clock, reverse painted glass front, in the art deco style, electric, rare, 1930s, 22" x 17", VG........................$2,950.00 C

**Dr. Pepper,** door pull, aluminum, in shape of bottle, 3½" x 10", VG........................$275.00 C

**Dr. Pepper,** menu board, tin, "Good For Life," embossed bottle at left corner, 17¼" x 23¼", EX........................$225.00 C

**Dr. Pepper,** menu board, tin, rounded corners and company logo at top of board, 20" x 28", EX........................$115.00 C

**Dr. Pepper,** picnic cooler, metal, with top wire bail handle, "Drink," 18" x 12" x 9", white on green, G........................$85.00 D

**Dr. Pepper,** picnic cooler, metal, with top wire bail handle, "Drink," 18" x 12" x 9", white on green, VG........................$115.00 D

**Dr. Pepper,** poster, "Have a Picnic," New York World's Fair, picnic scene, EX........................$40.00 D

**Dr. Pepper,** radio, wood case in shape of drink cooler, company logo on front, 12" x 8" x 8½", G........................$1,500.00 C

**Dr. Pepper,** shotglass, glass, "America's Oldest Soft Drink," 1989, EX........................$5.00 D

**Dr. Pepper,** sign, "Drink...Good for Life...Drink a bite to eat at 10–2–4," 3" x 3" x 6", NM........................$182.00 B

**Dr. Pepper,** sign, cardboard, diecut, fan hanger, smiling brunette opening a bottle, 1940s, 5" x 7", EX........................$55.00 D

**Dr. Pepper,** sign, cardboard, double-sided, in original wood frame, "A lift for life," 10, 2, and 4 o'clock at top, 1950s, 31½" x 19", NM........................$425.00 C

**Dr. Pepper,** sign, cardboard, hands making a Dr. Pepper float, "Try A Frosty Pepper," 25" x 15", VG........................$25.00 C

**Dr. Pepper,** sign, cardboard, hanging, clock face 10, 2 & 4 hands, 13" x 13", circa 1920s, EX........................$3,600.00 D

**Dr. Pepper,** sign, cardboard, self-framing, ladies watching cooking, EX........................$350.00 D

**Dr. Pepper,** sign, glo glass, "Energy-up Drink Dr. Pepper, Good For Life, Ice Cold," 1930s, 14" x 11", G........................$750.00 C

**Dr. Pepper,** sign, plastic, window, 13" x 9½", EX........................$45.00 C

**Dr. Pepper,** sign, porcelain, 10, 2, 4 image, 10" dia., EX...$210.00 C

**Dr. Pepper,** sign, porcelain, "Drink Good for life," 26½" x 10½", EX........................$215.00 C

**Dr. Pepper,** sign, porcelain, early block background, "Drink Dr. Pepper...good for life," 26½" x 10½", EX........................$275.00 C

**Dr. Pepper,** sign, porcelain, round, white center, "Drink Dr. Pepper," 10" dia., EX........................$725.00 C

**Dr. Pepper,** sign, porcelain, rounded corners, Dr. Pepper Bottling Co., 21½" x 12", VG........................$225.00 D

**Dr. Pepper,** sign, porcelain, self-framed, "Drink," 24" x 9¼", VG........................$95.00 B

**Dr. Pepper,** sign, tin, embossed, "Good for Life," "tacker" style, 19½" x 4", 1945, EX........................$250.00 D

**Dr. Pepper,** sign, tin, embossed, "Good for Life," "tacker" style, 19½" x 4", 1945, VG........................$220.00 B

**Dr. Pepper,** sign, tin, embossed, litho, "good for life," 19¼" x 7", EX........................$375.00 C

**Dr. Pepper,** sign, tin, embossed, self-framing, trademark 10, 2 & 4 dial and embossed bottle with dial, 18" x 53½", VG........$300.00 C

**Dr. Pepper,** sign, tin, litho, "Drink," chevron under product message, 27¾" x 11¾", NM........................$71.00 B

**Dr. Pepper,** sign, tin, litho, emergency plate with original paper insert for emergency numbers, "Drink...Good For Life," 4" x 8", EX........$235.00 C

**Dr. Pepper,** straw holder, glass with chrome top, 11½" tall, EX .$35.00 D

**Dr. Pepper,** thermometer, metal, "Drink, Frosty Cold," 10" x 25½", white, red, and black, F........................$200.00 C

**Dr. Pepper,** thermometer, metal, "Drink, Frosty Cold," 10" x 25½", white, red, and black, G.....................................................$250.00 D

**Dr. Pepper,** thermometer, metal, in shape of bottle cap, EX.$115.00 D

**Dr. Pepper,** thermometer, metal, painted, "When Hungry, Thirsty or Tired," with bottle at right of scale, 10–2–4 dial at bottom left, G .......................................................$75.00 C

**Dr. Pepper,** thermometer, metal, painted, scale-type, "Hot or Cold," 8¼" x 27", VG.....................................................$120.00 C

**Dr. Pepper,** thermometer, metal, painted, with Dr. Pepper logo in oval at bottom center, "Hot or Cold," red & white, G .........$65.00 D

**Dr. Pepper,** thermometer, metal, scale-type, "Frosty Cold," 9¾" x 25.675", VG.....................................................$135.00 C

**Dr. Pepper,** thermometer, tin, "Hot or Cold," NOS, 5⅛" x 26⅝", NM .......................................................$275.00 C

**Dr. Pepper,** thermometer, tin, bottle shaped, "Drink Dr. Pepper," EX.......................................................$325.00 C

**Dr. Pepper,** thermometer, tin, embossed, die cut, bottle and scale in neck of bottle, 5⅛" x 17¼", EX .......................................$325.00 C

**Dr. Pierce's Auric Tablets,** sign, cardboard, "Oh My Back! The Newest Discovery," VG ...............................................$135.00 D

**Dr. Pierce's Favorite Prescription,** sign, paper, litho, girlhood, womanhood, and motherhood, "For Sale Here," great colorful graphics, 11¼" x 48", G...................................................$1,200.00 B

**Dr. Pierce's Prescription,** decal on window glass, woman in a flared glass with a glass holder, 1890s, EX ................$2,800.00 D

**Dr. Roberts Dental Powder,** canister, metal and cardboard, EX .......................................................$25.00 D

**Dr. Russell's Pepsin Calisaya Bitters,** sign, paper, nymph with cornucopia over the product information, 15" x 21½", EX .$2,000.00 D

**Dr. Scholl's,** display, glass front metal case, store countertop, with products that are carried inside, complete with Dr. Scholl's Plant Jr. Massage and Foot Strengthener, 14½" x 10¾" x 23", VG...$450.00 B

**Dr. Scholls Foot Soap,** container, tin, with contents, shaker type top, 5" tall, EX .......................................................$12.00 C

**Dr. Schoop's Health Coffee Imitation,** match holder, metal, product name and founder, 4½" high, VG................................$215.00 C

**Dr. Shoop's Health Coffee,** match safe, tin, litho, package, never used, 3½" x 4⅞", NM .................................................$375.00 B

**Dr. Siegert's Bitters,** sign, tin, bottle, framed in vintage frame and under glass, 12" x 16", 1890s, NM ......................................$550.00 B

**Dr. Stevenson Dentist,** sign, light-up, original hanging arm, 25" x 14"x 2", 1930s, VG ...................................................$135.00 C

**Dr. Strong's Tricora Corset,** trade card, cardboard, woman in bustle dress, "Affords Great Relief and Comfort," 5½" x 2½", VG....$35.00 D

**Dr. Swett's,** sign, tin, embossed, "The Original Root Beer," 24" x 9", G.......................................................$600.00 C

**Dr. Townsend's Sarsaparilla,** thermometer, wood, Brooklyn, NY, 5⅞" x 24", EX.......................................................$120.00 B

**Dr. Warner's Health Corset,** statue, chalkware on plaster base product displayed around statue, patented Feb., 13, 1877, copyright 1886, Hennecke & Co., Milwaukee, Wis., base 72" tall, statue 28" tall, 1880s, EX...................................................$5,500.00 C

**Dr. Wells,** menu board, metal, "The Cooler Doctor," 19" x 27", EX.......................................................$55.00 C

**Dr. Wells,** menu board, tin, single-sided, "The Cooler Doctor," 18½" x 27", VG.......................................................$75.00 C

**Dr. Wells,** thermometer, tin, "The Cooler Doctor," scale type with rounded corners, 6" x 15", VG .......................................$45.00 C

**Dr. White's Cough Drops,** container, tin litho, extremely pleasant, hinged top for product, hard-to-find item, 3½" x 2¼" x ¾", EX.......................................................$600.00 B

**Drake's Palmetto Wine,** match holder, goose in flight, 3½" x 4¾", VG.......................................................$145.00 D

**Drako Coffee,** tin, litho, slip-on lid, duck on front label, 1-lb., EX .......................................................$185.00 C

**Dreibus Juanette Chocolates,** sign, cardboard, die cut, easel back, woman in bonnet, 8" x 14", EX...........................................$47.00 B

**Dri-Powr,** thermometer, dial, dri-powr genie, from the Pam Clock Co., 12" dia., 1958, EX.......................................................$150.00 B

**Drigga Milk & Cream,** thermometer, tin, die cut, cow on circle over scale, 15" dia., EX...................................................$195.00 C

**Drink City Club,** wheel cover, West Union, IA, 28", EX .$85.00 D

**Drobish Bros.,** cabinet, nickel drop cigar, trade stimulator in oak 14½" x 19½", 1897, NM .................................................$3,000.00 D

**Droste's Cocoa,** tin, Dutch girl on front, 1-lb., VG .............$25.00 C

**Drucker's Revelation For The Teeth and Gums,** container, tin, oval, 1" x 2½", VG.......................................................$40.00 C

**Drug Store,** sign, porcelain, message is in yellow on green, "Drug Store," 1930s, 16" x 11", VG .............................................$175.00 C

**Drugs,** sign, neon with neon border, 31½" x 10", EX .................$175.00 C

**Drummond Tobacco Co.,** sign, Enterprise Mfg. Co., Philadelphia, Pat. April 13, 1875, EX .....................................................$135.00 D

**Drummond Tobacco Company,** sign, paper, woman with bouquet, 1890s, 19" x 26¾", VG ...................................................$155.00 D

**Drummond's Horse Shoe,** sign, cardboard, die cut, in frame, 17" x 21", EX..................................................................$170.00 B

**Dry-Kold Refrigerator Company,** sign, porcelain, 22" x 11¾", EX ...................................................................$250.00 C

**DS Brown & Co Soaps,** sign, paper, women bathing in stream, 20" x 13", EX ...................................................................$2,800.00 C

**Du Bois Beer,** sign, curved glass front panel, light-up, Du Bois Brewing Co., Du Bois, Pa., 11" x 9¾", EX.................................$195.00 C

**Du Bois Budweiser** sign, metal back with curved glass front, light-up, 11" x 9¾", EX ..................................................$175.00 C

**Du Bois Budweiser,** clock, electric, light-up, 15" dia., EX ...$325.00 C

**Du Bois Budweiser,** clock, metal and glass, name on face, 15" dia., VG ...................................................................$255.00 D

**Du Bois Budweiser,** sign, tin, painted, 6" x 4", EX...................$35.00 D

**Du Bois Budweiser,** sign, tin, single-sided, embossed, bottle, 13½" x 19½", G.................................................................$65.00 B

**Du Bois Expert Beer,** sign, tin, self-framing, wood backed, "Ask for – Du Bois Expert Beer," 70" x 35½", EX.................................$145.00 C

**Du Bois,** sign, tin, embossed, "Try The Original...," 13¼" x 19¼", VG ...................................................................$50.00 C

**Du Pont Authorized Agency,** sign, porcelain, die cut, double-sided, 16" x 17¾", NM..................................................$395.00 C

**Du Pont Auto Polishes,** poster, cardboard, three-piece litho, young black boy seeing his reflection in auto trunk, 37½" x 46", EX..................................................$2,400.00 C

**Du Pont Ballistite,** sign, paper, ducks in flight, 1910s, 20" x 30", EX ...................................................................$2,000.00 C

**Du Pont Car Polish,** sign, cardboard, window display, young woman in shiny vintage convertible, 35" x 34½", VG........$595.00 C

**Du Pont Denatured Alcohol Anti Rust Anti-Freeze,** thermometer, metal, painted, scale in vertical arrow, messages at top and bottom, 8" x 38½", black, orange, and red, EX...............................$135.00 C

**Du Pont Explosives Dept.,** calendar, three months at a glance, bird dog and short artist bio, 1960, 15" x 31", EX.........$35.00 C

**Du Pont Generations,** sign, tin, self-framed, bird dogs in the field and different generations teaching and learning about hunting, by Edmund H. Osthaus, 23" x 33", VG.............................$1,200.00 C

**Du Pont Gun Powder,** sign, tin, litho, self-framed, father and son in field with bird dogs, 23" x 32½", NM ...................................$2,000.00 C

**Du Pont Paints,** sign, neon, oval, "DuPont Paints," 23" x 16", EX ...................................................................$250.00 C

**Du Pont Powders for Firearms,** booklet, paper, treed leopard, 1920s, 28 pages, EX ........................................................$50.00 C

**Du Pont Powders,** sign, cardboard, litho, part 2 of a six-piece set, general store scene, 13" x 8", 1909, EX ...................................$70.00 B

**Du Pont** sign, paint, hanging arm, 15" x 11½", EX ...........$240.00 B

**Du Pont Smokeless Shotgun Powder,** calender, The End of a Good Day, hunting scene, framed, 1911, 18" x 27", VG.............$595.00 C

**Du Pont Smokeless Shotgun,** shell box, American Litho, 3½" x 3½", 1910, EX ...................................................................$175.00 C

**Du Pont Smokeless,** pinback, celluloid, hunting dogs, "The Champion's Powder," 1¼" dia., NM...................................................$95.00 C

**Du Pont Sterling,** spoon, trap shooting in spoon bowl, marked Tiffany & Co., EX ...................................................$150.00 C

**Du Pont Zerex,** sign, cardboard, die cut, easel back, countertop, of service man holding large can of anti-freeze, 25½" x 32½", 1940s, EX...................................................................$150.00 C

**Du Pont,** calendar, paper with original metal strips, hunters with dogs, for DuPont Powder, partial calendar pad, 1907, 15" x 29¼", EX...................................................................$633.00 B

**Du Pont,** calendar, paper, full monthly pad, battle of Santiago, 1900, 14" x 28", VG ...................................................$575.00 D

**Du Pont,** poster, paper litho, Du Pont Sporting Powders, older man and young boy resting on snow-covered log after hunting, 17" x 25⅜", EX...................................................$850.00 B

**Du Pont,** poster, paper, litho, young boys in a snowy field hunting, 14½" x 20¼", 1909, EX...................................................$625.00 B

**Du Pont,** sign, cardboard, pointers at point, "Hunter's Inspiration," 13" x 8", EX ...................................................$165.00 C

**Du Pont,** sign, tin, self-framing edge, youngster being shown how to hunt by older man, "Generations Have Used DuPont Powder," 1910 – 20s, VG ...................................................$525.00 C

**Du Pont,** stickpin, setter bird dog, rare item, 1880s, EX.....$225.00 C

**Ducky Dubble,** sign, paper over cardboard, with popsicle, 18½" x 8", 1956, EX ...................................................$135.00 C

**Duke Beer,** clock, electric, light-up, diamond-shaped, 15¼" sq., EX...................................................................$100.00 C

**Duke of York Cigarettes,** charger, tin, litho, curved, Duke in the center, rare item, 16" dia., EX...................................................$525.00 B

**Duke's Cameo,** cigarette package, W. Duke & Sons, EX....$110.00 B

**Duke's Mixture,** door push, porcelain, hard-to-find, "the roll of fame," tobacco pouring from bag into man's hand, 5¼" x 8", VG ......**$350.00 C**

**Duke's Mixture,** poster, paper, litho, black men and an old buggy, 22½" x 20", VG .....................................................................**$425.00 B**

**Duke's Mixture,** poster, paper, litho, buggy with black men "For de lawd! Dis mus be what date nigger ment when he said he'd float de stock," 22½" x 20", VG .......................................................**$475.00 B**

**Duke's Mixture,** sign, blacks in a vehicle out of control going down a hill, 17" x 14", NM................................................................**$195.00 C**

**Duke's Mixture,** sign, paper, litho, four black men in a buggy while the mule stands behind the buggy, 22½" x 20", VG ..........**$300.00 B**

**Duke's Mixture,** sign, porcelain, raised metal surface, Belt Enamel Co., drawstring bag, 8¾" x 12", EX....................................**$525.00 B**

**Duke's Tobacco Mixture,** poster, 20" x 29¾", 1913, EX.**$100.00 D**

**Duluth Flour,** sack, black chef holding a platter of bread, 11" x 16", EX ........................................................................................**$75.00 B**

**Duluth Imperial Flour,** sign, tin, baker using product, 18" x 25", VG ......................................................................................**$2,200.00 C**

**Duluth Imperial Flour,** sign, tin, litho, beveled edge, black chef holding the finished product hot from a bakers' pan, hard-to-find piece, 18" x 25", EX ......................................................**$800.00 B**

**Dunham's Cocoanut,** sign, paper, die cut, lady with cake, 1915, 13" x 11", NM .....................................................................................**$84.00 B**

**Dunkin' Donuts,** tea set, plastic, child's toy set, 1970s, EX..**$100.00 C**

**Dunlap's Seeds,** poster, paper, child holding a large cabbage, 16" x 24", EX ....................................................................................**$625.00 C**

**Duquesne Brewing Company Duke Beer,** clock, metal back, curved glass front, light-up, 16" x 16", EX....................**$135.00 C**

**Duquesne Pilsener,** print, signed by Walt Otto, "The Finest Beer in Town," Duquesne Brewing Co., Pittsburgh, Pa., 1934, 29" x 32", EX...........................................................................................**$140.00 D**

**Duquesne Pilsner,** print, framed signed by Walt Otto, "The Finest Beer in Town," Duquesne Brewing Co., Pittsburgh, Pa., 1934, 29" x 32", G ........................................................**$125.00 D**

**Duquesne Pilsner,** sign, metal and glass, light-up, 24" x 6", EX...**$125.00 C**

**Duquesne,** clock, light-up, reverse painted face, "The Finest Beer in Town," 24½" x 5½" x 18½", VG ....................................**$425.00 B**

**Duracell Batteries,** bunny, cloth and metal, with the drum banging rabbit, 14" tall, EX................................................................**$35.00 D**

**Dutch Boy Paints,** display, tin, die cut, Dutch Boy with a bucket of paint, 6½" tall, VG................................................................**$275.00 C**

**Dutch Boy Paints,** match safe, tin, embossed, Dutch Boy with bucket which serves as the match holder, 3¼" x 6¼", EX .................................................................................................**$1,200.00 D**

**Dutch Boy Paints,** poster, cardboard, framed, Atlantic, Pure White Lead Paint, Dutch boy with paint bucket and brush sitting on shelf, 20¾" x 35", F .........................................................................**$165.00 C**

**Dutch Boy Paints,** puppet, cloth body and vinyl head, 1950s, F .**$33.00 C**

**Dutch Boy Paints,** sign, metal, Atlantic, boy sitting on a shelf with a paint brush, 20¾" x 35", 1906, G..................**$325.00 C**

**Dutch Boy Paints,** sign, porcelain, double-sided, flange, Dutch Boy with paint can and brush, 14" x 21", EX ............................**$325.00 C**

**Dutch Boy Paints,** string holder, metal, double-sided, "Atlantic White Lead," boy in the swing, heavy construction, 14" x 26", 1925, F .................................................................................................**$1,800.00 C**

**Dutch Boy White Lead Paint,** display, papier mache, Dutch Boy with a paint can, 12" x 30", G ..........................................**$625.00 C**

**Dutch Boy White Lead,** sign, litho on cloth, Dutch Boy and painter, 26½" x 50", 1933, NM..................................**$275.00 C**

**Dutch Boy,** statue, papier-mache, full figure holding a pail of Dutch white, 9" x 8½" x 28", EX.......................................................**$695.00 D**

**Dutch Cleanser,** decal on transom glass, trademark cleaning woman on both sides, 35½" x 14½", VG ......................................................**$55.00 B**

**Dutch Girl Coffee,** cardboard can, tin top and bottom, "Roasted and Packed by The Eureka Coffee Co., Buffalo, NY," Dutch girl on front, 3" x 6½" x 4¼", EX...................................................**$130.00 B**

**Dutch Java Blend Coffee,** tin, cardboard litho, die cut, young boy holding basket, 6¾" x 8½", EX ..................................................**$190.00 B**

**Dutch Java Coffee,** pocket mirror, "Secret of Happiness" on back, 2" dia., EX .....................................................................................**$75.00 B**

**Dutch Java Coffee,** sign, cardboard, die cut, farm scene and touring car, 7" x 8¾", EX .......................................................................**$145.00 D**

**Dutch Master Cigar,** can, metal, well known scene of Dutchmen seated around table, slip lid with company name on banner around the top of the can, 5¼" x 5¼", VG...................**$35.00 C**

**Dutch Master,** sign, porcelain, paint, single-sided, trademark Dutchman in center, 26" dia., EX ......................................**$325.00 B**

**Dutch Masters Cigars,** sign, tin, self-framed, litho, hanging, Dutch pilgrims, 11" x 9", EX............................................................**$75.00 B**

**Duxbak & Kamp-it,** sign, tin, self-framing, peaceful camp scene of man fishing and woman cooking, 1930s, 17" x 12", EX .....**$300.00 C**

Edelweiss Beer, serving tray, litho metal, 1913, 13½" dia., EX, $165.00 C.

Edgeworth Smoking Tobacco, sign, tin, heavily embossed, "Extra High Grade," 27" x 11", EX, $475.00 B. *Courtesy of Muddy River Trading Co./Gary Metz.*

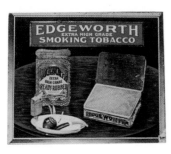

Edgeworth Smoking Tobacco, sign, tin over cardboard, pipe image, 11" x 9", 1930s, VG, $225.00 B. *Courtesy of Muddy River Trading Co./Gary Metz.*

Edison Mazda playhouse, from General Electric, designed to have Christmas lights placed inside for the illusion of interior lighting, 8" x 5½" x 9½", 1930s, EX, $65.00 B. *Courtesy of Buffalo Bay Auction Co.*

Egertsen Brothers Co Cypress, pocket mirror, "...yards & plg. mill, Cairo, ILL...", 3½" dia., VG, $95.00 C.

Egg-O-See Cereal, sign, paper, youngster and pets, "Dere ain't goner be no leavins," 16" x 10", EX, $1,100.00 C. *Courtesy of Buffalo Bay Auction Co.*

E. Robinsons Pilsner Beer, tray, serving, tin, litho, factory scene, 13⅛" dia., VG .....................................................$230.00 B

E.F. Young Jr. Pressing Oil, can, hair dressing oil to be used when pressing hair to keep hair from catching fire, young black woman, EX......................................................................$55.00 D

Eagle Brand Coffee, can, metal, screw lid, 1 lb, EX ..........$245.00 C

Eagle Brand Condensed Milk, sign, cardboard, little girl pointing to company information on picket fence, VG .........................$500.00 D

Eagle Liqueur Distilleries, print, paper, nude woman draped on company sign, 20" x 25", EX .......................................$625.00 C

Eagle Lye, pot scraper, VG.................................................$90.00 B

Eagle Oil, can, metal, Eagle lettering and logo, 1920s, 2 gal., VG....................................................................................$55.00 C

Eagle Stamps, sign, tin, "We Give...," 35" x 12", VG .........$75.00 A

Early Times Distillery, sign, plaster, painted and embossed, familiar oxen pulling a cart with whiskey barrels, 23" x 28", VG....$135.00 C

Early Times Whiskey, statue, plaster, man in old touring car, 1950s, 14" x 12", VG .......................................................$95.00 C

Early Times, sign, great bridge with product name and log cabin across creek, Brown Foreman Distilling, Louisville, KY, 15½" x 12", 1939, EX.............................................................$325.00 B

East Buffalo Brewing, tray, metal, serving size, company lettering, 14" dia., EX................................................................$85.00 C

Eastern Briar Pipe Co., store display board, cardboard, litho, Whiz Mfg. Co., 12 Bakelite cigar holders, NOS, 9" x 10¼", EX .....$75.00 D

Eisenhower Cigarettes, pack, unopened, with President Eisenhower on front label, 1950s, EX, $75.00 C. *Courtesy of Buffalo Bay Auction Co.*

EIS Parts Brake Fluid, sign, metal, single-sided, 15" x 15", VG, $35.00 D.

Ell-Ell Whiskey, sign, tin, litho, self-framed, ship at dock about to be loaded with the product, from Lemle Levy Co., San Francisco, an H.D. Beach litho, 28" x 22", EX, $1,450.00 B. *Courtesy of Buffalo Bay Auction Co.*

Emerson Television and Radio, clock, light-up, 14" x 10¼", EX, $350.00 B.

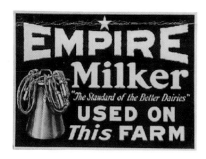

Empire Oil Works, oil painting, framed, from Reno, PA, 23½" x 18¾", VG, $235.00 C.

Empire Milker, sign, tin, litho by Shonk Works, American Can Co., "...used on this farm," 19½" x 13½", EX, $120.00 B.

Easy Bright Stove Polish, can, metal, boy and hat, 3¾" x 1", VG..................................................................$30.00 D

Eatmore Vacuum Packed Coffee, can, metal, slip lid and paper label with company information, 1 lb, VG ......................................$85.00 C

Ebbert Wagons, sign, tin, girl with apples and farmer, "In The Shade of the Old Apple Tree," BEWARE OF REPRODUCTIONS, 37½" x 27½", EX..................................................................$925.00 C

Ebbert Wagons, sign, tin, litho, self-framing, "In The Shade of the Old Apple Tree," with horse-drawn wagon being filled with fruit, 37½" x 25½", EX ..............................................................$2,900.00 B

Ecco Rolled Oats, tin, barefoot boy with hands at mouth to yell, EX .........................................................................$85.00 C

Echo Cut Plug Tobacco, container, metal, hunting scene, 6" x 4", EX..................................................................$125.00 D

Ecko, catalog, paper, with all the necessary supplies for the 1957 kitchen, 1957, 186 pages, VG ............................................$65.00 C

Eclispe Coffee, can, metal, name lettering diagonally across front of can, 1 lb, VG ................................................................$175.00 D

Eclispe Yeast Cakes, can, cardboard, metal lid, company product name diagonally on front of the container, VG ....................$15.00 D

Economy King Separators, postcard, paperboard, from Sears, Roebuck showing that new models ran from $1.85 to $5.75, 1916, 3½" x 5½", VG ................................................................$55.00 C

Empire Tobacco, cutter, EX, $125.00 C.

Empson's Ketchup, ad, cardboard, die cut, framed, 14" x 10", VG, $145.00 B. *Courtesy of Collectors Auction Services.*

Enders Dollar Safety Razor, sign, paper, 9" x 35", VG, $65.00 B.

England Electric Service, lighter, metal, in original box, never used, 1960s, 1½" x 2½" ⅜", NM, $35.00 C. *Courtesy of B.J. Summers.*

Enterprise Stoves and Ranges, sign, metal, double-sided, flange, stove and company information, 18½' long, EX, $275.00 B.

ES-KI-MO Rubbers, string holder, steel, litho, double-sided, 17¼" x 19¾", EX, $4,000.00 B. *Courtesy of Richard Opfer Auctioneering, Inc.*

Esso Oil, sign, tin, single-sided, die cut, Drop Lady, 5¼" x 15¾", G, $275.00 B.

---

**Eddy's Plows,** sign, wooden, logo and portrait of Mr. Eddy, 60" x 24", EX ..............................................................$575.00 C

**Edelweiss Beer,** serving tray, metal, litho, pretty woman and Schoenhofen Brewing Co., 13" dia., 1913, G...................................$125.00 C

**Edgeworth Extra High Grade Smoking Tobacco,** sign, tin, deeply embossed, couple of older gents, 27¼" x 11¼", G...........$200.00 C

**Edgeworth Flake Tobacco,** container, tin, round, company logo, 3" dia., EX .............................................................................$35.00 C

**Edgeworth Plug Slice,** container, tin, pocket sized, top contains good strong ornate graphics, hinged lid, 3¼ " x 2¼ ", EX ..$15.00 C

**Edgeworth Ready Rubbed Tobacco,** container, tin, sample size, some lettering and product name empossed over the lettering, EX ................................................................................$85.00 C

**Edgeworth Smoking Tobacco** container, tin, vertical, pocket, "Edgeworth Ready-Rubbed Smoking Tobacco," 2" wide, EX...........$95.00 C

**Edgeworth Smoking Tobacco,** canister, metal, square design with curved corners and concave sides, slip lid with finial, EX ..$115.00 C

**Edgeworth Smoking Tobacco,** flier, paper, 9" x 12", EX ..$55.00 C

**Edgeworth Smoking Tobacco,** sign, tin over cardboard, pipe image, 11" x 9", 1930s, VG ........................................................$225.00 B

Esso, poster, cardboard, black musician with bass, "Swing along with Esso," 1930 – 40s, 28" x 43", VG, $750.00 C.

Eureka Centre Draft Mower, handbill, paper, small kids playing ring around the rosie, 1880s, 10" x 6", VG, $135.00 C.

Eureka Harness Oil, sign, tin, embossed, 20¼" x 5¼", EX, $195.00 D.

Eveready Batteries, counter display, metal, 16" tall, EX, $325.00 B.

Evening Star, sign, tin, paper, single-sided, embossed, 13¾" x 9¾", VG, $75.00 C.

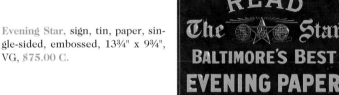

Eveready Flashlight Batteries, poster, paper, litho, 22¼" x 32½", VG, $195.00 C.

Eveready Prestone, anti-freeze can, metal with front of old car beside thermometer, 1920s, 1 gal., G, $60.00 C.

---

**Edgeworth Smoking Tobacco,** sign, tin, "Extra High Grade," heavily embossed, 27" x 11", VG ..............................$425.00 C

**Edgeworth Smoking Tobacco,** sign, tin, with painted lettering and background, "Mild, Slow Burning, Cool," G ..............$45.00 D

**Edgeworth Tobacco,** container, tin, pocket size, "...Junior Light Mild Tobacco...," EX............................................$95.00 C

**Edison Battery Oil,** bottle, glass, "Edison" embossed diagonally on bottle, EX....................................................$5.00 C

**Edison Mazda Lamps,** calendar, cardboard, Parrish- style litho of young girl in chair reading, with full calendar pad, 1917, 4" x 9", EX...............................................................$175.00 C

**Edison Mazda Lamps,** display, metal and glass, in shape of bell boys holding trays of lights, 13" x 7" x 20¼", EX ..............................$425.00 C

**Edison Mazda Lamps,** display, metal, curved top displays different style bulbs, reverse painted glas panels, 20½" x 13" x 7", EX .$475.00 C

Eveready Radio Batteries, poster, paper, litho, 1930s, 24" x 32", VG, $235.00 C.

Ever-Ready Safety Razor, countertop display, tin, litho, with glass and wood, still contains early razor blades, 9½" x 11½", EX, $1,100.00 B.

Evinrude Parts & Service, clock, metal and glass, double-bubble, light-up, 15" dia., $950.00 B.

Excelsior Brewing Co., serving tray, metal, tin, litho, pretty young lady with glass of the product, 16¾" x 13¾", VG, $425.00 C.

Ex-Lax, thermometer, metal, scale reading, VG, $225.00 B.

Ex-Lax, thermometer, porcelain, unusual horizontal scale, "Keep regular with Ex-Lax, the chocolated laxative," great graphics, 10" x 36" x 1", EX, $550.00 B. *Courtesy of Muddy River Trading Co./Gary Metz.*

---

**Edison Mazda,** calendar, advertising light bulbs, 1926, 18" x 30", EX.............................................................$1,300.00 C

**Edison Mazda,** display, metal, in shape of light bulb with various styles of the bulbs surrounding the display, 15½" x 11½" x 24", EX..............................................................$1,800.00 C

**Edison Mazda,** playhouse from General Electric designed to have Christmas lights placed inside to give the illusion of interior lighting, 8" x 5½" x 9½", 1930s, NM ...................................$125.00 C

**Edison Mazda,** sign, tin, light for car, "For Your Car," 3" x 2" x 1½", EX..............................................................$35.00 C

**Edison Phonograph,** sign, litho, woman listening, 20¾" x 28", EX..............................................................$3,100.00 B

**Edison Star Metal Polish,** container, tin, 2" dia. x 5½" h, VG.$30.00 C

**Edison Star Metal Polish,** container, tin, screw lid, company logo, NOS, 2" dia. x 5" tall, EX ...................................$15.00 C

**Edison-Mazda,** service station counter display box, "Name your car...I'll light it," woman holding box of bulbs, EX .........$695.00 D

**Edsel,** sign, neon and porcelain, with neon just showing name, 72" x 32", EX ..............................................................$1,500.00 C

**Edward Heuer Bottler,** calendar, paper, waitress beside a large bottle, full monthly pad, 12" x 19", EX...............................$1,000.00 B

**Edward's Coffee,** can, tin, "Regular Grind" under company name, ½ lb, EX..............................................................$40.00 C

**Effecto Auto Finishes,** color display, in the shape of wood-rimmed wheel with message in center, 25" dia., EX.....$595.00 C

**Egg-O-See Cereal**, sign, paper, youngster and pets, "Dere ain't goner be no leavins," 16" x 10", VG .................................$700.00 C

**Egyptian Diety Cigarettes**, sign, paper, pretty Egyptian girl in front of mirror, 1908, 9½" x 14", EX ...............................$105.00 C

**Egyptian Straights Cigarettes**, sign, metal, oval, pretty lady in bonnet, "Absolutely Pure 100% Turkish Tobacco," VG...........$525.00 C

**Eichberg Foot Wear**, calendar, cardboard, die cut, young children, 7¾" x 14½", 1910, VG .......................................$125.00 C

**Eight Brothers Tobacco**, pail, metal, "Long Cut," EX ..$95.00 C

**Eight O'Clock Coffee**, bank, metal, company logo, 4" tall, VG .$12.00 D

**Eisenhower Cigarettes**, pack, unopened, with President Eisenhower on front label, 1950s, VG.........................................$50.00 C

**Eisenlohr's Cinco 5¢ Cigar**, sign, metal, painted, 24" x 12", G ..$65.00 D

**Eisenlohr's Cinco & Webster Cigars**, box opener, metal, hammer shaped with engraved lettering, 6¼ " long, VG......$75.00 C

**Eisman & May**, ad, die cut, embossed, fashionable shoes, horse-drawn sleigh, 10" x 7½", EX .....................................$165.00 C

**El Amor Cigar Box**, label, paper, cat couple brought to life-like presence by the advertiser, 4½" x 4½", VG........................$45.00 B

**El Bubble Bubble Gum Cigars**, display box, cardboard, landscape with Indian, VG..............................................$75.00 D

**El Captian Coffee**, can, metal, with only product wording and key-wind lid, 1 lb, VG .................................................$55.00 D

**El Gallo Cigars**, art plate with rooster, 1905, 10" dia., EX...$610.00 B

**El Grande Cigar box**, label, paper, King of Sweden, VG...$85.00 C

**El Macco Cigars** sign, tin, self-framing, litho, simulated wood grain surrounding center cameo of couple sitting together, 20¼" x 24", EX ...............................................................$550.00 B

**El Moriso Guaranteed Hi-Grade Cigar**, sign, cardboard, 13½" x 10¼", EX.......................................................$75.00 C

**El Regit Long Filled 5¢ Cigar**, pennant, felt, Alabama, with tiger in tropics scene, 26" long, EX....................................$135.00 C

**El Teano Cigar**, Liberty tin, 6¼" x 4" x 5½", VG ...............$75.00 D

**El Tino**, cigar cutter, store counter, reverse painting on glass, 8¼" x 6¾" x 5", VG...........................................................$300.00 C

**El Verso** tip tray, cigar, man relaxing at home enjoying a cigar, 6½" x 4½", EX.................................................................$145.00 C

**El Verso**, tip tray, metal, "The Sweet & Mellow Cigar," with man in easy chair enjoying product, 6⅝" long, EX........................$75.00 B

**El-Bart Dry Gin**, sign, paper, pretty girl on beach with bottle in lower left corner, 33" x 46", EX....................................$3,500.00 D

**El-Myra Cigarettes**, sign, paper, litho, store, "for goodness sake smoke...10 for 5¢," 13½" x 10", EX .................$150.00 C

**Eldred Motor Oil**, can, metal, triangular logo, 1 gal., G .......$145.00 D

**Electric Appliance Company**, thermometer, wood, "San Francisco...Electric Supplies...Automotive Equipment," 3" x 11½", EX...............$40.00 B

**Electric Brand Spinach**, can, label, paper, woman with light, NM ............................................................... $10.00 D

**Electric Face Massage**, sign, heavy paper, litho, in old gesso frame, "sure death to all wrinkles and blackheads...35¢," with well-attired young man, 24½" x 28½", EX .....................$110.00 C

**Electrolux**, bank, plastic, in shape of vacuum cleaner, 1950s, EX .................................................................$35.00 D

**Elephant Salted Peanuts**, container, glass, tin screw on lid, 1lb, EX .................................................................$85.00 C

**Elephant Salted Peanuts**, container, tin, lid showing an elephant from the side, 4" x 4" x 2", EX .........................................$325.00 C

**Elgin Nat. Road Races**, pennant, felt, old vintage race car, Aug. 29 – 30, 1913, 29½ x 11½", G............................................$350.00 B

**Elgin Watches**, clock, neon, metal body and reverse painted face, from Glo-Dial Clock Sales, 580 Fifth Ave., New York, N.Y., 22" dia., EX....................................................................$375.00 C

**Elgin Watches**, clock, round, light-up, "Arthur J. Nyman and Sons Jewelers," message in center, number positions occupied by silver points, red, white, and cream, EX..................................$350.00 D

**Elgin Watches**, sign, glass, reverse painted, "Full Ruby Jeweled...The World's Standard," 24" x 30", VG................$275.00 D

**Elgin Watches**, sign, glass, reverse painted, in frame, the trademark "Full Ruby Jeweled," 23" x 29½", VG ..................$475.00 B

**Eljer**, clock, Pam, glass face and metal back, "Eljer, fine plumbing fixtures," 15½" x 15½", 1963, EX ......................................$125.00 C

**Elk Cigar Box**, label, paper, scene of elk, 1910s, 9" x 6", EX ........$65.00 C

**Elkins Brewing Co.**, beer mug, pint, Elkins W. Va. Brewery on the front, 3¾" x 4¼", VG .........................................................$50.00 C

**Ell-Ell Whiskey**, sign, tin litho, self-framed, ship at dock about to be loaded with the product, from Lemle Levy Co., San Francisco, an H.D. Beach litho, 28" x 22", VG ....................................$1,000.00 C

**Ellison's Flour**, sign, cardboard, easel back, store countertop, swan in center between product packages, 24" x 13", EX...........$130.00 B

**Ellwood Whiskey**, ad, oil on wood, out of Louisville, Ky., 1909, 26¼" x 32⅛", VG.........................................................$575.00 C

**Elmer's Glue-All,** container, plastic, trademark Elmer, by the Borden Chemical Co., 6½" tall, EX..............................................$65.00 D

**Elmore,** automobile pocket mirror, celluloid and glass, early open auto, 3" x 2", VG.....................................................................$995.00 C

**Elreco Re-formed Gasoline,** globe, glass, Gill body with black and white lettering, EX ...........................................................$550.00 C

**Elreco Special Gasoline,** globe, wide glass body with two glass lenses, "The El Dorado Refining Co.," 13½" dia., VG...$425.00 C

**Emancipator Cigar Box,** label, paper, workers in the field, EX..$75.00 D

**Emerson's Ginger Gum,** countertop display, 4¼" x 1" x 6", 1928, NM .......................................................................................$450.00 B

**Emerson,** radio clock, metal and glass, "EMERSONRADIO," EX.$300.00 D

**Emila Garcia 5¢ Cigar,** cigar holder, reverse glass and tin litho that slips over a 50-count cigar tin, EX .......................................$85.00 D

**Emilia Garcia Cigars,** container, metal, round with slip lid, EX .$45.00 C

**Emilia Garcia Cigars,** display, cardboard, man in five point star, 38" x 31", EX.....................................................................................$125.00 C

**Emmerlings Beer,** sign, tin, litho, vintage German couple enjoying the product, 28" x 19½", EX..............................................$400.00 B

**Empire Anti-Freeze,** thermmeter, wood, Empire logo, "Never Rusts Your Radiator," and "The Right Anti-Freeze," 36" tall, G....$55.00 C

**Empire Cream Separator Co.,** calendar, paper, girl in a pink bonnet, 12" x 20", EX.................................................................$155.00 D

**Empire Cream Separator Company,** calendar top, paper, Fisher Building, Chicago, Ill., mother and daughter, 1902, 12" x 20", EX..$137.00 B

**Empire Cream Separator,** pinback, celluloid over metal, product in center, 1¼" dia., VG.......................................................$55.00 B

**Empire Milker** sign, "used on this farm," with milker, 19" x 13½", EX..........................................................................................$135.00 C

**Empire State Building, New York City,** license plate attachment, cast aluminum with shape of Empire State Building in left corner, 11" x 5¾", EX ...........................................................................$200.00 C

**Empire Tobacco,** cutter, VG................................................$95.00 D

**Empress Chocolates,** sign, celluloid, queen in robe and crown and the company name, 16" x 20", EX....................................$350.00 C

**Empress Coffee,** can, metal, key wind lid, 1 lb, EX.............$55.00 D

**Empress Coffee,** pail, tin, wire metal handle, from Duluth, MN, 7½" x 9", VG..........................................................................$135.00 C

**Empress Toilet Powder,** can, tin, litho, sample size, Empress Powder Co., New York, NY, 1⅝" x 2⅜" x ⅞", EX.....................................$450.00 B

**Empson's Ketchup,** ad, cardboard, die cut, framed, 14" x 10", EX .............................................................................................$165.00 C

**En-Ar-Co C-1 Motor Oil,** sign, tin, embossed, Enarco boy at bottom with chalkboard, 10" x 36¼", EX .....................................$235.00 C

**En-Ar-Co Motor Oil,** bank, metal, oil can with red & white label on yellow background, 3½" T, EX....................................................$85.00 D

**En-Ar-Co Motor Oil,** can, metal, trademark blackboard boy in lower right, Qt., EX ...............................................................$65.00 C

**En-Ar-Co Motor Oil,** sign, iron, boy holding blackboard, 28" x 46", EX ...........................................................................................$2,200.00 C

**En-Ar-Co Motor Oil,** thermometer, tin, painted, scale-type, Enarco boy with chalkboard at top of scale, NOS, 8" x 38¾", EX ..$325.00 B

**En-Ar-Co Oil,** bottle, glass, embossed lettering and a funnel pouring spout, Qt., EX .................................................................$65.00 C

**En-Ar-Co Road Maps,** sign, tin, the En-Ar-Co boy holding a sign, "Free En-Ar-Co Road Maps," 1930s, 12" x 16", EX...........$450.00 D

**En-Be-Co Strup,** can label, paper, boy eating bread, 1910s, EX.$95.00 C

**Enameline Stove Polish,** sign, litho, young girl and puppy in front of the product, 13" x 23", EX..................................................$275.00 B

**Enders Dollar Safety Razor,** sign, metal and cardboard, stand up razor, 13" x 9", EX.............................................................$175.00 D

**Enders Razor,** sign, cardboard, Enders Man and "Enders Ends Your Shaving Troubles...," 8" x 12", VG .......................................$95.00 D

**Energee True Gasoline,** sign, metal, flange, The Pure Oil Co., 17½" x 20", EX...................................................................................$475.00 C

**English Bird's Eye Smoking Tobacco,** container, tin, rectangular, EX..................................................................................................$65.00 C

**English Walnut Smoking Tobacco,** container, tin, vertical pocket size, EX.........................................................................................$450.00 D

**Enrico Projetti & Sons,** calendar, Italian and American Grocery, family and Santa Claus around the Christmas tree, full tear sheet, 14" x 20", 1915, EX ...............................................................................$255.00 B

**Enterprise Brewery,** sign, litho, old cavalier seated in pub, by Meek & Beach Litho, 17" x 24", 1901, EX ...................................$975.00 C

**Enterprise Meat Choppers,** sign, paper, meat chopper being demonstrated by Uncle Sam, 20" x 18", VG......................$525.00 C

**Enterprise,** salesman sample stove No/115, gold raised lettering, 4" x 2¾", 1870s, VG.................................$95.00 C

**Epicure Coffee,** can, metal, screw on lid, waiter on center of can, 1 lb, EX.................................$325.00 C

**Erickson's Pure Rye Whiskey,** sign, tin, self framed, floating whiskey bottles attacking a submarine, 32" x 22", EX.................................$675.00 C

**Erlanger Beer,** tray, "Classic 1893," 13" x 10½", EX.................................$15.00 D

**ES-KI-MO Rubbers,** string holder, steel, litho, double-sided, 17¼" x 19¾", VG.................................$3,200.00 C

**Eskimo Pie,** sign, porcelain, rare item, 36" x 6½", EX..$275.00 C

**Esser's Paint,** clock, light-up, painter in center, Pam Clock Co., 15" dia., VG.................................$225.00 C

**Essex Rubber Co.,** clock, "Now is the time for magic rubber heels and soles," 14½" sq., VG.................................$195.00 C

**Esso Aviation Products,** sign, tin, round Esso over Aviation Products, double-sided, 1940 – 50s, EX.................................$650.00 D

**Esso Blue,** sign, porcelain, flange, "We Sell Esso Blue," 18" x 18", EX.................................$275.00 C

**Esso Elephant Kerosene,** sign, pump, porcelain, one-sided, elephant, 12" x 24", VG.................................$600.00 B

**Esso Extra Ethyl,** gas, globe, metal and glass, Ethyl logo in lower center of lens, 16" dia., EX.................................$455.00 C

**Esso Extra,** gas globe, glass, one piece, oval, red & blue on white, 20" x 15", EX.................................$425.00 C

**Esso Extra,** gas globe, metal and glass, blue lettering on white, 16" dia., EX.................................$450.00 C

**Esso Lubrication Service,** sign, cardboard, die cut, "Your Car Needs A Lift," 29" x 45", EX.................................$135.00 C

**Esso,** advertising block, embossed glass, "watch your savings grow," square EX.................................$65.00 D

**Esso,** bank, hard rubber, in likeness of tiger, 8" tall, EX.....$40.00 D

**Esso,** bank, plastic, "Fat Man," NOS, 5" tall, NM.................................$100.00 B

**Esso,** bank, plastic, "Save At Your Esso Dealer," 6" x 4", EX.$35.00 C

**Esso,** bank, plastic, figure, product name on front, 6½" tall, red, EX.................................$95.00 C

**Esso,** bank, plastic, in form of tanker truck, top coin slot, "Save At Your Esso Dealer," EX.................................$55.00 C

**Esso,** banner, canvas "World's First Choice," 36" x 83", G..$130.00 C

**Esso,** banner, plastic, "Put a Tiger in your tank," Esso tiger, 42" x 83", EX.................................$135.00 D

**Esso,** calendar, dealer, full monthly peel, "P.P. Cassetty, Difficult, Tennessee," 9¾" x 16", NOS, NM.................................$45.00 C

**Esso,** coloring book, paper, American landmarks, "Happy Motoring," 24 pages, VG.................................$35.00 C

**Esso,** globe, glass, metal bank and glass lens, 16½" dia., EX.........$325.00 C

**Esso,** letter opener, silver, relief image of Oil Drop Man on handle, 9" long, NM.................................$375.00 D

**Esso,** lighter fluid dispenser, metal, shape of gas pump, 8¼ " long, EX.................................$450.00 D

**Esso,** pocket knife, metal, in shape of gas pump, 2½" long, EX $125.00 C

**Esso,** sign, porcelain, double-sided, company logo in center, 22" x 22", 1939, EX.................................$225.00 C

**Esso,** sign, tin, die cut, shape of Esso Drop Girl, 7" x 16", EX.$325.00 D

**Esso,** sign, tin, litho, die cut, Esso girl waving, 5¼" x 16", EX..$130.00 B

**Essolene,** gas globe, metal body with glass lens, high profile, 15" dia., VG.................................$425.00 C

**Essolube Motor Oil,** puzzle, cardboard, ailing autos, 1926, 17" x 11", VG.................................$135.00 D

**Estabrook & Eatons,** ashtray, porcelain, Key West Cigar, 4" x ¾", VG.................................$45.00 C

**Estabrook's Red Rose Coffee,** sign, metal, in shape of large can with red rose in center oval, 18" x 16", EX.................................$200.00 D

**Esterbrook Pens,** dispenser, metal, round, rotating name sign above, 12" dia. x 14" tall, EX.................................$450.00 C

**Estey Organ Work,** ad, paper, showing the factory, gesso frame, from Ottmann Lith. Co., Puck Building, NY, 17" x 21", VG.........$110.00 B

**Ethyl Gasoline,** gas globe, wide hull body, 13½", EX.................................$550.00 C

**Eureka Harness Oil,** sign, metal, work horses, 19" x 13", VG.$55.00 D

**Eureka Spool Silk,** display cabinet, wood, glass front, clock on top of elaborate fretwork, 24" x 23" x 16", EX.................................$1,600.00 D

**Eureka Stock Food, Shrader Drug Co., Iowa City, Iowa,** advertisement, paper, 15⅜" x 20¼", G.................................$95.00 C

**Evans' Pastilles,** sign, porcelain, single-sided, "for all infections of the throat," 24" x 11", VG.................................$350.00 B

**Even Steven Cigars,** tin, square, slip lid, 3" x 3" x 5½", EX..........$400.00 D

**Ever-Ready Safety Razor,** clock, tin, company trademark in round face center, 1920s, 13" x 19", EX.................................$1,200.00 C

**Ever-Ready Safety Razor,** countertop display, tin, litho, glass and wood, still contains early razor blades, 9½" x 11½", F.........$325.00 D

# E

**Ever-Ready Shaving Brushes** display, tin, die cut, large brush and compartments for products, 15" x 12", EX..................$1,050.00 D

**Eveready and Mazda Lamps,** product cabinet, batteries being placed in flashlight, 11" x 9" x 11½", EX...........................$195.00 B

**Eveready Batteries,** puzzle, cardboard, young boy, flashlight asking "Is That You Santa Claus?," 1930s, 9" x 12", EX.................$75.00 C

**Eveready Batteries,** sign, paper, boy and dog, 20" x 30", VG.$95.00 D

**Eveready Battery,** display, metal, glass front, extra long life flashlight batteries, 9" W x 14" H x 10½" D, EX............$100.00 C

**Eveready Battery,** display, metal, glass front, extra long life flashlight batteries, 9"W x 14"H x 10½"D, G..........................................$75.00 B

**Eveready Flashlight Batteries & Mazda Lamps,** display, tin, front slanted compartments for storage, 12" tall, EX.................$250.00 C

**Eveready Mazda Automobile Lamp Kit,** metal case, spare lamps, product on both sides, NOS, EX...................................$65.00 C

**Eveready Prestone,** can, metal, gallon, original paper information sheet for car and radiator tag, 1-gal., EX..............$175.00 D

**Eveready Prestone,** container, tin, vintage automobile and thermometer, 1 gal., EX...........................................$110.00 B

**Everett Piano,** trade card, paper, scene of a recital, 1890s, VG..$29.00 C

**Everfresh Coffee,** can, metal, key wind lid, 1 lb, EX...........$55.00 C

**Everhart Confections,** sign, tin, litho, self-framing, young girl, 13" x 19", EX.......................................................................$350.00 B

**Eversweet,** pin tray, vintage accessory for lady's dresser, pretty young lady, 3½" x 5", VG.................................................................$231.00 B

**Evervess Sparkling Water,** clock, glass and metal, parrot, 1940s, EX.......................................................................................$385.00 C

**Evervess Sparkling Water,** sign, celluloid, "for your table at every meal," a Pepsi-Cola product, 9" dia., EX.................................$250.00 B

**Evervess Table Water,** sign, cardboard, "Sparkles Like Diamonds In Your Glass," 11" x 18", EX.......................................$185.00 D

**Evervess,** tip tray, metal, "Yes, Yes!...Thank You...Evervess Sparkling Water," Evervess bird with top hat and cane, EX..$75.00 C

**Everybody's Handsoap,** ad, paper, product can, 20" x 8", EX.$95.00 B

**Evinrude Detachable Motor,** pennant, cloth, company logo, 29" long, EX....................................................................$175.00 C

**Evinrude Motor Co.,** tip tray, metal, woman in boat, 4" dia., EX.................................................................................$425.00 C

**Evinrude Rowboat & Canoe Motors,** tip tray, metal rowboat, "On The Crest Of The Wave," 4" dia., VG...................$400.00 D

**Evinrude Rowboat and Canoe Motors,** tip tray, metal, round, "On The Crest Of The Wave," product in action, 4" dia., EX....$250.00 B

**Evinrude,** sign, metal, painted, double-sided, flange, "first in outboards," 26¼" x 15¾", EX.................................................$850.00 B

**Ex-Lax,** door push, porcelain, package in center, 4" x 8", G..$150.00 C

**Ex-Lax,** push and pull door signs, 4" x 8", VG.................$265.00 C

**Ex-Lax,** sign, porcelain, round, "Keep Regular...EX-Lax...The Chocolate Laxative," 20" dia., VG....................................$155.00 D

**Ex-Lax,** thermometer, porcelain, "the chocolate laxative millions prefer," 8⅛" x 36⅛", EX.................................................$175.00 D

**Ex-Lax,** thermometer, porcelain, "the chocolate laxative," small scale in center of sign, 8" x 36" x 1¼", EX.........................$235.00 C

**Ex-Lax,** thermometer, porcelain, scale type, "The Chocolate Laxative...Keep Regular With," 36" tall, EX..............................$225.00 D

**Ex-Lax,** thermometer, porcelain, unusual horizontal scale, "Keep regular with Ex-Lax, the chocolated laxative," great graphics, 10" x 36" x 1", G.........................................................................$275.00 C

**Ex-Lax,** thermometer, porcelain, vertical scale in center, "the chocolate laxative...millions prefer...," EX.................................$135.00 D

**Excide Batteries,** sign, metal, embossed, double-sided, "When Its An..." over battery graphics, 12" x 15", VG...........................$155.00 C

**Exide Batteries,** sign, tin, painted, tacker, NOS, 19¾" x 9¼", NM...................................................................................$125.00 C

**Exide Battery,** sign, metal, double-sided, flange, die cut to battery image, 14" x 14", 1953, EX...................................................$275.00 C

**Exide,** sign, metal, double-sided, flange, in shape of battery, 15" x 13", EX...........................................................................$215.00 D

**Extron,** gas globe, glass body and lens, 13½", EX...................$425.00 C

**Eye-Fix,** tip tray, metal, round, "The Great Eye Remedy," woman being attended by angel image, 4⅛" dia., EX.......................$250.00 B

**Eze-grape Drink,** sign, string hanger, bundle of grapes and bottle of product, 7½" x 9¾", EX...............................................$75.00 C

Fairbanks Gold Dust, sign, tin, embossed, twins in tub, 27½" x 40", VG, $2,100.00 B. *Courtesy of Collectors Auction Services.*

Fairbanks Gold Dust Washing Powder, sign, cardboard, round, string-hung, double-sided, 6½" dia., EX, $120.00 B. *Courtesy of Muddy River Trading Co./Gary Metz.*

Fairway Golf Balls, store display for floor use, young black caddy pulling the flag, United States Rubber Co., 25" x 48", 1920s, EX, $550.00 B. *Courtesy of Buffalo Bay Auction Co.*

Farmers Burley Warehouse, Paducah, KY, complimentary 20 package Chesterfield cigarettes, Liggett & Myers Tobacco Co., still sealed , 2" x 3" x ¾", EX, $35.00 C. *Courtesy of B.J. Summers.*

Fashion Cut Plug Tobacco, lunch pail, top handle, smartly dressed couple walking, 7½" x 5" x 4½", EX, $350.00 B. *Courtesy of Buffalo Bay Auction Co.*

Fatima, sign, metal, self-framing, veiled woman, 24" tall, G, $300.00 B.

---

F & M Herbs Cigars, sign, paper, woman in Victorian scene, 16½" x 25", VG ..............................................................$225.00 B

F & M Schaefer Brewing Co's Bock Beer, sign, metal, resting rams, 23" x 34", VG .........................................................$1,100.00 B

F A Poth & Son Brewers, calendar, paper, full monthly pads, hunting scene, 1898, 20½" x 30", EX .............................................$875.00 C

F.F. Lewis, sign, "Cash Dealer Groceries and General Merchandise, Mansville, N.Y.," small boy standing in boat wearing a blue coat, 5¾" x 8½", EX..............................................................$25.00 B

Fab, box, cardboard, sample size, ocean wave scenes, 4" x 3" x 1", EX.................................................................................$10.00 D

FAD Cigars, sign, tin, "Always Good," 46" x 11", EX ........$95.00 C

Fagg's Wire Cut Linament, sign, paper, "For Wire Sores, Sore Shoulders, Saddle Sores...," 5" x 6", EX..............................$65.00 B

Fairbank's Gold Dust Scouring Cleanser, can, metal, company logo on paper label, 14 oz., VG ...................................................$65.00 C

Fairbank's Gold Dust Scouring Cleanser, sign, paper, Gold Dust twins greeting Uncle Sam and President Roosevelt, 20" x 11", EX...$450.00 C

Fairbank's Gold Dust Washing Powder, box, cardboard, free sample size, twins logo, EX.......................................................$45.00 C

Fairbank's Gold Dust Washing Powder, box, cardboard, the twins and logo, 2 lb, VG.................................................................$30.00 D

Fairbank's Gold Dust Washing Powder, sign, cardboard, die cut in shape of product name, designed to be a string hanger, 15½" x 7¼", G .............................................................................$2,500.00 D

Fairbank's Gold Dust, display, cardboard, die cut, with twins on both sides of box, 14¼" x 3⅞" x 12¾", 1890s, VG .........$1,690.00 B

Fairbank's Gold Dust, trade card, cardboard, the twins and "Cleans Everything, 3" x 4", EX ...................................................$125.00 C

Fairbank's Standard Scale, sign, wood, company carved lettering, 40½" x 18¾ " x 1½", VG.......................................................$500.00 D

Faust on Draught, globe, one-piece, 8" dia., EX, $250.00 C.

Favorite Straight Cut Cigarettes, sign, tin, hunting dog, double-sided flange, 18" x 9" EX, $2,100.00 B. *Courtesy of Muddy River Trading Co./Gary Metz.*

Fehr's Famous F.F.X.L. Beer, serving tray, tin, litho, from Louisville, Ky., 1910, 13" dia., EX, $425.00 C.

Federal Cartridges, sign, tri-fold store counter, birds in field and flight, EX, $595.00 B. *Courtesy of Buffalo Bay Auction Co.*

Fehr's Malt, sign, metal, self-framing, pretty young lady, scantily clad, surrounded by cherubs with bottle on table beside her, 22" x 28", EX, $950.00 B. *Courtesy of Buffalo Bay Auction Co.*

Fern Glen Rye, sign, tin, self-framing, black man with watermelon and hen with a bottle of the product on the road in front of him, 23" x 33", EX, $3,000.00 B. *Courtesy of Collectors Auction Services.*

**Fairbank's Washing Powder**, sign, paperboard, small girl and baby boy on front of product box, 16" x 14½", VG.....................$275.00 D

**Fairbanks Gold Dust Washing Powder**, crate, wooden, "The N.K. Fairbank Company...Chicago St. Louis New Orleans New York Montreal," 27½" x 19½" x 12", VG................................................$65.00D

**Fairbanks Gold Dust Washing Powder**, watch fob, metal, embossed and enameled scene of twins with pans, EX .......................$55.00 D

**Fairbanks Morse Pumping Machinery**, sign, porcelain, single-sided, weight in hand in center of message, 20" dia., VG...............$60.00 B

**Fairbanks Morse Sales and Service**, sign, reverse painted face and metal housing, light-up, colors rotate in background, 15½" dia., EX........................................................................$775.00 D

**Fairbanks Morse Scales**, sign, porcelain, white company name on blue background, 50" x 9", EX ..................................$225.00 C

**Fairbanks Soap**, plate calendar, die cut, fairy by artisit Paul Moran, Litho by American, NY, 9½" dia., 1903, EX .......................$30.00 B

**Fairbanks Soap**, trade cards, set of eight cards from N.K. Fairbanks, Gold Dust twins, 3¼" x 5", 1885, EX .................$313.00 B

**Fairbanks-Morse**, sign, illuminated motion display, sales & service, 15½" dia. x 5" D, EX.............................................................$550.00 B

**Fairway Coffee**, container, tin, litho, key-wound, young children on front, 1-lb., EX................................................................$300.00 B

**Fairway Golf Balls**, store display for floor use, young black caddy pulling the flag, United States Rubber Co., 25" x 48", 1920s, VG..........$425.00 C

**Fairy Soap**, print, paper, great scene of woman watching a girl blowing bubbles, small children inside the bubbles, 1890s, 18" x 24", EX .................................................................................$255.00 D

**Fairy Soap**, sign, paper on cardboard, young mother and daughter at dressing table, 32½" x 43", 1919, G ..............................$355.00 B

**Fairy Soap**, tip tray, metal, round, "Have You a Little Fairy In Your Home?," little girl sitting on bar of soap, 4⅛" dia., EX..........$65.00 B

**Fairy Soap**, tip tray, metal, young girl sitting on top of a bar of soap, 1930s, 4" dia., VG .........................................................$100.00 D

**Fairy**, sign, cardboard, die cut, easel back, "Have You a Little Fairy in Your Home," fairy on bar of soap, 19" x 23½", NM ..............$1,850.00 B

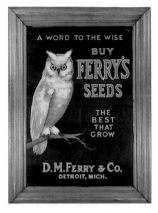

Ferry's Seeds, poster, framed, "A word to the wise...The best that grow," 27" x 36", NM, $475.00 C.

F.F.N. Gardner Jr., premium plate, china, painted lady on front side and store info on back, 1910 – 20s, 8" dia., VG, $45.00 C. *Courtesy of B.J. Summers.*

Field & Stream Outdoor Clothing, sign, cardboard, die cut, 3-D counter, 15¾" x 11¾", EX, $95.00 D.

Fireman's Fund Insurance Co., poster, cardboard, perils of the road, 22½" x 12½", VG, $500.00 B.

Fire Prevention Week, poster, paper, framed, 18¾" x 23¾", VG, $125.00 C.

---

**Falcon Motor Oil,** can, metal, falcon with company information both above and below the center, 1 qt, EX..........................$20.00 D

**Fall River Line,** sign, paper, steamer named the Bristol, 13" x 10½", EX..$625.00 C

**Falls City Beer,** nodder, plastic, "Falls City Gentleman" on a base that carries the product name, 1970s, 14" tall, EX.............$175.00 D

**Falls City Beer,** sign, cardboard, majorette with a glass of the product, 34" x 46", 1940s, EX .................................................$110.00 B

**Falls City Beer,** take-out bag with handles, paper, 6-pack, "It's pasteurized, it's bitter free," 7¾" x 9¾", EX .................................$15.00 D

**Falstaff Beer,** sign, metal, horizontal, painted, "An old Friend," medieval man with stein being served by waitress, 17½" x 15", EX.............................................................................................$100.00 D

**Falstaff Beer,** sign, metal, self-framing, large sized man in front of a window with a bottle of the product, 1910s, 30" x 24", EX .$1,500.00 D

**Falstaff Beer,** sign, paper, "an old friend!," G ....................$45.00 D

**Falstaff Beer,** sign, paper, "an old friend!," VG ...................$65.00 C

**Falstaff Bottled Beer,** sign, metal, man in an early open touring car offering a farmer a beer, 30½" x 22½", VG ......................................$2,200.00 D

**Falstaff,** charger, metal, medival man sitting at a table with friends, 24" dia., EX .....................................................................................$175.00 D

**Falstaff,** sign, metal, die cut, litho, trademark Falstaff man in a sitting position with product from the Wm. J. Lemp Brewing Co., St. Louis, U.S.A., 7" x 18", 1900s, EX..............................$1,200.00 D

**Falstaff,** sign, metal, two-piece, painted, "Enjoy Beer," 17½" x 15", EX .....................................................................................................$105.00 D

**Falstaff,** stein, china, lid, 10½" tall, EX ............................$135.00 D

**Famous Dukes Smoking Tobacco,** sign, paper, two midgets carrying the product, 17½" x 13", EX ................................$235.00 D

**Fan Tan Gum,** tray, Oriental scene on front, 13¼" x 10½", EX .$250.00 B

**Fanny Farmer Candy,** tin, litho, Uncle Sam, 1944, 3" x 10", EX ..$120.00 B

**Faries Starch,** sign, paper, "Makes Ironing Easy...," 15" x 10", VG .........................................................................................................$15.00 D

Firestone Gum-Dipped Motorcycle Tires, blotter, paper, motorcycle and rider, 3⅛" x 6", VG, $125.00 D.

Fisk Balloon Tires, calendar, framed, die cut, familiar boy in P.J.s, 3¼" x 5½", VG, $65.00 B.

Five Brothers Plug Tobacco, sign, tin litho over cardboard, 16" x 16", EX, $975.00 C. *Courtesy of Wm. Morford Investment Grade Collectibles.*

Florsheim Shoe, store display, neon, "for the man who cares, Shoes For Men," men's shoes over neon, Art Deco style, NM, $395.00 D. *Courtesy of Rare Bird Antique Mall/Jon & Joan Wright*

Flying A Associated Gasoline, sign, "chicken wing" logo, hard-to-find item, 27¾" dia., EX, $750.00 B. *Courtesy of Autopia Advertising Auctions.*

---

**Farmer Boy Pop Corn**, box, cardboard, boy's face and "Pop Corn None Better," 4½" x 7", EX .................................................$15.00 D

**Farmer's Hybrid**, license plate attachment, tin, painted, die cut, 9⅞" x 5⅝", NM.................................................$105.00 C

**Farmer's Pride Brand Coffee**, banner, canvas, arched name and tilted can, EX .................................................$250.00 D

**Farmers Ice Cream**, display, metal and cardboard, light up ice cream cone on top, 31½" w, VG .................................................$325.00 D

**Farmers Pride Brand Steel Cut Coffee**, tin, paper label, small child and man with cup of coffee, 4⅛" x 6", EX..............$300.00 B

**Fashion Cut Plug Tobacco**, lunch pail, top handle, smartly dressed couple walking, 7½" x 5" x 4½", VG..................$275.00 C

**Fashion Cut Plug Tobacco**, pail, metal, couple in car, 8" x 5" x 4½", EX .................................................$175.00 D

**Fatima Cigarette**, sign, tin, embossed, "The Turkish Blend," 20⅛" x 20⅛", VG.................................................$245.00 C

**Fatima Turkish Blend Cigarettes**, sign, glass, reverse painted, lettering with a chain hanger, 14" x 6", EX .............................$25.00 D

**Fatima Turkish Blend Cigarettes**, thermometer, porcelain, product name at top and bottom, featuring a barometer, 27" tall, EX.$225.00 D

**Fatima Turkish Cigarettes**, sign, wood frame, veiled woman in center, 27" x 26½", 1909, NM.................................................$275.00 D

**Fatima Turkish Cigarettes**, sign, veiled woman in center of message, in original frame, 27" x 26½", EX.............................$200.00 D

**Faust Blend Blanke's Drip Coffee Pot**, stoneware, with advertising on side and lid, 9" tall, EX.................................................$5750.00 B

**Favorite Straight Cut Cigarettes**, sign, tin, double-sided, flange, hunting dog, 18" x 9", G.................................................$1,000.00 C

**Fawn Beverages**, sign, tin, name in script in background, 28" x 14", VG .................................................$55.00 C

**Fayette's Ice Cream**, sign, porcelain, double-sided, die-cut, 28" x 20", VG .................................................$315.00 B

Flying A, pump sign, porcelain, for the "Super Extra" pump, 10" dia., G, $210.00 B.

Flying Red Horse, first aid kit, by Mobil-gas-Mobiloil, 3¼" x ¾" x 2¾", VG, $165.00 C.

Fogg's Ferry, poster, paper, litho, 21" x 28", VG, $275.00 C.

Ford, poster, paper, "Smart New Interiors," 46" x 35", G, $80.00 B.

Forest & Stream Tobacco, tin, men fishing, 3" x 4¼" x ¾", VG, $350.00 B.

FE Meyers & Bros Equipment, catalog, paper, tools for painting, disinfecting and spraying, 1910, 64 pages, VG .................$35.00 C

Federal Cartridge Sample Shells, box, cardboard, cutout for 5 shells, 5" x 3", VG .................$135.00 B

Federal Cartridges, sign, tri-fold store counter, birds in field and flight, VG .................$375.00 C

Federal Monark Target Load, shotgun shell box, G .................$10.00 D

Federal Sporting Ammunition, sign, cardboard, counter top, Monark shell, EX.................$65.00 C

Federal Tires, sign, porcelain, "Authorized Sales Agency," 36" x 18", EX.................$450.00 C

Federal Trucks, calendar, bottom tear sheets, colorful image of young lady in very short dress standing in front of fleet of trucks, 16" x 34", 1942, EX.................$60.00 B

Feen-A-Mint Laxative, dispenser, metal, oval mirror at top, lady, 16" tall, VG.................$355.00 D

Feen-a-Mint Laxative, dispenser, tin with wood back, woman poised to take the product, mirror at top, 7½" x 5½" x 16¼", EX ....$175.00 C

Feen-A-Mint Laxative, sign, porcelain, "Feen-A-Mint For Constipation," and product, 29" x 7", VG .................$85.00 D

Feen-a-Mint, sign, porcelain, "for constipation," blocks tumbling out of package, 29¼" x 7", VG.................$375.00 C

Feen-a-Mint, sign, porcelain, single-sided, "for constipation," package of product, 29½" x 7", EX.................$650.00 B

Fehr's Malt, sign, metal, self-framing, pretty young lady, scantily clad, surrounded by cherubs with bottle on table beside her, 22" x 28", G .................$500.00 C

Fehr's Malt-Tonic, sign, metal, self frame, topless maid reaching for a glass, oval, 28" x 22", EX.................$1,800.00 B

Fell Brewing Co., sign, paper, girl in festive clothing, "Season's Greetings," 1900s, 16" x 22", VG .................$1,200.00 B

The Foster Hose Supporters, sign, celluloid, litho on cardboard, woman with garter belt, 17" H, NM, $310.00 B. *Courtesy of Richard Opfer Auctioneering, Inc.*

Fountain Tobacco, tin, litho, fountain, strong colors, 6¼" H, EX, $375.00 B. *Courtesy of Richard Opfer Auctioneering, Inc.*

Fowler's Cherry Smash, dispenser, ceramic, metal top pump, 9½" x 15", EX, $2,300.00 B. *Courtesy of Wm. Morford Investment Grade Collectibles.*

Free Land Overalls, sign, porcelain, 30" x 10", EX, $475.00 B. *Courtesy of Wm. Morford Investment Grade Collectibles.*

French Wine of Coca, sign, tin, sidewalk, original legs and frame, 20" x 28", 1880s, NM, $10,000.00 B. *Courtesy of Muddy River Trading Co./Gary Metz.*

Fellow Citizens Cigars, sign, glass, reverse painted lettering and oval cameo of Lee & Grant, 16" x 7", EX..............$800.00 B

Fellow Society of American Florists, globe, high metal profile body, two glass lenses, light-up, 16½" dia., EX ............$390.00 B

Fern Glen Rye, sign, metal, self-framing, black man and watermelon, 23" x 33", EX ............................................................$2,000.00 C

Fern Glen Rye, sign, tin, self-framing, black man with watermelon and hen with a bottle of the product on the road in front of him, 23" x 33", F ..................................................................$975.00 C

Ferndell, counter display bin, painted, wooden rear doors, 25¼" x 11½" x 12", VG ...............................................................$275.00 C

Ferndell-Remus Tea, tin, tranquil bridge over stream, 3⅛" x 3⅛", VG ...................................................................................$35.00 D

Feronia Cigars, paperweight, glass, 4¼" x 2½" x ¾", EX .....$45.00 B

Ferris Corset, sign, tin, litho, self-framing, two girls, 16½" x 22½", NM ...........................................................................$2,300.00 B

Ferris Corset, sign, tin, litho, self-framing, two girls, 16½" x 22½", VG...............................................................................$1,200.00 D

Ferris Woolens, display box, cardboard, folks in Ferris clothing, 19" tall, VG ...................................................................................$275.00 D

Ferro-Phos. Co., tip tray, non-narcotic, non-alcoholic, "Pottstown, PA...Drink Ferro-Phos...The Favorite Beverage, Five cents," product in tray center, 4⅛", EX.........................$200.00 B

Ferry's Seeds, poster, framed, "A word to the wise...The best that grow," 27" x 36", EX ..........................................................$425.00 B

Ferry's Seeds, sign, paper, hands of a clock being tied by a young lad, "Don't Tie Your Hands...," 1900s, 25" x 34", VG..................$300.00 D

Festival, crate label, paper, California lemons, 1920s, 12" x 9", VG............................................................................................$12.00 D

Fidelity-Phenix Insurance, sign, tin, 23¼" x 11¾", VG ..$125.00 C

Fiendoil, tin, litho, "The enemy of corrosion," cleans and protects firearms, EX................................................................................$55.00 C

Frick Machinery, sign, tin, machinery list down both columns, 24½" tall, VG, $225.00 B.

Frictionless Metal Co., sign, tin, single-sided, self-framing, 16" x 22¼", VG, $325.00 C.

Friedman, Keiler & Co., sign, paper, framed, under glass, bestselling label Brook Hill Whiskey and A.N. Matthews, Eureka Springs, Ark., rough edges, tough to find this sign, 1900s, 15½" x 19½", G, $225.00 C. *Courtesy of B.J. Summers.*

Friedman Keiler & Co., souvenir flask, glass and leather, Brook Hill, 1900 – 1910s, ½ pint, VG, $125.00 C. *Courtesy of B.J. Summers.*

Frostie Root Beer, sign, porcelain, "You'll Love...," 1940 – 50s, 23" x 36", VG, $250.00 B.

**Fifth Avenue Coffee,** tin, litho, Cleveland, O., 4" x 6", EX ..**$60.00 B**

**Fig Newtons,** doll, vinyl, articulated head and arms, 1983, 4½" tall, VG ....................................................................**$55.00 C**

**Finest Rolled Oats,** container, grocer on front label, Boston, MA, EX ........................................................................**$85.00 C**

**Finck's Detroit Special Overalls,** pocket mirror, metal and glass, pig on back side, "Wears Like A Pig's Nose," 2¾ " oval, VG ....**$135.00 B**

**Finck's Detroit-Special Overalls,** pocket mirror, celluloid, "Wear Like a Pig's Nose," 2¾" x 1¾", EX ..................................**$350.00 B**

**Fink Brewing Co.,** tray, metal, man pouring beer into glass, 1910s, 12½" x 16", VG..................................................**$85.00 D**

**Finotti Beverage Co.,** calendar, paper, pretty young woman in sundress, full monthly pad, 1961, 16" x 33", EX ..............**$35.00 C**

**Finotti Beverage,** calendar, paper, girl with globe, 16" x 33⅓", 1961, EX ........................................................................**$39.00 D**

**Finotti,** calendar, paper, tear sheets at bottom, pretty girl sitting next to globe with message in center, 1961, EX................**$35.00 C**

**Fire Brigade Cigar,** box, inner lid litho from the Courier Litho Co., NY, fire being fought by comical brigade, 50-ct., EX ......**$1,200.00 C**

**Fire Chief Gasoline** sign, "Localized for you," 16" x 18¼", VG...**$75.00 B**

**Fireman's Fund Insurance Co.,** sign, paper, a fireman rescueing a girl from a fire, 22" x 29", VG....................................**$575.00 C**

**Firestone Battery Cables,** display, tin, company name above hooks to hold cables, 20" x 8", VG............................................**$45.00 D**

**Firestone Cycle Tires,** sign, metal, painted, "For Sale here," 22" x 11½", EX....................................................................**$250.00 C**

**Firestone Cycle Tires,** sign, painted metal, "For Sale Here," 22" x 12", VG .................................................................$350.00 B

**Firestone Delux Champion,** ashtray, rubber, in shape of tire, clear glass inset, EX .......................................................$25.00 D

**Firestone Gum-Dipped Tires,** calendar, paper, full monthly pad and scene of traveling car on a road with pine trees, also courtesy panel for dealer, 1928, VG......................................................$200.00 D

**Firestone Rims,** sign, paper, traveling scene, "Quick, Detachable, Demountable," 21" x 40", VG .........................................$925.00 D

**Firestone Spark Plugs,** cabinet, tin, painted, large spark plug and other advertising, 1940 – 50s, 20¼" x 15¼", EX...............$375.00 D

**Firestone Steel Radial Tires,** ashtray, rubber, clear glass insert, EX ...............................................................................$15.00 D

**Firestone Tires Batteries,** clock, wood and glass, spark plug advertising on face, 15" sq, EX...........................................$225.00 C

**Firestone Tires,** calendar, paper, bottom tear sheets, early touring car on winding road in forest, 1928, EX...................$175.00 D

**Firestone Tires,** clock, "Batteries, Spark Plugs, Brake Lining and Accessories," square, lettering in center, 15¼" x 15¼", orange, white, and dark blue, VG ................................$235.00 D

**Firestone Tires,** desk accessory, molded rubber, black man beside a rubber plant, "Firestone, Liberia," 3" dia. x 5¾", EX.........$375.00 D

**Firestone Tires,** sign, metal, embossed, "Most Miles Per Dollar, Butternut Valley Hdwe...," 1930s, 36" x 12", VG .....................$45.00 C

**Firestone Tires,** sign, porcelain, double-sided, flange, tire outlined, 1940s, 21" x 16", EX ..............................................$175.00 C

**Firestone Tires,** sign, porcelain, one-sided, self-framing, 72" x 23½", G...........................................................................$425.00 C

**Firestone Tires,** sign, tin, painted, "Most miles per dollar...Butternut Valley Hdwe. Co...Gilbertsville, N.Y.," 35½" x 11½", EX .......$125.00 D

**Firestone Tractor,** ashtray, rubber, clear insert, Firestone D embossed on tire, VG........................................................$18.00 D

**Firestone,** sign, porcelain, one-sided, "Universal Sales Co....Tire Service," 60" x 30", G.................................................$250.00 C

**Firestone,** sign, tin, embossed, 15¾" x 71½", 1947, EX ....$575.00 C

**Firestone,** sign, tin, one-sided, self-framing, 25" x 10", G....$45.00 C

**Firestone,** statue, countertop, man, molded rubber, 3" x 5¾", EX ................................................................................$50.00 B

**First Aid Syrup,** bottle, die cut cover, 13" x 6", EX.................$55.00 C

**First Aid,** sign, paper, "For Your Health's Sake Drink First Aid, Orange Fruity Flavor," 9" x 5½", EX................................$10.00 D

**First Banner Cigars Box,** label, paper, Washington, Jefferson, and Adams, 9" x 6", EX..............................................................$30.00 C

**First National Bank,** calendar, paper, sailing ship, 1899, NM .$295.00 D

**First National Bank,** sign, reverse painted glass in wood frame, metal corners, 24" x 24", VG.............................................$495.00 B

**Fischer's Coffees,** bin, metal, fancy emblem along with company and product name, 20¼" x 19¼" x 13", G....................$175.00 C

**Fisher Peanuts,** vendor case, curved front glass, reverse painting on glass, EX ..............................................................$225.00 B

**Fisher's Blend Flour,** pinback button, metal, flour sack and message, VG .................................................................$30.00 D

**Fishers Peanut,** tin, litho, peanuts all around canister, 12½" x 20¼", G..................................................................$55.00 C

**Fisk Red Tops,** ad, paper, older model touring car with kids looking at product on car, 12½" x 17", EX.....................................$85.00 D

**Fisk Tire,** sign, cardboard, Fisk boy holding a tire and candle, mounting panel for price of tire, 24" x 11", EX .............$150.00 C

**Fisk Tires & Tubes,** sign, wood, sandblasted finish, sleepy boy and product name over him, 31" x 47", VG...............................$475.00 D

**Fisk Tires Radiator,** sign, cardboard, Fisk Boy, candle and tire, 21¼" x 11", 1926, VG.........................................................$255.00 D

**Fisk Tires,** display, cardboard, circus theme, cutouts never removed, 62" x 35", EX ................................................$725.00 D

**Fisk Tires,** sign, porcelain, double-sided, flange, "Gasoline...Auto Supplies," "Ingram Richardson Beaver Falls, Pa.," 24" x 18", G .$175.00 B

**Fisk Tires,** sign, tin, litho, logo youngster and tire, 6¾" dia., EX.$115.00 D

**Fisk,** sign, metal, double-sided, die cut, "Time to Re-tire...Tires," boy with tire and candle ready for bed, 36" x 29", VG.......$450.00 C

**Fisk,** sign, paper, Fisk boy watching as another boy crosses the street, "Time To Re-Tire...," 1926, 11" x 14", EX.............$75.00 C

**Fitch's Standard Heart Chewing Gum,** sign, cardboard, die cut, young girl in Victorian dress and hat, 8" x 10", 1910, EX ....$165.00 D

**Fitwell Hats,** light, metal and glass, "Wear Fitwell Hats" on two milk glass sides, EX...........................................................$1,500.00 D

**Five Brothers Plug Tobacco,** tin, litho over cardboard, 16" x 16", VG ................................................................................$750.00 D

**Five Roses Flour,** menuboard, cardboard, Indian holding flour bag, 20" x 16", EX ............................................................$750.00 D

**Five Roses Flour,** sign, porcelain, Indian shouldering a bag of flour, 1910s, 24" x 40", EX........................................$2,500.00 D

**Flag Tobacco**, pillow cover, cloth, VG......................$25.00 D

**Fleckenstein Brewing Co.**, sign, tin over cardboard, beveled edge, from Fairbault, MN, brewery, men enjoying the product, "choicest malt and hops," 13¼" x 19", EX........................$600.00 B

**Fleet Motor Oil-Grease**, sign, tin, painted, airplane and auto, 23" x 11¼", NM.....................................$325.00 B

**Fleet-Wing** gas globe, plastic body, glass lens, 13½" dia., VG..$450.00 C

**Fleetwood Aero Craft Motor Oil**, can, metal, single engine plane, top metal handle and screw cap, 2 gal., EX......................$250.00 C

**Fleetwood Motor Oil**, can, metal, four engine plane, "2500 miles of lubrication," 2 gal., EX.................................$350.00 C

**Fleischmann Preferred Whiskey**, rug, composition, product, 12" x 14", EX..........................................$15.00 D

**Fleischmann's Yeast**, pocket calendar, celluloid, pretty woman on one side and product information and calendar on reverse side, 1911, 3" x 2", VG...........................$35.00 D

**Fleischmann's Yeast**, sign, reverse glass, "The Only Genuine – Beware of Imitation," 21¼" x 27¾", G...............$100.00 B

**Fleischmann's Yeast**, sign, tin, embossed lettering "...for health," product packaging, 9" x 6", VG......................$55.00 D

**Fleischmann's**, pitcher, glass, company name lettering, EX..$10.00 D

**Flexo Chocolate and Vanilla Flavored Confection**, two-piece box, men in rowboat off tropical beach, National Licorice Co., 12" x 8" x 3½", EX......................................$55.00 B

**Floress Lipstick and Nail Lacquers**, store display, cardboard, die cut, litho, 40" x 30", VG.............................$55.00 D

**Florida** souvenir spoon, black boy and an alligator, back of handle has boy's head and palm branches, 4¼", VG...............$115.00 B

**Florida Water Perfume**, sign, paper, tropical setting with fountains, 10" x 14", EX..........................$500.00 C

**Florist Telegraph Delivery**, clock, metal back, curved glass front, light-up, Interflora-Worldwide, FTD runner in center, 16" x 16", EX......................................$175.00 B

**Florsheim Shoe**, display, neon, "for the man who cares, Shoes For Men," pair of men's shoes over neon, Art Deco style, EX......$375.00 C

**Florsheim Shoe**, sign, reverse painted glass, easel back, "for the man who cares," 5⅜" x 7½", G...........................$155.00 C

**Florsheim Shoes**, display, composition, man's oxford, 5" long, EX...........................................$55.00 D

**Flying A Associated Gasoline**, sign, "chicken wing" logo, hard-to-find item, 27¾" dia., VG...................$675.00 C

**Flying A Credit Service**, machine, metal, service station stamps, 14" x 12" x 6", VG.............................$85.00 D

**Flying Red Horse**, first aid kit, by Mobilgas-Mobiloil, 3¼" x ¾" x 2¾", G.....................................$150.00 D

**Flying Wheel Firecrackers**, package, paper, winged wheel, 2" x 3", VG............................................$10.00 D

**Foley Kidney Pills**, door push, porcelain, black lettering on yellow background, 3" x 6½", VG...........................$115.00 D

**Foley Kidney Pills**, door push, porcelain, oval, EX...............$330.00 B

**Foley's Coffee**, can, tin, litho, key-wound lid, St. Paul MN, 1-lb., VG............................................$75.00 C

**Folger's Coffee**, container, cardboard, holds free puzzle, ship, "Free when you buy Folger's Vacuum or Flaked Coffee," 2¾" x 3½", NM...................................$35.00 D

**Folger's Coffee**, thermometer, tin, dial type, can, "Served Here Exclusively," 6" dia., EX..........................$250.00 D

**Folger's Golden Gate Steel Cut Coffee**, can, metal, slip lid, view of the bridge in oval, 1 lb, EX..........................$175.00 D

**Folger's Golden Gate Steel Cut Coffee**, tin, paper label of ships in San Francisco Bay, hard-to-find-item, 2½-lb., 6" x 6", EX......$90.00 B

**Folger's**, store mirror, colorful, J.A. Folger & Co., 13" x 9", EX..$50.00 B

**Forbe's Golden Cup Coffee**, tin, several scenes around container with small lid, 3-lb., EX..........................$75.00 C

**Ford Colvin Motor Sales**, sign, dealer, tin, one-sided, embossed, 27¾" x 9¾", VG...................................$225.00 B

**Ford Genuine Parts**, clock, metal and glass, neon, octagon, 18" dia., EX............................................$850.00 D

**Ford Motor Company**, spoon, metal, company logo in handle, 1930s, EX........................................$15.00 D

**Ford Sales/Service**, thermometer, wood, Fordson tractor, 4" x 14¼", VG............................................$275.00 C

**Ford Studebaker & Maxwell**, screwdriver, metal, chrome plated handle, 8½", EX...................................$55.00 D

**Ford V-8 Deluxe Sedan Coupe**, display, cardboard, "A New 1947...," 19" x 16" x 6", EX..........................$275.00 D

**Ford**, brochure, fold-out, new models of that year, front end of 1941 Ford, 8½" x 11", 1941, EX......................$65.00 C

**Ford**, calendar, paper, woman with stole over her arm, full monthly pads, 10" x 16", VG.............................$35.00 C

**Ford**, pin back, metal, 32 Ford, "A Ford Year," ¾" dia., EX..$25.00 D

**Ford**, sign, heavy tin, tacker style, "Service Station...Sales Agency," 35½" x 11⅝", EX.................................$775.00 C

**Ford**, sign, porcelain, blue script blue background, 39" x 25", EX..........................................$1,000.00 D

**Ford,** sign, porcelain, one-sided, "Genuine...parts Used Here," 26" x 9¾", VG .....................................................................$360.00 B

**Ford,** sign, porcelain, two-sided, oval, "Genuine...Parts," 24" x 16½", VG .............................................................................$475.00 C

**Foreman Co. Distillers,** serving tray, metal, dog listing for his master, 13" dia., EX .........................................................$300.00 D

**Foremost Milk,** sign, metal, die cut, single-sided, shape of milk carton, 11" x 22", EX ..............................................................$120.00 B

**Forest & Stream Rod Gun,** sign, paper, various sporting scenes, 15½" x 10", EX ...................................................................$1,050.00 D

**Forest & Stream Tobacco,** canister, tin, litho slip-lid, man fishing in stream in cameo on front, EX ..........................$146.00 B

**Forest & Stream Tobacco,** container, tin, litho, man fishing in stream, G ...............................................................................$100.00 B

**Forest & Stream,** pocket tin, litho, two men fishing out of a canoe, EX .................................................................................$600.00 B

**Forest & Stream,** pocket tobacco tin, goose taking flight, EX ..$105.00 C

**Forest & Stream,** tin, litho, two men fishing out of a canoe, EX.$600.00 B

**Forest Flower Tobacco,** hinged box, tin, girl swinging in the forest, from the S.F. Hess Co., Rochester N.Y., 6" x 4" x 2", EX .......$375.00 B

**Fort Bedford P-Nuts 5¢,** pocket mirror, "Does the party on the other side want...," box of product on cover, 1¾" dia., EX.$300.00 B

**Fort Cumberland Brew,** sign, metal, litho, two men in car being served by waiter, 24" x 16", EX ......................................$850.00 D

**Fort Pitt Beer,** sign, metal, embossed, painted, wood frame, couple sitting at table with bottle of product, 26" x 22¾", VG................$900.00 B

**Fort Pitt Special Beer,** sign, cardboard, litho, ball player, 26" x 18", NM ...........................................................................$875.00 B

**Fort Pitt Special Beer,** sign, metal, light-up, glass face, can be counter or wall displayed, 14½" dia., EX......................$300.00 B

**Fort Pitt,** clock, metal body, glass front and face, Telechron Inc., Ashland, Mass., 15" dia., EX ...................................................$155.00 C

**Fort Pitt,** clock, tin face and housing and reverse painted strip on top, light-up, 25" x 16", VG............................................$135.00 C

**Fortune Ethyl Gasoline,** sign, one-sided, painted, Mercury, 12" x 9", G..................................................................................$500.00 B

**Fountain Tobacco,** container, metal, counter top unit for old general store, 7¼" x 8½"x 6", EX...............................................$325.00 B

**Fountain Tobacco,** tin, litho, strong colors on fountain, 6¼" H, NM ....................................................................................$435.00 D

**Four Roses Smoking Tobacco,** container, metal, vertical, pocket size, with red roses on front, 3½" x 4", VG ......................................$25.00 D

**Four Roses Whiskey,** sign, metal, self-framing, two men with cock fighters, 1920s, 57" x 43", EX............................$1,000.00 D

**Four Roses,** clock, plastic, white face and roses atop product name, 13" x 12", EX ...............................................................$125.00 C

**Four Roses,** sign, tin, painted, self-framed, couple of guys playing cards while the chickens drink the Four Roses, 20" x 24", 1912, EX ...............................................................................$575.00 C

**Foursome Mixture Tobacco,** tin, men golfing, 4¼" x 3¼" x 1", EX ...........................................................................................$275.00 C

**Fowler's Cherry Smash,** dispenser, metal top, ceramic pump, 9½" x 15", G ...............................................................................$1,100.00 C

**Fox Bread,** calendar, young boy and girl with flowers, partial tear sheet, 1913, EX ...............................................................$110.00 B

**Fox Deluxe Beer,** serving tray, hunter with horn, G ........$45.00 D

**Fox Guns,** catalog, paper, price list and scene of fox on front, 38 pages, EX ...............................................................................$175.00 C

**Fox Valley Brewing Co.,** packet watch, metal and glass, company and label on front, 2½" dia., EX............................................$275.00 D

**Francisco Auto Heater,** sign, self-framing, "Summer Here All the Year," people in cut-away touring car on snow-covered roads at night, 40" x 18", EX..........................................................$575.00 D

**Frank Coe's Fertilizer Co.,** calendar, paper, lady at edge of plowed field, 9" x 13", VG..................................................................$45.00 D

**Frank Jones Brewing Co.,** sign, paper, factory and name in arch over smokestacks, 40" x 30", VG .......................................................$800.00 D

**Frank's Choice Cigar,** sign, tin, embossed, moveable hands to signal store hours, Freeport, Ill., 6½" sq., 1900s, EX .................$225.00 D

**Frank's Dhooge,** calendar, embossed, die cut, full pad, youngster, from Milwaukee, Wisconsin, grocer, 13" x 17", 1908, EX ..$140.00 B

**Franklin Baker Company Inc. Snowdrift Coconut,** container with paper label, round, tin, sweetened fancy shred, 12" x 14½", EX..........$45.00 D

**Franklin Glass & Mirror,** pocket mirror, 3½" dia., EX...$45.00 C

**Franklin Glass and Mirror Co.,** pocket mirror, metal and glass, company advertising on rear side, 3⅜" dia., EX ............$20.00 D

**Fred Krug Brewing Co.,** plate, 50th Anniversary, with factory on one side and Mr. Krug on other side, 1909, NM ..............$85.00 B

**Fred Krug Brewing Co.,** plate, china, 50th Anniversary special, image of founder, 1859 – 1909, 10" dia., EX..................................$675.00 D

**Frederick's Premium Beer,** serving tray, metal, "Brewed with pure artesian well water," round, with bottle in center, 13¼" dia., EX ....**$95.00 D**

**Free Lance,** cigar sign, cardboard, "Smoke a...and be Convinced," 11" x 9½", EX .................................................................**$71.00 B**

**Free Land Overalls,** sign, porcelain, 30" x 10", VG ...............**$395.00 C**

**Freedom Perfect Motor Oil,** sign, porcelain, double-sided, 23½" dia., G.................................................................................**$250.00 B**

**Freeman Headbolt Engine Heater,** thermometer, metal, painted, messages to right of vertical scale, rolled edges, 6" x 15", G ...**$95.00 D**

**Freeman,** sign, metal and glass, light-up, "shoes for men," 20" x 9", EX.......................................................................................**$95.00 C**

**Freeway Nevr-Nox Ethyl,** sign, porcelain, gas pump, bold product lettering, 1940s, 13½" x 12", EX ...............................................**$175.00 C**

**Freihofer's Cake,** counter display unit, tin litho sides and glass front, "A cake for every taste...pound, sponge, fruit," 14¾" x 17" x 22", EX ..................................................................................**$895.00 C**

**Freihofer's Cakes,** store counter display rack, glass front, 14¾" x 27½", VG ................................................................................**$600.00 B**

**French Bauer Ice Cream,** globe, glass, light-up, 13½" dia., EX .**$425.00 B**

**French Champaign,** sign, cardboard, stone litho, young lady at table being served, 41½" x 57", NM ...............................**$360.00 B**

**French Marker Coffee and Chicory,** tin, litho, key-wound, 1-lb., EX .......................................................................................**$30.00 B**

**French Wine of Coca,** sign, tin, sidewalk, original legs and frame, 20" x 28", 1880s, VG.........................................................**$3,000.00 C**

**Fresh Bond Bread,** broom display, metal, bread logo and sign in center surrounded by brooms, 19" x 41", EX....................**$415.00 D**

**Friedman Keiler & Co. Distillers,** sign, framed, woman reclining on day bed while looking into hand mirror, 1900s, 20" x 14", EX ..................................................................................**$2,000.00 C**

**Friedman Keiler & Co. Distillers,** thermometer, wooden, scale type, Brook Hill Whiskey, 1900s, 5½" x 20½", F ...............**$135.00 C**

**Friedman, Keiler & Co.,** invoice, paper, company letterhead and best selling label in spotlight "Brook Hill...Newport...J.W. Palmer," 1900s, 6¼" x 9", VG .........................................................................**$10.00 C**

**Friends Tobacco,** container, metal, man & dog, EX .........**$40.00 D**

**Frigidaire,** bank, metal, in shape of refrigerator, 2" x 4", EX .**$55.00 D**

**Frigidaire,** sign, porcelain, promoting its line of dairy milk coolers, with cow, 19½" x 13¾", EX.................................................**$175.00 C**

**Frisch's Big Boy,** cigarette lighter, metal, in likeness of the Big Boy, 1960s, 2" x 1¾ ", EX.......................................................**$275.00 D**

**Frisco Line Railroad,** pocket mirror, metal and glass, speeding train on back, 2¼" dia., EX......................................................**$195.00 D**

**Friskies,** clock, metal and plastic, light up, electric, dog that winks, EX ..........................................................................................**$175.00 D**

**Froehlich's Sausage Hams & Bacon,** sign, tin over cardboard, string hung, 19" x 13", NM..........................................................**$325.00 C**

**Frontier Rarin' to Go,** gasoline globe on gill body, NM..**$2,200.00 C**

**Frostie Root Beer,** thermometer, metal, painted, "the smooth one," Frostie at top over the vertical scale, EX .............**$45.00 D**

**Fruit Bowl,** sign, metal, painted, flange, "Drink Fruit Bowl," 18½" x 14", 1950s, EX.................................................................**$75.00 C**

**Fruit Bowl,** sign, tin, embossed, "Drink, Nectar for a Nickel," tilted bottle under product message, 6¼" x 19½", EX.................**$65.00 B**

**Fruit of the Loom,** mannequin, rubber, painted in likeness of person and fitted with a girdle, 29" tall, EX ...........................**$275.00 D**

**Fry's Chocolate,** sign, porcelain, single-sided, probably foreign, young boy crying until he gets his Fry's Chocolate, 36" x 30", VG ...........................................................................................**$790.00 B**

**Fry's Hot Chocolate,** dispenser, tin, litho, product logo, 6½" x 7", EX..........................................................................................**$175.00 C**

**Fry's Pure Breakfast Cocoa,** sign, porcelain, single-sided, can in center, 18" x 24", VG .....................................................................**$170.00 B**

**Fuller Morrison Co.,** container, tin, logo on front, 25-ct., 3¾" x 5½", G.........................................................................................**$65.00 C**

**Fulton County Fair,** poster, cardboard, litho, Jamestown, NY, Sept. 5, 6, 7, 8, 1904, 15" x 29", VG ...............................**$125.00 C**

**Fun-To-Wash Washing Powder,** box, unopened, Mammy on front, EX...........................................................................................**$85.00 C**

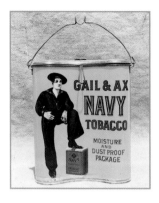

Gail & Ax Navy Tobacco, pail, bail handle, rare kidney-shaped 7" x 8½", EX, $2,300.00 B. *Courtesy of Morford Auctions.*

Galt House Coffee, tin, paper label container, roasted and packed by Norton & Curd Co., 1-lb., 1908, EX, $450.00 B. *Courtesy of Past Tyme Pleasures.*

Game Fine Cut, store cabinet, metal, litho, Jno. J. Bagley & Co., EX, $425.00 B. *Courtesy of Buffalo Bay Auction Co.*

Garcia Grande Cigars, sign, paper on cardboard, easel back, die cut, woman with box of product, 30" x 35", EX, $275.00 C.

Garcia Grande, countertop display and cigar lighter, paper litho on box, 8¾" x 9¼", G, $110.00 B.

Gardner Furniture Premium, china, "Made In Germany," store front on vase between handles, 1900s, 2¼" x 4" x1½", NM, $55.00 C. *Courtesy of B.J. Summers.*

G E Mazda Lamps, display, cardboard, three-dimensional, original real bulb, "Avoid Bulbsnatching," 8½" x 12¾", G..............................$65.00 D

G. Marconi, sign, porcelain, double-sided, die cut, the world in center of sign, 16" x 15", VG....................................$300.00 B

G. Washington Coffee, display case, tin, store counter, painted, glass front, three shelves for product display, 11½" x 13", VG...........$95.00 D

G. Washington Instant Coffee, can, metal with paper label in sample size, pry lid, 2½ oz, EX.................................$75.00 D

Gail & Ax Navy Tobacco, pail, bail handle, rare kidney-shaped, 7" x 8½", VG..................................................$1,700.00 C

Gail & Ax's Little Joker Tobacco, trade card, cardboard, little joker on cart with impaled bear, 3" x 6", EX................................$90.00 D

Gail & Ax's Little Joker Tobacco, trade card, cardboard, little joker with colonial man, 3" x 6", EX...............................$65.00 D

Gainer Feeds, sign, single-sided painted, rolled edges, "More Gains Per Dollar," 20" x 20", EX ...............................$135.00 D

Galiker's Ice Cream, sign, metal over cardboard, flavor holders at bottom, 9½" x 24", EX.............................$65.00 C

Gallagher & Burton Fine Whiskey, tip tray, tin, litho, bottle in center, 4½" dia., EX....................................$85.00 C

Gallagher & Burton Fine Whiskies, ashtray, metal, round, bottle in center, 4½" dia., EX .............................$65.00 D

Gallagher & Burton Whiskey, tip tray, "I am well preserved you see, many thanks to G & B," 4½" dia., NM........................$65.00 C

Gallagher & Burton Whiskey, tip tray, metal, older gentleman with bottle, 4¼" dia., EX.............................$95.00 B

Gallagher & Burton, ashtray, tin, litho, bottle in center, 4½" dia., G ...............................................$55.00 C

Gallagher & Burton, tip tray, tin, litho, bottle of whiskey in center, 4½" dia., EX.........................................$135.00 C

Gallaher's Honeydew Tobacco, tin, striker on side, 3¼" x 2" x ¾", EX.......................................................$75.00 C

Gallus Cigar Box, label, paper, crowing rooster, 9" x 6", EX .$45.00 D

Galt House Coffee, container, tin, paper label, roasted and packed by Norton & Curd Co., 1-lb., 1908, VG........................$400.00 C

GE Mazda, calendar, paper, National Lamp Works by Hayden Hayden, 1927, 8½" x 20¼", EX, $255.00 B. *Courtesy of Collectors Auction Services.*

Gem Safety Razor, clock, metal, lithoed to make case resemble wood grain, perpetual calendar at bottom, 28½" tall, VG, $850.00 B.

General Electric Lamps, general store lamp tester, original early lamps, "They stay brighter longer," with message on reverse painted glass, G, $550.00 E. *Courtesy of B.J. Summers*

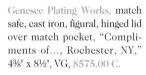

Genesee Plating Works, match safe, cast iron, figural, hinged lid over match pocket, "Compliments of..., Rochester, NY," 4⅜" x 8½", VG, $575.00 C.

Geo. Evans Honey Boy Minstrels, poster, paper, litho, 1912, 38½" x 77", G, $1,700.00 B.

Galva Creamery Co., sign, cardboard, for Peterson's Butter, Galva, Ill., Kansas City, Mo., St. Paul, Minn., 20¼" x 13", VG.........$95.00 C

Gamble's Super Quality Coffee, jar, glass, Gamble Stores, Minneapolis, 1-lb., EX .........................................................$20.00 D

Gambrinus Cincinnati Beer, sign, glass, reverse painted, "in Bottle & Keg" with king on throne, 16⅝" x 8", EX................................$235.00 C

Game Fine Cut Tobacco, tin, bird scene, manufactured by Jno J. Bagley E. Co., Detroit, Mich., 11½" x 6½" x 8", EX...............$255.00 C

Game Fine Cut Tobacco, tin, grouse in field, 11½" x 8" x 6½", VG ....................................................................................$325.00 D

Game Fine Cut, container, metal, counter top, grouse in brush, Jno J. Bagley & Co., VG ...................................................$500.00 C

Game Fine Cut, store cabinet, metal, litho, Jno. J. Bagley & Co., NM ....................................................................................$625.00 C

Game Fine Cut, tobacco bin, counter, birds in cover, Jno. Bagley & Co., Detroit, Mich., 11½" x 8" x 7", EX .........................................$525.00 B

Gansett Pilsner, stem ware, glass, etched lettering, 9" tall, EX .$55.00 D

Garcia Grande Cigar, tip tray, metal, rectangular, joker on stool to right of message, 6⅛" L, EX .......................................$85.00 C

Garcia Grande Cigars, box holder & lighter, metal, "Hole In Head, Just Lite!," EX.................................................................$125.00 D

Garcia Grande Cigars, sign, paper on cardboard, die cut, easel back, woman with box of product, 30" x 35", VG .............................$235.00 C

Garden City Brewery, cigar holder, merschaum, silver inlay, pro prohibition, EX ....................................................................$300.00 D

Garden Rolled Oats, container, from John Price & Co., Philadelphia, Pa., house and garden scene, EX ...........................................$185.00 C

Gardner Salted Peanuts, store jar, glass, "Always in Good Taste, Gardner Salted Peanuts, 5¢," 7" x 7¾", VG ..........................$95.00 C

Garland Stoves & Ranges, postcard, paperboard, fancy stove on front, 1910s, 5" x 3½", EX...................................................$65.00 D

Garland Stoves and Ranges, sign, cardboard, litho, boy and dog, 10¼" x 14", EX.................................................................$925.00 B

Garrett & Co., tray, metal, serving size, "Virginia Dare...Pure Garrett's Special...Norfolk VA, St. Louis, MO," 12" dia., EX....$325.00 D

Gasoline Globe, globe, glass, one-piece, etched and painted lettering, 12" x 5" x 12½", VG................................................$1,250.00 B

Gates Wintersafe Tire, sign, one-sided, tire going through the snow, 15" x 10¼", VG ................................................................$35.00 C

Geo. H. Goodman Company, brush, wood and fiber, embossed, Whiskies-Brandies-Wines, with locations in Paducah, KY., New Orleans, LA., Cairo, IL., Evansville, IN., main office was in Paducah, 1900 – 1910s, 7⅝" x 2⅜" x 1½", EX, $35.00 C. *Courtesy of B.J. Summers.*

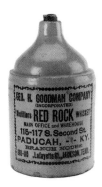

Geo. H. Goodman, jug, stoneware, stencil for Red Rock Whiskey, his most popular brands, 1900s, 1 qt., EX, $250.00 C. *Courtesy of B.J. Summers.*

Geo. Weidemann Brewing Co., sign, tin, hard-to-find die cut, easel back, man reading the newspaper while a young girl and boy look on and a bottle of beer on the table beside the man, Meek and Beach Litho, 9¾" x 13¾", 1901, EX, $1,450.00 B. *Courtesy of Buffalo Bay Auction Co.*

Gibbs Barber Shop, sign, porcelain, die-cut, double-sided, flange, 24⅛" x 12", VG, $170.00 B.

Gilbarco, clock face pump restored as an Esso pump, great example of the Art Deco influence, NM, $2,650.00 D. *Courtesy of Riverview Antique Mall.*

---

**GE Edison Mazda Automobile Lamps,** counter top display box, metal, "Name Your Car...I'll Light It," 24" x 12" x 14", EX...**$975.00 B**

**GE Edison Mazda Lamps,** playing cards, plastic, "Ecstact" by Maxfield Parrish, complete deck and in original box, 1930s, VG..........**$325.00 D**

**GE Mazda Lamps,** display, countertop unit, tin, litho, front display, various sizes of light bulbs, 27½" x 25½" x 22½", VG ..........**$495.00 C**

**Gelfands Mayonnaise,** sign, cardboard, die cut, 10" x 13½", EX..**$30.00 B**

**Gem Safety Razor,** container, metal, rectangle with slip lid and rounded corners, EX..........................................................**$145.00 D**

**Gem,** sign, tin on cardboard, promoting pantaloons and overalls, 13¼" x 9¼", EX....................................................................**$115.00 B**

**Gen. Steedman 5¢ Cigar,** sign, cardboard, embossed, girl climbing out of coach, Hettermann Bros. Co....Makers...Louisville, KY, in old gesso frame, 13" x 16½", EX.............................................**$400.00 B**

**General Arthur Cigar,** sign, reverse painted, bust of man in black jacket, 27" x 34½", EX...................................................**$255.00 C**

**General Arthur Cigars,** trade card, paperstock, "Spread Yourself & Smoke," 4" x 8", VG ...............................................**$225.00 D**

**General Electric Lamps,** sign, glass, reverse painted, "They stay brighter longer," general store lamp tester, original early lamps, G ..............................................................................**$550.00 E**

**General Electric,** ashtray, ceramic, likeness of flourscent light bulb, 1950, VG .......................................................................**$55.00 D**

**General Electric,** calendar, "Solitude" by Maxfield Parrish, 1932, 9" x 19", EX ..........................................................................**$675.00 D**

**General Miles Cigar,** sign, reverse chipped lettering on beveled glass, framed, Chicago, 22" x 12", NM ..............................**$355.00 B**

**General Mills Cheerios,** cereal bowl, Melmac, Sue and the Cheerios Kid, 1969, EX .........................................................................**$15.00 D**

**General Mills Cheerios,** plate, Melmac, Bullwinkle and Cheerios Kid, 1969, EX ..........................................................................**$20.00 D**

**General Mills Count Chocula,** doll, vinyl, 1977, 8" tall, EX ........**$150.00 D**

**General Motor Fuel,** globe, low profile metal body, two glass lens, 15" dia., VG ...........................................................................**$1,200.00 B**

**General Motors Fuel,** gas globe, metal and glass, knight in center and "General" diagonally across the front, 15" dia., EX.............**$700.00 C**

Gilliam's Candies, box, cardboard, "Good To The Last Bite," 1940 – 50s, 8" x 10½" x 3¾", G, $20.00 C. *Courtesy of B.J. Summers.*

Gilmore Lion Head Motor Oil, sign, tin, embossed, single-sided, 29½" x 11½", VG, $2,500.00 B.

Girard Cigar, cutter, metal bottom with stamped name, cardboard sign with cigar labels on top, also has match holder and ashtray, 5½" x 5" x 8", NM, $425.00 B.

Gladiator Coffee, large store bin for Brewster, Crittenden & Co., 13¼" x 21½" x 13¼", EX, $395.00 C. *Courtesy of Wm. Morford Investment Grade Collectibles.*

Glendale Cheese, box, wooden, "...Manufactured by Pauly & Pauly Cheese Co....," 5 lb., VG, $25.00 C.

General Motors, sign, metal, embossed, yellow "General Motors" on blue background, 3¼" x 29", EX .........................$95.00 D

General Petroleum Corporation, oil can, rare item, 1-gal., 10" tall, VG ......................................................$275.00 C

General Sherman Cigar Box, label, paper, salesman sample with the general's likeness surrounded by patriotic scenes, EX ..........$235.00 D

General Violet Ray Anti-Knock Gasoline, sign, porcelain, double-sided, 30" dia., VG..........................................$500.00 C

Genesee Beer, sign, tin on cardboard, two people sitting on box, 14½" x 7", EX.......................................$50.00 B

Genesee Beer, sign, tin over cardboard, 14⅝" x 7⅛", 1960s, EX .$55.00 C

Genesee Plating Works, match safe, earlier cast iron with hinged lid over match pocket, "Compliments of..., Rochester, NY," 4⅜" x 8½", EX.................................................$625.00 B

Geneva on the Lake, ashtray, metal, painted, stand-up, black boy smoking a cigar, made in Japan, 4¼" H, VG .....................$300.00 B

Genuine Ford Parts, sign, porcelain, double-sided, top-hung, 24" x 17", 1930s, EX................................................$1,800.00 C

Geo A Moss Union Star Paste Stove Polish, container, metal, oval with portrait in center, 4¼" x 3¼" x 1", EX ..........................$55.00 D

Geo Ehret's Beer, tray, metal, round, Extra Draught Beer, 13" dia., EX.................................................................$85.00 D

Geo H Goodman Co., mini jug, stoneware, "Compliments of...Geo H. Goodman Co....Distillers...Red Rock Whiskey...Paducah, Ky...Shreveport, LA...Jackson, Tenn," extremely hard to find, 3½" tall, EX ................................................$1,500.00 C

Geo Renner Brewing Co., tray, metal, rectangular, Old "Grossvater" Beer, 1930s, 10" x 13", EX .................................$115.00 D

Geo. E. Sawyer's Electric Cough Drops, display box, tin, litho, originally held 5¢ packages, 8½" x 7¼" x 4¼", EX..........................$400.00 C

Geo. H. Goodman Co., shotglass, glass, showing company offices, 1900s, 2" x 1⅞" dia. at widest point, EX ......................$35.00 C

GMAC, sign, National Credit Service Cards Honored Here, 24" x 12", VG, $275.00 C.

GMC Trucks, clock, metal and glass, neon, "sales, service," 1940 – 50s, 18½" x 18½", VG, $675.00 C.

Gold Bloom, milk bottle, glass with painted label of company name on front and war time "snap shot" on the back, "You Can Keep'Em Flying, By Buying, U.S. War, Bonds and Stamps," war plane, most war bottles are in demand more than the ordinary bottles, 1940s, 1 qt, VG, $45.00 C. *Courtesy of B.J. Summers.*

Gold Bloom Steel Cut Coffee, can, metal, pry lid, couple enjoying a cup of the product, 1 lb., VG, $95.00 C. *Courtesy of B.J. Summers.*

Gold Dust Tobacco, pocket tin, with great graphics, EX, $2,650.00 B. *Courtesy of Morford Auctions.*

**Geo. H. Goodman Company,** guarantee, paper, $1,000 to anyone who buys "Old McHaney" or "Smoky Mountain Corn Whiskey" and finds it not as represented, 1900s, 7¾" x 4", EX....................................$75.00 C

**Geo. H. Goodman Company,** whiskey jug, stoneware, blue stencil, shoulder jug, 1900s, 1 qt., EX ...........................................$350.00 C

**Geo. Weidemann Brewing Co.,** sign, tin, die cut, easel back, man reading the newspaper while a young girl and boy look on and a bottle of beer on the table beside the man, hard to find, Meek and Beach Litho, 9¾" x 13¾", 1901, G ....................................$450.00 C

**George Benz Liquors,** sign, couple having a cocktail, 21" x 17", 1910s, EX .................................................................................$235.00 C

**George H. Goodman Company Incorporated,** whiskey crock, 1-gal. message in outline box on front, cream, EX .....................$155.00 C

**George Lawrence Co. Dog Chains & Leads,** sign, metal, a dog and a method of displaying the products, 10" x 10", EX ........$155.00 D

**George Potter Cigars,** photogravure, George Potter smoking a cigar with a box of the product in background, 20½" x 24½", EX ..$45.00 C

**George Washington Cut Plug Tobacco,** pail, side wire bail handles, G ........................................................................................$115.00 D

**German American Brewing Co. Beer,** sign, "Matosia Beer," 5" dia., EX.........................................................................................$65.00 D

**German Fire Insurance Company Pittsburgh, Pa.,** calendar, cardboard, patriotic theme, 1905, 10½" x 13½", EX ....................$65.00 C

**German Insurance Co.,** calendar, six-pages with different scenes, 10¼" x 13¼", 1902, EX........................................................$40.00 B

**German Syrup,** sign, cardboard, double-sided, die cut, litho, black boy holding sign with advertising on hat, 9" x 17", VG....................$450.00 B

**Germantown Dye Works,** sign, cardboard, painted, factory, 14" x 11", 1920s, EX ...............................................................$85.00 C

**Gerst Brewing Co.,** notebook, leather and celluloid, 1897 calendar, William Gerst, Nashville, Tenn., 2¾" x 5¼", 1897, EX ..........$175.00 C

**Gettelman Beer,** sign, metal, stand up, ducks coming up out of the water, 1950s, 16" x 10", EX.................................................$65.00 D

**Getty,** sleeve patch, cloth, 4½" x 2⅞", G.............................$10.00 C

**Gevelot Ammunition,** sign, tin, one-sided, rolled edges, man holding game taken using the product, 17" x 22½", VG.............$75.00 C

Golden Bear Oil Co. Petroleum Products, pump sign, porcelain, one-sided, bear in center, 15" dia., VG, $1,900.00 B. *Courtesy of Collectors Auction Services.*

Golden Girl Cola, sign, tin, die-cut, embossed, bottle-cap shape, 33" dia., EX, $175.00 C.

Goldenrod Ice Cream, clock, reverse painted on glass, light-up, 15" dia., VG, $185.00 B. *Courtesy of Autopia Advertising Auctions.*

Gold Medal Flour, poster, paper, litho, kernel of wheat, 28" x 42", EX, $150.00 C.

---

**Ghirardellis Chocolate,** container, metal, sample size, "Sweet Ground" chocolate, EX ........................................................$175.00 D

**Ghostley Pearl,** sign, tin, one-sided, embossed, "Our Choice...the...Assured Poultry Profits," 18" x 12", VG .......$160.00 B

**Gibbons Beer Ale,** clock, Bakelite, electric, 14⅝" dia., NM.$135.00 C

**Gibbs,** sign, porcelain, flange, shop with die cut of barber pole, 20" x 24", VG ...........................................................................$425.00 B

**Gibbsons,** clock, metal and glass, on face "Gibbsons Is Good! Anytime," 15" dia., EX...........................................................$125.00 D

**Gibson Girl Cigarette,** tin, young lady on front, 3¼" x 3" x ⅝", EX ....................................................................................$285.00 C

**Gibson Girl,** tin, vertical, Gibson Girl on front, 3¾" x 3¾" x ¾", VG ....................................................................................$240.00 B

**Gibson Straight Rye Whiskey,** paperweight, glass, five "liars' dice" inside, 3" x 3" x 1", EX........................................................$65.00 C

**Gilbert Rae Aerated Waters,** sign, tin, embossed, litho, self-framed, bottles and the factory, 19¾" x 28", EX................................$675.00 B

**Gilcrest Animal Food,** sign, paper, in dialect "Golly! It Makes De Mule Go & Chickens Fly" with black man in a cart pulled by a mule, 21" x 16", VG ....................................................$950.00 C

**Gilette Safety Tires,** watch fob, metal, "A Bear For Wear," 1920s, NM .........................................................................................$155.00 C

**Gill Mortuary/ Emergency Ambulance** calendar, tin over cardboard, number cards at bottom and Pierce-Arrow automobile, 13" x 19", G ....................................................................................$375.00 C

**Gill's Hotel Special Coffee and Chicory,** container, tin, key-wound, litho, 1-lb., EX ....................................................................$37.00 B

**Gillette Blue Blades,** dispenser, metal, coin-operated, "10 for 50¢," works only with solid 50¢ pieces, 1950s, NM.............................$135.00 D

**Gillette Blue Blades,** sign, tin, single-sided, die-cut, advertising foreign, 5¾" x 7" x 4¼", scarce, F ...........................................$50.00 B

**Gillette Safety Razor,** pocket mirror, "No Stropping! No Honing!," 1913 mirror, 2⅛" dia., EX ..............................................................$140.00 B

**Gillette Safety Razor,** pocket mirror, celluloid, baby using razor, with 1909 calendar around outside of artwork, 2¼" dia., EX.......$160.00 B

Gold Seal Boots and Overshoes, sign, tin, double-sided, litho, boots and shoes, 18¼" L, G, $170.00 B.
*Courtesy of Richard Opfer Auctionering, Inc.*

Gold Seal Champagne, tip tray, manufactured by American Artworks, Coshocton, Ohio, 4½" x 6½", NM, $95.00 C.

Gold Seal Rubbers and Overshoes, sign, tin, products pictured, "We Sell...," 1910 – 20s, 18" x 9", VG, $275.00 B.

Gollam's Lebanon Ice Cream, sign, metal, painted, double-sided, sidewalk, "We Serve," 1940s, EX, $250.00 B. *Courtesy of Muddy River Trading Co./Gary Metz.*

Gillette Tires, sign, cardboard, bear with bowl and running from bee, "An Exclusive...Tire...No Chains Needed," 13" x 17", EX ....$675.00 D

Gillette's Flavoring, display case, metal, wood, and glass with curved glass front, 21" x 34", VG ...................................$1,200.00 D

Gillette, blade dispenser, metal, "Look Sharpe...Feel Sharpe...Be Sharpe," 18" x 8" x 3", EX ...................................$185.00 D

Gillette, sign, porcelain, die cut, double-sided, flange, razor and package of blades, 21½" x 19½", VG..........................$3,350.00 B

Gilmer Moulded Rubber, store countertop display unit, vintage man on front, back is open and has four shelves for storage, 16½" x 25" x 21½", G..................................................................$110.00 B

Gilmer, product box, cardboard, super-service molded rubber fan belt, EX..............................................................$425.00 C

Gilmore Blu-Green Gasoline, trade card, paper stock, with the trademark lion, EX...................................................$195.00 D

Gilmore Lion Head Motor Oil, pencil, metal with calendar near the top and oil sample on end, EX .........................................$210.00 D

Gilmore Lubricant, can, metal, with pry lid and round lion logo, 1 lb., EX........................................................................$350.00 B

Gilmore Motor Oil, pennant, cloth with company name and lion logo, 21" x 10", EX.........................................................$425.00 B

Gilmore, calendar, paper, young lady with Scottie dogs on leash tangled around her legs, 7" x 15¼", EX...............................$45.00 C

Gin Seng, serving tray, metal, rectangular, "The Beverage of Purity," EX.................................................................$125.00 C

Gin Seng, serving tray, metal, rectangular, "The Beverage of Purity," VG.................................................................$100.00 C

Ginta Cigar, sign, product box that has a pretty woman on the lid, G....................................................................................$55.00 B

Gladiator Coffee, store bin, large, Brewster, Crittenden & Co., 13¼" x 21½" x 13¼", EX .........................................................$395.00 C

Glendale Fresh Daily, sign, reverse painted on glass, farmyard scene, product container lights up, 15¼" x 11¼", EX...$195.00 C

Goodrich Company Hipress Boot, sign, cardboard, die cut, man ready to pull on a real boot on the foot of the display, easel back, 1917, 44" x 18½", NM, $435.00 B.

Goodrich Sport Shoes, poster, cardboard, framed, Indian, 26" x 41", EX, $270.00 C.

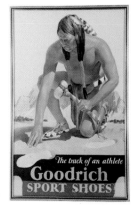

Good Year Tires, radiator cover, cardboard, from Ned Lambert, Hagerstown MD, directions on reverse side for installing on Model T radiator, 18½" wide, VG, $100.00 B.

Gordon's Potato Chips, can, metal, with Gordon's delivery truck at top, 7½" x 11½", red and cream, VG, $65.00 C. *Courtesy of B.J. Summers.*

Grand Old Party 1856 to 1908, tip tray, with Taft & Sherman in center of tray under White House, great strong graphics, 4⅛" dia., EX, $95.00 B.

Grant's Whiskey, sign, tin, litho, "...Cherry Whisky," English made for the American sales, 9¾" x 12½", EX, $240.00 B.

Glendora Coffee, sign, tin, embossed, NOS, 20" x 6½", NM .....$375.00 C

Glendora Coffee, tin, litho, container from the Glendora Products Co., Warren, Pa., 6⅝" x 8", EX ......................$55.00 C

GLF Quality gas globe, wide glass body with two lenses, 13½" dia., VG.................................$350.00 C

Globe Evaporated Milk, trade card with Uncle Sam barometer, 3½" x 6", EX...........................$50.00 C

Globe Gasoline, sign, metal, round, globe with name ribbon across the center, 30" dia., EX ...............................$475.00 D

Globe Tobacco Co., tin, Hand Made Tobacco, with small lid featuring hand with plug of tobacco, 5" x 6½", EX ..............$390.00 B

Globe Wernicke, tip tray, metal, litho, couple in front of bookcase at home, 4¼" dia., VG.........................$85.00 D

Globe White Seal Motor Oil, sign, tin, litho, double-sided, flange, early metal oil can, 12" x 19½", VG ..............................$1,100.00 B

Globe, sign, porcelain, "...The Universal..." with lion logo, 30" dia., VG ..............................................................$675.00 C

Gloco Ethyl, pump sign, porcelain, round, company name and Ethyl logo, 14" dia., EX.....................................$675.00 C

Gloco Hi'R Octane, pump sign, porcelain, "Use...," scalloped edge, 15" x 9", EX ......................................$425.00 C

Gloco, gas globe, plastic body with glass lens, 13½" dia., VG .$425.00 C

Gluck's Beer, sign, cardboard, designed to be used on bus benches, 12" x 7", VG.........................................$75.00 D

GMC Gasoline Trucks, sign, porcelain, logo in center dot, 30" dia., EX .............................................................$350.00 D

GMC Trucks Sales Service, clock, metal and glass, neon, G .$800.00 B

GMC Trucks, sign, metal and neon in art deco shape, 72" x 44" x 8", VG.....................................................$5,000.00 D

Grape Crush, dispenser, glass, very unusual, shaped like a grape, made with transalucent material, top pump is original and is sitting in original rubber base, 1920s, EX, $4,200.00 B.

Grape Dee-Light, sign, cardboard, hang-up, "Gee but it's good, Jacob Onuschak, Northampton, PA," 1920s, 10½" x 14", EX, $45.00 B. *Courtesy of Muddy River Trading Co./Gary Metz.*

Grape-Nuts, sign, tin, self-framing, "To school well fed on...There's a reason," little girl walking with St. Bernard, 20¼" x 30¼", EX, $1,350.00 D. *Courtesy of Antiques Cards & Collectibles/Ray Pelley*

Grape Ola, sign, tin, delicious looking bunch of grapes, 20" x 14", NM, $500.00 B.

Grape Smash, sign, tin, "Better Than Straight Grape Juice," 13½" x 9½", EX, $325.00 B. *Courtesy of Muddy River Trading Co./Gary Metz.*

---

GMC Trucks, sign, porcelain, double-sided, dealer, "Sales & Service," 42" dia., EX .................$1,175.00 C

GMC Trucks, sign, porcelain, two-sided, 48" x 24", VG.......$520.00 B

Goal Cigars, box, metal, slip lid and rounded corners, VG..........$125.00 C

Gobblers Cigars, container, metal, round, slip lid, "The Latest Smoke, Gobblers," 5" x 5" dia., EX ...................................$775.00 C

Goblin Soap, container, cardboard, elf-like figure on front, 2½" x 1½" x 4", EX.....................................................................$85.00 C

Goebel 22 Beer, calendar, 1887 baseball image, 18" x 27¼", 1953, EX......................................................................................$135.00 C

Goebel Bantam Beer, cardboard, die cut, "Enjoy, rooster," "tootin" his own horn, 9" x 11", EX....................................................$30.00 B

Goebel Private Stock Beer, calendar, Civil War-era baseball game, 18" x 27¼", 1951, NM..........................................................$150.00 C

Gold Bell, sign, metal, gift stamps advertising, painted, 19½" x 28", G.........................................................................$165.00 D

Gold Bond Smoking Tobacco, container, pocket size, "Old Reliable," EX....................................................................................$175.00 C

Gold Coin Coffee, container, metal, 1 lb., EX....................$15.00 D

Gold Cross Talc, foot powder container, tin, litho, 4½" x 2½", EX ................................................................................$180.00 B

Gold Dust Tobacco, pocket tin, with great graphics, EX.......$2,650.00 B

Gold Dust Twins Washing Powder, litho, cardboard, twins and box of product, "Let the Gold Dust Twins Do Your Work," 13¾" x 21¼", VG .............................................................$600.00 B

Gold Dust Twins Washing Powder, sign, cardboard, round, string-hung, double-sided, 6½" dia., G................................................$75.00 C

Gold Dust Twins Washing Powder, trade cards, cardboard, twins in washtub, 3" x 3¾", NM ......................................................$75.00 D

Gold Dust Twins, alarm clock, wind-up, cardboard face, metal body, and plastic front with graphics of washing powder box, 3¼" dia., EX.........................................................................$550.00 B

Grapette Soda, sign, porcelain, "Enjoy," 27" x 16", NM, $650.00 B.

Gray Line, sign, porcelain, "Sight Seeing Everywhere," 1930s, 20" dia., EX, $575.00 C.

Great Heart Coal, thermometer, porcelain, scale reading, good strong colors, 8" x 38½", VG, $250.00 B.

Great Majestic Ranges, sign, gesso bas-relief, woman cooking on product, great details, 1915, 37" x 49" x 4¼", EX, $3,000.00 B.

Great Western Line, sign, metal over cardboard, Smith Manufacturing Co., Chicago, IL, 27½" x 19", G, $1,200.00 B. *Courtesy of Collectors Auction Services.*

Gold Dust Twins, banner, cardboard, double-sided, twins and washing powder boxes, The Table and Ticket Co., Chicago & New York, 71½" x 17", EX ....................................................$3,800.00 B

Gold Dust Twins, banner, cloth, washing powder box and "GOLD DUST cleans everything," 58" x 24½", VG ........................$1,000.00 D

Gold Dust Twins, box, cardboard, litho of Gold Dust Twins cleaning, 10" x 18" x 12", VG ....................................................$110.00 B

Gold Dust Twins, can, cardboard, tin top and bottom, paper label, twins, 3" dia. x 4¾", VG ........................................$85.00 C

Gold Dust Twins, display, cardboard, die cut, twins on both sides of box, 14¼" x 3⅞" x 12¾", 1890s, VG ...............................$1,690.00 B

Gold Dust Twins, powder box, cardboard, twins, 4¾" x 8¾", VG .$50.00 C

Gold Dust Twins, sheet music for "Twins Rag," twins at piano and dancing, EX .....................................................................$55.00 C

Gold Dust Twins, sign, cardboard, double-sided, litho, store counter, twins doing various chores, 14" x 14", VG........$2,450.00 B

Gold Dust Twins, sign, tin, embossed, twins in tub, 27½" x 40", NM ..........................................................................$3,000.00 C

Gold Dust Twins, sign, tin, self-framing, from Meek & Beach Co., Coshocton, O., twins doing a variety of chores, "Let the GOLD DUST twins do your work," 25½" x 38", VG...............................$7,500.00 C

Gold Dust Twins, sign, trolley car, house cleaning in progress, "For Spring House Cleaning," 26" x 10½", NM........................$1,200.00 B

Gold Dust Twins, sign, washing powder advertising with cooking utensil on counter, "Quickly Clean with GOLD DUST," 22" x 12", EX ..................................................................................$150.00 B

Gold Hunter, cigar box label, railroad and Klondike prosecutor, 4½" x 4½", EX...........................................................................$65.00 D

Gold Leaf Distilling Co., tray, metal, rectangular, "Old Gold Leaf Rye," pretty woman, 12" x 17", EX....................................................$150.00 D

Gold Medal Coffee, can, metal, key wind lid, white company lettering, 1 lb, EX...................................................................$75.00 D

Gold Medal Flour, sign, paper on cloth, a kernel of wheat dissected and named, 28" x 42", G....................................................$95.00 B

Gold Medal, watch fob, celluloid and metal, 1½" dia., VG .......$75.00 C

Green River, sign, cardboard, counter stand-up, "first for thirst...Green River," with original bottle and cap, EX, $60.00 B. *Courtesy of Buffalo Bay Auction Co.*

Green-Wheeler Shoes, sign, tin on cardboard, "For Ladies, None Better," woman in vintage dress by stone wall, by American Artworks, 11¾" x 14¼", 1911, EX, $600.00 B. *Courtesy of Buffalo Bay Auction Co.*

Greenwich Ice Cream, sign, cardboard, die cut, store display, people around table eating different flavors of the product, 30" x 29", VG, $155.00 B.

Greenwich Insurance Co., calendar, paper, 8" x 12½", VG, $20.00. B. *Courtesy of Collectors Auction Services.*

Gregory Piping Co., lighter, metal, by Park Lighter, 1950 – 60s, 1½" x 2¼" x ⅜", F, $10.00 C. *Courtesy of B.J. Summers.*

Gregory, vinegar pitcher, stoneware, front stencil, "The O. L. Gregory Vinegar Co., Elko County, Pure Apple Juice Vinegar, Paducah, KY," handle on back, 1900s, 5" x 3", VG, $95.00 C. *Courtesy of B.J. Summers.*

---

**Gold Seal Boots and Overshoes,** sign, tin, double-sided, litho, boots and shoes, 18¼" L, EX............................................$250.00 C

**Gold Seal Champagne,** tip tray, manufactured by American Artworks, Coshocton, Ohio, 4½" x 6½", EX..............................$50.00 D

**Gold Soap,** sign, porcelain, curved, soap bar and "Extra large... Gold Soap...Extra Good," 1910s, 19" x 26", VG................$625.00 C

**Gold Standard Pure Allspice,** container, metal, 1½ oz., EX........$45.00 D

**Gold Star Coffee,** jar, glass, David G. Evans Coffee Co., St. Louis, 3-lb., G..................................................................$40.00 D

**Gold Star Pure Pennsylvania,** sign, porcelain, oil derrick, 29" dia., EX ....................................................................$1,950.00 C

**Gold Tip Gum,** gum package, cardboard, Peppermint, Sterling Mint Co., Inc., New York, EX..............................................$20.00 D

**Gold-Pak,** condom tin, litho, 3 for $1.00, Crown Rubber Co., Akron, OH, 1½" x 2", EX ...............................................$400.00 B

**Golden Bear Oil Co.,** pump sign, porcelain, one-sided, Petroleum...Products, with bear in center, 15" dia., EX....................$2,400.00 C

**Golden Burst Popcorn,** three tier countertop display with tin litho marquee, 7½" x 18" x 16", EX ...........................$225.00 C

**Golden Cup Coffee,** can metal, with key wind lid, 1 lb., NM........$65.00 D

**Golden Dawn Coffee,** can, metal with key wind lid and rose logo on front, 1 lb., EX.................................................$75.00 D

**Golden Eagle,** label, paper, for wooden crate of California oranges, EX.....................................................................$10.00 D

**Golden Eagle,** pump sign, porcelain with "Golden Eagle," 13" x 13", EX.....................................................................$575.00 C

**Golden Eagle,** pump sign, porcelain, one-sided of eagle, 13" x 13", VG .....................................................................$350.00 B

**Golden Glow Beer,** label, paper, Golden West Brewing Co., EX.$15.00 B

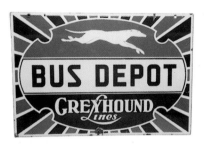

Greyhound Lines Bus Depot, sign, porcelain, running dog at top of lettering, 30" x 20", VG, $525.00 C.

Griffith & Boyd Co. Fertilizers, sign, paper, litho, framed, pretty young woman, 19¾" x 24¼", G, $295.00 C. *Courtesy of Collectors Auction Services.*

Gripwell Tires, sign, wooden, 12" x 16", G, $425.00 B.

Grocery and Meat Market, clock, glass and metal, Electric Clock Co., Chicago, 22½" dia., G, $325.00 B.

Gulf & Shell, salesman sample gas globes, glass and metal in carrying case, light up, 1950s, 21" tall, EX, $2,400.00 C.

---

**Golden Grain Smoking Tobacco,** bag, Brown & Williamson with Raleigh wrapping papers on back, G..................................$35.00 D

**Golden Grain Whiskey,** sign, metal, Lenore, a pretty bare shouldered lady, 15" x 15", VG .................................................$475.00 C

**Golden Light Coffee,** sign, metal, "Enjoy...It's Really Good," 16" x 9", VG .............................................................................$95.00 C

**Golden Pheasant Coffee,** tin, litho with bird on blue background, 1-lb., EX .........................................................................$1,500.00 C

**Golden Quality Ice Cream,** sign, metal with crown in clouds design, 44" x 28", VG ..........................................................................$85.00 B

**Golden Rail Beer,** sign, porcelain, curved, old steam locomotive, only 50 produced, 24" x 18", EX.....................................$775.00 C

**Golden Shell Motor Oil,** driveway sign, double-sided, 26½" x 34½", G ..............................................................................$325.00 D

**Golden Shell Motor Oil,** driveway sign, double-sided, 26½" x 34½", VG .............................................................................$375.00 C

**Golden Spring Beverages,** sign, celluloid over metal, chain-hanging, promoting Golden Spring Sarsaparilla, Smith Co., New Bedford, Mass., bottle pouring into glass, 11" x 8", EX .....................$375.00 C

**Golden State Beer,** tray, metal, rectangular, serving size with eagle on top of the Pan Am Expo shield, EX .........................................$125.00 D

**Golden Tip Gasoline,** sign, porcelain, single-sided, 60" x 38", VG..........................................................................................$775.00 C

**Golden Wedding Coffee,** can, key-wound vaccum pack 1- lb., G ..............................................................................................$35.00 D

**Golden Wedding Pure Rye,** sign, glass with reverse painted message in fancy lettering, 36" x 24", VG...............................$475.00 C

**Golden West Brewing Co.,** sign, porcelain, single-sided, Oakland, California, Bull's Eye Beer, 18" x 18", EX..........................$320.00 B

**Golden West Coffee,** can, metal with key wind lid, cowgirl, 1 lb., EX..............................................................................................$125.00 C

Gulf, banner, cloth, Irvin S. Cobb and Will Rogers, 66" x 30", EX, $375.00 B.

Gulf, gas globe, glass body and lens, 17" high, VG, $375.00 B.

Gulf, gas station photo, full color, matted and framed, 41" x 22¾", NM, $145.00 B.

Gulf, Heating Oils, sign, three-dimensional on hanging arm, NM, $325.00 C.

Gulflex, sign, tin, self-framing, embossed, 48" x 24", VG, $275.00 C.

---

**Golden West Coffee,** can, metal, key wind lid, cowgirl from shoulders up, 1 lb., VG ......................................................$165.00 D

**Golden West Coffee,** Clossett & Devers, Portland and Seattle, 5-lb, EX ....................................................................$125.00 B

**Golden-Rod Oats,** tin with slip lid, Chicago, IL, EX..........$125.00 C

**Goldenmoon Buckeye Root Beer,** syrup can, 5½" x 10" x 4½", VG ........................................................................$25.00 C

**Goldenrod Beer,** label, paper, Rock River Brewing Co., Rockford, Ill, 1930s, 12oz. bottle, VG ......................................$35.00 D

**Goldenrod Ice Cream,** clock, light-up, reverse painted on glass, 15" dia., EX................................................................$235.00 C

**Golf Girl Talcum Powder,** container, paper label, woman golfing, 2½" x 5½", EX................................................................$625.00 B

**Gollam's Ice Cream,** sidewalk sign, porcelain, double-sided, framed, youngster carrying a large cone, EX ...............$415.00 B

**Gollam's Lebanon Ice Cream,** sidewalk sign, metal, painted, double-sided, "We Serve," 1940s, VG.....................................$200.00 D

**Good Gulf Gasoline** globe, one-piece etched construction, 16", G............................................................................$500.00 C

**Good Humor,** badge, cloisonne, with name space in center of cloud shaped piece, 2½" x 1½", EX...............................................$400.00 C

**Good Humor,** sign, porcelain, product in pints, 56" x 5", EX .$275.00 D

**Good Year Bicycle Tire,** sign, paper, litho, vintage bicycle, 13" x 21", EX.............................................................$275.00 D

**Goodrich Batteries, Tires, Accessories,** sign, porcelain, self-framing, 60" x 20½", EX..............................................$195.00 C

**Goodrich Safety Tires,** sign, porcelain, one-sided, probably Canadian, Canadian Mountie, 18¼" x 62¾", VG.....................$6,000.00 B

**Goodrich Silvertown,** ashtray, rubber with glass insert, in shape of tire, 6½" dia., EX .........................................................$275.00 B

Gulf No-Nox Motor Fuel, poster, cardboard, "Now Aviation Grade," early auto and airplane, with a clock face pump, 1930s, 28" x 34", VG, $395.00 C.

Gulf, sign, porcelain, "Authorized Dealer," 1930s, 40" x 9", VG, $155.00 C.

Gulley & Co., pants, cloth, salesman sample of early clothing article, store tag sewn on inside of waist band, EX, $85.00 C. *Courtesy of B.J. Summers.*

Gurd's Distilled Water, sign, tin, single-sided, embossed, 21½" x 6", VG, $350.00 B.

G. W. Katterjohn Contractor, concrete stamp, brass with wooden handle on back side, used to place the contractor's name on completed projects, image appears in reverse to be correct when viewed in place, Paducah, KY, 1910s, 11¾" x 4¼", EX, $150.00 C. *Courtesy of B.J. Summers.*

Gypsy Hosiery, tip tray, metal, with gypsy camp scene and gypsy woman inset in center, George H. Buschmann, Owensville, Mo., 6" dia., EX, $210.00 B.

Goodrich Silvertowns, sign, cardboard, die cut, litho, cars and ocean, "Are Durable," 50" x 36", VG ............................$425.00 B

Goodrich Silvertowns, sign, porcelain, die cut, double-sided, flange, 23½" x 19", VG.......................................................$325.00 C

Goodrich Silvertowns, sign, porcelain, one-sided, 72" x 24", VG .........................................................................$425.00 C

Goodrich Sport Shoes, poster, cardboard, die cut, featuring Indian, framed, 26" x 41", VG .............................................$245.00 C

Goodrich Sport Shoes, sign, cardboard, die cut, easelback display, boy running with tie blowing in the breeze, 16½" x 23¼", NM......$195.00 C

Goodrich Tires, blotter, cardboard, Goodrich rain rubber with front zippers, scenes of people in winter landscape, 1950s, 6½" x 3½", VG ..............................................................$12.00 C

Goodrich Tires, sign, porcelain, single-sided, "Slow Down...Safety First," 26" dia., EX..........................................................$325.00 C

Goodrich Tires, sign, porcelain, supplies, flange, white lettering on blue background, 18" dia., G..............................................$265.00 D

Goodrich Tires, sign, porcelain, supplies, flange, white lettering on blue background, 18" dia., VG ...........................................$295.00 C

Goodrich, ad, paper, early model auto heater, "You'll get more and quicker heat with this hot water heater," 57" x 34", EX......$30.00 D

Goodrich, print, paper, "The Goodrich Rubber Man's Vacation...," 32" x 26", EX .................................................................$600.00 D

Goodstock Shirts, sign, tin, litho, applied glitter, 20" x 14", 1900s, EX..............................................................................$300.00 C

Goodyear Authorised Dealer, sign, porcelain, notice mispelling, lettering on yellow background, 24" x 21", EX................................$125.00 D

Goodyear Authorized Dealer, sign, porcelain, with company logo and name lettering below logo, 24" x 21", VG .......$185.00 C

**Goodyear Batteries,** sign, porcelain, one-sided, 47" x 26½", G ..$200.00 C

**Goodyear Camelback and Repair Materials,** clock, 7½" x 7½", VG ....................$55.00 C

**Goodyear Rubber Tires,** sign, porcelain, winged foot and "Agency...Akron Ohio," 16" x 24", EX..................$1,325.00 D

**Goodyear Service Station,** sign, porcelain, one-sided, with graphics circled by a tire, 71½" x 24", G ........................$325.00 C

**Goodyear Tires,** sign, metal, framed glass front light-up with fleet foot at top center, G ..............................................$95.00 C

**Goodyear Tires,** sign, porcelain, one-sided, fleet foot in center, 72" x 24", G ......................................................................$275.00 C

**Goodyear Tires,** sign, tin, painted, directional arrow, dealer, Scranton, PA, 35¼" x 11⅜", NM .......................................$235.00 C

**Goodyear Tires,** thermometer, wooden, painted with tire surrounding the earth at top, dealer message at bottom, vertical scale, 3¼" x 11½", G ..................................................$65.00 D

**Goodyear Wingfoot Heels,** trolley sign, cardboard, lady's feet in dainty french heels, "...The Comfort of Them," 1920s, 21" x 11", VG ..................................................................$45.00 D

**Goodyear,** award medal, molded with images of transportation growth, 1930s, 12" x 17", EX ........................$1,800.00 D

**Goodyear,** sign, metal, die cut in shape of blimp, "#1 in Tires," 39" x 17½", VG .............................................$2,500.00 C

**Goodyear,** sign, porcelain, die cut, winged foot, 46" x 16" x 1", 1940s, EX .......................................................$325.00 C

**Googh's Sarsaparilla,** ad, "Take for all blood diseases," small girl angel, 11" x 14", EX...........................................$125.00 D

**Googh's Sarsaparilla,** ad, paper, "Endorsed by the Best Chemists and Physicians in the United States," young girl angel, 11" x 14", EX...........................................................$95.00 D

**Gordon's Fresh Foods,** truck, store jar, clear glass with original metal lid, Serving The Best, 7½" dia., EX.............................$130.00 C

**Gordon's Fresh Potato Chips,** can, metal, potato chip on old panel delivery truck over message, 11¼" tall, EX..........................$65.00 C

**Gordon's Potato Chips,** can, delivery panel truck at top of container, 1-lb., 11¼" T, EX......................................$85.00 D

**Gordon's Potato Chips,** can, metal, Gordon's delivery truck at top, 7½" x 11½", red and cream, NM .........................$130.00 C

**Gorton's Codfish,** door push, porcelain, "Eat...in cans ready to use," 6" x 3½", EX ...........................................$525.00 B

**Goudy & Kent's Biscuit,** tin, paper label with pry lid, seaman at ship's wheel, 3" x 4½", EX ...................................$65.00 C

**Gowan Drug Co.,** sign, plastic, in the shape of morter & pestal, 37" x 24" x 18", G.......................................................$80.00 B

**Grads Cigarettes,** thermometer, metal, silhouette of graduate at top with company name, Canadian item, 39" tall, EX.................$125.00 C

**Graf's Beverages,** sign, tin, litho, spotlighted Graf man to left of message, "The Best What Gives," 29½" x 11½", EX........$175.00 C

**Graf's Zep,** sign, wood, die-cut in shape of zeppelin, 48" x 13½", G....................................................................$325.00 B

**Graham's Ice Cream,** box, waxed cardboard, with old delivery truck, 3½" x 2¾", EX..........................................$55.00 C

**Graham,** brochure, four-page foldout for their automobile with car front on the cover sheet, 11" x 8½", 1938, VG...................$65.00 C

**Grain Belt Beer,** sign, porcelain, "Drink...on tap" with diamond logo in center, 1940s, 48" x 36", VG .........................$625.00 B

**Grain Belt Brewing Co.,** litho on canvas depicting wilderness scene of hunters, horses, wolves, and deer, Minneapolis, 31" x 26", NM ...............................................................$130.00 D

**Grain Director cigar box,** label, paper, image of composer Franz Liszt, 9" x 6", EX ..........................................$145.00 D

**Grains of Gold,** box, cardboard, wheat grains on box, Scientifically Prepared Breakfast Cereal, 1929, 20-oz., EX.....................$20.00 D

**Grand Champion Special Motor Oil,** can, metal, tall, rectangular, grip handle, racing scene, 2 gal, VG .....................$145.00 C

**Grand Old Party 1856 to 1908,** tip tray with Taft & Sherman in center of tray under White House, 4⅛" dia., VG.....................$85.00 B

**Grand Order Cigars,** sign, tin, litho, self-framing, "Mild and Excellent," top mounting bracket, 37½" x 13", EX ...................$115.00 B

**Grand Prize Beer,** clock, wood and metal, from the Texas Brewery, 12½" x 3½" x 14½", EX...........................................$240.00 B

**Grand Republic 5¢ Cigar,** pocket cutter, 1" x 2", VG .........$50.00 B

**Grand Union Coffee,** tin, key-wound litho container, 1-lb., EX .$60.00 B

**Grand Union Tea Company** calendar, young girl on front, 13" x 29", 1903, EX.................................................................$525.00 C

**Grand Union Tea Company,** baking powder tin with paper litho label of two children, 3¼" x 5¼", VG ..................................$75.00 C

**Grand Union Tea Company,** trade card, with Mrs. Cleveland, Lady of the White House, and WI product locations on reverse side, 7" x 13½", EX ..........................................$75.00 C

**Grandy & Hoge,** tire cover, stenciled leather from Oakland-Pontiac-Paris Idaho, EX.........................................................$45.00 C

**Granger Pipe Tobacco,** sign, cardboard, master sergeant lighting up a pipe, 16¼" x 11½", EX .................................................$75.00 C

**Granger Pipe Tobacco,** tin, back side has a message explaining why this tobacco is cooler to smoke, G............................................$45.00 C

**Granger Rough Cut Tobacco,** sign, cardboard with old gentleman with horse and buggy, 15" x 20¼", EX ...................................$85.00 C

**Grant Batteries Service,** sign, metal, double-sided, flange, "Recharging," NOS, 18" x 14", EX.......................................................$275.00 C

**Grant Batteries,** clock, metal and glass with name in center dot, 15" dia., VG ...........................................................................$450.00 D

**Grape Crush,** dispenser, glass with metal pump, 6½" dia. x 12½", VG..................................................................$3,000.00 B

**Grape Dee-Light,** sign, cardboard, "Gee but it's good," Jacob Onuschak, Northampton, PA, with hang-up 1920s, 10½" x 14", VG ............................................................................$35.00 C

**Grape Ola,** sign, metal with wood sign, "Drink...It's Real Grape...For Sale Here," 19" x 13", EX ...................................................$250.00 D

**Grape Ola,** sign, tin with delicious looking bunch of grapes, 20" x 14", NM ..............................................................................$500.00 B

**Grape Smash,** sign, tin, "Better Than Straight Grape Juice," 13½" x 9½", G...........................................................................$150.00 C

**Grape Sparkle,** sign, tin litho over cardboard, young woman enjoying a bottle of the product, 13⅜" x 6", EX.........................................$170.00 C

**Grape-Nuts,** cereal tin, Postum Cereal Company, 5½" H, EX .$140.00 B

**Grape-Nuts,** sign, tin, self-contained frame, young girl carrying a basket of flowers, "To school well fed on Grape-Nuts...There's a reason," 20¼" x 30¼", EX ...............................................$1,595.00 C

**Grape-Nuts,** sign, tin, self-framing, little girl walking with St. Bernard, "To school well fed on...There's a reason," 20¼" x 30¼", EX ...........................................................................$1,350.00 D

**Grapette Soda,** sign, tin, self-framing, embossed, strong colors, 24" x 11½", EX .........................................................................$145.00 C

**Grapette,** clock, metal and glass with bottle from twelve to six, 1940s, 15" dia., EX ...................................................................$450.00 C

**Grapette,** sign, metal, oval, "Enjoy Grapette Soda," EX.........$395.00 D

**Grapette,** sign, metal, oval, painted, "Enjoy...Soda," F.....$125.00 C

**Grapette,** sign, porcelain, oval, "Grapette Soda," 17" x 10", EX.$350.00 C

**Grapette,** thermometer, metal, dial type, "Remember To Buy...," 15" dia., VG ...........................................................................$125.00 C

**Gray Line,** sign, porcelain, diamond shape, "The Gray Line," 36" x 18", VG...............................................................................$350.00 D

**Great Atlantic & Pacific Tea Co.,** trade card, cardboard, "The Great Demand For A & P Baking Powder," 7" x 9", VG .....$65.00 D

**Great Majestic Ranges,** sign, artist canvas, gesso bas relief, cook in front of vintage oven, 1910s, 37" x 49" x 4", EX ....$3,300.00 D

**Great Majestic Ranges,** sign, gesso bas-relief, woman cooking on product, great details, 1915, 37" x 49" x 4¼", VG ........................$1,900.00 C

**Great Northern Railroad,** sign, paper, "New Great Domes," scenes of train traveling in the mountains, 25" x 14", VG ...................$55.00 C

**Great Northern Railway,** calendar, "Lazy Boy," a Blackfoot medicine man, Glacier National Park, MT, "Route of the Empire Builder," with both top and bottom metal bands, 16" x 33", 1948, NM ......................................................................................$165.00 C

**Great Northwestern Railroad,** calendar, Indian in full headdress, metal strip at top and bottom with full tear sheet, 15½" x 33", 1944, EX .............................................................................$305.00 B

**Great Slice Plug,** tobacco cutter, country store countertop, 16" x 6", EX .................................................................................$155.00 C

**Green Giant,** doll, vinyl, in likeness of the giant, 1975, 9½" tall, NM......................................................................................$225.00 D

**Green River Whiskey,** ad, paper, litho, old man and horse, copyright 1889, J.W. McCulloch Owensboro, Kentucky, 22⅝" x 18¾", VG .....................................................................................$275.00 D

**Green River Whiskey,** ashtray with match holder at top, 5" x 5" x 4½", EX.................................................................................$75.00 C

**Green River Whiskey,** backbar statue, full-figure of elderly black man and sway-backed horse carrying whiskey, 14" x 10½" x 4", NM ......................................................................................$485.00 B

**Green River Whiskey,** blotter, "Blots out all your troubles," 9½" x 4", 1890s, NM .........................................................................$55.00 C

**Green River Whiskey,** charger, metal, bottle, 24" dia., VG .$575.00 D

**Green River Whiskey,** charger, tin, litho, horse, old man, and jug, 24" dia., EX ..........................................................................$425.00 B

**Green River Whiskey,** good luck token with the trademark black man and mule, "the Whiskey without regrets," "It's lucky to Drink Green River Whiskey," EX...................................................$30.00 B

**Green River Whiskey,** serving tray, tin, litho, black man and horse with jug scene, litho by Chas. Shonk, 12" dia., EX.........................$605.00 B

**Green River Whiskey,** sign, metal, old Black man and horse with saddle bags full of product, "She Was Bred In Old Kentucky," 45" x 33", EX ..............................................................................$1,300.00 C

**Green River Whiskey,** tin, litho, wood frame, old man, horse, and Green River Whiskey jug, Chas. Shonk Co., Litho Chicago No. C. 1203, 41" x 31", EX ....................................................$600.00 C

**Green River Whiskey,** token, metal, embossed, 1¼" dia., EX .......$75.00 D

**Green River Whiskey,** watch fob with the usual logo on front and product info on back, 1½", EX .............................................$85.00 B

**Green River Wines Liquors,** sign of label, trademark Green River Jug, old black man, and horse, 19" x 7", VG .......$130.00 B

**Green River,** display, store countertop, bottle, "The favorite of millions 5¢ a bottle," 7½" x 11¼", EX ......................................$65.00 B

**Green River,** ink blotter, "The Whiskey Without a Headache," old black man and sway-backed horse with jug of product on saddle, 9¼" x 4", EX.............................................................$75.00 C

**Green River,** sign, cardboard, counter stand-up, "first for thirst...Green River," with original bottle and cap, EX ...................................$60.00 B

**Green River,** sign, celluloid, oval, "A Quality Drink For A Quick Pick-Up," scene of moonlit river, 20" x 12", EX............................$375.00 D

**Green River,** sign, metal and cardboard with gold debossed company name, 1910s, 12" x 5", EX..............................$150.00 D

**Green River,** statue, resin, countertop, old black man and horse, 13¾" x 3½" x 9½", VG.......................................$225.00 C

**Green Spot Orange Drink,** chalk board, one-sided, embossed with glasses having the product poured, 17¼" x 27¼", VG ............$45.00 B

**Green Spot,** sign, cardboard, orange halves and bottles of product, 21" x 11", 1936, EX ..........................................$95.00 C

**Green Spot,** sign, tin, litho, embossed, promoting orange-ade with tilted bottle in center, 20" x 12", EX............................$145.00 D

**Green Tree Brewery,** sign, paper, tavern scene, 30" x 22", VG..$300.00 C

**Green-Wheeler Shoes,** sign, tin on cardboard, "For Ladies, None Better," woman in vintage dress by stone wall, by American Artworks, 11¾" x 14¼", 1911, G .........................................$125.00 C

**Greenfield Gasoline Service,** globe, light-up pump, with glass inserts in metal band, 18" x 19", EX .............................$485.00 C

**Greensmith's Derby Dog Biscuits,** sign, cardboard, dog & clown act, 23" x 19", VG...............................................$375.00 D

**Greensmith's Derby Dog Biscuits,** sign, cardboard, string-hung, dogs doing tricks for a clown, 24" x 19", 1920s, NM.....$195.00 C

**Greenwich Ice Cream,** sign, cardboard, die cut store display, people around table eating different flavors of the product, 30" x 29", VG ......................................................................$155.00 B

**Greyhound Lines,** calendar, horse and woman and bus in background, partial tear sheet, 20" x 30", 1938, EX ..............$175.00 C

**Greyhound Lines,** sign, porcelain, station with running dog in center, 36" x 20½", EX.............................................$325.00 C

**Greyhound,** calendar, paper, "Biscayne Key, Miami, Florida," only one monthly pad, 19½" x 32", EX ........................................$85.00 C

**Greyhound,** clock, light-up, wall, EX .....................................$175.00 C

**Greyhound,** sign, metal, double-sided, flange, "Greyhouse Package Express," 28" x 18", VG....................................................$150.00 C

**Greyhound,** sign, metal, double-sided, flange, dog and company name, 15" x 9", EX..........................................................$675.00 C

**Greyhound,** sign, porcelain, double-sided, "Ticket Office...Greyhound Lines," 25" x 30", VG.................................$2,500.00 D

**Greyhound,** sign, porcelain, double-sided, dog and company name, 40" x 20", EX ..............................................................$375.00 C

**Greyhound,** sign, porcelain, two-sided with racing greyhound, "Super Motor Fuel," 58" x 34", VG..................................$785.00 C

**Griesedieck Bros,** clock, metal frame, "Premium Light...Beer...It's De-Bitterized," in center of face, 15" dia., G .................$135.00 D

**Griffon Safety Razor,** container, tin, litho, 1⅜" x 2¼", EX.....$220.00 B

**Griffon Safety Razor,** tin, man shaving with product, 1¾" x 2¼" x 1⅛", EX............................................................$600.00 B

**Grisdale Coffee,** screw-top container, 4" x 6", VG .......................$40.00 C

**Grit,** calendar, heavy stock paper, frame, "America's Greatest Family Newspaper," 1904, VG ................................$120.00 B

**Grizzly Brake Lining,** sign, plastic and metal, light-up, bears, 25¼" x 10¼" x 4¼", EX .......................................................$325.00 C

**Grof Distilling Co.,** sign, cardboard, George Washington in outdoor scene with a child, 1906, 22" x 29", EX ...............................$475.00 C

**Grohman's Drug Store,** thermometer, wood, scale-type, "prescription druggist," 4" x 15⅛", G.................................................$110.00 B

**Groub's Belle Coffee,** tin, litho container, young woman in center cameo, screw lid, from the John C. Groub Co., NY, NY, litho by the Passaic Metal Co., 1-lb., VG ..............................$300.00 B

**Groub's Belle Oats,** tin, slip-lid, young woman in flower bonnet, EX.........................................................................$275.00 C

**Gruen Watch Time,** clock, light-up, "Post's Jewelry Store," local message on bottom, ad on plate, EX ...............................$425.00 C

**Gruen,** display case, wooden, watch with gold lettering at top of case, 8¾" x 15", VG................................................$135.00 C

**GSU Power Center,** sign, porcelain, with Reddy Kilowatt figure in center, one-sided, 44" x 33", G...........................................$125.00 C

**Guardian Taxi Corporation,** sign, metal, in shape of shield designed to place on door of car, 14" x 16", EX....................................$1,100.00 D

**Gulf Aircraft Oil,** can, metal, dark blue with orange, 1 qt, EX.**$85.00 C**

**Gulf Gasoline,** blotter, paperboard, "There Is More Power In That Good...From The Orange Pump," 6" x 4", VG ........................**$75.00 D**

**Gulf Heating Oils,** sign, three-dimensional on hanging arm, with sign in flames, EX........................................................**$295.00 D**

**Gulf Marine,** globe, small wide glass body with glass lens, white gasoline, 12½" dia., VG ......................................**$700.00 B**

**Gulf Marine,** pump sign, porcelain, 11⅜" x 8½", NM ...................**$300.00 C**

**Gulf Marine,** pump sign, porcelain, white gasoline, 10½" dia., EX .........................................................................**$350.00 B**

**Gulf Service Station,** gasoline price rack, panels for Gulftane, No-Nox, and Good Gulf, 43" x 57" x 62", VG ..........................**$350.00 B**

**Gulf Solar Heat,** sign, cardboard, die cut, bird-like cartoon figure with "No Large Bills" on beak, 1950s, 6" x 8", VG..................**$65.00 D**

**Gulf Supreme Motor Oil,** sign, porcelain, single-sided, "Slow," Courtesy of Gulf Refining Co., 14" x 45", G....................................**$400.00 B**

**Gulf Valvetop Oil Display,** service station metal rack for oil, 10¾" x 4" x 25½", EX..................................................**$95.00 C**

**Gulf,** gas globe, glass, one piece, "That Good Gulf Gasoline," 16" dia., VG...........................................................**$800.00 B**

**Gulf,** hat, service station attendant's, summer, NOS, Brokfield Uniforms, 6¾", NM................................................**$135.00 C**

**Gulf,** paperweight, glass with felt bottom, Gulf oil emblem in the center, super piece of petroleum advertising, 1960 – 80s, 3" x 4¼" x ¾", EX...............................................................**$25.00 C**

**Gulf,** patch, cloth, sleeve, 2½" x 2¼", G ...........................**$12.00 C**

**Gulf,** pocket lighter, metal, by Zippo with flip top and Gulf emblem on side, 2¼" tall, EX.........................................**$95.00 C**

**Gulf,** poster, paper, "Fill up with Stepped Up No-Nox," 27¾" x 42", VG ..............................................................**$75.00 C**

**Gulf,** pump plate, porcelain, "Dieselect Fuel," rare sign, 10½" , NM ...........................................................**$435.00 B**

**Gulf,** sign, "Look How They've Stepped Up No-Nox!...Better try this Better Fuel," with built-up muscle man, 27¾" x 42", VG .......**$110.00 B**

**Gulf,** sign, metal, lettering in blue with white shadows, 28" dia., EX........................................................**$135.00 C**

**Gulf,** sign, paper, "Winter's Ahead...Change To...Now," NOS, 28" x 42", NM................................................**$140.00 D**

**Gulf,** sign, plastic letters on metal strip, blue, EX ............**$115.00 C**

**Gulf,** sign, plastic, light up, shape of Gulf emblem, 1980s, 24" dia., EX ............................................................**$225.00 D**

**Gulf,** sign, plastic, light-up, lettering across center, 31" dia., EX.**$165.00 D**

**Gulf,** sign, porcelain, "Authorized Dealer," 1930s, 40" x 9", VG..**$225.00 B**

**Gulf,** sign, porcelain, "That Good Gasoline, At the sign of the orange disc," early touring car driving up hill, 27½" x 60", F ..........**$750.00 C**

**Gulf,** sign, porcelain, one-sided, touring car on road, "That Good...Gasoline...At the sign of the orange disc...Gulf Refining Co.," 27½" x 60", VG........................................**$2,400.00 B**

**Gulf,** sign, salesman sample for service stations, 7¼" x 21½", 1940 s, EX ..............................................................**$395.00 C**

**Gulf,** sign, "Singing with sweeter power...New No-Nox...New Good Gulf," 27¾" x 42", VG.........................................**$90.00 B**

**Gulf,** toy tanker, metal, friction type, orange and blue Gulf colors, Ford style truck, 12½" long, VG......................................**$500.00 D**

**Gulfex,** sign, light up in deco looking case with glass front, " Your Car Needs...Registered Lubrication," 1940s, 19" x 9", VG..........**$650.00 D**

**Gulflex Lubrication,** poster, paper, for posting Sept. 1 – 15, 1940, 27¾" x 42", VG ..................................................**$65.00 B**

**Gulflube,** sign, tin, self-framing, embossed, "The High Mileage Motor Oil Multi-Sol Processed," 48" x 24", 1948, EX......................**$350.00 C**

**Gulfpride,** poster, paper, with cat, "Change to...Here!," 27¾" x 42", VG................................................................**$150.00 B**

**Gypsy Hosiery,** tip tray, metal, gypsy camp scene and gypsy woman inset in center, George H. Buschmann, Owensville, Mo., 6" dia., F ...........................................................**$55.00 D**

**Gypsy Salmon,** can, label, paper, salmon, VG...................**$10.00 D**

**Gypsy Wine,** sign, celluloid over cardboard, promoting "E & K Gypsy Grape Wine," with pretty red-haired woman, 10" x 7", EX ...........................................................**$180.00 C**

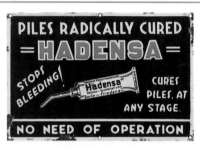

Hadensa, sign, porcelain, one-sided, "Piles Radically Cured,"18" x 22", G, $195.00 B.

Hamlin's Wizard Oil, sign, tin, embossed, with large bottle of product, "Great for Pain," 12" x 6½", EX, $230.00 B.
*Courtesy of Autopia Advertising Auctions.*

Handy Package Dyes, sign, paper, with cherubs and clothes on line, 17" x 13", VG, $75.00 C.

Hair Bobbing, sign, porcelain, "Ladies & Children Our Specialty," 24" x 12", VG, $400.00 C.

Hamm's Beer, sign, metal and plastic, motion light-up, "Born in the land of sky blue waters," great graphics, 31" x 18", EX, $275.00 D.

Hannan Supply Co. Inc., thermometer & barometer, celluloid and metal, desk stand on back, 1930 – 40s, 3¼" x 3¼", EX, $55.00 C.
*Courtesy of B.J. Summers.*

H. Sandmeyer & Co., match holder, tin, litho, Peoria, Ill., Golden Anniversary Hardware, 5" H, G..........................................$110.00 B

H.B Franklin & Co., cigar box, "Chicago, Ill., Each Cigar Is A Perfect Smoke And Extra Value," G..........................................$25.00 D

H.C. Carpenter Barber Shop, ad, paper, young girls feeding a pony, 12¼" x 16¼", 1922, EX..........................................$75.00 B

H.H. Marvin, calendar, die cut, give-away from Oregon, WI, hardware merchant, 7" x 13", EX..........................................$125.00 B

H.M. Pentz, Glen Hope, Penn. Milling Specialist, calendar, paper, die cut, young lady with large hat, full monthly pad, 1913, 14" x 23", NM..........................................$363.00 B

Ha Dees Auto Heater, sign, cardboard, die cut counter top display with easel back, female "devil" with vintage auto, NOS, 1930s, EX .$185.00 C

Ha Dees, license plate attachment, heated tin, devil in the center, 5⅞" T, EX..........................................$250.00 C

Haberle Brewing Co., match light, stoneware, 4¾" x 6½", EX.$165.00 D

Haffen Brewing Co., sign, paper, open touring car with driver and 3 pretty ladies wearing bonnets, 15½" x 20", VG..................$575.00 C

Hage's Ice Cream, sign, metal, die cut to resemble an ice cream square with company advertising, 9" x 8", EX..................$125.00 D

Hagerstown Brewing Co., tray, metal, girl with flowers, 1900s, 10½" x 13¼", VG..........................................$55.00 C

Hair Bobbing, sign, porcelain, "Ladies & Children Our Specialty," 24" x 12", G..........................................$350.00 B

Hales Midget Popcorn, container, metal, with likeness of one of the small people in tails,4½" dia., VG..........................................$15.00 D

Half and Half Burley and Bright Pipe Tobacco, jar, glass with cardboard lid, 1-lb., EX..........................................$55.00 C

Half and Half Burley and Bright Pipe Tobacco, jar, glass with cardboard lid, 1-lb., G..........................................$25.00 C

Half and Half Burley and Bright Tobacco, tin, 3" x 4¼" x 1", EX .$12.00 D

Hall's Chocolates, calendar, paper, partial pad, framed, 16¾" x 30", G..........................................$110.00 B

Hambone, tobacco pouch, cloth, black man chewing on hambone, 2" x 3" x 1", 1917, EX..........................................$65.00 C

Harbour & Wilson Department Store, Home Savings Department bank, metal with embossed lettering on front, drop slot on top and lock on side, 3¼" x 4¼" x 1½", VG, $110.00 C. *Courtesy of B.J. Summers.*

Harrison's Heart O' Orange, sign, tin, round, embossed, "sold here," 14¼" dia., EX, $250.00 C.

Hart & Son, hand made razor, celluloid and metal, in original Geo. O. Hart & Son box, razor is imprinted with Geo. Hart, Paducah, KY, 1890s, 6" long closed, VG, $75.00 C. *Courtesy of B.J. Summers.*

Hartford Fire Insurance Company, sign, metal, painted, flange, deer in center, 1950s, 18" x 28", VG, $375.00 C.

Harvard Beer, sign, tin, litho in gold frame, woman in a Turkish setting, 36" x 45", EX, $1,500.00 B.

Harvester Cigar, sign, tin, painted, self-contained, framed, "Heart of Havana," A.C. Co 71-A at bottom, 9" x 13", VG, $125.00 C.

---

Hamilton Brown Shoe Co., ad, paper, George and Martha Washington with shoe company emblem between them, 29¾" x 39¾", EX ............................................................$275.00 C

Hamilton Brown Shoe Co., ad, paper, litho, "The Prettiest Woman in America," 22" x 31", G..............................$275.00 B

Hamilton Brown Shoe Co., sign, paper, with girl and a load of fruit, "Compliments of...," 26" x 30", EX ...................................$175.00 D

Hamilton Brown Shoe Company, sign, metal, painted, flange, two-sided, 19½" x 14", G........................................$125.00 C

Hamm Brewing Co., B.P.O.E. guest, pinback, 2¼" x 1", 1897, NM.$95.00 C

Hamm's Beer, sign, paper, window, "in cans," 17¾" x 5½", 1930s, NM.................................................................$125.00 C

Hamm's, sign, electric motion, flip-type panels, 9" x 6" x 6½", EX .................................................................$145.00 C

Hancock Gasoline, pump sign, porcelain, 12" dia., EX ..$1,200.00 C

Hancocks Ale, sign, porcelain, "...the sign of Hospitality," 31½" x 41¾", VG ...........................................................$255.00 C

Hand Made Flake Cut, canister, tin, litho, small top, Globe Tobacco Co., Detroit, Mich., 4⅞" x 6¼", EX ..................$525.00 B

Hanlen Bros, tip tray, metal, "Harrisburg, PA...The Old Reliable Liquor Dealers," horse's head in tray center, 4⅛" dia., EX.$130.00 B

Hannum's Prevento Radiator and Gas Engine Compound, container, tin, litho, vintage auto on front, 3⅝" x 4½" x 2⅛", EX ....$275.00 B

Haverly's United Mastodon Minstrels, poster, paper, litho, 42" x 32½", VG, $500.00 B.

Havoline Motor Oil, sign, metal, double-sided, 21½" x 18½", EX, $275.00 C.

Hazle Club Tru-Orange, sign, metal, painted, flange, 14" x 20", EX, $145.00 C.

Headlight Overalls, sign, porcelain, store, train with light, "Agency for…," 32" x 10", VG, $395.00 C. *Courtesy of John and Vicki Mahan.*

Heinz 57 Varieties, string holder, die cut, double-sided, hard-to-find item, 17" x 14" x 7", EX, $5,400.00 B. *Courtesy of Buffalo Bay Auction Co.*

Heinz Home-Style Soups, sign, tin, litho, single-sided with rolled edges, 27½" x 10½", VG, $275.00 B.

**Hansen Hardware,** clock, metal, light-up, advertising on top of message, light-up strip, 26" x 18½", VG..................................$350.00 B

**Hanson's Drug Store,** calendar, cardboard, die cut, Hanson's Headache Powders, young woman in Panama straw hat, 1903, 7¼" x 13", NM.................................................................$75.00 B

**Happy Home Rolled Oats,** container, home scene on cover, from St. Louis, MO, 1-lb. 4-oz., EX.............................................$135.00 C

**Happy Hotpoint,** cardboard, easel back, die cut figure, 9¼" x 13¼", 1920s, NM....................................................................$85.00 C

**Happy Hour Coffee,** tin, litho, hot steaming cup of coffee on front label, 1-lb., EX.................................................................$125.00 C

**Hard A Port Tobacco,** tin, man at ship's wheel, Moore & Calvi, New York, 3¼" x 3¼", EX............................................$180.00 B

**Harding Cream Co.,** sign, porcelain, double-sided, die cut, flange, shaped like old milk can, "Cash For Cream," 15" x 27", EX.$1,700.00 B

**Harley-Davidson Motorcycle,** clock, metal body and glass face and cover, light-up, 15¼" sq., EX ............................$1,000.00 C

**Harley-Davidson,** bullet pencil, 75th anniversary, 1978, EX ...$50.00 C

**Harley-Davidson,** clock, one-day war alarm, promoting war bonds, original cardboard box, "Compliments of Harley Davidson Motor Co.," 1940s, EX.................................................$625.00 C

**Harley-Davidson,** Rider's Handbook, 4¾" x 6¾", 1929, VG...$65.00 C

**Harness Soap,** sign, paper, litho, man cleaning a harness, by International Food Co., Minneapolis, Minn., USA, 26¾" x 33½", VG.$975.00 D

Hendlers Ice Cream, sign, paper, litho, framed, 20" x 29", VG, $975.00 C.

Hero, fire extinguisher kit in original cardboard box, "Puts Out Fires Instantly," 5" x 8¼" x 2⅞", VG, $25.00 C.

The Hickman-Ebbert Co., sign, tin, one-sided, litho, self-framing, 34½" x 23⅜", VG, $975.00 C.

Hides-Franklin Mineral Water, small childs seat, wooden with company decal on back, "sold Here," 12½" tall, VG, $75.00 B.

Hills Bros. Coffee, sign, automated black youngster sitting on top of message box pouring and drinking a cup of the product, 21" x 18" x 41", VG, $2,750.00 B. *Courtesy of Collectors Auction Services.*

Hills Bros., puzzle, framed under glass with original box, 14" x 16", 1933, VG, $90.00 B.

**Harold's Club,** license plate attachment, metal, die cut, in likeness of covered wagon, "or bust...Reno, Nevada," 14" x 8", EX.**$135.00 C**

**Harrington & Richardson Arms Co.,** calendar, paper, hunter in snow scene, full calendar pad and top and bottom metal strips, 14" x 27", 1907, NM ............$275.00 C

**Harrington & Richardson,** calendar, paper, bottom tear sheets, woman, gun, and dog in hunting scene, full calendar pad, 14" x 26", 1905, NM..........$575.00 D

**Harrison's Heart O' Orange** sign, tin, round, embossed, "sold here," 14¼" dia., G..........$135.00 C

**Hart Brand Canned Foods,** sign, beveled tin, litho over cardboard, string-hung, product cans, 13" x 9", EX ...........$850.00 B

**Hartford Fire Insurance Company,** sign, metal, painted, flange, deer in center, 1950s, 18" x 28", G ............$325.00 B

**Harvard Ale,** sign, reverse on glass with cardboard backing, easel back for countertop display, product bottle and glass, 19" x 13", EX.....$145.00 C

**Harvard Ale,** sign, tin, litho, beer porter, 23¼" x 23¾", F.**$115.00 C**

**Harvard Beer,** serving tray, metal, manufactured by the H.D Beach Co., couple at table being served beer, 12" dia., VG.........$170.00 B

**Harvard Brewing Co.,** sign, tin, litho, woman enjoying cocktail in room overlooking garden courtyard, 36" x 45", EX.........$1,750.00 B

**Harvest Queen Coffee,** container, tin, key-wound, litho, crown on front, 1-lb., EX...........$37.00 B

**Harvester Cigar,** sign, tin, self-framing, litho, "Heart of Havana," young lady, 9" x 13", EX ...........$180.00 C

**Harvey's Coffee,** sign, glass, restaurant, "Serving Harvey's Coffee," 11" x 6", NM...........$65.00 C

**Hatchway Union Suits,** box, cardboard, man walking in product with robe over arm, 1915, 10" X 15" x 1½", EX ........$30.00 B

**Havana Blossom,** sign, cardboard, man promoting product, from P. Lorillard Co., 1910, 12" x 18", NM ........$185.00 B

Hires, dispenser, ceramic, with the correct metal pump, 14" high, VG, $625.00 C.

Hires, tray, oval, self-framing, litho, two pretty women enjoying the product, "Drink Hires," great graphics, rare item and hard to find, 23½" x 19½", VG, $1,000.00 B.

Hires, sign, cardboard, "Drink in Bottles," girl and flare glass, by Haskell Coffin, 1910s, 15" x 21", EX, $575.00 B.

Hires, sign, tin, embossed, man holding bottle, "Drink, It hits the spot, Try a bottle and you'll buy a case,"15¾" x 9¾", EX, $225.00 B. *Courtesy of Muddy River Trading Co./Gary Metz*

Hires Root Beer, sign, "Enjoy...Healthful Delicious," 1930s, 9½" x 27½", EX, $325.00 B.

Hires Root Beer, door push, tin, with beveled edges, "Finer Flavor because of Real Root Juices," EX, $150.00 B. *Courtesy of Muddy River Trading Co./Gary Metz.*

---

**Havana Plantation,** paperweight, metal, figural, 4" x 1½", EX..**$75.00 B**

**Have Some Junket,** tip tray, metal, small girl with a bowl of gelatin, 4¼" dia., EX.............................................................**$90.00 B**

**Havoline Marine Oil,** paperweight, tin, litho, "it makes a difference...Havoline Oil Company, New York City," made to resemble a 1-gal. oil can, filled with sand, 1½" x 2½" x 1", EX .........**$1,550.00 B**

**Hawken,** sign, tin, "Everything Musical...Pianos," Nipper listening to his master's voice, 28" x 19½", VG ...............................**$240.00 B**

**Hazel Club,** door push, tin, embossed, "Finer Flavor Drink," EX.............................................................................**$90.00 B**

**Hazle Club Tru-Orange,** sign, metal, painted, flange, 14" x 20", VG..............................................................................**$130.00 C**

**Hazle Club,** door push, tin, embossed,"Finer Flavor Drink," VG ................................................................................**$75.00 C**

**Headlight Overalls,** sign, porcelain, store, train with light, "Agency for...," 32" x 10", G .................................**$300.00 C**

**Headlight Shrunk Overalls,** sign, cardboard, tin surround, standard train headlight beam, "A New Pair Free If They Shrink," 20¾" x 10", G .............................................**$175.00 C**

**Headlight Work Clothes,** sign, metal, embossed, original wooden frame, 60" x 8", EX...........................................................**$325.00 D**

**Heaney, Magician,** sign, paperboard, 14" x 20", 1915, EX.**$195.00 D**

**Heath & Milligan Sunshine Finishes,** tip tray, two children and dog on floor, 4¼" dia., G ..............................**$75.00 C**

**Heide's Colored Coons,** candy box, 10¼" x 6¾" x 1¾", EX..**$350.00 C**

**Heide's Mints,** trade card, red-haired child advertising the product on the front and a testimonial on the back by Sarah Bernhardt, made for the Pan American Exposition, 3½" x 5½", 1901, EX..............**$95.00 C**

Hires Root Beer, sign, heavy cardboard, die cut, woman entertaining, "The Right Note for Home Refreshment," matted and framed, 34½" x 38½", VG, $475.00 B. *Courtesy of Autopia Advertising Auctions.*

Hires Root Beer, sign, porcelain, tilted bottle, "Drink..." in light burst, 1950s, 13½" x 42", EX, $325.00 B.

Hires Root Beer, sign, glass, reverse painted, chain-hanging, 7¼" x 8¼", NM, $2,100.00 C.

Hires, sign, cardboard, pretty lady, "Enjoy...," 1920s, EX, $475.00 B.

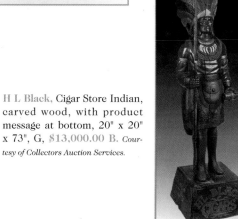

H L Black, Cigar Store Indian, carved wood, with product message at bottom, 20" x 20" x 73", G, $13,000.00 B. *Courtesy of Collectors Auction Services.*

H.M. Pentz, Glen Hope, Penn. Milling Specialist, calendar, paper, die cut, young lady with large hat, full monthly pad, 1913, 14" x 23", NM, $363.00 B. *Courtesy of Buffalo Bay Auction Co.*

---

Heineken Beer, sign, porcelain, one-sided, caricature of beer glass man, 16" x 23½", VG ......................$250.00 B

Heineken Beer, tapper handle, wooden, G ..........................$10.00 C

Heineken's Holland Beer, shoe, wooden, EX ....................$25.00 C

Heineken's Imported Holland Beer, sign, tin over cardboard litho, Holland graphics in left lower corner, 1950s, EX................$45.00 B

Heinsohn Bros. Dairy, calendar, paper, full month pad and original metal strips on top and bottom, baby in highchair, 1927, 15" x 19½", EX................................................$30.00 B

Heinz 57 Tomato Catsup, sign, trolley car, catsup bottle with a 1908 date, 21" x 11", 1908, EX..........................................$130.00 B

Heinz 57 Varieties, string holder, die cut, double-sided, hard-to-find item, 17" x 14" x 7", EX..........................................$5,400.00 B

Heinz Bros., catsup bottle, early glass with paper label, large tomato in center of label, 2¼" x 8¼", VG........................$140.00 B

Heinz, delivery truck, tin, litho, working lights and original box, 12" x 3½" x 5", EX.................................................................$550.00 B

Hello World Coffee, tin, paper, label with globe on center, 1-lb., EX.............................................................................................$150.00 B

Helmar Turkish Cigarettes, sign, cardboard on wood, "Quality Superb," 3½" x 21½", G .....................................................$25.00 C

Helmar Turkish Cigarettes, sign, cardboard, wood frame, 21⅝" x 3⅝", EX....................................................................................$55.00 C

Helmar Turkish Cigarettes, sign, paper, framed, young woman in western attire, 33" x 42½", G ...........................................$670.00 B

Helmar, tip tray, metal, Turkish scenes, 6" L, EX ..............$75.00 C

Hoffmann's Old Time Roasted Coffee, grinder, tin front with wood frame on cast iron, litho, 13½" H, EX, $1,200.00 B. *Courtesy of Richard Opfer Auctioneering, Inc.*

Hollingsworth Candies, poster, cardboard, couple ready for a kiss as a result of the product, 40" high, EX, $175.00 C.

Hollywoodglo, ad, cardboard, tri-fold, early motion picture cameras and actress, "For screen star loveliness use," VG, $85.00 C. *Courtesy of Illinois Antique Center/Kim & Dan Phillips.*

Holsum Bread, sign, tin, single-sided, self-framed, 7½" x 13", VG, $200.00 B.

Home-Run Stogie, tobacco tin canister, baseball scene on front, 4¼" dia., x 5¾", EX, $1,850.00 B.

Honey Moon Tobacco, sign, tin, one-sided, litho, from Penn Tobacco Co., couple sitting on quarter moon, 9¾" H, EX, $525.00 B. *Courtesy of Richard Opfer Auctioneering, Inc.*

Honey Scotch Candy, sign, tin, image of product, 1930s, 19½" x 7", EX, $250.00 B.

Hemmer's Ice Cream, serving tray, "Rich and Delicious," ice cream products in center of tray, 1920s, 13" x 13", EX................$235.00 C

Hendlers Ice Cream, sign, paper, litho, framed, 20" x 29", F .$625.00 B

Hendlers Ice Cream, window display, die cut, ice cream cones with message inside, 1950s, 36" x 23", NM .................................$85.00 C

Henkel's, pot scraper, tin, litho, Henkel's Flour, 3¼" x 3", red, blue, and white, EX.................................................................$300.00 B

Henkes' Beer, sign, porcelain, self-framed, "Taste The True Juniper Flavor," product bottles, 12½" x 19", VG ...........$450.00 C

Henry Claus Brewing Co Extra Beer, label, paper, with company name arched above logo, 1910s, VG ....................................$10.00 C

Henry Weilersbacher, paperweight, advertising beer, carbonated drinks, and fountain & bar supplies, 4" dia., EX ............$100.00 B

Hep, sign, tin, double-side, flange, "Get...for yourself," product bottle, NOS, 17⅝" x 13¼", NM ...............................................$325.00 C

Heptol Splits Laxative, tip tray, metal, cowboy riding a bucking horse, 4¼" dia., VG .........................................................$400.00 C

Heptol Splits Laxitive, tip tray, metal, cowboy riding bucking bronc, "For Health's Sake," 4⅛" dia., G .............................$170.00 B

166

Hood's Ice Cream, sign, metal, double-sided, painted, trademark cow's head in center, 19" dia., G, $1,200.00 B. *Courtesy of Collectors Auction Services.*

Hoodsies Ice Cream, sign, cardboard, die cut, young couple on swing, 12¼" x 18½", EX, $2,000.00 B. *Courtesy of Collectors Auction Services.*

Hood's Sarsaparilla, calendar, die cut, pretty girl in bonnet, 1894, 5½" x 8¾", EX, $55.00 C.

Hopkins & Allen Arms Co., poster, paper, litho, Prairie Girl, good graphics and difficult to locate, 10" x 26¾", 1910s, EX, $2,500.00 C. *Courtesy of Autopia Advertising Auctions.*

Hot Ball Tobacco, sign, tin, embossed, litho, jester holding package, rare piece, G, $900.00 B. *Courtesy of Richard Opfer Auctioneering, Inc.*

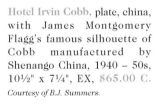

Hotel Irvin Cobb, plate, china, with James Montgomery Flagg's famous silhouette of Cobb manufactured by Shenango China, 1940 – 50s, 10½" x 7¼", EX, $65.00 C. *Courtesy of B.J. Summers.*

Hotel Palmer, Paducah, KY, honey pot, china, painted label and labeled spoon, pot made in Germany, 1930 – 40s, 2" x 2¾" dia., EX, $135.00 C. *Courtesy of B.J. Summers.*

Herbert Tareyton Cigarettes, tin, 100-piece, flat, F............$42.00 D

Hercules Coffee, tin with small top, Hercules in cameo on front, 1-lb., VG .......................................................$40.00 B

Hercules EC & Infallible Shotgun Powder, sign, paper, two black hunters loading a muzzle loader and one of them reporting "Dah He Goes!," 1920s, 16" x 24", EX .........................................$1,100.00 D

Hercules Explosives, calendar top, paper, hunt scene, EX........$100.00 D

Hercules Explosives, calendar, paper, full monthly pad, man and his dog, 1927, 13" x 20", EX................................$275.00 D

Hercules Gunpowder, poster, black man and youngster hunting in the snow with dog, complete with top and bottom metal strips, 15½" x 25⅛", EX .........................................$395.00 D

Hercules Gunpowder, poster, paper, black youngster and older black gentleman in snowy field loading a muzzle loader, 13½" x 19", 1924, VG.................................................$85.00 B

Hercules Powder Black Sporting, container, paper litho label on tin, Hercules on front cover, 1-lb., EX................................$60.00 B

Hercules Powder Co., badge, metal, Hercules above company name, 1½" x 2", EX.............................................$85.00 C

Hercules Powder Co., sign, paper, litho, pheasant in field setting, 20¼" x 23¼", VG................................................$700.00 B

Hercules Powder Company, calendar, boy and dog, 1941, 13" x 29½", EX................................................$95.00 C

Hrobak's Beverages, sign, tin, embossed, single-sided, 20" x 9¼", VG, $85.00 C.

Hougland Barge Line, lighter, metal with boat on side and company name on bottom, never used, 1950 – 60s, 1½" x 2¼" x ¼", NM, $55.00 C. *Courtesy of B.J. Summers.*

Houston Crick Dairy, pitcher, glass premium, front reading "Compliments Of Houston Crick Dairy, Paducah, KY," 1890s, 4¼" X 4¾", NM, $275.00 C. *Courtesy of B.J. Summers.*

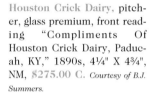

Howel's Root Beer, sign, tin, embossed, elf holding a bottle, 1940s, 28" X 20", VG, $750.00 B.

Hudepohl Beer and Ale, sign, cardboard, old man and dog, 29½" x 38", VG, $375.00 C.

Hummel Bros. Insurance paperweight, glass with business advertising inside, 3" dia., 1920 – 1930s EX, $95.00 C. *Courtesy of B.J. Summers.*

---

**Hercules Powder Company,** calendar, boy and dog, 1941, 13" x 29½", VG .......................................................$75.00 C

**Hercules Pure Coffee,** container, metal, square with pry lid, EX $50.00 C

**Hercules,** condom tin, litho, Hercules holding the globe, 2⅛" x 1⅝" x ¼", EX ..........................................................$130.00 C

**Hercules,** poster, hunting scene with two men and a dog, 15½" x 24½", EX...........................................................$825.00 B

**Herman Cortez Cigars,** sign, metal, die cut, girl holding an open box of cigars, 1910s, 12" x 16½", VG ...............................$575.00 D

**Henry Heeren,** calendar, farm machinery dealer, die cut, 5¾" x 11½", 1907, EX ...............................................$145.00 C

**Hero Coffee,** container, metal, Admiral Dewey and others, 4" x 7", VG .......................................................$185.00 C

**Hershey's Chocolate,** container, metal, boy cutting cake and girl eating, EX .......................................................$10.00 C

**Hershey's Cocoa,** pocket mirror, metal and glass, company trademark on back, 1¼" dia., EX ...........................................$1,000.00 D

**Hershey's Gum,** blotter, cardboard, 6 sticks for 5¢ cents, 5⅜" x 2⅞", EX .............................................................$475.00 B

**Hershey's Ice Cream,** menu board, litho, message, EX.....$100.00 C

**Hershey's Kisses,** container, metal, girl feeding boy, 1982, 2" x 5"dia., EX.............................................................$10.00 D

**Hershey's Krackel Milk Chocolate,** box that held 24 bars, 1-lb. 5-oz., EX .............................................................$10.00 C

**Hershey's Krackel Milk Chocolate,** box that held 24 bars, 1-lb. 5-oz., NM.............................................................$20.00 C

**Hershey's Mint Flavor Chewing Gum,** countertop display box, cardboard, 5¼" x 5⅞" x 4⅛", EX...................................$1,200.00 B

**Hi Energee,** gasoline globe, plastic body with two glass lenses, 13½" dia., VG .............................................................$375.00 C

Humphreys' Remedies, store display wooden cabinet with metal front, 18" W x 21" H x 7¼" D, EX, $295.00 D.

Huntley Palmers Biscuits, sign, single-sided, litho, foreign, 24" x 28½", F, $425.00 B.

Husky, sign, porcelain, two-piece, die cut, dog with Husky base, difficult item to find, NM, $3,000.00 C. *Courtesy of Autopia Advertising Auctions.*

H. Weil & Sons, whiskey bottle, glass with paper label and cork cap, "Three Rivers Bourbon Whiskey," 1890 – 1900s, ½ pt., VG, $45.00 C. *Courtesy of B.J. Summers.*

Hyde Propellers, sign, porcelain, "Sales and Service," 17" x 26", EX, $900.00 C.

Hy-Quality Coffee, sign, cardboard, die cut, young girl in swing with cup of product, 16" x 37", EX, $1,290.00 B. *Courtesy of Buffalo Bay Auction Co.*

---

Hi-D Ammonium Nitrate, thermometer, glass and tin, 12" dia., EX ........................................................$115.00 C

Hi-Gloss Auto Enamel, can label, paper, man painting an antique automobile, 1927, VG ..........................................$25.00 C

Hi-Plane Smooth Cut Tobacco, container, metal, pocket size, "For Pipe & Cigarettes," 3" x 4½", EX..........................................$75.00 D

Hi-Plane Smooth Cut Tobacco, sign, cardboard, "for pipe and cigarettes," die cut of airplane in flight, 23" x 22", G ................$75.00 C

Hi-Plane Tobacco, pocket tin, airplane on front label, EX ..$55.00 C

Hi-Plane Tobacco, pocket tin, litho, vertical with double prop plane, EX ..............................................$115.00 B

Hi-Plane Tobacco, sign, tin, embossed, package of product, 35" x 11¾", EX ................................................$75.00 B

Hiawatha Airway, box, shot shells, G .................................$15.00 C

Hiawatha Oil, can, tin, Hiawatha Harvester Oil from Fairwell Ozmun Kirk & Co., St. Paul, MN, 3" x 7½", EX..................................$110.00 B

Hiawatha, crate label, paper, California Oranges with Red Ball logo and iron faced Indian, 1930s, 11¾" x 10", EX ....................$65.00 D

Hickman's Silver Birch Chewing Gum, countertop display package, 5¢, 4½" x 6½" x 1", EX............................................$625.00 B

Hickman's Silver Birch Chewing Gum, display, cardboard, complete with unopened gum packs, bird on birch limb, 6¼" x 5¼" x 4¼", EX ........................................................$1,200.00 B

Hickory Children's Garters, display, wooden cut out of boy and girl under umbrella, 19½" x 13" x 5½", EX ..............................$350.00 D

**Hickory Garters,** display, countertop, die cut, litho, wood, children under umbrella, 13" x 19½", NM..........................$1,025.00 B

**Hicks Capudine,** tip tray, metal, round, "Its Liquid-effects immediately," 10¢, 25¢, and 50¢ cents a bottle, product in tray center, 6" dia., EX..........................$160.00 B

**High Admiral Cigarettes,** lapel pin, metal, image of Puritan lady under Pure & Sweet slogan, 1896, VG ..........................$20.00 D

**High Admiral Cigarettes,** pinback, featuring yellow kid, 1¼", 1890s, EX ..........................$75.00 C

**High Ball Ginger Ale,** sign, tin, litho, bottle in center, 9" x 9", EX..........................$145.00 B

**High Grade Sausage,** sign, metal, string-hung, from P.E. Rathjens & Sons, 9⅜" x 6⅜", NM ..........................$125.00 C

**Highest Grade Tobacco,** tin, good strong graphics, 4½" x 3" x 2", EX..........................$55.00 C

**Highland Evaporated Cream,** tip tray, metal, cream can in center of tray, 3⅝" dia., EX ..........................$120.00 B

**Highlight Overalls,** sign, metal and neon, with company name in locomotive head light beam, 28" x 14" x 4", VG..........................$825.00 C

**Hilbrich's Coffee,** pail, handle, from Hilbrich & Bastgen Co., Chicago, Ill., 7½" x 9", EX..........................$125.00 C

**Hildreth Varnish Co.,** sign, cardboard, Brooklyn Bridge, 15" x 20", EX ..........................$700.00 D

**Hill's Bros. Coffee,** can, metal, Hill's man drinking coffee, 2 lb, EX..........................$200.00 D

**Hills Bros. Coffee,** jar, glass, 1-lb., EX ..........................$25.00 C

**Hills Bros. Coffee,** sign, automated, black boy sitting on top of message box pouring and drinking a cup of the product, 21" x 18" x 41", VG ..........................$2,750.00 B

**Hills Bros. Coffee,** sign, roll down paper over cloth, "Coffee hungry folks prefer...," early scene in cabin around table with product, 61½" x 42", EX ..........................$375.00 B

**Hills Bros. Coffee,** tin "Drip Grind Coffee," Hills man drinking product on front, 20-lb., 9½" x 9½" x 13", EX..........................$45.00 C

**Himalaya Bouquet,** sign, porcelain, flange, 14" x 9", VG...$270.00 B

**Hinz's Eagle Brand Coffee,** tin, paper label, with slip lid, 1-lb., NM ..........................$30.00 B

**Hiram's General Store,** punch board, 12½" x 15", G..........$70.00 B

**Hiram's General Store,** punch board, 12½" x 15", VG ........$95.00 C

**Hire's Root Beer,** dispenser, paper label on front glass, 22", EX.$275.00 C

**Hires R-J Root Beer,** dispenser, glass and metal, 22" tall, EX.$300.00 C

**Hires R-J Root Beer,** sign, stamped and embossed, round, 14" dia., EX ..........................$155.00 B

**Hires R-J Root Beer,** sign, tin, embossed, "A Toast To Good Taste...Enjoyable In Bottles," R-J disc logo in center, NOS, 35¼" x 11¼", NM..........................$275.00 B

**Hires R-J Root Beer,** sign, tin, round, embossed, "with real root juices," 12" dia., EX..........................$150.00 B

**Hires Root Beer,** barrel, wood and metal with claw feet and metal spouts, Hires decal and message on front and back, 21" x 31", EX..........................$500.00 B

**Hires Root Beer,** door push, tin, beveled edges, "Finer Flavor because of Real Root Juices," EX..........................$150.00 B

**Hires Root Beer,** mug, German-made, 5" tall, EX ............$210.00 B

**Hires Root Beer,** pocket mirror, featuring the "ugly kid," G .$275.00 C

**Hires Root Beer,** poster, heavy paper, woman enjoying a glass of the product, "So Good With Food," 59" x 35½", NM..........$400.00 B

**Hires Root Beer,** sign, cardboard, plate of food and a cool mug of root beer filling a frosty mug with the Hires logo on the side, 1950s, 22" x 19", VG..........................$65.00 C

**Hires Root Beer,** sign, heavy cardboard, die cut, woman entertaining, "The Right Note for Home Refreshment," matted and framed, 34½" x 38½", VG..........................$475.00 B

**Hires Root Beer,** sign, reverse painted glass, chain-hanging, 7¼" x 8¼", EX ..........................$1,700.00 C

**Hires Root Beer,** sign, stainless steel, drugstore dispenser, "with Roots, Barks, Herbs," EX..........................$95.00 B

**Hires Root Beer,** sign, tin, double-sided, top mounting holes, rare R-J disc logo in center, "Fountain Service," "We Serve With Real Juices," 16" x 14⅝", EX..........................$600.00 C

**Hires Root Beer,** sign, tin, embossed, "in bottles-ice cold," 27¼" x 19⅜", F ..........................$60.00 B

**Hires Root Beer,** sign, tin, embossed, bottle, "For Pleasure and Thirst," 55¾" x 17¾", NM..........................$450.00 C

**Hires Root Beer,** sign, tin, self-framing, litho, oval, two young women enjoying the product from glasses with straws, made by Stelad Signs, 23¾" x 19¾", 1915, VG..........................$250.00 B

**Hires Root Beer,** sign, tin, self-framing, oval, the classic "ugly" kid holding a mug of the product and smiling, copyright date of May 21, 1903, by Beach Art Display, 1909, 20" x 24", 1900s, G........$850.00 B

**Hires Root Beer,** thermometer, die cut, bottle, 1950s, 28" tall, EX ..........................$165.00 B

**Hires Root Beer,** thermometer, tin, Hires bottle at bottom of scale, 8¼" x 27", NM..........................$325.00 B

**Hires Root Beer,** tray "Quenches any thirst up to a mile long...just what the doctor ordered," Josh Slinger, 1914, EX.........**$1,750.00 B**

**Hires,** banner, cloth, R-J logo, "It's So Good...In Bottles," 57" x 36", EX ..................................................................................**$175.00 D**

**Hires,** bottle carrier, cardboard, cold frosty mugs, NM .......**$15.00 D**

**Hires,** bottle dispenser, metal, round R-J logo at top, wall mounted with dispensing slot at bottom, 19" tall, VG .....................**$175.00 D**

**Hires,** bottle topper, logo and "Hires So Good With Food 5¢," 3½" x 6", EX ..................................................................................**$30.00 D**

**Hires,** charger, tin, litho, familiar Hires Boy holding a mug of Root Beer, 20" x 24", 1907, VG ............................................**$1,400.00 B**

**Hires,** clock, metal and glass, "Drink Hires Root Beer," EX .**$275.00 D**

**Hires,** cork fasteners, cardboard, store display for bottle tops, these were used for Hires home-brewed root beer, 11" x 9", G...**$350.00 B**

**Hires,** dispenser, china with metal pump, in the shape of an hourglass, "Drink...it is pure," 7½" dia. x 13½", VG .**$450.00 B**

**Hires,** door push bar, "It's High Time For Hires Root Beer," 30" long, EX ..................................................................................**$65.00 D**

**Hires,** door push, metal, painted, "It's high time for Hires...Root Beer," bottle cap to left of message, 29½" x 4", G.................**$55.00 B**

**Hires,** globe, glass, brown lettering reads "Drink Hires," 8½" dia., EX ..................................................................................**$200.00 D**

**Hires,** menu board with bottle image and message at top of blackboard, "Drink," 16" x 29", EX..............................................**$125.00 C**

**Hires,** menu board, glass, cardboard, and paper in chrome frame, Hires bottle at top of menu strips, 12" x 24", EX...............**$225.00 B**

**Hires,** menu board, metal, tilted bottle with "Drink Hires," 16" x 29", EX ..................................................................................**$150.00 D**

**Hires,** menu board, tin, tilted bottle at top, 15½" x 29½", EX.**$65.00 B**

**Hires,** mug, Ugly Kid, by Mettlach, 4¼" T, EX ..................**$220.00 B**

**Hires,** sign, cardboard, "Drink in Bottles," girl and flare glass, by Haskell Coffin, 1910s, 15" x 21", EX ..........................................**$575.00 B**

**Hires,** sign, cardboard, girl and paper label bottle, 22" x 12", EX..**$200.00 B**

**Hires,** sign, embossed, "Enjoy...Healthful...Delicious," "tacker" with image of product bottle, 9½" x 27½", 1930s, EX...............**$150.00 B**

**Hires,** sign, metal, embossed, "Ask For Hires In Bottles," 28" x 10", EX ..................................................................................**$350.00 D**

**Hires,** sign, metal, embossed, "Drink...It Hit's The Spot," Josh Slinger in white suit, 16" x 9", EX ..........................................**$400.00 D**

**Hires,** sign, metal, painted, "In Bottles," tilted bottle at right of message, 27" x 10", EX ............................................................**$95.00 D**

**Hires,** sign, metal, painted, "So refreshing," made with roots, barks, herbs, AAA Sign Co., Cottsville, Ohio, 13½" x 11½", EX.....**$95.00 D**

**Hires,** sign, oval, framed, "Say," Hires child holding early Hires mug, 1900s, 20" x 24", EX..................................................**$600.00 B**

**Hires,** sign, oval, framed, "Say," Hires child holding early Hires mug, 1900s, 20" x 24", VG..................................................**$450.00 C**

**Hires,** sign, paper, soda jerk with product, 11¼" x 7", 1914, EX..................................................................................**$375.00 D**

**Hires,** sign, tin, "In Bottles," embossed lettering and bottle, 27¾" x 9¾", VG ..................................................................................**$140.00 B**

**Hires,** sign, tin, die cut, embossed, bottle, 15½" x 57", VG..**$325.00 B**

**Hires,** sign, tin, double-sided, flange, "Made With Roots-Barks-Herbs, So Refreshing," rare item, 14" x 12", NM .............**$375.00 C**

**Hires,** sign, tin, double-sided, flange, "So Refreshing," EX .**$250.00 C**

**Hires,** sign, tin, embossed, "Drink, It hits the spot, Try a bottle and You'll buy a case," man holding bottle, 15¾" x 9¾", VG.......**$175.00 C**

**Hires,** sign, tin, embossed, "Drink," Hires bottle, 32" x 11", NM..**$155.00 B**

**Hires,** sign, tin, embossed, framed, "and it's always pure...in bottles," 21¾" x 16", VG..................................................**$395.00 C**

**Hires,** sign, tin, one-sided, embossed, "Drink," bottle to right side of message, 32" x 11", G..................................................**$110.00 B**

**Hires,** syrup dispenser, Mettlach in shape of urn and images of the Hires Boy pointing, "Drink Hires Root Beer," 19" x 10½", VG ......**$22,500.00 B**

**Hires,** thermometer, dial-type, with root beer mug in center of piece, 12" dia., EX ............................................................**$150.00 C**

**Hires,** thermometer, metal, scale type, "Hires...Root Beer," rounded ends, 5" x 17", EX..................................................................**$75.00 D**

**Hires,** thermometer, tin, die cut, bottle, embossed with scale in neck of bottle, 7⅝" x 28½", NM..................................................**$225.00 C**

**Hires,** tray, metal, "Things Is Getting Higher...Still A Nickel A Trickle," 1915, EX ............................................................**$425.00 D**

**Hires,** tray, metal, Hires Kid pointing and a frosty mug in the other hand, 1930 – 40s, 13½" dia., VG......................................**$500.00 D**

**Hires,** tray, oval, self-framing, litho, two pretty women enjoying the product, "Drink Hires," great graphics, rare item, hard to find, 23½" x 19½", EX ..................................................................................**$1,500.00 C**

**Hit Parade Cigarettes,** flip-top box, G ................................**$15.00 C**

**Hitchner Cookie Store,** bin cover, metal and glass, 10¼" x 10½", F ..................................................................................**$25.00 D**

**Hite's,** thermometer, wood, metal, and glass, pain remedy, scale from Roanoke, VA, 5⅛" x 24¼", VG..................**$95.00 C**

**HO Stanley & Son Rangely Spinner**, trade card, cardboard, showing bait, 1900-1910s, EX ........................................$95.00 D

**Hoffman House Cigar**, sign, cardboard, nudes by a stream, "The New ..½ Cents," 18" x 26", EX ........................................$675.00 C

**Hoffman House Cigar**, sign, paper, litho in wood frame, famous men smoking their cigars, 1901, 37½" x 24", G ................$695.00 C

**Hoffman's House Cigar**, sig, young patriotic girl with marching soldiers in background, 15½" x 25½", 1898, VG ......................$425.00 C

**Hoffman's Ice Cream**, sign, metal, double-sided, painted, 28" x 20", G ........................................................................$85.00 C

**Hoffman's Ice Cream**, sign, porcelain, die cut, outdoor, on original metal hanging arm, "First Choice...Sealtest Approved," 25¾" x 22", VG ........................................................................$250.00 C

**Hoffman's Ice Cream**, sign, porcelain, double-sided, designed to hang, product name and logo, 26" x 22", EX ......................$175.00 D

**Hoffman's Ice Cream**, sign, porcelain, double-sided, hanging, "First choice," 25¾" x 22", EX ........................................$225.00 D

**Hoffmann's Old Time Coffee**, container, tin, early, litho, pry lid, "granny" in center cameo, 1-lb., EX ................................$150.00 B

**Hoffmann's Old Time Coffee**, tin, 4¼" H, EX ..................$75.00 D

**Hoffmann's Old Time Roasted Coffee**, grinder, tin, litho, wood frame on cast iron, 13½" H, F ........................................$250.00 D

**Hofnar Cigar**, sign, porcelain, self-framing, foreign, 23" x 61", G ........................................................................$185.00 B

**Holiday Regular 94 Octane**, gas globe, light-up, narrow glass body, metal base with two lenses, 13½" dia., VG ......................$600.00 B

**Holland House Coffee**, container, tin, litho, key-wound, 1-lb., EX ........................................................................$25.00 B

**Hollywoodglo**, sign, cardboard, tri-fold, "For screen star loveliness use," early motion picture cameras and actress, EX .......$100.00 C

**Hollywoodglo**, sign, tri-fold, counter, 18" x 12", EX ..................$75.00 C

**Holman's Trailing Arbutus Face Powder**, container, tin, litho, designed to be used as trinket box after product is used, 1915, EX ........................................................................$50.00 D

**Holsum Bread**, sign, metal, yard-long, with strips at both top and bottom, man and woman reading, 11¾" x 35", EX ..............$95.00 B

**Holsum Bread**, thermometer, metal, scale type, "Ask For...," Holsum lettered vertically beside scale, 18½" tall, VG ...........$250.00 C

**Home Brewing Co's Monogram Ale**, label, paper, pre-prohibition with Monogram Ale under arched Home, 1910s, EX ...........$25.00 D

**Home Brewing Co.**, sign, paper, pretty girl in oval surrounded by flowers, "Brewers Of Fine Lager Beer," 23" x 29", EX...$400.00 D

**Home Lighting and Cooking Plant**, tip tray, metal, early kitchen scene, "The Incandescent Light and Stove Co., Cincinnati, OH," 4⅛" dia., EX ........................................................................$260.00 B

**Home Run Razor Blades**, box, cardboard, with original contents and picture of baseball player hitting a home run, EX ........$45.00 D

**Honest Long Cut Tobacco**, package, unopened, honest character on front and back, an early Duke Bros. piece, VG ................$175.00 C

**Honest Scrap Tobacco**, sign, cardboard, cat & dog pulling a pouch between them, 32" x 24½", EX ....................................$675.00 C

**Honest Scrap Tobacco**, sign, original frame, dog and cat on both sides of product package, 30" x 22½", EX ................................$1,800.00 B

**Honest Scrap Tobacco**, sign, original frame, dog and cat on both sides of product package, 30" x 22½", VG ..............................$1,300.00 C

**Honest Scrap Tobacco**, sign, tin, trademark forearm, hand with hammer, 6¾" x 8¾", VG ........................................$185.00 B

**Honest Scrap Tobacco**, store bin, metal, dog and cat image on the front, slanted top lid, 18" x 14" x 12", EX ......................$1,800.00 C

**Honest Scrap**, sign, porcelain, arm with hammer, 9" x 12", EX.$130.00 B

**Honest Tobacco**, sign, cardboard, in frame, man at table in hat, "Long Cut...Smoking...Chewing," 1890s, G ..................................$1,150.00 C

**Honest Tobacco**, sign, cardboard, wood frame, "Honest Long Cut Tobacco," 1890s, G ........................................$850.00 C

**Honest Tobacco**, unopened pack from American Tobacco Co., Factory #1, "Long Cut...smoking and chewing," NM ......$50.00 B

**Honest Wear-u-Well Shoes**, sign, porcelain over metal, double-sided, flange, 26¼" x 17½", VG ........................................$145.00 B

**Honey Bee Snuff**, sign, tin, embossed, framed, can of product prominently displayed, 13½" x 19¼", EX ............................$60.00 B

**Honey Moon Tobacco**, pocket tin, vertical, litho, man and woman sitting on crescent moon, rare variation, 3" x ⅞" x 4½", EX ........................................................................$1,950.00 B

**Honey Moon Tobacco**, sign, tin, litho, one-sided, Penn Tobacco Co., couple sitting on quarter moon, 9¾" H, F ................$100.00 C

**Honey-Fruit Gum**, sign, tin over cardboard, "Nothing Like It, Delightful Flavor," manufactured by Franklin-Caro Company in Richmond, Va., 16¼" x 9", EX ....................................$1,300.00 B

**Honey-Fruit Gum**, sign, tin over cardboard, "Nothing Like It, Delightful Flavor," manufactured by Franklin-Caro Company in Richmond, Va., 16¼" x 9", F ....................................$300.00 C

**Honey-Fruit Gum**, sign, tin, litho over cardboard, "Nothing Like It...Delightful Flavor," American Artworks, 9⅛" x 6¼", EX.$2,500.00 B

**Honeymoon Keen Cut Breakfast Coffee**, tin, litho, loving couple sitting on crescent moon, key-wound, 1-lb., EX ................$85.00 C

**Honeymoon Tobacco,** pocket tin, vertical, trademark man on the moon, 1910s, G ....................$130.00 B

**Hood Tire Dealer,** sign, tin, die cut, litho, Hood man, 11" x 35½", VG ....................$1,125.00 C

**Hood Tires,** sign, porcelain, die cut, Hood man, 1930 – 40s, 10" x 35½", VG ....................$1,200.00 B

**Hood Tires,** thermometer, wooden, Hood man with stop flag at top center over vertical scale, Hood Tires message in circle at bottom, 4" x 15", orange, white, and black, G ....................$325.00 C

**Hood's Ice Cream,** sign, metal, double-sided, painted, trademark cow's head in center, 19" dia., EX ....................$2,000.00 D

**Hood's Ice Cream,** sign, tin, litho, embossed, Donaldson Art Sign, "The flavor's there," 20" x 28", EX ....................$335.00 C

**Hood's Sarsaparilla,** calendar, "The Sewing Circle," children sewing, 1892, NM ....................$165.00 C

**Hood's Sarsaparilla,** calendar, cardboard, die cut, unused calendar pad, young girls on front, NM ....................$95.00 B

**Hood's Sarsaparilla,** calendar, die cut, pretty girl and roses, full calendar pad, 1904, EX ....................$75.00 B

**Hood's Sarsaparilla,** calendar, die cut, pretty girl in bonnet, 1894, 5½" x 8¾", G ....................$30.00 C

**Hood's Sarsaparilla,** calendar, full calendar pad, 7" sq., 1892, EX ....................$55.00 B

**Hood's Sarsaparilla,** calendar, full calendar pad, pretty woman titled "Donna Inez, The Spanish Beauty," 1912, NM ....................$65.00 C

**Hood's Sarsaparilla,** calendar, girl wearing a flowery bonnet, 1886, 7¼" x 14¾", EX ....................$65.00 C

**Hood's Sarsaparilla,** calendar, girl wearing a flowery bonnet, 1886, 7¼" x 14¾", VG ....................$50.00 C

**Hood's Sarsaparilla,** calendar, paper, die cut pictures of 2 young girls, 1900, VG ....................$95.00 D

**Hood's Sarsaparilla,** calendar, paper, with product coupons, embossed image of pretty little girl, 1898, 5" x 7½", EX ....................$95.00 D

**Hood's Sarsaparilla,** calendar, paperboard, die cut young lady wearing a full bonnet, full monthly pad, 1888, EX ....................$200.00 D

**Hood's,** calendar, cardboard, die cut, full pad of tear sheets and information sheets, young woman in bonnet, 4¾" x 8", 1888, EX ....................$165.00 B

**Hood's,** calendar, die cut, young pretty girl, full unused monthly tear sheets, 4¾" x 7", 1897, NM ....................$225.00 C

**Hood's,** calendar, full tear sheet pad, young boy and girl in front of world globe, 6" x 8½", 1893, EX ....................$200.00 B

**Hood's,** calendar, pretty young girl with bow in hair, 7" x 7½", 1910, VG ....................$175.00 B

**Hood's,** calendar, two young children playing with kittens, 7" x 8", 1913, EX ....................$175.00 B

**Hood's,** calendar, young girl with animals, full calendar pad, "Four Friends," 4½" x 15½", 1903, EX ....................$220.00 B

**Hood's,** calendar, young woman with fur hat, 5½" x 9¾", 1889, EX ....................$165.00 C

**Hoods Tires,** sign, metal, Hood man standing beside courtesy panel for dealer, 1930 – 40s, 24" x 12", VG ....................$250.00 D

**Hoodsies Ice Cream,** sign, cardboard, die cut, young couple on swing, 12¼" x 18½", EX ....................$2,000.00 B

**Hoop-La Cigars,** box label, paper, with circus scene, 1880s, 9" x 6", VG ....................$85.00 C

**Hopalong Cassidy's Popcorn,** can, metal, Hopalong and his favorite popcorn, 10 oz., VG ....................$125.00 C

**Hopalong Cassidy,** popcorn container, Hoppy on front, 10-oz., EX ....................$255.00 C

**Hopalong Cassidy,** wrist watch, original box, VG ....................$125.00 C

**Hopkins & Allen Arms Co.,** mug, Mettlach, produced for the Rochester 1911 Police Chief's Convention, 1911, NM ....................$400.00 D

**Hopkins & Allens Arms Co.,** print, paper, young boy aiming at an apple on his dog's head, 20" x 14", VG ....................$475.00 C

**Horlacher Brewing Company,** calendar, pretty woman and a penguin, 16" x 33½", EX ....................$125.00 C

**Horlick's Malted Milk,** pocket mirror, metal & glass, cow and a milkmaid, 2⅛" dia., EX ....................$150.00 C

**Horlick's Malted Milk,** pocket mirror, young girl with calf, 2" dia., EX ....................$100.00 C

**Horlick's Malted Milk,** tin, litho, small canister top lid, cow on front, #10 can, EX ....................$45.00 B

**Horlick's Malted Milk,** trade card, die cut, dimensional, stand-up, in shape of pretty lady and cow, 4" x 5" x ¾", EX ....................$70.00 B

**Horlick's,** sign, bottle, "for Strength and Energy," 18½" x 28½", VG ....................$170.00 B

**Horrigan Supply Co.,** calendar, pretty young woman, 15" x 20", 1906, EX ....................$235.00 B

**Horse Shoe Tobacco,** sign, porcelain, flange, "We Sell," 18" x 8", G ....................$200.00 B

**Horse Shoe,** sign, metal, embossing for the cut plug tobacco with litho of 3 gunboats, 36" x 24", EX ....................$900.00 D

**Horseshoeing, Wheelwrighting, and Painting,** sign, painted and carved for F. Poitras & Co., 14" x 6", EX ........$1,500.00 B

**Horton Brewing Co.,** sign, glass with reverse painting, company name and logo on front, 10" x 10½", EX ................$85.00 D

**Horton's Ice Cream,** sign, porcelain, single-sided, "The Premier Ice Cream of America," 20" x 28", EX ..................$375.00 C

**Horton's Ice Cream,** sign, porcelain, single-sided, "The Premier Ice Cream of America," 20" x 28", VG ................$275.00 B

**Hoster's Famous Beer,** charger, metal, crow in graduation cap, "Something To Crow About," 24" dia., EX ................$395.00 C

**Hostess,** container, tin, litho, holiday fruit cake, 6³½" x 3¼" x 3", VG ..............................$40.00 B

**Hot Ball Chewing and Smoking Tobacco,** sign, tin, embossed, litho, jester holding package, rare piece, EX ............$1,800.00 C

**Hot Springs, Arkansas,** souvenir spoon, black boy eating a watermelon, marked "Sterling," 5" l, VG ................$300.00 B

**Hotel Ardmore,** paperweight, glass, with mirror that has image of hotel in Ardmore, OK, 3½" dia., EX ................$50.00 D

**Hotel McAlpin Coffee,** container, tin, litho, small canister-type lid on top, hotel scene, 1910, 6" x 11", EX ................$60.00 C

**Hotel Statler,** pocket mirror, metal and glass, outside image of hotel on back side of mirror, 2¾" oval, EX ................$65.00 D

**Houdaille Shock Absorber Service,** sign, tin, double-sided, flange, 26" x 19¾", ................$275.00 B

**Housatonic Inn,** sign, wood, inn on the Housatonic River in Conn., 42" x 28", 1900, VG ................$600.00 B

**Household,** match striker, match striker, tin, litho, wall-hung, "Your credit is good...The Household," by Kaufmann & Strauss Lithographers, 4¾" x 7¾", 1915s, G ................$65.00 C

**Household,** match striker, tin, litho, wall hung, "Your credit is good...The Household," by Kaufmann & Strauss Lithographers, 4¾" x 7¾", 1915s, EX ................$130.00 B

**Houstonia Liniment,** sign, cardboard, die cut, EX ............$110.00 B

**Howard Co. Fair Aug 31 – Sept. 1-2-3...Horse Races,** license plate attachment, tin, embossed, sulky racing at top of attachment, 5¾" x 6¼", NM ................$115.00 C

**Howard Johnson's,** toy, dairy bar and soda fountain, neat, still in original box, EX ................$75.00 C

**Howard's Perfection Oil,** can, metal, photo of vintage combine, 1910s, 2" x 3", VG ................$75.00 D

**Howdy Doody Washington Apples,** plastic bag, NOS, Howdy Doody and friends on front, 3-lb., EX ................$15.00 D

**Howdy Doody Washington Apples,** plastic bag, NOS, Howdy Doody and friends on front, 3-lb., NM ................$18.00 D

**Howdy Doody,** ice cream box, unused with Howdy on lid, 12-oz., 1950s, EX ................$55.00 C

**Howdy Orange Soda,** display, paper, die cut, bottle at right of Howdy, 1930s, 42" x 15", EX ................$65.00 D

**Howdy Orange Soda,** sign, cardboard, hanger, bottle, "Don't Say Orange...Say...," 1920s, 6" x 12", VG ................$55.00 C

**Howdy,** bottle topper, cardboard, die cut, sandwich in hand, 6½" x 10½", NM ................$75.00 C

**Howdy,** sign, tin, embossed, "The Nose Knows," "tacker" style of bottle and boy, NOS, 19½" x 9¼", NM ................$350.00 B

**Howel's Orange Julep,** dispenser, ceramic with base, 9" x 15", VG ................$1,600.00 B

**Howel's Orange Julep,** pedestal glass, 1920s, EX ................$120.00 B

**Howel's Root Beer,** sign, tin, embossed, die cut, bottle, 8⅜" x 29½", EX ................$275.00 C

**Howertown Sanitary Dairy,** serving tray, metal, 13¼" sq., VG .$75.00 C

**Hoyt & Co. Buffalo Peanut Butter,** pail with wire bail handle, tin, litho, 3¾" x 3¼", EX ................$325.00 B

**Hubig's Pie Co.,** tip tray, tin, litho, factory and horse-drawn delivery wagon, "A guarantee against cellar made pies," 3⅝" dia., 1906, EX ................$240.00 B

**Hubley Guns,** display, metal, for displaying toy guns, "Buy Hubley," 23" x 17", VG ................$75.00 C

**Hudson Essex Serviced,** sign, porcelain, double-sided, 30" x 16", EX ................$400.00 B

**Hudson Terraplane Authorized Service,** sign, porcelain, single-sided, 42" dia., EX ................$1,100.00 C

**Hudson's Bay Co's Tea,** container, metal, graphics on all four sides, 8½" x 6" x 6", VG ................$75.00 D

**Hudson's Bay Co.,** calendar, men at lake with canoe by artist Phillip R. Goodwin, 11½" x 6½", 1928, NM ................$425.00 B

**Hudson,** auto catalog, new cars on front cover, 11" x 6", 1938, EX ................$40.00 B

**Hudson,** sign, porcelain, "Rambler...Sales...Service," 1940s, 42" x 30", EX ................$525.00 C

**Hully-Gee Pepsin Gum,** wrapper, from the Buckeye Gum Co., Salem, Ohio, famous Yellow Kid in a cameo at left of message, 3½", EX ................$575.00 B

**Hully-Gee Pepsin Gum,** wrapper, from the Buckeye Gum Co., Salem, Ohio, famous Yellow Kid in a cameo at left of message, 3½", G ................$300.00 C

**Humble Gasoline,** knife sharpening stone, celluloid, product message on back, 1⅝" x 2⅞", EX ................$110.00 B

**Humble Rest Rooms,** sign, metal, die cut, "Top Rated," 1960s, 30" x 30", EX.............................................................$145.00 C

**Humble,** pump sign, porcelain, continuously improved, single-sided, 10¾" x 18", G...............................................$115.00 C

**Humphreys Specifics,** medicine product cabinet, with tin front, back has drawers that hold product, complete with original product, 21¾" x 8" x 28¼", EX .....................................$900.00 B

**Humphreys' Remedies,** store display cabinet, wooden with metal front, 18" W x 21" H x 7¼" D, G.......................................$175.00 C

**Hunter Arms Co.,** envelope, paper, photo of dead game in dogs mouth, VG...................................................$125.00 D

**Hunter Red Dog Shells,** box, empty, 12 gauge, dog on front, 4⅛" x 4⅛" x 2½", NM .....................................$75.00 C

**Hupmobile,** calendar, paper, sailboat scene, full calendar pad, 14¼" x 31", 1926, EX ...............................................$275.00 C

**Hurtz,** sign, tin, painted, "100% pure black salve," black man in center, 22" x 22", VG.................................$200.00 B

**Husemann's Soda, Clear and Sparkling,** sign, tin, embossed, painted, from Red Bud, Ill., 19½" x 13½", VG.........................$85.00 C

**Husemann's Soda,** sign, tin, embossed, painted, "Clear and Sparkling," from Red Bud, Ill., 19½" x 13½", G.................$65.00 D

**Husky Gasoline,** lighter, etched, painted, 1¾" tall, NOS, M...$110.00 B

**Husky Hi Power,** pump sign, porcelain, one-sided, husky dog, 12" x 12", G.................................................$375.00 B

**Husky Hi-Power,** gas globe, metal and glass, company name just below a Husky dog, 15" dia., EX.........................$85.00 D

**Husky Motor Oil,** container, metal, floral design, Husky, 1 qt, EX .$80.00 D

**Husky,** sign, porcelain, two-piece, die cut, dog with Husky base, difficult item to find, G.......................................$750.00 C

**Huyler's Candies,** sign, porcelain, flange, double-sided, "made to eat...not to keep," 20¼" x 7", VG .....................$235.00 C

**Hyde Propellers Sales and Service,** sign, porcelain, one-sided, large propeller in center, 18" x 26", G ...........................$900.00 B

**Hygia Coffee,** blotter, paper, with coffee can on a high billboard "A Sign Of Good Taste," 1920s, 6½" x 3½", VG.....................$10.00 C

**Hygienic Kalsomine,** sign, cardboard, "Germ proof your walls," housewife and painter, 1909, 11" x 15", EX.........................$47.00 B

**Hygrade Products Co.,** fuel pump rebuild kits, metal, lift-front door, original parts inside, New York, N.Y., 12¾" x 15" x 12¾", EX................................................................$195.00 D

**Hyroler Whiskey,** tip tray, metal, round, Louis J. Adler & Co., man in dress attire and top hat, 4¼" dia., EX ...............$75.00 C

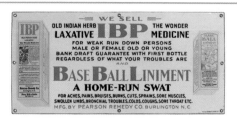

IBP Laxative and Base Ball Liniment, sign, porcelain, good strong colors, 26" x 12", EX, $795.00 C.

Illinois, watch, metal and plastic display, 11" x 15" x 35", G, $895.00 C.

Ideal Smokeless Shotgun Shells, box with paper litho, 4¼" x 4¼" x 2⅝", VG, $110.00 B.

Imperial Airways, poster, paper, litho, 28" x 43", VG, $800.00 B.

Imperial Airways, poster, paper, litho of cutaway of seaplane, 43" x 28", EX, $725.00 B.

Imperial Ice Cream, menu board, mirror and chrome, 28" wide, VG, $250.00 B.

I W Harper Whiskey, sign, canvas, showing a couple in an open touring car about to depart from friends and being handed a bottle of the product, titled "The Parting Gift," 1912, 46" x 34", VG....$2,000.00 D

I W Harper, sign, vitrolite, dog in cabin scene, framed, 1909, 22" x 28", VG .................................................................$2,200.00 C

I.W. Harper Oleograph, wood and canvas, honeymoon scene, from Bernheim Distilling Company, Inc., 46" x 34½", 1912, EX .$1,225.00 B

I.W. Harper Whiskey, print, framed, bird dog in front of log cabin with hunting gear on front porch, good, strong sign, 24" x 30", NM ..................................................................$1,000.00 B

I.W. Harper, sign, reverse glass in wooden frame, older gentleman watching young girl, 23½" x 35½", 1900s, EX ...............$6,500.00 B

I.W. Harper, sign, vitrolite, hunting dog and hunting gear inside warm cabin with a bottle of the product prominently displayed, 17" x 23", G................................................................$450.00 D

IBP Old Indian Laxative & Liniment, sign, porcelain, "We Sell IBP Old Indian Herb Laxative & Base Ball Liniment," product boxes, 26" x 12", EX ....................................................................$800.00 D

Ice Service, sign, cardboard, "Clean Courteous...Careful," service man carrying block ice on shoulder, 30½" x 20½", 1948, EX........$125.00 C

Idaho Power Company, sign, tin, Reddy Kilowatt, 40" x 24", NM..............................................................................$235.00 C

Ideal Alaska Down Bustles, trade card, cardboard, lady checking out a bustle in a mirror, "The Improved Genuine...," 3" x 5", EX ...................................................................................$85.00 D

Ideal Bread, sign, metal, rack, painted, "Ideal for every meal," 40" x 17½", F.............................................................................$195.00 D

Ideal Coffee, tin, litho, screw-on lid and silver serving coffee pot, 4" x 6", EX.............................................................................$130.00 B

Ideal Dog Food, sign, enamel, dogs face, "A Complete 7 Course Meal," 17" x 9", EX.....................................................$185.00 D

Ideal Quality chekd Dairy Products, clock, plastic, light-up, 15½" dia., G...............................................................................$95.00 C

Ideal Quality chekd Dairy Products, clock, plastic, light-up, 15½" dia., VG.............................................................................$135.00 C

Idle Hour Cut Plug Tobacco, container, metal, pocket size, EX .$85.00 D

Idle Moments Cigar, box label, paper, image of woman, 1900s, 9" x 6", EX .........................................................................$35.00 D

IGA Deluxe Coffee, can, metal with key wind lid, gold eagle on red background, 1 lb, VG .....................................................$25.00 C

IGA Deluxe Coffee, tin, key-wound litho, eagle on front, 1-lb., EX.................................................................................$40.00 D

Independent Cigar Co., box, wood, oval name on top "222, Paducah, KY," 8½" x 5¼" x 1½", VG, $45.00 C. *Courtesy of B.J. Summers.*

Independent Gasoline, gas globe, metal high profile body with two glass lenses, hard-to-find item, 15" dia., VG, $5,000.00 B. *Courtesy of Collectors Auction Services.*

Independent Local and Long Distance Telephone, sign, porcelain, double-sided, flange, 17" x 18", NM, $550.00 B. *Courtesy of Autopia Advertising Auctions.*

Indian Maid Coal, sign, porcelain, Pocahontas in spotlight, 24" wide, G, $250.00 B.

Indian Rock Ginger Ale, 5¢, syrup dispenser with Indian scenes on both sides, complete with ball pump, 12" tall, EX, $2,250.00 B.

Iron Fireman Coal, sign, porcelain, 20" dia., EX, $575.00 C.

---

**Illinois Bell Telephone Company, American Telephone & Telegraph Co.,** sign, porcelain, double-sided, flange, 12" x 11", NM .....$225.00 C

**Illinois Farm Bureau, Illinois Agricultural Mutual Insurance Co.,** license plate attachment, porcelain, 3¾" x 4½", EX ............$85.00 C

**Illinois Springfield Watches,** sign, tin, "Observatory of Illinois Watch Company Springwell," 24" x 18", VG .....................$575.00 D

**Illinois Valley Ice Cream,** sign, metal and plastic, light-up, EX...$155.00 D

**Illinois Valley Ice Cream,** sign, metal and plastic, light-up, NM ..$165.00 D

**Illinois Watch Co.,** sign, glass with reverse painting for sales and service steam engine and coal tender, "Authorized Watch Inspector," 22" x 13", EX.............................................................$500.00 D

**Illinois Watch Company,** print, framed, factory scene, 24½" x 16½", EX...................................................................................$75.00 D

**Illinois Watch,** photo, factory and early cars, 24⅜" x 16½", G.$55.00 C

**Illustrator Cigar,** container, metal with slip lid, man in powder wig on paper label, VG .......................................................$95.00 C

**Imperial Cigar,** sign, tin, embossed, litho, Club cigars for 5¢, "The Best For The Money," 13¾" x 10", EX .................$155.00 C

**Imperial Club 5¢ Cigar,** sign, tin, embossed, litho, full box of the product, 13¾" x 10", EX ...............................................$125.00 C

**Imperial Club 5¢ Cigar,** sign, tin, painted, embossed, Wolf & Co. Selling Agents, 13½" x 10", EX.........................................$150.00 C

**Imperial Club 5¢ Cigar,** sign, tin, painted, embossed, Wolf & Co. Selling Agents, 13½" x 10", G..............................................$95.00 C

**Imperial Dry Ginger Ale,** tip tray, metal, product bottle at right of message, 6⅛" L, NM....................................................$95.00 C

**Imperial Egg Food,** sign, paper, litho, black workers gathering eggs, from Kellogg & Bulkeley Co., Hartford CT, 29" x 35", G ......$300.00 C

**Imperial Egg Food,** sign, paper, litho, men feeding chickens while other men catch the eggs and load them on a train, 29" x 35", VG .......................................................................$650.00 C

**Imperial Egg Food,** sign, paper, litho, workers catching eggs and gathering hens and loading railroad freight cars, 29" x 35", EX ...$930.00 B

Iroquois Beer, sign, double-bubble, light-up, Indian in full headdress on woodgrain-look face, 15" dia., EX, $800.00 B. *Courtesy of Collectors Auction Services.*

Iroquois Indian Head Beer, serving tray, tin, litho of Indian, Buffalo, NY, 12" dia., EX, $95.00 C.

Ithaca Featherweight Repeaters, sign, cardboard, die cut, pheasant in flight, 21" x 14", G, $105.00 B.

Ivory Soap, ad, cardboard, early die cut string hanger with cherub holding a bar of Ivory overhead, probably having to do with early advertising that Ivory was the soap so pure it floats, 6" x 11", 1870s, EX, $1,050.00 B. *Courtesy of Wm. Morford Investment Grade Collectibles.*

I.W. Harper, sign, vitrolite, hunting dog and hunting gear inside warm cabin with a bottle of the product prominently displayed, 17" x 23", EX, $870.00 B. *Courtesy of Buffalo Bay Auction Co.*

Imperial Gasoline, gas globe, metal and glass, name in blue, 16" dia., VG .................................................$395.00 C

Imperial Gun Powder, container, metal, various animals, by Eureka Powder Works, 5" tall, EX .........................................$125.00 D

Imperial Premier Gasoline, gas globe, red metal body and glass lens, 16½" dia., VG .......................................$525.00 C

Imperial Service, sign, porcelain, art deco look, white lettering on blue background, 42" x 24", EX .....................................$750.00 D

Imperial, gas globe, plastic body with two glass lenses, no lead, 13½" dia., VG ........................................................$500.00 C

Imperiales Cigarettes, sign, framed, manufactured by The John Bollman Co., San Francisco, Calif., 16" x 20", EX ........................$225.00 C

Imps Breath Perfume 5¢, container, celluloid, round, devil's head in center, "For All Who Breathe," EX .................................$75.00 D

Inca Maidens, pail with wire handle, reel cut coffee, Inca Maiden and village in background, Bloomington, IL, 7½" x 7½", EX.......$295.00 C

Incuba Cigars, container, metal with slip lid, EX.............$135.00 D

Independence cigar box, label, paper, Miss Liberty, 4½" x 4½", EX...............................................................$95.00 D

Independent Brewing Co, tray, metal, round with high lip, bottle and goblet, 1900s, 12" dia., EX ........................................$165.00 D

Independent Cigars, sign, paper, George Washington with open boxes of cigars, 35" x 28", VG ..........................................$150.00 C

Independent Gasoline, gas globe, metal high profile body with two glass lenses, hard to find item, 15" dia., EX ....................$5,700.00 C

Independent Gasoline...Motor Oil, sign, porcelain, two-sided, 29½" dia., VG ........................................................$425.00 C

Independent Local and Long Distance Telephone, sign, porcelain, double-sided, "Pay Station," from Ing-Rich Beaver Falls, Pa., 100 Wm. St. NY, 18" x 18", EX...............................................$350.00 C

Independent Local and Long Distance Telephone, sign, porcelain, double-sided, flange, 17" x 18", G.....................................$135.00 C

Independent Malting Co., drinking glass with etched lettering, 3½" tall, EX .........................................................$125.00 D

**Independent Radio and TV Service,** clock, light-up, message in center of clock face, 16" dia., EX.................................................$95.00 C

**Independent Stove Co. Owosso, Mich.,** paperweight, cast iron, enameled, shape of alligator, 5½" L, NM ..........................$118.00 B

**Independent Tea Co,** calendar, cardboard, embossed image of pretty girl in front of lilacs, 1909, 15" x 20", EX......................$375.00 D

**India Tires,** sign, porcelain, single-sided, owl, 60" x 18", G...$275.00 B

**Indian Crown 10¢ Cigar,** sign, tin, litho, embossed, Indian in full headdress at left of info, McCoy & Co. Makers, New York, 20¾" x 15", EX.................................................$975.00 B

**Indian Gas Indian Refining Co., Incorporated,** sign, die cut, hanging, held by metal brackets over round extension arm, double-sided, 45" x 36", VG ..........................$675.00 C

**Indian Gasoline Pump,** sign, porcelain, straight for later pump styles, Indian head, 12" x 18", VG ...................................$450.00 C

**Indian Gasoline,** sign, porcelain, designed for pump attachment, Indian, 11" x 18", VG ..........................................$275.00 C

**Indian Gasoline,** sign, porcelain, Indian, gas logo at top of message, Indian Refining Co., New York, New York, 1940s, 12" x 18", VG ..........................................$185.00 C

**Indian Head Overalls,** sign, porcelain, Indian in cameo, 14" x 10", VG ..........................................$850.00 B

**Indian Motorcycle Agent,** button, metal, "Agent Indian Motorcycle" around Indian head, 1¼" dia., EX.........................$1,000.00 D

**Indian Motorcycle,** cigar cutter, Hendel Manufacturing Co., Springfield, Mass., J.E. Mercot Co. Newark, N.J., 2½" x 1", EX ....$400.00 B

**Indian Motorcycle,** clock, metal and glass with reverse painting of Indian head, 1910s, 20" dia., EX.........................$3,500.00 D

**Indian Motorcycles,** ad, paper, promoting the new 1935 line of motorcycles, 1935, 45" x 14", EX...................................$500.00 D

**Indian Motorcycles,** clock, metal, glass, and neon with black numbers and red company lettering on white face background, 18" dia., EX ..........................................$1,800.00 C

**Indian Motorcycles,** lapel pin, metal, round Indian head in goldtone, ½" dia., EX..........................................$225.00 C

**Indian Motorcycles,** match holder, metal, embossed Indian face in center of lettering, 1½" x 2", VG ..........................$600.00 C

**Indian Motorcycles,** sign, metal, double-sided, flange, trademark Indian head and "Indian Motorcycles" in red, 1940s, 26" x 24", VG ..........................................$625.00 D

**Indian Motorcycles,** watch fob, metal, in shape of arrowhead with trademark Indian head, considered to be difficult to find, 2" long, EX ..........................................$150.00 D

**Indian Premium Motorcycle Oil,** can, metal, logo above company name lettering, 1 qt., EX..........................................$300.00 C

**Indian Queen Chewing Tobacco,** sign, paper, bare breasted Indian maiden and tobacco leaves, 13" x 10", VG ..........................$525.00 D

**Indian Rock Ginger Ale 5¢,** syrup dispenser, complete with ball pump, Indian scenes on both sides, 12" tall, F ...........$1,100.00 D

**Indian Rock Ginger Ale,** sign, metal, bottle at each end and "Indian Rock Ginger Ale" in curves fashion, 36" x 12", EX.....$235.00 D

**Indian Rock Ginger Ale,** sign, tin, embossed, litho, bottle on both sides, 35½" x 11½", EX ..........................$325.00 C

**Indian,** gas globe, narrow glass body with glass lens, 13½" dia., VG.$800.00 B

**Indianapolis Brewing Co.,** notebook, celluloid cover with 1903 calendar, by Whitehead & Hoag, 2½" x 4¾", 1903, VG...........$95.00 C

**Indianapolis Brewing Co.,** pocket match safe, brass with embossing on both sides, 1½" x 3", VG..........................$175.00 C

**Indianapolis Brewing Co.,** sign, metal, self-framing, Venice canal with two bottles and a cherub, 26" x 38", VG ...............$2,000.00 C

**Indianapolis Brewing Co.,** sign, paper, "Progress Brand," 30" x 40", EX ..........................................$1,000.00 D

**Indianapolis Brewing Co.,** tray, metal, tip size, bottle on a red background, lettering around the rim, 1900s, VG ...........$150.00 D

**Indianapolis Glove Co.,** thermometer, wood, scale type with keyhole design, logo at top of thermometer, 4" x 11", VG ......$150.00 C

**Indianapolis Speedway,** checkered flag, silk, 17" x 17", EX...$125.00 C

**Indianapolis Speedway,** leather jacket, limited edition, #33/50, XL, NM ..........................................$1,300.00 B

**Indianapolis Speedway,** pennant, cloth, single-sided, 29" x 10½", VG.$135.00 C

**Industrial Supplies Corp.,** calendar, young woman on beach in swim suit, full pad, 16" x 33½", 1953, EX ..........................$30.00 B

**Infallible Shotgun,** pinback, celluloid, smokeless, 1¼" dia., G ..$50.00 B

**Infallible Smokeless Powder,** sign, linen, company lettering over a pair of ducks sitting in a marsh, 1909, 18" x 24", VG ......$1,850.00 C

**Ingersol Watches,** sign, porcelain, company name lettering in white on blue background, 24" x 3", EX...................................$200.00 C

**Ingersol Watches,** sign, porcelain, double-sided, die cut in shape of pocket watch, 8" x 12", EX...................................$475.00 D

**Ingersol Watches,** sign, porcelain, double-sided, flange, die cut in shape of pocket watch, "We Have Reliable Watch For One Dollar...Look For The Name," 9" x 17", EX..........................$425.00 C

**Ingersol Watches,** store display case, metal, brown with woodgrain look, manufactured by the H.D. Beach Co., Coshocton, Ohio, U.S.A., 9½" W x 14¼" H x 6" D, VG ..........................$120.00 C

**Ingersol Watches,** store display case, metal, brown woodgrain look, manufactured by the H.D. Beach Co., Coshocton, Ohio, U.S.A., 9½" W x 14¼" H x 6" D, G ..........................$100.00 B

**Ingram Perfumed Talcum Powder,** tin, litho, woman in center cameo, 2" x 4⅞", EX .................................................. **$190.00 B**

**Interlux Marine Paint,** sign, porcelain, single-sided, boats being painted, 24" x 14", G .................................................. **$400.00 B**

**International Harvester Co.,** sign, metal, double-sided, die cut to resemble a gasoline engine, 16" x 23", VG .................... **$2,000.00 D**

**International Harvester Co.,** watch fob, metal, round, embossed initals encircled by wheat wreath, EX .............................. **$475.00 C**

**International Harvester,** clock, metal body and glass face and cover, light-up, Pam Clock Co., 15½" sq., VG ................................ **$325.00 B**

**International Harvester,** clock, metal body with tin face and glass cover, neon, IH symbol in center, 15½" x 15½", EX ......... **$650.00 B**

**International Louse Killer,** container, metal, young girl among chickens in chicken yard, 7" x 3" dia., E ......................... **$425.00 D**

**International Motor Trucks,** sign, tin, single-sided, embossed, 27½" x 10⅛", VG .................................................. **$95.00 C**

**International Triple Diamond Service,** sign, porcelain, lettering around company logo, 42" dia., VG .............................. **$575.00 C**

**International Trucks Parts Service,** sign, porcelain, lettering around company logo, 42" dia., EX .............................. **$575.00 D**

**Interwoven Socks,** sign, cardboard, litho, die cut, 3-D effect, stand-up with easel back, has Santa in Christmas tree, 14" x 21", VG .................................................. **$455.00 B**

**Interwoven Socks,** sign, cardboard, litho, die cut, stand-up, man in front of street light, 18" x 36", 1935, VG .................... **$75.00 C**

**Interwoven Socks,** sign, elderly lady in chair with sewing basket, Norman Rockwell signature, 28" x 38", EX ...................... **$275.00 C**

**Interwoven Socks,** sign, paper-linen, woman in overstuffed chair knitting, by Norman Rockwell, 28" x 38", EX ................. **$95.00 C**

**Invincible Motor Insurance,** sign, tin, painted, spotlight on vintage auto, NOS, 20" x 9½", EX .................................. **$375.00 C**

**Invincible Schley,** cigar box label, paper, with likeness of Commander Schley Schmidt, VG .................................. **$200.00 C**

**Iris Brand Majoram,** spice tin with windblown flowers, 2¼" x 3¼" x 1", EX .................................................. **$110.00 B**

**Iris Coffee,** can, metal with key wind lid, "5¢ Off Regular Price," 1 lb, EX .................................................. **$60.00 D**

**Iris Coffee,** tin, litho, key-wound lid, Los Angeles, CA, 1-lb., EX... **$55.00 C**

**Iron City Beer,** display, chalkware with customer wearing a top hat talking with a bartender, 15" x 10" x 3", VG .................... **$95.00 D**

**Iron City Beer,** sign, metal and neon, product lettering on clock face, round, 1950s, EX .................................. **$295.00 D**

**Iroquois Beer,** sign, cardboard, "Catch'um Fresh...While In...," Indian with canoe, 1960s, 22" x 11", EX ...................... **$55.00 D**

**Iroquois Beer-Ale,** clock, light-up, Indian head outlined by arrowhead, 17" dia., EX .................................................. **$450.00 C**

**Iroquois Beer/Ale,** clock, metal and glass, light up, Indian head profile on clock face, 15" dia., EX ...................... **$695.00 C**

**Iroquois Indian Head Beer & Ale,** tray, metal, Indian head in profile, 13" dia., VG .................................................. **$110.00 C**

**Iroquois,** sign, double-bubble, light-up, Indian in full headdress on woodgrain-look face, 15" dia., F .............................. **$100.00 C**

**Iroquois,** tip tray, lithographed, Indian head in center, 4½" dia., VG .................................................. **$65.00 B**

**Irvin Ethyl Gasoline,** globe, high profile body with two glass lenses, 15" dia., G .................................................. **$550.00 C**

**Irving Cigars,** spitton, porcelain with black "Irving Cigar" on white background, VG .................................................. **$225.00 D**

**Isbrandtsen Red Label,** tin, litho, key-wound, large ship on front, 1-lb., EX .................................................. **$75.00 B**

**Ithaca Featherweight Repeaters,** sign, cardboard, die cut, wall-hanging, goose in flight, 15" x 17" x 1", VG .................... **$275.00 B**

**Ithaca Gun Catalog,** shotgun on cover, 11" x 8½", 1936, EX .. **$140.00 B**

**Ithaca Gun Co.,** sign, cardboard, die cut, goose in flight, 16½" x 14½", VG .................................................. **$190.00 B**

**Ithaca Guns,** sign, paper, "Extinct Passenger Pigeon...Outshoot Them All/ Authorized Agent," courtesy strip for dealer's name, metal strips at top and bottom, 17" x 28", VG ................. **$700.00 D**

**Ithaca Guns,** sign, paper, "Extinct Passenger Pigeons Ithaca Guns" product, 19" x 27", VG .................................. **$575.00 D**

**Ivory Soap,** ad, paper, litho, gesso frame, "A Busy Day," 20" x 22½", VG .................................................. **$235.00 B**

**Ivory Soap,** sign, cardboard, "Purity...It Floats," 26" x 34", EX .**$500.00 D**

**Ivory Soap,** sign, cardboard, early, die cut, string hanger, cherub holding a bar of Ivory overhead, probably having to do with early advertising that Ivory was the soap so pure it floats, 6" x 11", 1870s, EX .................................................. **$1,050.00 B**

**Ivory Soap,** sign, metal, die stamped, "99 44/100 Per Cent Pure," 11" x 9", EX .................................................. **$225.00 D**

**Ivory Soap,** sign, porcelain, 21" x 3¼", EX ...................... **$175.00 C**

**Ivory Soap,** sign, porcelain, white lettering on blue, 21" x 3", VG .................................................. **$250.00 C**

**Izaak Walton Cigars,** container, metal, round, slip lid, "2 for 5¢," EX .................................................. **$125.00 C**

Jackson Restaurant China Co., salesman's sample plate with the salesman's name C.W. Young incorporated into the message on the plate center with images of various serving pieces around the border, 3¾" dia., EX, $300.00 B. *Courtesy of Wm. Morford Investment Grade Collectibles.*

Jack Sprat Peanut Butter, tin with pry lid, walking Jack on front, 25", VG, $1,665.00 B.

J.A. Johnston & Co., sign, tin, successors to C.D. Daniel, 29⅝" x 11¾", EX, $135.00 C.

Jarvis D-X, knife, celluloid and metal, "Compliments Cletus Jarvis, Agent Paducah, KY," two blades, 3¼" long closed, EX, $15.00 C. *Courtesy of B.J. Summers.*

Jas. Pepper, tray, metal, patriotic scene promoting sour mash whiskey, by American Art Works Co., 16½" x 13¾", VG, $220.00 B.

J & P Coats Best Six Cord Spool Cotton, sign, hardboard, painted, framed, "For Hand & Machine," 18" x 30", F ..................... $75.00 D

J & P Coats Best Six Cord Spool Cotton, sign, hardboard, self-framing, gold lettering, 18" x 30", VG..................... $325.00 D

J & P Coats Spool Cotton, cabinet, oak with thread racks under roll top, 31" x 24" x 11", EX ............................................. $750.00 D

J & P Coats Spool Cotton, cabinet, oak, revolving base with four hinged panels, 22¾" tall, EX ......................................... $1,500.00 C

J & P Coats Spool Cotton, sign, paper, woman watching a man fishing, 22" x 17½", VG................................................. $250.00 D

J & P Coats, sign, wood frame and gold embossed lettering and spool cotton in center, 18" x 30", EX ................................. $425.00 C

J A Cigars, sign, die cut, easel back, man in suit enjoying a cigar, 17½" x 29½", EX.................................................... $235.00 C

J A Cigars, sign, porcelain, "Smoke JA Cigars," EX....... $135.00 B

J C Johnson & Co., sign, paper, horses being roped, framed, "Harness, Saddles, Leather...," 30" x 24", EX ........................ $2,800.00 B

J Devar & Sons Whiskey, print, cardboard, Highland Whiskey bottles and two men in a library, 31¼" x 22¼", EX ............................. $20.00 D

J G Dill's Lookout Tobacco, container, metal with slip lid, lighthouse, "Rough & Ready," EX ............................................. $675.00 C

J H Friedwald Wines & Liquors, shot glass, glass, etched "Compliments Of...," EX ................................................................. $20.00 C

J H Johnson Great Western Gun Works, catalog, paper, engraved illustrations, 1889, 64 pages, EX...................................... $175.00 D

J Hungerford Smith Co., tray, metal, serving size, "True Fruit Flavors Make Our Fountain," VG ......................................... $100.00 D

J I Case Threshing Machine Co., sign, metal, embossed lettering, steam threshing machine, 19½" x 13½", EX............... $3,000.00 D

J Krauss & Co. Washing Machine Mgf., trade card, cardboard, factory scene and train, VG...................................................... $40.00 C

J L Taylor & Co. Tailors, thermometer, wood, scale type, rounded top, company name at left of scale and at bottom, 22" tall, VG....... $55.00 C

J C Soda, sign, gloglas, bottle and "Drink," 1940s, EX, $1,000.00 B.

Jesse James, poster, paper, litho, "The Sensational Western Life Drama," black couple, 30" x 44", G, $1,700.00 B. *Courtesy of Collectors Auction Services.*

Jewelry Watch Repairing, sign, porcelain, double-sided with iron holder, 11¼" x 16½", G, $910.00 B.

John J. Bleich Jewelry, oyster plate premium by Wheelock China, "A Busy Day at the Warph, Paducah, KY," 1900s, 6" x 4½", EX, $100.00 C. *Courtesy of B.J. Summers.*

Johnnie Walker Red, backbar statue, F, $45.00 C. *Courtesy of B.J. Summers.*

---

J M Pratt & Co., blotter, paperboard, pretty young lady removing her skirt, 1940s, 4" x 9", VG.................................$15.00 C

J R Hewitt Saddle Harness & Trunk Maker, sign, paper, picture of early storefront, 10" x 14", EX .................................$175.00 D

J Schriber & Co's Prairie Flower Chewing Tobacco, sign, metal, Indian princess with flowers, 28" x 20", EX .....................$975.00 C

J Stevens & Co., letterhead, paper, a large revolver, 1881, EX.$75.00 A

J Stevens Arms & Tool Co., ad, paper, hunters gathering, 1907, EX .................................................................$125.00 B

J Stevens Arms & Tool Co., ad, paper, rifle, "We Shall Exhibit...Auto show," 1905, EX.................................................$100.00 D

J W M Field's Whiskey, sign, metal, elegant woman with a serving tray, 19½" x 28", EX......................................$100.00 D

J Widman brewery, match safe, metal, embossed elk, 1½" x 2¾", VG .................................................................$225.00 C

J. B. Barnaby Co., pocket mirror, Providence, promoting Collegian cut clothing, 1¾" dia., EX .........................................$425.00 B

J. Devar & Sons Whiskey, print, cardboard, in wood frame that appears to be original, 31¼" x 22¼", EX .........................$75.00 C

J.B. Lewis Shoemaker, sign, tin, litho, single-sided, cobbler at work at his bench, 13½" x 19½", VG .........................$375.00 B

J.D. Mahoney, sign, paper, line of clothes, 5¼" x 7¼", EX..$75.00 C

J.G. Dill's Best Cut Plug Tobacco, tin, G.........................$35.00 C

J.G. Hoffman & Sons Co., ad, paper, their buildings, manufacturer of "Star-Oak-Harness Leather," 48½" x 36", G.........................$405.00 B

J.S. Brown Mercantile Co. Denver, Colo., sign, advertising on both sides for Mount Cross Coffee, 5½" x 9½", VG.........................$120.00 B

J.T. and Drummond Natural Leaf Chewing Tobacco, ad, paper, litho in wood frame, "Compliments of Drummond Tobacco Co., St. Louis, MO, manufactures of Horse Shoe J.T. and Drummond Natural Leaf Chewing Tobacco, copyright 1894," 28" x 33", 1890s, VG .....................$160.00 B

Jac Jic Soda, sign, metal, double-sided, flange, "Drink Jac Jic," 18" x 14", EX .........................................................$195.00 D

Johnson Outboard Motor, sign, paper on cardboard, "Sea Horse" line, 1954, 42¼" x 25¼", VG, $165.00 B.

Johnson's Log Cabin, store bin, tin litho resembles log cabin, 24" x 18" x 28", EX, $2,750.00 B.

Johnson's Powder Wax, can, wax for dance floors, 14-oz., G, $30.00 D.

Johnston Brokerage Company, knife, celluloid and metal, marked Paducah, KY, on other side of handle, blade marked Murcott Germany, in original box, these long thin bladed knives were often referred to as "Mellon" knives and were used to cut plugs out of watermelons, 4" long closed, NM, $55.00 C.
*Courtesy of B.J. Summers.*

Just Suits Tobacco, lunch pail, metal, with wire bail handle, 8" long, VG, $70.00 B.

**Jack Daniel's Whiskey,** thermometer, wooden, rounded top and square bottom, 22" x 12", VG.................................$75.00 C

**Jack Frost Baking Powder,** tin, paper label of snow and cabin scene, 3" x 5½", EX...............................................$350.00 B

**Jack Frost Sugar Co,** doll, cloth, Jack with blond hair, 17" tall, EX ........................................................................$55.00 D

**Jack Sanitary Barber Shop,** sign, paper, litho, scantily dressed woman, great strong colors, 1890s, 14" x 20", NM ............$325.00 B

**Jackie Coogan Kid Candy,** pail, metal with slip lid, Jackie Coogan, 7 oz, EX ...................................................................$825.00 C

**Jackie Coogan Peanut Butter,** pail, metal with slip lid, Jackie Coogan straight on, 1 lb, VG.............................................$250.00 C

**Jackie Coogan Salted Nut Meats,** container, metal, Jackie on elephant, 11" x 8" dia., EX ....................................................$325.00 C

**Jackson Restaurant China Co.,** salesman's sample plate with the salesman's name C.W. Young incorporated into the message on the plate center with images of various serving pieces around the border, 3¾" dia., VG.....................................................$225.00 C

**Jackson's Best Chewing Tobacco,** sign, paper, 2 men with tobacco plugs and money bag, 11" x 14", EX..................................$950.00 D

**Jackson's Best Chewing Tobacco,** sign, paper, C.A. Jackson & Co., Petersburg, VA, 12" x 14½", EX....................................$100.00 B

**Jackson's Best Chewing Tobacco,** sign, paper, litho, boy sneaking a bite of a chaw, VG........................................................$325.00 C

**Jackson's Best Sweet Navy Chewing Tobacco,** trade card, cardboard, from Petersburg, Va., with old black man, "Tole You Chilon," 1890s, 3¼" x 5", NM.................................................................$55.00 B

**Jacob Hoffman Brewery,** sign, paper, smoking cigar in ashtray, glass of beer and a table of flowers, 1900s, 21" x 31", EX..$135.00 D

**Jacob Hoffman Brewing Co.,** sign, paper, litho, flowers and a glass of the product, J. Ottmann Litho Co. Puck Building, N.Y., 25" x 32", VG ............................................................$100.00 B

**Jacob Ruppert Beer & Ale,** sign, metal, "Famous For Flavor," 1940s, 23½" x 11¾", VG.....................................................$95.00 C

**Jacob Ruppert Beer Ale,** serving tray, metal, litho, two beer mugs with a full head of the product, 14½" x 10¾", 1939, EX ......$85.00 C

**Jacob Ruppert,** serving tray, oval, 1930s, 10¾" x 14½", G .$85.00 C

**Jacob Schmidt Brewing Co.,** sign, metal, factory scene, 40" x 28", VG ......$650.00 C

**Jacobson Bros Ginger Ale,** sign, cardboard, large bottle on red background, "delicious! Try It, Jacobson Bros. Lakewood NJ," 9" x 24", VG ......$35.00 D

**Jacobson Bros Wholesale Liquors,** pocket mirror, metal and glass, child getting ready to be spanked, 1¼" x 2¾", EX ......$300.00 C

**Jake Shaefer Havana Cigars Box,** label, litho proof, billiards scene, 1900s, EX ......$350.00 C

**Jam-Boy Coffee,** tin, litho, pry-type lid, young man at table with cup of product, 1-lb., EX ......$352.00 B

**Jam-Boy Coffee,** tin, screw lid, young boy with toast and jam at breakfast table, from Jameson-Boyce, Binghampton, NY, 1-lb., EX ......$305.00 B

**James Buchanan & Co. Ltd. Scotch Whisky Distillers,** sign, Black & White Scotch Whisky, dogs in field, note spelling of "whisky," 23" x 24½", EX ......$225.00 D

**James Buchanan & Co. Ltd. Scotch Whisky Distillers,** sign, Black & White Scotch Whisky, dogs in field, note spelling of "whisky," 23" x 24½", G ......$125.00 D

**Janney Best Paints,** clock, metal body and reverse glass decaled front, electric, light-up, 15½" sq., EX ......$155.00 C

**Janney Best Paints,** clock, metal, light-up, authorized dealer, paint can, 26" x 18½", VG ......$350.00 B

**Jap Lily Talc,** container, metal with shaker type top, Orential lady on front, VG ......$40.00 D

**Jap Rose Bath Soap,** display, metal, counter display that holds bars of soap, 18" x 14", EX ......$1,000.00 C

**Jap Rose Soap,** thermometer, porcelain, cobalt, "Kirk's...Toilet, Bath, Shampoo," scarce, 1915, EX ......$260.00 B

**Jap Rose Soap,** tip tray, metal, couple of kids bathing a doll, 4¼" dia., EX ......$135.00 C

**Jap Rose Soap,** tip tray, metal, litho, youngsters and Chinese lantern, 4¼" dia., EX ......$190.00 B

**Jap Rose Talcum Powder,** tin, litho, sample size, Japanese girl on front, EX ......$59.00 B

**Japalag Wood Finish,** banner, cloth, The Glidden Varnish Co., 61½" x 24", VG ......$275.00 B

**Japan Air Lines,** hand fan, plastic, paper, and wood, advertising for the airline in both Japanese and English, VG ......$55.00 C

**Japp's Hair Rejuvenator,** sign, metal over cardboard, actual hair samples, 1910s, 13¼" x 9¼", EX ......$175.00 B

**Japp's Hair Rejuvenator,** store card, metal and cardboard, self-framing, 13¼" x 9¼", EX ......$55.00 C

**Javotte Cigars Box,** label, paper, young woman surrounded by florial border, 9" x 6", EX ......$10.00 D

**Jaw Teasers Bubble Gum,** pail with handle, tin, litho, gumball on sides, 5" x 7½", EX ......$54.00 B

**Jaxon Soap,** string holder, cast iron, shape of rendering kettle with hole in bottom, embossed lettering, 4½" x 4½", EX ......$75.00 B

**Jay-Bee's Cigars Box,** label, paper, beehive and a blue jay, 9" x 6", EX ......$20.00 D

**Jayne's Expectorant & Tonic Vermifuge,** sign, paper, John Adams, 14" x 28", EX ......$150.00 D

**Jayne's Hair Tonic,** sign, paper on cardboard, women admiring their hair and product message, 1880s, 12" x 15", EX ......$147.00 B

**Jeep,** sign, metal and glass, light up, "Jeep...Parts-Service," 24" x 19", VG ......$275.00 B

**Jell-O,** recipe book, paper, "Jell-o and The Kewpies," 1915, 5" x 6", VG ......$85.00 D

**Jell-O,** sign, paper, the product dessert mix, 15" x 40¼", EX..$135.00 D

**Jena Glass,** door push plate, porcelain, "The Famous...Quality Imports," 1930 – 40s, 3" x 8", EX ......$195.00 D

**Jenne Lind Cigars,** sign, cardboard, from the National Cigar Co., Bristol, Indiana, center of stamped sign has inside cigar box label, 14½" x 8¼", EX ......$120.00 B

**Jennessy Ginger Ale,** sign, cardboard, 11" x 14", 1940s, EX..$65.00 B

**Jenny Aero,** gas pump sign, porcelain, name in center, blue border, 12" x 9", VG ......$275.00 C

**Jenny Gasoline,** playing cards, linen-finish, early service station and car on each card with original box, full deck, EX ......$130.00 B

**Jenny Super Aero Gasoline,** globe, narrow hull body with two glass lenses, 13½" dia., G ......$575.00 C

**Jergens Crushed Violet Talcum Powder,** tin, litho, flower on front, EX ......$40.00 B

**Jergens Oriental Talc,** container, metal, an Oriental nature, shaker style top, VG ......$115.00 D

**Jergens Violet Miss Dainty Talcum,** tin, Miss Dainty around the label, 2½" x 1¼" x 4½", EX ......$55.00 C

**Jerome B Rice & Co. Garden Seeds,** print, children picking flowers, 1895, 23" x 17", EX ......$225.00 D

**Jerome Flachat Gun Maker's,** sign, paper, early guns, 10½" x 8", EX ......$75.00 D

**Jersey Cream,** dispenser, ceramic, with metal lid and pump, red & green lettering, 11¼" tall, EX.............................$475.00 D

**Jersey Ice Cream,** sign, porcelain, double-sided, sandwich on saucer, 20" x 28", EX.............................$150.00 C

**Jersey Lane Ice Cream,** sign, porcelain, double-sided, hanging, 28" x 20", VG.............................$375.00 C

**Jersey-Creme,** serving tray, pretty young lady, 12" dia., VG ..$155.00 B

**Jersey-Creme,** serving tray, tin, litho, girl in period dress, "At Founts, The Perfect Drink, In Bottles," 12" dia., EX.........$300.00 B

**Jersey-Creme,** serving tray, tin, litho, young lady in pretty hat, 12½" dia., EX.............................$180.00 B

**Jersey-Creme,** sign, cardboard, die cut, string-hung, two girls in swing reading product ad, EX .............................$425.00 C

**Jesse James,** playbill, stone, litho, cowboys, 19" x 29", EX ..$460.00 B

**Jesse James,** poster, paper, litho, "The Sensational Western Life Drama," black couple, 30" x 44", P .....................$225.00 C

**Jesse Oakley's Transparent Toilet Soap,** sign, tin, one-sided, 13¾" x 9¾", EX.............................$80.00 B

**Jetrol 100+ Octane Premium,** pump sign, porcelain, single-sided, Canadian item, 12" sq., VG.............................$225.00 B

**Jewel Coffee,** puzzle, cardboard, with several scenes of manufacturing, to table, 13" x 10", EX.............................$45.00 C

**Jewett White Lead Paint,** calendar, Dutch Boy, 14¾" x 38", 1917, VG ..........................................................................$425.00 C

**Jim Hogg Cigars,** sign, paper, "New Governor Size," with James Stephen Hogg, 20" x 9", NM.............................$30.00 B

**Jim Hogg Cigars,** sign, paper, Governor of Texas, James Stephen Hogg, 20" x 9", EX .............................$50.00 D

**Jimmy Murphy Cigars Box,** label, paper, lithographer's proof of a country scene and Mr. Murphy smoking a cigar, EX ..........$65.00 D

**JJ G Dill's Best Cut Plug,** container, metal, elegant pretty woman in center, 6" x 4", EX.............................$35.00 D

**Jno Gund Brewing Co. Extra Pale,** label, paper, company logo, pre-prohibition item, 1900 – 1920, EX.............................$35.00 D

**Jno T. Barbee and Co.,** sign, tin, litho, beer with log cabin scene, Louisville, Ky., 16½" x 13½", EX.............................$235.00 C

**Joan of Arc Brand Red Kidney Beans,** thermometer, wood, stenciled black lettering on a white background, 15" tall, G ................$55.00 C

**Jockey Cigars,** box label, paper, jockey and horse jumping stream, 4½" x 4½", VG.............................$15.00 D

**Jockey,** display, countertop, composition, for underwear, Coopers, Kenosha, WI, EX.............................$80.00 B

**Joe Anderson Havana Cigars,** match dispenser, "Peace Time," The Universal Match Corporation, with Joe Anderson on front, 9" dia., x 14½", VG.............................$800.00 B

**Joe Lewis World Champion,** clock, electric, molded copper, "United Self Starting," 12" H, EX.............................$500.00 B

**Joe Palooka,** lunch box, 1946, EX.............................$60.00 C

**John Adams Cigars,** label, paper, John Adams along with the Capital and his homestead, 9" x 6", VG.............................$20.00 D

**John Bull Tyres,** sign, porcelain, one-sided, foreign, "made for the man who will have the best," 48" x 15½", VG .............................$300.00 B

**John C. Stocker Brewer,** sign, paper, three women in boat looking for help, 22" x 17", VG.............................$675.00 C

**John D. Jr. Hand Soap,** tin, 3-lb., G .............................$20.00 D

**John Deere Farm Implements,** sign, porcelain, double-sided, hanging, JD logo at center top, 72" x 23¾", EX.............................$950.00 D

**John Deere Quality Farm Impliments,** sign, metal, Deere logo and courtesy panel for dealer, 24" x 12", VG .............................$115.00 C

**John Deere,** calendar, paper, wildlife scene, full monthly pad, 1955, VG.............................$55.00 D

**John Deere,** sign, metal and glass with neon, "Authorized Dealer," tractor, 75" x 37", EX.............................$3,000.00 D

**John Deere,** sign, paper, deer pulling a John Deere buckboard, "Deere vehicles are allright," in original wooden frame, 31½" x 23½", EX .............................$1,610.00 B

**John Deere,** thermometer, metal, 150th Anniversary edition, VG.............................$55.00 D

**John Deere,** tractor, metal, die cast with plastic tires, 8" long, EX.............................$145.00 D

**John Deere,** watch fob, brass, VG.............................$30.00 C

**John Dewar & Sons,** ad, cardboard, Old World scene in original oak frame, 31¼" x 22¼", EX.............................$50.00 C

**John Drew,** sign, tin, litho, man in center, "Berdan the Mark of a Good Cigar," 18½" dia., VG.............................$400.00 B

**John Finzer & Bros Tobacco,** clock, wood, raised lettering, round face with one key wind and glass pendelum door at bottom, 1900 – 1910s, 30½" tall, VG .............................$1,800.00 C

**John Finzer & Bros.,** tobacco cutter, Louisville, Ky., EX .$160.00 D

**John G. Watts,** calendar, meat market from Albion, NY, full calendar pad, women shopping at meat market, 14" x 18", 1900, EX .............................$165.00 B

**John Gessert Shoes,** sign, metal, "tacker" style, man examining vintage shoe, "Rubber & Leather Goods Store," 19¾" x 13½", EX.............................$250.00 C

**John Gund Brewing Co.,** sign, paper, little girl with ribbon in her hair, 20½" x 47", EX .......................................... $400.00 C

**John Hancock Insurance,** calendar, paper, horse drawn carriage, full calendar pages, 1893, 12½" x 16", EX .......................... $65.00 D

**John Hancock Life Insurance Co.,** calendar, girl asleep beside a large dog, 1902, 9½" x 10½", EX ................................. $225.00 D

**John Hauck,** pocket match safe, metal, embossed, 1½" x 3", VG ........................................................... $175.00 C

**John Krider Gun Maker,** trade card, cardboard, resting hunters, 1845, EX ............................................................ $625.00 C

**John M. Miller & Sons Wholesale Confectioners,** countertop store display jar, great paper label of elephant and peanuts for 5¢, 5⅝" x 5⅝" x 9¼", 1915, EX ................................... $120.00 C

**John Milton Cigars,** box label, paper, medieval man, 1908, 9" x 6", VG ........................................................... $45.00 C

**John P Squire & Co.,** puzzle, cardboard, pig diagramed for cuts of meat, 1899, 11" x 7", VG ...................................... $195.00 D

**John Rinchy Wines Liquor & Cigars,** pocket mirror, metal and glass, cancan girl doing a high kick, 2¼" dia., VG ........................... $55.00 C

**John Roots Bitters,** sign, metal, sick man being helped by girl while an angel comes out of a fountain, 1870s, 21½" x 27½", EX ..... $3,300.00 D

**John Ruskin Best and Biggest Cigars,** sign, tin, embossed, cigar, NOS, 29⅝" x 9⅜", NM ...................................... $200.00 C

**John Ruskin Best and Biggest,** sign, tin, single-sided, embossed, 29½" x 9⅜", EX .................................................. $175.00 C

**John Ruskin Cigars,** sign, paperboard, action image of rider reaching for a box of cigars from a running horse, 19" x 26", VG ....... $1,550.00 D

**John Ruskin Cigars,** tin, litho, John Ruskin on front, 3½" x 3½" x 5", EX .............................................................. $155.00 C

**John Ruskin,** sign, tin, single-sided, embossed, "Best and Biggest," lit cigar, 29¾" x 9½", VG ...................................... $155.00 C

**John W Masury & Son Motor Vehicles,** pocket mirror, metal and glass, vintage touring car on reverse side, 3½" dia., EX .... $95.00 D

**John Weisert Tobacco Co.,** box, cardboard, mule on front, St. Louis, U.S.A., EX ........................................................ $20.00 C

**John Wieland's Bock Beer,** label, paper, rams head in center, 1930s, EX ........................................................ $30.00 D

**Johnnie Walker Red,** backbar statue, EX .......................... $135.00 C

**Johnson & Johnson,** decal, molded pressboard, "Baby Needs...," message stenciled and J & J baby in center, 32" x 6", EX .... $50.00 B

**Johnson & Johnson,** sign, cardboard, "For Babies," baby in diaper under moonlit sky with product box, 14½" x 22", G .......... $95.00 D

**Johnson and Melaa's Dry Goods Stoughton, WI,** tip tray, young black child eating watermelon, 2½" x 3¼", EX ................. $165.00 B

**Johnson Bros. Funeral Directors,** thermometer, metal, painted, vertical scale between messages, "Call Our Ambulance Phone 45, Boaz, Ky.," 1910 – 1920s, 8½" x 38½", white on blue, F ..... $85.00 C

**Johnson Halter Store,** sign, papier-maché, horse head with product message embossed in halter, 23" x 21" x 10", EX ..... $425.00 B

**Johnson's Baby Powder,** container, 100th Anniversary edition, 2½" x 5¼", EX ................................................... $10.00 D

**Johnson's Cold Fudge Syrup,** soda fountain jar, 8½" T, 1950s, EX .............................................................. $95.00 C

**Johnson's Factory Seconds,** cigar box, wooden, from the Tunis Johnson Cigar Co., Grand Rapids, Mich., 12" x 4", EX ......... $20.00 D

**Johnson's Log Cabin,** store bin, tin, litho, resembles log cabin, 24" x 18" x 28", VG .................................................... $1,900.00 C

**Johnson's Nuts Vendor,** countertop display unit, porcelain and glass "eat the best," 24" x 14" x 15", EX .................................. $445.00 B

**Johnson's Peacemaker Coffee,** store bin, cardboard, die cut, 13½" x 14", EX .............................................................. $455.00 B

**Johnson's Peacemaker Coffee,** store bin, metal, in form of a cabin with a door that opens to reveal a 1915 calendar, 1915, 27½" x 24" x 18", EX .............................................................. $700.00 D

**Johnson's Wax,** container, metal, pretty woman polishing a table, 1920s, 2½" dia., VG .................................................. $25.00 D

**Johnston Milwaukee, Charm,** box, cardboard, Soda Crackers, 1-lb., EX .............................................................. $25.00 C

**Johnston's Cold Fudge,** display, ceramic with embossed name, 10" x 9" dia., EX .......................................................... $95.00 D

**Johnston's Hot Fudge,** dispenser, aluminum with pottery insert, art deco graphics, 12" x 8½" dia., EX ................................... $150.00 D

**Johnston's Instant Hot Fudge,** soda fountain fixture with hinged lid, lettering on band around center of item, VG .......... $175.00 C

**Jolly Pops,** dispenser, metal, "Those Good Suckers 1¢," sunburst on front, green panel on red background, 9½" x 20", EX .. $105.00 D

**Jolly Pops,** dispenser, metal, painted, two suckers on front, 9½" x 20", VG .............................................................. $125.00 C

**Jolly Roger Hulless Pop Corn,** pail, metal, boy and girl bending over the popping corn, 1 lb, EX ....................................... $95.00 D

**Jolly Roger,** crate label, paper, Florida citrus with a smiling pirate, 9" x 9", EX .............................................................. $5.00 D

**Jones & White Artificial Teeth,** trade card, cardboard, directions of four locations, EX .................................................. $65.00 D

**Jones Dairy Farm Sausage**, sign, tin over cardboard, farm building and snow-covered tree, 12" x 8", EX ....................................$86.00 B

**Jos Doelger's Sons Lager Beer**, sign, metal, die cut gnome with beer stein, 19½" x 28", EX .............................$1,200.00 D

**Jos Grim's Grand Central Hotel**, trade card, cardboard, man's growing beer belly, EX .......................................$45.00 D

**Jos Schlitz Brewing Co.**, tray, metal, factory and inset of Mr. Schlitz, 15" x 18", VG.....................................$95.00 D

**Jos Stoeckle Brewing Co.**, sign, metal, self-framing, two founders, 38" x 25½", EX .............................................$225.00 D

**Jos Suffrin Clothier**, match holder, metal, "Compliments Of..." embossing, 4" x 5½", EX .....................................$175.00 D

**Jos Yund & Son Furniture**, trade card, cardboard, name and images of furniture, EX ........................................$55.00 D

**Joseph Hajicek Hitchinson Brewery**, tray, metal, Grandpa telling a tale, very rare item, 16¾" x 16½", EX ...............$2,500.00 D

**Josephine Baker Follies**, tray, 12" dia., G .........................$500.00B

**Judge Best Cigars**, box, label, paper, old judge with white hair and beard, 9" x 6", EX .................................................$35.00 D

**Juicy Fruit**, match holder, "The Man Juicy Fruit Made Famous," 3¼" x 4¾" x 1¼", EX .........................................$140.00 B

**Juicy Fruit**, match holder, metal, image of the founder, VG..$250.00 D

**Julep**, sign, metal, "Drink Julep, Six Delicious Flavors," 27¼" x 19", EX ...............................................................$125.00 D

**Juliet Perez Cigars**, box label, paper, little girl in pink dress, EX ..........................................................................$10.00 D

**June Kola**, sign, tin, "Now in Quarts...6 Full Glasses," bottle of the product, 23" x 11½", VG ..........................................$75.00 D

**June Kola**, sign, tin, embossed, "Now in quarts...6 full glasses," vertical of bottle, 23" x 35¼", 1953, EX .........................$155.00 B

**June Kola**, sign, tin, single-sided, "Now in quarts...6 full glasses," 23½" x 11½", 1936, VG ......................................$65.00 B

**Junge's Bread**, door push, porcelain, "For Better Health," 4" x 9½", VG ......................................................................$75.00 D

**Junket Pot Scraper**, metal, litho, for Junket dessert powder, 3¼" x 2⅝", EX.........................................................................$135.00 C

**Just Born Nuts Brazil & Almonds**, display case, glass, framed case with original front display papers, 7¼" x 7½" x 11", VG....$175.00 B

**Just Suits Cut Plug Tobacco**, pail, metal, Buchanan & Lyall of New York, N.Y., U.S.A., G .......................................$75.00 D

**Just Suits Cut Plug**, container, metal, company logo, 6" x 4", EX ............................................................................$65.00 D

**Just Suits Tobacco**, lunch pail with wire handle, Buchanan & Lyall, New York, 7¾" x 5" x 4¼", EX............................$175.00 C

**Just the Thing Brand Tobacco**, box, label, paper, older man being handed the product by a young lad, 6" x 12½", EX.................$45.00 D

Kayo, sign, tin, single-sided, embossed, "Tops in Taste," 13⅞" x 27⅜", VG, $230.00 B.

Karo Syrup, sign, paper, Dionne Quintets, VG, $125.00 C.

Keen Kutter Safety Razor, ad, cardboard, man shaving, "Always Ready to Shave, The Razor That Fits the Face," good graphics, 20¾" x 10¾", EX, $75.00 C.

Katter Blox, whiskey bottle, glass with paper label, screw on lid, bottled by Medley Distilling Co., Owensboro, Ky, Bottled Especially for GEO W. KATTERJOHN, Paducah, Ky, 4/5 qt, EX, $100.00 C. *Courtesy of B.J. Summers.*

Kellogg's All-Bran, sign, cloth, roll-down, metal strips at top and bottom, young woman displaying different products on the sign, 10" x 40½", 1920s, VG, $2,300.00 B. *Courtesy of Wm. Morford Investment Grade Collectibles.*

---

Kaffee Hag Coffee, tin, litho, key-wound, unopened, 1-lb., EX $37.00 B

Kaffee Hag Coffee, tin, metal, vaccum packed, key wind lid, unopened, 1 lb, EX ............................................................$37.00 B

Kaffee Hag Coffee, tin, metal, vacuum pack, key-wound lid, 1-lb., G......................................................................................$20.00 D

Kaier's Special Beer, sign, cardboard, die cut, horse, foreign, 19½" x 16½", VG .......................................................................$90.00 B

Kaiser Approved Service, sign, porcelain, double-sided, for dealer use, 57" x 42", VG................................................................$200.00 B

Kamo Peanut Butter, can, metal, with pry lid, duck sitting on a body of water in can center, 1 lb., NM ..........................$2,100.00 B

Kamo Rolled Oats, container, cardboard, paper label, ducks on front, Paxton & Gallagher, Omaha, Nebraska, 3 lb, VG.....$190.00 B

Kanotex, gas globe, wide body with two glass lenses, 13½" dia., VG ..................................................................................$500.00 B

Kansas City Brreweries, pocket mirror, metal and glass, EX.$135.00 D

Kar-A-Van Coffee, can, metal, with pry lid, 1 lb., VG .........$35.00 D

Kar-A-Van Famous Coffee, can, metal, with snap lid, yellow and black, 1 lb., EX ................................................................$145.00 B

KASCO Feeds, scale, metal, debossed "Weight The Milk...Weight The Feed," 5" x 16", EX.....................................................$150.00 C

Kaweah Maid, crate label, paper, California Lemons, pretty Indian maiden, EX................................................................$15.00 D

Kayo, menu board, metal, over writting area "Tops In Taste...Kayo...It's Real Chocolate Flavor" with bottle, 14" x 27", VG ..................................................................................$145.00 D

Kayo, sign, metal, bottle and "Delightful...Refreshing," 4" x 12", VG ..................................................................................$275.00 B

Kellogg's, sign, paper, litho, Kellogg's Corn Flakes, Camp Fire Girl with a bowl of the product 23" x 28", 1920s, EX, $725.00 B.

Kellogg's, Toasted Corn Flakes, sign, cardboard, young girl with box, "Fine With Berries, Peaches or Bananas," 1915, 11" x 20", NM, $550.00 B.

Kellogg's, Toasted Corn Flakes, sign, steel, double-sided, flange, great graphics of small girl in basket, 13½" x 19½", EX, $3,400.00 B. *Courtesy of Richard Opfer Auctioneering, Inc.*

Kelly Tires, sign, metal, painted, flange, Kelly girl waving from older model touring car, 24" dia., VG, $2,200.00 C.

Kendall the 2000 Mile Oil, clock, neon spinner, 20" dia., EX, $1,200.00 C.

---

Kayo, sign, metal, bottle at left of message, "Drink Kayo In Bottles...The Milky Chocolate Malted Drink...When Your Thirsty," 20" x 9", VG ............................................................$175.00 D

Kayo, sign, metal, Kayo running with a bottle of the drink, "Tops In Taste...It's Real Chocolate Flavor," 1930s, 14" x 24", EX ..$200.00 D

Kayo, sign, tin, embossed, Kayo boy holding a large bottle of the product, "Tops In Taste, It's Real Chocolate," 14" x 27⅜", EX.....$175.00 C

Kayo, sign, tin, one sided, Kayo boy with boxing gloves, "K-O your thirst with...," 25" x 9", VG ..............................................$125.00 D

Kayo, sign, tin, single-sided, boy boxer "K-O your thirst with Kayo," 25" x 9", VG.................................................................$145.00 D

KC 25¢ Baking Powder, pocket mirror, metal and glass, with product on back, EX ...............................................................$500.00 B

Keck's Sparkling Beverages, menu board, metal, self-framing, "Enjoy," 17" x 23½", VG .....................................................$75.00 B

Keen Kutter E.C. Simmons Cutlery Tools, sign, cardboard, in shape of KK logo, 10¼" x 13", NM ........................................$35.00 C

Keen Kutter E.C. Simmons Cutlery, Tools, sign, cardboard, die cut, in shape of Keen Kutter logo, 10¼" x 13", EX .....................................$35.00 C

Keen Kutter Tools, sign, tin, embossed but with an unusual look, instead of the usual dealer banner this one has crossed saw and axe image, 21" x 7½", EX.................................................. $195.00 D

Keen Kutter Tools, sign, tin, embossed, "Hank Bros, Paducah, KY.," 27" x 10", EX .................................................................$125.00 C

Ken-L Ration Meal Biskit, door push, tin, super strong colors, dog licking his chops, 1950s, EX, $325.00 B.

Kenny's Maid Coffee, can, metal, Dutch maid on front, 4 lbs., VG, $200.00 B.

Kenny Teas Coffees, tip tray, metal, pretty red headed woman in center, 4" dia., VG, $180.00 B.

Kentucky's Pride Tobacco for pipe or cigarette, bag, cloth, paper label with tobacco plant, from the National Tobacco Co., Paducah, KY, never opened, 2½" x 4¼" x 1½", VG, $25.00 C. *Courtesy of B.J. Summers.*

Kentucky Power Co., sign, porcelain, one-sided, Redi-Kilowatt, 48" x 36", G, $230.00 B.

**Keen Kutter**, calendar, cardboard and paper, die cut in shape of axe with mountain scene, dealer information panel, 1935, 12" x 16½", NM ................................................................**$95.00 C**

**Keen Kutter**, calendar, cardboard, die cut, axe head with two sitters at work in the field, 1935, 12" x 17", EX.........................................**$150.00 D**

**Keen Kutter**, calendar, cardboard, with full monthly pad, top of calendar has scene of a cabin in the winter, and partially framed by a pair of Keen Kutter scissors, 1940, 10" x 17", EX ...............**$75.00 D**

**Keen Kutter**, calendar, die cut, axe head with mountain stream, 12" x 16½", 1935, NM .....................................................**$95.00 C**

**Keen Kutter**, calendar, paper and cardboard, die cut, axe, bottom tear sheets present, dealer information panel, 1935, 12" x 16½", EX...............................................................................**$95.00 D**

**Keen Kutter**, display case, wood, hinged lid, containing some original flatware, EX...............................................................**$125.00 D**

**Keen Kutter**, sign, cardboard, "Always ready to shave, the razor that knows the face," man shaving, 20¾" x 10¾", VG ... **$70.00 C**

**Keen Kutter**, sign, cardboard, man shaving at sink, "Keen Kutter Safety Razor," 20¾" x 10¾", VG .........................................**$65.00 C**

**Keen Kutter**, sign, cardboard, various products, 10¼" x 13", EX.**$75.00 C**

**Keen Kutter**, sign, tin, embossed, unusual configuration with the saw and axe, "Keen Kutter Tools," 21" x 7½", NM..........**$225.00 C**

**Kellogg Iron Works**, calendar, cardboard and paper, stand up features, 12" x 8", EX .............................................................**$150.00 C**

**Kellogg's All-Bran**, sign, cloth, roll-down, metal strips at top and bottom, young woman displaying different products on the sign, 10" x 40½", 1920s, F ............................................................**$895.00 D**

Kentucky Wagon Mfg Co., sign, tin, litho, by Chas Shonk, factory and grounds, 31" x 12", EX, $475.00 B.

Kerr-View's Milk, sign, porcelain, bottle-shaped, "From our own herd," 19" x 48", G, $1,850.00 D. *Courtesy of Riverview Antique Mall.*

King Midas, string holder, tin, litho, general store advertising "King Midas...The Highest Priced Flour in America," 15" x 19¾", EX, $2,000.00 B. *Courtesy of Wm. Morford Investment Grade Collectibles.*

Kingan's Reliable, sign, cardboard, original wood frame, with sailor at the wheel of a ship in a storm, 17" x 27", G, $250.00 C.

King Cole Tea & Coffee, door push, porcelain, used in the days of screen doors to help save the screens, 1940s, 3" x 11", EX, $150.00 B.

King's Pure Malt, tip tray, metal, Panama and Pacific Exposition awards, 6" long, EX, $160.00 B.

Kellogg's Cereal, box, cardboard, Corn Flakes, war time period with three fighter planes, "let's go USA keep 'em flying," 1940s, 11 oz., EX ....................................................$110.00 B

Kellogg's Cereal, box, cardboard, Corn Flakes, war-time with small identification of three fighter planes, "let's go USA keep 'em flying," 1940s, 11-oz., EX ............................................. $95.00 D

Kellogg's Cereal, box, cardboard, Rice Krispies, featuring all three Snap, Crackle, and Pop, 1948, 5½ oz., EX..........................$65.00 C

Kellogg's Cereal, box, cardboard, Rice Krispies, with three Krispie creatures, 1948, 5½ oz., EX............................................. $50.00 B

Kellogg's Cereal, display, aluminum, countertop unit for individual cereal boxes, 20½" x 27" x 6", EX ...................$395.00 C

Kellogg's Corn Flakes, sign, cardboard, trifold window display, 1917, 12" x 39½" each, EX...............................................$450.00 C

Kellogg's Corn Flakes, sign, paper, litho, Camp fire Girl with a bowl of cereal, 1920s, 23" x 28", VG..........................................$575.00 C

Kellogg's Corn Flakes, sign, paper, litho, three-piece window display shows two women in a cornfield and a product writer with "Kellogg's, The original toasted corn flakes," 12" x 39½" each, 1917, VG .......................................................................................$435.00 B

Kellogg's Corn Flakes, sign, paper, litho, woman by lake with a bowl of cereal, 23" x 28", EX.................................$1,200.00 C

Kellogg's Corn Flakes, watch fob, metal, shaped like a cereal box, 1¼" x 1½", EX................................................................. $60.00 B

**Kirkman's Borax Soap,** match holder, tin, litho, die cut, woman doing wash in wooden tub, 7" H, NM, $5,700.00 B. *Courtesy of Richard Opfer Auctioneering, Inc.*

**Kirchhoff's Bread,** door push, heavy metal, adjustable, used on screen doors before the days of air conditioning, G, $95.00 C.

**"Kis-Me,"** sign, cardboard, die cut, easel back, embossed, Kis-Me Chewing Gum, hard to find, 6½" x 10½", EX, $1,550.00 B. *Courtesy of Wm. Morford Investment Grade Collectibles.*

**Kist Beverage,** sign, paper, litho, pretty girl with product bottle, 13½" x 17½", VG, $225.00 C.

**Knox Sparkling Gelatine,** sign, carboard, litho, die cut, children standing on slanted platform and holding a plate of gelatin, with trademark cow, 14" x 10" x 16", EX, $3,500.00 D. *Courtesy of Collectors Auction Services.*

**Kodak,** display, cardboard, life-size, die-cut of pretty woman, "Stop Here for...Kodak Verichrome Film," 21" x 64", G, $125.00 C.

---

**Kellogg's Corn Flakes,** watch fob, metal, shaped like a cereal box, 1¼" x 1½", EX........................$65.00 C

**Kellogg's Kaffee Hag Coffee,** can, metal, with key wind lid, "97% of the caffeine removed," 1 lb, VG........................$35.00 D

**Kellogg's puzzle,** framed and matted, young boy on scooter with running dog, 6" x 8", EX........................$85.00 C

**Kellogg's Supreme Quality Coffee,** tin, litho, key-wound, 1-lb., EX........................$28.00 B

**Kellogg's Toasted Corn Flakes,** sign, cardboard, "...Fine with Berries, Peaches or Bananas," young girl with box, 1915, 11" x 20", EX........................$475.00 C

**Kellogg's Toasted Corn Flakes,** sign, cardboard, "Fine With Berries, Peaches or Bananas," young girl with box, 1915, 11" x 20", VG..$300.00 C

**Kellogg's Toasted Corn Flakes,** sign, cardboard, hanging, "A Hit and A Miss," girl eating cereal, Look for this Signature, W.K. Kellogg, 1915, 10½" x 15½", G........................$250.00 B

**Kellogg's Toasted Corn Flakes,** sign, cardboard, hanging, "A Hit and A Miss," girl eating cereal, Look for this Signature, W.K. Kellogg, 1915, 10½" x 15½", NM........................$500.00 C

**Kellogg's Toasted Corn Flakes,** sign, steel, double-sided, flange, small girl in basket, 13½" x 19½", G........................$1,200.00 C

Kodak, sign, porcelain, die cut triangle with film box at bottom, "Developing, Printing, Enlarging," 1930s, 16" x 17", 1930s, VG, $525.00 C.

Koken Shop, sign, porcelain, advertising barber shop, originally held light bulbs on the outside of rare find, 31" dia., G, $1,800.00 B.

Kools, clock, metal and glass, electric, light up, by Pam Clock, with Chilly Willy, 1950s, VG, $525.00 B.

Kotex, countertop display, litho, nurse on both ends holding product package, 8½" x 13½" x 14", VG, $335.00 C.

Kreso Dip No. 1, sign, tin, litho, different animals and the medicines for each, Parke, Davis & Co., 28" x 18", EX, $1,350.00 B. *Courtesy of Wm. Morford Investment Grade Collectibles.*

Kuhn's Climatized Paints, sign, porcelain, die cut, double-sided, raccoon on limb with can of the product, 18" x 24", NM, $1,500.00 C. *Courtesy of Autopia Advertising Auctions.*

Kellogg's, blotter, cardboard, "Toasted Corn Flakes...," 6" x 3", EX......................................................................$35.00 D

Kellogg's, cereal box, cardboard, All Bran, 1952, EX..........$20.00 C

Kellogg's, cereal box, cardboard, Cocoa Krispies, Snagglepuss on front, 1963, NM ..............................................................$375.00 D

Kellogg's, cereal box, cardboard, Corn Flakes, contest to Win A Pair of Fords with Huckleberrt Hound, 1960, EX.......................$75.00 C

Kellogg's, cereal box, cardboard, Corn Flakes, funny face mask cut out on back, 18 oz., EX ......................................................$75.00 C

Kellogg's, cereal box, cardboard, Corn Flakes, W K Kellogg signature the first wax tight box with inner seal, 8 oz., EX .......$185.00 D

Kellogg's, cereal box, cardboard, Corn Flakes, Yogi Bear, unopened, 1962, EX...............................................................................$350.00 C

Kellogg's, cereal box, cardboard, Frosted Flakes, Tony the Tiger, for the Canadian market, 1966, EX........................................$275.00 D

Kellogg's, cereal box, cardboard, Frosted Flakes, Tony's mug, spoon & bowl deal on side of package, EX......................................$85.00 D

Kellogg's, cereal box, cardboard, Fruity Pebbles, offer to purchase a pencil holder, 1974, EX ......................................................$75.00 D

Kellogg's, cereal box, cardboard, Pep, man in ball cap, 1963, 1 oz., EX..........................................................................................$35.00 D

**Kellogg's,** cereal box, cardboard, Raisin Bran, offer for space age Sonic Gun, 1960, EX........................................$75.00 D

**Kellogg's,** cereal box, cardboard, Rice Krispies, a treasure hunt with Dennis the Menace, 1960, VG........................$35.00 D

**Kellogg's,** cereal box, cardboard, Rice Krispies, bike contest featuring Woody Woodypecker, 1960, VG ....................$55.00 D

**Kellogg's,** cereal box, cardboard, Rice Krispies, early Snap, Crackle, and Pop, 1948, 5½ oz, VG...........................$65.00 D

**Kellogg's,** cereal box, cardboard, Rice Krispies, offer for squeeze toys of Snap, Crackle, and Pop, 1976, EX...........$50.00 D

**Kellogg's,** cereal box, cardboard, Sugar Pops, Jingles and his horse with a free giveaway of pilots' wings inside the box, 8 oz., EX........$100.00 D

**Kellogg's,** cereal box, cardboard, Sugar Smacks, Quick Draw McGraw Road eace game on back, 1964, EX....................$375.00 D

**Kellogg's,** cereal box, cardboard, Toasted Corn Flakes, W K Kellogg signature and dated, 1915, 8 oz., EX .................$325.00 C

**Kellogg's,** decoder, plastic, "Dig'em" in green, 1985, EX.....$15.00 D

**Kellogg's,** doll, soft squeeze vinyl, Pop, 1978, EX.....................$40.00 D

**Kellogg's,** doll, vinyl, Fruit Loops Toucan Sam, NRFB, 1984, 6¼", NM ....................................................$75.00 D

**Kellogg's,** doll, vinyl, set of Snap Crackle and Pop, NRFB, 1984, 6¼ tall, NM....................................................$200.00 C

**Kellogg's,** jigsaw puzzle, cardboard, "keep going with KELLOGG'S" and boy throwing a baseball, NOS, 6" x 8", M....$90.00 C

**Kellogg's,** jigsaw puzzle, cardboard, boy throwing a baseball, 6" x 8", EX..................................................$75.00 C

**Kellogg's,** jigsaw puzzle, cardboard, boy throwing a baseball, NOS, 6" x 8", NM..........................................$100.00 C

**Kellogg's,** paper doll, "Daddy Bear" holding a cereal box, 1925, NM ..........................................................$95.00 C

**Kellogg's,** paper doll, "Daddy Bear" holding cereal box, uncut, 1925, NM..........................................................$82.00 B

**Kellogg's,** patch, cloth, Snap, Crackle, and Pop, glow in the dark iron on, 1974, NM ....................................$15.00 D

**Kellogg's,** patch, cloth, Tony the Tiger, glow in the dark iron on, 1974, 2" dia, NM..........................................$15.00 D

**Kellogg's,** sign, canvas, "Toasted Corn Flakes," 19" x 29", VG .$210.00 D

**Kellogg's,** sign, cardboard, designed for counter top or point of sale use, die cut, pretty young lady in bonnet with a box of the cereal and a bowl that's full, 1948, EX .......................$195.00 D

**Kellogg's,** sign, cardboard, die cut, image of kids on bicycles, "I Go For Kellogg's Corn Flakes," 37" tall, VG....................$475.00 D

**Kellogg's,** sign, cardboard, Toasted Corn Flakes, small girl fixing a bowl on top of a product box, "Fine With Berries...," 1915, 11" x 20", EX....................................................$600.00 D

**Kellogg's,** sign, paper, litho, Kellogg's Corn Flakes, Camp Fire Girl with a bowl of the product, 23" x 28", 1920s, G ............. $300.00 C

**Kellogg's,** sign, paper, litho, Kellogg's Corn Flakes, young woman by lake and a bowl of cereal, 23" x 28", EX ............................. $1,150.00 B

**Kellogg's,** watch fob, brass, box of Toasted Corn Flakes and W K Kellogg signature, hard to find item, VG..........................$175.00 C

**Kelly Builds Quality, Quality Builds Kelly,** sign, metal, single-sided, 8" H, G..............................................................$315.00 B

**Kelly Springfield Tires,** sign, cardboard, die cut, lady and her dog watching her service station attendant, 1920s, 26" x 33", EX............$475.00 D

**Kelly Springfield Tires,** trade card, cardboard, "The Only Complaints About...Are Their Scarcity," Lotta Miles framed by tire, 2" x 4", EX ..........................................................$30.00 D

**Kelly Tires,** sign, metal, double-sided, flange, waving Kelly girl, 24" dia, EX..........................................................$1,850.00 C

**Kelly Tires,** sign, metal, painted, flange, Kelly girl waving from older model touring car, 24" dia., G ........................................ $900.00 C

**Kemp's Balsam,** sign, cardboard, octagonal, hanger, self-framing, bottle in the center, double-sided, 11" x 11", VG .............$75.00 C

**Kemps Nuts,** dispenser, glass and metal, designed to be used as a counter top unit, rotates to keep the product warm, 32" x 21½" x 21", EX ..........................................................$100.00 C

**Ken-L-Ration Dog Food,** sign, tin, die cut, dog "lickin his chops," 14" x 21", EX ....................................................$95.00 C

**Ken-L-Ration Dog Food,** sign, tin, die cut, dog "lickin his chops," 14" x 21", NM....................................................$125.00 C

**Ken-L-Ration,** thermometer, metal, scale type, can and "For best Results! Feed Your Dog Ken-L-Ration," to left of scale, rounded corners, 7" x 27", EX ....................................................$145.00 D

**Kendal Motor Oil,** clock, metal and glass, checkered flag and Kendall GT-1 Racing on clock face, EX ............................$165.00 C

**Kendall De-Luxe,** gas globe, plastic and glass, 13½" dia, VG .$395.00 C

**Kendall De-Luxe,** gas globe, plastic body with two glass lenses, 13½" dia., VG ....................................................$350.00 B

**Kendall Motor Oil,** clock, metal and glass light up, logo and derrick in center of clock face, 1960s, 18" dia, EX ......................$175.00 D

**Kendall Motor Oil,** license plate attachment, metal, small salesman sample, rare with company logo, 3" x 6", EX ....................$135.00 C

**Kendall Motor Oil,** sign, metal, vertical message with logo at top, "The Dealer Sign of Quality," G........................................$115.00 C

**Kendall Motor Oil**, sign, metal, vertical, oil can at bottom, 12" x 72", VG .................................................................$950.00 B

**Kendall Motor Oil**, thermometer, metal, dial type, familiar red two finger logo, "Kendall The 2000 Mile Oil," 12" dia, EX.......$185.00 C

**Kendall Motor Oils**, clock, plastic, electric light up, 10½" dia, EX..................................................................$210.00 C

**Kendall Motor Oils**, clock, plastic, fired-on lettering, light-up, 10½" dia., EX................................................ $195.00 B

**Kendall Motor Oils**, sign, metal, double-sided, NOS, 23¾" dia, EX.................................................................$125.00 C

**Kendall Motor Oils**, sign, metal, painted, double-sided, NOS, 23¾" dia., EX................................................ $110.00 B

**Kendall Motor Oils**, sign, metal, vertical, embossed, painted, with logo at top of message, "The Dealer Sign of Quality," G......$95.00 C

**Kendall Outboard Motor Oil**, sign, metal, double-sided, flange, 18" x 13", EX................................................$295.00 C

**Kendall Outboard Motor Oil**, sign, tin, double-sided, flange, 18" x 13", EX ................................................ $275.00 C

**Kendall**, sign, porcelain, "Kendall The 2000 Motor Oil" in curved can shaped, 19" x 30", EX ...................$1,700.00 C

**Kendall**, sign, tin, self-framing, vertical, bottom insert of oil can in hand, 12" x 72", VG .................................................$950.00 B

**Kenny's Maid Coffee**, tin pail, with wire handle, C.D. Kenny Co., Baltimore, MD, 7½" x 8", 4-lb., EX.................................. $525.00 C

**Kenny's Teas & Coffees**, tip tray, metal, litho, three "no evil" monkeys, 4¼" dia, VG .................................................$240.00 B

**Kenny's Teas & Coffees**, tip tray, metal, three "no evil" monkies, 4½" dia, EX...........................................$250.00 C

**Kenny's Teas & Coffees**, tip tray, tin, litho, pretty girl, 4½" dia, EX.................................................$175.00 C

**Kenny's Teas & Coffees**, tip tray, tin, litho, pretty young woman, 4¼" dia., EX ................................................. $160.00 B

**Kent Cigarettes**, sign, metal, painted, 30" x 12", EX...........$20.00 C

**Kent Cigarettes**, sign, tin, painted, 30" x 12", EX.................. $15.00 D

**Kentucky Cardinal**, 1¢ match dispenser, paper label, two birds, in working order, 6" x 13" x 5", EX...........................................$375.00 D

**Kentucky Cardinal**, crate label, paper, red bird sitting on a branch, VG .................................................................$35.00 D

**Kentucky Cardinal**, match dispenser, metal, paper label, two birds, ¢1 drop, 6" x 13" x 5", EX...........................................$400.00 C

**Kentucky Club Tobacco**, thermometer, metal "For Real Pipe Smoking Enjoyment," EX ........................................................$145.00 D

**Kentucky Club Tobacco**, tin, pipe and cigarette cut, EX ....$20.00 C

**Kentucky Club Tobacco**, tin, pipe and cigarette, G............$15.00 D

**Kentucky Fried Chicken**, bank, plastic, Colonel Sanders, 10" tall, EX...............................................................$65.00 D

**Kentucky Fried Chicken**, sign, molded plastic, the Colonel, 32½" x 36", F ..................................................................$50.00 B

**Kern's Bread**, door push, porcelain, "Take Home...Bread," 27" x 3", NM ..................................................................$195.00 C

**Kern's Bread**, door push, porcelain, "Take Home...," 27" x 3", EX....................................................................$175.00 C

**Kern's Bread**, thermometer, tin, litho, "Take it Home," 5¾" x 13½", VG .................................................. $100.00 B

**Kern's Bread**, thermometer, tin, litho, "Take it Home," 5¾" x 13½", EX.......................................................$115.00 C

**Kerr's Hotcake Flour**, container, cardboard, red sailing ship in center, 2 lb 8 oz, EX ...................................................$125.00 C

**Kerr-View's Milk**, sign, porcelain, die cut, bottle shape, "From Our Own Herd," 19" x 48", EX...............................................$2,100.00 C

**Kessler Brewery**, sign, metal, the US Gunboat Helena, 26" x 20", VG ................................................................$750.00 C

**Kessler Whiskey**, back bar statue, rubber, football, 18" x 46", VG................................................................$365.00 C

**Kessler Whiskey**, display figure, composition, football, 46" long, EX ................................................................$950.00 D

**Key West Extras**, cigar box label, paper, cigar production, 4½" x 4½", EX ................................................................$50.00 D

**Key West Havanas**, cigar box label, with company image, EX..$125.00 C

**Keystone Agricultural Implements**, trade card, cardboard, Uncle Sam showing people of all nations our products, 6" x 4", EX.........$135.00 C

**Keystone Ice Cream**, sign, porcelain, company logo in center, 28" x 20", EX ..................................................................$225.00 C

**Keystone Ice Cream**, sign, porcelain, original iron hanger, logo in center, 28" x 20", EX.......................................... $225.00 D

**Keystone Ice Cream**, sign, porcelain, outdoor hanging on original metal arm, 28" x 20", EX................................................$165.00 C

**Keystone Powerfuel Ethyl**, pump sign, porcelain, 12" x 14", EX.......................................................... $275.00 B

**Keystone Powerfuel Ethyl**, pump sign, porcelain, 12" x 14", EX..................................................................$295.00 C

**Keystone Powerfuel**, pump sign, porcelain, "More Power To You," 1920s, 12" x 14", VG .....................................................$325.00 C

**Keystone Varnishing,** sign, tin, die cut, child in rain coat, 1890s, 8" x 14", EX ........................................................................$295.00 D

**Kickapoo Joy Juice,** bottle carrier, cardboard, Lil Abner and Dog Patch characters, with full 10 oz bottles, 1965, VG ..........$145.00 D

**Kim-Bo Tobacco,** container, cardboard, pocket size, pretty young maiden on front, EX.....................................................$275.00 C

**Kinfsley Harness Co.,** calendar, cardboard, die cut, girl in bonnet and vintage dress, 1900, 8" x 9", EX ............................$225.00 D

**King Arthur Flour,** container, King Arthur in armor on horseback, 10" x 21", G..........................................................$97.00 B

**King Arthur Flour,** container, King Arthur on horseback, 10" x 21", VG .......................................................................$100.00 C

**King Arthur Flour,** sign, porcelain, King Arthur on his horse, double-sided, 17⅞" x 17⅞", EX..............................$1,100.00 C

**King Arthur Flour,** sign, porcelain, king on horse back, 40" x 36", EX...........................................................................$225.00 C

**King Coal,** cigar box label, paper, miners in tunnel, 9" x 6", EX.$45.00 D

**King Cole Coffee,** thermometer, metal, scale with working tube, 5" x 17", VG ......................................................................$40.00 C

**King Cole Coffee,** tin, litho, King Arthur holding up a cup, pry lid, 1 lb., EX....................................................................$500.00 C

**King Cole Coffee,** tin, litho, pry-lid, king holding cup of product, 1-lb., EX..................................................................... $484.00 B

**King Cole Tea & Coffee,** door plate, porcelain, company lettering only, rounded ends, Canadian, 3" x 14", EX ....................$150.00 D

**King Cole Tea, Coffee,** door push, porcelain, 31½" x 3", VG .$135.00 C

**King Edward Smoking Tobacco,** pocket tin, metal, vertical, EX ...........................................................................$900.00 D

**King George Cross Cut,** pocket tin, metal, vertical, VG ...$575.00 C

**King Koal Stripped Tobacco,** lunch box, metal, oval logo KK, EX ...................................................................................$40.00 D

**King Midas Flour,** pot scraper, tin, litho, small girl in bonnet, "the highest priced flour in America and worth all it costs," 2⅞" x 3⅝", EX ............................................................... $135.00 D

**King Midas Flour,** scoop, tin, litho, 1¾" x 4", VG.................$150.00 B

**King Midas Flour,** string holder, tin, litho, "The Highest Priced Flour in America," 15" x 19¾", VG.................................$1,100.00 C

**King Midas Tobacco,** can, metal, curved corners, vertical, EX ..$95.00 D

**King Midas,** string holder, tin, litho, general store advertising "King Midas...The Highest Priced Flour in America," 15" x 19¾", G. $1,000.00 D

**King Mogul Coffee,** can, metal with key wind top, 3 lb., EX..$60.00 D

**King Othon Coffee,** can, metal with paper label, king in center oval, 1 lb., EX..........................................................................$65.00 D

**King Polly,** cigar box, cardboard, with bird and "A Cigar That Talks For Itself," EX..............................................................$95.00 C

**King Tut,** crate label, paper, California lemons, with lemons and lemonade, VG.........................................................................$12.00 D

**King's Castle Flour,** sample bag, paper, small village on front, 3¼" x 5", EX..................................................................................$40.00 C

**King's Castle Flour,** sample bag, small village, 3¼" x 5", EX........ $35.00 D

**King's Court Beverage,** sign, cardboard, bottle, 14" x 45", 1940s, VG ..........................................................................$70.00 B

**King's Court Beverage,** sign, cardboard, bottle, 1940s, 14" x 45", VG ..........................................................................$75.00 C

**King's Herald 5¢ Cigar,** store bin, metal, for use on store counter, 20" x 15", VG...................................................................$550.00 D

**King's Peanut Butter,** pail, tin, litho, King Arthur holding the product, 1 lb., EX.........................................................$795.00 C

**King's Puremalt,** tip tray, bottle in center, "good, for insomnia...strengthening...heathful," 6⅛" L, EX ............ $120.00 B

**King's Puremalt,** tip tray, metal, bottle in center, 6⅛" long, VG .$125.00 C

**Kingan's Butterine,** sign, tin, litho, man being served product with meal, 1920s, EX.................................................... $33.00 B

**Kingan's Butterine,** sign, tin, man being served product with meal, 1920s, EX..........................................................................$40.00 C

**Kingman's Meat Proof,** sign, paper, litho, meat products, 42" x 28", EX..................................................................................$100.00 C

**Kings Peanut Butter,** pail, tin, litho, king with product in hand, 1-lb., EX.................................................................... $786.00 B

**Kingsbury Pale Beer,** sign, tin, embossed, bottle at left of message panel, 27½" x 19½", VG ...................................................$145.00 C

**Kingsbury Pale Beer,** sign, tin, embossed, bottle of beer, 27½" x 19½", G...........................................................................$130.00 B

**Kips Bay Pure Ales and Lager Beer,** sign, porcelain, one-sided, 28" x 20¼", VG..........................................................................$380.00 B

**Kirchhoff's Bread,** door push, metal, heavy and adjustable, used on screen doors before the days of air conditioning, EX ........$135.00 C

**Kirk's Flake Soap,** door plate, porcelain, "Come In For Kirk's Flake Soap," 4" x 9", EX.........................................................$325.00 B

**Kirk's Pancake Flour,** sign, tin, embossed, chef carrying tray, 1930s, 20" x 14", VG .........................................................$265.00 C

**Kirkman's Borax Soap,** match holder, tin litho, die cut, woman doing washing on washboard, 7" tall, G .........................$1,850.00 D

**Kirkman's Floating Soap,** sign, cardboard, for trolley car use with bar of soap and message, 21" x 11", EX............................$155.00 C

**Kis-Me Gum,** fan, cardboard, litho, by Feigenspan & Co., 10" dia, EX.....................................................................$500.00 C

**Kis-Me Gum,** fan, folding, litho, by Feigenspan & Co., 10" dia., EX................................................................. $475.00 B

**Kis-Me Gum,** jar, glass, embossed lettering, square with beveled edges, 11" tall, EX ........................................$175.00 D

**Kis-Me Gum,** sign, cardboard, die cut, easel back, embossed, hard to find, 6½" x 10½", VG..................................... $1,050.00 C

**Kis-Me Gum,** sign, cardboard, die cut, Yellow Kid walking while holding a leather satchel with product name on side of case, 3" x 6½", EX..................................................... $925.00 B

**Kis-Me Gum,** sign, cardboard, waist length stand up of woman in boa and hat, 1890s, 7" x 11", EX.........................$275.00 D

**Kis-Me Gum,** sign, cardboard, Yellow Kid walking with a leather satchel, 3" x 6½", EX ........................................$950.00 C

**Kis-Me,** sign, cardboard, "Kis-Me" gum, easel back, 6½" x 10½", EX.............................................................$1,600.00 C

**Kiss Beverages,** sign, paper, close up of pin up girl in black dress, 14" x 18", EX ..............................................$65.00 D

**Kissel's Garage,** calendar, paper, "towing and lifting capacity 25 tons," 16¾" x 21¼", VG....................................$65.00 C

**Kissel's Garage,** calendar, paper, vintage wrecker on front that boasts of "towing and lifting capacity 25 tons," 16¾" x 21¼", VG ....$55.00 B

**Kist Beverages,** menu board, tin, litho, message panel at top, 8¾" x 19½", VG ..........................................$75.00 C

**Kist Beverages,** sign, cardboard and tin, bottle, 6" x 13¼", EX.$230.00 C

**Kist Beverages,** sign, cardboard, die cut, pretty woman with bottle, VG ............................................................$165.00 C

**Kist Beverages,** sign, cardboard, woman at ship's wheel, 13" x 18¼", EX.............................................................$295.00 C

**Kist Beverages,** sign, metal, die cut, bottle cap shape, 1959, 15" dia, EX............................................................$195.00 D

**Kist Beverages,** sign, metal, double-sided, "Enjoy," 21¾" x 17½", EX ..........................................................$300.00 C

**Kist Beverages,** sign, porcelain, "Drink" over red lips lettered Kist, 23" x 17", EX .............................................$345.00 D

**Kist Beverages,** sign, store countertop, woman at ship's wheel, 13" x 18½", EX......................................................... $275.00 B

**Kist Beverages,** sign, tin over cardboard, embossed and flat, bottle, and "Drink," 6" x 13¼", NM ..................................$225.00 C

**Kist Beverages,** sign, tin, bottle cap shaped, orange, 1940 – 50s, 48" dia, EX............................................................$450.00 D

**Kist Beverages,** sign, tin, double-sided, flange, 22" x 17½", EX. $225.00 B

**Kist Beverages,** sign, tin, double-sided, flange, 22" x 17½", EX.$235.00 C

**Kist Beverages,** sign, tin, embossed bottle cap design, 1959, 14¾" dia, VG ............................................................$175.00 C

**Kist Root Beer,** sign, cardboard, single-sided, bottle, G......$35.00 C

**Kist,** menu board, tin, self-framing, litho, message at top and menu lines below, 8¾" x 19½", EX............................... $65.00 B

**Kist,** sign, cardboard, die cut, dimensional, pretty woman with bottle, "Orange and Other Flavors," easel back, 12" x 9" x 5", NM ......$155.00 C

**Kist,** sign, tin, embossed, bottle cap, "The Drinks With Real Flavor," 14¾" dia., 1959, EX .............................................. $170.00 B

**Kleinert's Dress Shield Guimpe,** pocket mirror, product on back side, 2" dia., EX.................................................. $44.00 B

**Klondike Fizz,** sign and matching trade card, paperboard, man and dog sled at North Pole, 10½" x 7", 1890s, EX..................... $155.00 B

**Klondike,** cigar box label, paper, two men panning for gold, EX..............................................................$275.00 C

**Klong's Pros't,** tray, metal, tip size, "In Kegs & Bottles," deep lip, 4" dia, VG ............................................................$125.00 C

**Knapsack Matches,** dispenser, wood, metal and glass, one-cent, tin box, 10" x 10½", EX............................................. $675.00 C

**Knapsack Matches,** vendor, wooden, octagonal with lettered glass panels, 1892, 11" tall, VG ...............................$650.00 D

**Knickerbocker Beer,** tray, metal, tip size, lettered "The Beer Drinker's Beer," profile of colonial man, VG ....................$75.00 D

**Knight of Pythias,** cigar box label, paper, knights helping knights, 4½" x 4½", EX..........................................................$45.00 C

**Knox Gelatin,** box, cardboard, trademark cow, from the "Charles B. Knox Gelatine Co., Inc, Johnstown, N.Y., Camden N.J., U.S.A.," 3½" x 2¾" x 5", VG.................................................$100.00 B

**Knox Gelatin,** display, cardboard, die cut, litho, with advertising on all four sides, with children holding product and cow in center at top, hard-to-find item, 14" x 10" x 16", G........................ $750.00 B

**Knox Gelatin,** sign, canvas, girl putting strawberries on dessert, 1901, 27" x 20", VG.................................................$250.00 D

**Knox Gelatin,** sign, canvas, litho, little girl with mammy, 1901, 29¾" x 22¾", VG .................................................$2,000.00 B

**Knox Gelatin,** sign, canvas, litho, nanny and young girl working on a dessert, 20" x 16", EX ...................................... $430.00 B

**Knox Gelatin,** sign, litho, great detail, older black woman with young girl working on dessert at table, double matted and framed, 1901, 26" x 20", NM......................................................$1,250.00 B

**Knox Gelatin,** slanted platform, cardboard, die cut, litho, children standing with trademark cow and holding a plate of gelatin, 14" x 10" x 16", G ...................................................... $900.00 D

**Knox Sparkling Gelatine,** sign, cardboard, pyramid shaped, die cut, black and white girls and a cow's head at top, 10" x 15" x 16", VG......................................................$2,200.00 D

**Kochenderfer Oil Co Motor Oil,** can, metal, screw on lid, oval image of #8 race car, 1/2 gal., EX......................................$450.00 D

**Kodak All Supplies,** sign, porcelain, round, 20" dia., EX . $475.00 C

**Kodak Film,** sign, metal, shape of film box, 1915, 7" x 17", VG.$275.00 C

**Kodak Film,** sign, porcelain, die cut, triangle shape, double-sided, film box, 23" x 26", EX ......................................................$700.00 B

**Kodak Film,** sign, tin, double-sided, die cut, in shape of box, hanging arm, 17" x 6½", 1914, EX ........................................ $455.00 C

**Kodak Supplies,** sign, porcelain, "Kodak...All Supplies," 20" tall, EX......................................................$450.00 B

**Kodak Verichrome Film,** sign, porcelain, triangle with film box in center, double-sided, 22" x 12", EX...................................$325.00 B

**Kodak Verichrome Safety Film,** sign, porcelain, in shape of box of film, 24½" x 12½", EX ...................................... $250.00 C

**Kodak Verichrome,** sign, porcelain, double-sided, likeness of a box of film, 21¼" x 12½", EX ...................................... $225.00 B

**Kodak's,** sign, porcelain, double-sided, die cut, different image angles on each side, top hung, 26" x 22½", EX.............................. $215.00 C

**Kodak,** clock, light-up, older plastic body, "America's Storyteller," 19" dia., VG ......................................................$45.00 B

**Kodak,** clock, light-up, package of film under number 12, 15¼" x 15¼", EX. ...................................... $120.00 B

**Kodak,** film display, metal, countertop case, Ed Sullivan, 12½" x 7½", VG ......................................................$85.00 C

**Kodak,** sign, metal and glass, reverse painted lettering for developing & printing, 21" x 7" x 8", EX.......................................$325.00 D

**Kodak,** sign, metal, double-sided, die cut, advertising of box of film at bottom, "Developing...Printing...Enlarging," 17" x 17", G ....$300.00 B

**Kodak,** sign, metal, flange, double-sided, 21½" x 25½", EX...$55.00 C

**Kodak,** sign, porcelain, double-sided, roll of product, "Developing & Printing," 20" x 14", EX ...................................... $425.00 C

**Kodak,** sign, porcelain, self-framing, single-sided, foreign, 11" x 71", VG ......................................................$500.00 B

**Koehler's Pilsener Beer,** salt & pepper shakers, in the shape of amber paper label beer bottles, 4" tall, VG .........................$20.00 D

**Koehler,** salesman sample bath tub, porcelain and iron, 11" x 5" x 3¼", VG ......................................................$95.00 B

**Koken Shop,** barber shop sign, porcelain, originally held light bulbs on the outside of sign, rare find, 31" dia., EX...................$2,200.00 C

**Koken,** barber pole, porcelain and glass construction with paper cylinder, 14" x 28", G ......................................................$325.00 B

**Kolb's Roughs Mild Cigar,** container, metal, yellow with red bands, EX ......................................................$65.00 C

**Kolynos Dental Cream,** sign, cardboard, die cut, man and woman clowns, 13" tall, VG......................................................$325.00 C

**Kool Cigarettes,** case, cardboard, flat, holiday version, holds 50 cigarettes, EX......................................................$250.00 D

**Kool Cigarettes,** display, cardboard, for carton, EX...................$50.00 D

**Kool Cigarettes,** fan, images of penguins skating around product package, EX ...................................... $35.00 B

**Kool Cigarettes,** push plate, metal, "They're So Refreshing," EX......................................................$85.00 D

**Kool Cigarettes,** salt and pepper, Millie & Willie, promotional items, 3¼" H, VG ......................................................$65.00 D

**Kool Cigarettes,** sign, cardboard, die cut, easel back, Willie playing the trumpet, 9¼" x 12¹¹⁄₁₆", 1940s – 1950s, NM .....................$135.00 C

**Kool Cigarettes,** sign, cardboard, die cut, girl in scarf holding mask, "Mild Menthol, Cork Tipped," 32" x 47", VG ................... $155.00 C

**Kool Cigarettes,** sign, cardboard, die cut, Willie standing playing a trumpet in front of a package of Kool cigarettes, 9" x 13", 1940 – 1950s, EX ........................................................ $135.00 D

**Kool Cigarettes,** sign, metal, double-sided, flange, 4" x 12", EX.$120.00 B

**Kool,** cigarette holder, metal, Kool penguin and product pack, "Menthol Magic...Smoke Kool," EX ...........................................$45.00 D

**Kool,** sign, metal, horizontal, embossed, painted, Kool penguin to left of message, "Smoke We Sell Cigarettes," 25" x 10½", EX..... $59.00 D

**Koolmotor,** sign, porcelain, die cut, double-sided, "The Perfect Pennsylvania Oil," 23¾" x 23¾", EX.............................. $325.00 B

**Koolmotor,** sign, tin, "Refill with...The Perfect Pennsylvania Oil" "Refill with Cities Service Oils" on reverse side, double-sided with top mounting holes, 20¾" x 12", EX.............................. $375.00 B

**Koppitz Victory Beer,** label for 12 oz bottle, 1930 – 40s, VG ..$30.00 D

**Korbel Sec California Champagne,** sign, metal over cardboard, "Fermented in the Bottle," lady growing grapes, 19" x 13", VG..$165.00 D

**Korbel Sec California Champagne,** sign, metal, painted, 19" x 13", EX.............................................................$175.00 D

**Korbel Sec California Champagne,** sign, metal, painted, 19" x 13", NM.............................................................$200.00 C

**Korbel Sec Champagne,** sign, tin over cardboard, beveled edge, self-framing, woman, grapes, and bottle at right of artwork, 19" x 13", NM.........................................................$365.00 B

**Kow-Kare,** sign, metal, double-sided, flange, "Sold Here," 12" x 9", EX.............................................................$255.00 C

**Kozy Cup Roasted Coffee,** box, cardboard, embossed lettering, 1 lb., EX.............................................................$45.00 D

**Kraeuter Tools & Pliers,** sign, cardboard, "Ask Any Mechanic," 1910s, 14" x 18", EX.........................................$50.00 C

**Kraft Macaroni & Cheese,** bank, vinyl, Cheese Rex, EX.....$45.00 D

**Kraft Pex,** sign, metal, die cut, embossed, painted, chicken, 14¼" x 19½", EX.............................................. $110.00 B

**Krantz Brewing Corp.,** pinback with bar scene, Old Dutch Beer, 1¼" dia., NM.............................................$75.00 C

**Kreger's Bakery and Ice Cream Parlor,** calendar, paper, litho, two young girls on burro being led by young boy, 1907, 15" x 20", EX .............................................. $75.00 C

**Kreso Dip No 1,** sign, metal, farm animals, "Helps Keep All Livestock & Poultry Healthy," 28" x 16", EX......................$1,250.00 D

**Kreso Dip No. 1,** sign, tin, litho, different animals and the medicines for each, Parke, Davis & Co., 28" x 18", G.............. $500.00 C

**Kreso,** sign, tin, one-sided, embossed, "Disinfectant Kills Germs Everywhere," 23" x 12", G ...................................$45.00 C

**Kreuger Beer/Ale,** sign, metal over cardboard, embossed gold lettering and company logo, 13" x 6", EX ................................$125.00 C

**Kroger's Coffee,** can, metal, key wind lid, white lettering "...Country Club Regular Grind," 1 lb., EX .....................................$35.00 C

**Krout's Baking Powder,** tin, paper on cardboard, pry lid, from Albert Krout Co., Philadelphia, 3" x 6", EX....................................... $425.00 C

**Krueger Beer & Ale,** sign, in bottles and keg-lined cans, 10" x 15", EX................................................................. $150.00 B

**Krug,** plate celebrating the fiftieth anniversary of the brewery, photo of founder on front and brewery on reverse, 10" dia., 1909, EX................................................................. $125.00 C

**Kuhn's Climatized Paints,** sign, porcelain, die cut, double-sided, raccoon on limb with can of the product, 18" x 24", G............................$500.00 C

**Kuhn's Climatized Paints,** sign, porcelain, die cut, racoon holding onto a can, double-sided, 18" x 24", EX....................................$1,400.00 C

**Kum-Seald,** display, wood and glass, back opens for refilling, 22" W x 12" H x 8" D, EX ............................................. $140.00 D

**Kurfees Paint,** sign, porcelain, double-sided, flange, can in center, "Saves the Surface," 18¼" x 13¼", VG ............................$395.00 D

**Kynoch's Sporting & Military Cartridge,** board, of cartridges, 18½" x 27", 1897, EX................................................................. $875.00 B

Lack Sporting Goods Paducah Kentucky lighter, premium by Wind Master, sporting goods store advertising in shield on front, 1950 – 60s, 1½" x 2¼" x ¼", EX, $45.00 C. *Courtesy of B.J. Summers.*

Lack Sporting Goods, drinking glass, painted label showing shield of sports equipment, 1950s, 5" x 2¾" dia., EX, $35.00 C. *Courtesy of B.J. Summers.*

Lagomarsino's Kentucky Whiskies, thermometer, wood, scale type, "Speciality In JUG TRADE, Best $2.00 Whiskey in City," instructions printed on the back, 1910s, 15" x 4", EX, $325.00 C. *Courtesy of B.J. Summers.*

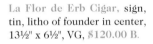

La Flor de Erb Cigar, sign, tin, litho of founder in center, 13½" x 6½", VG, $120.00 B.

Lance, store jar, glass, crossed lances on front & back with hard-to-find metal Lance bottom, 1940s, EX, $195.00 C. *Courtesy of Rare Bird Antique Mall/Jon & Joan Wright.*

---

**L & M Cigarettes,** sign, metal, image of cigarette pack, VG........$65.00 B

**L & M Cigarettes,** thermometer, metal, self-framing, embossed, scale-type indicator, 5¾" x 13¼", EX.................................$110.00 B

**L.B. Silver Co.,** Cleveland, Ohio, pinback, celluloid over metal, 2" dia., VG..................................................................$25.00 B

**L.C. Smith Gun,** paperweight, glass, breech-loading gun, 4" x 2½" x ¾", EX ................................................................$135.00 C

**L.E. Graybill,** calendar, paper, three-dimensional, die cut, animals in background with tear sheets at bottom, 1923, 15" x 15", EX ................................................................$75.00 C

**L.F.S. Cigars,** poster, paper, young girl and flowers, from L.F. Stander, Greencastle, Ind., 15" x 19", 1900s, NM.................$135.00 B

**L.P. Thomas & Son Co. High Grade Fertilizer,** calendar, paper, framed, Hiawatha's Wedding Journey, 16" x 25½", VG........$160.00 B

**L.S. DuBois, Son & Co. Wholesale Druggist, Paducah, Ky.,** jug, crock, block advertising on front, brown top with cream bottom, EX...........................................................$135.00 C

**La Belle Creole Tobacco,** pocket tin, metal, woman in center outlined by coins, 1890s, EX.................................$275.00 C

**La Britanica,** cigar box label, paper, a woman with a harp in a sunrise setting, 4½" x 4½", VG .................................$20.00 D

**La Corna Cigar,** tin, round, with 1932 tax stamp, "Havana Cigar & Tobacco Factories Ltd. Grown in Cuba Blended in Havana, Rolled and Packed in the United States of America," 2¼" dia., x 5¼", VG ....................................................$45.00 C

**La Corona Tobacco,** tin, metal, woman holding globe, 50 ct., EX..$65.00 D

**La Fendrich Cigar,** thermometer, metal, scale type with wording to the left of the tube, "Always A Cool Smoke," EX..............$235.00 C

**La Palina,** jar, cigar counter display, embossed lettering on jar, 6½" x 8" EX.......................................................$130.00 C

**La Penserosa,** cigar box label, paper, printers proof of girl in hat with flowers, EX ................................................$65.00 C

**La Preferencia Seconds,** ad, paper, framed, "My! This IS a Mild Cigar, 5¢ Straight," 23¼" x 19¼", EX ..........................$35.00 C

La Preferencia Seconds, paper, framed, "My! This IS a Mild Cigar, 5¢ Straight," 23¼" x 19¼", NM, $55.00 C.

Larro SureRaise and Sure-Calf Feed, sign, metal, double-sided, flange, "Raise Better Calves," 22" x 20", VG, $425.00 C.

Lead Mine Cigar Factory, sign, paper, litho, pretty young girl, framed, 1920s, 14" x 18", VG, $165.00 B.

Leak-Proof Piston Rings, clock, light-up, by Telechron, 15" dia., NM, $495.00 C. *Courtesy of Autopia Advertising Auctions.*

Lear & Oliver Ice Cream, menu board, cardboard, wood frame, 20" tall, G, $50.00 B.

Leavision, bottle, embossed on front "To Retain This Bottle From A.M. Leavision, Paducah, KY Subjects You to Prosecution," great air bubbles, 1890 – 1900s, 11½" x 3½" dia., EX, $55.00 C. *Courtesy of B.J. Summers.*

**LaAzora Cigars,** charger, metal, great Nubian slaves and Turkish princess, 24" dia., EX .........................$385.00 C

**Labatt's,** serving tray, porcelain, 16" x 12", EX .................$65.00 D

**LaBelle Creole Cigarettes,** poster, cardboard, litho, mammy and children at fence, 22¼" x 17¼", VG .....................$2,000.00 C

**LaBelle Creole Cigarettes,** sign, paper, stamped and embossed, black kids trying to hide from mammy, S. Hernsheim Bros. & Co., New Orleans, 1890s, EX .....................$850.00 B

**Lablatt's,** tray, porcelain, name in script, 16" x 12", VG .........$65.00 B

**Labor King,** cigar box label, paper, salesman sample, EX.$185.00 C

**Lacquerwax,** sign, metal, "Motorists Relax With...," 20" x 14", EX.............................$195.00 D

**Lacquerwax,** sign, tin, embossed, can and vintage car, "Lasts Twice As Long," 19½" x 13½", VG.................$195.00 C

**Laddies Short Smokes,** sign, cardboard, two men in hats and tails with the product in front of an opera house, 21" x 33", EX .$195.00 D

**Ladies & Children Hair Bobbing,** sign, porcelain, double-sided, flange, "...Our Speciality," 24" x 12", EX .........................$375.00 C

**Ladies' Home Journal,** banner, cloth, "for spring fashion read...," framed with Irene Bordoni at left of message, 46" x 34", EX.$350.00 C

**Ladies' Home Journal,** sign, porcelain, double-sided, LHJ pattern, 18" x 7½", EX.............................$350.00 B

**Lady Churchill,** cigar box, wooden, fan design on top lid, EX..$45.00 C

**Lady Hellen Coffee,** container, cardboard, pretty girl in center, top and bottom are metal, 1 lb., EX .........................$90.00 C

**Lady Hellen Coffee,** tin, paper label on container, pry lid, 1-lb., EX.............................$110.00 B

Lee Overalls, sign, tin, litho, embossed, hard to find item, 23" wide, EX, $350.00 B.

Lehigh Anthracite, sign, porcelain, single-sided, 21" x 11", VG, $300.00 B. *Courtesy of Collectors Auction Services.*

Leinenkugel & Rheim Cigar, calendar, cardboard, die cut, embossed, 19" x 20", 1917, EX, $275.00 B. *Courtesy of Past Tyme Pleasures.*

Lemon Chill Cure, sign, metal, taker type, "No Cure — No Pay," 1920s, 14" x 5", G, $55.00 C. *Courtesy of B.J. Summers.*

Lemon-Kola, sign, tin over cardboard, girl with flared glass with straw, rare, 6¼" x 9¼", EX, $400.00 B. *Courtesy of Muddy River Trading Co./Gary Metz.*

Lady Hellen Coffee, tin, paper label, pry lid, woman on front, 1-lb., EX ............................................$175.00 C

Lady Macbeth, cigar box label, paper, woman in red, 4½" x 4½", VG ......................................................$30.00 D

Lafin & Rand Smokeless Powder, sign, paper, rough rider with revolver, 1899, 8½" x 13", EX ..........................$250.00 C

Laflin & Rand Orange Extra Sporting Powder, tin, paper label, 3½" x 4" x 1", EX ...................................$70.00 C

Laflin & Rand Powder Co, tin, litho, flying flag, "Orange...extra...sporting," 4" x 6" x 1¼", 1900s, EX ..............$100.00 C

Lake Ridge, crate label, paper, California pears, mountain view scene, 11" x 8", VG.................................$10.00 C

Lake Shore Ice Cream Co., tray, metal, pretty lady in center in white outfit, lettering on rim, 16" tall, EX............$95.00 C

Lakeland Quick Cooking Rolled Oats, container, cardboard, superb moon shining on lake silhouette, 3 lb., EX ............$65.00 C

Lakeside Club Bouquet, sign, vitrolite, couple of gentlemen and a lady, 1900s, 30" x 26", EX.............................$2,200.00 D

Lakeside Grape Juice, serving tray, metal, from selected grapes, The Beverage of Quality, with grapes and bottle, 13½" dia., EX .$110.00 B

Lambertville "Snag-Proof" Boots, sign, metal, double-sided, flange, brownies inspecting boots and shoes, 18" x 13", EX ............$4,000.00 B

Lambertville Rubber Co., calendar, paper, Brownies working on boot, full months, 1901, 7" x 10", EX ...............................$145.00 C

Lambertville Rubber Co., sign, paper in roll down fashion, Brownies working on large boot, 15" x 22", EX.......................$1,100.00 C

Lance, store jar, clear glass, embossed on both sides of handle on top and on bottom of jar, "From the House of Lance," 7" x 8½", EX .........$85.00 C

Lewis Hunter Rye, sign, celluloid, easel back, bottle,
"Bottled in Bond," 1915 –
20s, 7" x 12", EX, $170.00 B.

Libby's, Rolled Ox Tongues, sign,
paper, litho, framed, under glass, EX,
$425.00 B. *Courtesy of Richard Opfer Auction-
eering, Inc.*

Liggett's Cherraide, bottle,
enamel name on glass, 10"
high, EX, $275.00 B.

Lift Beverage, sign, tin, painted,
"Drink, It's Good For You," 12" x
24", EX, $175.00 C.

Lilly's, gas globe, gill body
with glass lens, lilies at bottom of face, 13½" dia., VG,
$1,800.00 B. *Courtesy of Collec-
tors Auction Services.*

Lily White Flour, sign, tin,
curved, embossed, can, made
by Sentenne & Green, 19" x
35½", 1890s, EX, $4,800.00 B.
*Courtesy of Buffalo Bay Auction Co.*

Lance, store jar, glass, crossed lances on front & back with hard-to-find metal Lance bottom, 1940s, F ......................................$95.00 C

Lance, store jar, glass, our 75th anniversary, with original lid, EX ......................................$115.00 C

Land O' Lakes, thermometer, metal, dial type, Indian princess, 1968, 10" dia., EX ......................................$50.00 D

Land O' Lakes, thermometer, tin, litho, Indian maid at bottom of vertical scale, 1960s, NM ......................................$145.00 C

Land O' Lakes, thermometer, tin, litho, sweet cream butter with trademark Indian at bottom, 8" x 27", EX ......................................$235.00 B

Land O' Lakes, tin, key-wound, powdered milk, Indian maiden, 4¼" x 4", 1940s, EX ......................................$95.00 C

Lane Bryant, catalog, paper, for Spring & Summer 1969, 166 pages, EX ......................................$22.00 D

Lane Cedar Chest, sign, cardboard, die cut, easel back, moth in clothes drawer, 19" x 29¾", EX ......................................$47.00 B

Lane's Cold Tablets, sign, die cut, lady with a pill box of the prod-uct, 14" tall, EX ......................................$75.00 B

Laquerwax, sign, cardboard, die cut, clouds bringing in different weather conditions, 22" x 30", EX ......................................$170.00 B

Lincoln-Zephyr V 12, brochure, three-page, 11" x 8½", 1939, NM, $75.00 C. *Courtesy of Past Tyme Pleasures.*

Lions International, sign, porcelain, 30" dia., EX, $135.00 C.

Lipton's Tea, string holder, tin, double-sided, die cut, litho, "Always Satisfactory," 13¾" x 19½", EX, $1,512.00 B.

Liquid Green Soap, sign, paper, litho, bottles ascending up into the mountains while a floating female figure watches, top has been trimmed, but still an unusual item, 16" x 23", G, $200.00 C.

L.N. Meadows & Co. store sign, tin, painted and stenciled, information on supplies and woman behind a vintage camera, 36" tall, EX, $575.00 B.

Larco Gasoline, globe, metal and glass, product name and logo on company shield, 1935, 15" dia., EX ................................$1,500.00 C

Lash's Bitters, cribbage board, wood with stenciling, "For Headache, Malaria...," 13" x 4½", EX ................................$75.00 B

Lash's Orangeade, dispenser, metal, 21½" T, VG ...................$500.00 B

Lash's Root Beer, mug, stoneware, black logo, 4" x 6", EX ........$75.00 C

Lash's Syrup, dispenser, Depression glass, round, green, 7" x 8", EX ................................................................$75.00 B

Lasico Medicinal, sign, tin, embossed, a cure for "nervous debility and sexual weakness," 7" x 10", EX....................................$250.00 B

Lauenstrin sign, wines and liquor, die cut, man with sandwich board promoting Old Kentucky Whiskey, 8½" x 14½", VG .$75.00 C

Laughing Eyes, cigar box label, paper, salesman sample, "From Finest Selected Tobacco," EX ...........................................$60.00 B

Laurier Premier Cigar Co., sign, metal, shaped like a horse shoe with man's portrait in center, 19" x 24", EX .....................$245.00 D

Lautz Bro's & Co Soaps, sign, paper, man washing a black boy with the soap until he turns white, 21" x 27", EX..........................$630.00 B

Lava Soap, fan pull, cardboard, double-sided, product in center, 11" sq., EX .................................................................$95.00 C

Lava Soap, sign, cardboard, one-sided, diamond-shaped litho, "Better than a Turkish Bath," 8" x 8", VG .................................$25.00 B

Lavine Laundry Soap, sign, woman at table with box of product, from the Hartford Chemical Company, 13" x 28½", 1890s, EX ......$335.00 C

Lawrence Barrett Cigar, sign, porcelain, die cut, bust of man over product lettering, 18" x 20", EX ....................................$2,400.00 B

Lawrence Barrett Cigar, sign, porcelain, founder in center oval, 21" x 31", EX................................................................$700.00 B

Log Cabin Syrup, store counter display, cardboard, super colors, Pioneer Co., St. Paul, MN, 31½" x 21¾" x 2", VG, $1,500.00 B.

Long's Ox-Heart Chocolates, poster, cardboard, double-sided, 11⅓" dia., VG, $30.00 C.

Look Better, Feel Better, barber pole, porcelain, 7½" x 48", red, white & blue, VG, $395.00 C.

Lorillard's Redi-Cut Tobacco, tin with round wire bail top handle, 7½" tall, G, $50.00 B.

Lowe Brothers Paint, sign, metal and glass, neon, 30" x 11", VG, $350.00 C.

---

**Lawrence Tiger Brand Paints & Varnishes,** sign, cardboard, metal frame, 30" x 42", VG .......................................................$160.00 B

**Lax-ets Candy,** sign, celluloid, bowel laxative, 17" x 14", EX ...$400.00 B

**Laxol Castor Oil,** tip tray, metal, "Like Honey," bottle, 4¼" dia., EX ...................................................................................$85.00 C

**Lay or Bust Feeds Fresh Eggs,** chalkboard, price, 20" x 26", VG .$350.00 B

**Le Roy Cigarettes,** sign, paper, "Smoke The Le Roy" with cherubs, EX ..................................................................$75.00 C

**Leader Rolled Tip Spark Plugs,** store countertop display, with spark plug on front of unit, 15" x 4" x 10¼", G .................$350.00 B

**Leadway Rolled Oats,** container, bowl of hot oats, 3-lb., EX.........$65.00 C

**Leaf Spearmint Chewing Gum,** sign, tin, litho, single-sided, 25⅛" x 8⅞", VG .................................................................$135.00 C

**Leaf Spearmint Gum,** store counter display, with unopened packages of gum, 6⅛" x 4¼" x 3", 1930s, EX ............................$400.00 B

**Leak-Proof Piston Rings,** clock, light-up, by Telechron, 15" dia., G..................................................................................$195.00 C

**Lee Jeans,** sign, neon, 36" x 24", EX ................................$375.00 B

**Lee Overalls,** sign, cardboard, die cut, young boy in overalls holding hammer, 10" T, EX ............................................................$90.00 B

**Lee Riders,** sign, double-sided, man riding on bucking bronc, 17½" dia., EX .....................................................................$200.00 B

**Lee Tires,** sign, metal, framed glass front, light-up, 32" x 7½", EX .........................................................................$195.00 C

**Lee Tires,** sign, tin, embossed, self-framing, 72" x 17½", VG...$275.00 C

**Lee,** banner, cloth, authentic western wear EX................$145.00 C

**Lee,** display, country store, overalls, 4' x 12', EX .....................$160.00 B

**Lefevre-Utile Biscuits,** sign, paper, woman surrounded by dogwood blooms, 1900s, 20" x 27", EX .............................................$300.00 B

Löwenbräu, back bar statue, lion, with bottle, EX, $135.00 C. *Courtesy of B.J. Summers.*

Lowney's Chocolate Bars and Cracker Jack, thermometer, porcelain, 8" x 30¼", VG, $235.00 B. *Courtesy of Collectors Auction Services.*

Lucke's Telescopes, cigar box, wood, 100-count, litho, man at telescope, 1880s, NM, $405.00 B. *Courtesy of Buffalo Bay Auction Co.*

Lucky Curve Plug Cut Tobacco, tin, man getting ready to throw a baseball on front, 7" x 4½" x 4¼", G, $295.00 B.

Lucky Strike Cigarettes, sign, cardboard, die cut, 3-D, 1920s, EX, $435.00 B.

Lehnert's Beer, tip tray, metal, large dog sporting eyeglasses and smoking a cigar, "Drink...Made in Catasauqua, Pa.," 4¼" dia., EX ...........................................................$300.00 B

Leinenkugel & Rheim Cigar, calendar, cardboard, die cut, embossed, 19" x 20", 1917, F ...............................$75.00 C

Leinenkugel's Beer, clock, double-bubble, Indian head, 15" dia., VG .......................................................................$485.00 B

Leland McNamee's Ministrels, poster, paper on cardboard, black man's head, 41" x 80", VG ...............................$300.00 B

Lemon Dry Beverages, door push, tin, litho, 4" x 10", EX.$195.00 C

Lemon Kola, tip tray, tin, litho, 4¼" dia., EX ...................$180.00 B

Lemon-Julep, sign, tin, "Drink Lemon-Julep In Bottles," 32" x 10", VG ..................................................................$175.00 D

Lemon-Kola, sign, metal over cardboard, pretty red headed woman in a large hat holding a glass of the product, lettering at bottom, 6" x 9", VG ....................................................................$400.00 B

Lemon-Kola, sign, tin over cardboard, girl with flared glass with straw, rare, 6¼" x 9¼", VG.......................................$325.00 C

Lenox Soap, sign, porcelain, 10" x 6", EX .........................$175.00 C

Lenox Soap, sign, porcelain, 10" x 6", G...........................$120.00 B

Lenox Soap, sign, porcelain, with product name, 10" x 6", EX.$120.00 B

Lenox Tobacco, pocket tin, metal, open touring car on front, VG...............................................................................$850.00 B

Leonard Skins, cigarette papers package, paper, VG..........$12.00 D

Leopold: The Clothier, Miffinburg, PA, tip tray, metal, round with scalloped edges and three white horses in center, 4¼" dia., EX ....$175.00 D

Levenson Hair Shop, pocket mirror, celluloid, red-haired woman on front, 1¾" x 2¾", EX.....................................................$250.00 B

Levering's Coffee, container, paper, litho on cardboard, message and product image on back and a checker board on reverse side, 1910s, 4¾" x 9½", EX.......................................................$75.00 C

Lucky Strike, pocket mirror, similar to package, 2" x 3", 1938, EX, $135.00 C.

Lucky Strike, sign, cardboard, heavy easel back, litho, "Luckies – a light smoke...it's toasted," man and woman at ship porthole enjoying a smoke, 27½" x 36", 1940s, VG, $165.00 C. *Courtesy of Collectors Auction Services.*

Luden's Chewing Gum, change receiver, gum packages in center, 1920s, 11" dia., G, $180.00 B. *Courtesy of Muddy River Trading Co./Gary Metz.*

Luden's Cough Drops, sign, tin, embossed, litho, box of menthol drops, 35½" x 19½", EX, $210.00 B.

Lydia E. Pinkham's Vegetable Compound, calendar, framed, full monthly pad, short bio, 15" x 22¾", VG, $145.00 C.

---

Levi's, poster, showing cowboy lore, 25" x 36½", 1933, EX. **$355.00 C**

Levi's, sign, molded plastic, embossed, man carrying saddle, 16" x 32", 1960s, EX.................................................**$925.00 B**

Levi's, sign, paper. "...The real thing" with image of cowboy and horse, 24" x 36", EX.............................................................**$225.00 C**

Levy's Bread, poster, paper, litho, young black man eating a sandwich made with Levy's bread, "You don't have to be Jewish to love Levy's...real Jewish rye," 29½" x 45¼", VG .........................**$550.00 B**

Lewis 66 Whiskey, tray, metal, tip size, pretty girl in plummed hat, 4" dia., EX.............................................................................**$100.00 B**

Libby's, sign, paper, litho under glass, rolled ox tongues, framed, G..........................................................................................**$275.00 C**

Liberty Beer, tip tray, metal, with Indian logo in center of tray, "In Bottles Only," American Brewing Co., 4⅛", EX................**$160.00 B**

Liberty Bond, cigar box label, paper, promoting government bonds, 4½" x 4½", EX ....................................................................**$10.00 D**

Liberty Ice Cream, serving tray, hard plastic, rectangular, "Superior, Improved," EX .............................................................**$25.00 C**

Licenses & General Motor Insurance Policy, sign, foreign, single-sided, 19" x 29¼", F............................................................**$200.00 B**

Lictonic, sign, tin, embossed, litho, cow eating at left and dealer strip at bottom, 20" x 9", EX ................................................**$165.00 C**

Lieber's Gold Medal Beer, tip tray, bottle in center of tray, 5" dia., EX............................................................................................**$95.00 C**

**Life Belt,** cigar box label, paper, salesman sample, swimming women that have surrounded a young sailor, EX .............$400.00 B

**Life Saver,** license plate attachment, tin, die cut, jewel-type reflector attached to center of unit, "Drive Safely," 5" x 6½", EX .........$250.00 C

**Life Savers,** display rack, tin, litho, three-tier, would display 9 different flavors, 1920s, 15½" x 14" x 10", EX.............$600.00 B

**Life Savers,** display unit, tin, litho, 18½" x 24" x 11", G......$70.00 C

**Life Savers,** display, counter, polished aluminum, three tiers for merchandise display, 9¼" x 12" x 9", EX ...........................$125.00 C

**Life Savers,** display, tin, litho, counter unit with two shelves holding the product, 3" x 6½" x 7", VG ......................................$85.00 C

**Lifebuoy Soap,** ad, trolley car, framed, youngsters in school scene, 22¼" x 12¼", EX...............................................................$120.00 B

**Lift Beverage,** sign, tin, painted, "Drink, It's Good For You," 12" x 24", G.................................................................................$85.00 C

**Lift Beverage,** sign, tin, single-sided, embossed, bottle, "It's Good for You," 7" x 12", VG ........................................................$135.00 C

**Lift,** Three Star Bottling Works, sign, porcelain, bottle "Drink, It's good for you," 12" x 24", NM ...............................................$200.00 B

**Liggett & Meyers Star Brand Tobacco,** box, wooden, unopened with 1910 Federal Stamp, 13" x 7" x 3", 1910s, EX...........$85.00 C

**Liggett & Meyers Tobacco Co. Velvet Pipe & Cigarette Tobacco,** tin with press on lid, EX .....................................................$25.00 C

**Liggett & Meyers Tobacco Co.,** pail, tin, with wire bail handle, product information in oval on front, G .......................................$55.00 C

**Liggett & Meyers Tobacco Co.,** store tin, "Sweet Cuba...Fine, Cut...the kind that suits," ocean and lighthouse, F ...............$45.00 D

**Liggett's Coffee,** tin, promoting Java coffee, small top, 5¼" x 9½", EX .................................................................................$275.00 C

**Light Horse Squadron,** tip tray, metal, "The Aristocrat of 10¢ Cigars," camp scene in center, 6⅝" L, EX ...........................................$95.00 B

**Lilly's,** gas globe, gill body with glass lens, lilies at bottom of face, 13½" dia., F ...........................................................................$500.00 C

**Lily Cigarettes,** box, cardboard, lily surrounded by product name, 16 ct, EX .................................................................................$45.00 B

**Lily White Flour,** sign, tin, curved, embossed, product can, made by Sentenne & Green, 19" x 35½", 1890s, G.................$1,000.00 C

**Lily White,** display, metal, "Bias Fold Tape...Extra Fine Quality," 15" x 8¼" x 8", G .......................................................$35.00 D

**Lily White,** display, metal, counter unit, "Bias Fold Tape," 15" x 8" x 8¼", VG ...............................................................$75.00 C

**Lily,** tip tray, metal, bottle in center with sandwich and glass, "A Beverage...Rock Island Brewing Co., Rock Island, Ill.," 6½" L, EX ...............................................................................$110.00 B

**Lime Cola,** menu board, tin, painted, "We Serve...It's Definitely Good," NOS, 14" x 20", NM ............................................$160.00 B

**Lime Cola,** sign, celluloid over cardboard, disc, string-hung, 9" dia., NM .............................................................................$150.00 C

**Lime Cola,** sign, celluloid, "Drink," 1950s, 9" dia., VG ....$110.00 C

**Lime Cola,** sign, celluloid, product bottle, 1950s, 9" dia., EX..$130.00 B

**Lime Cola,** sign, celluloid, round, "Drink,"1950s, 9" dia., EX...$150.00 C

**Lime Cola,** sign, tin embossed, strip, "Drink," 24" x 8", NM...$110.00 B

**Lime Kiln Club,** tobacco box label, paper, group of Black men, 7¾" x 6", EX.............................................................................$75.00 D

**Lime-Crush,** sign, cardboard, string hanger, "Like Limes? Drink," woman in hat, 9" x 12", EX...............................................$535.00 B

**Lime-Crush,** sign, tin, "tacker" style, "Drink," 19½" x 14", EX.$210.00 B

**Lime-Julep,** string hanger, cardboard, couple enjoying a bottle of the product with two straws, 8" x 11", 1940s, EX .............$155.00 B

**Linco Motor Oil,** calendar, paper, plane sky-writing about product, 19½" x 26½", 1936, VG ......................................................$65.00 C

**Lincoln Cab Co.,** thermometer, wood, vintage cab at top, 4" x 15", G..............................................................................$95.00 C

**Lincoln Flour,** sign, paper, Abraham Lincoln in center, with metal top and bottom strips, "Ask Your Grocer," "Traders Meat Market, Polaski, Iowa and Standard, St. Paul," 16" x 22½", EX......$225.00 C

**Lincoln Steel Cut Coffee,** tin, paper label, Abraham Lincoln, pry-lid, from Capitol Grocery Co., Springfield, IL, EX.............$135.00 D

**Lincoln-Zephyr V 12,** brochure, three-page, 11" x 8½", 1939, VG...........................................................................................$50.00 C

**Lion Coffee,** card set, vinyl, coffee beans being picked by black workers, 1800s, EX................................................................$55.00 C

**Lion Coffee,** sign, cardboard, lion smoking a pipe and wearing a blue uniform, 20" x 31", EX.................................................$400.00 B

**Lion Coffee,** store bin, lion pulling chariot on lift-top lid, 32¼" H, EX..............................................................................$450.00 B

**Lion Coffee,** store bin, lion pulling chariot on lift-top lid, 32¼" H, NM.............................................................................$500.00 D

**Lion Gas,** globe, metal and glass, roaring lion and product name, 13½" dia., EX ............................................................$1,200.00 C

**Lion Heat Resistant Lubricant,** can, metal, lion logo, 1 lb, EX...**$95.00 B**

**Lion Naturalube,** license plate attachment, embossed, painted with die cut, trademark lion at top, "The New Type Motor Oil," 6" x 6¼", VG .....................................................**$125.00 C**

**Lions International,** sign, porcelain, 30" dia., G.................**$20.00 B**

**Lions International,** sign, porcelain, lions' heads on both sides of message, 30" dia., EX .......................................**$150.00 D**

**Lipton's Tea,** sign, porcelain, "None Genuine Without The Signature" and product name, 60" x 12", EX...........................**$195.00 D**

**Lipton's Tea,** string holder, tin, double-sided, die cut, litho, "Always Satisfactory," 13¾" x 19½", VG.........................................**$1,000.00 C**

**Lipton's Teas & Coffees,** sign, cardboard, pretty lady surrounded by product name and information, 14" x 20", EX.....................**$395.00 B**

**Lipton's Teas,** sign, paper, litho, young lady with tea tray in front, "Will You Have Some?," strong colors and great depth, 1899, NM .............................................**$1,324.00 B**

**Lipton's Teas,** stone litho on paper, young girl at table with the product ready to serve, Ceylon, 1899, VG ....................................**$675.00 B**

**Listerated Gum,** sign, cardboard, "10 Nuggets 5¢" people watching biplanes, 26" x 42", EX.....................................**$2,500.00 B**

**Litchfield Ice Cream,** sign, metal, framed, plastic front, G..**$145.00 D**

**Litholin Waterproof Linen,** pocket mirror, metal and glass, red bow tie and collar on back of mirror, 2¾" dia., EX.....................**$65.00 C**

**Litholin Waterproofed Linen,** trolley sign, cardboard, man surrounded by a collar and red bow tie with product lettering, 21" x 11", EX.......................................................**$215.00 C**

**Little Beauties,** cigar box, kids dressed as adults, 50-ct., EX..**$225.00 C**

**Little Boy Blue,** dispenser, metal, for bluing, bottle with boy on label, 1920s, 4" x 19", EX ................................................**$250.00 B**

**Little Dutchman Beer,** label, paper, from the Vienna Brewing Co. with an Internal Revenue Tax, 1930 – 50s,12 oz., EX ........**$30.00 C**

**Little Fairies Baking Powder,** container, cardboard, man's photo in center cameo with product lettering, 2¼" x 4", EX...............**75.00 C**

**Little Giant Elevators,** sign, metal, painted, giant holding ball with farm equipment, EX ...........................................**$95.00 C**

**Live-Well Pure Cocoa,** container, cardboard, Joyce-Laughlin Co., Peoria, Ill., 2-lb., P................................................. **$40.00 D**

**Lively Limes,** mirror, metagolio, 18⅛" x 12", VG ..............**$145.00 C**

**Lockwood Taylor Hardware Co.,** tip tray, metal, litho, pretty woman in center and "incandescent mantles," 4¼" dia., VG ............**$75.00 C**

**Lodge & Davis Machine Tool Co.,** sign, paper, name surrounding bust of pretty lady, 14½" x 30", VG....................................**$275.00 B**

**Loft Brand Midget Candy Sticks,** sign, tin, litho, children feeding candy stick to squirrel, 6" x 4¾", EX.....................**$300.00 B**

**Log Cabin Coffee,** can, tin, litho, key-wound, cabin in clearing in woods, Shaffer Stores, Altoona, PA, 1-lb., 4" x 5", EX.........**$1,550.00 B**

**Log Cabin Frontier Inn,** container, people on front porch with horse tied to rail, 5-lb., NM .............................................**$207.00 B**

**Log Cabin Syrup,** box, cardboard, shipping, young girl holding a syrup tin, 16½" x 11" x 10½", 1918, EX...........................**$375.00 C**

**Log Cabin Syrup,** container, tin, litho, Frontier Jail, NM..**$141.00 B**

**Log Cabin Syrup,** container, tin, litho, quart-size, boy at door and hat, 1914, EX .....................................................**$100.00 C**

**Log Cabin Syrup,** container, tin, litho, Stockade School, children playing in front of school, NM .........................**$187.00 B**

**Log Cabin Syrup,** container, tin, litho, table sized, boy in blue with hat, 1914, EX .....................................................**$70.00 B**

**Log Cabin Syrup,** container, tin, litho, table-sized, boy in black at door, 1914, EX................................................**$75.00 B**

**Log Cabin Syrup,** container, tin, litho, table-sized, frontier house bank, EX.............................................................**$115.00 C**

**Log Cabin Tobacco,** sign, paper, "Smoke...," with cabin and pioneer, 18" x 22", EX ............................................**$300.00 B**

**Log Cabin,** cigar box, wood, in shape of log cabin, paper litho inside lid showing family dancing and smoking, 8½" x 5" x 5½", VG .........................................................**$775.00 D**

**Log Cabin,** cigar box, wood, inside label of black family entertaining themselves beside a log cabin, 100-ct., EX..................**$165.00 B**

**Log Cabin,** cigar box, wood, paper litho, wagon, in shape of log cabin, 8½" x 5" x 5½", VG.................................................**$750.00 D**

**Logan Brew/Columbia Brewing Co.,** label, paper, from a 22 oz. bottle, company logo and name, 22 oz, EX............................**$20.00 D**

**Lohrey's Silver Star,** sign, glass, company's logo in blank at top of sign, "Silver Star sausage, ham and bacon," 13" x 19", EX ..**$85.00 C**

**Lolita Talcum Powder,** container, tin, oval, "Lolita" on front, 4¼" x 7" x 9", EX ................................................**$145.00 D**

**Lolita Talcum Powder,** container, tin, oval, "Lolita" on front, 4¼" x 7" x 9", VG................................................**$115.00 C**

**London House Coffee,** container, tin, litho, Silver Banner, key-wound, 1-lb., EX ............................................**$44.00 B**

**Lone Jack Tobacco,** container, metal, EX.........................**$85.00 D**

**Lone Jack,** sign, etched stained glass, "smoke the...seg-ars," 4" x 9¾", EX.............................................................**$900.00 B**

**Lone Star Beer,** monkey, mechanical, 25" dia., x 39" H, VG ..**$1,225.00 B**

**Long Chew Gum,** trade stimulator, metal and wood, clown and giraffe, EX.........................................................**$5,400.00 B**

**Long Tom Smoking Tobacco,** container, metal, black man, EX.**$240.00 B**

**Longfellow,** cigar box label, paper, Indians, old white haired pioneer, and Indian maiden, 1903, EX ....................................**$45.00 B**

**Longhorn Pure Lard,** pail, metal, rolled bail handle, pry lid, 8 lb., EX.........................................................................**$135.00 D**

**Look Better, Feel Better,** barber pole, porcelain, 7½" x 48", red, white & blue, G ........................................................**$350.00 D**

**Look Out Cut Plug Tobacco,** pocket, tin, flat pocket, lighthouse, from J.C. Dill's, Richmond, VA, 4½" x 2" x 1", EX ..............**$95.00 C**

**Lorain Creamery,** sign, porcelain, double-sided, Jersey Lane Ice Cream, 28" x 20", VG .................................................**$325.00 B**

**Lord Baltimore,** cigar box label, paper, "Try Then, Tastes Good," 13" x 7", EX ..................................................................**$45.00 B**

**Lord Delaware,** cigar box label, paper, seashore and shipyard scene, 9" x 6", EX ...............................................................**$50.00 D**

**Lord Grasby,** cigar box, wood, Indians with tobacco leaves, 100-ct, 1915, EX ..................................................................**$40.00 D**

**Lord Salisbury Turkish Cigarettes,** container, metal, flat, gold lettering and gold border, 50 ct, EX ........................................**$75.00 D**

**Lord Tennyson Puritanos Cigars,** container, tin, litho, Canadian, 5" x 5⅛", EX ...............................................................**$110.00 B**

**Lorillard Indian Snuff,** bottle, glass, complete contents, unbroken seal, 1898, NM ............................................................**$65.00 D**

**Lorillard's Redicut Tobacco,** lunch box, metal, "Just Break Off A Piece To fit," EX .............................................................**$95.00 D**

**Lorillard's Stripped Smoking Tobacco,** lunch box, metal, product, EX.............................................................................**$25.00 D**

**Lorillards "49" Cut Plug Tobacco,** trade card, litho, miners at water plume panning for gold, litho by Grocer & Canner, SF, 4½" x 3¼", EX .....................................................................**$230.00 B**

**Los Angeles Brewing Co.,** jug, ceramic, company name lettering, VG .............................................................................**$265.00 B**

**Louisville Tin & Stove Co.,** catalog, paper, company wares, 1938, 80 pages, VG ...................................................................**$65.00 D**

**Love Nest Coffee,** container, key-wound, cozy home scene, 1-lb., EX.............................................................................**$210.00 B**

**Lowe Brothers Paints for All Purposes,** sign, porcelain, 27¾" x 19¾", VG ..........................................................................**$65.00 C**

**Lowe Brothers Paints,** sign, porcelain, "...For All Purposes," 28" x 20", EX ......................................................................**$75.00 D**

**Lowe Brothers Paints,** sign, porcelain, for all purposes, store, 27¾" x 19¾", G...............................................................................**$90.00 C**

**Löwenbräu,** bar statue, lion bottle, F..........................................**$45.00 C**

**Lowney's Cocoa,** sample tin, litho, Victorian woman on front, 1⅝" x 1⅜" x 1", EX ...............................................................**$250.00 B**

**Lowney's Cocoa,** string holder, metal, fancy graphics, EX ........**$3,630.00 B**

**Lowney's Cocoa,** tin, children eating the product, 3" x 4¾" x 2⅛", EX.............................................................................**$55.00 C**

**Loyl Coffee,** container, metal, screw lid, eagle and product lettering, 1 lb., EX .....................................................................**$200.00 B**

**Lubri-Gas,** sign, tin, self-framing, embossed, "Tractor-Diesel-Aviation or Marine Fuel," 56" x 32", VG ...................**$300.00 B**

**Lubrite Motor Oil, Socony-Vacuum Oil Company, Inc.,** sign, metal, double-sided, painted, 20" x 11", F.....................**$85.00 C**

**Lubrite Sky-Hy,** gas globe, metal and glass, red name, and blue Sky-Hy in speed lettering, 15" dia., EX ...................................**$785.00 C**

**Lubrite,** gas globe, metal and glass, name in red lettering, 15" dia., EX.............................................................................**$575.00 C**

**Luck Ghost,** poster, paper, litho, movie starring Mantan Moreland and F.E. Miller, 28½" x 40½", EX .....................**$125.00 D**

**Lucke's Telescopes,** cigar box, wood, 100-count, litho, man at telescope, 1880s, NM.................................................**$405.00 B**

**Lucke's Telescopes,** cigar box, wood, telescope looking to the heavens inside label, 100-ct., 1883, EX ...............................**$355.00 C**

**Lucky B,** cigar box, shaped like a book, "Works of Nietzsche and Kuhn" on spine, 50-ct., EX.........................................**$85.00 C**

**Lucky Club Cola,** sign, cardboard, die cut, cowboy, "Ace For Thirst," 12" x 24", VG ........................................................**$110.00 D**

**Lucky Cup Coffee,** tin, key-wound top, steaming cup of coffee with horseshoe, 1-lb., EX .................................................**$33.00 B**

**Lucky Hit Tobacco,** label, paper, girl deep in thought with cupid's arrow in her heart, 6" x 12", VG.......................................**$65.00 C**

**Lucky Lager,** sign, paper, Happy Holidays, chef presenting holiday dinner, 27" x 13½", VG ....................................................**$25.00 D**

**Lucky Penn Motor Oil,** can, metal, name and product information in yellow & red, 1 qt, VG.................................................**$45.00 C**

**Lucky Star Ginger Ale,** sign, metal, large bottle, 12" x 24", VG ..**$115.00 D**

**Lucky Strike Apples,** crate label, paper, lakeside scene complete with hunter and a deer, 12" x 9", VG ...............................**$10.00 D**

**Lucky Strike Filter 100s,** carton, never been opened, EX ..**$50.00 C**

**Lucky Strike,** cigarette tin, flat, fifties cigarettes, hinged, "Lucky Strike...It's toasted," 5½" x 4½", EX .......................................**$25.00 C**

**Lucky Strike,** container, metal round, "Cigarettes" in gold and familiar company logo, 100 ct., EX......................................$85.00 D

**Lucky Strike,** container, metal, pocket, vertical, familiar company logo and "Genuine...Roll Cut Tobacco," 4" tall, NM ......................$645.00 B

**Lucky Strike,** container, metal, rounded corners, company logo in center, 5" x 3" x 2", VG ........................................$60.00 D

**Lucky Strike,** display box, cardboard, holiday sales "Merry Christmas," designed for point of purchase use, 12½" x 10" x 2", VG........$135.00 D

**Lucky Strike,** display, cardboard, die cut, easel-back, countertop, Santa Claus, 8¼" x 13¼", VG ............................................$140.00 B

**Lucky Strike,** fan, cardboard, die cut, in shape of tobacco leaf, Frank Sinatra, EX......................................................$250.00 B

**Lucky Strike,** pocket container, tin, litho, vertical, white Lucky package, 3" x 1" x 4¼", EX .............................$225.00 D

**Lucky Strike,** pocket mirror, similar to package, 2" x 3", 1938, F .$70.00 C

**Lucky Strike,** sign, cardboard, "Luckies A Light Smoke...," couple of men offering woman a cigarette as she is getting on an airplane, 13" x 21", EX....................................................$65.00 B

**Lucky Strike,** sign, cardboard, heavy, easel back, litho, "Luckies-a light smoke...it's toasted," man and woman at ship porthole enjoying a smoke, 27½" x 36", 1940s, EX ..................................$175.00 C

**Lucky Strike,** sign, metal, pretty woman holding a product pack in her hand, 15" x 21", EX.....................................$300.00 C

**Lucky Strike,** sign, tin, girl in spotlight, signed by "Bazz," 1950s, 17" x 24", EX ..................................................$300.00 B

**Lucky Strike,** sign, tin, painted, pin-up girl, 15" x 21", EX$250.00 B

**Lucky Strike,** sign, tin, painted, pin-up girl, 15" x 21", G..$175.00 D

**Lucky Strike,** trolley sign, paper, Harry Heilmann, Detroit Tigers...World's Leading Batter, sign, "I smoke Luckies because they are the best," 21" x 11", EX ............................$1,250.00 C

**Lucky Tiger Dandruff,** tin, paper label, screw-top on lid, 1-qt., VG..............................................................$55.00 C

**Lucky Tiger,** sign, cardboard, easel back, "For Hair and Scalp...with oil or without," pretty woman with tiger bust, 22" x 33½", NM...$235.00 C

**Luden's Chewing Gum,** change receiver, gum packages in center, 1920s, 11" dia., EX...........................................$225.00 C

**Luden's Cough Drop,** tip tray, package in center of tray, 3½" dia., VG ..............................................................$360.00 B

**Luden's Cough Drops,** tip tray, metal, early cough drop box, "Give Instant Relief," Reading, Penna., 3½" dia., EX.................$900.00 B

**Ludwig Pianos,** tip tray, metal, pretty girl with a rose in her teeth, 4" dia., VG .............................................$35.00 D

**Ludwig Pianos,** tip tray, metal, pretty woman, New York, 4¼" dia., EX..............................................................$125.00 C

**Lunch Ice Cream Soda,** sign, porcelain, die cut, EX ....................$280.00 C

**Luntin Cigar Factory,** sign, paper, portrait and flowers, Canadian, hard to find especially in good shape, 26" x 20", EX........$1,200.00 D

**Lush'us Rolled Oats,** container, cardboard, product being served, 3-lb., VG .............................................$180.00 B

**Luter's Pure Lard,** pail, tin, litho, "The Smithfield Packing Company, Inc., Smithfield, Virginia," 10" dia., x 11¾", VG.......$175.00 C

**Luxury Tobacco,** counter sign, cardboard, easel back, man enjoying a pipe, 9" x x 11", EX......................................$325.00 C

**Luxus Cigars,** sign, tin, ostrich in center from F. Tuchfarber Co., Cincinnati, OH, 13½" x 9¾", 1890, EX .............................$125.00 B

**Luzianne Coffee & Chicory,** can, metal, sample size, "mammy" serving the product, round screw lid, EX .........................$195.00 D

**Lydia E Pinkham,** trade card, cardboard, vegetable compound, florial design, EX..........................................$20.00 D

**Lykens Dairy Milk and Cream,** sign, tin, one-sided, 30" x 14", VG..............................................................$85.00 C

**Lyons' Tea,** sign, porcelain, 36" x 12", EX ......................$225.00 C

**Lysol,** booklet, paper, "The Country Doctor Talks To Women," Dionne Quints, 1937, 32 pages, VG....................................$25.00 D

Madison Cigar, sign, paper, store, risque Indian maiden, by Hayes Litho Co., Buffalo, NY, 15" x 30", 1906, EX, $1,200.00 B.
*Courtesy of Buffalo Bay Auction Co.*

Maestro, sign, cardboard, die cut, litho, 14" x 17", NOS, EX, $85.00 B.

Mabry, Brown & Bigelow, lighter, metal, "A Light Reminder of Juett S. Mabry, Brown & Bigelow, Paducah, Ky," never used, 1½" x 2¼" x ⅜", NM, $30.00 C. *Courtesy of B.J. Summers.*

Magic Baking Powder, door push, porcelain, "Use...For All Your Baking," 1910 – 20s, 3¼" x 12", EX, $425.00 B.

Mail Pouch Chew Tobacco, thermometer, metal, painted, embossed, "treat yourself to the best," 1950s, 3" x 9", EX, $395.00 C.

M & M Premium Regular Gas, globe, metal and glass, blue lettering and trim, 13½" dia., VG ....................................$350.00 C

M & S Soda, sign, tin over cardboard, beveled edge, bottle at right of message, 13" x 9", NM.........................................$45.00 C

M & S, gas globe, low profile metal body, two glass lenses, "The Best" 15" dia., VG...............................................$335.00 C

M Hohner's Harmonicas, display case, wooden, people playing the product, EX .......................................................$60.00 B

M Robinson Brewery, match safe, metal, company name engraving, EX ....................................................................$85.00 C

M Samuels Specialmarke, cigar box label, paper, couple riding horses, EX .....................................................$100.00 B

M. Hohner Harmonica, display, wooden with paper label on lid, fold-out, VG............................................................$115.00 C

M. Stachelberg & Co's, sign, cardboard, die cut, Raphael Clear Havana Cigarettes, 17¼" x 21", VG.........................$115.00 B

M. Stachelberg & Co.'s Raphael Clear Havana Cigarettes, sign, die cut, pretty woman, 17¼" x 21", VG..................$115.00 B

M.K. Goetz Brewing Co., sign, tin, litho, "Jerry's Smile," black man smiling and enjoying a glass of beer, self-framing, 22½" x 28", EX...................................................$4,400.00 B

Ma's Old Fashion Root Beer, bottle topper, cardboard, "Demand the best," die cut arrow and the image of "Ma," EX.............$45.00 C

Ma's Root Beer, sign, tin, single-sided, die cut, bottle, 6" x 9¾", VG ...................................................................$145.00 C

Ma-Belle, cigar box label, paper, rather buxom woman wearing a feathered hat, 4½" x 4½", EX...............................$25.00 D

Mac Cigars, sign, tin, single-sided, 14" x 10", VG ....................$125.00 C

Machados Collins, sign, porcelain, double-sided, die cut, advertising foreign, 11½" x 18", EX....................................$75.00 C

Mack Trucks, paperweight, glass, very early Mack gasoline truck, 2½" dia., EX.............................................................$415.00 B

Mack, pocket mirror, celluloid, "Leading Gasoline Truck of America," 2½" x 3⅛", EX .........................................................$550.00 B

Mackie's White Horse Whisky, sign, porcelain, white lettering with horse on background, 36" x 30", EX..................$155.00 C

Mail Pouch, thermometer, metal, scale type, 38½" high, G, $135.00 C.

Mail Pouch Tobacco, sign, tin on wood, painted and cut to resemble a barn, neat item, 56" wide, EX, $350.00 B.

Makin's Tobacco, sign, metal, double-sided, flange, "No Premiums But More Good Tobacco For ¢5 Sold Here" under a package of the product, 17" tall, F, $100.00 B.

Malt-Nutrine, sign, cardboard, one-sided, litho over tin, "A Hurry Call," 12½" x 7¾", VG, $95.00 C.

Marie Tempest Cigars, poster, paper, stone litho, young maiden, 16" x 22", 1900s, NM, $1,900.00 B. *Courtesy of Buffalo Bay Auction Co.*

**Macmillan Ring Free Motor Oil,** sign, tin, double-sided, Scotsman pinching a penny, "Saves Fuel...Saves Wear," 11" x 11¾", EX.$95.00 C

**Macmillian Ring Free Motor Oil,** sign, tin, die cut, embossed, hand holding a can of the product, 27¼" x 34", EX........$135.00 C

**Madam Lindsey Hair Dressing,** can, metal, silhouette lettering, VG ........$25.00 D

**Madison Cigar Manufacturing Co.,** sign, paper, Indian maiden in profile with clothes draped off shoulder, 1900s, 15" x 30", VG....$800.00 B

**Madison Cigar,** sign, paper, store, risque Indian maiden, by Hayes Litho Co., Buffalo, NY, 15" x 30", 1906, G ........$400.00 C

**Madras,** cigar box label, paper, Indians, trains, and ship, 9" x 6", VG ........$45.00 D

**Maduro Chewing Tobacco,** label, paper, Spanish lady encircled by flowers, S.F. Hess Co., 11" x 11", EX ........$140.00 B

**Magic Chef,** countertop display figure, composition, man with wand and one hand with card slot, 11½" x 9" x 28", EX..........$100.00 B

**Magic Leather Belt,** store bin, tin, die cut, litho on wood, man with belt, "No Binding-No Pressure," 1915, 15" x 14¼" x 4", EX .$200.00 B

**Magic Rust Eraser,** display, cardboard, rubber erasers, 13⅞" x 16¼", VG ........$40.00 D

**Magic Yeast,** sign, cardboard, 1893 Columbian Expo ribbon that surrounds an oval with a girl's likeness, 10" x 12", EX ........$95.00 C

**Magic Yeast,** sign, cardboard, die cut, black person with dog, 5" x 10", EX ........$115.00 C

**Magic Yeast,** sign, cardboard, stone litho, young man in turban, 10" x 15", 1906, EX ........$225.00 C

**Magic Yeast,** sign, paper, stone litho, ladies by the fireplace, 20" x 15", 1909, EX ........$725.00 C

**Magic,** sign, tin, one-sided, embossed, gasoline globe, "Use...Gasoline," "Ellwood Myers Co., Springfield, O.," 18" x 24", F...$135.00 C

**Magnolia Brand Condensed Milk,** box, wooden, Bordon's Condensed Milk Co., N.Y., embossed block printed letters, 19" x 7" x 13", EX........$35.00 C

**Magnolia Brand Condensed Milk,** wooden shipping box, painted debossed lettering, 19" x 7" x 13", EX ........$55.00 C

**Magnolia Coffee,** can, metal, key wind lid, 1 lb., EX........$160.00 B

Marigold Dairy Products, clock, double-bubble, light-up, EX, $600.00 C.

Marsh Wheeling Stogies, clock, light-up, Pam, 15¼" x 15¼", VG, $275.00 B.

Marvels, thermometer, tin, scale-type, "The Cigarette of Quality," 4" x 12", EX, $155.00 B.

Ma's Cola, sign, tin, single-sided, embossed, bottle, 22½" x 31", VG, $75.00 C.

Mason's Root Beer, thermometer, glass and metal, 12" dia., EX, $200.00 C.

Mass & Steffer Inc. Furs, poster, paper, litho, 17" x 23½", G, $90.00 B.

---

**Magnolia Gasoline**, sign, porcelain, "Motor Oil" in center and "Magnolia Gasoline" around edges, round sign, 42" dia., VG.......**$375.00 C**

**Magnolia Metal Company**, pocket mirror, celluloid over metal, 3½", VG .........................................................................**$75.00 C**

**Magnolia Petroleum Company**, sign, porcelain, one-sided, Pegasus each side of top, "Private Road...Unauthorized Personnel...Keep Out," 15" x 8", G.................................................................**$160.00 B**

**Magnolia**, cigar box label, paper, 9" x 6", EX .....................**$75.00 B**

**Magnolia**, sign, porcelain, red flying horse and dealer courtesy panel, 27" x 16", EX.............................................................**$450.00 C**

**Magnus Root Beer**, dispenser, ceramic, in shape of a barrel, VG.....................................................................................**$500.00 B**

**Magnus Root Beer**, dispenser, ceramic, top-mounted metal pump in the shape of a barrel, label on front and back, 14½" tall, 1915, NM ...............................................................**$825.00 B**

**Maier Brewing Co.**, sign, tin, litho, California's finest 102 beer, Los Angeles, CA, 27" x 17", EX ....................................................**$235.00 C**

**Maier Brewing Co.**, tray, metal, "Standard of Perfection," VG **$125.00 C**

**Mail Pouch Chew Tobacco**, thermometer, metal, painted, embossed, treat yourself to the best, 1950s, 3" x 9", VG ...**$155.00 C**

**Mail Pouch Tobacco**, catalog, paper, products for premiums, 1910, 32 pages, VG.........................................................................**$50.00 C**

**Mail Pouch Tobacco**, packet, paper, sample size, "Sweet Chewing," VG ...............................................................................**$20.00 C**

**Mail Pouch Tobacco**, sign, cardboard, curved top standup, "He Punished the Sea," signature by J.Ropen, 21" x 34", VG.....**$75.00 D**

**Mail Pouch Tobacco**, sign, cardboard, curved top, "They Ducked the Ducks," 21" x 34", EX................................................**$105.00 C**

Massasoit Coffee, presentation sign with the trademark Indian Chief, "Fine Aroma, Delicious Flavors," 27" x 34", EX, $825.00 B. *Courtesy of Collectors Auction Services.*

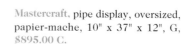

Mastercraft, pipe display, oversized, papier-mache, 10" x 37" x 12", G, $895.00 C.

Mattil, Efinger & Roth, brush, wood and fiber, embossed, "Ambulance, Funeral Directors, Chapel, 5th & Monroe Sts., Both Phones 126, Paducah, KY," 1900s, 7⅝" x 2¼" x 1¾", VG, $45.00 C. *Courtesy of B.J. Summers.*

Mavis It's Real Chocolate, sign, tin, embossed lettering and image, 28" wide, VG, $180.00 B.

Maxwell House Coffee, tray, metal, serving size, old couple in center enjoying the product, oval, 17" long, VG, $195.00 B.

Mail Pouch Tobacco, sign, cardboard, standup style, "The First Hunter Was Also the Game," signed by J Ropen, 21" x 34", VG ..........$65.00 C

Mail Pouch Tobacco, sign, cardboard, title "Their Stone Lips Will Never Tell," with J Ropen signature, 21" x 34", VG ............$95.00 C

Mail Pouch Tobacco, sign, metal, double-sided, flange, boy holding the product, "For Dad Chew Smoke," 21" x 16", VG ......$4,250.00 B

Mail Pouch Tobacco, sign, paper, Indian with his arms crossed and wearing a full headress, "Bloc Tobacco Co," 1909, 15" x 20", EX..................................................................$2,200.00 C

Mail Pouch Tobacco, sign, porcelain, "chew and smoke," 42" x 12", EX.......................................................................$295.00 C

Mail Pouch Tobacco, sign, porcelain, "Treat Yourself To The Best," 36" x 11", EX ...............................................................$175.00 D

Mail Pouch Tobacco, store bin, metal, designed to hold product on counter close to point of purchase, VG .............................$450.00 D

Mail Pouch Tobacco, string holder, metal, mechanism that causes product pouch to rise as string is pulled, 1908, 15" x 20", G .........$2,350.00 B

Mail Pouch Tobacco, thermometer, porcelain, 8" x 38¼", EX .$235.00 D

Mail Pouch Tobacco, thermometer, porcelain, "Chew" in circle logo, 9" dia., EX ...............................................................$200.00 C

Mail Pouch Tobacco, thermometer, porcelain, "treat yourself to the best," 8" x 38½", VG.................................................$225.00 C

Mail Pouch Tobacco, thermometer, porcelain, scale type, "Treat Yourself To The Best" top and "Chew Mail Pouch Tobacco" at the bottom of scale, rounded top and bottom, 39" tall, EX..............$325.00 D

Mail Pouch, sign, cardboard, single-sided, men looking for Davy Jones's locker, "The Real Man's Choice," 14½" x 21", VG...$75.00 C

Mail Pouch Tobacco, thermometer, porcelain, messages at top and bottom, vertical scale, "treat yourself to the best...chew," 8" x 38¾", blue, orange, and white, G .....................$145.00 D

Maine Brace Cut Plug, container, metal, round, slip lid, VG ........$95.00 D

Maine Sardine Council, container, tin, litho, 4th Boy Scout Jamboree Special, 1957, 4-oz., EX .........................................$145.00 C

Majestic Batteries, sign, tin, painted, embossed, "Sales and Service," 19½" x 26", NM.......................................................$350.00 C

Majestic Bottling Company, seltzer bottle, Lynchburg, VA, EX .$45.00 C

Majestic, cigar box label, paper, ocean liner, 9" x 6", NM..$60.00 B

Major Cola, tray, metal, oval, band in a parade, 1930 – 40s, 16", EX...............................................................................$150.00 D

Maxwell House High Grade Coffee, sign, cardboard, container and cup, "the last drop," NOS, 11" x 8¾", 1921, NM, $275.00 C. *Courtesy of Autopia Advertising Auctions.*

Mayo's Plug, sign, porcelain, rooster standing on plugs of tobacco, "Smoking cock o' the walk," 1910s, 6½" x 13", NM, $2,300.00 B. *Courtesy of Muddy River Trading Co./Gary Metz.*

Mazda Lamps, sign, cardboard, "How are you fixed for Mazda lamps?," display being held by bellman, G, $150.00 C.

Mazda Lamps, store display, "How are you fixed for lamps?," box of National Mazda Lamps over message, VG, $125.00 C.

McCord Motor Gaskets, clock, metal and glass, 14½" x 14½", G, $100.00 B.

**Malkin's Best**, sign, metal, light up, coffee cup and "Malkin's Best...Better Foods," 27" x 25" x 10", VG ......................$325.00 B

**Mallard Whiskies**, sign, metal, hunter in boat, 28" x 23", EX.$625.00 B

**Mamma's Choice Rolled Oats**, container, cardboard, paper label, 4¼" x 7⅝", EX.......................................................$65.00 C

**Mamma's Choice Rolled Oats**, container, from Samuel Mahon, Ottumwa & Ft. Madison, IA, young red-haired girl on front cover, 1-lb., EX.......................................................$325.00 C

**Mammoth Peanuts**, container, metal, round, large elephant with huge tusks in oval on front of can, 10 lb., EX.................$225.00 D

**Mammoth Salted Peanuts**, store tin, wooly mammoth on front, Kelly Co., 10-lb., EX.......................................................$165.00 C

**Mammy Brand Salted Peanuts**, tin, litho, mammy on front, "Prepared & Packed By Murray-Roll Co. Pittsburgh, PA," 8" dia. x 9¾", VG.......................................................$1,500.00 D

**Mammy Salted Peanuts**, can, metal, 10 lb, EX..............$2,300.00 B

**Mammy's Favorite Brand Coffee**, pail, metal, from C D Kenny Co., 4 lb., EX .......................................................$365.00 D

**Mammy's Favorite Coffee**, container, tin, litho, metal handle, C.D. Kenny Co., Baltimore, MD, 6¼" dia. x 10½", VG ..............$220.00 B

**Mammy's Favorite Coffee**, from C.D. Kenny, Baltimore, Md, black mammy on front and back, 4-lb., EX................................$275.00 B

**Mammy's Shanty**, matchbook, woman doing wash, "The world's best Apple Pie," front strike, 30 ct., EX .............................$15.00 D

**Manager Hotels Coffee**, can, metal, key wind lid, 1 lb., VG.........$75.00 D

**Manbru Coffee**, tin, litho, screw lid, Schreiber Products Corporation, Buffalo, NY, 1-lb., EX......................................$25.00 B

**Mandarin Salmon**, can label, paper, salmon, EX......................$25.00 D

**Mandeville & King Co Superior Flower Seeds**, sign, paper, pansies in center, 17" x 27", VG .......................................$275.00 D

**Mandeville and King Co. Superior Flower Seeds**, sign, paper, litho, signature Raphael Beck, Rochester, N.Y., young woman and windmill, 23" x 35½", VG.......................................................$275.00 B

**Mandeville and King Co.**, sign, large bouquet of flowers, Rochester NY, 15¾" x 27½", VG.......................................$100.00 D

McCormick-Deering Service, sign, porcelain, double-sided on original hanger arm, 2" x 24", VG, $210.00 C.

McFadden's Spice & Coffee Co., Dubuque, Iowa, sign, cardboard, tin litho, child with a flower, "Select Ground Spices," 13⅜" x 19", EX, $1,450.00 B. *Courtesy of Wm. Morford Investment Grade Collectibles.*

Meadow Gold Ice Cream, sign, porcelain, "Serving...," 20" x 30", EX, $425.00 C.

Meadow Gold Milk, sign, wood and masonite, 13" x 12", G, $115.00 C.

Meat Market, light up globe, milk glass, cow and message on both sides, 16" dia., EX, $795.00 C.

---

**Manhattan Cigar Co.,** box label, lithographer's proof of Indian, 9" x 6", EX............................................$165.00 B

**Manhattan Gasoline,** sign, porcelain, double-sided, 30" dia., EX ........................................................$1,775.00 C

**Manning's Coffee,** can, metal, key wind lid, NM ................$45.00 D

**Manobra,** cigar box label, paper, Indian Chief holding a tomahawk, 9" x 6", EX............................................$55.00 C

**Manru and Nilo Beer,** sign, tin, litho, self-framed, A. Schrriber Brewing Co., Buffalo, N.Y., young woman, glass of the product, "King and Queen of Bottled Beer," 20½" x 24", G...............................$130.00 B

**Mansco Perfume Talc,** container, tin, litho, baby in cameo in center, 2⅛" x 1¼" x 5⅞", EX ................................$180.00 B

**Mansfield Tires Becker Texaco Service,** clock, plastic, round, light-up, metal ring around glass face, EX.....................$245.00 C

**Mansfield's Pepsin Gum,** dispenser, automatic clerk, tag on top, 6½" W x ½" D x 11½" H, EX...............................$400.00 B

**Mansfield's Pepsin Gum,** dispenser, automatic clerk, tag on top, 6½"W x ½"D x 11½"H, VG .........................................$300.00 C

**"Mantan Morehead, Come On Cowboy,"** poster, paper, litho, cowboy on horseback, all-star cast, with Mauryne Brent, Johnny Lee, and F.E. Miller, 28" x 40½", VG...........................................$50.00 B

**Manuel Silvia,** calendar, die cut, from Newport, RI, Boot, Shoe and Rubbers retailer, woman and two young girls, 1905, 12½" x 18", NM .........................................................$325.00 B

**Mapacuba Cigars,** can, metal with embossed lettering and curved corners, 5" dia., EX...............................................$75.00 C

**Mapco Genuine Ignition Parts,** sign, tin, embossed, 36" x 10", 1949, NM.........................................................$250.00 D

**Mapco Speedway Coils,** sign, metal, coil, "The Coil with the Original One Year Guarentee," 10" x 13", EX..........................$450.00 D

**Mapco Speedway Coils,** sign, tin, embossed, vintage auto and product, 9⅛" x 13⅛", NM...........................................$475.00 C

**Maquoketa Cuban Hand Made Cigars,** pinback, celluloid over metal, vintage automobile, 1¾" dia., VG.........................$75.00 B

**Marathon Motor Oil,** hand-soldered can, tin, litho, Transcontinental Oil Co., logo flame runner, 8½" x 6" x 5½", EX.............$135.00 C

Mecca Cigarettes, sign, framed, pretty lady in a wide brimmed hat, 11" x 20", VG, $275.00 C.

Mennen, sign, tin, litho, flange, young child holding Mennen's product, 22¾" W x 14¼" H, EX, $1,250.00 B. *Courtesy of Richard Opfer Auctioneering, Inc.*

Mennen's Toilet Powder, sign, paper, logo of Mennen's man, 1919, 9" x 14", VG, $55.00 B.

Mentholatum, A.A. Hyde, display, cardboard, die cut, nurse showing the many uses for the product, 31" x 43", NM, $235.00 C. *Courtesy of Muddy River Trading Co./Gary Metz.*

Mentholatum, window display, cardboard, tri-fold, great graphics and strong colors, 48" x 35", G, $275.00 C. *Courtesy of Wm. Morford Investment Grade Collectibles.*

---

Marathon Motor Oil, sign, tin, double-sided, flange, "For Good Running," Marathon runner, hard-to-find item, 13½" x 23½", EX ...............................................................$975.00 C

Marathon Oil Co., pocket knife, EX ..................................$20.00 C

Marathon Oil Co., thermometer, runner at top, 5" x 16", EX .$215.00 C

Marathon, gas globe, metal and glass, runner image and logo, 13½" dia., EX ....................................................................$375.00 C

Marathon, oil can, metal, spout and grip handle, "Best In The Long Run," 1 gal., VG................................................................$75.00 C

Marathon, sign, metal, runner logo and "Get Marathon Motor Oil," 30" x 12", VG.................................................................$250.00 C

Marathon, sign, pressed board, painted, "Disarm Winter," snow figure with rifle, 48" x 48", G ........................................$45.00 C

Marathon, thermometer, metal, scale type, company logo at bottom, square corners, 5" x 16", EX .....................................$145.00 C

Marbest Turmeric, can, metal, 2 oz., EX...........................$20.00 D

Marburg Bros. Louisiana Perique Tobacco, tin, "grown in St. James Parish, La.," 3½" x 2" x 1¾", EX...............................$75.00 B

Marburg Brothers Tobacco, tin, small lid, two women and "seal of North Carolina, plug cut," 5" x 6", EX.............................$225.00 C

Marc Anthony, crate label, paper, California oranges, helmeted soldier image, EX....................................................................$10.00 D

Marguerite Cigar, sign, cardboard, paper litho, in center cameo, Havana Cigar, 12" x 15", VG.............................................$57.00 B

Marie Tempest Cigars, poster, paper, stone litho featuring young maiden, 16" x 22", 1900s, NM .......................................$1,900.00 B

Marie Tempest Cigars, sign, litho on paper, pretty woman, head scarf, B. Newmark & Co., New York, 1900s, 16" x 22", EX ...............$968.00 B

Marigold Dairy Products, clock, double-bubble light-up, metal body, glass cover and face, 15½" dia., VG...................$450.00 C

Marine Band, large hanging store harmonica, made of high quality cardboard, 24" x 5" x 7", EX...............................................$300.00 C

Merrick Six Cord Soft Finish Spool Cotton, cabinet, wood and glass, product message on front glass, VG, $2,100.00 C.

Metzger Packing Co. Inc. playing cards, plastic coated, full deck in original box, company name on each card, 2½" x 3½", VG, $20.00 C. *Courtesy of B.J. Summers.*

Meyer Distributing Co., lighter, metal, Falstaff Beer shield on side, made by Park Lighter, 1¼" x 2¼" x ¼", F, $10.00 C. *Courtesy of B.J. Summers.*

Michelin, sign, cardboard, die cut, easel back, stand-up, foreign, 14¾" x 17½", VG, $1,200.00 C.

Michigan Bell Telephone, sign, porcelain, flange, 11¾" x 11", NM, $295.00 C. *Courtesy of B.J. Summers.*

---

Marine Special Outboard Motor Oil, can, metal, boat, 1 qt., EX .$75.00 D

Market Basket Coffee, can, metal, key wind lid, 1 lb., EX........$50.00 B

Market Coffee, tin, litho, key-wound lid, from San Francisco, CA, 1-lb., EX ...................................................................$55.00 C

Marklin Trains, sign, cardboard, stand up, train engine, 1939, 16" x 12", EX ...................................................................$55.00 D

Marks Bros. Dramatic Co., "The Canadian Kings of Repertoire," poster, paper, litho, cast, 40" x 27", 1905, EX..................$180.00 B

Marlin, razor blades, in original box, G ..............................$15.00 C

Marlin Firearms Co., catalog, paper, front cover of man cleaning a rifle, 1926, 24 pages, EX.....................................................$65.00 C

Marlin Firearms Co., catalog, paper, Marlin products illustrated, 1911, 122 pages, EX.........................................................$175.00 C

Marlin Firearms Co., catalog, paper, small carry along size full of rifles and shotguns, 1922, 20 pages, EX.............................$50.00 C

Marlin Firearms Co., stationary, paper, engraved Marlin shotgun on the letterhead, 1890s, EX....................................................$120.00 C

Marlin Firearms, sign, paper, hunter hidden behind rock, "A Gun For The Man Who Knows...," 1905, 13" x 23", EX ............................$850.00 B

Marlin Razor Blade, display, with all blade packages present, 9" x 13½", EX...............................................................................$95.00 C

Marlin Repeaters, sign, cardboard, campfire with Indian brave holding a rifle while he keeps watch, Marlin Fire Arms Co., 8" x 11", EX...............................................................................$550.00 B

Marlin Repeating Rifles & Shotguns, sign, paper, hunting and downed Mallards, 1908, 15" x 24", EX ...............................$150.00 C

Marlin Rifle and Shotgun, banner, cloth, vertical, 20" x 29", VG.............................................................................................$75.00 C

Marmon Roosevelt, sign, porcelain, "Authorized Service," double-sided, 30" x 24", EX........................................................$2,750.00 B

Marquette Club Ginger Ale, sign, cardboard, 14" x 3" x 15", EX .$25.00 B

Marquette Club Ginger Ale, sign, die cut, easel back, man has attached glass eyes, 1940s, 8" x 11", EX............................$140.00 B

Marquette Club Ginger Ale, sign, die cut, easel back, man has attached glass eyes, 1940s, 8" x 11", NM..........................$200.00 C

Michigan Propellers, thermometer, metal and glass, 12" dia., VG, $350.00 B.

Midwest Ice Cream, sign, porcelain, a bonnet-clad lady with a serving tray, 20" x 30", EX, $325.00 C.

Midwest Milk, clock, metal body with reverse painted glass front cover, light-up, 15½" x 15½", white and red, EX, $200.00 C. *Courtesy of B.J. Summers.*

Mil-Kay, sign, metal, black man with serving tray with product, "Drink...The Vitamin Drink...Large Bottle 5¢," scarce, 1941, 55" x 31½", G, $825.00 D. *Courtesy of Rare Bird Antiques Mall/Jon & Joan Wright.*

Miller Genuine Draft, display, light-up, three-dimensional, bottle in ice block, NM, $95.00 C. *Courtesy of Pleasant Hill Antique Mall & Tea Room/Bob Johnson.*

---

**Marquette Club Pale Dry Ginger Ale**, sign, cardboard, die cut, woman in front of icebox, 22" x 26", EX ..............................$75.00 B

**Marshall Cubana**, cigar box label, paper, medieval wars, 9" x 6", EX.................................................................................$45.00 D

**Martin Cigar**, shoe horn, give-away item, 4¼", EX ...................$55.00 C

**Martin Diesel**, No. 1 H.I. globe, plastic body with glass lens, 13½" dia., VG ..............................................................................$350.00 C

**Martin**, gas globe, plastic and glass, Martin logo and "Xtra Special Ethyl," also has Ethyl logo at bottom, 13½" dia., EX.........$375.00 C

**Martin-Senour Paints**, sign, porcelain, paint being applied with a brush, "Sold Here" in die cut at bottom, double-sided, 19" x 21", EX.................................................................................$650.00 B

**Marvel Brand Coffee and Food Products**, display case decal, product in front of window scene, 1925, 8½" x 11", EX..............$80.00 B

**Marvel Brand Coffee**, decal, vinyl, steaming cup of coffee, 1920s, 9" x 11", EX............................................................................$125.00 D

**Marvel Oats**, box, cardboard, early with mountains and waterfall scene, from the Webster Grocery Co., Danville, IL, 5⅜" x 9½", EX.................................................................................$120.00 B

**Marvells**, thermometer, metal, "the cigarette of quality," painted, product package at top of vertical scale, message at bottom, blue background, G.......................................................................$55.00 C

**Marvels Mild Cigarettes**, carton, G ...................................$40.00 D

**Marx Old Style Bread**, sign, "Famous for Flavor," bread wagon being pulled by oxen, 36" x 24", EX............................................$450.00 B

**Marx Old Style Bread**, sign, "Famous for Flavor," bread wagon being pulled by oxen, 36" x 24", G ..............................................$200.00 C

**Maryland Club Coffee**, can, metal, sample size, unopened, 1½ oz, EX ....................................................................................$95.00 D

**Maryland Club Mixture**, container, metal, vertical, pocket sized, large building in center oval, EX .......................................$250.00 B

Miller High Life, sign, light-up, "Buy it now" with bottle and can on either side of message, EX, $95.00 C. *Courtesy of B.J. Summers.*

Milwaukee Harvesting Machines, match holder, tin, litho, worker with bandana and wide brimmed hat, "Always Reliable," 5½" H, EX, $395.00 C. *Courtesy of Richard Opfer Auctioneering, Inc.*

M. Livingston & Co. Inc. Mince Meat, box, cardboard, 2½" x 3¼" x 2", EX, $35.00 C. *Courtesy of B.J. Summers.*

M. Livingston & Co., washboard, wood and metal, company information at top of metal board, 1910 – 20s, 12½" x 23½", VG, $55.00 C. *Courtesy of B.J. Summers.*

Mobil Car-Care, thermometer, metal with curved glass face, "at all temperatures," 11¾" dia., VG, $325.00 C.

---

**Marylin Monroe,** playing cards, display, cardboard, die cut, heart, 1955, 8" x 6" x 9", EX ..........................$350.00 D

**Mascot Tobacco,** tip tray, metal, animals at water, 5" L, EX .$75.00 C

**Mason & Stout,** sign, glass, reverse painted, wood frame, "Bill posters...orders left at wood's exchange promptly executed," 23½" x 19.33", EX ........................................................$225.00 C

**Mason & Stout,** sign, glass, reverse painted, wood frame, city bill posters 23½" x 19½", EX....................................$135.00 C

**Mason and Hamlin Piano,** sign, tin, embossed, baby grand piano in center, 32" x 24", VG..................................$175.00 B

**Mason's Blacking Box,** box, wood, paper litho on inside lid and front of box, boot shiner, 11¾" x 9" x 3", G..................$145.00 B

**Mason's Old Fashioned Root Beer,** sign, cardboard, bottle rack with beach scene, "Everybody's Favorite," 10" x 10", EX...$95.00 C

**Mason's Old Fashioned Root Beer,** sign, cardboard, bottle rack with beach scene, "Everybody's Favorite," 10" x 10", NM ..$110.00 C

**Mason's Root Beer,** chalkboard menu, G...........................$65.00 C

**Mason's Root Beer,** thermometer, tin, embossed, tilted bottle, 10¼" x 25", 1960s, EX ........................................................$90.00 B

**Mason-Heflin Coal Co.,** puzzle, cardboard, finished image of very early company coal truck, 1930s, 6½" x 4.75", EX.............$75.00 D

**Massasoit Coffee,** presentation sign, trademark Indian chief, "Fine Aroma, Delicious Flavors," 27" x 34", F...........................$300.00 C

**Massey Ferguson,** sign, metal, self-framing, "World Famous Farm Equipment," 40" x 20", G...................................................$155.00 C

**Master Feeds,** sign, porcelain, "We sell ...," 26½" x 16", VG .$75.00 C

**Master Feeds,** sign, porcelain, oval, "We sell ...," 26½" x 16", EX ......................................................................................$155.00 C

**Master is Good Bread,** door push, tin, embossed, double-sided, 3" x 29½", EX.............................................................................$115.00 C

Mobil-flame, sign, porcelain, Pegasus, "bottled gas service," double-sided, on metal arm, 32½" x 40½", VG, $2,000.00 C. *Courtesy of Collectors Auction Services.*

Mobilgas, sign, porcelain, double-sided, shield with iron hanger at top, 48" x 48", EX, $1,300.00 C. *Courtesy of Collectors Auction Services.*

Mobilgas Special, pump globe, glass and metal, 1940 – 50s, 20" high, EX, $875.00 C.

Mobil Oil, Pegasus, porcelain, die cut, 36" tall, red, NM, $1,800.00 C.

Modox Drink, tip tray, tin, litho, die cut, "Indian Herbs," strong colors, 5⅝" x 5", EX, $500.00 B. *Courtesy of Richard Opfer Auctioneering, Inc.*

**Master Locks,** display, metal, Strength Security Padlock, 5½" dia.., G ..$45.00 C

**Master Mason Plug Smoking Tobacco,** tin, "It's good tobacco," Quebec, 3-lb., G .................................................................$65.00 D

**Master Mason Ready Tobacco,** can, metal, pocket size, EX .$1,075.00 B

**Master Padlocks,** emblem, metal, round, embossed lion head and lettering, 6" dia., EX .......................................................$75.00 C

**Master Trucks Inc.,** ink well, cast iron, embossed lettering, Chicago, USA, 7" x 5½" x 2¾", EX...............................................$210.00 B

**Masterpiece Fertilizers,** sign, tin, single-sided, embossed, 20" x 13½", VG ..............................................................$185.00 C

**Masury Paints-Varnishes,** sign, metal, painted, "Masury is Good Paint," English-style soldier in spotlight at lower left of message, 36" x 24", G...........................................................$70.00 C

**Masury Paints-Varnishes,** sign, metal, painted, flange, 36" x 24", EX.........................................................................$55.00 C

**Mathie Brewing Co.,** tray, metal, deep rim and lettering, girl playing ukuele in center, 13" dia., EX.....................................$525.00 B

**Mavis Chocolate,** sign, cardboard, standup for counter use, "Cooling Refreshing Drink...Real Chocolate Flavor," 1930s, 20" x 30", EX.........................................................................$125.00 D

**Mavis,** sign, tin, double-sided, litho, flange, bottle, "Real chocolate flavor," by the American Artworks, 12½" x 9½", EX.......$180.00 B

**Max-I-Mum Coffee,** can, metal, key wind lid, 2 lb, EX........$85.00 D

**Maxine Shoes Sign,** sign, tin, die cut, litho, woman in high top shoes, 13¼" x 19½", EX....................................................$275.00 B

**Maxwell Automobiles,** tray, metal, dealer name on rim, 4" dia., EX ..........................................................................$360.00 B

**Maxwell House Coffee,** cup, heavy paper, sample, tilted coffee cup on front, "Good to the Last Drop," 2½" x 2½", EX ...............$3.00 D

Mogul Egyptian Cigarettes, sign, tin, litho, self-framing, Mogul with a cigarette, temple, in background 20" x 24", EX, $2,200.00 B. *Courtesy of Buffalo Bay Auction Co.*

Mojud Supp-hose, ad, plastic, three-dimensional, woman in yellow outfit sitting in ladder-back chair, EX, $195.00 C. *Courtesy of Creatures of Habit.*

Molloy Marine Service Paducah Ky, lighter, metal, made by Park Lighter, advertising on one side only, 1¼" x 2¼" x ¼", EX, $25.00 C. *Courtesy of B.J. Summers.*

Monarch Coffee, container, cardboard, super lion in center cameo, from Reid, Murdoch & Co., Chicago, 1930s, 3 lb., G, $145.00 C.

Monarch Finer Foods, clock, metal and glass, good colorful image of logo lion's head in center by Telechron, 15" dia., EX, $300.00 B.

---

Maxwell House Coffee, factory cafeteria cup and saucer with cup in front of factory, EX............................................................$110.00 B

Maxwell House Coffee, serving tray, metal, "since 1892," 15" x 12½", EX.............................................................................$30.00 C

Maxwell House Coffee, sign, cardboard, string-hung, 1920s coffee container, 1920s, EX...........................................................$325.00 B

Maxwell House Coffee, sign, cardboard, upturned coffee cup, the last drop on the rim and a can of the product, 1920s, 11" x 9", EX.............................................................................$250.00 D

Maxwell House Coffee, sign, celluloid, upturned coffee cup, "good to the Last Drop," 12" x 6", EX..........................................$125.00 B

Maxwell House Coffee, thermometer, metal and glass, dial type, cup and saucer in center, 13" dia., EX..............................$100.00 C

Maxwell House High Grade Coffee, sign, cardboard, container and cup, "the last drop," 11" x 8¾", 1921, G ............................$95.00 C

May-Day Coffee, tin litho, key-wound, unopened, "You'll Like The Flavor," 1-lb., NM................................................................$34.00 B

Mayo's Cut Plug "Brownie," tin, litho, mammy smoking a pipe with product in dress pocket, 6" dia. x 7¼" h, VG ....................$400.00 B

Mayo's Cut Plug Smoking and Chewing Tobacco, pail, tin, with wire, G ................................................................................$75.00 C

MoPar, clock, neon, lighted, "Parts...Accessories," 18¼" x 18¼", EX, $975.00 C. *Courtesy of Autopia Advertising Auctions.*

Motor Club Coffee, tin, paper label, couple in vintage touring car, for Beiderman Bros., Chicago, pry lid, 1-lb., EX, $1,350.00 B. *Courtesy of Wm. Morford Investment Grade Collectibles.*

Mountain Dew, sign, porcelain, "Drink...," 1965, 5' x 3', EX, $375.00 B.

Moxie, globe, glass, light up, painted, "Drink Moxie" in center color band, 10" dia., EX, $500.00 B.

Moxie, tip tray, metal, litho, woman with glass of product and leaf border, "I just love...don't you," 6" dia., EX, $235.00 B.

---

Mayo's Mammy, roly-poly, in likeness of black mammy, G.$250.00 B

Mayo's Plug Smoking Tobacco, poster, canvas, rooster crowing, 60" x 24", EX....................$155.00 B

Mayo's Plug Tobacco, sign, cardboard, rooster crowing about the product, "light and dark," 18½" x 31", VG.......................$200.00 B

Mayo's Plug, sign, porcelain, rooster standing on plugs of tobacco, "Smoking cock o' the walk," 1910s, 6½" x 13", G...............$900.00 C

Mayo's Tobacco, banner, cloth, Mayo's Plug Smoking Tobacco, rooster, 59" x 23", EX.......................$150.00 D

Mayo's Tobacco, can, metal, round, slip lid, ½ lb, EX.......$100.00 B

Mayo's Tobacco, roly poly in likeness of a Dutchman, EX ..$550.00 B

Mayo's Tobacco, roly poly in likeness of Black mammy, EX .$850.00 B

Maytag, display, composition and wood, in likeness of the lonely Maytag man, 10" tall, EX.....................................$95.00 D

Maytag, Newton, Iowa, sign, porcelain, single-sided, 9" x 12", EX .................................................................$275.00 B

Mazawattee Tea, tin, litho, 3 boys with empty cups, 8½" x 5½" x 6", VG .................................................................$500.00 B

Mazda Lamps, display, cardboard, "How are you fixed for Mazda lamps?," display being held by bellman, EX.....................$300.00 C

Mazda Lamps, store display, "How are you fixed for lamps?," box of National Mazda Lamps over message, G...........................$85.00 D

MBC Mixed Paint, bill hook, celluloid and metal, can of American Varnish, 2" dia., EX ..........................................$110.00 B

McAvoys Malt Marrow Beer, serving tray, tin, litho, boy with a bottle and a dog, 12" dia., G ....................................$220.00 B

McCord Gaskets, thermometer, metal, "Hot or Cold You Can Depend On," square with arched scale type, 15" x 15", EX..............$275.00 C

Moxie, thermometer, metal, scale-type, "It's Always A Pleasure to Serve You," 6¾" x 12⅛", G, $170.00 B.

Moxie, match holder, tin, litho, die cut, resembling Moxie drink bottle, 7" H, EX, $500.00 B. *Courtesy of Richard Opfer Auctioneering, Inc.*

Moxie, sign, metal, double-sided, flange, 18" wide, EX, $325.00 B.

Moxie, sign, tin, litho, white horse in the touring car with a Moxie billboard in background, 24" x 13", 1933, EX, $575.00 C. *Courtesy of Buffalo Bay Auction Co.*

Moxie, thermometer, tin, litho, great graphics on this piece, 1920s, 12" x 9½", EX, $1,500.00 B. *Courtesy of Muddy River Trading Co./Gary Metz.*

---

**McCormick Bee Brand Teas, Spices, Extracts, Drugs,** pocket mirror, celluloid, 1¾" x 2⅞", EX.................................................$800.00 B

**McCormick Deering,** calendar, full calendar pad, young boy playing a horn, 13" x 20", 1942, EX .........................................$40.00 B

**McCormick Farm Machinery,** calendar, paper, horse drawn machinery and girl with roses, 1912, EX.........................$155.00 D

**McCormick Farm Machinery,** sign, paper, girl greeting returning soldier, ""Back From The War," 1940s, 27" x 18", EX ...............$135.00 D

**McCormick Harvester,** sign, paper, litho, field scene showing the new product, 33¼" x 27½", 1831, VG ................................$750.00 B

**McCormick Harvesting Machines,** sign, paper, the Battle of Atlanta, July 28, 1864, 28" x 27", VG .............................................$490.00 B

**McCormick,** calendar, full pad of tear sheets, young women with children in front of Dutch windmill, 1933, EX .........................$175.00 C

**McCormick-Deering Farm Machines,** sign, tin, painted, 27½" x 10", EX ..........................................................................$95.00 C

**McCormick-Deering Farm Machines,** sign, tin, painted, from Baldwinsville Farm Supply, Baldwinsville, N.Y., 27½" x 10", EX $75.00 B

**McCormick-Deering,** sign, tin, self-framing, embossed, "We Use Only Genuine Parts," 16" x 12", VG...........................$210.00 B

**McCulloch Chain Saws,** sign, tin, embossed, goose in flight, 47" dia., G...................................................................$135.00 D

**McCulloch Chain Saws,** thermometer, metal and glass, arched dial type, "Hot or Cold...Start Fast," 1950s, 14" dia., VG .............$125.00 D

**McCulloch Chain Saws,** thermometer, reverse on bubble glass, dial-type, 1950s, 14" dia., NM .................................................$135.00 C

**McDonald's,** bank, plastic, "Ronald's Singing Wastebasket," 1975, EX .................................................................$15.00 D

**Muchlebach's,** match holder, tin, litho, die cut, shaped like bottle, "special brew," 7" H, EX, $195.00 C. *Courtesy of Richard Opfer Auctioneering, Inc.*

**Mullen Motor Co. Inc.,** lighter, metal, premium for Ray H. Mullen Buick, car logo on lid, 1960s, 1½" x 2¼" x ¼", EX, $35.00 C. *Courtesy of B.J. Summers.*

**Munsing Wear,** store display, cardboard, easel back, small red-haired girl, "Miss Particular," 1910, 8½" x 11", NM, $95.00 C. *Courtesy of Muddy River Trading Co./Gary Metz.*

**Munsing Wear Union Suit,** sign, tin, die cut, litho, small boy and girl in their union suits, 20½" x 21", EX, $3,400.00 B.

**Murad The Turkish Cigarette,** sign, tin, self-framing, simulated wood frame, 28" x 39", 1906, EX, $550.00 B. *Courtesy of Buffalo Bay Auction Co.*

---

**McDonald's,** hand puppets, vinyl and cloth, set of three, Hamburgler, Ronald, and Grimace, 1993, EX .......................$35.00 C

**McDonald's,** postcard, cardboard, also a coupon for free food, early building, 5" x 3½", EX .......................$35.00 C

**McFadden's Spice & Coffee Co. Dubuque, Iowa,** sign, tin over cardboard, vintage litho, child with a flower, "Select Ground Spices," 13⅜" x 19", EX .......................$1,450.00 B

**McFadden's Spices,** sign, tin on cardboard beveled edge, young girl with flower, 13¼" x 19", 1904, G .......................$500.00 C

**McGarvey Atwood Coffee,** sign, cardboard, steaming hot cup of coffee, "We Serve...of Course," 12" x 6", EX .......................$25.00 B

**McKesson's Asprin,** thermometer, porcelain, scale type, with product at bottom, "Best for Pain..." at top, rounded top & bottom, 27" tall, EX .......................$350.00 B

**McLaughlin Bros.,** game board "Parlor Football Game" vintage football game in progress, 19¾" x 10½" x 1", 1900s, EX .......$1,150.00 B

**McLaughlin's Coffee,** store bin, slant top, cup and saucer, 16¾" x 13" x 19¼", EX .......................$275.00 C

**McLaughlin's Columbian Coffee,** container, tin, litho, sailing ship on side, pry-type lid, 1-lb., EX .......................$74.00 B

**McLaughlin's Manor House Coffee,** can, metal, keywind lid, and landscape scene, 1 lb, EX .......................$50.00 B

**McLaughlin's Manor House Coffee,** tin, key-wound lid, 1-lb., F .$12.00 C

**McNish, Johnson and Slavins Refined Minstrels,** poster, paper, litho, two men on front, 1920s, 30½" x 42", EX .......................$425.00 B

**Meadow Gold Ice Cream,** display board, masonite, "Please Pay When Served," manufactured by Kay Displays, 11" x 16", VG .........$75.00 C

**Meadow Gold Ice Cream,** display board, masonite, "Please Pay When Served," manufactured by Kay Displays, 11" x 16", EX .......$135.00 C

**Meadow Gold Products,** sign, porcelain, self-framing, 30" x 26", VG .......................$175.00 C

Murattis After Lunch Cigarettes, tin, man at table with the product, 3¼" x 2¾" x ½", VG, $80.00 B.

Muriel Cigars, sign, cardboard, die cut, pretty Edie Adams holding a box of the product, 8½" x 20¼", VG, $45.00 B.

Mustang Liniment, sign, metal, "Use...Man or Beast," 20" wide, VG, $225.00 B.

M/V Cindy Celeste Christening, stemware glass, by B & H Towing, 1992, 9" tall, NM, $35.00 C. *Courtesy of B.J. Summers.*

Myrick's Boat Store, lighter, metal, premium, by Park Lighter, 1¼" x 2¼" x ⅜", G, $20.00 C. *Courtesy of B.J. Summers.*

---

Meadow Gold Vanilla Ice Cream, tin, round, half-gallon ice cream, EX .................................................................$15.00 D

Mecca Flake Cut Plug Tobacco, container, tin, litho, by the Daniel Scotten Co., 4½" x 3¼" x 1½", EX.......................................$50.00 C

Meiers Ice Cream, sign, porcelain, double-sided, "We Serve... Meiers Ice Cream...Waukesha," 35¾" x 24", VG ...............$325.00 B

Melachrino Cigarette, sign, cardboard, "The one cigarette sold the world over," 28" x 4", EX ........................................$55.00 C

Melachrino, sign, cardboard with wooden frame, "The one cigarette sold the world over," 28" x 4", EX .........................$55.00 C

Melachrino, sign, tin on cardboard, young woman with the product, "The Cigarette Elect of all Nations, by the New York Metal Ceiling Co., 11¼" dia., EX .............................................................$110.00 B

Mello Ice Cream, sign, metal, double-sided, cone carature proclaiming "For Goodness' Sake! eat...," 36" x 24", EX .................$275.00 C

Mellor & Rittenhouse Licorice, tin, White House on lid, 5" x 5" x 6¾", 1880s, VG.......................................................$95.00 C

Melox Dog Food, sign, porcelain, dog on large ball, 18" x 26", EX ...............................................................................$875.00 D

Melox Dog Food, sign, porcelain, dog on Melox ball, "The Foods that Nourish," 18" x 26", EX.................................................$525.00 C

Memory, cigar box label, paper, old man by fireplace, 9" x 6", EX $45.00 D

Mennen Talcum for Men, container, metal, sample size, flower basket design, 2¼ " tall, EX ................................................$50.00 D

Mennen's Violet Toilet Powder, tin, litho, vintage era man on front, 2½" x 4⅝" x 1⅜", VG ...............................................$300.00 B

Mennen's, sign, paper, framed, promoting toilet powder, 9½" x 13¼", EX......................................................................$85.00 C

Mennen, sign, tin, litho, flange, young child holding Mennen's product, 22¾" W x 14¼" H, VG................................................$475.00 C

Mentholatum, sign, cardboard, die cut, nurse showing the many uses for the product, A.A. Hyde, 31" x 43", VG..............................$175.00 C

**Mentholatum,** sign, cardboard, trifold design, redheaded girl in center, "...For Head Colds," 48" x 35", EX.............................$675.00 D

**Mentholatum,** window display, cardboard, tri-fold, 48" x 35", EX..$625.00 B

**Mercantile,** calendar, die cut, from Eilers & Bolton, Monticello, IA, with full pad and young girls in boat, 10¼" x 18"x, 1900, EX.$280.00 B

**Mercurochrome,** sign, cardboard, die cut, counter, man doctoring arm with product, 15" x 22", VG.........................................$95.00 C

**Meriden Fire Arms Co.,** box, cardboard, empty, two-piece, "Pointer Loaded Shells, Conn., " 4" x 4" x 2½", NM.........................$200.00 C

**Merion Hair Net,** display box, metal, store, bobbed hair woman with mirror on lid, G...............................................................$95.00 D

**Merita Bread,** sign, self-framing, embossed, Lone Ranger, 24" x 36", G...........................................................................................$375.00 B

**Merriam Bulldog Segars,** figure, cast metal, 3" x 2" x 1½", EX..$85.00 B

**Merrick Six Cord Soft Finish Spool Cotton,** cabinet, wood and glass, message on front glass, G................................$975.00 C

**Merrill Transport Company,** thermometer, dial-type, resembling a tire, 15" dia., EX.......................................................................$250.00 D

**Messeroll Cough Drops,** store jar, glass, vintage, embossed lettering, 5⅛" x 5⅛" x 8¼", EX..............................................$170.00 B

**Metro,** pump sign, porcelain, red Pegasus over lettered Metro, 13" x 13", EX ........................................................................$550.00 C

**Metz Beer,** tin, litho, face, square tin frame, beer bottle on left side of face, "The Old Reliable," 15" sq., VG.............................$175.00 B

**Meyer Brewing Co.,** tip tray, young woman, same image as found on Old Reliable Coffee tip tray, "Compliments of...Bloomington, Ill." 4¼" dia., EX ...................................................................$201.00 B

**Meyer's Ice Cream,** tray, metal, boy & girl eating ice cream, 13" dia., EX.............................................................................$935.00 B

**Meyers Pumps,** sign, paper, complete line of pumps and products, metal bottom and top strips with calendar tear sheets in center of paper, limited issue due to WWII, 17" x 51", 1944, EX ........$275.00 B

**Meyers,** calendar, paper, heavy stock, "Pumps, Hay Tools, Door Hangers," distributed by FF Meyers & Bro Co., 1929, 20" x 50", EX...................................................................................$265.00 B

**MFA,** gas globe, plastic and glass, company lettering on shield design, EX ................................................................$300.00 C

**MH & M Shoes,** sign, tin, embossed, die cut, in the shape of an arm and hand, 28" x 6½", black on yellow, EX .........$225.00 C

**MH & M,** sign, tin, die cut, embossed, cut-out of hand with finger pointing to the right direction, 28" x 6½", VG.............$275.00 C

**Mi Favorita Cigars,** tip tray, metal, "A Solace For Busy Minds...Clear Havana," 1⅛" L, EX .................................$130.00 B

**Miami Beach, World's Playground,** license plate attachment, cast aluminum with die cut images of palm trees and fish, 12" x 4¾", EX.$95.00 C

**Miami Powder Co,** sign, paper, mallards in flight, 1891, 18" x 25", EX.........................................................................$2,500.00 B

**Mica Wheel Grease,** sign, cardboard, countertop display, 11" x 14¾", EX....................................................................$135.00 C

**Michael-Leonard Seed Co.,** thermometer, tin, salesman sample, featuring three different Indian images, with original box, 9" dia., 1930s, NM ..........................................................$325.00 C

**Michelin Man,** ashtray, molded with Michelin Man standing in ashtray, 1940s, 6" x 4¾", EX...................................................$85.00 C

**Michelin Man,** sign, porcelain, Michelin Man on a speeding bike, 15" x 19", EX .......................................................$425.00 B

**Michelin Man,** sign, porcelain, one-sided, with tire, NOS, 27" x 31½", EX................................................................$300.00 B

**Michelin Man,** sign, tin, one-sided, on motorcycle, foreign, 14½" x 20", VG............................................................$500.00 C

**Michelin truck,** ornament, metal, in likeness of the Michelin Man, 9" tall, EX...........................................................$75.00 C

**Michelin,** sign, porcelain, one-sided, motorcycle tire, 38" x 57½", G.....................................................................$950.00 B

**Michelob Beer,** bar sign, plastic and metal light up, pretty smiling woman at a bar and a tall mug of Michelob beer in front of her, 1970s, 19" x 16", VG ..................................................$15.00 C

**Michelob Classic Dark,** tapper handle, EX.........................$15.00 D

**Michelob Light,** tapper handle, with skier on top, EX ........$20.00 D

**Michelob,** sign, metal and glass, light up, neon, name and bow tie, Anheuser-Busch eagle at top of sign, 1940s, 40" long, EX.....$235.00 D

**Michigan Ammonia Works,** container, tin, Excelsior Carbonate of Ammonia, with small snap lid, 5-lb., 7⅞" x 4½" dia., EX.....$25.00 C

**Michigan Bell Telephone,** sign, porcelain, flange, 11¾" x 11", EX .$250.00 B

**Michigan Stove Co.,** match holder, cast iron, "Michigan Stove Co. Stoves are the best," 4" x 7", EX.........................................$215.00 B

**Mickey Mouse Cookies,** box, cardboard with string carrier, Mickey Mouse on side, from Nabisco, 1940s, 6" x 3" x 2", EX........$165.00 B

**Mickey Mouse Shoe Polish,** hat, paper, scenes of Mickey Mouse polishing shoe next to product, 12" x 6", VG......................$95.00 D

**Midwest Ice Cream,** store sign, porcelain, bonnet-clad lady with a serving tray, 20" x 30", VG................................................$275.00 C

**Midwest Milk,** clock, metal body with reverse painted glass front cover, light-up, 15½" x 15½", white and red, VG............$175.00 C

**Mil K Botl,** display, cardboard, die cut, countertop, "Double Size 5¢," 8½" x 10", EX ................................................................$55.00 B

**Mil-Kay Soda,** sign, cardboard, die cut, black waiter with a tray holding a bottle and a glass, 28" x 17", EX ........................$215.00 C

**Mil-Kay Soda,** sign, cardboard, die cut, black waiter with a tray holding a bottle and a glass, 28" x 17", VG ......................$145.00 C

**Mil-Kay,** sign, metal, black man with serving tray with product, "Drink...The Vitamin Drink...Large Bottle 5¢," scarce, 1941, 55" x 31½", EX ......................................................$1,295.00 C

**Mil-Kay,** sign, tin, Black waiter, "Drink Vitamin Drinks...," EX .$750.00 B

**Milburn Wagon Co.,** sign, metal, "The Demand For The Milburn Wagon," bandits and wagons, 28" x 20", VG ...................$1,600.00 B

**Milcor Steel Company,** sign, cardboard, paper, products, from Canton, Ohio, 22" x 28", 1931, NM ........................................$285.00 C

**Military Brand,** cigar box label, paper, campsite scene of soldiers during the war of northern aggression, EX ........................$250.00 B

**Milking Shorthorns,** license plate attachment, tin, embossed, "The Breed that Fills Every Need," 10¼" x 5¼", VG....................$50.00 B

**Millar's Home Blend Coffee,** container, tin, key-wound, litho, 1-lb., NM ........................................................................$37.00 B

**Millar's Magnet Cocoa,** container, tin, litho, harvesting of cocoa on each side, 3¼" x 3¼" x 6", EX ................................$65.00 C

**Millar's Magnet Coffee,** tin, F.B. Millar & Co, Chicago, Denver, 1-lb., G............................................................................$25.00 D

**Millar's Mountain Brand Coffee,** tin, paper label of Turkish tent scene, 2-lb., EX ......................................................$210.00 B

**Millar's Nut Brown Coffee,** tin with paper label, 3-lb., EX .$125.00 C

**Millard's Vanilla Chocolate & Breakfast Cocoa,** sign, metal, boy standing on box while holding sign, "Give Strength & Nourishment...They Are The Best," 16" x 21", EX ....................................$950.00 B

**Miller Beer,** pinback, Miller Girl on crescent moon, Whitehead & Hoag, ¾" dia., VG ....................................................$35.00 C

**Miller Genuine Draft,** display, light-up, three-dimensional, bottle in ice block, EX ......................................................$65.00 D

**Miller High life Beer,** display figure, plastic, Miller girl with glass, EX............................................................................$65.00 D

**Miller High Life,** sign, neon, new, EX................................$145.00 C

**Miller High Life,** serving tray, metal, round, lady on crescent moon, "The champagne of bottled beer," 12" dia., EX..................$65.00 C

**Miller High Life,** sign, light-up, "Buy it now," bottle and can on either side of message, VG ..................................................$75.00 C

**Miller High Life,** sign, neon, new, VG ..............................$100.00 C

**Miller's Crown Dressing,** trade card, cardboard, die cut in shape of woman's shoe, 7½" x 5", NM................................................$50.00 B

**Miller's Finer, Flavor-Rich Milk,** Delicious Ice Cream, sign, reverse painted glass front, F................................................$45.00 D

**Miller's Finer, Flavor-Rich Milk, Delicious Ice Cream,** sign, reverse painted glass front, G................................................$60.00 C

**Millers Falls,** sign, metal framed plastic front, light-up, "The safest name in tools," 25" x 8", G....................................$55.00 C

**Mills Bros. 27th annual tour, three-ring circus,** poster, trapeze act and horsemanship, 14" x 41", EX......................................$45.00 C

**Milwaukee Crane,** sign, porcelain, single-sided, 18" x 18", VG.$225.00 C

**Milwaukee Harvesting Machines,** match holder, tin, litho, worker with bandana and wide-brimmed hat, "Always Reliable," 5½" H, VG ..........................................................................$350.00 B

**Milwaukee Journal 1923 Tour Club,** radiator grill attachment, die cut, etched brass, in the shape of arrowhead with frog-faced driver with "Gatsby" type hat and glasses, 4" x 5½", NM ............$500.00 C

**Minneapolis Underwear,** sign, cardboard, die cut, "Baby Mary," "Knit Underwear for All the Kiddies," 7" x 10", EX..........................$275.00 D

**Minneapolis Universal,** pocket mirror, celluloid, early farm tractor on reverse side, 2⅛" dia., EX............................................$135.00 C

**Minstrels, McNish, Johnson and Slavins,** poster, paper, litho, 30½" x 42", EX..............................................................$425.00 B

**Miss Detroit Broad Leaf Cigars,** box, cardboard, store display, Miss Detroit on front, 8¼" x 9½" x 9¼", EX ..............................$700.00 B

**Miss Minneapolis Highest Quality Flour,** menu board, die cut, girl holding blackboard, 1918, 19" x 28", EX ........................$95.00 C

**Miss Princine Baking Powder,** cup with paper label, Miss Princine in the center of the can, 3½" x 3⅞", VG ..............................$45.00 D

**Mission Orange,** dispenser, countertop, cooler no. 9672 California Crushed Fruit Corporation, Los Angeles, California, 13½" x 25½", VG ....................................................................$225.00 B

**Mission Orange,** sign, metal, painted, bottle 8¾" x 25", G..$75.00 D

**Mission Orange,** sign, metal, painted, bottle 8¾" x 25", VG ..$95.00 C

**Mission Orange,** sign, tin, litho, self-framing, bottle in center, 10" x 25½", EX..............................................................$225.00 C

**Mississippi Pacific Lines,** calendar, metal back and tear sheets at bottom, speeding locomotive at top, 13" x 19", EX.............$95.00 C

**Missouri Pacific Lines,** calendar, paper, tear sheets at bottom, steam engine moving on tracks, no year, only daily sheets, G......$135.00 C

**Missouri Smoking Pipes,** blister pack from country store with full sheet of pipes, NOS, EX....................................................$65.00 C

**Mister Donut Exclusive Blend Coffee,** container, tin, litho, Mr. Donut, key-wound lid, 1-lb., EX ........................................................$250.00 B

**Mit-Che Ice Cold,** sign, tin, embossed, 23½" x 15½", VG ...$65.00 C

**Mo-Sam Coffee,** tin, litho, pry-lid, pyramid on both sides, 1-lb., EX ........................................................................................$975.00 B

**Mo-Sam Coffee,** tin, paper label, Morton Coffee Co., Baltimore, MD, Egyptian scene on front label, 1-lb., EX............................$250.00 C

**Mobil Freezone,** thermometer, tin, painted, scale-type, Pegasus at top of scale, 8" x 36", NM.....................................................$825.00 B

**Mobil Oil,** calendar, large shop with fishing scene on front in center of message, "follow the magnolia trail," 1933, EX ........$95.00 C

**Mobil Oil,** curb sign, porcelain, cast iron base, Pegasus, 36½" x 65", EX.$500.00 C

**Mobil Oil,** curb sign, porcelain, double-sided, cast iron base, Gargoyle, 30" x 63", EX ........................................................$450.00 C

**Mobil Oil,** Pegasus, porcelain, die cut, 36" tall, red, EX..............$900.00 C

**Mobil Oil,** sign, cardboard, one-sided, 43" x 22", VG........$35.00 C

**Mobil Radiator Flush,** metal rack with cardboard, 25" x 40", G.$80.00 B

**Mobil Service,** clock, Pegasus in center of face, 13" dia., EX .$165.00 C

**Mobil Tire,** clock, foreign, 4" dia., ...................................$210.00 B

**Mobil,** attendant display, life-size painted wood in likeness of station attendant with easel back, 21" x 72", VG............$650.00 B

**Mobil,** attendant's summer hat, all original, EX ......................$175.00 C

**Mobil,** clock, metal body with glass face and front, light-up, Pegasus on the clock face, 15" dia., EX ...........................................$500.00 B

**Mobil,** cloth sleeve patch, 3⅛" x 1¼", G ...............................$10.00 C

**Mobil,** dealer sign, porcelain, single-sided, Pegasus at bottom of sign, 81" x 39", VG.........................................................$280.00 B

**Mobil,** license plate attachment, tin, die cut, embossed, Pegasus, 4½" x 6¼", VG ...................................................................$75.00 C

**Mobil,** license plate attachment, tin, die cut, embossed, Pegasus, "California World's Fair," 5½" x 6¼", NM....................$175.00 C

**Mobil,** playing cards with original leather carrying case, NM...$20.00 C

**Mobil,** sign, plastic, die cut, embossed, red neon, Pegasus, 53" l, VG ..........................................................................................$600.00 B

**Mobil,** sign, porcelain, die cut, one-sided, in shape of Pegasus, 44" L, G.............................................................................$1,100.00 B

**Mobil,** sign, porcelain, die cut, Pegasus, 44" L, G...........$1,100.00 B

**Mobil,** sign, porcelain, restroom with key outline, NOS, 8¾" x 3½", NM .......................................................................$500.00 C

**Mobil,** thermometer, dial, 12" dia., VG........................$400.00 B

**Mobil-flame,** sign, porcelain, bottled gas service, double-sided on metal arm, Pegasus, 32½" x 40½", G ..............................$1,600.00 B

**Mobilfuel Diesel,** globe, low profile metal body with glass lens, Pegasus trademark, 16½" dia., VG ....................................$900.00 C

**Mobilgas Ethyl,** gas globe, metal body with 4 lenses, square, 22½" x 22½" x 16", VG.................................................................$850.00 C

**Mobilgas Marine Gasoline,** globe, wide body glass body, Pegasus, 13½" dia., NM..................................................................$1,200.00 C

**Mobilgas Special Gasoline,** pump sign, porcelain, Pegasus, outlined in black, hard-to-find, 11½" x 12", EX ..............................$275.00 C

**Mobilgas Special,** pump sign, porcelain, die cut, Pegasus at top of message, 1947, 12" x 12", EX ......................................$135.00 C

**Mobilgas Super Speed,** gas globe, low profile metal body with two glass lenses, greyhound racing dog on lens, 15" dia., G .....$600.00 C

**Mobilgas,** clock, light-up, Pegasus the winged horse in the trademark Mobil shield, manufactured by the Pam Clock Co., 15" dia., EX ......................................................................................$650.00 B

**Mobilgas,** Ford tanker truck, tin, 1940s, 2½" x 9", red & white, G .........................................................................................$225.00 C

**Mobilgas,** sign, porcelain, die cut, restroom pledge in shape of shield, 7⅝" x 8", NM ...........................................................$475.00 C

**Mobilgas,** sign, porcelain, truck topper of Pegasus, 24" x 10", EX ........................................................................................$875.00 B

**Mobilgas,** thermometer, porcelain, "Friendly Service," Pegasus at top center, vertical scale, 4¼" x 34½", EX...............................$250.00 C

**Mobilgas,** uniform badge, enameled cloisonné, Pegasus over name, screw-on attachment, ⅝" x 1⅝", EX........................................$375.00 B

**Mobiloil Vacuum Oil Company,** thermometer, porcelain, vertical scale, Pegasus at top in shield, 8" x 23", white, red, and blue, EX ........................................................................................$225.00 C

**Mobiloil,** calendar, "Magnolia Trail," ocean scene at sunset in center of message, 1933, EX ......................................$95.00 C

**Mobiloil,** curb sign, porcelain, two-sided, die cut, Pegasus in center on heavy cast base, "Property of Socony Vacuum Oil Company, Inc." on base, 30½" x 64", VG........................................$700.00 B

**Model 10¢ Tobacco,** sign, tin, litho, cigar store Indian, 6" x 15", NM .....................................................................................$127.00 B

**Model Smoking Tobacco For Pipe or Cigarette,** tin, Model man on front, key-lift lid, 1926 tobacco stamp on lid, G .................$35.00 C

**Model Smoking Tobacco,** sign, metal, "Did You Say 10¢," Model Man, 7" x 16", EX................................................................$265.00 B

**Model Smoking Tobacco,** sign, porcelain, Model Man "Yes I Said Model," 36" x 12", VG .................................................$295.00 D

**Model Tobacco,** sign, tin, litho, Model logo man in cigar store Indian attire, 6" x 15", EX ..............................................$80.00 C

**Model Tobacco,** tin, litho, free sample pocket 3" x 4¼" x ⅞, EX .$400.00 C

**Modena,** cigar box label, paper, EX ...................................$100.00 B

**Modern Girl Beautiful Stockings,** box, woman pulling on stockings, 7½" x 9¾" x 1½", EX............................................................$30.00 C

**Modern Home Series,** tip tray, metal, room setting in tray center, Peaslee-Gaulbert Co...Louisville, Ky., 6¼", G.....................$40.00 B

**Modox Drink,** tip tray, tin, litho, die cut, strong colors, "Indian Herbs," 5⅝" x 5", VG ...........................................................$250.00 C

**Modox,** tray, metal, die cut in shape of Indian in full headress, "...Made from Indian Herbs," EX.....................................$800.00 B

**Mogul Egyptian Cigarettes,** sign, tin, litho, self-framing, Mogul, cigarette, and a temple, 20" x 24", EX.....................$2,200.00 B

**Mohawk Gasoline,** paperweight, glass and copper, company name on band around base and profile of Indian head in center, 3" dia., EX............................................................................$360.00 B

**Mohawk Gasoline,** pocket lighter, die cut Indian head, 1¼" x 2¼" x ⅜", NM.................................................................$300.00 C

**Mohawk Gasoline,** sign, metal and glass, neon lettering and Indian head profile, 48" dia., EX.............................$4,250.00 B

**Mohawk Refrigerator,** sign, metal and glass, Indian head profile in reverse painting, 18" x 10", EX.......................................$75.00 D

**Mohawk Tool Works,** sign, brass, raised detail featuring Indian bust, NOS, 10" x 16", NM............................................$650.00 C

**Mohican Coffee,** tin, litho, slip-lid, Indian in full headdress on front, 1-lb., G...............................................................$40.00 D

**Mohican,** sage spice container, tin, Indian head in war bonnet on front label, 2-oz., EX..................................................$95.00 C

**Mojud Supp-hose,** display, plastic, three-dimensional, woman in yellow outfit sitting in ladder-back chair, G ...........................$125.00 D

**Mojud Thigh-Mold,** display, stretch top garter belt, 11" x 11½", EX.....................................................................................$125.00 C

**Mokaine Liqueurs,** tip tray, tin, litho, old gent at cafe table, 3¾" x 4" x ½", EX.........................................................................$75.00 C

**Monadnock Coffee,** tin, screw-lid, mountain lake scene, from Keene, NH, 1-lb., EX.............................................................$200.00 B

**Monadnock Peanut Butter,** pail with wire handles on side, tin, litho, lake scene in center, 1-lb., EX........................$236.00 B

**Monarch Coffee,** tin, Chicago, L.A. & Boston, 1-lb., EX......$55.00 C

**Monarch Green Tea,** tin with lid, teapot on front, EX ........$12.00 D

**Monarch Light of Asia Tea,** container, metal, pretty lady in front of mountains, 3" x 6", EX........................................................$45.00 D

**Monarch Toffies,** tin, key-wound lid, 1-lb., EX.................$125.00 C

**Monastic,** backbar decanter, ceramic, monks testing the product, metal spigot at base, 9" x 13" x 13", EX.............................$700.00 B

**Monogram Coffee,** tin, paper label from F.W. Wagner & Co., Charleston S.C., with small top, 5½" x 7½", EX ...............$275.00 C

**Monogram High Grade Coffee,** tin, paper label, shaped like a milk can with side handle bail 2-lb., EX................................................$135.00 C

**Monogram Motor Oil,** sign, cardboard, "Stands Up," marching soldiers, 35½" x 11¼", VG ..........................................$135.00 C

**Monogram Uniform Motor Lubricants,** sign, metal, double-sided, flange, 18" dia., EX ..........................................................$360.00 B

**Monogram Uniform Quality Motor Lubricants,** sign, porcelain, double-sided, 18" dia., EX .................................................$375.00 B

**Monroe Beer,** tip tray, metal, banner across the globe, 4⅛" dia., EX..............................................................................$65.00 C

**Monroe Brewing Co,** tray, metal, tip size, king of Rochester holding up a tankard of beer, 4" dia., EX .........................................$95.00 C

**Monroe,** clock, light-up, "the ultimate in shock absorbers...America rides...Monroe," G................................................................$115.00 D

**Monroe-Matic Shock Absorbers,** clock, metal body with glass face and front, double-bubble, "Load Levelers," NOS, 16" dia., EX......$575.00 C

**Montana Frank Western Show,** sign, paper, litho, Indians attacking a home, 20¼" x 27½", 1929, EX ...............................................$625.00 C

**Montgomery Ward Java & Arabian Coffee,** tin with large lid, 7" x 9", 3-lb., 1900s, EX.........................................................$175.00 C

**Montgomery Ward, Red Head,** box, cardboard, two-piece, paper litho with geese, 4⅛" x 4⅛" x 2½", F ...................................$35.00 C

**Monticello Special Reserve,** tip tray, metal, "It's All Whiskey," Monticello along with men on horseback, 6¼", EX.............$80.00 C

**Moore's Supreme Ethyl,** pump sign, porcelain, single-sided, NOS, 10" x 15", EX .................................................................$350.00 B

**Moose Beer,** sign, wood, embossed, 15" x 6⅛", EX..................$125.00 C

**Moose Beer,** sign, wooden, painted, "Better Than Ever," 15" x 6⅞", G.............................................................................$95.00 C

**Moosehead Beer,** sign, tin, EX..........................................$25.00 D

**Moosehead,** sign, neon, moose, "Imported on Tap," EX...**$175.00 D**

**MoPar Parts Accessories,** clock, metal and glass, octagonal, 18" x 18", EX.............................................................................**$550.00 B**

**MoPar Parts Accessories,** clock, neon, lighted, 18¼" x 18¼", VG.............................................................................**$500.00 C**

**MoPar Parts,** sign, porcelain, double-sided, flange, 26" x 18¼", G.............................................................................**$1,100.00 B**

**Morgan & Wright Tire,** sign, paper, young boy in yellow trench coat, 15" x 20", EX.............................................................**$150.00 B**

**Morning Glow Coffee,** can, tin, litho, featuring ship, 5" x 4", EX .............................................................................**$170.00 B**

**Morning Joy Pure Coffee,** can, tin, litho, key-wound, singing bird in front of sunrise, 5" x 3½", EX.........................**$250.00 B**

**Morrell's Boiled Ham,** sign, litho, string-hung, double-sided, ham being lifted out of cauldron being watched by sad pig, 1900s, 10¼" x 11¼", NM.............................................................**$333.00 B**

**Morrell's Pride Meats,** pocket mirror, 2" dia., EX..................**$55.00 C**

**Morris Evans Remedies,** sign, cardboard, litho, 10¼" x 14¾", NM.............................................................................**$58.00 B**

**Morris Supreme Peanut Butter,** pail, tin, litho, children at beach, 12-oz., EX.............................................................**$75.00 B**

**Morse's Candy,** tin, young lady with wide brim hat, screw-on lid, 4½" sq. x 9", EX.............................................................**$125.00 C**

**Morton House Coffee,** tin, litho, screw-lid container, 1-lb., EX .**$61.00 B**

**Morton Salt,** dispenser, tin, wall mount, "Miniatures," Morton girl at top, 3" x 19½" x 2", NM...................................**$135.00 D**

**Morton's Salt,** sign, tin, single-sided, embossed, "It Pours," 27½" x 9¾", VG.............................................................**$55.00 C**

**Mother's Oats,** sign, paper, "The Naughty Boy," 16" x 23", EX .**$300.00 D**

**Mother's Oats,** sign, paper, litho, "Our Boy," young boy, 16" x 22", 1906, EX.............................................................**$180.00 B**

**Mother's Oats,** sign, youngster in pajamas holding a bowl of the product, Akron Oats Co., 15½" x 21", EX.....................**$50.00 B**

**Mother's Worm Syrup,** wall match holder, tin, litho, good, strong colors, mother giving youngster medicine, 2¼" x 6¾", EX .......**$975.00 C**

**Motor Club Coffee,** tin, paper label, couple in vintage touring car, from Beiderman Bros, Chicago, pry-lid, 1-lb., EX...........**$1,350.00 B**

**Motorcycle Equipment Co.,** Ford Supplies catalog, paper, 14th annual catalog, 72 pages, VG.............................**$195.00 C**

**Motorists 5¢ Cigars,** sign, canvas, litho, a man helping a lady motorist, 20" x 16", EX.............................................**$75.00 C**

**Motorola,** clock, metal body, tin face, white neon light, light-up spinner, 21" dia., VG.............................................................**$650.00 B**

**Motorola,** clock, reverse painted glass face, neon spinner, "Radio...For Home or Car," 21½" dia., EX .................**$675.00 C**

**Motorola,** license plate attachment, tin, embossed, Auto Radio Drive Safety, 4⅝" x 4¾", EX.............................................**$95.00 C**

**Motorola,** sign, metal, painted, "Service...Car Radio," G .**$135.00 D**

**Motoroma, Boston, Mass.,** pennant, felt, 28¼" x 12", G.....**$75.00 C**

**Mound City Paints & Brushes,** calendar, cardboard, distributed by BZ Harrison Druggist, lady pilgrim, 1912, 12" x 16", EX ...**$145.00 D**

**Mount Cross Coffee,** tin, litho, embossed tin lid, 5½" x 9½", VG .............................................................................**$120.00 B**

**Mount Cross,** coffee can, metal, key wind lid, 3 lb., VG ...**$190.00 B**

**Mountain Dew,** sign, metal, "Drink...It'll Tickle Your Innards," 60" x 36", EX.............................................................**$395.00 C**

**Mountain States Telephone,** ashtray, glass, blue advertising in flat center, EX .............................................................**$100.00 C**

**Mountain States Telephone,** sign, porcelain, bell logo in center, double-sided flange, 18" x 18", EX.....................**$175.00 B**

**Movie Guide,** display, painted wood, die cut, slug, plate, "Philadelphia Enameling Works, 25¢ N. 13th St., Phila, PA," 13½" x 58½" x 23", G .............................................................**$1,900.00 C**

**Moxie Pureoxia Ginger Ale,** sign, cardboard, "Drink Pureoxia Ginger Ale / Frank Archer Invites You To Visit Moxieland," 39" x 28", EX.............................................................**$450.00 B**

**Moxie,** ashtray, "Drink," Frank Archer promoting product, EX .**$70.00 B**

**Moxie,** ashtray, ceramic, Moxie Man in center, EX............**$95.00 C**

**Moxie,** clock, wood and glass, Baird in the figure 8 shape, face has Roman numerals, "Moxie...Of Course You Will Have Some... It's So Healthful," 31" tall, EX.............................................**$2,200.00 D**

**Moxie,** dish, china, center, Moxie Man, oval shaped, 10" x 5", EX .............................................................................**$175.00 D**

**Moxie,** fan, cardboard, Francis Pritchard, 1918, VG......**$75.00 D**

**Moxie,** fan, young cowboy on rocking horse and Frank Archer on reverse side, EX.............................................................**$225.00 C**

**Moxie,** Lowell bottle, nerve food, EX.................................**$65.00 C**

**Moxie,** match holder, die cut, litho, bottle of product, 2½" x 7⅛", VG ................................................................$300.00 C

**Moxie,** match holder, tin, litho, die cut resembling Moxie drink bottle, 7" H, EX ...........................................$500.00 B

**Moxie,** sign, cardboard, die cut, easel back, "Learn to Drink...Very Healthful," Frank Archer, sitting on product box, 19" x 40", EX ....................................................$790.00 B

**Moxie,** sign, die cut, Moxie girl in center of circle, "I like it," 6¼" dia., EX ...................................................$325.00 C

**Moxie,** sign, die cut, promoting benefits of Moxie as proclaimed by FDR, good, full image of FDR, 12" x 4", EX ....................$305.00 B

**Moxie,** sign, metal, "Drink Moxie," 27" x 19", EX ...........$250.00 D

**Moxie,** sign, tin litho over cardboard, string-hanger, also has easel back for countertop applications, 10" x 2⅝", NM.............$175.00 C

**Moxie,** sign, tin, die cut, girl with glass of Moxie, "I like it" at bottom, 6" dia., EX ..........................................$725.00 B

**Moxie,** sign, tin, embossed, "Drink," 1938, 27" x 19", white on red with yellow outline, EX .....................................$125.00 B

**Moxie,** sign, tin, litho, flange, double-sided, "Drink," 18" x 9", EX ..........................................................$225.00 B

**Moxie,** sign, tin, litho, girl on the white horse in the touring car with a Moxie billboard in background, 24" x 13", 1933, VG.......$250.00 C

**Moxie,** thermometer, girl at top and man at bottom, "The H.D. Beach Co., Coshocton, O," 9" x 26½", VG .........................$235.00 B

**Moxie,** tip tray, "I like it," woman with glass of product, 6" dia., EX ..........................................................$170.00 B

**Moxie,** tip tray, metal, "Drink...Very Healthful," in center of tray, 6" dia., EX ......................................................$75.00 C

**Moxie,** tip tray, metal, "I Just Love...Don't You," leaf border and woman with glass of product in center, 6" dia., VG .............$95.00 C

**Moxie,** tip tray, metal, "makes you eat, sleep, and feel better," 6" dia., EX ........................................................$65.00 C

**Moxie,** tip tray, metal, "the National Health Beverage," 3½" dia., EX ..........................................................$195.00 B

**Mr. Cola,** sign, tin, single-sided, embossed, 18" x 18", EX...$75.00 C

**Mr. Peanut,** ashtray, bisque composition, Mr. Peanut standing behind ashtray shell, 4½" x 3", NM ......................$55.00 C

**Mr. Peanut,** costume, EX................................$650.00 C

**Mr. Peanut,** peanut butter maker, plastic figural, complete with box, 12½" tall, EX ......................................$45.00 C

**Mr. Peanut,** store jar, plastic head display, 7½" x 12", EX ..$65.00 D

**Mr. Thomas,** tip tray, metal, "5¢ Cigar...None Better," "tom" cat on tray, 4⅛" dia., EX ...........................................$650.00 B

**Mrs. Tucker's Shortening,** sign, porcelain, pail with Mrs Tucker's likeness in the center, 32" x 46", EX ........................$750.00 B

**Mt Clemens Brewing Co.,** ashtray, glass, with match holder, EX..$65.00 B

**Mt Hood,** crate label, paper, Oregon Apples, Mt. Hood and Hood River, EX ...........................................$35.00 D

**Mt. Cabin,** sign, tin, embossed, "Just Sweet Enough...Just Tart Enough," man in uniform with sign, 11⅞" x 17⅞", NM............$205.00 B

**Mt. Rushmore,** license plate attachment, tin, die cut, "See," shape of the four presidents, 11¼" x 5½", NM.....................$195.00 C

**Muchlebach's,** match holder, tin, die cut, litho, shaped like bottle, "special brew," 7" H, VG ...................................$185.00 C

**Mulford's Tiolet Talcum,** container, metal, sample size, EX .$100.00 D

**Munsing Union Suits,** sign, cardboard, stand up, die cut, toddler at a blackboard, "Recommended by Millions of Satisfied Munsingites," 1907, EX ........................................$245.00 D

**Munsing Union Suits,** sign, metal, double-sided, flange with scrolled edges, mother and daughter in product, 19" x 15", EX...........$4,000.00 B

**Munsing Wear,** sign, "Ask for...Fashion Books Take One," woman and child, 12" x 14", EX.......................................$800.00 B

**Munsing Wear,** sign, cardboard, easel back, woman at table with flowers, 20" x 30", EX ......................................$90.00 C

**Munsing Wear,** sign, metal, die cut, stand up, "Perfect Fitting..." 6 children in suits, 24" x 16", EX .......................$2,800.00 B

**Munsing Wear,** sign, tin, litho, die cut, "Perfect Fitting...Union Suits," children playing with mother, EX.................$3,100.00 B

**Munsingwear,** sign, metal, young girl in Munsingwear looking at herself in mirror, 25" x 37", EX ...............................$860.00 B

**Munyon's Homeopathic Home Remedies,** counter top storage cabinet, wood, founders image on slanted top, EX..................$700.00 B

**Munyon's Homeopathic Home Remedy,** store cabinet, tin, litho, salesman on top, EX ........................................$506.00 B

**Murad Cigarette,** sign, paperboard, embossed product box, 21" x 3", EX ..........................................................$70.00 B

**Murad the Turkish Cigarette,** sign, metal, woman holding up the product on a tray, 28" x 39", EX.................................$700.00 B

**Murad the Turkish Cigarette,** sign, tin, self-framing, simulated wood frame, 28" x 39", 1906, G .................................$325.00 D

**Murdoch's Mustard,** tin, paper label, 2-oz., EX..................$75.00 C

**Muriel Cigars,** change receiver, glass, label under glass, Muriel Cigars woman, EX ................................................................$100.00 D

**Muriel Tobacco,** container, tin, litho, woman wearing a veil, 5¾" x 6", G................................................................$30.00 B

**Murray's Root Beer,** dispenser, ceramic, barrel shaped on a tree stump, EX.......................................................$200.00 B

**Murry's "Warrior" Plug Tobacco,** sign, cardboard, pirate over lettering, 22" x 30", EX.......................................................$225.00 D

**Musgo Gasoline,** sign, porcelain, two-sided, "Michigan's Mile Maker," Indian in full headdress in center, 48" dia., EX.$6,500.00 B

**My Baby's Talc,** container, tin, litho, good, strong colors, cherub on both sides, Sears Roebuck and Co., 2¼" x 6" x 1¼", EX....$400.00 B

**My-Cola,** door kick plate, tin, embossed, "The Best Ever 5¢ Founts and Bottles," early imitator of Coca-Cola, 36" x 12", 1908, EX.....$800.00 C

**My-Cola,** door kick plate, tin, embossed, "The Best Ever 5¢ Founts and Bottles," early imitator of Coca-Cola, 36" x 12", 1908, VG.....$700.00 B

Nap-Hold Velvet Finish Shell Horse Hide, razor strop, supplied by the Paducah Barber Supply, Paducah, KY, 2¼" x 24", VG, $45.00 C. *Courtesy of B.J. Summers.*

National Eagle Whiskey, bar statue, papier-mache, 16½ x 33½", VG, $175.00 C.

National Fire Insurance Company of Hartford, sign, tin, one-sided, framed, 21" x 12", VG, $105.00 C.

National Sportsman Fishing Tackle, sign, metal, double-sided, flange, "...Sold Here," 26" wide, VG, $625.00 B.

Nature's Remedy, thermometer, brass body with paper face, unusual dial type reading, 9" dia., EX, $115.00 B.

Nature's Remedy Tums, thermometer, metal, dial reading, unusual item advertising both NR and Tums, also lighter color blue background than normally seen, 1930s, 9" dia., EX, $425.00 B.

**N.A. Jordon Sporting Goods,** calendar, gambling goods, 10" x 14", 1905, EX.................................................$95.00 C

**N.V. Van Melle's Toffee,** store counter bin, great bright graphics, 9½" x 8" x 10", EX.................................$1,495.00 C

**Nabisco National Biscuit Company,** store bin cover, gold metal frame with glass cover, "Patented March 13, 1923" embossed on side, EX................................................................$40.00 D

**Nabisco National Biscuit Company,** store bin cover, gold metal frame with glass cover, "Patented March 13, 1923" embossed on side, NM................................................................$55.00 C

**Nabisco Pretzels,** doll, cloth, Mr. Salty, 11" tall, EX...........$15.00 D

**Nabisco Shredded Wheat,** biscuit box, cardboard, presidential offer on front, 1949, 12-oz., 12-biscuit, EX..................$35.00 C

**Nabisco Uneeda Bakers,** store jar, glass with embossed lettering, ball shaped, 10" dia, EX.....................................................$65.00 D

**Nabisco,** cookie jar, pottery, barrel shaped with Nabisco lettered across the front, 1974, EX..................................................$95.00 D

**Nabisco,** letter opener, tin, litho, die cut, Uneeda boy on handle, 1½" x 8", EX......................................................................$165.00 C

**Nabisco,** sign, Christmas, Santa Claus delivering Nabisco products, 24½" x 17", 1940s, EX............................................$295.00 C

**Nabisco,** sign, porcelain, die cut, in shape of Nabisco TM, 48" x 33¼", EX............................................................................$600.00 C

**Nabob Baking Powder,** tin, litho, from Vancouver, BC, 5" x 8¾", EX.........................................................................................$85.00 C

**Nabob Brand Baking Powder,** tin, litho, freshly cut cake on front, 5" x 7½", VG.............................................................................$35.00 C

**Nachtegall & Veit Bar Room Fixtures and Furniture,** door push, glass, reverse painted, hard-to-find item, 3" x 10", EX .....$400.00 C

The Navy, poster, cloth-backed, recruiting, signed by artist, Howard Chandler Christy, "I want you," girl in uniform, 1917, 26½" x 41", EX, $450.00 C.

Nebo Cigarettes, sign, cardboard, pretty girl in center and price ¢5 in corners, 1915, 17" x 14", EX, $60.00 C.

Nehi Beverages, sign, tin, embossed, litho, bottle in oval, 44" long, VG, $300.00 C.

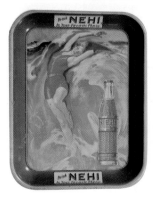

Nehi, Drink, tray, serving, "In Your Favorite Flavor," girl on wave with bottle of Nehi in foreground, G, $160.00 B. *Courtesy of Muddy River Trading Co./Gary Metz.*

Neitzey & Ballenger, Fresh and Salt Fish, sign, framed and matted, 14⅝" x 19¾", G, $375.00 B.

Nesbitt's, thermometer, metal, spot-lighted bottle under message and at top of scale, "a soft drink made from real oranges," not an easy piece to find, 7" x 23", yellow and orange on blue, G, $160.00 D. *Courtesy of Patrick's Collectibles.*

Nanga Saki Cigars, box label, paper, Japanese man in a garden, EX ........................................$45.00 D

Nanty-Glo, sign, painted arrow, Edelstein's for clothing, 5" x 20", EX ........................................$65.00 D

Nanty-Glo, sign, painted arrow, Edelstein's for clothing, 5" x 20", VG ........................................$55.00 D

Naples Velvet Finish, sign, paper on cardboard, rabbit with pointer showing off different colors, Adams & Elting Co., 1920s, 16" x 9", EX ........................................$110.00 B

Napoleon Flour, sign, Napoleon on front, 18" x 35", EX ........$510.00 B

Napoleon Flour, sign, Napoleon on front, 18" x 35", G .....$275.00 C

Napoleon Tobacco Clippings, package, unopened, Napoleon on front, EX ........................................$175.00 C

Napoleon's Condom, tin, litho, crossed swords, complete with original products, 1⅞" x 1⅝" x ⅜", EX ........................................$300.00 B

Narragansett Lager & Ale, tray, serving, tin, litho, Indian with tray of product, 12" dia., VG ........................................$135.00 C

Nash Authorized Service, sign, double-sided, hanging, 22" x 36", EX ........................................$2,500.00 C

Nash Auto, playing cards, vinyl coated, Nash automobiles, in original box, EX ........................................$65.00 C

Nash Bonded Select Used Cars, sign, porcelain, double-sided, 42" dia., VG ........................................$775.00 C

Nash's Drip Grind Coffee, tin pail with wire handle, 7½" x 8", 1920s, EX ........................................$135.00 C

Nash, booklet, paper, promoting the new Nash auto, 1950, 4 pages, VG ........................................$20.00 D

Nash, catalog, new Nash automobile on the cover, 12" x 10", 1938, EX ........................................$45.00 C

Nesbitt's Soda, clock, metal and glass, electric light up, tilted bottle in center, 1956, VG, $1,050.00 C.

Nevada Bell Telephone Co., sign, porcelain, logo promoting both "Local & Long Distance Telephone," 12" x 18", EX, $2,200.00 C.

Newbro's Herpicide, sign, canvas, pretty girl using the product in her hair, "A Delightful Hair Dressing," 11½" x 17", EX, $375.00 C.

New Era Ice Cream, sign, neon light-up store display 24¾" x 14¾", VG, $450.00 C. *Courtesy of B.J. Summers.*

Niagara Shoes, sign, tin over cardboard, "for youthful feet," Niagara Falls, 9" x 19", EX, $145.00 C.

Nine O'Clock Washing Tea, sign, tin, litho, embossed, made by Tuscarora Company, Coshocton, Ohio, 13½" x 13", 1895, EX, $1,800.00 B. *Courtesy of Buffalo Bay Auction Co.*

---

**Nash,** pin back button, metal, "There's None As New As Nash," EX..................................................................$35.00 D

**Nash,** sign, porcelain, "Authorized Service," 42" x 42", EX .$625.00 C

**Nash,** thermometer, plastic, dial-type, P.K. Williams, calendar tear sheet receptacle at bottom, no sheets, 7½" x 15", EX..........$15.00 C

**Nation's Choice Whiskey,** flask, glass, paper label, Parker-Davis, VG .............................................................................$525.00 C

**National Ales Brew'g Co., Syracuse, NY,** match striker, heavy enamel porcelain 4" x 6", EX.............................................$500.00 B

**National Batteries,** sign, metal, embossed lettering and eagle and battery, 20" x 12", EX.....................................................$225.00 C

**National Beer,** tray, metal, rim lettering, cowboy on horseback charging through paper with a bottle of the product in his hand, 13" x 16", EX.....................................................................$850.00 C

**National Beer,** tray, metal, tip size, cowboy on horseback, 4½" dia, EX....................................................................$275.00 C

**National Beer,** tray, tip, metal, cowboy riding horse with bottle of product, "The Best in the West," 4½" dia., EX..................$625.00 B

**National Biscuit Co,** box, cardboard, Graham crackers, VG .......$55.00 D

**National Biscuit Co,** sign, wood, "National Biscuit Company" with shadow type lettering, double-sided, EX..........................$475.00 D

**National Biscuit Co.,** clock, wood case, product name and Uneeda Kid in yellow rain slicker on clock face, EX .....................$600.00 D

**National Biscuit Co.,** display rack, metal and wood, gold stenciling on racks, 55½" tall, EX.......................................................$600.00 B

**National Biscuit Co.,** sign, Uneeda Kid in yellow rain coat, 1901, 13¼" x 16¾", VG..............................................................$135.00 C

None Such, clock, paper, litho, pumpkin-shaped, embossed in pie tin, 9½" H, EX, $925.00 B. *Courtesy of Richard Opfer Auctioneering, Inc.*

North-Star Refrigerator, agency sign, porcelain, 8" x 16", EX, $165.00 B.

Noxie Kola, sign, tin, embossed, single-sided, strip, 13¾" x 3⅛", VG, $85.00 C.

NuGrape, Drink, tray, serving, woman and child in front of fountain and pool, "A Flavor You Can't Forget," VG, $275.00 B. *Courtesy of Muddy River Trading Co./Gary Metz.*

NuGrape, sign, tin, bottle in hand, "...Demand It In This Bottle," 1930 – 40s, 12" x 45", EX, $375.00 B.

NuGrape, thermometer, metal, bottle at left of scale, 6" x 16¼", yellow, grape, and white, EX, $135.00 C.

**National Biscuit Company,** sign, paper, litho, framed, silent film star Diana Allen, "does my baking," 20" x 27", 1920s, VG.......**$1,500.00 B**

**National Brand Cocoa,** tin, litho, Capitol building and kids at table, Geo. Rashmussen Co., 2½" x 2½" x 4⅞", EX ....................**$275.00 B**

**National Brewery Co.,** tray, metal, factory scene, 14" x 10", EX .........................................................................**$195.00 D**

**National Brewing Co.,** stamp holder, celluloid, cowboy on horseback with a bottle of the product, San Francisco, 1½" x 2½", VG....................................................................**$100.00 B**

**National Brewing Co.,** tray, metal, large man and small child that resembles Satan playing golf, 4¼" dia, EX ........................**$450.00 B**

**National Brewing Co.,** tray, metal, tip size, bearded man and gun with a hunting dog, 4½" dia, EX.........................................**$145.00 D**

**National Cash Register Co.,** receipt holder, pressed metal, 3¼" x 6½", EX.................................................................**$145.00 B**

**National Cigar Stand Co.,** light, metal and mica, lettering on front panel, EX...................................................................**$2,900.00 C**

**National Cigar Stand Co.,** tray, metal, tip size, classical look of scantily dressed lady with daisies in hair, lettering on rim, 6" dia, EX ...................................................................**$195.00 D**

**National Cigar Stands,** tray, metal, tip, lady with early off-the-shoulder dress, "Our Brands," 6" dia., EX..........................**$75.00 C**

**National Cigar Store,** light fixture shaped like cigar store with leaded glass dome, 23" x 22½" x 11", EX.........................................**$3,200.00 C**

**National Cream Separator,** stick pin, metal, products, EX ..**$50.00 D**

**National Dairy Council,** sign, paper, extolling the virtues of dairy products, American Litho Co., N.Y., 20" x 31", EX .......**$325.00 B**

**National Fire Insurance Co.,** ledger marker, cloth ribbon, Columbia and flag, patirotic scene, 3" x 12½", VG..............................**$75.00 D**

NuGrape Soda, door push bar, aluminum, painted, reverse side says, "Thank You Call Again," 30" x 4½", EX, $300.00 B. *Courtesy of Autopia Advertising Auctions.*

Nu Icy, sign, tin, embossed, bottle in center, "Drink...," 1930 – 40s, 9" x 20", EX, $200.00 B.

NuGrape Soda, thermometer, metal, marching bottles, 6¾" x 16", G, $90.00 B.

Nu Icy Soda, sign, porcelain, bottle, "...Flavors You Can't Forget," 1930 – 40s, 35" x 18", EX, $375.00 B.

Nutriola Blood & Nerve Food, sign, cardboard, early, great graphics, 14" x 18", EX, $975.00 B. *Courtesy of Morford Auctions.*

---

**National Life & Accident Insurance Co.,** calendar, barnyard animals playing musical instruments, all months shown at once, 10½" x 13½", VG .......................$45.00 D

**National Oats Co.,** box, cardboard, paper label with Donald Duck on front promoting Donald Duck Oats, 3-lb., VG............$275.00 B

**National Premium Brewing Co.,** globe, glass, reverse painted logo, 15" x 17", EX ....................................$950.00 D

**National Premium,** gas globe, one-piece, fired-on lettering with decal for company, diamond-shaped globe, foreign, 22½" x 19", G..........................................$525.00 C

**National Protective Legion,** calendar, cardboard, logo and child with sword, 1908, 21" x 26½", VG .......................$95.00 C

**National Royal,** gas globe, wide glass body with glass lens, 13½" dia., G...........................................$350.00 C

**National Tobacco Co.,** cutter, National Specialty Mfg. Co., Philadelphia, Pa., EX..........................................$135.00 C

**National Wax Thread Sewing Machine,** sign, "Best In The World," 23" x 21", EX ....................................$450.00 D

**National White Rose Ethyl,** gas globe, wide glass body with two glass lenses, 13½" dia., VG...............................$450.00 C

**National White Rose,** gas globe, wide glass hull body with two lenses, 13½" dia., G ....................................$395.00 C

**Nationwide Food Stores,** sign, porcelain, die cut, single-sided, 32" x 36", VG ..........................................$110.00 B

**Nature's Remedies,** menu board, self-framed and embossed, litho by H.D. Beach, 17" x 22", EX....................................$265.00 C

**Nature's Remedy,** clock, wood, wall, Gilbert, paper sign under glass door, 15" x 4½" x 33", EX..............................$610.00 B

**Nature's Remedy,** sign, cardboard, man with large stacks of money and name lettering, 26" x 41", EX .......................$95.00 C

**Navy Brand Firecrackers,** package, paper, a sailor, 1928, VG .**$25.00 D**

**Neato Wintergreen Pepsin Gum,** sign, litho, two different size glass counter jars, 6¼" x 4¼", NM...............................................**$95.00 C**

**Nebo Cigarettes,** sign, paperboard, woman with hand to ear in bare shouldered dress, large product labeling at top, 19" x 27", EX...............................................................................**$275.00 D**

**Nebraska Seed Co.,** display rack, wood, slanted shelves for seed packages, 29" x 45", EX.................................................**$495.00 D**

**Necco Coffee Soda,** lapel pin, metal, name and smiling boy, EX.**$30.00 D**

**Necco Wafers,** display rack, metal, product information on top and bottom of revolving rack, 19" tall, VG............................**$295.00 C**

**Nectar Cigars,** box label, paper, wine glass being held by a woman, 9" x 6", EX ...................................................................**$45.00 D**

**Nectar Tea,** sign, porcelain, die cut, in shape of cup, foreign, 21" x 12½", VG ...................................................................**$160.00 B**

**Nehi Beverages,** sign, tin, die cut, double-sided, flange, "Drink...Ice Cold," bottle, 18" x 13½", NM .....................................**$525.00 C**

**Nehi Orange,** clock, glass and metal, "Drink...and other Nehi flavors," 15" dia., EX ....................................................**$325.00 B**

**Nehi Orange,** sign, paper, "Drink...and other Nehi flavors," 7¼" x 12", EX.....................................................................**$40.00 C**

**Nehi,** sign, metal, self-framing, painted, "Drink Beverages," bottle to right of message, Robertson 1504, 17¾" x 53½", red, white, and gray, EX.................................................................................**$345.00 C**

**Nehi,** sign, paper, litho, pretty lady with hat holding Nehi bottle, 16⅞" x 23⅝", VG ..........................................................**$75.00 C**

**Nehi,** sign, tin, embossed, "Curb Service...Sold Here Ice Cold," NOS, 19⅝" x 27¾", NM..............................................**$95.00 C**

**Nehi,** sign, tin, embossed, tacker style, "Drink...Beverages," bottle at right of message, 29½" x 11¾", 1932, EX ..................**$240.00 B**

**Nehi,** sign, tin, painted, "Drink," bottle in spotlight at right of message, 45" x 18", EX...............................................**$125.00 C**

**Nehi,** sign, tin, painted, bottle in oval in right side portion of sign, 45" x 18", EX ......................................................**$155.00 C**

**Nehi,** tray, metal, woman in ocean wave, VG.........................**$195.00 D**

**Nesbitt's California Orange,** poster, cardboard, litho, family outing, 36" x 25", EX ..............................................................**$155.00 C**

**Nesbitt's California Orange,** sign, tin, embossed lettering and bottle, 27¼" x 11", 1938, EX ..............................................**$135.00 C**

**Nesbitt's California Orange,** sign, tin, embossed lettering and bottle, 27¼"x 11", 1938, P ............................................**$35.00 C**

**Nesbitt's,** sign, cardboard, "...A Soft Drink...," and woman with a bottle, 26" x 19", VG......................................................**$375.00 C**

**Nesbitt's,** sign, cardboard, girls and their dolls seated at a small table having a party with the product, 36" x 25", EX........**$425.00 D**

**Nesbitt's,** sign, metal, painted, "a soft drink made from real oranges," in spotlight, 32" x 32", white, orange, black on yellow, P.......**$50.00 D**

**Nesbitt's,** thermometer, "Nesbitt's Made From Real Oranges," 27" tall, EX ...........................................................................**$115.00 D**

**Nesbitt's,** thermometer, metal, "Drink Nesbitt's California Orange" with slanted bottle, 27" tall, EX .......................................**$125.00 D**

**Nesbitt's,** thermometer, metal, painted with vertical scale, "the finest soft drink ever made...Don't say orange say...," EX ..**$95.00 C**

**Nesbitt's,** thermometer, metal, painted, logo at top of vertical scale and bottle to left of scale, rolled sides and corners, orange & white, EX .............................................................................**$125.00 C**

**Nestea,** dispenser, glass, in shape of upright barrel on stoneware base with product name, 16½" tall, EX............................**$125.00 D**

**Nestle's Hazelnut Chocolate,** dispenser, metal and glass with paper labels, EX ...........................................................................**$145.00 D**

**Nestle's Original Toll House Cookies,** cookie jar, pottery, gold trim, EX ........................................................................**$135.00 D**

**Neuweiler's Beer,** sign, cardboard, two men in bar, "Watch the place awhile...," 17¼" x 13¾", EX ......................................**$45.00 C**

**Neva Myss Flour,** sack, cloth, bird dogs flushing birds, 6-lb., EX.**$35.00 C**

**Neversink Distillery,** sign, glass, reverse painting, brewery and busy street scene, 28" x 20", VG...............................................**$300.00 C**

**New Bachelor Cigar,** tin, man on front, 4¼" x 5⅝" x 2¼", EX..**$75.00 C**

**New Burch Plows,** sign, wood, "Made at Chrestline Ohio," 72" x 17", EX ............................................................................**$150.00 D**

**New Century & Mushroom 5¢ Cigars,** knife and corkscrew, 3¾" x 1" x ¼", VG ......................................................................**$45.00 C**

**New Chief Ammunition,** poster, paper, litho, framed, man getting ready to go hunting and wife reminding him to take the product with him, 17" x 22", EX ......................................................**$600.00 B**

**New England Brewing,** tray, metal, elk in high grass, 16½" x 13¾", EX...........................................................................**$125.00 C**

**New England Telephone & Telegraph,** sign, porcelain, company in border surrounding trademark bell, "Local and Long distance," 11" x 11", VG .............................................................................**$175.00 B**

**New Era Coffee,** tin, litho, from G. Thealheimer, Syracuse NY, slip-on lid, good, strong colors, 3½" x 6" x 3½", 1900s, EX ......**$155.00 C**

New Era Dairy Velvet Rich Ice Cream, clock, metal body, plastic face, message panel to right of clock face, light-up, 1960s, 24¾" x 11¾", EX.....................................................................$225.00 C

New Era Dairy Velvet Rich Ice Cream, clock, plastic front light-up, metal back, F .................................................................$95.00 C

New Era Dairy Velvet Rich Ice Cream, clock, plastic front light-up, metal back, VG ..............................................................$190.00 C

New Era Ice Cream, sign, neon light-up, 24¾" x 14¾", G.....$375.00 D

New Era Potato Chip, container, tin, 1-lb., EX.........$50.00 D

New Haven Dairy Ice Cream, sign, porcelain "Quart & Pint Bricks," 21" x 27", EX ................................................................$135.00 D

New Home Sewing Machine, sign, cardboard, man getting paints sewed up, 30½" x 44½", EX ......................................$975.00 D

New Home, poster, paper, litho, foreign, 1900s, 17½" x 25", G .$110.00 B

New King Snuff, pocket mirror, metal and glass, snuff pouch on back, 1920s, VG ...............................................................$135.00 D

New Method Self Starting Lighter, display box, cardboard, die cut, man lighting a cigar with the product, VG...........................$45.00 D

New Pullman Cigars, sign, cardboard, die cut, pretty young woman, 10" x 15", EX .......................................................................$85.00 C

New Sharon Iowa's City of Roses, license plate attachment, tin, painted, roses, 110" x 5½", EX..................................$110.00 C

New Tydol, banner, cloth, woman behind the wheel of an auto, "First In Milage Power Anti-knock," 59" x 36", VG ........$325.00 C

New York Central-Hudson Type, locomotive, printed in the U.S.A, H.O. Bailey Studios, 1934, 29" x 14", G......................$110.00 B

New York Coach Oil, can, metal, from Marshall Oil Company, coach, 3" x 3¼" x 6¾", VG ..............................................$130.00 C

New York Stineware Co., jug, pottery, floral design, 13" T, EX.$195.00 C

New York Times Newspaper, clock, composition, pendulum base, "Have You Read The Times This Morning," 18½" x 31", EX.$675.00 D

New Yorker Cigars, box label, paper, pilgrim, 4½" x 4½", VG .$10.00 D

Newberry Shoe, match holder, metal, die cut, "Wear The Newberry Shoe," EX .......................................................................$95.00 C

Newly Wed, Sugar Stick Candy, pennant, young man and woman eating candy, while a young child watches, 25" L, NM ......$122.00 B

Newport Gasoline Oils, globe, one-piece, etched, hangs instead of sitting, 16½" dia., G...........................................................$770.00 B

Newsboy Cut Plug Tobacco, trade card, cardboard, man seated on tackle box, "Waiting For The Fishing Party," 1892, 3" x 6", VG........$25.00 C

Newsboy Tobacco, card, early stage actress Agnes Reily likeness on front, 6" x 9", 1893, EX.....................................................$35.00 B

Ni-Tro Ethyl, gas globe, metal body with two glass lenses, high profile, 16½" dia., G..............................................................$800.00 B

Niagara Fire Insurance Co., sign, paper, small Niagara Falls, "Niagara Falls...Cash, Capital, New York, 1,000,000," 21½" x 16", EX ......................................................................$250.00 B

Niagara Fire Insurance Company, sign, reverse painted on glass, Niagara Falls, 33¼" x 25¼", EX...................................................$375.00 C

Niagara Punch, sign, tin, litho, bottle, 19½" x 9¼", EX .............$225.00 C

Niagara Punch, sign, tin, painted, "Drink," bottle at left, 20" x 9", EX.............................................................................$110.00 C

Niagara Shoes, sign, metal over cardboard, embossed image of Niagara Falls in center, 9" x 19½", EX...................................$500.00 D

Niagara Shoes, sign, tin over cardboard, "for youthful feet," Niagara Falls, 9" x 19", G.............................................................$75.00 C

Niagara Shoes, sign, tin over cardboard, self-framing, Niagara Falls, from The American artworks, Coshocton, Ohio, 9" x 19", VG...........$190.00 B

Niagara Shoes, sign, tin over wood, self-framing, "Niagara Shoes for Youthful Feet," the falls over message, 8⅝" x 19", VG......$125.00 C

Nichol Kola, door push, metal, embossed, "Drink America's Taste Sensation," 8" x 24", EX............................................$125.00 D

Nichol Kola, sign, "Drink...America's taste sensation," embossed bottle in center, 8" x 24", EX...........................................$110.00 C

Nichol Kola, sign, cardboard, die cut, pretty red head beauty holding a bottle, EX....................................................................$195.00 C

Nichol Kola, sign, metal, painted, "America's taste sensation 5¢," The Parker Metal Dec. Co., Baltimore, Ohio, 27½" x 11¼", white, orange, and black, EX .......................................................$110.00 C

Nichol Kola, sign, metal, painted, "Drink...Vitamin B1 added," America's taste sensation, marching soldier at lower left, 20" x 28", EX...........................................................................$115.00 C

Nickel King Cigars, sign, cardboard, single-sided, 18" x 6", VG..$65.00 C

Niehoff Automobile Products, sign, metal and glass, light up, "Authorized...Distributor," 11" dia, VG ..............................$75.00 D

Nigger Baby Oranges, paper litho for shipping crate, 24" x 10", 1930s, NM ........................................................................$125.00 C

Nigger Hair Tobacco, tin litho, black man with ring in nose and ear, 5½" x 6½"h, VG.........................................................$800.00 B

Nigger Head Oysters, can, paper label, black man holding an oyster, strong colors, unopened, 4-oz., NM..........................$135.00 D

**Nigger Head Oysters,** label, early version, envelope from company, hard-to-find 1933 Chicago Century of Progress stamp, 8" x 2¾", 1930s, EX ..............................................................$175.00 C

**Nigger Head Oysters,** sign, paper, litho, die cut, clown holding a wooden looking sign promoting Baltimore Fresh Oysters from the Aughinbaugh Canning Co., 11" x 12½", EX......................................$675.00 B

**Night Rider,** crate label for peaches, cowboy on horse, 8" x 7", VG ............................................................................$18.00 D

**Nikolai Vodka,** backbar statue, plaster, likeness of Russian dancing, 1970s, 12" tall, EX.............................................$115.00 D

**Nine O'Clock Washing Tea,** sign, tin, embossed, wood frame, 15¼" x 15", VG ...............................................................$950.00 B

**Nine Star Lager,** label, paper, large 9 surrounded by stars, VG..$45.00 C

**Nitro Club Loaded Paper Shells,** empty cardboard box, mallard on front, 4" x 4" x 2½", NM .................................................$100.00 C

**Nobel's Empire Smokeless Sporting Powder,** container, tin, litho, 3½" x 6" x 1½", EX ..........................................$240.00 B

**Noble 5¢ Cigar,** display, metal, designed to sit on counter, "Everybody's Smoking It," 18" x 12" x 15", EX..........................$475.00 D

**Nochol Kola,** sign, metal, embossed, "Twice As Good," 12" x 35½", EX ........................................................................$95.00 D

**None Such Mince Meat,** clock, metal and cardboard, resembles a pumpkin, 9½" dia, EX ..........................................$500.00 C

**None Such Mince Meat,** sign, cardboard, die cut, woman holding a freshly prepared pie, 8¾" x 11", EX ..............................$195.00 C

**None Such,** clock, paper, litho, embossed, in pie tin, pumpkin-shaped, 9½" H, VG .....................................................$650.00 C

**Noon Day Stove Polish,** sign, paper, baby and dog looking at stove, "Most Brilliant," 17" x 21½", EX .................................$4,000.00 B

**Noonan's Hair Petrole for Falling Hair,** sign, porcelain, double-sided, flange, Zepp's Hair Dressing advertised on other side, 16" x 12", EX.........................................................................$400.00 B

**Nor'way Antifreeze,** thermometer and chalk board, Nor'way man at bottom, 15¼" x 22¼", VG ..............................$120.00 B

**Norco Feeds,** sign, tin, single-sided, pig sharpening a knife, 24" x 12", VG ...........................................................................$220.00 B

**Norfolk,** sign, paper, litho, "food of strength," young child's development, 33½" x 23½", 1900s, EX .................$355.00 C

**Norka Ginger Ale,** sign, metal, tilted bottle, "...Tastes Better," 1930s, 24" x 12", VG ...........................................$45.00 D

**Normans Ink,** sign, porcelain, single-sided, bulldog, 21" x 37½", EX.........................................................................$900.00 B

**Norse Coffee,** pail, metal, scrolled company logo and slip lid, rolled bail, 7" x 9", VG ...........................................................$75.00 D

**North American Savings Company,** calendar, cardboard, embossed, Indian bust, 14" x 19", EX ..............................$95.00 B

**North Pole Smoking Tobacco,** lunch pail, metal, man and bear at pole, 4" x 6" x 6", VG ..............................................$375.00 C

**North Pole Tobacco,** lunch pail with top wire bail handle, 6" x 4" x 6", EX.......................................................................$350.00 B

**North Star Tobacco,** pocket container, metal, flat, extremely hard to find, VG.................................................................$575.00 C

**North Star Tobacco,** pocket tin, litho, goddess in clouds, EX .$750.00 B

**North Western Cigars,** box label with gold leaves embossed, 9" x 6", VG ............................................................................$5.00 D

**North Woods,** tin, litho, key-wound lid, 1-lb., EX ..............$50.00 C

**Northampton Brewing Co. Lager Beer,** tray, metal, tip, hand holding 3 bottles, 4⅛" dia., EX................................................$140.00 B

**Northampton Brewing Co.,** tray, metal, tip size, 3 bottles, 4½" dia, VG ...........................................................................$100.00 C

**Northern Navigation Division,** sign, celluloid over metal, Ticket and Information Canadian National Route, steamship at dock, 8" x 9", EX.........................................................$650.00 B

**Northland Oils Lubes,** sign, tin, painted, 24" x 24", EX ....$175.00 C

**Northwestern National Bank Portland Trust Co. of Oregon,** tip tray, bank building in center, 6⅛" L, EX ..............................$95.00 B

**Nosler Bullets,** display, wood, various game animals and size bullet needed, 19" x 13", EX.........................................................$150.00 D

**Notary Public,** sign, celluloid over metal, bonded by Hartford Accident and Indemnity Company with the Hartford deer in lower center, 8¾" x 4½", VG.....................................................$65.00 C

**Nourse Motor Oil,** sign, metal, double-sided lubster, Nourse warrior, 6½" x 8½", G .........................................................$300.00 C

**Nu Icy,** sign, metal, self-framing, bottle and lettering embossed, "Flavors You Can't Forget," 60" x 36", EX................................$550.00 C

**Nugget,** sign, porcelain, shoe polish, 1920 – 1930s, 42" x 17", G ................................................................................$900.00 C

**NuGrape Pepsi-Cola, Orange-Crush,** plate, all three logos, by Wellsville China, 7" dia, EX..........................................$150.00 C

**NuGrape Soda,** clock, convex glass front, light-up, by Swihart, 1940s, 13" x 14", G ...............................................$195.00 C

**NuGrape Soda,** clock, convex glass front, light-up, by Swihart, 1940s, 13" x 14", VG ...........................................$235.00 C

**NuGrape Soda,** door push bar, aluminum, painted, reverse side says "Thank You Call Again," 30" x 4½", VG .................................$225.00 C

**NuGrape Soda,** sign, tin, die cut, double-sided, flange, "A Flavor You Can't Forget," bottle in hand, 19½" x 13½", VG ......$350.00 B

**NuGrape,** calendar, paper, all months complete, 1957, VG $35.00 C

**NuGrape,** clock, bottle in center, 1940 – 1950s, 13¼" x 16", EX..$195.00 C

**NuGrape,** clock, light-up, "If you only knew what goes into…you'd never drink anything else!," message panel to right of clock face, EX.................................................................$275.00 C

**NuGrape,** menu board, metal, "NuGrape," and tilted bottle above writting area, VG ...............................................$75.00 C

**NuGrape,** sign, metal, round, painted, "More Fun With Soda," bottle cap, EX ........................................................$110.00 C

**NuGrape,** syrup dispenser, metal and glass, 11½" x 8" dia, VG.$125.00 D

**NuGrape,** thermometer, metal, bottle at left of scale, 6" x 16¼", yellow, grape, and white, G .......................................$60.00 C

**NuGrape,** thermometer, metal, embossed bottle, 16" tall, VG .$155.00 C

**NuGrape,** tray, metal, lettering on rim and a bottle, a burst of light in center, 10" x 13", G .......................................$95.00 C

**NuGrape,** tray, metal, serving, rectangular, "A Flavor You Can't Forget," girl with bottle, EX ....................................$120.00 B

**NuGrape,** tray, metal, serving, rectangular, "A Flavor You Can't Forget," girl with bottle, G.............................................$85.00 C

**NuGrape,** tray, metal, woman in moonlight, 10½" x 13¼", EX..$115.00 D

**Nutmeg State Beer,** label, paper, for the Eastern Brewing Co., 1940s, EX ........................................................$25.00 D

**Nutmeg,** sign, tin, painted, "Ice Cold Club Beverages," bottle at left, 28" x 10", EX ........................................................$100.00 D

**Nutriola Blood & Nerve Food,** sign, cardboard, 14" x 18", G...$375.00 C

**Nuvana Cigar,** door push, aluminum, embossed lettering, 2" x 6", VG ........................................................$110.00 C

**NY Central,** sign, "Twentieth Century Limited," titled As Centuries Past In The Night, 1923, VG ...............................$95.00 C

**Nyal Service Drugstore,** sign, porcelain, oval, single-sided, 36" x 23½", EX........................................................$150.00 B

**Nyal's Family Remedies,** sign, metal, embossed, "Nyal's Family Remedies Good For You," 20" x 10", VG ...........................$35.00 D

**Nylotis Baby Powder,** container, tin, litho, three babies on front, unopened, NM ........................................................$169.00 B

Oakite, sign, cardboard, for store display, woman holding up product, "...cleans a million things," 22" x 36", VG, $500.00 C.

Octagon Kirkman Coupons Redeemed Here, sign, metal, double-sided, flange, 18" long, VG, $250.00 B.

Odin 5¢ Cigar, sign, tin, embossed, 19½" x 27½", VG, $380.00 B.

Office Equipment Co., Inc., playing cards, plastic covered, company advertising on the backs, still in original box, all cards present, EX, $35.00 C. *Courtesy of B.J. Summers.*

Ogden's St. Bruno Flake, sign, porcelain, "...A Man's Tobacco," 24" x 36", G, $50.00 B.

Ohio Valley Fire & Marine Insurance, sign, solid brass, embossed lettering and copper flashing on front, from Paducah, Kentucky, framed and restored, 24" x 9", EX, $675.00 C. *Courtesy of B.J. Summers.*

---

**O & F Star,** counter dispenser, tin, litho, pure spices, star between O & F, 7" x 7" x 8", EX..................................................$100.00 B

**O U Cut Plug Tobacco,** container, metal, paper label, round, slip lid,1909, EX........................................................................$75.00 C

**O'Brien's Candies,** sign, cardboard, die cut, young boy and girl at fence gate, the girl is holding a package of the product, from Omaha, NE, 6½" x 9", NM ..........................................$100.00 B

**O'day Pep,** gas globe, metal body with two glass lenses, high profile, 15" dia., G .................................................... $1,200.00 C

**O'Malley's Havana Fives Cigar,** sign, paper, image of container, "Buy Your Havana Fives Here...The best 5¢ Cigar in America," 17" x 7", EX ..............................................................$115.00 C

**O'Neill Creamery,** sign, double-sided, die cut, in shape of milk can, 15" x 27", F............................................................ $125.00 D

**O-Baby,** box, cardboard, countertop display, pop-up die cut marquee, young girl holding an O-Baby candy bar, 6¾" x 4½" x 8¼", EX................................................................................$400.00 B

**O-Cedar Mops,** store display, tin, litho, die cut, "cleans as it polishes," 20¼" x 18½" x 4¼", EX ............................................$375.00 B

**O-Cedar,** store display rack, metal, woodgrain look, advertisement from 1925, 14"W x 40½"H x 11½"D, G.............................................$120.00 B

**O-Cedar,** store display rack, metal, woodgrain look, advertisement from 1925, 14"W x 40½"H x 11½"D, VG.........................................$135.00 C

**O.F.C. Rye,** sign, paper, framed, black butler with product on tray, "Massa's Favorite," 26" x 30¼", EX ....................................$110.00 B

**O.F.C. Whiskey,** sign, metal, cabin and deer, 30" x 43", EX ..$500.00 C

Ohio Valley Supply Co. Incorporated, calendar, metal and paper, rotating months and days and a flip date pad, use this one a very long time, 1950s, 10" x 15", VG, $65.00 C. *Courtesy of B.J. Summers.*

O Jayco Paints, sign, metal, large paint can and painter, 17" x 20", VG, $95.00 C. *Courtesy of Autopia Advertising Auctions.*

Old Cold Springs Hand Made Sour Mash Whiskey, jug, stoneware, distilled by Dreyfuss & Weil, 1900 – 1910s, 8" tall, EX, $225.00 C. *Courtesy of B.J. Summers.*

Old Crow Medium Mild Tobacco, pouch, cloth, paper label, rooster getting ready to crow, "For Pipe or Cigarettes," 2½" x 3¾" x 1", VG, $35.00 C. *Courtesy of B.J. Summers.*

Old Export, sign, metal, "Mountain Water Makes The Difference," 42" dia., G, $110.00 B.

Old Gold Cigarettes, sign, porcelain, Regular and King Size, "Same Famous Quality," 1950s, VG, $250.00 B.

Old Hickory Clay Co., knife, celluloid and metal, company name with P.O. Box 271, Paducah, Ky, reverse side Mines: R.F.D. 2 Mayfield, KY , 31 Years of Service to the Industry, 3⅛" long closed, VG, $25.00 C. *Courtesy of B.J. Summers.*

---

O.F.C., sign, cardboard, black waiter with a tray of the product, litho by Stecher Litho Co., Rochester, N.Y., 15" x 26", EX..........$200.00 B

Oak Motor Oil, sign, porcelain, oak tree logo, Canadian, 20" dia., EX ..................................................................$1,500.00 B

Oakland Pontiac Sales-Service, sign, porcelain, double-sided, 35½" x 23¾", EX.......................................................................$425.00 C

Obald & Son, sign, metal, pair of hunters drinking by moonlight, for Old Coon Sour Mash, 28" x 23", NM .............................$800.00 B

Obermeyer & Leibmann's, vendor's cart, wood, bottled beer with metal handle and wheels, 16" x 43", EX.........................$2,500.00 C

OCB Cigarette Papers, paper holder, tin, "Roll Your Own with" on front, yellow lettering on black, EX ....................................$30.00 D

Occident Flour, sign, metal & cardboard, with spotlights that show the process from start to finish, 14" x 9", EX......................$75.00 D

Ocean Spray cigar, box label, paper, EX ...........................$165.00 B

Oceanic Cut Plug, can, metal, horizontal, curved corners, 6" x 4", EX ................................................................................$100.00 D

Oceanic Oysters, sign, tin over cardboard, "in Season," 9¼" x 13¼", yellow lettering on green, EX.................................................$75.00 B

Oconto Brewing Co., tray, metal, tip size, Compliments Of... courtesy panel, 1908, EX .......................................................$165.00 D

Oertel's 92 Beer, ashtray, plaster, company logo at top of bowl, EX................................................................................$55.00 D

OFC Bourbon, sign, paperboard, "A Stag Party," 1880s, 25" x 34", EX ................................................................................$300.00 C

Officers Club Cigars, container, metal, vertical, "8¢...2 For 15¢," EX................................................................................$50.00 D

Old Honesty Plug Tobacco, sign, paper, framed, older couple looking at paper, Calvert Litho Co., 20" x 20", EX, $195.00 C.

Old Irvin Cobb Kentucky Straight Bourbon Whiskey, bottle, glass, paper label, screw on lid, no federal stamp, label has the Flagg Cobb silhouette, rear label "Distilled and Bottled By HEAVEN HILL DISTILLERIES, Inc., Bardstown, Nelson County, Kentucky," ⅘ qt, EX, $125.00 C. *Courtesy of B.J. Summers.*

Old Judson, match holder, tin, litho, J.C. Stevens, 518 Delaware St., Kansas City, MO, USA, 5" H, EX, $200.00 B. *Courtesy of Richard Opfer Auctioneering, Inc.*

Old Ken-Tuck Medium Mild Tobacco, pouch, cloth with paper label, old gent smoking a pipe, "For Pipe or Cigarettes," never opened, seal unbroken, 2¼" x 3¼" x 1½", G, $25.00 C. *Courtesy of B.J. Summers.*

Old Paduke Distillery Co., wallet, leather, "send #3¼ for 4 full quarts of their Old Paduke Whisky, Ten years old," established 1865, 6" x 7½" open, F, $35.00 C. *Courtesy of B.J. Summers.*

Old Reliable Coffee, sign, tin, "Always Good,"1910s, 6½" x 9", EX, $350.00 B. *Courtesy of Muddy River Trading Co./Gary Metz.*

Old Reserve Whiskey, bottle, glass, paper label, Kolb Bros. Drug Co., 1 qt., VG, $100.00 C. *Courtesy of B.J. Summers.*

**Official National Automobile Club,** sign, porcelain, double-sided, hanging, 18" x 21", EX......................................$250.00 C

**Offutt & Pierce,** calendar, die cut, souvenir from "the Reliable Home Furnishers, Lowell, Mass.," promoting household ranges, young girl and her pet, missing calendar pad, 9½" x 14½", EX............$120.00 B

**Ogburn, Hill & Co. Tobacco,** sign, cardboard, Indian maiden in canoe that's full of flowers, "rich and waxy tobacco," 10¾" x 14", EX......................................................................$160.00 B

**Oh Boy 1¢ Gum,** sign, tin, litho, young boy holding samples of the product, 7¼" x 15¼", 1920s, EX ......................................$425.00 B

**Oh Boy Gum,** sign, metal, elf whispering in boys ear, "It's Pure," 7" x 16", EX ......................................................................$350.00 D

**Ohio Match Co.,** paperweight, glass, mirrored view of the company factory, EX ......................................................................$125.00 C

**Ohio Rake Co., Dayton,** sign, paper, litho, Statue of Liberty and patriotic farming type scenes, 34½" x 28½", EX............$2,100.00 B

**Ohio Rake Co., Dayton,** sign, paper, litho, Statue of Liberty and patriotic farming type scenes, 34½" x 28½", F .................$425.00 C

**Ohio State Cigars,** container, metal, round, slip lid, EX ........$125.00 C

**Ohio Tobacco,** display, plaster, Indian at rest with pipe, EX.$275.00 D

**Ohio Valley Fire & Marine Insurance,** sign, solid brass, embossed lettering and copper flashing on front, from Paducah, Kentucky, framed and restored, 24" x 9", VG ......................................$395.00 C

**Oil Well Supply Co.,** paperweight, glass, rectangular, rounded corners, "Everything For Oil Wells," 4" x 2½", EX ......................$30.00 D

**Oilzum 2 Cycle Motor Oil,** sign, metal, "Choice of Champions!," 36" x 15", EX ......................................................................$195.00 C

246

Oldsmobile Service, sign, porcelain, double-sided, dealer with coat of arms in center, 42" dia., EX, $1,000.00 C.

Old Sport Tobacco, print, framed, 10½" x 10½", EX, $75.00 C. *Courtesy of Collectors Auction Services.*

Old Virginia Cheroots, sign, cardboard, matted, framed, and under glass, 1900s, 6½" x 10½", EX, $350.00 B. *Courtesy of Muddy River Trading Co./Gary Metz.*

Oliver Chilled Plows, sign, tin, litho, self-framed, embossed, youngster on horseback and the products in foreground, 27¼" x 36½", 1890, EX, $1,000.00 B. *Courtesy of Buffalo Bay Auction Co.*

Omar Turkish Cigarette, sign, paper, litho, framed, father and son enjoying a smoke, engraving on frame bottom "American Tobacco Co., Omar Turkish Blend Cigarettes," 18½" x 25", VG, $405.00 B. *Courtesy of Collectors Auction Services.*

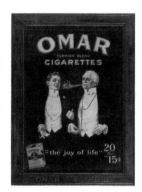

O'Neill Creamery, sign, double-sided, die cut, in shape of milk can, 15" x 27", VG, $600.00 B. *Courtesy of Collectors Auction Services.*

Oilzum Motor Oil, banner, cloth, "Escape to No Wear," Oilzum Man, 1950s, 26" x 12", EX ..................................................$575.00 C

Oilzum Motor Oil, can, metal, handle in an elongated shape to fit under seat, ½ gal., EX ......................................................$675.00 C

Oilzum Motor Oil, clock, light-up,"Choice of Champions," Oilzum Man in center, 14½" dia., EX .........................$1,100.00 C

Oilzum Motor Oil, clock, square, "Choice of Champions," 16" sq., EX................................................................................$235.00 C

Oilzum Motor Oil, sign, metal, two-sided, Oilzum Man, "If motors could speak we wouldn't need to advertise," 20" x 10", VG. $1,600.00 B

Oilzum Motor Oil, sign, tin, die cut, flange, Oilzum Man, 15¾" x 17", EX................................................................................$455.00 C

Oilzum Motor Oils, sign, porcelain, "America's Finest Oil," head of Oilzum Man, double-sided, 20" x 28", EX.........................$1,200.00 C

Oilzum, oil can, tin, Oilzum Man, 1-gal., EX ......................$75.00 C

Oilzum, service station attendant cap, leather, Oilzum Man on both sides, , EX.........................................................................$100.00 C

Oilzum, sign, metal, "Winter Oilzum...The Cream...For Easy Starting," 1947, 22" x 14",EX..................................................$375.00 C

Oilzum, sign, metal, double-sided, flange, painted, 20" x 14", 1950s, EX...................................................................................$625.00 B

Oilzum, sign, porcelain, double-sided, "America's finest choice," Oilzum Man in the upper part of this sign, 19¾" x 27½", G ...$290.00 B

Onondaga Brand Glass, sign, metal, flange, painted, Indian in center, 18½" x 13½", EX, $250.00 C.

Optimo Cigars, Very Mild, F. A. Bronchain, sign, reverse imaging under beveled glass, 11¼" H, EX, $225.00 C. *Courtesy of Richard Opfer Auctioneering, Inc.*

Orange-Crush, sign, tin over cardboard, "Drink, The National Fountain Drink, Color Added," girl with glass of Orange Crush, 1920s, 6¼" x 9¼", VG, $750.00 C. *Courtesy of Muddy River Trading Co./Gary Metz.*

Orange Crush, menu board, glass and chrome, big name circle in center, 1930s, 25" x 14½", EX, $1,900.00 B.

Orange Crush, sign, tin, single-sided, embossed, rolled lip edge, "Enjoy The Fresh Taste," 35¼" x 34¼", G, $100.00 B.

Orange Crush, poster, cardboard, straight sided bottle, "Served here," 1929, 11" x 14", EX, $170.00 B.

Orange Crush, sign, cardboard, little girl drinking product with a straw, matted and framed, 1920s, EX, $425.00 B.

---

Oilzum, sign, tin, double-sided, painted, "America's Finest Oil," Oilzum Man at lower left, 60" x 36", G .......................... $1,800.00 C

Oilzum, sign, tin, litho, "Choice of Champions," 72" x 36", EX .$325.00 B

Oilzum, sign, tin, litho, Oilzum Man in upper left corner, "If motors could speak we wouldn't need to advertise," 72" x 32", EX..$950.00 B

Oilzum, sign, tin, vertical, painted, Oilzum Man inside the O in the name, 10¾" x 43½", NM .....................................$575.00 B

Oilzum, thermometer, tin, painted, "The Choice of Champion Race Drivers," Oilzum Man to left of vertical scale, message at top & bottom, 7½" x 15", EX ..........................................$450.00 C

Ojibwa Fine Cut Tobacco, store container, for counter use, round, slip lid, EX.......................................................$825.00 D

OK Tire, sign, tin, litho, die cut, saluting man, 34" x 60", EX $235.00 C

OK Used Cars and Trucks, sign, metal, painted, one-sided, Chevy trucks, 48" x 36", G ......................................... $350.00 B

OK, sign, metal and neon, large O K flashes, 1950 – 60s, 24" dia., VG ................................................................$1,800.00 C

OK, sign, porcelain and neon, Chevrolet Used Cars, 24" dia., x 8" d, NM .....................................................................$1,500.00 C

Oklahoma Vinegar, glass, etched, from Fort Smith, Arkansas, 5" H, G................................................................... $55.00 C

Old Abe Chewing Tobacco, tin, litho, Abe and slaves, "Manufactured by B. Leidersdorf & Co. Milwaukee, Wis.," 8" dia., VG .......... $750.00 B

Old Barbee, Vienna art plate, old man pouring product and women conversing beside log house, Louisville distillery, 1908, 10" dia., NM ............................................................$594.00 B

Orange Crush, sign, metal, embossed, self-framing, bottle in center, 17" x 53¼", NM, $525.00 D.

Orange Crush, counter dispenser, stainless steel with sides, 11" x 17" x 20", EX, $2,100.00 B. *Courtesy of Muddy River Trading Co./Gary Metz.*

Orange Crush, sign, tin, flange, Crushy at the bottom of the diamond, 1930s, 18" x 18", EX, $450.00 B. *Courtesy of Muddy River Trading Co./Gary Metz.*

Orange-Julep, sign, cardboard, hang-up, man and woman drinking from a single bottle with two straws, 1930s, 7¾" x 11", EX, $140.00 B. *Courtesy of Muddy River Trading Co./Gary Metz.*

Orange Julius, sign, "A Devilish Good Drink," devil figure in center, rare, 1920s, 24" x 35", G, $800.00 B. *Courtesy of Muddy River Trading Co./Gary Metz.*

Orts Bread, thermometer, porcelain, scale type reading, 27" tall, VG, $120.00 B.

Osh Kosh B'Gosh, mirror, reverse painted glass, oak frame, for store display, 1920s, EX, $240.00 B.

---

Old Boone Whiskey, tip tray, metal, log cabin distillery, Thixton, Millett & Co., Louisville, Ky., 4⅛" dia., EX..........................$210.00 B

Old Bridgeport Monongahela Rye Whiskey, sign, metal, man in tux, "You've Tried The Rest, Now Try The Best," 17" x 23", VG..$795.00 D

Old Cabinet Whiskey, sign, canvas, cancan girl resting, for Lindley Distributors, 1900s, 30" x 26", EX.....................................$3,200.00 B

Old Chum Tobacco, container, metal, vertical, curved corners, 3½" x 5" x 1", EX ...........................................................................$75.00 D

Old Colony, gas globe, wide glass body with glass lens, beehive on face, 13½" dia., G ............................................................. $550.00 B

Old Colony, sign, tin, litho, center hanger, colonist, 15½" x 5", EX...............................................................................................$85.00 C

Old Company's Lehigh, sign, porcelain, single-sided, die cut, "anthracite...It lasts longer!," 12" x 12", VG................. $200.00 B

Old Coon 5¢ Cigar, sign, porcelain, horse head, "Union Made...Hand Work," 18" x 7", EX.......................................$775.00 C

Old Crow Rye, sign, metal, monk in leaves, "A Straight Hand Made Sour Mash Whiskey," 1903, 22" x 29", EX.......................$1,000.00 B

Old Crow Whiskey, decanter, figural, complete, cane and spats, EX.................................................................................................$65.00 C

Old Crow, backbar display, composition figural, 3½" x 11½", EX .................................................................................................$95.00 C

Old Dutch Beer, pinback, by Bastian Bros., "The good, Beer," 1¼" dia., VG................................................................................... $55.00 C

Old Dutch Beer, sign, embossed, die cut, man holding mug, EX..$75.00 C

Old Dutch Cleanser, sign, porcelain, "We Sell Large Sifter Can 10¢," 14" x 20", EX............................................................$475.00 C

Oshkosh R.R. Suits, Union Made, sign, reverse painted glass in wood frame, oil worker at left side of 48¼" x 18½", EX, *$3,800.00 B. Courtesy of Richard Opfer Auctioneering, Inc.*

Our Game, cigar box, vintage baseball game, scarce item, 1900s, VG, *$600.00 B. Courtesy of Buffalo Bay Auction Co.*

Outboard Motor Shop, silhouette, plastic, John G. Billow, Owner, 1950s, 10¾" x 6¼", EX, *$15.00 C. Courtesy of B.J. Summers.*

Overland Motor Car, sign, tin, single-sided, 13¾" x 9¾", VG, *$195.00 C.*

Owen Bros Quality Cleaners, ad, glass, reverse painted, baby, candlestick phone and customer information, 2¾" x 4¼", VG, *$125.00 C. Courtesy of B.J. Summers.*

Owl Cigars, sign, cardboard, double-sided, die cut, string hanger, 7" x 9½", EX, *$300.00 B. Courtesy of Wm. Morford Investment Grade Collectibles.*

Old Dutch Cleanser, sign, tin over cardboard, "for Healthful Cleanliness," old "Dutch" cleaning woman, 18" x 9¼", EX ............$275.00 C

Old Dutch Cleanser, sign, tin over cardboard, hands shown scrubbing pan and product container in lower right, EX............$450.00 B

Old Dutch Cleanser, sign, tin, litho, double-sided, good strong colors, 12¾" L, NM ................................................................$160.00 B

Old English Curve Cut, store bin with slanted front with product on all sides, "A Slice to a Pipeful, It Fits the Pocket," 13" x 10¼" x 8½", G........................................................ $125.00 B

Old Faithful, lighter fluid can, geiser on the front, 4-oz., NM.$135.00 C

Old Fitzgerald, lamp, motion, 14" H, EX.........................$175.00 C

Old Forrester, display, plaster statue of Man-O-War, EX ....$125.00 C

Old Fort Feeds, sign, porcelain, one-sided, die cut, wagon wheel, 40" x 47½", VG ..................................................................... $425.00 B

Old Fort Feeds, sign, porcelain, one-sided, wagon wheel, from Marion, Ohio, and Harrisburg, PA, 40" x 47½", EX..............................$420.00 B

Old Gold Cigarettes, flat tin, F...........................................$33.00 D

Old Gold Cigarettes, sign, paper on cardboard, easel back, Dick Powell promoting product, 10½" x 13½", EX ................................$35.00 C

Old Gold Cigarettes, sign, paper, actor Dick Powell seated enjoying an Old Gold cigarette, 11" x 14", VG..................................$20.00 D

Old Gold Cigarettes, sign, porcelain, 36" x 12", VG.................... $195.00 C

Old Gold Cigarettes, sign, porcelain, "Not a cough in a carload," 36" x 11", G ...................................................................... $295.00 C

**Old Gold Cigarettes,** sign, porcelain, horizontal, 36" x 12", F..**$95.00 C**

**Old Gold Cigarettes,** sign, porcelain, self-framing, single-sided, "Not a Cough in a Carload," 36" x 12", VG ..................... **$395.00 C**

**Old Gold Cigarettes,** sign, tin, litho, self-framed, embossed, cigarette packages, 33" x 14", EX.................................**$125.00 B**

**Old Gold Cigarettes,** tin, round vacuum pack, "the treasure of them all," 50-count, F ......................................**$65.00 C**

**Old Gold Special Cigarettes,** sign, cardboard, litho, street car scene, 29" x 41", G ....................................... **$250.00 B**

**Old Gold,** sign, die cut, easel back, cigarette girl with product vendor tray, 14" x 32", EX....................................**$140.00 B**

**Old Gold/Kent/Camels,** sign, metal, "Cigarettes Buy The Carton...Popular Brands," 12" x 34", VG.............................**$50.00 D**

**Old Grandad Whiskey,** sign, canvas, litho, old man in chair beside table with bottle of Old Grand Dad on table, 29½" x 23½", EX..........**$325.00 C**

**Old Green River Tobacco,** stoneware container in shape of whiskey jug, paper label, information about Old Green River Tobacco, top comes off jug for product access, 6" dia., x 8¼" h, EX .......**$400.00 B**

**Old Harvest Corn Whiskey,** sign, tin, litho, man holding child reaching for glass, 19½" x 13", VG ................................. **$750.00 B**

**Old Hickory Distillers Co.,** thermometer, bottle next to dial-type face, 8⅞" dia., VG................................... **$95.00 C**

**Old Hickory Distillery,** crock jug, Madisonville, Ky., 1-gal., EX ..**$185.00 C**

**Old Hickory,** store bin, shoe lace for product, 12½" x 6" x 11", EX..................................................................**$175.00 C**

**Old Hickory,** typewriter ribbon, tin, litho, black man resting under tree, 2½" x 2½", EX.....................................................**$170.00 B**

**Old Hill Side Tobacco,** sign, paper, older man smoking a pipe with a pouch of the product, "Some Smooth Smoke Believe Me," 15" x 20", EX ........................................................**$295.00 D**

**Old Home Brand Candies,** pail, wood bucket, paper label, "Manufactured Expressly for Ridenour-Baker Grocery Co., Kansas City, Mo." man cooking over a fire with cabin and mammy in background, 35-lb., VG.............................................. **$250.00 D**

**Old Honesty Plug Tobacco,** sign, cloth, "Chew...Always Reliable," 52" x 19", EX ..................................................**$195.00 D**

**Old Judge Cigarettes,** trade card, cardboard, "An Interesting Interview," 4" x 7", EX ................................................**$125.00 C**

**Old Judge Coffee,** can, metal, owl logo, slip lid, 1 lb., VG .........**$85.00 D**

**Old Judge Coffee,** sample cup, paper, product can on front, 2½" x 2½", EX....................................................................**$4.00 D**

**Old Judge Coffee,** sample cup, paper, product can on front, 2½" x 2½", NOS, NM..............................................................**$5.00 D**

**Old Judge Rye,** statue, carved wood, yarn hair, man is holding a cane and bottle of the product, 9½" x 12" x 47½", VG ............. **$1,000.00 B**

**Old Judson Whiskey,** match holder, tin, litho, man pulling on coat in front of roaring fire, 3½" x 5", NM..................................**$230.00 B**

**Old Judson,** match holder, tin, litho, 3" x 5" x 1¼", G..... **$125.00 D**

**Old Judson,** match holder, tin, litho, J.C. Stevens, 518 Delaware St., Kansas City, MO, USA, 5" H, F .................................................**$75.00 C**

**Old Kentucky's Boss,** whiskey bottle, paper label, G ........ **$25.00 C**

**Old King Cole Cigars,** box label, embossed, Maxfield Parrish art, 10" x 6", EX.................................................................**$195.00 C**

**Old King Cole Smoking Mixture,** pocket tin, paper label, artwork by Maxfield Parrish, rare and hard-to-find, 3½" x 1½" x 4½", EX.**$575.00 C**

**Old Manse Syrup,** tin, house in winter, 6" x 3½" x 11", EX.**$135.00 C**

**Old Master Coffee,** tin, old master on the front, 5½" x 9½", EX.**$75.00 C**

**Old Mill Cigarettes,** sign, paper, farmer leaning on fence and product lettering on barn behind her, 19" x 26", EX.................**$450.00 D**

**Old Mission Lager,** tray, metal, old mission in landscape, 12" dia., EX .................................................................**$250.00 D**

**Old Mr. Boston Fine Liquors,** clock, metal, cut in likeness of bottle, 22" tall, EX ................................................................**$250.00 C**

**Old Mr. Boston,** clock, embossed, shape of flask, made by Gilbert at Winstead, Conn., 10" x 5½" x 21¼", VG ........................... **$125.00 B**

**Old North State Tobacco,** sign, canvas, barn with package on blue background, framed in quarter-sawn oak frame, 30" x 20", EX .................................................................**$120.00 B**

**Old Overholt Rye,** sign, tin, litho, original wood frame, hunters in field with dog, 37" x 28", EX..............................................**$745.00 B**

**Old Overholt Whiskey,** oleograph, canvas, wood frame, man with bottle of product and a fishing rod, 1913, 27½" x 38½", EX .......**$350.00 D**

**Old Overholt Whiskey,** sign, metal, hunter and farmer, 36" x 28", EX.................................................................**$855.00 C**

**Old Overholt,** oleograph, old gentleman in stream fly fishing and pouring whiskey from a bottle into a container, signed R. Bohunck, 27½" x 38½", 1913, EX .................................**$575.00 C**

**Old Plantation Steel Cut Coffee,** bag, heavy paper, black man with sack of product in front of paddle wheeler, 1-lb., EX............**$25.00 C**

**Old Quaker Straight Whiskey,** display, Scottie dog on cardboard box, 13" x 11" x 6", EX......................................................**$75.00 C**

**Old Reading Beer,** serving tray, metal, "Traditionally Pennsylvania Dutch," 12" dia., EX ........................................................**$35.00 D**

**Old Reliable Coffee,** pocket mirror, dock scene on back side, EX .................................................................**$125.00 C**

**Old Reliable Coffee,** sign, cardboard, "A Real Breakfast, Always The Same, Always Good," breakfast scene and product box, trolley car, 21" x 11", NM ..................................................................$97.00 B

**Old Reliable Coffee,** sign, logo gentleman, litho by H.D. Beach Co., 6¼" x 9¼", EX ...............................................................$425.00 C

**Old Reliable Coffee,** sign, paper, litho, trademark old Russian and package of product, "Always the same...Always good," 11½" x 21½", VG .................................................................... $95.00 B

**Old Reliable Coffee,** sign, tin, "Always good," 1910s, 6½" x 9", F .$95.00 C

**Old Reliable Coffee,** sign, tin, embossed, litho, "Always Good...Go to G.M. Law's General Merchandise," 6½" x 13¾", EX..................$40.00 B

**Old Reliable Coffee,** sign, tin, single-sided, embossed, raised lettering, "always good," 13¾" x 6½", VG.....................................$95.00 C

**Old Reliable Coffee,** sign, trolley car, "Welcome as April showers," man with cup of coffee, 21" x 11", EX.............................$175.00 D

**Old Reliable Coffee,** tip tray, metal, "Guaranteed Pure," Russian man and package of product, 4¼" dia., EX .........................$100.00 B

**Old Reliable Coffee,** tip tray, metal, pretty woman with flower in hair, 4¼" dia., NM................................................................$143.00 B

**Old Reliable Coffee,** tip tray, tin, litho, old Cossack man, 4¼" dia., EX ...........................................................................$155.00 B

**Old Reliable Peanut Butter,** pail, wire side-mounted bail, tin, litho, 1-lb., EX................................................................................$75.00 C

**Old Reliable,** crate label, paper, for Colorado apples, EX ...$35.00 D

**Old Reliable,** pocket mirror, celluloid back, old logo gentleman in center, 2" dia., G...........................................................$100.00 C

**Old Reliable,** pocket mirror, celluloid back, old logo, gentleman in center, 2" dia., EX.........................................................$175.00 C

**Old Rip Long Cut Smoking Tobacco,** pocket tin, metal, vertical, 7" tall, EX.................................................................................$125.00 C

**Old Seneca Stogies,** can, metal, Indian Chief, "3 for 5¢," EX.$295.00 D

**Old Seneca Stogies,** tin, litho, Indian bust on front, 4" dia., x 5½", EX.................................................................................$240.00 B

**Old Soldier Tobacco,** pail, metal, "Extra Sweet Smoke & Chew," paper label, EX.........................................................................$345.00 D

**Old Southern Coffee,** can, metal, screw lid, 1 lb., EX ........$115.00 C

**Old Southern Coffee,** container, tin, litho, slip-lid, woman in chair with cup of product, Larkin Co., Buffalo, NY, 1-lb., EX..........$75.00 D

**Old Southern Coffee,** tin, litho, slip-lid, woman in chair with cup of product, Larkin Co., Buffalo, NY, 1-lb., G..........................$55.00 D

**Old Southern Molasses,** tin, litho, label, Packed by J. Stromeyer Co., Philadelphia, Pa., 9" x 9" x 15", VG.......................$100.00 B

**Old Squire Tobacco,** pocket tin, from Tuckett Tobacco Co., Canada, 3⅛" x 4½" x ²⁵⁄₃₂", EX ....................................................$700.00 B

**Old Style Lager,** cigarette vendor, wooden, backbar, point of sale, "We don't aim to make the most beer: just the best," 21½" x 4" x 12¾", EX............................................................$55.00 B

**Old Style,** sign, plastic light-up, "Brewed with water from when the earth was pure," 15" x 10¼", EX.........................................$25.00 D

**Old Style,** thermometer, tin, litho, die cut, musketeer holding a mug of the product, 6" x 13¼", EX...................................$725.00 B

**Old Taver Brew,** label from bottle, for the Rock Island Brewing Co., 12 oa., EX..................................................................................$45.00 C

**Old Virginia Catsup,** Halloween mask of Mammy, cardboard, giveaway, products information on reverse, 9" x 10¼", EX........$225.00 B

**Old Virginia Cheroots,** sign, cardboard, litho, couple greeting each other, 20½" x 20½", VG ...................................................... $150.00 B

**Old Virginia Cheroots,** sign, cardboard, matted, framed, and under glass, 1900s, 6½" x 10½", G.........................................$125.00 D

**Old Virginia Cheroots,** sign, paper, Uncle Sam, 17" x 25", EX....$750.00 C

**Old Virginia Cheroots,** sign, tin, litho, cigar box image on front, 8½" sq., VG ............................................................... $185.00 D

**Old Windsor Whisky,** sign, paper, black servant pulling a bottle from a treasure chest, 1870 – 80s, 12" x 23", VG .............$395.00 C

**Olde Philadephia Coffee,** tin, key-wound lid, Philadelphia landmarks, 5" x 3½", EX .........................................................$75.00 D

**Oldfield Tires,** sign, metal, flange, double-sided, tire graphics, 21" x 16", EX.................................................................................$2,530.00 B

**Oldfield Tires,** sign, porcelain, double-sided, flange, 21¼" x 16½", VG.................................................................................. $800.00 B

**Oldsmobile Service,** clock, neon circle on outside, 21" x 6", VG ................................................................................. $600.00 B

**Oldsmobile Service,** sign, porcelain, double-sided, dealer with coat of arms in center, 42" dia., G ............................$425.00 C

**Oldsmobile Service,** sign, porcelain, one-sided, 42" dia., VG. $875.00 C

**Oldsmobile,** clock, light-up, electric, by Pam Clock Co., 15½" sq., VG ................................................................................. $475.00 B

**Oldsmobile,** clock, metal and glass neon accents, "Oldsmobile Service," 18" x 18", EX .........................................................$795.00 D

**Oldsmobile,** sign, porcelain, globe with ring, no lettering, 15" x 20", EX......................$595.00 C

**Oldsmobile,** sign, porcelin, "Oldsmobile Service," globe with ring, double-sided, 60" dia., EX ..................$950.00 C

**Olin Winchester,** display, flashlight and battery, store counter 34" T, VG .......................... $95.00 C

**Oliver Chilled Plows,** sign, metal, self-framing, man on horse back at old general store, 23" x 32", EX..................................$7,000.00 B

**Oliver Chilled Plows,** sign, tin, litho, self-framed, embossed, youngster on horseback and the products in foreground, 27¼" x 36½", 1890, VG ...............................................$395.00 C

**Oliver Implements,** sign, tin, flange, "Plowmakers for the world," globe in center, 18" x 18", EX ..........................$175.00 C

**Oliver Implements,** sign, tin, painted, die cut, flange, "plowmakers for the world," earth in center, 18" x 18", EX ...................$225.00 C

**Olixir,** sign, tin, "Feel the Difference," vintage auto moving up a hill, JB Clark Oil Co., Buffalo, NY, 17⅝" x 18", G .......................$140.00 B

**Ology Quality Cigar,** sign, cardboard, die cut, easel back, man with golf club, 1930s, 25" x 37", EX...............................$145.00 B

**Ols English Curve Cut Pipe Tobacco,** store countertop bin, slant top, country gentleman enjoying a smoke from the product, 13" x 10¼" x 8", EX....................................................$370.00 B

**Olympia Beer,** tray, metal, cavalier image in center, pre-prohibition, 12" dia., EX .................................................$150.00 D

**Olympian Coffee,** tin, litho, pry-lid, 1-lb., EX ...........$88.00 B

**Olympic Ice Cream,** sign, metal, "The Pure Food Cream," 15" x 14", EX ............................................$375.00 C

**Omar Baking Co.,** sign, Indianapolis, "Fresh at your door every day," 6½" x 8", EX..................................................$525.00 B

**Omar Cigarette,** sign, cardboard in original frame, two older gentlemen enjoying a smoke, 18¼" x 25", EX ............................$575.00 C

**Omar Turkish Cigarette,** sign, paper, litho, framed, father and son enjoying a smoke, engraving on frame bottom, "American Tobacco Co., Omar Turkish Blend Cigarettes," 18½" x 25", F ....... $110.00 D

**Omar Turkish Cigarettes,** sign, paper, "Like the World of a Gentleman," 28" x 36", EX ..........................................$350.00 D

**Omega,** sign, porcelain, large pocket watch, 1910 – 20s, 28" x 18", EX .............................................................$595.00 D

**Omin Giano Tonic Vigor,** display, chalkware, cow, 5" x 6" x 9", VG ...........................................................$75.00 D

**On Parade Fine Tobacco,** label, paper, "Made in America," image of soldier, 7" x 14", EX.........................................$45.00 D

**On the Stroke of Twelve,** poster, paper, litho, two men getting ready to box, 24½" x 32½", VG ........................ $185.00 B

**On Time Gum,** tin, stenciled chewing gum, top-mounted wire handle, 7¾" x 5¼" x 2", EX.....................................$900.00 B

**One Eleven American Cigarette,** full pack, Indian bust in full headdress, 2" x 2¾", NM.....................................$80.00 B

**Oneida,** cigar box label, paper, river scene, VG ...............$145.00 D

**Onondaga Brand Glass,** sign, metal, flange, painted, Indian in center, 18½" x 13½", VG........................................$165.00 C

**Onyx,** gas globe, plastic body with glass lens, 13½" dia., VG..$550.00 C

**Opal Powdered Sugar,** box, cardboard, woman making desserts with the product, 8" tall, EX.......................................$180.00 B

**Opex Lacquers Enamels,** sign, porcelain, flange, Sherwin Williams Paint logo at top left and right, 22" x 16", EX.....................$275.00 C

**Opex Paints,** sign, porcelain, two-sided, flange, "Sherwin Williams, The Modern Automobile Lacquer Finish," 22" x 16", EX...$250.00 C

**Optimo Cigars,** sign, reverse imaging under beveled glass, "Very Mild, F. A. Bronchain," 11¼" H, VG.................................$135.00 C

**Optomertist,** sign, glass, reverse painted, eyebrow with the lettering curved below, 28" x 16", EX ...............................................$650.00 B

**Orange Crush Carbonated Beverages,** sign, tin, embossed, Crushy at bottom, diamond-shaped, 21¼" x 21¼", 1938, EX ..............$275.00 B

**Orange Crush Soda,** thermometer, tin, die cut, embossed, bottle, 7" x 28¾", 1950s, NM.....................................................$300.00 B

**Orange Crush Ward's Orange Crush, Lemon Crush, and Lime Crush,** sign, metal, single-sided, embossed lettering and bottles, 19¾" x 9¼", VG ....................................................... $375.00 B

**Orange Crush,** blotter, cardboard, "Compliments of...," 1930s, VG ....................................................................$35.00 D

**Orange Crush,** clock, metal and glass, bottle cap on clock face, Pam Clock Co., 15" dia., EX.......................................$350.00 D

**Orange Crush,** clock, plastic, light-up, "Taste," 15" sq., EX .$135.00 C

**Orange Crush,** clock, tin, litho, electric, face and wooden body, 15½" sq., 1940s, VG........................................ $425.00 C

**Orange Crush,** counter dispenser, stainless steel, porcelain sign sides, 11" x 17" x 20", F....................................$500.00 D

**Orange Crush,** display, cardboard, "At Ease...Always In The Krinkly Bottle!," image of service men, 1940s, 16" x 10", VG ........$700.00 B

**Orange Crush,** display, cardboard, real bottle, "Drink O-C & O-C Beverages...," 1930s, EX .................................$375.00 D

Orange Crush, glass, Bakelite and frosted glass, Art Deco style, rare, EX ..................................................................$450.00 C

Orange Crush, glass, flared top and etched syrup line, NM........$195.00 C

Orange Crush, menu board, metal, Crushy logo, "Drink Orange-Crush Frosty Cold," 1950s, 19" x 28", EX.........................$250.00 B

Orange Crush, menu board, metal, painted, message and bottle at top, 19" x 27¼", G ............................................... $125.00 D

Orange Crush, menu board, metal, painted, message and bottle at top, 19" x 27¼", VG.............................................$145.00 C

Orange Crush, menu board, tin, embossed, Crushy figure at top, 19¼" x 27", EX................................................$280.00 B

Orange Crush, pitcher, glass, orange bottom, slide handle and metal spout, 1920 – 30s, EX.....................................$350.00 B

Orange Crush, sign, "Drink," bottle in snow at outer edge, 17½" x 11½", NM ............................................................$75.00 D

Orange Crush, sign, cardboard, cut out, pretty girl on the beach at the ocean, "Drink Orange-Crush...Made from Ripe Oranges," 1920s, 12" x 18", EX ...............................................$500.00 B

Orange Crush, sign, cardboard, die cut, krinkle bottle with Crushy, 14" x 30", EX ................................................$175.00 C

Orange Crush, sign, cardboard, lady and her dog, 14" x 19", EX...............................................................$190.00 B

Orange Crush, sign, cardboard, stringer hanger, die cut, clear bottle and hotdog, 1920 – 30s, EX .......................................$295.00 D

Orange Crush, sign, metal, "Feel Fresh...," Crushy logo at bottom, 1930s, 21" x 21", EX.............................................$295.00 C

Orange Crush, sign, metal, double-sided, flange, "There's Only One...Sold Here Ice Cold," 18" x 12", EX .........................$450.00 B

Orange Crush, sign, metal, embossed, self-framing, bottle in center, 17" x 53¼", EX ................................................$460.00 D

Orange Crush, sign, metal, raised lettering strip, "ask for a ...natural flavor...natural color," 26½" x 3½", VG ...................$75.00 C

Orange Crush, sign, metal, single-sided, bottle, 31½" x 11¾", VG................................................................$125.00 C

Orange Crush, sign, mirror, "Feel Fresh...Drink O-C Carbonated Beverage," 1930 – 40s, 9" x 11", VG..................................$275.00 B

Orange Crush, sign, paper on cardboard, woman and dog, 13½" x 19¼", EX...............................................................$150.00 B

Orange Crush, sign, tin over cardboard, "Drink, The National Fountain Drink, Color Added," girl with glass of Orange Crush, 1920s, 6¼" x 9¼", G .......................................... $500.00 B

Orange Crush, sign, tin, clear ribbed bottle, "Come In...," 1930s, 3" x 10", EX...............................................................$500.00 B

Orange Crush, sign, tin, flange, Crushy at the bottom of the diamond, 1930s, 18" x 18", F ................................................$125.00 C

Orange Crush, street marker, cast brass, "National Safety Eng. Bham, ALA" on back side, 3¾" dia., EX....................$325.00 B

Orange Crush, thermometer, aluminum and plastic, dial-type scale, half-sliced orange above product name in center of dial, 1950s, 12½" dia., EX .......................................$135.00 C

Orange Crush, thermometer, metal and glass, dial, "Taste," 12" dia., VG .................................................... $120.00 B

Orange Crush, thermometer, metal, painted, bottle cap at top of scale, 5¾" x 16", NM.............................................$145.00 C

Orange Crush, thermometer, metal, painted, "Thirsty...Crush that thirst," Crush cap at top of vertical scale, EX...........................$85.00 C

Orange Crush, thermometer, metal, scale type, bottle cap graphics at top, rounded top & bottom, 1950s, 6" x 15", EX....................$165.00 D

Orange Crush, tray, metal, foreign lettering, Crushy logo, 12" dia., VG...............................................................$95.00 C

Orange Drink, barrel, wooden, painted on lettering, 14" x 20", G .............................................................. $75.00 B

Orange Julius, sign, "A Devilish Good Drink," devil figure in center, rare, 1920s, 24" x 35", F..............................................$300.00 C

Orange Kist, cooler, metal and tin, "Drink Orange Kist," 31" x 22" x 31", VG .................................................... $350.00 B

Orange Kist, sign, cardboard, die cut, standup, girl bending at the waist, 9" x 12", EX ...........................................$300.00 D

Orange Kist, sign, metal, "Drink Orange Crush and other Kist flavors," 20" x 13", NM .......................................$275.00 B

Orange-Crush, electric drink box, other versions of this box were made for other drinks, most were embossed, PELCO 510-E, 1940 – 1950s, 10-case, orange, NM ....................$2,995.00 D

Orange-Crush, sign, cardboard, die cut, bathing beauty on dock, "Drink Delicious O-C," 1920s, EX ...................................$695.00 D

Orange-Julep, bottle topper, "Drink, It's JULEP Time," EX ..$65.00 B

Orange-Julep, bottle topper, "Drink, It's JULEP Time," G .$55.00 D

Orange-Julep, serving tray, metal, "Drink," girl at beach with umbrella, and holding a glass of Orange-Julep, G ............. $130.00 B

Orange-Julep, sign, cardboard, hang-up, man and woman drinking from a single bottle with two straws, 1930s, 7¾" x 11", G......$95.00 C

Orbit Gum, valentine card, cardboard, black boy with a sample box of the product, EX................................................$125.00 D

Orchard Park Coffee, can, metal, key wind lid, 1 lb., EX ........$30.00 D

Orchid, crate label, paper, for Florida citrus, EX ...............$10.00 D

**Orcico Cigar,** tin, litho, Indian on front, 2 for 5¢, 6" x 5½" x 4", 1919, EX ...............................................................$350.00 B

**Oregon Association of Nurserymen,** sign, porcelain, double-sided, member, 18½" x 15¼", NM ...............................................$165.00 C

**Oregon Chief Gasoline,** sign, porcelain, Indian chief surrounded by Washington-Idaho-Montana, 72" dia., EX.........................$4,300.00 B

**Oregon Winter Sports Association,** license plate, tin, embossed, ski jumper in action, 12" x 5", 1942, EX.................................$275.00 C

**Oregon Winter Sports Association,** license plate, tin, embossed, ski jumper in action, 12" x 5", 1942, F....................................$100.00 D

**Oretel Brew,** tray, metal, tip size, woman seated in profile, 5" dia., EX .................................................................................$100.00 D

**Oriental Special Auto Oil,** sign, porcelain, large oil can, 17" x 21", EX...................................................................................$1,760.00 B

**Original Hoffman House Rye,** sign, stone, litho, paper, nudes cavorting around Satyr, in original stamped wood frame, Buckeye Distillery Co., 24½" x 32½", EX .....................................$1,025.00 B

**Orioles,** cigar box label, paper, birds in tree, EX....................$95.00 C

**Orphan Boy Smoking Tobacco,** sign, cardboard, cut out, pouch with donkey on label, 12" x 17", EX....................................$150.00 C

**Orsborne Plow Co.,** sign, paper, pretty girl looking at all of company implements on advertising board, 24" x 31", EX .................$675.00 B

**Ortlieb's Laeger Beer – Ale,** sign, tin, litho, self-framing, 14" dia., VG.....................................................................................$135.00 C

**Osborne Farm Impliments,** catalog, paper, farmer and wife on front, 24 pages, EX .............................................................$80.00 B

**OshKosh B'Gosh Overalls,** display, cardboard, cut out, Uncle Sam wearing an actual pair of the product, 1936, 27" x 77", EX.$2,150.00 B

**Oshkosh R.R. Suits,** sign, reverse painted glass in wood frame, "Union Made," oil worker at left side of sign, 48¼" x 18½", P ...........$100.00 C

**OshKosh Tools,** calendar, cardboard, pinup girl on ladder, 1952, 16" x 32", EX .............................................................$115.00 D

**Oshkosh Work Clothes,** clock, neon, octagonal, 1930s, EX ..$495.00 C

**Oster Electric Scalp Massage,** clock, plastic, light-up, 16" x 16" x 3¾", G ..............................................................................$110.00 C

**Ottumwa Brewing Co.,** shell, clear, gold rim, company logo, pre 1911, NM ...............................................................................$140.00 B

**Our Advertiser Smoking Tobacco,** bag, OCB papers, G .........$8.00 D

**Our Advertiser Tobacco,** display box, cardboard, "5¢ A Cool Sweet Smoke For Cigarette Or Pipe," complete with 24 unopened packages, EX................................................................$340.00 B

**Our Alderman,** cigar box label, paper, man in top hat, EX..$150.00 B

**Our Game,** cigar box, vintage baseball game, scarce item, 1900s, EX............................................................................ $775.00 C

**Our Hobby Sliced Plug,** pocket tin, tin, litho, early, rare, Taylor & Co., Burlington, VT, 4⅝" x 2¾" x ⅞", EX ..............................$300.00 B

**Our Jewel Roasted Coffee,** tin, litho, knob handle top, young child in cameo on front, scarce, Ericsson's Mills, New York, 1-lb., G ...... $159.00 B

**Our Mutual Friends,** cigar box, wood, paper litho labels, 3 young boys, 8¼" x 4¾" x 2¼", VG............................................... $170.00 B

**Our Pride,** cigar box label, paper, Panama Canal, 9" x 6", EX..$25.00 D

**Ovaltine,** sign, metal, men jumping hurdles, 12" x 18", EX..$170.00 B

**Ovaltine,** sign, tin, litho, "For Health Strength and Energy," 12" x 18", G ...................................................................... $300.00 B

**Overholt Whiskey,** sign, tin in wood frame, metal slug plate, "It's Old Overholt," folks and dog, 36½" x 27¼", VG..................... $1,000.00 B

**Overland Co. Garage,** sign, tin, painted, service, 23½" x 12", EX .................................................................................$200.00 C

**Overland Service,** sign, porcelain, oval, "Genuine Parts," 40" x 30", EX................................................................................$650.00 B

**Overland,** cigar box label, paper, locomotive pulling a load through the mountains, 9" x 6", EX ...................................................$85.00 D

**Owl Cigars,** sign, cardboard, die cut, hanger, birdcage, owl, perch is cigar, 10" x 7", EX............................................................$300.00 B

**Owl Cigars,** sign, cardboard, double-sided, die cut, string hanger, 7" x 9½", F ................................................................$125.00 D

**Ox-Heart Brand Peanut Butter,** door push plate, porcelain, "We Sell...," 4" x 7", EX .................................................................$700.00 B

**Ox-Heart Cocoa,** door push, porcelain, Dutch Process Cocoa, 4" x 6½", EX ...............................................................................$175.00 D

**Ozark Mountain Spring Water,** sign, tin, embossed, "tacker" style, "Drink Million Smiles," 20" x 9", G ................................... $95.00 C

**Ozonite,** sign, paper, "The Complete Detergent," 22¾" x 19¾", VG..................................................................................$50.00 C

Pabarco Rose Hair Oil, bottle, glass, paper label, Paducah Barber Supply Co., 6¼" tall, EX, $45.00 C. *Courtesy of B.J. Summers.*

Pabst Blue Ribbon, backbar, statue, boxer in ring with bottle, NM, $165.00 C. *Courtesy of Pleasant Hill Antique Mall & Tea Room/Bob Johnson.*

Pabst Blue Ribbon Beer, poster, cardboard, framed, waiter in uniform carrying a tray of beer and glasses, older version, 26½" x 36", EX, $675.00 C.

Pabst Blue Ribbon, display, light-up motion train, "Old Time Beer Flavor," VG, $265.00 C. *Courtesy of B.J. Summers.*

Pabst Brewing Co., sign, paper, litho, pre-Prohibition, worker elves tapping into a barrel of the product in the factory storage cellar, 34¾" x 26¾", EX, $2,700.00 B. *Courtesy of Wm. Morford Investment Grade Collectibles.*

P Lorillard Fine Cut, sign, paper, angelic figure giving a tobacco leaf to an Indian, 8½"x 11", EX .........................................$220.00 B

P. Lorillard & Co. Tobacco, store display cabinet, wood with etched glass and brass lettering, great piece, 43" H, G..$1,500.00 C

P.O.N., sign, glass, reverse painted, for Pride of Newark quality brews, 16"x 13", EX.......................................................$135.00 C

Pabst Beer, sign, cardboard, die cut, beer bottle, easel back, 9½" x 32", EX.....................................................................$35.00 C

Pabst Beer, sign, Spanish-American war heroes around table celebrating with product, 1899, EX ...........................$610.00 B

Pabst Blue Ribbon Beer, can, flat top, Internal Revenue Paid note, 12 oz., EX .....................................................................$20.00 D

Pabst Blue Ribbon Beer, clock, molded plastic, light-up, 17" dia., VG ...............................................................................$80.00 B

Pabst Blue Ribbon Beer, cup and saucer set, logo on rim, VG .$75.00 C

Pabst Blue Ribbon Beer, display, a man in an old open car, product sign on brick wall behind car, real beer bottle in front of car, 16" x 17", VG .................................................................$135.00 C

Pabst Blue Ribbon Beer, display, chalkware bust of girl, "What'll You Have?...Finest Beer Served," 10" x 12", EX ...............$125.00 D

Pabst Blue Ribbon Beer, display, metal and glass, boxer with sign overhead, "On Tap," EX .................................................$100.00 D

Pabst Blue Ribbon Beer, display, metal and glass, light up, bartender, 3 deminsonal figures, "We Serve The Finest People Everyday," EX .......................................................................$115.00 D

Pabst Blue Ribbon Beer, display, metal and plastic, dimensional engineer in train that moves and smokes when plugged in, "Old Time Beer Flavor, Original," 1961, EX ...........................$195.00 C

Pabst Blue Ribbon Beer, display, molded plastic, barbershop quartet with a bottle and barber pole, VG...................................$95.00 D

Pabst Blue Ribbon Beer, menu board, new, EX.......................$45.00 D

Pabst Blue Ribbon Beer, menu board, new, NM ................$65.00 C

Pabst Blue Ribbon Beer, poster, cardboard, framed, waiter in uniform carrying a tray of beer and glasses, older version, 26½" x 36", G.................................................................................$225.00 C

Pabst's Okay Specific Medicinal Remedy, sign, tin, embossed, 6" x 9", EX, $115.00 C. *Courtesy of Muddy River Trading Co./Gary Metz.*

Paducah Cooperage Company, Inc., the Padco barrel in its stand and vaseline shot glasses, 1910 – 20s, 10" x 6½" dia., EX, $275.00 C. *Courtesy of B.J. Summers.*

Paducah, Ky, souvenir cup and saucer, river and steamboats, "Scene on the Ohio at Paducah, Ky by moonlight," Dresden, made in Germany, 1890 – 1900s, NM, $125.00 C. *Courtesy of B.J. Summers.*

Paducah, Ky, souvenir, cup, custard with gold rim and red lettering, 1903, 3" x 2½", EX, $125.00 C. *Courtesy of B.J. Summers.*

Paducah Laundry & Cleaners, Inc., playing cards, plastic coated, cook with large cooked turkey on a platter and company information at bottom on back of each card, full deck in unopened sealed box with stamp on top, 1940 – 50s, 2½" x 3½", NM, $35.00 C. *Courtesy of B.J. Summers.*

---

Pabst Blue Ribbon Beer, print, paper, 6 horse team wagon and a dog running along side, "Pabst Famous Blue Ribbon Winners," 31"x 11", EX..................................................................$95.00 C

Pabst Blue Ribbon Beer, sign, cardboard, black waiter with tray, 24" x 33¼", 1931, EX .....................................$375.00 C

Pabst Blue Ribbon Beer, sign, cardboard, black waiter with tray, "Yes Suh," 27" x 36", EX .....................................$650.00 B

Pabst Blue Ribbon Beer, sign, cardboard, litho, black waiter, 30"x 39½", 1938, VG..................................................................$275.00 B

Pabst Blue Ribbon Beer, sign, metal, embossed bottle with "Pabst," 1930s, 12" x 18", VG .........................................$115.00 C

Pabst Blue Ribbon Beer, sign, porcelain, "Pabst Blue Ribbon," 42" x 30", EX..................................................................$235.00 C

Pabst Blue Ribbon Beer, sign, tin, "at popular prices...6 for...," PBR can at bottom, 26" x 60", EX .................................$75.00 C

Pabst Blue Ribbon Beer, sign, tin, painted, "at popular prices," beer can with message at top, 26" x 60", EX .......................$95.00 C

Pabst Blue Ribbon, backbar statue, boxer in ring with bottle, EX ...........................................................................$135.00 C

Pabst Blue Ribbon, display, light-up, motion train, "Old Time Beer Flavor," EX ....................................................................$325.00 C

Pabst Blue Ribbon, serving tray, Pabst Brewing Company, Milwaukee, Wisc., EX...............................................................$25.00 C

Pabst Blue Ribbon, sign, tin, litho, Rip Van Winkle, "The Beer that brings back Memories," 17½" x 11½", EX .........................$200.00 D

Pabst Brewery, booklet, paper, company scenes, 1907, 40 pages, EX...........................................................................$65.00 D

Pabst Brewing Co., match safe, metal, embossing on both sides, 1½" x 2⁹⁄₁₀", VG.................................................................$225.00 C

Pabst Brewing Co., sign, paper, litho, pre-Prohibition, worker elves tapping into a barrel of the product in the factory storage cellar, 34¾" x 26¾", G....................................................$1,100.00 C

Pabst Extract, calendar, cardboard and paper, woman with yellow scarf, 1917, 7¼" x 36", NM ...........................................$380.00 B

Paducah Sash & Door Co., lighter, metal, by Dundee, company truck, "It Pays To Call Paducah First," bright colors, reverse side reads "Paducah Sash & Door Company, Paducah, Kentucky," 1950 – 60s, 2⅛" x 1⅞" x ⅜", EX, $45.00 C. Courtesy of B.J. Summers.

Page & Shaw Chocolates, sign, cardboard, standup, Santa Claus, 39" tall, G, $55.00 B.

Palmolive Soap, poster, cardboard, easel back, stand up, "Keep that Schoolgirl complexion," 10" x 15", VG, $245.00 C.

Pan-Am, ink blotters, "Keep Pace with Pan-Am Gasoline," 6¼" x 3", EX, $160.00 B.

Parlor Chair Long Cut Tobacco, sign, paperboard, young lady on front, H.F. Hess & Co., 8" x 11", VG, $230.00 B.

---

Pabst Extract, calendar, paper, yard long print of pretty girl in red dress looking over her shoulder, full monthly pads, 1907, 10" x 37", EX .................................................................$330.00 B

Pabst Extract, sign, yard-long American Girl, in long dress with top strip, bottom strip missing, 1914, 35½"L, EX ...................$100.00 B

Pabst's Okay Specific Medicinal Remedy, sign, tin, embossed, 6" x 9", G.................................................................$55.00 C

Pabst, display, plaster and composition, young lady with a bonnet with inset for bottle of product, 9½" x 4" x 11½", VG........$135.00 C

Pabst, sign, neon, window, 21" x 19", EX..........................$110.00 C

Pacer 200 Hi-Test, pump sign, porcelain, lettered in red & black diagonally, 8½" x14", EX ....................................................$250.00 C

Pacer 400 Ethyl, pump sign, porcelain, lettered diagonally in red with ethyl logo, 8½" x 14", NM ..........................$550.00 B

Pacer Cigar, box label, paper, harness race, 1909, 4½" x 4½", VG.................................................................$55.00 D

Pacific Brewing & Malting Co., art plate, china, with 2 children at play, EX.................................................................$155.00 D

Pacific Brewing & Malting Co., calendar, cardboard, pretty red-headed lady with large hat and roses, partial monthly pads, 19" x 33", EX.................................................................$500.00 B

Pacific Coast Steamship Co., tip tray, metal, company flag in tray center, 3⅝" dia., EX.................................................................$75.00 B

Pacific Inter-Mountain Express, calendar, tin over cardboard, tear sheets at bottom and truck at top, 12½" x 19", G..............$130.00 B

Pacific Power & Light Co., sign, porcelain, Reddy Kilowatt in center surrounded by company name, 36"dia., EX ................$750.00 B

Packard Automobile Cable, display, metal, counter rack, gold lettering, 18" x 36", EX.................................................................$75.00 D

Page Baby Talc, tin, litho, woman holding baby on front label, 4½"T, EX.................................................................$375.00 C

Pearl Lager Beer, clock, neon, 18⅜"
x 18⅜" x 6⅝", VG, $450.00 C.

Pedigree Whiskey, sign, tin, litho, self-
framing, horse and rider in center oval,
27" x 19", EX, $325.00 B.

Pennsylvania Rubber Co., ash-
tray, vaseline glass, non-skid with
CV logo, Jeannette, PA, NM,
$145.00 D. *Courtesy of Antiques, Cards
& Collectibles/Ray Pelley.*

Pennsylvania Rubber Company,
sign, paper, litho, oil-proof tires,
pretty woman with hat, "Euphemia"
under artwork, Jeannette, PA, 25¼"
x 35½", VG, $400.00 B. *Courtesy of Col-
lectors Auction Services.*

Pennzoil, sign, metal, early
brown bell in center, lollipop,
original heavy embossed stand,
"Safe Lubrication," 1920s, G,
$675.00 D. *Courtesy of Illinois
Antique Center/Kim & Dan Phillips.*

---

**Page Borated Baby Talc,** container, tin, litho, woman with baby,
2½" x 1¼" x 4½", EX ..........................................................$45.00 C

**Page's Ice Cream,** folding chair with name and message embossed
on wooden back, 16" x 20" x 32½", EX ..............................$300.00 B

**Paige Sales & Service** globe, milk glass, "Sales and Service," 1920s,
EX..............................................................................$1,100.00 B

**Pal Ade,** calendar, cardboard, boy at bat, image of Babe Ruth "Let's
Go Pal," 1950, 11" x 23", EX .............................................$525.00 B

**Pal Ade,** door push, tin, EX................................................$95.00 C

**Palace Brand Coffee,** container, tin, litho, slip-lid, Winter Carnival
Ice Palace, from Atwood & Co., Minneapolis, 3-lb., G..........$236.00 B

**Paladin,** lunch box, Paladin on horseback, 1960s, EX.........$85.00 C

**Palethorpes Royal Cambridge Sausage,** sign, porcelain, single-
sided, foreign, , 36" x 24", EX............................................$325.00 B

**Pall Mall Cigarettes,** sign, metal, package in corner with seductive
lady, 15" x 21", EX.............................................................$65.00 D

**Pall Mall Cigarettes,** sign, tin, pin-up girl, same set-up used in
Lucky Strike advertisement, 1950s, 15" x 21", EX.........$230.00 B

**Pall Mall Cigars,** poster, paper, litho, by Currier & Ives, two black
sailors dancing on a vintage sailboat, "The Pall Mall Yacht Club-On
the Winning Tac," 19¼" x 17¼", 1885, G.........................$325.00 D

**Pall Mall Cigars,** sign, paper, litho, by Currier & Ives of the Pall Mall
Yacht Club "The Cup Secure," 15" x 11½", 1885, VG..........$245.00 B

**Pall Mall Famous Cigarettes,** box, Christmas motif, 7" x 8½" x
2", EX...............................................................................$75.00 D

**Pall Mall Menthol 100s,** pack, green, unopened 20-count, EX...$20.00 C

**Pall Mall Menthol 100s,** pack, green, unopened 20-count, VG ..$10.00 C

Pepsi-Cola, bottle cap, sign, metal, double-sided, flange, 1950s, 15" x 14", VG, $475.00 B.

Pepsi-Cola, sign, tin, oval, double-sided, flange, "Buy...Here," 16" x 12", VG, $550.00 B. *Courtesy of Autopia Advertising Auctions.*

Pepsi-Cola, clock, metal and glass, light-up, bottle cap in center, good strong colors, 9¼" x 12½", red, white, blue cap on yellow, EX, $195.00 C.

Pepsi-Cola, clock, metal, glass, "say...please," rainbow banner at top, VG, $450.00 C.

Pepsi-Cola, cooler, metal, top hinged lid, correct Pepsi opener, 1920s, 27" long, G, $575.00 C.

---

**Pall Mall,** display rack, wooden, countertop, debossed message on each side, dovetailed joints, EX .........................................$135.00 C

**Pall Mall,** display rack, wooden, countertop, debossed message on each side, dovetailed joints, VG ................$115.00 D

**Pall Mall,** display rack, wooden, countertop, paper message at top, "Streamlined for better smoking...A Cooler Smoother Smoke," debossed sides, EX .......................................................$95.00 D

**Pallas Peanut Butter,** pail, tin, litho, wire bail handle, Kansas City, MO, with slip-lid, EX .........................................................$95.00 C

**Palm Cigars,** sign, metal, embossed, "3 for 5¢," 19" x 6½", EX...$75.00 D

**Palm Cigars,** sign, tin, embossed, from the De Nobili Cigar Company, Long Island City, N.Y., 19" x 6", EX..............................$35.00 C

**Palmer & Goodrich Tires,** print, paper, signed and dated portrait of Aida of Verdi's opera, 1900, 18" x 24", EX ........................$300.00 B

**Palmer House Key West Cigars,** paperweight, glass, round, crown in center, 3" x 1½", EX .........................................................$50.00 B

**Palmer Method Writing Position,** sign, paper, litho, two children at their desks, 17¾" x 21⅝", VG .........................................$155.00 B

**Palmer Tires,** sign, pretty woman in bonnet, 19¾" x 28", VG.$525.00 C

**Palmer's Root Beer,** sign, barrel, NOS, 19" x 14", NM.......$375.00 C

**Palmolive Soap,** sign, cardboard, pretty little girl, "Palmolive Soap 3 for 25¢," 10" x 15", EX.....................................................$245.00 D

**Palmolive Soap,** sign, paper, little girl washing behind her ear, "Keep Clean," 17" x 28", EX..............................................$900.00 B

**Pan American Exposition,** clock, by C.F. Chouffer, Jeweler Buffalo, NY, scantily clad young ladies, in shape of frying pan, 6" x 11½", EX...............................................................$165.00 C

**Pan-Am Motor Oils,** pump sign, porcelain, one-sided, 15" dia., VG ..........................................................................$425.00 B

**Pan-Am Quality Gasoline,** pump sign, porcelain, with torch logo and "Quality Gasoline," 10½" x 12½", EX .......................$215.00 C

**Pan-American Airlines,** hat box, airplanes on all sides, 11½" x 14" x 6¾", EX...............................................................$175.00 B

**Pan-American Airlines,** table lighter, EX ........................$100.00 C

**Pan-Handle Scrap Tobacco,** tin, litho, Currier & Ives, black man rolling the dice while the cops wait to make a bust, 1890s, EX...........$490.00 B

**Panhandle,** gas globe, low profile body with two glass lenses, 15" dia., VG ......................................................................$1,100.00 B

Pepsi-Cola, door pull handle, 2¾" x 12", EX, $235.00 C. *Courtesy of Muddy River Trading Co./Gary Metz.*

Pepsi-Cola, crossing guard, tin and cast iron, 62" tall, VG, $450.00 B.

Pepsi-Cola, display, mechanical, monkey with can of Pepsi that spins when plugged in, 26" dia. x 37", VG, $1,100.00 B. *Courtesy of Collectors Auction Services.*

Pepsi-Cola, store display, cardboard, die cut stand that holds a paper label 12-oz. Pepsi bottle, "Double Size," NOS, 6½" x 13½", EX, $380.00 B. *Courtesy of Autopia Advertising Auctions.*

Pepsi-Cola, script hat pin, employee, "Drink...Delicious Heathful," EX, $50.00 D. *Courtesy of Antiques, Cards & Collectibles/Ray Pelley.*

**Panhandle,** gas globe, metal and glass, with inverted triangle logo, 15" dia., EX....................$1,000.00 B

**Panton Plows,** watch fob, metal, with interwined plow and initials, EX....................$125.00 B

**Par-t-pak,** sign, metal, self-framing, "full flavor...Beverages," 52" x 34", VG....................$95.00 C

**Paraland,** gas globe, plastic body with two glass lenses, 16½" x 5½" x 12½", VG....................$350.00 C

**Parisian Novelty Co.,** brush, wood and bristle, advertising on the handle, "Makers of Advertising Specialities," 3½" long, EX.$100.00 B

**Park Brewing Co.,** sign, charger with game birds and products in foreground on table, 24" dia., EX....................$751.00 B

**Parke Davis Wormwood Drug,** tin, turn-of-the-century house on all four sides, 1900s, 4½" x 4" x 9", EX....................$77.00 B

**Parke's Newport Coffee,** can, tin, litho, factory scene on front cameo, with pry-lid, 1-lb., EX....................$130.00 B

**Parker Bros.,** picture puzzle, "The Darktown Fancy Ball," black people in horse-drawn sleigh, 9⅜" x 7¾" x 1¼", 1890s, EX.......$575.00 B

**Parker Brothers, Inc.,** card game, "Touring...Improved Edition," automobile in original package, complete, VG....................$35.00 C

**Parker Pen,** display, wood and glass, light-up, original key, 20½" x 9" x 9", EX....................$145.00 C

**Parker's Cold Cream,** sign, cardboard, fancy woman's bust, 7½" x 11½", EX....................$120.00 B

**Parker's Foot Powder,** container, tin, litho, foot on front, 2-oz., EX....................$35.00 C

**Parrot & Monkey Baking Powder,** container, cardboard with tin top and bottom, paper label with trademark monkey and parrot, 2½" x 5", EX....................$215.00 B

**Pastum J. Sarubi, Hair Dressing,** sign, tin, double-sided, litho, flange, 18½" x 7", EX....................$125.00 C

Pepsi-Cola, fan, "Drink," 1912, 8" x 9", G, $1,000.00 B. *Courtesy of Muddy River Trading Co./Gary Metz.*

Pepsi-Cola, sign, tin, self-framed, painted, "Drink Iced," 55" x 17½", NM, $925.00 C.

Pepsi-Cola, cooler, metal, gull wing, by Heintz Manufacturing, restored condition, somewhat scarce, 44" tall, EX, $500.00 B.

Pepsi-Cola, sign, tin, embossed, sidewalk, "Hot Dogs Hamburgers, Ice Cold Bigger – Better, 5¢," 1930s, 20" x 28", G, $325.00 B. *Courtesy of Muddy River Trading Co./Gary Metz.*

Pepsi-Cola, sign, metal and plastic, bottle cap and popcorn, "Hot Pop Corn," 1940s, 19" x 9" x 6", VG, $700.00 B.

---

**Pat Hand,** tobacco container, metal, pocket size, "Cube Cut Granules & Price Five Cents," VG ..........................$100.00 B

**Pate Challenge,** pump sign, porcelain, single-sided, shield, 12" x 15", VG ..........................$450.00 B

**Pathfinder Coffee,** watch fob, metal with celluloid center, image of coffee can, EX..........................$55.00 C

**Patterson Sargent Paint,** sign, porcelain, die cut, "For Better Results," 33" x 24", EX ..........................$135.00 C

**Patterson Sargent Paint,** sign, porcelain, die cut, "For Better Results," 33" x 24", NM..........................$155.00 C

**Patterson's Recut Tobacco,** sign, paper, "10¢ value for 5 cents," with product image on both sides of message in center, 36" x 18", NM ..........................$55.00 B

**Patterson's Tuxedo Tobacco,** canister, metal, screw top, "Specially Prepared For Pipe or Cigarette," EX ..........................$125.00 B

**Paul Jones & Co. Whiskey,** sign, rolled tin, "The Temptation of St. Anthony," woman with a watermelon and a man holding a bottle of the product, 19½" x 13½", VG ..........................$550.00 B

**Paul Jones & Co.,** sign, metal, firearms and game in cabin with a glass and bottle of the product, 31" x 45", EX..........................$400.00 B

**Paul Jones & Co.,** sign, metal, man choosing whiskey over watermelon, "The Temptattion of Saint Anthony," 20" x 12", EX ......$550.00 B

**Paul Jones Havana Cigars,** tin, litho, wood grained, self-framing, cameo of Paul Jones in center, also self-framed, this type sign is difficult to find, 20" x 24", EX ..........................$725.00 B

**Paul Jones Pure Gin,** sign, tin, litho, young boys at a split rail fence, 13¼" x 19½", 1905, EX..........................$550.00 B

**Paul Jones Whiskey,** sign, litho by H.D. Beach, a big name in early, old gent with bottle and glass, "Comrades for 81 years," 1903, EX .$525.00 C

**Paul Jones,** sign, paper, litho on wood, black woman with watermelon and older gentleman with bottle, VG ..........................$275.00 B

**Paul Jones,** sign, wooden, promoting Rye Whiskey with black family, 20" x 13¾", 1900s, EX..........................$475.00 C

**Pay Car Scrap Chewing Tobacco,** sign, cardboard, railroad man with the product, "Hey There Get Your Chewing Tobacco," 13" x 20", VG..........................$85.00 D

Pepsi-Cola, box cooler, metal, salesman sample, "Ice Cold...Hits The Spot," embossed bottle caps on lid & sides, logo on front, rare item, NM, $3,200.00 D. *Courtesy of Rare Bird Antique Mall/Jon & Joan Wright.*

Pepsi-Cola, mileage chart, metal and plastic, measuring mileage from Paducah, Ky., to various parts of the country, 1950s, 7" x 31", yellow, white, and black, EX, $65.00 C. *Courtesy of B.J. Summers.*

Pepsi-Cola, sign, celluloid and metal, light up, Pepsi disc and cup, 20½" wide, VG, $275.00 B.

Pepsi-Cola, sign, cardboard, die cut, 1930s, 21" x 15", EX, $375.00 B. *Courtesy of Muddy River Trading Co./Gary Metz.*

Pepsi-Cola, sign, cardboard, self-framed, girl with lace hat and an early bottle of Pepsi-Cola, 1930s, 30" x 20", EX, $800.00 B. *Courtesy of Muddy River Trading Co./Gary Metz.*

---

**Pay Car Scrap Tobacco,** sign, tin, litho, "Chew...the best flavor," product package in center, 13¾" x 17¾", EX......................$225.00 D

**Pay Car Tobacco,** sign, cardboard, two men fishing in boat, "Hook Onto Pay Car Tobacco, Chews Good Anyhow," 1920 – 30s, 40" x 27", NM......................$700.00 B

**Peachey Double Cut Tobacco,** pocket tin, metal, vertical, large peach, EX......................$150.00 D

**Peachy,** pocket tin, vertical, peach in bloom, VG.......$160.00 B

**Peacock Condom,** container, tin, litho, peacock in full feathers, 1⅝" x ⅝", EX......................$250.00 B

**Peacock Condom,** tin, peacock with tail feathers spread, 1½" dia. x ¾", F......................$65.00 C

**Peacock Ice Cream,** Cleveland Indians license plate attachment, tin, Indian on attachment, 9⅞" x 4¾", EX......................$155.00 C

**Peak's Coffee,** can, metal, mountain scene, and slip lid, EX....$50.00 D

**Peak's Coffee,** tin, packed for Independent Grocers Alliance Dist. Co., Chicago, Ill., EX......................$35.00 D

**Pear's Soap,** ad, paper, "He Won't Be Happy Til He Gets It," baby crawling out of tub, from the *Ladies' Home Journal,* 1912, 10" x 14", EX......................$90.00 B

**Pear's Soap,** plate, center, youngster in countertop bathing tub, 15½" x 10¼", 1909, EX......................$50.00 B

**Pear's Soap,** sign, cardboard, die cut, mother cleaning son's ear, 6½" x 12½", VG......................$75.00 B

**Pear's Soap,** sign, paper, die cut, woman scrubbing child's ear, 5½" x 9½", EX......................$141.00 B

**Pear's Soap,** sign, paper, die cut, young child trying to climb out of wash tub, 10" x 6¼", EX......................$135.00 C

**Pear's Soap,** sign, paper, framed, young child sitting on towel, 9½" x 14", 1910s, EX......................$85.00 C

**Pear's Soap,** sign, paper, young girl holding a candle, 1905, 12" x 15", EX......................$605.00 B

**Pearl Oil,** sign, string-hung, "We Sell...Heat and Light," family in warm well-lit house, 10⅜" x 14", EX......................$135.00 C

Pepsi-Cola, sign cover, plastic, polar bear with company name, 1950 – 60s, 22" x 18" x 3", VG, $1,250.00 B.

Pepsi-Cola, sign, die cut, bottle, 1930s, 12" x 45", EX, $625.00 B. *Courtesy of Muddy River Trading Co./Gary Metz.*

Pepsi-Cola, sign, gloglas, bottle, "Refreshing and Healthful," 1935 – 40s, 12" x 10", EX, $5,500.00 B.

Pepsi-Cola, sign, metal, double-sided, flange, "Buy...Here," 1940s, 16" dia., EX, $800.00 B.

Pepsi-Cola, sign, metal, painted sidewalk or curb with original metal base, Stout Sign Co., St. Louis, MO, 24" x 50½", VG, $450.00 B. *Courtesy of Collectors Auction Services.*

**Pearless Majestic,** tip tray, metal, with see, hear, and speak no evil monkeys, American Brewing Co., Phil., 4¼" dia., EX ........$185.00 B

**Pedro Cut Plug Tobacco,** bag with graphics on both sides, 2¾" x 4¼" x ⅞", G.................................................................$230.00 B

**Pedro Smoking Tobacco Cut Plug,** pail, tin, Wm. S. Kimball & Co., The American Tobacco Co., EX.......................................$145.00 C

**Peerless Tobacco,** pail, tin, litho, wire handles, factory scene on front, NM ............................................................$110.00 B

**Peerless Weighing Machine Co.,** sign, porcelain, company name and "Did You weigh Yourself Today," EX .........................$195.00 C

**Peerless Weighing Machine Co.,** sign, porcelain, curved penny scale, "Did you weigh yourself today," 5½" x 9", EX.......$245.00 C

**Peerless Weighing Machine Co.,** sign, porcelain, curved, penny scale, "Did you weigh yourself today," 5½" x 9", G........$170.00 B

**Peg Top Cigar,** door push, porcelain, "The Old Reliable," cigar, 4" x 13", EX.................................................................$135.00 B

**Peg Top,** door push, metal, "The Old Reliable," 4" x 12½", EX...$150.00 C

**Peidmont Cigarettes,** sign, porcelain, cigarette pack in center, 30" x 49", VG.................................................................$155.00 C

**Peidmont Cigarettes,** sign, tin, litho, George Washington at Mount Vernon, from Liggett & Myer Co., 30" x 24", 1911, EX...$1,000.00 B

**Penn Cigars,** store bin, metal, "30¢ plugs," G ...................$75.00 D

**Penn City Motor Oil,** can, old Quaker on the front, 2-gal., EX..$175.00 C

**Penn Drake,** menu board, tin, one-sided, 19⅜" x 27½", VG.$175.00 C

**Penn Tobacco Co.,** pocket tin, litho, Honey Moon Tobacco, 3" x 4½" x ⅞", EX .................................................................$1,950.00 B

Pepsi-Cola, sign, metal, bottle cap at top of courtesy panel, 56" tall, EX, $200.00 B.

Pepsi-Cola, sign, cardboard, string hung, "Buy...Today!" Pepsi Pete, 1940s, 13" tall, VG, $110.00 C.

Pepsi-Cola, sign, tin, line of double dot bottle caps, 1940s, 36" x 14", EX, $625.00 B.

Pepsi-Cola, syrup dispenser, rare and hard-to-find, 1900s, EX, $3,700.00 B. *Courtesy of Muddy River Trading Co./Gary Metz.*

Pepsi-Cola, clock, plastic, light-up, "The light refreshment," 1950s, NM, $600.00 B. *Courtesy of Muddy River Trading Co./Gary Metz.*

**Penn's Spells Quality,** tin box, metal, hinged lid, 6½"W x 2½"H x 6½"D, G .............................................................$330.00 B

**Penn-Beel Motor Oil,** can, metal, bees on hive, 1 qt, EX ..$210.00 B

**Penn-Drake Motor Oil,** sign, tin, embossed, well tower at left of message, 27¾" x 9¾", NM.....................................$280.00 B

**Penn-Valley Gasoline,** gas globe, metal and glass, "Independent Oil," 15" dia., EX .............................................$525.00 C

**Pennsey Select Beer,** tip tray, tin, litho, young serving woman with bottle, 4¼" dia., VG .............................................$125.00 C

**Pennsylvania Motor Oil,** early tin container, "100% Pure," 8-qt., EX..............................................................$110.00 B

**Pennsylvania Railroad,** calendar, Conway rail yard at top with tear sheets at bottom, 28½" x 28½", 1958, EX .............................$75.00 C

**Pennsylvania Railroad,** calendar, paper, 3-month tear sheets at bottom, "Vital Lines To The World," ship/rail loading facility, 1957, G .............................................$50.00 C

**Pennsylvania Railroad,** calendar, paper, "Conway Yard," 3-month tear sheets at bottom, rail yards at top, 1958, G ...............................$65.00 C

**Pennsylvania Railroad,** calendar, paper, "Mass Transportation," 3-month tear sheets at bottom of artwork, 1955, EX..............$65.00 C

**Pennsylvania Railroad,** calendar, paper, no pad, "Dynamic Progress," modern train passing piggy-back freight traffic, 1956, EX .............................................$75.00 C

**Pennsylvania Rubber Co.,** ashtray, vaseline glass, non-skid with CV logo, Jeannette, PA, EX.......................................$125.00 D

**Pennsylvania Rubber Company,** sign, paper, litho, oil-proof tires with pretty woman with hat, "Euphemia" under artwork, Jeannette, Pa., 25¼" x 35½", F .............................................$210.00 D

**Pennsylvania Transformer,** sign, porcelain, company logo, 12" dia., EX.............................................$95.00 D

**Penny Post Cut Plug Tobacco,** lunch pail, metal, bail handle, from Strater Tobacco Co., EX.......................................$350.00 B

Pepsi, thermometer, metal, painted, "More Bounce to the Ounce," 8" x 27", VG, $295.00 C.

Pepsi-Cola, clock, double bubble, light-up, "think young, Say Pepsi please," 1955, EX, $800.00 B. *Courtesy of Muddy River Trading Co./Gary Metz.*

Pepsodent, sign, cardboard, die cut, Andy holding tube of product, "Um! Um! Ain't dis sumpin," 22½" x 62", 1930s, VG, $925.00 B. *Courtesy of Collectors Auction Services.*

Pepsodent, sign, cardboard, die cut depicting Andy holding a tube of Pepsodent, "Oh! Sho-Sho-Pepsodent! Check an' DOUBLE CHECK," 21" x 54½", 1930s, VG, $825.00 B. *Courtesy of Collectors Auction Services.*

Perfect Brew, tray, metal, serving size, bull dog on front, "The Purest and Best Bottled beer," 13" x 13", VG, $180.00 B.

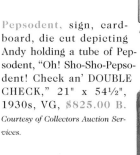

Perfection Cigarettes, sign, cardboard, litho, pretty young woman, 20" x 26", G, $200.00 C.

---

**Penny Post Cut Plug**, pail, tin, wire handle, good bright colors, EX ............................................................$275.00 C

**Pennzip**, gas globe, wide body, 13½" , G ..........................$650.00 C

**Pennzoil Lubrication**, menu board, tin, self-framing, 17½" x 24", EX ..........................................................$135.00 C

**Pennzoil Safe Lubrication**, display rack, metal, "Sound Your Z," 1940s, 39" tall, EX ..........................................$180.00 B

**Pennzoil Safe Lubrication**, sign, metal, company lettering on die cut bell, 22" x 24", EX .........................................$1,300.00 B

**Pennzoil**, oil can, tin, logo owls and airplane, 1-qt., EX .$85.00 B

**Pennzoil**, sign, metal, lollipop, "Safe Lubrication," early brown bell in center, original heavy embossed stand, 1920s, EX ....$1,200.00 C

**Pennzoil**, sign, metal, lubster, 9½" x 3⅞", VG....................$200.00 C

**Pennzoil**, sign, metal, vertical, painted, "Sound Your Z," logo at bottom, G ............................................................$105.00 D

**Pennzoil**, sign, porcelain, "Safe Lubrication," bell in center, 62" x 35", black & orange on yellow, G ....................................$195.00 C

**Pennzoil**, sign, porcelain, double-sided, flange, "Safe Lubrication," still in original crate, 26½" x 26", VG..........................$2,500.00 B

**Pennzoil**, sign, porcelain, oval, bell logo, 20" x 13", EX.....$390.00 B

**Pennzoil**, sign, porcelain, rainbow-shaped, double-sided, originally was used over the oval curb, "Bonded Dealer," 29½" x 3½", 1930s, NM ......................................................................$325.00 C

**Pennzoil**, thermometer, metal body, glass front, dial-type, "Get Protection Reserve...Motor Oil," in center, 12" dia., EX.$150.00 C

**Pennzoil**, tin, with airplane, 5-qt, EX ..............................$145.00 C

**Penreco**, gas globe, metal and glass, 1920s, 15" dia., EX...$800.00 B

**Pensupreme Ice Cream**, sign, porcelain, single-sided, old Quaker at bottom, 24" x 13", G ....................................................$300.00 B

**Pep Boys 600 Transmission Oil**, can, metal, with black and orange lettering, 1 gal., EX ..........................................................$160.00 B

**Pep Boys Hand Soap**, can, metal, slip lid, images of Manny, Joe & Jack, 6" tall, EX ............................................................$450.00 B

Perfection Cigarettes, sign, wood framed, young lady in pirate dress, 1909, 24" x 30", EX, $675.00 B.

Perfection Cigarettes, sign, porcelain, double-sided, flange, "Simply Perfect," 19½" VG, $275.00 B.

Permit to smoke, sign, litho, framed, "a good cigar," 1910s, 25" x 31½", EX, $285.00 C.

Perry's Quality Beverages, door push, tin, "triple filtered, nothing finer," EX, $55.00 B. *Courtesy of Muddy River Trading Co./Gary Metz.*

Peter Cooper Rye, backbar bottle, glass, gold lettering, ribs on neck and base, good clear glass, not seen very often, 1900 – 10s, 9" x 4" dia., NM, $145.00 C. *Courtesy of B.J. Summers.*

**Pep Boys Handy Bulb Kit,** tin, boys on the front, 4" x 2¼" x 2½", EX ..............$55.00 C

**Pepsi,** clock, plastic, light-up, "The light refreshment," 1950s, G ..............$350.00 C

**Pepsi,** menu board, metal, "say "Pepsi," EX..............$75.00 C

**Pepsi,** menu board, metal, self-framing, bottle top, at top, 20" x 30", G..............$135.00 C

**Pepsi,** menu board, tin, embossed, "Enjoy," 19¼" x 27¼", EX.$165.00 B

**Pepsi,** menu board, tin, self-framed, bottle cap logo, "Have a," 19½" x 30", 1950s, VG..............$120.00 C

**Pepsi,** poster, cardboard, "Be Sociable...Serve," woman in hat holding six-pack in palm with bottle cap logo at left, double-sided, 36" x 24¾", VG..............$175.00 C

**Pepsi,** poster, cardboard, "Be sociable...Serve," woman in hat holding six-pack in palm with bottle cap logo at left, double-sided, 36" x 24¾", G ..............$135.00 C

**Pepsi,** sign, cardboard, horizontal, litho, "it's got a lot to give," young couple enjoying a bottle of Pepsi, in original metal Pepsi frame, 37¼" x 25½", EX ..............$110.00 B

**Pepsi,** sign, cardboard, wood frame, hard-to-find piece even in less than perfect condition, 25" x 32", P ..............$250.00 C

**Pepsi,** sign, metal, painted, sidewalk or curb, original metal base, Stout Sign Co., St. Louis, MO, 24" x 50½", EX............$1,100.00 C

**Pepsi,** sign, metal, single-sided, self-framed, "say Pepsi please," bottle cap, 31" x 11½", VG ..............$110.00 B

**Pepsi,** sign, porcelain, "Enjoy," bottle cap at right, 29¼" x 12¼", NM ..............$400.00 B

**Pepsi,** sign, porcelain, double-sided, "Have a. . .," 28" x 25½", G ...$145.00 C

**Pepsi,** sign, porcelain, single-sided, "enjoy" on bottle cap in center, 29" x 12½", VG ..............$125.00 B

**Pepsi,** sign, tin, easel back, "Say...Please," bottle of the product, 8½" x 12", EX ..............$110.00 B

**Pepsi,** sign, tin, self-framing, bottle and cap, 17" x 47", VG .$210.00 B

**Pepsi,** thermometer, tin, embossed, "The light refreshment," bottle cap at top of scale, 7" x 27", G..............$40.00 B

**Pepsi,** thermometer, tin, litho, self-framing, "say Pepsi please," scale-type bar, 7¼" x 28", VG..............$90.00 B

Peter Pan Peanut Butter, sign, cardboard, framed and matted, original artwork, 1940 – 50s, 16" x 13", VG, $275.00 B.

Peter Rabbit Peanut Butter, pail with litho of rabbit on front, 1 lb., VG, $900.00 B.

Peters Weatherbird Shoes, thermometer, procelain, 1915, 7" x 27", VG, $225.00 C.

Petter Anniversary, paperweights, metal, each has the likeness of the founder, Henry A. Petter, the smaller one is for the 50th anniversary in 1940, while the larger one is for the 75th anniversary, 1940 & 1965, 2½" dia., & 3" dia., EX, $40.00 C pair. *Courtesy of B.J. Summers.*

Pepsi, thermometer, tin, vertical scale, "say...please," at top and logo at bottom, painted red, white, yellow, and blue, EX.$55.00 C

Pepsi-Cola, sign, tin, self-framing, painted, "Drink," bottle cap in center of sign, G......$1,150.00 D

Pepsi-Cola sign, tin, single-sided, embossed, "Ice Cold," 30½" x 27", VG ......$275.00 C

Pepsi-Cola, 45 rpm record, original paper cover, original mailing package, "Your Man In Service," EX......$65.00 C

Pepsi-Cola, animated cardboard boy and girl, EX......$675.00 C

Pepsi-Cola, ashtray, ceramic, bottle cap in center, square shape, EX......$65.00 B

Pepsi-Cola, banner, canvas, "Drink Pepsi-Cola, Double Size 5¢," 33" x 36", EX......$275.00 B

Pepsi-Cola, banner, canvas, double-sided, hand-stenciled, "Drink, Double Size 5¢," rare piece, 1930s, G......$275.00 B

Pepsi-Cola, banner, canvas, double-sided, hand-stenciled, "Drink, Double Size 5¢," rare piece, 1930s, P......$75.00 C

Pepsi-Cola, base for patrol boy, cast iron, 1950s, 24" dia., G..$150.00 B

Pepsi-Cola, blotter, cardboard, "Drink Pepsi-Cola Delicious Healthful," EX......$120.00 B

Pepsi-Cola, bottle cap, light-up, 16" dia., EX......$575.00 C

Pepsi-Cola, bottle carrier, wood, "Buy Pepsi-Cola," 1940s, EX.$100.00 D

Pepsi-Cola, bottle opener, metal, logo and "Sparkling Satisfying Pepsi-Cola," 1930s, 4⅛" long, EX......$90.00 B

Pepsi-Cola, bottle radio, Bakelite, "Have a Pepsi," 24" T, 1940s, VG......$135.00 C

Pepsi-Cola, bottle radio, Bakelite, bottle on round base, 1940s, 24" tall, EX......$500.00 B

Pepsi-Cola, bottle radio, older paper label bottle, 24", 1940s, VG......$425.00 C

Pepsi-Cola, calendar, complete with full pad, "Hits The Spot," girl with bottle, 1941, 15" x 23", NM......$340.00 B

Pepsi-Cola, calendar, paper, 1919 and 1921 calendars, signed Rolf Armstrong, 1920, 5" x 7", EX......$2,600.00 B

Pepsi-Cola, calendar, paper, "Pepsi=Cola Competition For American Artists," 1945, EX......$40.00 B

Petter, playing cards, plastic coated "redi-slip finish," full deck in unopened sealed container, famous "Petter Blue Book" on each card, this company was founded over a hundred years ago and is still in business with their home office in Paducah, KY, 2½" x 3½", NM, $25.00 C.
*Courtesy of B.J. Summers.*

Philco, sign, cardboard, die cut, standup, Don McNeill of the "Breakfast Club" showing all the features of the refrigerator, 1940s, 32" x 64", VG, $55.00 C.

Philip Morris, sign, cardboard, die cut, Johnny, 1950s, 16½" x 49", VG, $250.00 C.

Philip Morris, sign, porcelain, Johnny and the trademark "Call For...," 1950 – 60s, EX, $175.00 B.

Phillips 66, salt & pepper shakers, plastic, on back "L.B. Vaughn Motor Co., Phone 4400, Paducah, KY," 1940s, 1" x 2¾" x ¾, EX, $75.00 C. *Courtesy of B.J. Summers.*

---

Pepsi-Cola, can, metal, early cone top with original cap, 1940s, 12 oz., VG..................................................$240.00 B

Pepsi-Cola, cash register topper, cardboard, resembles art deco style billboard, 1930 – 40s, EX.......................................$550.00 B

Pepsi-Cola, cigarettes, paper sealed package with Pepsi-Cola over bottle cap logo, EX ..........................................$100.00 C

Pepsi-Cola, clock, double dot light-up, by Telechron, 15" dia., 1940s, NM .......................................................$425.00 C

Pepsi-Cola, clock, double-bubble, light-up, "say Pepsi please," made by Products, 15" dia., NM...................................$850.00 C

Pepsi-Cola, clock, light-up, "think young, Say Pepsi please," 1955, G ...........................................................$400.00 C

Pepsi-Cola, clock, light-up, bottle cap in the center, yellow face, 1970s, EX .......................................................$325.00 B

Pepsi-Cola, clock, metal and glass, counter top, "Drink Pepsi Anytime" and Pepsi logo, 1970s, EX .........................................$75.00 C

Pepsi-Cola, clock, metal and glass, light up, "Drink Pepsi-Cola Ice Cold," bottle cap center, 1950s, 15" sq., EX .....................$350.00 B

Pepsi-Cola, clock, metal and glass, light-up, bottle cap in center, good strong colors, 9¼" x 12½", red, white, blue cap on yellow, VG .........................................................$160.00 D

Pepsi-Cola, clock, metal and glass, light-up, Telechron, 15½" dia., EX ...........................................................$505.00 B

Pepsi-Cola, clock, metal body, glass face and cover, light-up, "Say Pepsi please," gold outside ring and white face, 16" sq., VG .$245.00 C

Pepsi-Cola, clock, plastic and metal, light-up, "say Pepsi please," 16" x 16", G ........................................................$135.00 C

Phillips 66, clock, light-up, double-bubble, "Tires Batteries," great color, 18" dia., NM, $750.00 C.

Piedmont Cigarettes, sign, canvas, "The Quality of Virginia," unusual item, 28" x 45", F, $350.00 C.

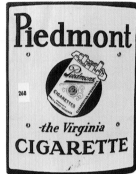

Piedmont Cigarettes, sign, porcelain, "...the virginia...," curved shape, 15¾" high, EX, $250.00 C.

Piedmont Cigarettes, sign, framed, matted, and under glass, "the cigarette of quality," man in moon, 1907, 14" x 20", EX, $425.00 B. *Courtesy of Muddy River Trading Co./Gary Metz.*

Pinkerton's, sign, metal, "caution," reflective, 12" x 14", VG, $75.00 C.

Pippins 5¢ Cigar, tip tray, tin, litho, 5½" L, EX, $210.00 B. *Courtesy of Richard Opfer Auctioneering, Inc.*

---

Pepsi-Cola, concentrate drum, metal, "Nickel Drink-Worth A Dime...Pepsi-Cola Bigger & Better 5¢," 1941, 10 gal., EX ....$85.00 B

Pepsi-Cola, cooler radio, 1950s, EX .................................$550.00 C

Pepsi-Cola, cooler, metal, salesman sample, embossed bottle caps on lid & sides, logo on front, "Ice Cold...Hits The Spot," rare item, EX ..........................................................................$2,500.00 D

Pepsi-Cola, cooler, metal, similar to Glascock, "Pepsi-Cola Double Size 5¢," 1920 – 30s, 31" x 22" x 34", EX......................................$1,200.00 B

Pepsi-Cola, cooler, salesman sample, "Ice Cold," rare and hard-to-find, G ................................................................$1,200.00 C

Pepsi-Cola, cooler, slide, original Pepsi colors with logo on left side of front, 31" x 20" x 32", VG ...............................$200.00 B

Pepsi-Cola, dispenser, china, tree decoration and embossed lettering, 1960s, NM..................................................................$500.00 B

Pepsi-Cola, dispenser, syrup, rare, hard-to-find, 1900s, EX ..$3,700.00 B

Pepsi-Cola, display rack, metal, designed for counter top use, capacity is two cases, 1930s, EX......................................$500.00 B

Pepsi-Cola, display, cardboard, "New Single Drink Size," 14" x 10", EX....................................................................$215.00 B

Pepsi-Cola, display, countertop, Pepsi and Pete and early bottle, 12" x 13½", EX.................................................................$290.00 B

Pepsi-Cola, display, mechanical monkey with can of Pepsi that spins when plugged in, 26" dia. x 37", F............................$325.00 C

Pepsi-Cola, display, mechanical seal, seal moves as if balancing the Pepsi-colored ball on his nose, 37" x 39" x 40", VG ........$1,675.00 B

Pepsi-Cola, door pull handle, 2¾" x 12", VG......................$195.00 C

Pepsi-Cola, door pull handle, metal, "Enjoy...Pepsi-Cola," bottle cap logo, 1940s, 3" x 12", EX .................................................$210.00 B

Pepsi-Cola, door pull, metal, painted, "Bigger Better," 2¾" x 12", EX..................................................................................$190.00 B

Pirelli Tire, sign, tin, single-sided, embossed, 19¼" x 27¼", EX, $3,200.00 B.

Planters Peanut Butter, tin, bail handle, lettering superimposed over the Mr. Peanut man figure, 25 lb., G, $190.00 B.

P. Lorillard & Co. Tobacco, store display cabinet, wood with etched glass and brass lettering, great piece, 43" H, EX, $6,000.00 B. Courtesy of Richard Opfer Auctioneering, Inc.

Pocahontas Norfolk and Western Railway, sign, glass, reverse painted, Indian with feather, 24" dia., G, $395.00 C.

Pointer Brand Overalls, sign, paperboard, pointer hunting dog in field, 17" x 10½", NM, $190.00 B.

---

Pepsi-Cola, door push plate, metal, "Pick a Pepsi," 1940s, 3½" x 13½", EX ...............................................$165.00 B

Pepsi-Cola, fan, "Drink," 1912, 8" x 9", EX ...................$2,000.00 C

Pepsi-Cola, fan, cardboard, die cut, girl sipping Pepsi from a bottle sitting beside a flared glass with a straw, 1910s, 8" x 9", EX....................................................$1,000.00 B

Pepsi-Cola, fountain dispenser, plastic and metal, counter, "Have a Pepsi," EX .......................................................$250.00 D

Pepsi-Cola, game, cardboard, "Vest Pocket Baseball," 1941, EX.........................................................$145.00 B

Pepsi-Cola, glass, syrup line and double dot, NM ...............$45.00 C

Pepsi-Cola, glass, syrup line, "Hits The Spot," NM..............$75.00 C

Pepsi-Cola, menu board, tin, litho, self-framing sides, 19½" x 30", 1930s, EX .........................................................$275.00 C

Pepsi-Cola, menu, paper, logo banner at top and items for the day, 7" x 10½", EX .......................................................$10.00 D

Pepsi-Cola, mileage chart, metal and plastic, measuring mileage from Paducah, Ky., to various parts of the country, 1950s, 7" x 31", yellow, white, and black, VG.........................................................$45.00 C

Pepsi-Cola, mirror, glass, chain-hung reverse, with cap logo, 1950s, 9½" dia., EX.......................................................$295.00 C

Pepsi-Cola, notebook, paper, "Get The Flavor There's a Difference," EX .......................................................$65.00 C

Pepsi-Cola, opener, metal, figural bottle "America's Biggest Nickel's Worth," 2¾" L, 1930s, G ...................................................$45.00 C

Polar Bear Tobacco, counter display bin, large polar bear with product package, 18" x 14" x 12", VG, $900.00 B.

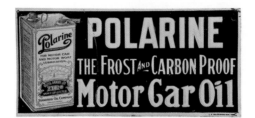

Polarine Motor Car Oil, sign, tin, embossed, vintage Polarine can, 19⅝" x 9¼", EX, $475.00 B. *Courtesy of Autopia Advertising Auctions.*

Poll-Parrot, display, motorized so parrot and shoes revolve, 20" x 33", EX, $425.00 C.

Poll-Parrot, shoe bench, wooden, Poll-Parrot painted on one end, animal heads cut out between seat sections, unusual item, 96" wide, VG, $6,700.00 B.

Poll-Parrot Shoes, sidewalk sign, wooden, cut to resemble parrot at top, double-sided, 46" tall, G, $300.00 B.

Pepsi-Cola, radio, fountain dispenser, 1950s, EX .........................$675.00 C

Pepsi-Cola, radio, upright vending machine, 1960s, G .....$300.00 C

Pepsi-Cola, script hat pin, "Drink...Delicious Heathful," emblem for employee, VG........................................................................$40.00 D

Pepsi-Cola, serving tray, 12" dia., G ...............................$150.00 C

Pepsi-Cola, serving tray, girl with glass of Pepsi, 1908, EX .$2,900.00 C

Pepsi-Cola, serving tray, metal, 13¾" x 10⅜", G .................$90.00 B

Pepsi-Cola, serving tray, metal, "Coast to Coast, Bigger and Better," United States map Pepsi bottle, EX....................................$410.00 B

Pepsi-Cola, serving tray, tilted bottle over a map of the US, rectangular, 1939, EX...............................................................$425.00 C

Pepsi-Cola, sign, cardboard, "Be Sociable...Serve...," 1960s, 37" x 26", EX...................................................................................$130.00 B

Pepsi-Cola, sign, cardboard, "Buy Here," 21" dia., G .....$95.00 C

Pepsi-Cola, sign, cardboard, "Why Take Less, Pepsi's Best," trolley car use, 1940s, 25" x 11", EX ...........................................$775.00 B

Pepsi-Cola, sign, cardboard, a 12 oz bottle, "Reputation Follows High Quality," 1930s, 8" x 16", EX....................................$270.00 B

Pepsi-Cola, sign, cardboard, die cut, couple enjoying the product, 16¾" x 22½", EX.................................................................$200.00 B

Pepsi-Cola, sign, cardboard, die cut, couple enjoying the product, 16¾" x 22½", G .............................................................$150.00 C

Pepsi-Cola, sign, cardboard, die cut, older cardboard 6-pack, 1930s, 21" x 15", VG ...............................................$275.00 D

Pepsi-Cola, sign, cardboard, die cut, stand up, Pete and Pepsi, the Pepsi cops with an older 6 pack of beverage, 1930s, 21" x 15", EX .............................................................$375.00 B

Popeye, sign, cardboard, stand-up, "Drink, I Yam what I yam and I yam tops," Popeye Brand soda, rare, 1929, 22" tall, EX, $550.00 B. *Courtesy of Morford Auctions.*

Possum Cigars, canister, possum on front cameo, 5¼" dia., x 5¼", VG, $405.00 B.

Postal Telegraph, sign, porcelain, double-sided, flange, superb example of a hard to locate collectible, 10½" long, VG, $140.00 B.

Postal Telegraph, sign, porcelain, double-sided, flange, "The International System," 29½" x 16", EX, $325.00 D. *Courtesy of Riverview Antique Mall.*

Post Office Smoking Tobacco, tin, litho, large building in center cameo, 3½" x 4¾" x 2", EX, $2,200.00 B. *Courtesy of Wm. Morford Investment Grade Collectibles.*

Pepsi-Cola, sign, cardboard, for trolley car use, "Big shot," young boy offers a Pepsi to a young girl, 1930 – 40s, 28" x 11", EX........$240.00 B

Pepsi-Cola, sign, cardboard, lady at a lift top cooler, "Obey That Impulse / Drink...Iced / at this Sparkling Cooler," Canadian, 1940s, 60" x 30", EX .................................................$2,000.00 B

Pepsi-Cola, sign, cardboard, man with bottle beside Pepsi-Cola bottle top logo, "Here's Energy," 1940s, 28" x 11", EX.$105.00 B

Pepsi-Cola, sign, cardboard, pretty girl in hat holding a bottle of Pepsi, self-framing, 30" x 20", EX .....................................$800.00 B

Pepsi-Cola, sign, cardboard, self-framed, girl with lace hat and an early bottle of Pepsi-Cola, 1930s, 30" x 20", G ....................$300.00 D

Pepsi-Cola, sign, cardboard, stand-up, girl with product, easel back, 1940s, 20" x 15", EX.....................................$775.00 C

Pepsi-Cola, sign, cardboard, stringer, die cut, "Refreshing Big Big Bottle 5¢," 1930s, EX.....................................$1,100.00 B

Pepsi-Cola, sign, cardboard, trolley car use, bottle and glass, bottle cap logo, "Pepsi's Best, Drink It At The Fountain Too!," 1940s, 21" x 11", EX.....................................$550.00 B

Pepsi-Cola, sign, cardboard, trolley use, girl skiing with a bottle of the product, 1940s, 42" x 11", EX .....................................$850.00 B

Pepsi-Cola, sign, celluloid, "Ice Cold, Sold Here," 9" dia., EX.$250.00 B

Pepsi-Cola, sign, celluloid, "More Bounce to the Ounce," 9" dia., EX .....................................$225.00 B

Pepsi-Cola, sign, countertop, light-up, "Drink," 1950s, 14" dia., EX .....................................$175.00 B

Pepsi-Cola, sign, die cut, bottle, 1930s, 12" x 45", F .........$125.00 D

Pepsi-Cola, sign, fiberboard, "A nickel drink worth a dime," early Pepsi bottle, 1930s, 12¾" x 14¾", G .................$140.00 B

Pepsi-Cola, sign, foil-backed, "Hot Popcorn," G..................$95.00 B

Post Toasties, sign, child sleeping in rocker by the glow of the fire with her dog at her feet, absolutely great general store item, 1900s, 16½" x 23½", VG, $450.00 B.

Post Toasties, string dispenser, tin, self-framing, metal string holder, 11½" dia., 1916, VG, $645.00 B.

Postum, string holder, metal, "Health...First," 11" dia., VG, $225.00 C.

Powell, Rogers & Co., pouch, leather with draw string, reverse side is addresses and has a canceled stamp, "Wagons, Buggies, and Farm Machinery," 1910s, 3½" x 5¼", VG, $45.00 C. Courtesy of B.J. Summers.

Prairie Rose Coffee, tin, litho, key-wound, from E-H-B Coffee, Kansas City, young girl in center cameo, 1-lb., EX, $850.00 B. Courtesy of Wm. Morford Investment Grade Collectibles.

Pratts Poultry Food, sign, paper litho, framed, "A Guaranteed Egg Producer," 21" x 28", EX, $675.00 B. Courtesy of Morford Auctions.

Pepsi-Cola, sign, glass mirror, cap logo, chain-hung, reverse, 1950s, 9½" dia., G.............................................................$130.00 B

Pepsi-Cola, sign, glass of Pepsi in snow, "say please," 1970s, EX ..$65.00 B

Pepsi-Cola, sign, glass, light-up, convex glass, "Drink...The Light Refreshment," 1950, 16" dia., NM .................................$1,350.00 B

Pepsi-Cola, sign, glass, light-up, convex glass, "Drink...The Light Refreshment," 1950S, 16" dia., EX ................................$1,250.00 B

Pepsi-Cola, sign, metal and glass, light-up, "The Light Refreshment," 19" x 9" x 6½", 1950s, EX ...........................................$235.00 C

Pepsi-Cola, sign, metal and plastic, light up, bottle cap logo, 1950 – 60s, 16" x 20", EX.......................................................$1,750.00 B

Pepsi-Cola, sign, metal, "More Bounce To The Ounce!," 1940s, 18" x 48", VG ...............................................................$325.00 B

Pepsi-Cola, sign, metal, bottle and cap, "say Pepsi please," 1950s, 16" x 46", EX ......................................................$325.00 D

Pepsi-Cola, sign, metal, embossed, painted, self-framing, "Drink...5¢," 58½" x 36", G ...........................................$195.00 C

Pepsi-Cola, sign, metal, self-framing, "Drink," the price 5¢, 1950s, 40" x 34", F.......................................................$330.00 D

Pepsi-Cola, sign, plastic, light-up, bottle cap, "Drink...Ice-Cold," 1950s, 16" dia., EX .......................................$500.00 B

Pepsi-Cola, sign, porcelain, "Drink Iced," 60" x 36", G........$525.00 C

Pepsi-Cola, sign, porcelain, "Enjoy Pepsi," bottle cap logo, 1950s, 30" x 12", EX ....................................................$250.00 B

Pepsi-Cola, sign, porcelain, double-sided, "Hit the spot," 56" x 23", G..............................................................$700.00 B

Primley's Gum, sign, cardboard, die cut bear promoting California Fruit Gum, 6½" x 2¾", EX, $305.00 B. *Courtesy of Buffalo Bay Auction Co.*

Prince Albert Crimp Cut, sign, metal, double-sided, flange, likeness of tin, 17" tall, VG, $300.00 B.

Procter & Gamble Co., sign, die cut, "Crisco...Better than Butter," produced by Baltimore Enamel Nov. Co., 14" x 20", EX, $4,500.00 B.

Providence Washington Insurance Company, sign, tin, wood frame, 20½" x 26¼", EX, $375.00 C.

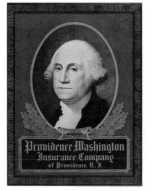

Public Telephone, sign, metal, lettering and bell emblem painted on, double-sided, flange, extremely tough to find one in this good condition, 1950s, 13" wide, EX, $110.00 B. *Courtesy of B.J. Summers.*

Public Telephone, The Lincoln Telephone and Telegraph Company, sign, porcelain, flange, 16" dia., NM, $450.00 B. *Courtesy of Riverview Antique Mall.*

Pepsi-Cola, sign, tin, bottle cap button, embossed, "Drink," Stout Sign Co., St. Louis, Mo., Made In U.S.A., M-104, 30" dia., G .........$250.00 B

Pepsi-Cola, sign, tin, die cut, embossed, bottle cap, double dot style, 13¼" x 17⅞", EX......................................................$325.00 C

Pepsi-Cola, sign, tin, double-sided, flange, "Buy...Here," 16" x 12", EX..................................................................................$695.00 C

Pepsi-Cola, sign, tin, embossed, 1950s, 3½" x 4", EX........$135.00 C

Pepsi-Cola, sign, tin, embossed, "Drink..½¢," 58½" x 36", EX .$195.00 D

Pepsi-Cola, sign, tin, embossed, "Drink...Delicious Delightful," 1910s, 3½" x 9¾", EX......................................................$275.00 B

Pepsi-Cola, sign, tin, embossed, bottle cap, 19¼" dia., NM..$200.00 B

Pepsi-Cola, sign, tin, embossed, die cut, bottle in double dot pattern, NOS, 8" x 29½", NM...................................................$475.00 C

Pepsi-Cola, sign, tin, embossed, painted, "America's Biggest Nickel's Worth," 40" x 12", EX..................................................$785.00 C

Pepsi-Cola, sign, tin, embossed, painted, "America's Biggest Nickel's Worth," 40" x 12", VG .......................................................$600.00 B

Pepsi-Cola, sign, tin, embossed, sidewalk, "Hot Dogs Hamburgers Ice Cold Bigger Better, 5¢," 1930s, 20" x 28", EX..........................$525.00 C

Pepsi-Cola, sign, tin, litho, embossed, "Drink...Delicious Delightful," 1910, NM ..............................................................$395.00 C

Pepsi-Cola, sign, tin, one-sided, embossed, "More Bounce to the Ounce," 57" x 33", G.........................................................$150.00 B

# P

Pur-ox, Syrups, Beverages, thermometer, wooden, 5" x 21", EX, $400.00 B. *Courtesy of Muddy River Trading Co./Gary Metz.*

Pulver's Kola-Pepsin Chewing Gum, box, cardboard, two-piece with vending machine on both sides, 6⅞" x 5¼ x 5" x 1⅜", G, $3,000.00 B.

Pure Gas, radio, wood, shaped and stenciled to resemble an early filling station, 1930 – 40s, 14" high, G, $575.00 C.

Putnam Dyes, wooden store display box, General Putnam litho on outside cover, also litho on inside cover, strong colors, with original dye packages, EX, $350.00 B. *Courtesy of Richard Opfer Auctioneering, Inc.*

Pyrene, sign, cardboard, die cut, father putting out auto fire while mother and child wait, "Pyrene kills auto fires," 21" x 31½", VG, $750.00 B. *Courtesy of Collectors Auction Services.*

Pepsi-Cola, sign, tin, painted, bottle breaking through sign beside bottle cap logo to right of message, "More Bounce to the Ounce," unusual and hard-to-find, 36" x 14", G ...........................$195.00 C

Pepsi-Cola, sign, tin, round, double-sided, flange, "Buy...Here," 17" x 16", EX.......................................................................$575.00 B

Pepsi-Cola, sign, tin, self-framed, painted, "Drink Iced," 55" x 17½", EX.......................................................................$775.00 C

Pepsi-Cola, sign, trolley car, boy and girl with early bottles of Pepsi, 28" x 11", EX .......................................................$240.00 B

Pepsi-Cola, sign, wood, double-sided, "Drink...," 23¼" x 18½", VG.........................................................................$45.00 C

Pepsi-Cola, soda jerk hat, cloth, Pepsi-Cola and bottle cap logo, NM .........................................................................$75.00 B

Pepsi-Cola, store rack, single case, countertop, 1930s, EX .$500.00 B

Pepsi-Cola, straws, in original unopened box with 5¢ bottle, NM .........................................................................$540.00 B

Pepsi-Cola, thermometer, bottle cap at top of scale, embossed lettering, "the Light Refreshment," 7¼" x 27¼", EX..............$195.00 C

Pepsi-Cola, thermometer, metal, "sat Pepsi please," slanted bottle and bottle cap logo, square corners, 1960s, EX................$145.00 D

Pepsi-Cola, thermometer, metal, embossed, bottle cap over scale, "The Light Refreshment," 27" tall, VG ............................$125.00 D

Pepsi-Cola, thermometer, metal, pretty girl drinking with a straw from a bottle, "Weather Cold...Weather Hot," Pepsi-Cola at top, 27" tall, EX...................................................$1,125.00 B

Pepsi-Cola, thermometer, tin, "Bigger, Better," 6¼" x 15¾", G...$175.00 D

Pepsi-Cola, thermometer, tin, painted, "Bigger Better," double dot bottle at right of scale, 6¼" x 15¾", NM ..........................$475.00 B

Pepsi-Cola, thermometer, tin, painted, "Bigger Better," double dot bottle at right of scale, 6¼" x 15¾", VG ..........................$225.00 C

Pepsi-Cola, tip tray, "The Pepsin Drink," 6" round, VG....$175.00 C

**Pepsi-Cola,** tip tray, Gibson Girl at soda fountain with glass of Pepsi, 1909, VG......................................................**$1,200.00 B**

**Pepsi-Cola,** tip tray, woman with glass of Pepsi, 9½" x 9¾", 1908, NM......................................................**$3,000.00 C**

**Pepsi-Cola,** toy truck, plastic, flat bed, decals of double dot name, 7½" long, EX......................................................**$195.00 D**

**Pepsi-Cola,** tray, milk glass, small, about the correct size for a tip tray, 4¼" x 3¼", EX......................................................**$200.00 B**

**Pepsi-Cola,** umbrella, canvas, red & white with bottle cap logos, 1950s, large beach size, EX......................................................**$120.00 B**

**Pepsi-Cola,** vending machine, metal, vendorlater #3D-33, 1950s, G......................................................**$750.00 D**

**Pepsodent,** display, cardboard, die cut, Andy holding a tube of Pepsodent, "Oh! Sho-Sho-Pepsodent! Check an' DOUBLE CHECK," 21" x 54½", 1930s, F......................................................**$300.00 D**

**Pepsodent,** sign, cardboard, die cut, litho, Andy holding tube of product, "Um! Um! Ain't dis sumpin," 22½" x 62", 1930s, G........**$250.00 C**

**Pepto-Bismol,** display, cardboard, die cut, young boy and dog, 31" x 31½", VG......................................................**$110.00 B**

**Pepto-Bismol,** sign, cardboard, die cut, bottle, 10⅞" x 27¼", EX..**$65.00 D**

**Pepto-Bismol,** sign, cardboard, die cut, in the shape of a bottle, 10⅞" x 27¼", EX......................................................**$75.00 C**

**Pepto-Bismol,** sign, cardboard, die cut, man rubbing his stomach, "Upset Stomach...Take Soothing...," 20" x 30", VG .............**$75.00 D**

**Perfect Circle Piston Rings,** sign, metal, embossed, "Don't Drive An Oil Hog," 30" x 36", EX......................................................**$700.00 B**

**Perfect Circle Piston Rings,** sign, tin, double-sided, hanging, "Home of...The Doctor Of Motors," mechanic in center, complete with wrought iron hanging arm, NOS, 24" x 24", NM ..................**$650.00 C**

**Perfection Beer,** label, paper, 11 oz., EX.............................**$10.00 D**

**Perfection Distilled Water Co.,** sign, porcelain, 26" x 15", EX...**$135.00 D**

**Perfection Dyes,** dye cabinet, tin, embossed front door, "For Silk, Woolen, Cotton and Feathers," 10" x 14", EX...............**$115.00 B**

**Perfection Oil,** sign, metal, 3 families using the product, "Brilliant & Odorless," 19" x 13", EX......................................................**$325.00 B**

**Permit to Smoke,** sign, litho, framed, "A Good Cigar,"1910s, 25" x 31½", F......................................................**$95.00 D**

**Perry's Quality Beverages,** door push, tin, "triple-filtered, nothing finer," G......................................................**$55.00 C**

**Pet Cigarettes,** sign, cardboard, young girl at well, "are the best," Allen & Ginter, 4" x 9½", EX .............................................**$77.00 B**

**Pet Cigarettes,** sign, die cut, easel back, "are the best," young girl sitting on tree limb swinging her straw hat, 1905, EX ......**$155.00 B**

**Peter Bold's "Prudencia,"** sign, wood, in likeness of cigar, 4½" x ¾" x ¾", EX......................................................**$75.00 B**

**Peter Doelger,** tip tray, metal, "Bottled Beer," with eagle in center, 4⅛" dia., EX......................................................**$160.00 B**

**Peter Pan Bread,** broom holder, tin, front is stenciled with product message, wooden top has holes for brooms, EX........**$350.00 B**

**Peter Pan Cottage,** sign, cardboard, item that came with variety of products, all products listed on reverse side, 10½" x 12" x 9", EX......................................................**$70.00 B**

**Peter Pan Ice Cream,** sign, metal, Peter Pan, "Demand...Take Home a Pint," 24" x 28", EX......................................................**$195.00 D**

**Peter Pan Ice Cream,** sign, tin, embossed, 23½" x 32", G .**$350.00 B**

**Peter Rabbit Peanut Butter,** pail, tin litho, wire side-mounted handles, 1-lb., EX......................................................**$484.00 B**

**Peter Schuyler Perfecto Cigars,** tip tray, Peter Schuyler in tray center, 6" dia., EX......................................................**$200.00 B**

**Peter Schuyler,** sign, porcelain, "Get a heck of a cigar," silhouette of man's head smoking a cigar at top center, 36" x 12", EX .....**$125.00 C**

**Peters Ammunition,** sign, easel back, elk in sight, 13" x 9", EX..**$85.00 D**

**Peters Big Game Ammunition,** sign, paper, moose, company logo, 18" x 29", VG......................................................**$700.00 B**

**Peters Cartridge Co.,** calendar, paper, hunting dogs in field, 1909, 13¾" x 27", G......................................................**$165.00 B**

**Peters Cartridge,** wooden case, black debossed lettering, 8½" x 14½" x 7⅛", G......................................................**$70.00 D**

**Peters Cartridges,** pin back, celluloid, bullet and capital letter P, ⅞" dia., NM......................................................**$75.00 C**

**Peters Cartridges,** postage cover, hunter taking aim, 6½" x 3½", 1904, VG......................................................**$85.00 B**

**Peters Diamond Brand Shoes,** sign, cardboard, hi-top shoe cutaway to show construction, 1910, 18" x 10", EX........................**$95.00 D**

**Peters Diamond Brand Shoes,** sign, tin, embossed, single-sided, 23½" x 12", VG......................................................**$55.00 C**

**Peters High Velocity,** shotgun shell box for .410 gauge, duck leaving water, 25 shell size, EX......................................................**$75.00 C**

**Peters No. 12,** pin back, celluloid, target in likeness of shell brass, ⅞" dia., EX......................................................**$155.00 B**

**Peters Rustless Metallic Ammunition,** sign, cardboard, die cut, easel back, moose and package of the product, 13½" x 9", EX........**$95.00 C**

**Peters Shells & Cartridges,** pin back button, metal, company logo, "The Perfect Ammunition," EX.................................$35.00 C

**Peters Weatherbird School Shoes,** thermometer, wood, scale type reading, boy and the product, 2⅛" x 8½", NM.....................$70.00 B

**Peters Weatherbird Shoes,** thermometer, porcelain, "Pat. March 16, 1915, Mfg. by Beach, Coshocton, O," 7" x 27", EX ......$375.00 C

**Peters Weatherbird Shoes,** whistle, metal, "Best for Boys-Best for Girls," keyhole shaped, EX .............................................$35.00 D

**Peters,** sign, die cut, countertop, stand-up, new belted bullet and a charging bear, "The New 50 Caliber Belted Bullet," 17" x 18", EX......................................................................$145.00 C

**Peters,** sign, paper chart, "Packs the Power, Know your game," with top and bottom metal strips, 24" x 35", EX.....................$176.00 B

**Peterson's Rose Butter,** sign, cardboard, litho, easel back, plastic coating, 20¼" x 13", VG...............................................$40.00 B

**Petter,** clock, electric, double-bubble, "Use the Petter blue book," great graphics, 1950s, 15" dia., EX.................................$525.00 C

**Pexwear Clothing,** sign, paper on wood, die cut, easel back, man in lab coat, 17" x 40", EX ...............................................$60.00 B

**Pflueger Fishing Tackle,** sign, cardboard, die cut, stand up, three large fish trying to get the bait, 1937, 22" x 23", EX.............$460.00 B

**Phelax Rain Resisting Coat,** sign, porcelain, single-sided, a man shooting a gun, 16¾" x 60", VG .......................................$675.00 B

**Phelps Shoe Shop,** sign, glass window, pretty lady with cats, for Cat's Paw Heels, 27¼" x 35¼", VG.....................................$235.00 C

**Philadelphia Brewing Co.,** print, paper, sheep in tranquil country setting, matted and framed with company name on matte, 1920s, 19" x 15", EX ....................................................................$75.00 C

**Philco,** sign, cardboard, die cut, stand-up, Don McNeill of the "Breakfast Club" showing all the features of the refrigerator, 1940s, 32" x 64", EX.............................................................................$110.00 C

**Philip Morris Cigarettes,** sign, metal, bellboy image, "Get'em Here," 12" x 14", EX ...........................................................$195.00 B

**Philip Morris Cigarettes,** sign, tin, litho, self-framed, embossed, Johnny, 27" x 14½", EX ...................................................$150.00 B

**Philip Morris,** sign, metal, painted, Philip Morris boy holding a metal cigarette pack, 1940s, 27" x 15", G.........................$195.00 D

**Philip Morris,** sign, porcelain, strip, "do you inhale-Is call for Philip Morris...smoking pleasure with smoking penalties," 22½" x 3¼", EX...........................................................................$725.00 B

**Philip Olin & Co. Whol. Grocers,** tobacco cutter, Sheffield, Anniston, Ala., EX ...................................................................$95.00 D

**Phillies Cigar,** sign, tin, rolled edge, embossed, "America's No. 1 cigar," cigar, 20¼" x 13", VG..............................................$65.00 B

**Phillips 66 Agricultural Ammonia,** menu board, tin, litho, application information and price lines, 30" x 20", EX............$75.00 C

**Phillips 66,** clock, light-up, double-bubble, "Tires Batteries," great color, 18" dia., EX.........................................................$600.00 C

**Phillips 66,** clock, metal and glass, light-up, double-bubble, "Tires...Batteries," trademark shield in center of clock face, 15" x 4", VG ..................................................................................$475.00 C

**Phillips 66,** doll, composition, Buddy Lee in company uniform, no hat, EX...................................................................................$275.00 B

**Phillips 66 Farm Service,** cooler, metal, white lettering on side, lift off lid, 12" x 19" x 14", EX .................................................$75.00 B

**Phillips 66,** map rack, rotating base, holds 48 assorted maps with Phillips 66 shield at top, 12" x 10" x 22", VG ....................$650.00 B

**Phillips 66 Motor Oil,** sign, metal, double-sided, painted, "our finest quality...100% paraffin base," 22" x 11", F.............$240.00 B

**Phillips 66,** pocket mirror, silver anniversary, Phillips Petroleum Co., Chicago Division, 1955, 3½" dia., EX ..................................$130.00 C

**Phillips 66,** service station attendant's hat, cloth top with embroidered patch, this is the type that comes without the vinyl bill and has snap for attaching the bill, VG ..................$210.00 B

**Phillips 66,** sign, porcelain, die cut, embossed, neon shield, "Federal Electric Co.," 46" x 48", VG .......................................$1,600.00 B

**Phillips 66,** sign, porcelain, shield, die cut, 29½" x 29½", VG.$350.00 C

**Phillips Ethyl,** sign, porcelain, double-sided, shield-shaped, 29" x 29", G...............................................................................$700.00 B

**Phinney-Walker,** cardboard, "Clocks For Automobiles...," 15" x 20", EX...................................................................................$395.00 C

**Phinney-Walker,** clock in front of city scene, cardboard, "Clocks for automobiles...'On Time,'" models for every type of car, 15" x 20", VG..................................................................................$325.00 C

**Phoenix Rolled Oats,** container, cardboard, trademark Phoenix rising from the flames, little girl with cereal bowl on front, 4 oz., EX.............................................................................................$110.00 B

**Phoenix,** match safe, metal body, embossing on sides, from St. Louis Brewery, 1¾" x 3", EX .................................................$275.00 C

**Phurnod Smokeless Coal,** sign, porcelain, single-sided, "For all Types of Hot-Water Boilers," 15" x 22½", EX....................$160.00 B

**Picaninny Freeze,** sign, paper on cardboard, 14" x 11", VG .$135.00 D

**Pickaninny Peanut Butter,** pail, tin, litho, black girl sitting on front, slip-lid and side-mounted pail handles, 1-lb., EX ...............$214.00 B

**Pickwick Ale,** serving tray, "Ale that is Ale," Copyright Hoffenreffer & Co., Inc., ale barrels being drawn by team of horses, 12" dia., EX...................................................................................$100.00 C

**Pickwick Ale,** sign, tin over cardboard, painted, Copyright Hoffenreffer & Co., Inc., 23" x 6½", VG.............................$95.00 C

**Pickwick Coffee,** container, metal, "Flavor Fresh," portrait in oval, key wind lid, 1 lb., EX ..............................$50.00 B

**Pickwick Coffee,** tin, litho, Mr. Pickwick on front, 3-lb., EX...$90.00 B

**Piedmont Cigarettes,** display, cardboard, in shape of large oversized pack with pretty woman with hat, 1910s, 10" x 17" x 4", EX.$495.00 D

**Piedmont,** sign, "the cigarette of quality," woman with big hat and fancy hair style, 1910s, 19" x 25", EX ................................$350.00 C

**Piedmont,** sign, "the cigarette of quality," woman with big hat and fancy hair style, 1910s, 19" x 25", G ..................................$175.00 C

**Piedmont,** sign, porcelain, "For cigarettes Virginia Tobacco is the best," package in center of message, 30" x 49", EX ..............$235.00 C

**Piedmont, The Virginia Cigarette,** folding chair, porcelain, double-sided, back, wooden, VG.....................................$130.00 C

**Piel's Beer,** straw and napkin dispenser, die cast, bar top, a couple of elves getting beer from a keg, 6½" x 7" x 6", EX ........................$30.00 B

**Piel's Real Lager Beer,** sign, porcelain, "on draught," 24" x 12", EX...........................................................$195.00 C

**Piels Real Lager Beer,** sign, porcelain, self-framing, "on Draught, Made in America," 24" x 12", EX ....................................$185.00 B

**Pierce Oil Corporation,** sign, porcelain, one-sided, "Pennant Oils," 14½" dia., G...............................................$450.00 B

**Piff's Beverages,** sign, tin, litho, embossed, "The Perfect Refreshment In Bottles," 30" x 14", EX........................................$155.00 C

**Pigmeat Almo Markham House Rent Party,** poster, paper, litho, by Ted Toddy Pictures, 28½" x 43", VG.........................$325.00 B

**Pilot Brand Typewriter Ribbon,** can, metal, red background with dark company lettering, image of an airplane, 2½" x 2½" x ¾", EX.................................................$85.00 D

**Pilot Cigarette,** tobacco container, tin, litho, airplane, by W.C. McDonald, Montreal, 4½" x 4½", EX..............................$50.00 B

**Pilot Knob Coffee,** container with bail handle from Bowers Bros., Richmond VA, 5-lb., EX ......................................$275.00 B

**Pinch Hit Chewing Tobacco,** sign, paper, baseball fan, "The Hit Of The Day," 42" x 27", EX .......................................$525.00 B

**Pinch Hit Chewing Tobacco,** sign, tin, embossed, painted, 14" x 9", P .................................................$200.00 C

**Pinkerton's National Detective Agency,** sign, porcelain, 7¼" x 3⅜", EX.................................................$125.00 C

**Pioneer Auto Service Co.,** sign, porcelain, two-piece, double-sided, vintage iron hanging bracket, "Official Service Station," 18" x 24½", NM ........................................$775.00 C

**Pioneer Club,** license plate attachment, aluminum, die cut, "Downtown Las Vegas, Nevada," cowboy, 10⅝" x 7⅜", EX.............$250.00 C

**Pioneer Glass & Paint Co.,** calendar, Indian maiden in canoe, partial months pad, 1923, 10" x 14", EX.........................$30.00 B

**Piper Heidsieck Champagne,** sign, clay coat, litho, dogs chasing a rat, John Osborn & Sons, NY, 29" x 20", EX .....................$350.00 C

**Pippins Cigar,** sign, tin, litho, 21" L, G......................................$250.00 B

**Pittsburgh Brewing Company,** sign, cardboard, logo in upper right hand corner, 40½" x 22", VG..................................................$75.00 C

**Pittsburgh Paint,** sign, tin, self-framed, product container, "Satisfaction in service since 1855," 38" x 27", NM ...................$390.00 B

**Pittsburgh Paints,** clock, light-up, motion, 15½" dia., VG..$600.00 C

**Pittston Gazette,** sign, porcelain, manufactured by Ing-Rich, Beaver Falls, Pa., "Bright, Clean, Newsy," 16" x 8", VG .....................$100.00 C

**Plano Harvesting Machines,** calendar, Indian and full calendar pad, 1905, 13" x 19", NM ............................................$165.00 B

**Planters Novola Peanut Oil,** container, metal, litho, image and message on sides, 5-gal., EX...............................................$175.00 D

**Planters Peanut Butter,** pail, litho, Mr. Peanut, 3½" x 3⅞", EX..$900.00 B

**Planters Peanut,** 5 cent jar, embossed lettering and Peanut man, 9" x 9" x 12", G........................................................$110.00 B

**Planters Peanut,** barrel jar, glass, original lid peanut-shaped handle, EX.........................................................$250.00 C

**Planters Peanut,** barrel jar, glass, original lid, peanut-shaped handle, G........................................................$135.00 C

**Planters Peanut,** container, shaped to resemble a peanut, 11" long, EX ........................................................$75.00 C

**Planters Peanut,** container, shaped to resemble a peanut, 11" long, G........................................................$55.00 C

**Planters Peanut,** container, waxy, two-piece, scarce, globe version, 7¼" x 5¾" x 3⅜", 1930s, VG...........................$1,400.00 B

**Planters Peanut,** parade costume shaped like a peanut, made from a composition material, 24" x 48", 1950s, EX ...$2,300.00 B

**Planters Peanut,** top, tin, early key-wound, Mr. Peanut on front, 4¼" x 4¾", G .......................................................$95.00 C

**Planters Peanuts,** box, wax-coated, G ...............................$40.00 B

**Planters Peanuts,** box, wax-coated, VG.............................$55.00 D

**Planters Peanuts,** sign, cardboard, die cut, Mr. Peanut and small child in cowboy attire, easel back, 6½" x 14", NM .............$215.00 B

**Planters Peanuts,** store jar, etched lid, embossed Mr. Peanut running around jar, 1935, NM................................................$286.00 B

**Planters Peanuts,** store jar, fish bowl with decal of fish, product message on fish body, hard-to-find item, 1929, NM..........$220.00 B

**Planters Peanuts,** store jar, glass, football, embossed "Planters Salted Peanuts" on both sides, 1930, NM ......................................$302.00 B

**Planters Peanuts,** store jar, glass, leap-year with paper label, 1940, NM .................................................................$165.00 C

**Planters Peanuts,** store jar, glass, metal lid which has Mr. Peanut, 5¼" x 10" x 8½", VG......................................$275.00 B

**Planters Peanuts,** store jar, glass, streamlined, yellow metal lid, 1937, NM ...............................................................$155.00 B

**Planters Peanuts,** store jar, seven-sided, embossed, paper label, 1926, EX..................................................................$225.00 B

**Planters Peanuts,** store jar, six-sided, Mr. Peanut decals on all sides, etched glass lid, 1936, NM ...........................................$160.00 B

**Planters Salted Peanuts,** container, waxy cardboard, airplane, 6" x 9" x 3", 1944, EX ................................................$375.00 B

**Planters Suffolk Brand Salted Peanuts,** can, metal, original lid, gold, black, and white label, 10 lb., VG..........................$1,500.00 B

**Planters,** ashtray, metal, with Mr. Planter standing in the middle, 6" x 6", EX..........................................................$30.00 D

**Planters,** display, tin, litho, countertop unit, 14" x 4¾" x 7¾", EX ....................................................................$595.00 C

**Planters,** earrings, plastic clip-on, in original gift box, ⅞" x 1¼", EX................................................................$70.00 B

**Planters,** jar, glass, slanted front with painted on Mr. Planter and information on lid, EX...............................................$150.00 B

**Planters,** jar, tin, litho, paper label on each side with lady, 9¼" x 5" x 7¾", 1937, EX...............................................$225.00 C

**Planters,** jumbo block wax display, cardboard, countertop, die cut, 8" x 10¾" x 7", EX .............................................$350.00 C

**Player's Weights Cigarettes,** sign, cardboard, original wood frame, "Players" name stamped on the bottom of the frame, clown with musical instrument, 18¼" x 22¾", NM..........................$500.00 B

**Plow Boy Chewing & Smoking Tobacco,** can, metal, boy resting on plow in field, slip lid, 5" x 6", EX .......................................$50.00 B

**Plow Boy Chewing and Smoking Tobacco,** pail, side-mounted wire bail handle and paper label, G.............................................$95.00 D

**Plow Boy Tobacco,** counter store bin, tobacco package on front and sides, 8" x 10½" x 10½", EX...................................$1,200.00 C

**Plow Boy Tobacco,** sign, cardboard, farmer plowing while girl is picking apples from nearby tree, "Everybody Likes It," 15" x 20", EX...........................................................$410.00 B

**Pluto Water,** sign, celluloid, "Drink... America's Physic," 1940s, 6" dia., EX..................................................................$100.00 B

**Plymouth Binder Twine,** banner, cloth, litho, "Insures a successful harvest," 28" x 7", 1920, VG .........................$95.00 C

**Plymouth Dry Gin,** "Coates...Original," with monk bottle, 4⅛" dia., EX..................................................................$40.00 B

**Poehler,** quick rolled oats from Poehler Mercantile, Lawrence, Topeka, Emporia & McPherson Kansas, EX......................$575.00 C

**Poker Club Mixture,** can, metal, poker hand, S.F. Hess & Co., EX...............................................................$1,000.00 B

**Poker Cut Plug,** container, metal, four men playing poker, "The Rock city Tobacco Co.," EX..............................................$225.00 B

**Polar Bear Tobacco,** store bin, metal, slant top, large lettering, EX...............................................................$395.00 B

**Polar Bear Tobacco,** store counter display bin, large polar bear with product package, 18" x 14" x 12", G....................................$675.00 C

**Polarine Frost & Carbon Proof Motor Oil,** sign, metal, embossed, oil can and lettering, 19½" x 19½", EX ...........................$525.00 B

**Polarine Gasoline,** sign, tin, litho, painted, two vintage automobiles with young ladies at the wheel, 19¼" x 27½", 1913, G...$1,800.00 C

**Polarine Motor Oil,** watch fob, metal, polar bear and product name, EX................................................................$65.00 B

**Polaris Sno-Traveler,** sign, tin, self-framing, single-sided, 28" x 35", G......................................................................$485.00 B

**Polaroid Land Camera,** sign with clock in left side of display, light-up, 1960s, VG.............................................................$165.00 C

**Polaroid Land Camera,** sign, light-up display with clock in left side of display, 1960s, G...........................................$125.00 D

**Poll-Parrot Shoes,** lamp, metal and plastic, 8" x 19", VG....$85.00 D

**Poll-Parrot Shoes,** sign, glass, reverse painted, wood frame, 14½" x 25", VG..................................................................$560.00 B

**Poll-Parrot Shoes,** sign, metal, die cut, "for Boys, for Girls," cut-out of parrot at top, rare and hard-to-find, double-sided, EX .$1,250.00 D

**Poll-Parrot,** chalkware parrot on trapeze with name strip below parrot, 19" H, EX.........................................................$400.00 B

**Poll-Parrot,** radio, plastic and composition, "Poll-Parrot Shoes for Boys and Girls," 3¾' x 11", VG ..........................................$135.00 C

**Poll-Parrot,** sign, neon over porcelain, die cut, bird sitting on perch at top of sign, EX.........................................................$1,350.00 D

**Poll-Parrot,** sign, neon, EX...............................................$1,250.00 C

**Poll-Parrot,** sign, porcelain, neon, light up, parrot on perch, 21" x 41", EX................................................................$950.00 B

**Poll-Parrot,** thermometer, dial-type, Poll Parrot, rare item, 10" x 24", EX................................................................$325.00 B

**Polly Prim Cleaner,** sign, cardboard, litho, woman with cleaning to do and the product in hand,. N.K. Fairbank Company, 20½" x 28½", G......................................................................**$185.00 B**

**Ponoco Cayenne Pepper,** tin, Grand Union Co., New York City, Indian head with full war bonnet on label, 2½-oz., EX......**$165.00 C**

**Pontiac,** sign, neon, blue and white Indian logo, new, 26" x 18", EX.....................................................................................**$185.00 B**

**Pontiac,** sign, porcelain, "Authorized Service," with Indian head logo in center of sign, 41½" dia., EX ................................**$325.00 C**

**Pontiac,** sign, porcelain, die cut, embossed, Indian head, 25" x 18", EX ............................................................................**$1,100.00 C**

**Pony Brand Marshmallow,** tin, Canadian, ponies and flags all around top of tin, 12" x 5", EX..................................**$85.00 B**

**Pop Kola,** sign, metal, "Drink Pop Kola," 33" x 6", EX.....**$125.00 D**

**Pop Kola,** sign, tin, one-sided, embossed, "12 ounces of Pep," 14" x 15", VG.............................................................................**$110.00 B**

**Popel-Giller Co. Inc. High Grade Bottled Beer,** tip tray, metal, woman, glass of product and bouquet of flowers, 4¼" dia., EX.**$125.00 C**

**Popeye Paints,** sign, metal, Popeye, Olive Oyl, and Sweet Pea, 1933, VG ........................................................................................**$75.00 C**

**Popeye,** sign, cardboard, stand-up display, "Drink, I Yam what I Yam and I Yam Tops," rare, 1929, 22" tall, VG.............**$300.00 D**

**Popper's Ace Tobacco,** store counter display case with glass front lid, 6" x 7" x 8¾", VG.............................................**$675.00 D**

**Popper's Ace,** container, metal, vertical pocket tin, bi-plane, EX .........................................................................................**$675.00 B**

**Popper's Eight Center,** sign, tin, embossed, spotlight from cigar on eight-ball, 35¼" x 11¼", EX .........................................**$175.00 C**

**Popsicle,** sign, tin, litho, "Everybody Loves Popsicle" 27½" x 10", NM .....................................................................................**$150.00 C**

**Porter's Antiseptic Healing Oil,** sign, cloth, horse prancing, "For Cuts, Sores, & Burns," 20" x 36", EX ............................**$975.00 D**

**Portuondo Cigars,** thermometer, wooden, product at bottom, 5" x 21", VG .....................................................................................**$325.00 B**

**Possum 3 for 5¢ Cigar,** canister, white opossum on front, 5" x 5", EX .........................................................................................**$360.00 B**

**Possum Cigar,** tin, possum on front, 50-ct, EX ...................**$175.00 C**

**Post Cereals,** calendar, youngster enjoying a bowl of the product, 8" x 12", 1924, VG ....................................................................**$70.00 B**

**Post Office Smoking Tobacco,** tin, litho, large building in center cameo, 3½" x 4¾" x 2", F..............................................**$825.00 B**

**Post Toasties,** sign, paper, "with peaches and cream," milk being poured on bowl of cereal, framed, 15¼" x 12¼", EX .........**$135.00 D**

**Post-Standard Branch,** sign, metal, double-sided, flange, 13" x 9¾", VG ....................................................................................**$145.00 C**

**Postal Telegraph,** sign, porcelain, "Postal Telegraph The International System," 30" x 16", EX.........................................**$300.00 B**

**Postal Telegraph,** sign, porcelain, double-sided, flange, "The International System," 29½" x 16", F ....................................**$95.00 D**

**Postmaster Cigar,** tin, postmaster smoking a cigar, 5¼" x 5", VG.............................................................................................**$55.00 D**

**Postmaster Smokers,** container, metal, pipe smoking man, round, slip lid, VG.......................................................................**$80.00 B**

**Postum,** string holder, tin, "Drink...There's a Reason...Health First," in center, EX ......................................................**$280.00 B**

**Poth's Beer,** pinback, by Whitehead & Hoag, 1¼" , NM.......**$65.00 C**

**Potosi Brewing Co.,** sign, metal, self-framing, "The Cockfight," two older men watching a barn cockfight, 1912, 20" x 24", EX.**$195.00 D**

**Power House,** box, two-piece, 24-count candy, "Bigger," product bar on front, 9" x 5" x 2", EX ............................................**$15.00 C**

**Powerlube Motor Oil,** sign, porcelain, two-sided, tiger, 59½" x 36", G........................................................................................**$950.00 B**

**Prairie Farmer,** subscription form, paper, litho, 32¼" x 24½", G **$110.00 B**

**Prairie Farms Milk Ice Cream,** clock, plastic body and cover light-up 16" dia., EX.............................................................**$165.00 C**

**Prairie Farms, Milk, Ice Cream,** clock, plastic front cover on plastic base, light-up, VG..................................................**$135.00 C**

**Prairie Rose Coffee,** can, tin, litho, key-wound, from E-H-B Coffee, Kansas City, young girl in center cameo, 1-lb., rare, F.......**$175.00 D**

**Pralines, Genuine Creole,** box, cardboard, litho, silhouette couple in lower corner and mammy in other corner, 1-lb., EX.......**$75.00 C**

**Pratt & Lambert Paint,** sign, porcelain, double-sided, 36" x 24", EX..........................................................................................**$200.00 C**

**Pratt & Lambert Paint,** sign, porcelain, double-sided, 36" x 24", VG..........................................................................................**$85.00 C**

**Pratt & Lambert Paint,** sign, porcelain, logo on 3 color band, double-sided, 36" x 24", EX ....................................................**$75.00 B**

**Pratt & Lambert Varnish Makers,** sign, paper, girl on dock with framed sign, 13" x 20", EX .................................................**$880.00 B**

**Pratts Poultry Food,** sign, paper, litho, "A Guaranteed Egg Producer," 21" x 28", P ..............................................................**$75.00 D**

**Premium,** sign, metal and cardboard, "For Friendly Flavor," VG.............................................................................................**$70.00 B**

**Prescriptions,** sign, glass, reverse painted, wood frame, 17¼" x 11¼", VG........................................................................**$275.00 B**

**President Suspenders,** tip tray, metal, "Absolute Comfort," 4" dia., EX .................................................................$100.00 B

**President Suspenders,** tip tray, metal, "Absolute Comfort...J.H. Beamer," pretty woman in tray center, 4⅛" dia., EX..........$65.00 C

**Prest-O-Lite Hi-Level Batteries,** door push bar, porcelain, "The Battery With A Kick," 36" x 4", EX .........................................$160.00 B

**Prestone Anti-Freeze,** thermometer, dial-type, 10" dia., EX..$225.00 C

**Prestone Anti-Freeze,** thermometer, wooden, early, "the perfect anti-freeze," 7¾" x 39½", 1930s, EX .................................$275.00 B

**Price's Milk,** clock, glo-dial neon, chrome case, 14½" dia., NM...$575.00 C

**Pride of Aden Coffee,** canister, with small lid, refund for return of tin, The Ginter Grocery Co., 6¾" x 9", 4-lb., 1906, EX .....$185.00 C

**Pride of Virginia Sliced Plug,** tin, rectangular, cameo on front cover, G .......................................................................$25.00 C

**Primley's California Fruit and Pepsin Chewing Gum,** display case, oak framing and etched glass, 18¼ ", EX ...........................$525.00 B

**Primley's California Fruit and Pepsin Chewing Gum,** display case, oak framing and etched glass, 18¼", G ..............$325.00 D

**Primley's California Fruit Chewing Gum,** sign, cardboard, die cut, easel back, stand-up, "sweeter than honey," bear holding product package, 13⅞" x 10½", VG......................................................$325.00 C

**Prince Albert Crimp Cut,** sign, paper, framed, 1927, 29" x 15", EX ...................................................................$115.00 C

**Prince Albert Tobacco,** charger, metal, "...The National Joy Smoke," jolly old gent smoking the product, 24" dia., EX ...$45.00 C

**Prince Albert Tobacco,** sign, metal, "...National Joy Smoke," Chief Joseph Nez Perce, 19½" x 25½", F .........................$450.00 B

**Prince Albert Tobacco,** sign, tin, litho, Chief Joseph Nez Perce, from American Art Works, 19" x 25½", EX .................................$5,500.00 C

**Prince Albert,** banner, cloth, "The National Joy Smoke," promoting both pipe and roll your own uses for the product, 95" x 43", 1941, NM ...................................................................$375.00 C

**Prince Albert, Crimp Cut Tobacco,** jar, paper label, original lid, rare, EX .......................................................................$95.00 C

**Prince Albert, Crimp Cut Tobacco,** jar, paper label, original lid, rare, NM.......................................................................$145.00 C

**Princess Rolled Oats,** container, cardboard, princess looking over her shoulder, by the Gobel-Reid Grocer Co., 42 oz., VG...$160.00 B

**Princeton Farms Hybrid Pop Corn,** can, metal, 10 oz., NM..$65.00 B

**Princine Baking Powder,** tin, litho, woman and product, 3" x 3", 1916, EX .......................................................................$135.00 B

**Principe Alfonso Cigar,** tin, litho, "5 in bundle 25¢," 13½" x 10", NM ...................................................................$250.00 B

**Priscilla Crayons,** tin, litho, "High Quality Brilliant Colors," brilliant colors of crayons in hand, 1937, NM..........................$70.00 B

**Pro-To-Co Tank Car Gasoline,** globe, metal body with glass lenses, high profile, "The Standard Oil Co. of New York," 16½" H, VG ...................................................................$500.00 B

**Procter & Gamble Co.,** sign, die cut, "Crisco...Better than Butter," produced by Baltimore Enamel Nov. Co., 14" x 20", G ..$1,200.00 D

**Progress Beer,** tray, metal, 3 men around a fire place, by Indianapolia Brewing Co., pre 1920, VG .................................$95.00 C

**Prosper Lambert Automobiles,** serving tray, metal, scalloped edges, man in early auto, product message on reverse side, 5", G..$500.00 B

**Prosperity Ranges,** bank, metal and celluloid, in shape of barrel, Sears Roebuck & Co., VG......................................................$52.00 B

**Providence Washington Insurance Co.,** tin, litho, with artwork of George Washington, 18" x 24", VG....................................$300.00 C

**Prudential Insurance Co. of America,** paperweight, glass, home office building, "Claims Paid Over $17,000,000, rectangular, NM ...................................................................$75.00 D

**Prudential,** sign, paper, pretty Prudential girl in a bare shouldered outfit, 1904, 9" x 12", EX.....................................................$220.00 B

**Public Telephone, Bell System Connections,** sign, porcelain, double-sided, flange, white on blue, P .........................$295.00 D

**Public Telephone,** sign, porcelain, die cut, flange, older model 202 phone in center of message, 16" x 16", EX.....................$375.00 C

**Public Telephone,** sign, porcelain, flange, "The Lincoln Telephone and Telegraph Company," 16" dia., EX............................$375.00 C

**Puck Virginia Cigarette Tobacco,** can, metal, round with slip lid, scene of 2 hockey players, NM ..........................................$250.00 B

**Pulver's Cocoa,** tip tray, metal, 4½", VG..........................$135.00 C

**Pulver's Kola-Pepsin Chewing Gum,** box, cardboard, two-piece with vending machine on both sides, 6⅞" x 5¼" x 1⅜", F ........$1,200.00 D

**Pulver,** gum dispenser, porcelain, glass window at payout with traffic cop, 8½" x 20", EX.......................................................$775.00 C

**Punch Baking Powder,** tin with paper label, 2½" x 5", VG..$125.00 B

**Pur-ox Syrups & Beverages,** thermometer, wood, pretty girl with glass beside scale, 1910s, 5" x 231", NM............................$400.00 B

**Pur-ox Syrups, Beverages,** thermometer, wooden, 5" x 21", G ..$95.00 C

**Pure as Gold Motor Oil,** can, metal, three Pep Boys, screw top and handle, 1930s, 2 gal., EX.....................................................$165.00 B

**Pure as Gold Motor Oil,** can, tin, two-gallon, the Pep Boys, Manny, Moe & Jack, 1933 ................................................................$100.00 B

**Pure Beer,** label, paper, North Lake Brewery, pre-prohibition, 12 oz., EX ...................................................................$25.00 D

**Pure Oil Co.,** gas globe, metal & glass, "Products of the ...," 15" dia., EX.................................................................$300.00 B

**Pure Oil Co.,** license plate attachment, metal, "Drive Safely" banner, VG.................................................................$130.00 B

**Pure Stock Quality 5¢ Cigar,** can, metal, tobacco leaves with company name, round, EX.................................................$25.00 B

**Pure-Pep,** pump sign, porcelain, "Be Sure With Pure," 10" x 12", EX.................................................................$90.00 B

**Pureoxiz Ginger Ale,** sign, metal, large horizontal oval in center with product name, 1920s, NM.......................................$650.00 B

**Puritan Tobacco,** tin, crushed plug mixture, vertical pocket litho 3" x 4⅜" x ⅞", EX.................................................$275.00 B

**Purity Butter Pretzels,** sign, cardboard, die cut, stand-up, young boy and a giant pretzel, 12½" x 22", VG..........................$135.00 B

**Purity Cigarettes,** sign, cardboard, bust of lady with stole, "Smoke Purity Cigarettes," 1880 – 90s, 9" x 14", VG.....................$95.00 C

**Purity Kiss,** sign, metal, two children kissing in a wicker chair, National Biscuit Co., 8" dia., EX.................................$450.00 B

**Purol Gasoline,** sign, porcelain, one-sided with arrow in center of face, 14" dia., G...............................................$175.00 B

**Purolator Oil Filters,** display, cardboard, stand up, die cut, service station attendant holding up filter, 26" x 22", EX..............$180.00 B

**Purolator,** oil rack complete with top sign, 1950s, G........$125.00 C

**Putnam Dyes,** display box, wooden, General Putnam litho on outside cover, also litho on inside cover, strong colors, with original dye packages, G..............................................$165.00 D

**Putnam Dyes,** metal cabinet, Gen. Putnam charging on his horse, 1940s, G.................................................................$150.00 B

**Putnam Fadeless Dyes,** cabinet, wood, general on horeback escaping from the red coats on tin front, VG.....................................$185.00 B

**Putnam Fadeless Dyes,** display box, tin, woman admiring clothing, 16½" x 8" x 11¼", EX.................................................$135.00 D

**Putnam Fadeless Dyes,** fan, cardboard, wooden handle, peacock, "Putnam Fadeless Dyes and Tints," EX....................................$30.00 D

**Pyrene,** sign, cardboard, die cut, father putting out auto fire while mother and child wait, "Pyrene kills auto fires," 21" x 31½", EX.................................................................$825.00 C

Quickure Mfg. Co., sign, metal, stand-up counter display for radiator leak cure, 9¾" x 11¼", EX, $485.00 B. *Courtesy of Collectors Auction Services.*

Quinlan's Butter Pretzel, tin, slip lid, small boy with basket on front, 1920s, 26 ct., EX, $95.00 C.

---

Q Boid Cube Cut Pipe Tobacco, container, metal, vertical pocket tin, cabin, never opened, NM ...........................................$230.00 B

Q Boid Granulated Plug, container, metal, vertical pocket tin, concave, EX........................................................................$40.00 B

Quadriga Cloth, sign, wooden, die cut, "The girl who sews has better clothes," logo at left of message, 20" x 6½", EX ............$75.00 D

Quadroom Smoking Tobacco, pouch, cloth with paper label, 4 oz., VG........................................................................$225.00 B

Quail Cigars, sign, paper, a pair of quail, "A Standard Of Excellence For Over Forty Years," 1900s, 13" x 9", EX ...........$50.00 B

Quaker Coffee, can, metal, oval image on key wind lid, 1 lb., EX ....................................................................$40.00 B

Quaker Crackers, display, cardboard, for counter use, box with "Help Yourself To..., Stays Crisp In The Box, Dish," 21" x 23", EX ..................................................................$200.00 B

Quaker Crackers, sample dispenser, cardboard, Quaker on front, would dispense sample by moving lever on side, 21" x 22" x 5½", EX ...............................................................$225.00 B

Quaker Maid Milk, sign, porcelain, "First In Quality," with die cut emblem, 41" x 24", EX........................................$500.00 B

Quaker Maid Milk, sign, porcelain, die cut, Quaker woman in center, "First In Quality," 41¼" x 23¾", EX...........................$575.00 C

Quaker Maid Petroleum Products, thermometer, dial-type, 12" dia., EX.............................................................$225.00 C

Quaker Maid Rye, sign, metal, bottle on a tray being held by a barmaid in a bonnet, S. Mirsch & Co., 32" x 46", EX ......$950.00 B

Quaker Maid, sign, porcelain, die cut, "First In Quality...Milk," woman in maid attire, 41" x 24", NM ..................$575.00 C

Quaker Oats Cap'n Crunch, bank, plastic, in shape of treasure chest, 1984, EX ....................................................$15.00 D

Quaker Oats Cap'n Crunch, doll, vinyl, special prototype, only 6 known produced, EX....................................$300.00 D

Quaker Oats Dionne Quints, floor display unit, cardboard, die cut, 60" x 30", EX ...........................................$120.00 B

Quaker Oats Quality Products, display rack, metal, "The Best Cereal Food," 28" x 70", EX.................................$650.00 B

Quaker Oats, sign, cardboard, wood framed, silhouette Quaker Man and sunset, 21" x 11", EX ..................................$50.00 B

Quaker Oats, sign, porcelain, tilted box of oats, "Eat..., In Packages Only," 24" x 42", EX........................................$750.00 B

Quaker Puffed Rice Sparkies, cereal box, cardboard, airplane, 6" x 9", EX.......................................................$50.00 B

Quaker State Duplex Outboard Oil, sign, tin, double-sided, 24" x 12", VG........................................................$65.00 C

Quaker State Lubrication Service, sign, tin, wood frame, single-sided, 63½" x 33", VG..................................................$325.00 B

Quaker State Motor Oil, clock, plastic construction, "ask for," 16" sq., VG..........................................................$80.00 B

Quaker State Motor Oil, clock, plastic, light up, "Ask For...," all green lettering and numbers on white background, 16" x 16", EX .................................................................$155.00 D

Quaker State Motor Oil, display rack, metal, vertical christmas tree style, holds 12 oil cans, EX ...............................$275.00 B

Quaker State Motor Oil, sign, metal, arched ribbon with logo of 100% Pure, 1938, 16" x 18", EX...........................$135.00 C

Quaker State Motor Oil, sign, metal, double-sided, original metal frame, 28¼" x 29¾", EX........................................$110.00 B

Quaker State Motor Oil, sign, paper, older lady in hat with her change purse, "The Right Change...," 58" x 34", EX .....$100.00 B

**Quaker State Motor Oil,** sign, porcelain, double-sided, driveway, "Certified Guaranteed," with logo at top of sign 26½" x 29", G .......$95.00 D

**Quaker State Oils & Greases,** clock, metal and glass, art deco design, neon around face, 19" x 16", EX ...........................$550.00 B

**Quaker State Summer Oil,** sign, paper, small boy at bat, "Make A Hit With Your Motor, Change Now To...," 58" x 34", EX .$140.00 B

**Quaker State,** clock, metal body with glass face and cover, light-up, trademark clover leaf on face, 15" dia., VG ...........................$425.00 B

**Quaker State, Summer Oil,** banner, 57" x 33¾", VG ..........$65.00 B

**Quality Inn Coffee,** can, tin, key-wound, litho, horseback travelers arriving at inn, 1-lb., 5" x 4", EX ......................................$250.00 B

**Quasar,** thermometer, metal, painted, "Pete's Discount...Whirlpool," dealer information in bottom panel, G ....................................$25.00 C

**Queed Tobacco,** can, metal, vertical pocket tin, EX .........$120.00 B

**Queen Cola,** sign, tin, painted, 7" x 19⅞", G....................$100.00 D

**Queen Quality Beer,** sign, wood and glass, light up, bottle and elk at top, 13" x 25", EX ......................................................$700.00 B

**Queen Quality Shoes,** display, metal, wood and plastic, women's high top shoes on top of sign, 25" x 37" x 8", EX...............$500.00 B

**Queen Quality Shoes,** pocket mirror, metal and glass, pretty lady featured on back, EX.......................................................$45.00 B

**Queen Quality,** tape measure, celluloid, lady in white, 2" dia., EX .................................................................................$50.00 B

**Quick Meal Ranges,** tray, metal, tip size, chicks, "Ask Your Dealer," 5" oval, EX .......................................................................$230.00 B

**Quick Meal Steel Ranges,** booklet, paper, front and back information, inside has story of the 3 bears, by the Ringen Stove Co., 1910s, 10 pages, EX .......................................................$100.00 B

**Quick Meal Steel Ranges,** booklet, ten-page, Buster Brown and Tige on front and back with product information inside, 1910, NM ................................................................................$110.00 C

**Quick Meal,** sign, porcelain, oval, chick emerging from an egg shell in grass, 44¾" x 33⅛", EX.................................................$275.00 D

**Quick Meal,** sign, porcelain, oval, egg and chick chasing insect, 44¾" x 33½", EX .......................................................$215.00 C

**Quiky, Tart, Tangy, Terrific,** thermometer, metal, 8" x 16½", G.$150.00 B

**Quincey Brewing Co.,** pocketknife, with embossing "Compliments of Dick & Bros." on back, has corkscrew, 3¼". VG..............$75.00 C

**Quincy Mutual Fire Insurance Co.,** calendar, cardboard, cat watching 3 rats play with matches, all monthly sheets, 1889, 7" x 10", EX.........................................................................$5,750.00 B

Radiola, sign, porcelain, double-sided, flange, 19" x 17¾", EX, $130.00 C.

Railway Express Agency, sign, tin over cardboard, self-framing, 19¼" x 13¼", VG, $975.00 C.

Raleigh, poster, paper, "the all-steel bicycle," 40" x 60", VG, $3,500.00 C.

Rambler, clock, light-up, from the Pam Clock Co., New Rochelle, N.Y., "Rambler Time," 16" sq., VG, $375.00 C. *Courtesy of Collectors Auction Services.*

Ramon's Brownie Pills, thermometer, wood, scale type reading, product information for the backache pills, 21" tall, VG, $200.00 B.

R Dougherty's Carriage Works, sign, paper, carriages in front of factory, 14½" x 12", VG .................................................... $150.00 B

R-B Cigars, sign, metal, bare bottomed child reaching for the product, "Daddy Wants An A-B," 13" x 19", VG ........................ $650.00 B

R-KAO Coffee, tin, litho, slip-lid, scarce item, "For Lovers of True Flavor," 1-lb., EX .................................................... $85.00 B

R.A. Patterson Tobacco Co. Lucky Strike Tobacco, clock, wood case with brass and glass door, with eight-day wind-up mechanism, 12¼" x 19", VG .................................................... $650.00 C

R.G. Sullivan Co., sign, glass, reverse painted, light-up, 7-20-4 cigar, 24" x 8" x 3¾", EX .................................................... $355.00 B

R.G. Sullivan Inc. Cigar, box opener, metal, company name on one side and "7-20-4 Cigar" on the back side, item was necessary early in the 20th century to open cigar boxes for counter display, 1900 – 1930s, 8" long, EX .................................................... $25.00 C

R.G. Sullivan's Quality 10¢ Cigar, sign, porcelain, single-sided, 30" x 12", VG .................................................... $195.00 C

Radiant Coffee, tin, key-wound lid, Chris Hoerr & Sons, Peoria, Ill., 1-lb., F .................................................... $25.00 D

Ragtime Jubilee, poster, cardboard, 15" x 22½", EX .................... $35.00 B

Ragtime Jubilee, window card, cardboard, directed by Max Presnell a caricature of a large well-dressed black man, 15" x 22¾", VG .. $225.00 C

Railway Express Agency, sign, metal and fiberboard, arched lettering, 14" x 14", EX .................................................... $85.00 D

Railway Express Agency, sign, porcelain, one-sided strip, 120" x 5", NM .................................................... $325.00 B

Railway Express Agency, sign, porcelain, single-sided, diamond-shaped, 8" x 8", EX .................................................... $150.00 B

Railway Express, sign, porcelain, white & green lettering on green background, 23" x 6½", EX .................................................... $225.00 D

Rain Dears, sign, metal, self-framed, painted, "Finest Plastic Rainboots," 25" x 9½", EX .................................................... $65.00 C

Randolph Macon Cigars, sign, tin, litho, man and woman with a box of the product, self-framing, 20" x 24", G, $675.00 C.

R. Brand & Co. sign, tin, litho, "Fine Whiskies and Wines...Toledo, O," pretty young woman, in original period frame, 17" x 23", 1880s, EX, $3,700.00 B. *Courtesy of Buffalo Bay Auction Co.*

RCA, sign, porcelain, double-sided, "His Master's Voice," foreign, very rare sign, 16" x 18", VG, $3,200.00 C.

RCA, sign, porcelain scroll, "Radiola Dealer," 14½" x 19", G, $140.00 C.

RCA, watch fob, presentation, sterling silver with cloisonne enameled Nipper at the horn, 1⅜" x 1½", EX, $1,050.00 B. *Courtesy of Wm. Morford Investment Grade Collectibles.*

---

Rain Dears, sign, metal, self-framed, painted, "Finest Plastic Rainboots," 25" x 9½", VG..................................................$45.00 D

Rainbo Bread, door push bar, porcelain, "Good Bread," VG .$150.00 B

Rainbo, door push and pull handle, steel, "is good bread," NOS, 26½" x 8½", NM...............................................................$300.00 C

Rainbow / Peerless Rubber Manufacturing Co., sign, metal, show how gasket and packing made by the company were used on the battleship Oregon, 21" x 15", VG .......................................$140.00 B

Rainbow Dyes, cabinet, wooden with tin insert on door, "One Dye for All Fabrics," 11½" x 5" x 19", VG ..........................................$375.00 C

Rainbow Dyes, countertop display cabinet, wood, "one dye for all fabrics," paper label and complete with product packages, 6" x 12½" x 16¾", VG ....................................................................$850.00 C

Rainier Ale & Beer, sign, metal, die cut, embossed, 13" x 8⅜", 1940s, NM ....................................................................$135.00 C

Rainier Beer, barometer, metal and plastic, 9⅝" x 12½", VG .$75.00 C

Rainier Brewing Company, serving tray, metal, 12" dia., G .$75.00 C

Rainier Club, sign, metal, bottle and name over bottle, 7" x 12", VG .............................................................................$150.00 B

Rainier Pale Beer, serving tray, "Compliments of the season," snow scene on front, pre-Prohibition item, 9¼" dia., EX..$225.00 C

Rajah Motor Oil, sign, metal, "Double Milage...A Penn-O-Tex Product," 20" x 28", EX..........................................................$1,400.00 B

Raleigh Cigarettes, poster, cardboard, easel back, Douglas Fairbanks, Jr., 20" x 30", VG......................................................$55.00 C

Raleigh Cigarettes, sign, cardboard, free playing cards with Raleigh coupons, framed, 13½" x 19½", EX.......................................$35.00 C

Raleigh Cigarettes, sign, paper, "Playing Cards Free, Save The Coupon...Now 15¢," 14" x 20", EX....................................$100.00 D

Raleigh Cigarettes, sign, paper, framed, 14½" x 17½", G..$20.00 B

Raleigh Cigarettes, sign, paper, litho, framed, 16½" x 21½", EX ...$75.00 C

Rebel's Rest Antiques, sign, tin, litho, die cut, black man holding a sign an antique business, item is probably older than the advertiser, 35" x 56", 1915, VG, $475.00 B. *Courtesy of Buffalo Bay Auction Co.*

Record's Ale, globe, light-up, metal body and glass lenses, 15½", VG, $1,000.00 B. *Courtesy of Collectors Auction Services.*

Red Bell Motor Oil, can, red bell in center spotlight, 1 gal, EX, $45.00 B.

Red Crown Ethyl Gasoline, sign, porcelain, double-sided, with very strong colors, 30" dia., EX, $425.00 B. *Courtesy of Autopia Auctions.*

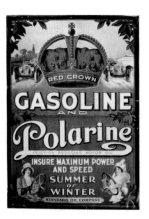

Red Crown, sign, tin, litho, painted, two vintage automobiles and young ladies at the wheel, 19¼" x 27½", 1913, EX, $7,000.00 B.

Red Goose Shoes, clock, light-up with goose in center, 1930s, Telechron, EX, $400.00 B. *Courtesy of Muddy River Trading Co./Gary Metz.*

Raleigh Tobacco, sign, cigarettes with filter tip, 28" x 14½", EX ...**$55.00 C**

Raleigh, change receiver, under glass on wood base, product package, 7¾" x 7½" x 2½", EX .................................................**$65.00 C**

Ralston Leather Wing Tip Shoes, display shoe, leather, "Smart Shoes For Men, They Need No Breaking In," 25½" long, EX ..........**$660.00 B**

Ralston Purina, ashtray, pottery, in the shape of a dog's bowl, 6" dia., VG ...............................................................**$35.00 D**

Rambler Cars, postcard, cardboard, photo of a family enjoying the freedom that only could come by owning a new Rambler, fantastic colors of a green and white four door Rambler in front of mountains, unused, 1961, 5½" x 3½", EX ...................................**$10.00 C**

Rambler Parts & Service, sign, porcelain, white lettering on red background, 42" dia., EX.................................................**$795.00 D**

Rambler, clock, light-up, Pam Clock Co., New Rochelle, N.Y., "Rambler Time," 16" sq., EX .....................................**$425.00 C**

Ramer's Chocolates, sign, tin, self-framing, products on table, 19" x 13", G..............................................................**$61.00 B**

Ramon's Brownie Pills, thermometer, wood, painted, little doctor at right of the scale, 9" x 21", EX...............................**$495.00 C**

Ramon's Brownie Pills, tin, litho, "The Little Doctor Brings Happy Days," the doctor at right of scale, in cream color, 9" x 21", NM ........................................................**$332.00 B**

Rand McNally Pocket Maps, display, pasteboard, 6 slanted slots for maps and names on front for each, 9" x 7" x 6", EX ............**$190.00 B**

Ranger Beer, label, paper, with revenue stamp, by Ahrens Brewing Co., 12 oz., VG .................................................**$22.00 C**

Rat Bis-Kit, display, die cut, easel back, for rat bait, NOS, rat eating product, 8¾" x 12", EX......................................**$300.00 B**

Rat-Tox, sign, cardboard, die cut, Pied Piper luring rates with a tube of the product, 24" x 19", EX....................................**$410.00 B**

Red Indian Gasoline, globe, Indian in full headdress with screw-on glass body, 13½" dia., EX, $1,300.00 B. *Courtesy of Autopia Advertising Auctions.*

Red Indian Motor Oils, sign, porcelain, Indian in full headdress, back mounting bracket, 17" x 24", EX, $2,000.00 C. *Courtesy of Autopia Advertising Auctions.*

Red Man sign, porcelain, "Mellow Chew," scarce, with pack and arrow, 22" x 10½", EX, $500.00 B. *Courtesy of Autopia Advertising Auctions.*

Red Ranger, cigar box, red fox on inside lid, 15½" x 4½" x 5", G, $70.00 B.

Red Rock Co., sign, tin, embossed, promoting their flavors, 19½" x 27½", VG, $125.00 C.

---

Rawleigh's Baking Powder, tin, free sample, 1" x 1½", EX..$175.00 C

Rawleigh's Cocoa, tin, sample size, "Free Sample," 1¾", EX.$125.00 C

Rawleigh's Good Health Cocoa, tin, litho, Mr. Rawleigh and outdoor scene, packed by The W.T. Rawleigh Co., Freeport, Ill., USA, 1¼" x 1¾" x ⅝", EX ............................................................$180.00 B

Rawleigh's Good Health Products and Service, sign, tin, double-sided, flange, dealer, 18" x 15¼", EX..................................$325.00 C

Rawleigh's Talcum, tin, litho, clown on unicycle, 7½" T, EX ..$55.00 C

Ray Cotton Company, inkwell, cast iron, heavily embossed lettering, Franklin, Mass., Agents Cotton Mills Waste Association, 8" x 3¾" x 3", EX.....................................................................$95.00 C

Ray's Standard Oil, license plate attachment, tin, painted, "Gas...Mt.Vernon, LA," 10" x 2½", EX...................................$95.00 C

Raybestos Brake Service, sign, metal, double-sided, flange, hand pulling early "on the floor" emergency brake lever, 18½" x 14", VG ................................................................................$495.00 C

Raybestos Fan Belt, sign, tin, "Avoid Breakdowns," service man holding a belt, 21" x 11⅞", EX..........................................$175.00 C

Raybestos, thermometer, metal, scale type, "Check Brakes!," 30½" tall, EX ...............................................................................$110.00 D

Raytheon Radio Service, sign, metal, flange, double-sided, Raytheon radio tubes, 18" x 14", EX.................................$145.00 C

Razzle Dazzle Tobacco, store barrel with paper label, mule kicking off shoe at black man, 15" x 21", EX.................................$795.00 C

Razzle Dazzle, wood barrel with paper label, mule kicking shoe off, 16" dia., x 21½", VG..............................................$995.00 C

RC, thermometer, metal, painted, with vertical scale under message, "Royal Crown Cola," EX.............................................$85.00 C

RCA Radiotrons, display figure, wood, man with lettering on chest and hat, 1950s, 15" tall, EX.........................................$1,800.00 C

RCA, bank, pot metal covered by felt, Nipper, marked Radio Corporation of American, 6", NM .................................................$185.00 B

RCA, Nipper dog, papier-mache, 5" x 11¼", 1920s, VG.$195.00 D

RCA, oleograph, early Nipper at phonograph, "Victor Records," "His Master's Voice," framed, 30" x 24", EX .............................$650.00 C

Red Rock Whiskey, mini jug, stoneware, front stencil reads "Compliments of GEO. H. Goodman Co., Distillers Red Rock Whiskey, Paducah, KY, Shreveport, LA, Jackson, Tenn.," rare and very scarce, 1900 – 1910s, 3⅛" tall, EX, $1,400.00 C. *Courtesy of B.J. Summers.*

Red Rose Tea, door push, porcelain, Canadian product, "it's good tea," 1940s, 3" x 9", EX, $200.00 B.

Red Seal Battery, thermometer, porcelain, large battery at top of scale, 27" tall, VG, $150.00 B.

Red Seal, sign, tin over cardboard, automotive ignition battery, strong colors, 27" x 19", EX, $1,500.00 B. *Courtesy of Wm. Morford Investment Grade Collectibles.*

Reed Oil Co., lighter, metal, premium for Phillips 66 distributor, made by Barlow, never used, advertising one side only, 1¼" x 2¼" x ¼", NM, $35.00 C. *Courtesy of B.J. Summers.*

RCA, oleograph, early Nipper at phonograph, "Victor Records," "His Master's Voice," framed, 30" x 24", G ...................$235.00 C

RCA, placemat, Nipper dog, with Donald Duck logo, G ....$35.00 C

RCA, sign, glass, reversed painted, "Tubes Tested Free...," EX...$145.00 D

RCA, sign, porcelain scroll, "Radiola Dealer," 14½" x 19", EX .$225.00 D

RCA, sign, porcelain, "His Master's Voice" Nipper at the gramophone, 23" x 17", EX........................................................................$450.00 C

RCA, sign, porcelain, single-sided, "His Master's Voice," 27" x 21½", G..........................................................................................$825.00 C

RCA, sign, porcelain, single-sided, "His Master's Voice...Radio," trademark Nipper, 24" x 15", NM .....................................$500.00 B

RCA, watch fob, sterling silver, Nipper at the horn, 1⅜" x 1½", EX...............................................................................$125.00 D

Reader's Digest & Campbell's Soup's, alarm clock, metal and glass, message on clock face, "Reader's Digest & Campbell's Soup's Go together," 1950s, 3" dia., EX .................................................$95.00 C

Real Penn Motor Oil, can, Quaker man in diamond insert in center, 1 qt., EX....................................................................$125.00 D

Rebel's Rest Antiques, sign, tin, litho, die cut, black man holding a sign advertising an antique business, item is probably older than the advertiser, 35" x 56", 1915, EX.........................................................$550.00 C

Recommended Hotel AAA, sign, porcelain, neon, double-sided, hanging, 48" x 31½", red, white & blue, EX....................................$500.00 C

Record's Ale, globe, light-up with metal body and glass lenses, 15½", G..................................................................................$475.00 C

Recruit Little Cigars, sign, cardboard, die cut, stand up, Civil War soldier with a product package, 20" tall, EX .....................$200.00 C

Recruit Little Cigars, sign, die cut, store, tri-fold, featuring scenes on each fold of places to enjoy product, 39" x 29", EX ......$225.00 B

Red & White Corn Flakes, box, cardboard, #2 Davy Crockett edition, bowl of cereal on front, 13-oz., EX ............................$75.00 C

Red Bell Motor Oil, can, metal, screw lid, bell, 2 gal., VG ..$125.00 D

Rees, A.F., sign, tin, single-sided, embossed, "We pay for dead stock," G, $175.00 C.

Rehkopf's Special, Straight Kentucky Whiskey, Paducah, Ky., jug, stone, 1-qt. EX, $325.00 C.
*Courtesy of B.J. Summers.*

Remington, UMC, Sportsmen's Headquarters, Firearms & Ammunition, sign, double-sided, die cut, flange, Remington bears, 7" x 8", EX, $2,200.00 B.
*Courtesy of Morford Auctions.*

Rexall, McFarlin, sign, porcelain, double-sided, arm-hung, 72" x 30" x 4¼", EX, $825.00 C.

Rex Flintkote Roofing, match holder, tin, litho, barn with message on roof, "For all roofs," 5" H, G, $350.00 B.
*Courtesy of Richard Opfer Auctioneering, Inc.*

---

**Red Belt,** pocket tin, vertical, belt and buckle from John J. Bagley & Co., 3" x 3" x 1", EX ............................................$90.00 B

**Red Bird Rolled Oats,** sign, from Highland Grocery Co. of Ohio, red bird on front, EX ............................................$175.00 C

**Red Bird,** container, rolled oats from Midland Groceries, Ohio, red bird on front, 20-oz., VG ............................................$70.00 B

**Red Cap,** candy box, cardboard, "At Your Service Everywhere 5¢," 24-count, two-piece, red-capped man carrying vendor box of product, 7" x 10" x 2½", EX ............................................$36.00 B

**Red Chief Plug Cut / H Bohls & Co.,** container, metal, George Washington and product lettering, 6" x 4", EX ..................$175.00 C

**Red Comb Poultry Feeds,** sign, metal, "Quality Feeds At Low Price," rooster, 20" x 27", EX ............................................$400.00 D

**Red Crest Tobacco,** lunch box, leather with strap closure, rooster on front label, hard-to-find, 8" x 5" x 4", VG ....................$275.00 C

**Red Cross Coffee,** container with paper label, from C.A. Cross Co., Fitchburg, MA, 1-lb., EX ............................................$65.00 C

**Red Cross Shoes,** sign, neon, manufactured by Lackner, Cin. O, 21" x 7", VG ............................................$185.00 B

**Red Cross Stoves Ranges & Furnaces,** pocket mirror, metal and glass, logo of the Co-operative Foundry Co. on back side, VG ...........$55.00 C

**Red Crown Ethyl,** gas globe, one-piece, shape of crown with embossed lettering at bottom band, 17½" dia., VG ...........$1,100.00 B

**Red Crown Gasoline,** globe, high profile metal body with glass lenses, painted lettering and crown, 15" dia., VG ......................$725.00 C

**Red Crown Gasoline,** sign, metal, crown logo, "Coupons Accepted Here," 24" x 9", EX ............................................$250.00 C

**Red Crown Gasoline,** sign, porcelain, circular, crown logo in center, 42" dia., EX ............................................$875.00 C

**Red Crown Gasoline,** sign, porcelain, circular, crown logo in center, 42" dia., NM ............................................$1,200.00 C

**Red Crown Gasoline,** sign, porcelain, crown logo and name, 14" dia., VG ............................................$550.00 B

Rhodes-Burford House Furnituring Co., brush, wood and fiber, embossed lettering, "You Furnish The Girl, We'll Furnish Your Home," 1910s, 7¾" x 2¼" x 1½", EX, $65.00 C. *Courtesy of B.J. Summers.*

Ridenour-Johnson Hardware Co., sign, cardboard, framed, litho, copyright 1922, 1920s, 16" x 26½", EX, $135.00 C.

Rit Dye, tin cabinet with six product drawers in back, 10" x 16¼", VG, $125.00 C.

Ritz Hotel Lounge, lighter, metal, by "My-Lite, Mopey," Budweiser logo on flip top, never used, 1960s, 1½" x 2¼" X¼", NM, $25.00 C. *Courtesy of B.J. Summers.*

Roanoke Rye, Thompson, Wilson & Co., Distillers Paducah, Ky., sign, paper, litho, framed, still has good colors, professionally restored, in original frame, 1900s, 14" x 19", EX, $1,500.00 C. *Courtesy of B.J. Summers.*

Red Crown Gasoline, sign, porcelain, double-sided, crown trademark in center, 30" dia., 1929, VG .................................$365.00 C

Red Crown Gasoline, sign, porcelain, double-sided, product name and crown logo, 30" dia., VG.............................................$395.00 C

Red Crown Tobacco, pail, wire bail handle on lid, 6½" x 5" x 4¼", VG ........................................................................$225.00 C

Red Crown, poster, paper, "You Can't Beat...for Mileage," 27¾" x 44", 1938, VG ...................................................$75.00 C

Red Devil's Lighter Fluid, thermometer, metal, scale type, can at top and "The Fluid With A Thousand Lights" at bottom, VG.....$180.00 B

Red Diamond Overalls & Shirts, watch fob, metal, man in product in front of D logo, VG ............................................$25.00 D

Red Dot Cigars, fan pull, cardboard, double-sided, 6½" x 8½", EX....................................................................$100.00 C

Red Dot Cigars, sign, cardboard, painted, lady in red dot and product in lower left corner, 9" x 12½", EX................................$95.00 C

Red Earl Cigars, tip tray, Red Earl in tray center, 3⅝" dia., EX..$110.00 C

Red Feather, cigar box label, paper, Indian in full headress, EX..............................................................................$530.00 B

Red Fox Cigarette Tobacco, pouch, cloth, paper label, EX...$35.00 D

Red Gate Mocha and Java Coffee, sign, cardboard, framed, EX.$101.00 B

Red Giant Oil, can, giant engine with company product lettering, 1 qt., EX .................................................................$45.00 D

Red Goose Paper, poster, Red Goose with the golden egg, 28" x 9", EX..............................................................................$85.00 C

Red Goose Shoes, carpet, store entry, two Red Goose images, "Half The Fun of Having Feet," 59" x 27", G ...............................$525.00 B

Red Goose Shoes, clock, metal body, glass front, light-up, Red Goose in center, message over goose, EX.........................$575.00 D

Red Goose Shoes, clock, metal, neon, logo Red Goose in center, 18" x 18", 1930s, EX....................................................$495.00 D

Red Goose Shoes, clock, plastic and wood construction, light-up, trademark Red Goose in center of face, 19½" x 18", VG.......$195.00 C

Robert Smith Ale Brewing Co., serving tray, tin, litho, self-framing, 19" x 23½", EX, $4,500.00 C.

Rock's Buster Brown Shoes, ruler, wood, for the business at 421 Broadway, Paducah, KY, 1920 – 40s, 12" long, VG, $15.00 C. *Courtesy of B.J. Summers.*

Rose-O-Cuba Cigars, sign, cardboard, vase of roses, 24" tall, VG, $130.00 B.

Ross, Jesse L., & Co., Druggists, serving tray, metal, litho, 13¾" x 16¾", VG, $265.00 C.

Roth, brush, wood and fiber, "Roth Funeral Directors, Ambulance Service, 5th and Monroe Paducah, Ky, Phone 126," 6" x 1¼" x 1½", VG, $35.00 C. *Courtesy of B.J. Summers.*

**Red Goose Shoes,** clock, Telechron, light-up, goose in center, 1930s, VG.................................$300.00 C

**Red Goose Shoes,** display, cardboard, counter, easel back, young girl and Red Goose, 7" x 10", EX.......................$45.00 C

**Red Goose Shoes,** display, composition, in shape of goose, 5½" x 11½", VG..........................$285.00 B

**Red Goose Shoes,** poster, cardboard, easel back, with the admonition to watch the Red Goose lay a golden egg every time you buy Red Goose shoes, 11" x 13, EX.........................$65.00 C

**Red Goose Shoes,** sign, porcelain, neon, die cut, trademark Red Goose, 20" x 36", VG.............................$450.00 C

**Red Goose Shoes,** store display, metal and cardboard, revolving rack with cardboard Goose, 32" x 36", EX.......................$350.00 D

**Red Goose Shoes,** string holder, metal, die cut, logo goose with string holder beneath goose, 18" x 36", VG....................$1,500.00 B

**Red Goose,** egg machine, papier-maché and cardboard, "Ask for a Golden Egg," eggs contain prizes, EX................................$325.00 B

**Red Hat Motor Oil and Gasoline,** gas globe, metal and glass, product lettering and top hat, 15" dia., NM..........................$2,100.00 B

**Red Hawks,** cigar box, wooden, Indian on inside lid 50-ct., 1895, VG.............................$40.00 B

**Red Head Hi-Octane Gasoline,** globe, glass wide body with two glass lenses, 13½" dia., G..............................$1,100.00 B

**Red Head,** bottle caps, resealable on blister pack from country store, NOS, 1940s, EX.......................................$50.00 C

**Red Indian Gasoline,** globe, glass body, Indian in full headdress, screw-on, 13½" dia., VG................................$725.00 C

**Red Indian Motor Oils,** sign, porcelain, profile of Indian in full headress and product name, 20½" x 18", EX.................$1,400.00 B

Royal Crown Cola, poster, cardboard, Shirley Temple, 29½" x 12¼", VG, $300.00 C.

Royal Crown Cola, clock, cardboard body with glass face and cover, light-up, Telechron Inc., Ashland, Mass., U.S.A. C.A.P., 15" dia., VG, $275.00 B. *Courtesy of Collectors Auction Services.*

Royal Crown Cola, thermometer and barometer, mirrored, "Drink... Best By Taste Test," rare piece, 12" x 24", G, $250.00 B. *Courtesy of Muddy River Trading Co./Gary Metz.*

Royal Crown Cola, scales, cast iron and plastic, top section in shape of bottle, 45" tall, VG, $950.00 B.

Royal Crown Cola, sign, gloglas, "we Serve...Highballs," 1935 – 4012" x 10", EX, $2,500.00 B.

---

**Red Jacket Smoking Tobacco,** container, metal, vertical pocket tin, jockey on horseback, EX ..................................................$135.00 D

**Red Man Chewing Tobacco,** display box, cardboard, lettering and Indian with headress on front, 15" tall, EX......................$175.00 D

**Red Man Chewing Tobacco,** sign, cardboard, "First In America," view of Fulton Steamship, 14" x 21", VG ...........................$40.00 D

**Red Man Chewing Tobacco,** sign, paper, "Fresh! Red Man Wax Wrapped," 18" x 8", EX......................................................$65.00 B

**Red Man,** sign, paper, litho, wax wrapped, 20½" x 10½", VG .$75.00 C

**Red Man,** sign, porcelain, "The Mild Mellow Chew," 22" x 10½", VG ..........................................................................$345.00 C

**Red Man,** sign, porcelain, "The mild mellow chew," hard-to-find, arrow through product package, 22" x 10½", EX ........$825.00 B

**Red Mill Rolled Oats,** tin, Winona, MN, EX ....................$175.00 C

**Red Raven Splits,** ashtray, porcelain, "Ask the man," 6" x 3½", EX ..............................................................................$110.00 B

**Red Raven Splits,** serving tray, tin, lithographed, "Ask the man," 13¾" x 10½", VG ............................................................$235.00 B

**Red Raven Splits,** sign, paper, small naked child climbing onto product box for a bottle, logo red raven in front, 14" x 25", EX...$450.00 B

**Red Raven Splits,** tip tray, metal, "For high livers' livers," red raven and bottle in center, 12" dia., EX ............................$440.00 B

**Red Raven,** tip tray, good graphics, 4¼", EX ......................$300.00 C

**Red Raven,** tip tray, metal, "Ask the Man," woman with red raven, 4" dia., NM ..............................................................................$376.00 B

**Red Raven,** tip tray, metal, "For Headache...For Indigestion," red raven and woman on tray center, 6⅛" L, EX ....................$170.00 B

**Red Raven,** tip tray, tin, litho, young girl hugging an oversized version of the logo bird, 4¼" dia., EX ....................................$350.00 B

**Red Raven,** tray, metal, "For Headache & For Indigestion" glass and bottle image, 1910, 13" x 13", EX......................................$145.00 B

**Red Rock Cola,** door opener, 24" x 3", VG......................$115.00 C

Royal Crown Cola, sign, heavily embossed, bottle, 15½" x 58½", EX, $185.00 C. *Courtesy of Riverview Antique Mall.*

Royal Crown Cola, sign, metal, self-framing, embossed, NOS, 31½" x 12", EX, $95.00 C.

The Royal Tailors, sign, tin, die cut, painted, stand-up, great graphics, 19½" x 9", EX, $550.00 B.

Russells' Ales, sign, metal, self-framing, men unloading wooden barrels of the product, 1910s, 29" tall, G, $350.00 C.

Ryzon, The Perfect Baking Powder, sign, tin, double-sided, baking powder can, arm-hung, 1940s, 12" x 16", EX, $475.00 B. *Courtesy of Muddy River Trading Co./Gary Metz.*

Red Rock Cola, sign, metal, "Enjoy Red Rock Cola," 19" x 4", EX .......$45.00 D

Red Rock Cola, sign, paper, product bottle directly beneath bouquet of flowers, 20" x 24", VG .......$85.00 D

Red Rock Ginger Ale, sign, glass, reverse painting of Annie Oakley look alike and company name, 5" x 10", EX .......$550.00 B

Red Rock Ginger Ale, sign, paper, litho, under glass, link chain frame, woman with product, 6" x 8", 1920s, EX.......$185.00 B

Red Rose Tea, sign, metal, embossed product package, 29" x 19", NM .......$250.00 B

Red Seal Battery, sign, metal, flange, painted, "A battery for every use," dry seal battery, EX .......$325.00 C

Red Seal Battery, sign, porcelain, die cut, curved, shaped in the the product, 14½" x 34¼", EX .......$575.00 C

Red Seal Battery, sign, porcelain, double-sided, die cut, the product, 13" x 24½", EX .......$925.00 C

Red Seal Bottlers Extracts, sign, heavy paper, litho, woman wearing red hat and red dress, St. Louis, Mo., 11½" x 16½", G.$140.00 C

Red Seal Peanut Butter, tin, litho, three fiddlers, 12-oz., EX.$196.00 B

Red Seal Snuff, container, metal, paper label, unopened, EX..$25.00 D

Red Seal, sign, tin over cardboard, automotive ignition battery, strong colors, 27" x 19", VG .......$1,000.00 C

Red Seal, thermometer, porcelain, battery at top, "The guarantee protects you," 7¼" x 27¼", EX .......$170.00 B

Red Spot Coffee, door push, tin, embossed, 19¾" x 2¾", NM ..$60.00 B

Red Star Cleaning Powder, box, cardboard, paper label, early family scene, 5" x 3½" x 1¼", 1880s, VG .......$95.00 D

**Red Top Steel Posts,** sign, metal, painted, 18" x 24", G......**$95.00 D**

**Red Wing,** pot scraper, tin, litho, Red Wing Flour, with flour bag on front, 3" x 2½", EX................................**$1,050.00 B**

**Red Wolf Coffee,** container, metal, wolf, slip lid, 3 lb., VG.**$95.00 B**

**Red Wolf Steel Cut Coffee,** tin, litho, wire handle, wolf in oval on front, 6-lb., EX................................**$200.00 B**

**Red-Ola Cigars,** tip tray, metal, pretty woman in center of tray, Edward D. Depew & Co., New York, 4¼" dia., EX..............**$175.00 B**

**Reddy Kilowatt,** display figure, plastic, in likeness of the electric figure, 1950s, 5½" tall, NM................................**$150.00 D**

**Reddy Kilowatt,** pencil, mechanical, EX ............................**$15.00 C**

**Redford's Celebrated Tobaccos,** sign, cardboard, wealthy land owner smoking a cigar and watching the hands at work in the field, 1900 – 10s, 25" x 20", EX................................**$245.00 C**

**Redmen Archery,** sign, wood, Indian in center, 24" x 34", VG.**$475.00 D**

**Redmen Archery,** sign, wood, painted, "Shoot," Indian head in center of message, 24" x 34", EX................................**$250.00 C**

**Reed & Bell Root Beer,** mug, glass, red logo and lettering, 4½" tall x 3" dia., EX................................**$25.00 C**

**Reed & Bell Root beer,** sign, porcelain, frosty cold mug of the product and company lettering, 39" x 30", EX ........................**$375.00 B**

**Reed Manufacturing Co.,** sign, tin over cardboard, bench vise, 19¼" x 13¼", VG................................**$175.00 C**

**Refiners,** gas globe, high profile metal body with two glass lenses, 16½" dia., G................................**$725.00 C**

**Regal Beer,** thermometer, metal, "Better Change to Better Taste," 6" x 14", EX................................**$75.00 B**

**Regal Cube Cut Smoking Tobacco,** container, metal, vertical pocket tin, lion logo in center circle, flip top, EX......................**$450.00 B**

**Rehkopf's Special Straight Kentucky Whiskey Paducah, Ky.,** jug, stone, 1-qt. G................................**$175.00 C**

**Reids Special Ice Cream,** sign, porcelain, double-sided, die cut, top hanger, 30" dia., VG ................................**$375.00 B**

**Reliable Coal,** pocket mirror, celluloid and glass, four digit phone number on the back side, VG art deco design around outer edge of of celluloid back, 1920 – 30s, 3½" dia., NM.........................**$45.00 C**

**Reliance Advertising Co.,** sign, porcelain, single-sided, advertising their enameled advertising signs, 24" x 13¼", VG .............**$170.00 B**

**Reliance Baking Powder,** match holder, tin litho, woman working in kitchen, 5¾" H, G................................**$425.00 B**

**Remer's Tea Store,** sign, cardboard, die cut, cat in cup, 10" x 6¼", EX................................**$45.00 C**

**Remer's Tea Store,** sign, cardboard, die cut, cup on edge with cat drinking from saucer, 10" x 6¼", EX................................**$35.00 D**

**Remington Ammunition,** sign, animals, 20" x 27", EX......**$125.00 C**

**Remington Firearms Ammunition,** catalog, paper, 1955, 12 pages, EX ................................**$35.00 C**

**Remington Game Loads,** print, paper, large buck surrounded by various birds, 21½" x 29½", EX................................**$195.00 B**

**Remington Household Knives,** sign, cardboard, "At last I've found a knife that cuts," ad of woman at kitchen table with product, 12" x 18", VG................................**$125.00 C**

**Remington Nitro Express Long Range Game Loads,** box, cardboard, shell with Remington UMC spotlight at top of message, full box, EX ................................**$135.00 C**

**Remington Sporting Cartridges,** sign, cardboard, wall-hanging, cartridges and their sizes. 13" x 20", EX ................................**$95.00 C**

**Remington UMC Auto Loading & Repeating Firearms,** sign, cardboard, display case of guns, "...Sold Here," 14" x 20", EX..**$625.00 B**

**Remington UMC Nitro Club,** shell box, cardboard, goose on front, 4" x 4" x 2½", NM ................................**$95.00 C**

**Remington UMC Sportsmen's Headquarters Firearms & Ammunition,** sign, double-sided, die cut, flange, Remington bears, 7" x 8", EX ................................**$1,200.00 C**

**Remington UMC,** sign, cardboard, "The Remington Idea, Solid Breech Hammerless," different guns, 13" x 24", EX....**$395.00 B**

**Remington UMC,** sign, cardboard, standup, man checking out a gun in front of a gun cabinet, 14" x 20", EX................................**$600.00 B**

**Remington,** calendar, "Old Mike" in boat ready for waterfowl hunting, 15" x 29", 1924, NM................................**$475.00 C**

**Remington,** poster, different long guns and the game for each, 13" x 25", VG................................**$200.00 C**

**Remington,** sign, "Let 'er Rain," hunter in boat, 1925, 15" x 28½", EX................................**$560.00 B**

**Remington,** sign, cardboard, window, .22 rifle, 20½" x 18½", G .**$200.00 D**

**Remington,** sign, metal and plastic, light-up, muzzle loader with powder horn, "the most famous name in shooting," 25" x 12", G.**$115.00 C**

**Repeater Fine Cut Tobacco,** container, metal, flat style, Mountie on horseback, 4" x 3" x 1", EX................................**$55.00 D**

**Resinol Soap & Ointment,** tip tray, metal, "For All Skin Diseases...At All Drug Stores," red-haired woman in center of tray, 4¼" dia., EX ................................**$170.00 B**

**Return of Mandy's Husband,** poster, paper, litho, starring Mantan Morehead and Flourney E. Miller, 26½" x 40½", G ..............$125.00 C

**Rev-O-Noc,** sign, tin, litho over cardboard, firearms, sporting goods, fishing tackle, 19¼" x 13¼", 1915, EX..........................$1,100.00 C

**Revelation Smoking Mixture,** container, metal, pocket tin, sample size, "The Perfect Pipe Tobacco," EX ..................................$95.00 B

**Rex Flintkote Roofing,** match holder, tin, litho, "For all roofs," barn with message on roof, 5" H, EX...................................$475.00 C

**Rex King's,** sign, cardboard, framed, belladonna, porous and kidney plasters, 16" x 25", VG........................................................$115.00 C

**Rex Mild Cool Burning Pipe & Cigarette Tobacco,** container, metal, vertical pocket tin, torches surround an oval bust portrait, EX ..........................................................................................$145.00 B

**Rexall Foot Bath Tablets,** sign, framed, litho, "for Foot Comfort," 22" x 47¼", VG.......................................................................$335.00 C

**Rexall,** clock, light-up, "Compare the price and save on...," to left of clock face, EX..........................................................................$105.00 C

**Rexall,** sign, metal, product name in script, 72" long, EX ...$75.00 D

**Rexall,** store bowl, glass, clear with heavily embossed lettering, "From The...Store," 4¼" x 4¾", EX .........................................$55.00 B

**Rexall,** tin, litho, baby talc with young baby in cameo shot in center, 2½" x 4½" x 1⅜", EX ..................................................$300.00 B

**Rhinelander Butter,** sign, tin over cardboard, 13¼" x 9¼", NM.$165.00 C

**Rib Mountain Lager,** label, with tax stamp, from the Wausau Brewing co., 12 oz., EX ......................................................................$45.00 D

**Rice Oil Co,** gas globe, high profile metal body with two glass lenses, Johnstown, O., 15" dia., VG.......................................$1,500.00 C

**Rice Shoes,** sign, cardboard, die cut shoe, compliments of C.W. Rice, Baldwinsville, N.Y., 9¼" x 6", EX....................................$45.00 D

**Rice's Seeds,** poster, stone litho, man lifting a very large turnip, 20½ x 28¼", 1890s, EX .................................................$805.00 B

**Richardson Root Beer,** display, electric animated bear and glass mug, papier-mache bear turns and spins on base simulating ice skating, 16½" x 16½" x 25", NM...............................................$425.00 B

**Richardson Root Beer,** mug, glass, barrel shaped with embossing, EX...................................................................................$35.00 B

**Richardson Root Beer,** sign, metal, die cut, barrel with name on front, 21" x 26", EX .........................................................$250.00 D

**Richardson Root Beer,** sign, tin, litho, "Rich in Flavor," 1950s, 14" x 10", red, white, and black, NM .........................................$75.00 C

**Richardson's Silk,** spool cabinet, wood, 8 drawers, 7 have glass fronts, solid drawer has product name, 22" x 18" x 19", EX.$700.00 D

**Richelieu Coffee,** Sprague, Warner & Company, Chicago, Ill., U.S.A., with screw-on lid, 1-lb., G ........................................$45.00 C

**Richfield Ethyl,** gas globe, metal and glass, ethyl logo and product name, 15" dia., EX................................................................$1,800.00 C

**Richfield Gasoline,** sign, tin, embossed, "Just Ahead," eagle in center, 70" x 56", EX.........................................................................$895.00 C

**Richfield Hi-Octane,** gas globe, low profile metal body with two glass lenses, Richfield bird in center, 15" dia., VG ..........$495.00 C

**Richfield Oil Company Game Reserve,** sign, tin, embossed, "No Hunting In This Closed Area," 13¾" x 9¾", NM..........$165.00 C

**Richfield,** calendar, paper, never used, 7⅜" x 7½", NM ..$135.00 C

**Richfield,** gas globe, metal and glass, name lettering in yellow on blue band across center of globe, 15" dia., EX...............$1,200.00 C

**Richfield,** poster, paper, "Here Soon," man in early model race car, 39½" x 54½", G .......................................................................$225.00 C

**Richfield,** sign, porcelain, two-sided, die cut, shield-shaped, "The gasoline of power," 48" x 48", G......................................$1,200.00 B

**Richfield,** weathervane, metal, eagle arrow and directional, 43" x 28", EX........................................................................................$1,200.00 C

**Richlube Motor Oil,** sign, metal, double-sided, 24" dia., EX..$1,300.00 B

**Richlube Motor Oil,** sign, metal, double-sided, attachment that spins in the wind that says "Richlube," message on main body, "Longer Wear Without Repair," 36" x 231", EX................$175.00 D

**Richlube Motor Oil,** sign, metal, pole, die cut, in shape of oil can, 9" x 15", VG..................................................................$155.00 C

**Richlube Motor Oil,** sign, porcelain, double-sided, 24" dia., F.$275.00 C

**Richlube,** rack sign, metal, double-sided, "All-Weather Motor Oil...30¢ per quart," 16" x 12", 1938, EX..........................$255.00 C

**Richmond Straight Cut Cigarettes,** cabinet card, cardboard, "...Are The Best," 6" x 9", VG........................................................$55.00 D

**Ridenour-Johnson Hardware Co.,** sign, cardboard, litho, framed, copyright, 1922, 1920s, 16" x 26½", G............................$75.00 C

**Rieck's Ice Cream,** sign, paper, lady at ice cream parlor with soda "jerk," "It's So delicious I'll Take Home A Brick Of...," 22" x 12", EX.............................................................................................$225.00 D

**Rienzi Beer,** tip tray, "In Bottles Only...Bartholomay Brewery, Rochester, NY," man on white horse with product bottle, 4⅛" dia., EX.............................................................................................$130.00 B

**Right Food Company,** watch fob, hog in gold wash, Moorman Mfg. Co. Quincy, Ill., EX .........................................................$85.00 C

**Right-Cut Chewing Tobacco,** wall dispenser, tin, litho, old gent, 4¼" x 10¼" x 2¼", EX ...........................................................$70.00 D

**Riley Bros.,** sign, tin, litho, "That's Oil," 13½" x 5½", EX ...**$85.00 C**

**Ringling Bros. and Barnum & Bailey,** poster, paper, "May Wirth, the greatest bareback rider of all time," 16¾" x 24½", VG........**$195.00 C**

**Ringling Bros. and Barnum Bailey Circus,** poster, paper, litho, leopard head, 29" x 43½", EX .....................................................**$190.00 C**

**Rinso Soap,** sign, cardboard, designed for trolley car use, "A Whiter Wash In Half The Time," 21" x 11", VG ..............................**$95.00 C**

**Rinso,** sign, porcelain, one-sided, "Soak the clothes – that's all...saves coal every wash-day," 24" x 18", VG ..............**$650.00 B**

**Rising Sun Stove Polish,** sign, store, 8¾" x 6", EX.................**$325.00 C**

**Ritz Crackers,** poster, cardboard, 26" x 14", VG.....................**$55.00 C**

**Rival Stove,** nickel-plated sample item, by J & E Stevens Co., Cromwell CT, 5½" x 7½" x 15½", 1895, EX ........................................**$1,500.00 C**

**River Front Coffee,** container, paper label, cardboard sides and metal top and bottom, waterport scene, from Reeves, Parvin & Co., Philadelphia, 1-lb., EX ......................................................................**$155.00 C**

**Rivera Brand Coffee / Sears Roebuck & Co.,** milk can, metal, bail handle, 5 lb., EX ..................................................................**$85.00 C**

**Road Runner Non-Detergent Motor Oil,** can, waxed cardboard, road runner on front, 1 qt., EX .........................................**$65.00 C**

**Roadfinder Cycle Tyres,** sign, porcelain, one-sided, 24" x 8", VG..**$135.00 C**

**Roanoke Rye, Thompson, Wilson & Co., Distillers, Paducah, Ky.,** sign, paper, litho, framed, still has good colors, professionally restored, in original frame, 1900s, 14" x 19", G ..............**$500.00 C**

**Roast Coffee,** container, metal, key wind lid, mountain scene, 1 lb., EX..................................................................................**$45.00 D**

**Robert Burns 10¢ Cigar,** charger, metal, Robert Burns, 24" dia., EX.......................................................................................**$250.00 D**

**Robin Hood Flour,** watch fob, metal, EX...........................**$45.00 D**

**Robin Hood Shoes,** display, plaster, in likeness of Robin Hood standing with arms crossed, 12" tall, EX..........................**$245.00 D**

**Robin Hood,** sign, reverse painted, "Tread Straight," 15" x 4", VG..................................................................................**$110.00 B**

**Robinson's Pilsner Beer,** serving tray, tin, litho, folks enjoying beer in canoes on lake at a dock, 12", EX .........................**$288.00 B**

**Rochester Percolator,** sign, paper, litho, woman enjoying the "new" product, 27" x 21", EX.......................................**$40.00 B**

**Rochester Photo Supply Co.,** pocket mirror, metal and glass, view of downtown Rochester, EX .............................................**$105.00 B**

**Rochester Root Beer,** dispenser with front tap with Rochester decals on back and side panels, made by Multiplex Faucet Co., St. Louis, MO, 16½" x 16½" x 25", G ...........................**$100.00 D**

**Rock Spring Sparkling Water...Ginger Ale, Kola,** serving tray, metal, 12" dia., EX.............................................................**$35.00 C**

**Rockford High Grade Watches, Oscar Holmes, Cambridge, Minn.,** tip tray, metal, woman sitting beside tree, 4⅞" L, G ..........**$65.00 C**

**Rockford Watch,** sign, metal, pocket watch being held by a pretty lady, 17" x 23", VG .............................................................**$550.00 B**

**Rocky Ford,** cigar box, "A new high in two for five cigars," 50-count, Indian looking with hand over eyes, EX............................**$45.00 C**

**Rocky Mountain Beer,** label, paper, mountains and company name, 12 oz., EX ...........................................................................**$55.00 C**

**Rocky Mountain Honey Co.,** sign, tin, embossed, child eating breakfast, 16" x 12", VG ................................................**$550.00 B**

**Rode-O-Cuba Cigars,** container, metal, product name and portrait of pretty lady in gold trim, EX .........................................**$135.00 D**

**Roe Feeds,** sign, metal, painted, 7" x 12", VG.....................**$85.00 C**

**Rogers Bros. Silverplate,** poster, paper, litho, 31" x 45", VG.**$115.00 D**

**Rogers Drugs,** sign, leaded glass, light-up, 63" x 27", VG ..**$600.00 B**

**Roi-Tan Cigars store,** sign, cardboard and plastic, "Take a ride with Sophie," "Sophie Tucker and her Roi-Tan show on the Radio, C.B.S., Mon. Wed. Fri., 1939 Wyandotte Chevy , NRFB, 1939, NM ...................................................................**$300.00 D**

**Roi-Tan,** sign, cardboard, die cut, cigarette girl, countertop size, easel back, NOS, 7" x 19", 1930s, EX ...............................**$375.00 C**

**Roi-Tan,** sign, original brass frame, reverse glass, "Man to Man...A Real Fine Cigar," 13" x 21¼", NM.......................................**$687.00 B**

**Roi-Tan,** sign, tin, litho, automobile, "Take a ride with Sophie Tucker and Roi-Tan," with double-sided marquee, 4¼" x 1½" x 4½", EX.................................................................................**$475.00 C**

**Rolling Rock Beer,** sign, wood, "Lucky Debonail," 10" x 14", VG.................................................................................**$75.00 D**

**Rolling Rock Extra Pale Beer,** thermometer, metal, painted, 8¼" x 27", EX.................................................................................**$75.00 C**

**Rolling Rock,** sign, glass, easel back, "The Premium Beer," cobalt, EX.................................................................................**$125.00 C**

**Rose Exterminator Co.,** sign, porcelain, die cut, oval, owl, "Wise Protection...Since 1860," 18¾" x 11¼", NM...............................**$175.00 C**

**Rose Exterminators,** sign, die cut, "spraying man," figural, 10¾" x 10¾", NM.....................................................................**$275.00 C**

**Rose Valley Whiskey,** sign, tin, self-framing, 1905, 28¾" x 22¼", VG .................................................................................**$500.00 C**

**Rose-O-Cuba Cigar,** tin, litho, roses and senorita on front and back, 5½" x 5¼", EX ...........................................................**$75.00 B**

**Rosemary Foods,** wagon with rubber tires, metal, the highest standard of purity and excellence, 15" x 14" x 34", G ................$95.00 C

**Roszell's Sealtest Homogenized Milk,** sign, plastic and neon, EX ...........................................................$200.00 C

**Rough Ridewr Baking Powder,** container, metal, paper label, unopened, 4¼ oz., NM ........................................$95.00 D

**Round Oak Stove,** calendar, Indian, 10½" x 20½", 1926, NM ..$410.00 B

**Round Oak Stoves Ranges & Furnaces,** mug, ceramic, Indian, "Doe-Wah-Jack," 1900s, EX...............................$100.00 C

**Round Oak Stoves, Ranges & Furnaces,** match safe, metal, pocket, celluloid on sides, 1½" x 3" x ⅜", EX.....................$325.00 B

**Round Up Coffee,** jar, glass, paper label, manufactured by the Round Up grocery Co., Spokane, WA, cowboy riding a bucking horse in center cameo, 4" x 6", EX ...............................$110.00 B

**Roundy's Coffee,** container, metal, hot cup of coffee, The peak of...," 2 lb., EX ....................................................$75.00 D

**Rowntree's Toffee,** tin, slip-on lid, 6½" x 4" x 8¼", EX .......$95.00 C

**Royal 99,** pump sign, porcelain, die cut, shield with diagonal name lettering, 7" x 9", EX ...............................$425.00 C

**Royal Baking Powder,** box, wooden, shipping, with good advertising on ends and sides, debossed and painted lettering, 14¾" x 8½" x 7¾", EX ...............................................$75.00 C

**Royal Baking Powder,** poster, paper, offering a free fairy tale book, 20" x 30", VG.................................................$275.00 D

**Royal Beer Ale,** sign, cardboard, 21" x 11", G ....................$65.00 C

**Royal Blend High Grade Roasted Coffee,** Granger & Co., Buffalo, NY, sign, paper, litho on cardboard, crown on lid and front, trolley on reverse, 1-lb., EX ...........................................$45.00 B

**Royal Club Cut Plug,** container, metal, company name and embossed lion and crown, EX .........................................$195.00 B

**Royal Crown Cola,** bottle, miniature, 1936, 3" tall, EX.......$75.00 C

**Royal Crown Cola,** bottle, miniature, 1936, 3" tall, G ........$50.00 D

**Royal Crown Cola,** calendar, paper, "RC Tastes Best! says Wanda Hendrix," Wanda holding a bottle of the product, 1950, 12" x 25", VG .........................................................$45.00 D

**Royal Crown Cola,** can, metal, flat top, large "RC" lettering, EX..$40.00 D

**Royal Crown Cola,** clock, cardboard body with glass face and cover, light-up, Telechron Inc., Ashland, Mass., U.S.A. C.A.P., 15" dia., NM..............................................$450.00 D

**Royal Crown Cola,** clock, light-up, Pam Clock Co., 14½" dia., EX .........................................................$235.00 C

**Royal Crown Cola,** menu board, metal, "Drink," logo at top, 19¾" x 28", red, blue, black, and white, EX..................................$125.00 C

**Royal Crown Cola,** poster, cardboard, one-sided, girl on phone, 28" x 11", EX......................................................$115.00 C

**Royal Crown Cola,** poster, paper on board, "Tastes Best," 20th Century Fox star Linda Darnell serving the product to two service men, 43" x 31", EX.........................................$225.00 C

**Royal Crown Cola,** poster, paper on board, "Tastes Best," 20th Century Fox star Linda Darnell serving the product to two service men, 43" x 31", VG.........................................$150.00 B

**Royal Crown Cola,** sign, "RC tastes best!" says Barbara Stanwyck, with actress holding a bottle of RC, trolley car 28" x 11", VG..........$225.00 C

**Royal Crown Cola,** sign, cardboard, "RC Tastes!" says Barbara Stanwyck, while she holds a bottle of the product, 28" x 11", EX................................................................$175.00 C

**Royal Crown Cola,** sign, cardboard, die cast, stand up, girl with crown, "Nothing Sparkles Like A Royal Crown," 1950s, 16" x 30", EX................................................................$150.00 C

**Royal Crown Cola,** sign, heavily embossed bottle, 15½" x 58½", NM.................................................................$225.00 D

**Royal Crown Cola,** sign, heavy paper, Jeanette MacDonald enjoying the product with three service men, 40" x 28½", VG ........$195.00 C

**Royal Crown Cola,** sign, metal, die cut, big 6 pack, "Take Home A Carton," 24" x 16", EX.........................................$600.00 B

**Royal Crown Cola,** sign, metal, die cut, painted, 1936 bottle, 15¾" x 59¾", EX ....................................................$395.00 D

**Royal Crown Cola,** sign, tin, stenciled, double-sided bracket-hung 6-pack, "Six Big Bottles 25¢," strong colors, 23¾" x 15¾", EX ..$525.00 B

**Royal Crown Cola,** thermometer, metal, "the fresher refresher," 10" x 26", white, red, and blue, EX .........................................$195.00 C

**Royal Crown Cola,** thermometer, metal, "the fresher refresher," 10" x 26", white, red, and blue, G..........................................$130.00 C

**Royal Crown Motor Oil,** can, metal, "100% Pure Pennsylvania" and company logo and name, 5 gal., EX ...............................$145.00 C

**Royal Crown,** sign, metal, "Relax and Enjoy," Art Deco style, tilted bottle in spotlight in center, 23¾" x 16", EX.........................$435.00 D

**Royal Crown,** thermometer/barometer, mirrored, "Drink... Cola Best By Taste Test," rare piece, 12" x 24", EX................................$395.00 D

**Royal Daylight Lamp Oil,** sign, porcelain, single-sided, "Best American Lamp Oils," horse-drawn oil wagon, 21" x 14½", VG..$800.00 B

**Royal Egypt,** cigar box label, paper, Egyptian dancer beside a tiger, 1900s, EX ...........................................................$185.00 C

# R

**Royal Portable Typewriter,** sign, paper, litho, Continental Litho Corp., Cleveland O., typewriter with a card that reads "Merry Christmas to The Family," 21½" x 27½", VG ...............................$100.00 B

**Royal Princess,** cigar box, Indian princess on inside lid and front label, 50-ct., 1930, EX ........................................................$95.00 C

**Royal Rose Talcum Powder,** tin, litho, rose, National Drug Co., 2¼" x 6" x 1¼", EX.......................................................$130.00 B

**Royal Scot Feeds,** sign, tin, single-sided, embossed, 16" x 23½", VG ...............................................................$125.00 B

**Royal,** gas globe, shape of crown, 11" x 13", NM............$1,400.00 C

**Royalty Club Whiskey,** sign, glass, painted, framed, A. Friedman Co...Sole Distributers, 31" x 21", EX ...............................$145.00 C

**Roza De Luzon Cigars,** sign, stone litho, Kurz & Allison, Chicago, Battle of Chattanooga, 34¼" x 27¼", 1888, EX..........................$975.00 C

**RPM Heavy Duty Motor Oil,** sign, porcelain, double-sided, 34" dia., EX ..............................................................$300.00 B

**RPM Motor Oil,** sign, porcelain, double-sided flange, "Thermo-Changed...100% Pure Paraffin Base," 22½" x 22", EX .......$800.00 B

**RPM Motor Oil,** sign, tin, painted, "A Knockout For Winter," Donald Duck and a snowman, 23⅝" dia., 1940s, NM............$2,250.00 B

**Ruhstaller's Lager,** tip tray, metal, "Best Beer Brew...Sacramento, Cal.," serving maid carrying steins of product, 4¼" dia., EX ..$170.00 B

**Ruhstaller's,** tray, gilt edge, metal, two ladies being served in an open car by a gentleman, 1920s, 13" x 13", VG...............................$85.00 D

**Runkel Brothers Breakfast Cocoa,** tin, litho, small top, 2½" x 2½" x 4¾", EX.......................................................$75.00 C

**Runkel's,** tin, screw-on lid, "Essence of chocolate," 6" x 6" x 9", EX....................................................................$375.00 C

**Ruppert's Beer,** globe, plastic and glass, name and eagle logo on face of lens, 1920s, 16" dia., EX .......................................$500.00 C

**Rusco Fan Belts,** display unit, countertop, 12½" x 22" x 16¾", VG....................................................................$175.00 B

**Rush Park Seeds,** display, shipping and countertop box, colorful paper labels, 31" x 16" x 5½", EX .......................................$95.00 B

**Ryan's Jet Regular,** gas globe, heavy milk glass. NOS, still in original shipping box, 16½", NM...............................................$350.00 B

**Ryzon,** sign, tin, double-sided, "The Perfect Baking Powder," baking powder can, arm-hung, 1940s, 12" x 16", VG.........................$200.00 C

Samoset Chocolates, sign, metal, Indian in canoe, "Chief of them all," 1940s, 22" x 4", VG, $300.00 C.

San Antonio Brewing Assoc., sign, paper, "The Famous Judge Roy Bean Horse Thief Trail," 1945, 26" x 21¼", VG, $135.00 C.

San Carlos Brand California Wine, sign, gloglas, 1930s, 8" x 10", EX, $225.00 B.

San Diego Bus Stop, sign, porcelain, one-sided, 16" x 12½", VG, $350.00 C.

Sanford's Inks, sign, tin, litho, embossed, jars and bottles, by the Tuscarora Advertising Co., Coshocton, OH, 19½" x 13½", 1890s, EX, $3,000.00 B. *Courtesy of Buffalo Bay Auction Co.*

S & H Green Stamps, clock, "We Give S & H green stamps," 15¼" x 22¾", EX.............................................$125.00 C

S & H Green Stamps, sign, porcelain, double-sided, hanging, EX .........................................................$225.00 C

S Babic Wholesale Liquor Dealer, tray, metal, gold letter on deep rim, 13" dia., EX ...................................$350.00 B

S.J. Tuft 178 Genesee St.,...Utica, N.Y., Dealers in ladies furnishing goods, dust pan, cardboard, die cut, 9½" x 9", EX .......$45.00 C

S.M. Hess & Brother, calendar, by Hayes Litho Co., "manufacturers of rich grade fertilizers," 1907, 15" x 22¼", G............................$130.00 C

S.M. Hess & Brother, calendar, by Hayes Litho Co., "manufacturers of rich grade fertilizers," 1907, 15" x 22¼", VG .........................$175.00 C

Saboroso Cigar Store, tape measure, celluloid, 1¾" x ½", EX..$40.00 B

Sailors Delight Tobacco, label, paper, with scene of dock, 13" x 7", VG .........................................................$95.00 D

Saint Louis Cigar, box label, paper, sample, 1893, EX .....$105.00 D

Salada Coffee, sign, die cut, single-sided, can of coffee, 12" x 12", EX..............................................................$450.00 B

Salada Tea, door push, porcelain, "Delicious Flavor," 34" x 3½", VG ..............................................................$125.00 D

Salada Tea, sign, porcelain, single-sided, Canada, 14⅞" x 6¾", VG ..............................................................$500.00 C

Salem Cigarettes, sign, metal, "Refreshes Your Taste," with lettering and product graphics, 9" x 9", VG ................................$25.00 D

Salem, change pad, rubber astro turf, "Change To," 10" x 10", G .$20.00 C

Salinas Brewing Co., plate, Sterling China Co., give-away, horse head in center, 9" dia., 1904, EX.........................................$50.00 B

Salisbury's New Car Rental, sign, cardboard, post-war auto, 23" x 12½", NM.........................................................$155.00 C

Sally Clover Coffee, tin, litho, screw-lid, 1-lb., NM .............$45.00 B

Sambo Axle Grease, can, metal, black boy, from Nourse Oil Co., VG .........................................................$195.00 B

Santa Bana Cigar, sign, paper, framed, young lady in thoughtful pose, EX, $850.00 B.

Satin Skin Cream & Powder, sign, cardboard, die cut, countertop, woman and cherub, 18" x 18", 1911, EX, $440.00 B. *Courtesy of Buffalo Bay Auction Co.*

Sauer's, Flavoring and Extracts, clock, wood case with reverse painting and lettering, 42½" H, EX, $1,550.00 B. *Courtesy of Richard Opfer Auctioneering, Inc.*

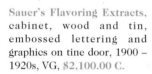

Sauer's Flavoring Extracts, cabinet, wood and tin, embossed lettering and graphics on tine door, 1900 – 1920s, VG, $2,100.00 C.

Schell's Carbonated Mead, sign, Prohibition advertising for August Schell Brewing Co., New Ulm, Mn., great artwork of woman with peacock, 16¼" x 33", EX, $1,350.00 B.

**Sambo's Fine Cigars,** clock, tin, litho face and wooden frame, with smoking Sambo in center of clock face, 15¼" x 15¼", 1930s, EX..................$250.00 C

**Sambo's Restaurants,** plate, china, palm tree and name next to the tree, 9¾" dia., VG..................$85.00 D

**Sambo's Restaurants,** token, wooden, "What This Country Needs Is A Good 10¢ Cup Of Coffee...," 1½" dia., VG..................$20.00 D

**Sambo,** display, counter, smoking Sambo standing enjoying a cigar, "Smoking Sambos Fine Cigars, Euclid, OH," 8½" x 16", 1930s, EX..................$155.00 C

**Sambo,** sign, tin litho, drink, black bell man, made by Carvin Bottle Cap Corporation, Brooklyn, N.Y., 13¾" x 19⅝", VG..........$300.00 B

**Samoset Chocolates,** pocket mirror, celluloid and glass, product and Indian in canoe on back, 2½" dia., EX..................$2,300.00 B

**San Alto Cigar,** sign, cardboard, 3 men and a black waiter, "Instantly Recognized By Its Rich Aroma & Mildness," 14" x 30", EX..................$275.00 D

**San Alto Cigar,** sign, cardboard, black servant serving product, 14" x 30", EX..................$230.00 B

**San Diego Beer,** tray, metal, eagle logo, by the American Art Works, pre prohibition, 13" dia., EX..................$195.00 C

**San Felice Cigar,** sign, cardboard, man and woman critiquing a painting, "for gentlemen of good taste," 18¼" x 23¾", VG...$170.00 B

**San Marto Coffee,** tin, litho, screw-on lid, horseback warrior, 1-lb., 1923, EX..................$225.00 C

**Sanders Court & Cafe,** postcard, cardboard, roadside cabins in Corbin Kentucky, 5" x 3½", VG..................$22.00 D

**Sandusky Gold Bread,** log holder, tin, "Radiant Baked," 36½" x 13½" x 3½", VG..................$135.00 C

**Sanford's Inks & Mucilage,** sign, metal, product bottles shown, "Faultness," 20" x 14", VG..................$2,450.00 B

Schmidt's, bronze bartender, embossed lettering, 7¾" H, EX, $235.00 C.

Schmidt's Beer, sign, gloglas, product bottle, "We Serve...," 1940s, 12" x 10", EX, $400.00 B.

Schmidt's Blue Ribbon Bread, door push, metal, shaped and painted to resemble a loaf of bread, 19" wide, VG, $160.00 B.

Schmidt's Blue Ribbon Bread, thermometer, metal and glass, dial reading, loaf of bread in center, Pam Clock Co., 12" dia., VG, $375.00 B.

Schrafft's Chocolates, sign, cardboard, trolley size, "Daintiest of Dainty Sweets," 1900 – 10s, 21" x 11", G, $215.00 C.

Sanford's Inks, sign, tin, litho, embossed, products in jars and bottles, by the Tuscarora Advertising Co., Coshocton, OH, 19½" x 13½", 1890s, P ............................................................$300.00 D

Sanita Malt Coffee, sign, paper, litho, two small girls at table, 10" x 15", EX.................................................................$50.00 C

Sanitary Ice Cream and Milk, clock, metal body with glass face and lenses, light-up, 15" dia., VG ...............................................$155.00 C

Sanitary Netted Spounge, container, metal, round, product lettering, VG ............................................................$55.00 D

Sanka coffee, can, square, slip lid, sample, EX...................$65.00 D

Santa Fe Cigar, box, cardboard, decorated with lady in white, EX ....................................................................$65.00 C

Santa Fe Coffee, can, metal, showing railroad workers, key wind lid, 1 lb, EX.......................................................$275.00 C

Santa Fe Pure Ground Mustard, spice tin, paper label, Indian beside trademark, 3¼" x 2⅛ x 1¼", EX...............................$55.00 C

Santa Fe Railroad, sign, porcelain, "The scout," Indian on horseback, 40" x 20", NM .......................................................$6000.00B

Santovin, sign, tin, litho, veterinary remedy, animals and sunrise, 20⅛" x 27⅛", NM ...............................................$195.00 C

Sapolio Soap, sign, paper, trolley, man and woman shown using the product, 21" x 11", EX.......................................................$165.00 B

Satin Luminall, thermometer, metal, painted, vertical scale in center with product messages at top and bottom, "one coat," 8½" x 38½", EX.......................................................................$75.00 C

Satin Skin Cream & Powder, sign, cardboard, die cut, countertop, woman and cherub, 18" x 18", 1911, VG ..........................$210.00 C

Satin Turkish Cigarettes, serving tray, metal, "20 for 15¢," 13¾" dia., EX .......................................................................$55.00 C

Sauer's Flavoring and Extracts, clock, wood case with reverse painting and lettering, 42½" H, VG .............................................$1,200.00 D

Scotch Woolen Mills, store sign, cardboard, wood, and tin, light up, 38" wide, VG, $100.00 B.

Scudder's, Brownie Brand Confection Butter Maple Flavor, can, Brownie characters, 1½-lb., EX, $240.00 B. *Courtesy of Morford Auctions.*

Scull's Coffee, store bin, tin, great stencil and litho graphics, 21½" H, EX, $925.00 B. *Courtesy of Richard Opfer Auctioneering, Inc.*

Seagram's, Canadian Hunter, poster, paper, wood frame, 34½" x 78¼", VG, $95.00 C.

Sealy Mattress, display, includes print with black workers picking cotton, and three die cut black figures working in cotton, unusual to find the die cut items, EX, $1,550.00 B. *Courtesy of Buffalo Bay Auction Co.*

---

Sauer's Flavoring Extracts, clock, wood and metal, New Haven regulator style with product information, EX.....................$1,300.00 C

Sauer's Flavoring Extracts, thermometer, wood, 7¾" x 23½", G .$185.00 C

Sauer's Flavoring Extracts, thermometer, wood, product box, VG .................................................................................$250.00 C

Sav'n Sam Ethyl Gasoline, pump sign, metal, cowboy with a wad of money, 10" dia., EX...........................................................$375.00 C

Sav'n Sam's Super Ethyl Gasoline, pump sign, porcelain, cowboy with a hand full of money, 10" dia., EX.............................$695.00 C

Sav-More System, regular gas globe, plastic body with glass lenses, 13½" dia., VG .................................................................$450.00 C

Savage Arms, firearms catalog, Indian with firearm, 28 pages, 1935, VG ......................................................................................$185.00 B

Savage Revolvers, watch fob, metal, revolver, EX.................$125.00 D

Savage Stevens Fox Shotguns, poster, cardboard, geese in flight, 16" x 12", NM.................................................................$150.00 C

Save More, pump sign, porcelain, name over dollar sign, 10" x 12", EX....................................................................................$495.00 C

Sayman's Soap, store box, lid that folds into display unit containing 12 full bars of vegetable soap, 7" x 6½" x 2½", EX.............$145.00 C

Scandinavian-American Lines, sign, metal, ocean line departing with seaport in background, 41" x 37", EX .......................$900.00 C

Schell's Carbonated Mead, sign, Prohibition advertising for August Schell Brewing Co., New Ulm, Mn., great artwork of woman with peacock, 16¼" x 33", VG....................................................$825.00 C

Seay's Breeze, peanut dish, glass photo of "Cousin Buster," this was a popular location located in a wet county on the county line of a dry county, 1950 – 60s, 4¾" dia., EX, $65.00 C. *Courtesy of B.J. Summers.*

Sellars & Gholson, letter opener, wood and metal, trowel shaped giveaway opener, 6¼" x 1½", G, $15.00 C. *Courtesy of B.J. Summers.*

Sensation Smoking Tobacco, lunch pail, metal, double swing handles, 7" long, VG, $50.00 B.

Seven Up, display, cardboard, easel back, "...Your Stand-By Always Likes You," 1940s, 18" high, EX, $300.00 C.

Seven Up, kick plate, porcelain, bottle with bathing beauty, 1951, 30" x 12", VG, $850.00 B.

---

Schell's Mead, sign, stone litho, August Schell Brewery in New Ulm, MN, featuring woman and peacock, very colorful, 16" x 32", 1910, G..........................$575.00 C

Schepps Cake, tin litho, embossed, vintage family scene, 13" x 13" x 14", VG ..........................$165.00 B

Schlaich Locks, box, tin, litho, store counter display for the Boyce MotoMeter, 13" x 2 x 8¾", VG..........................$325.00 C

Schlitz Beer, sign, litho, from Chas. Shonk Co., logo man in center, 13½" x 19", EX..........................$2,030.00 B

Schlitz Hotel & Palm Garden, pocket knife, complimentary, clown in center, "Milwaukee Carnival Knife," EX ..........................$95.00 C

Schlitz Jos Brewing Co's Milwaukee Buck Beer, sign, paper, king with a large goblet, 1890s, 24" x 37", EX..........................$600.00 C

Schlitz Jos Brewing Co., sign, metal, Statue of Liberty, "Loved By Millions," 1942, 22" x 28", EX ..........................$250.00 C

Schlitz, bottle flashlight, VG ..........................$45.00 D

Schlitz, display figure, chalkware, man holding bottle, 1950s, 18" tall, EX..........................$55.00 D

Schlitz, match and stamp safe, metal, embossed sides, two separate compartments, 1½" x 3", EX ..........................$195.00 C

Schlitz, match safe, metal, leather embossed logo and cigar cutter on bottom, VG..........................$95.00 D

Schlitz, radio, plastic, in likeness of trademark globe, 6" x 8", EX .$95.00 C

Schlitz, salt & pepper set, VG ..........................$20.00 C

Schlitz, sign, cardboard, factory scene, "The Beer That Made...," 1903, 38" x 26", EX ..........................$450.00 C

Schlitz, sign, glass, reverse painting, globe logo, "On Draught," 12" x 16", VG ..........................$250.00 B

Schlitz, sign, metal and cardboard, tilted bottle and pilsner glass, "For Great Occasions," 11" x 16", EX..........................$65.00 D

Seven Up, sign, tin, embossed, 13¾" x 18", 1947, EX, $190.00 B. *Courtesy of Buffalo Bay Auction Co.*

Seven Up, sign, tin, embossed, art deco style logo, "You Like It...It Likes You," 1940 – 50s, 28" x 20", VG, $400.00 B.

Seven Up, sign, tin, heavily embossed, large oval with side fans, 1958, 41" x 42", EX, $800.00 B.

Seven Up, sign, tin, outdoor, wooden frame, joined in center, 1971, 8' x 8', VG, $100.00 B.

Seven Up, sign, curb side, policeman, "Slow School Zone," 34" x 61½", VG, $1,000.00 B. *Courtesy of Collectors Auction Services.*

Seven Up, thermometer, aluminum, dial-type, "Likes You," 10" dia., NM, $225.00 C. *Courtesy of Autopia Advertising Auctions.*

---

**Schlitz,** sign, metal and glass, light up, trademark globe with bottle of the product, "Have A Bottle Now," EX..............................$95.00 D

**Schlitz,** sign, neon, original wood crate, three-color, red, blue, and green, 1930s, 17" x 29", NM ...............................................$490.00 B

**Schlitz,** sign, neon, plastic globe, 1970s, 20" x 19", EX..........$2,255.00 C

**Schlitz,** sign, paper, "Purity," in original frame, 28" x 28", EX .$1,650.00 B

**Schlitz,** sign, porcelain, in shape of globe, 14" dia., VG ....$185.00 D

**Schlitz,** tray, round, company logo, tip size, EX................$100.00 C

**Schmauss Garden Cafe, Milwaukee, Wis.,** tip tray, metal, very colorful restaurant interior scene, 6" dia., EX .........................$95.00 C

**Schmidt Jacob Brewing Co.,** sign, metal, "Schmidt Brg Co's Big Game," 32" x 24", VG.....................................................$1,600.00 C

**Schmidt's,** bartender, bronze, embossed lettering, 7¾" H, VG .$175.00 C

**Scholl's Axle Grease,** pail, tin, litho, metal handle, runaway wagon, "Independent Oil Co., Mansfield, Ohio," 6" x 9½", EX..............$80.00 B

**School Boy Peanut Butter,** pail, tin, litho, side-mounted wire bail, 2-lb., EX...............................................................................$110.00 C

**School Boy,** crate label, paper, boy with apples, EX.........$175.00 D

**School Days Sifted Early Variety Peas,** can, metal, paper label, football player, VG .............................................................$75.00 D

Sharples Cream Separator, sign, metal, "used on this farm," G, $325.00 C.

Sharples, pot scraper, woman at separator, "The 1909 tubulars are better than ever," 1909, EX, $280.00 B. *Courtesy of Buffalo Bay Auction Co.*

Sharples Separator, sign, metal, self-framing, cherub and lady operating separator, EX, $2,900.00 C. *Courtesy of Buffalo Bay Auction Co.*

Shaw & Truesdell Scratch & Chick Foods, sign, cardboard, farmyard scene, 21" x 31", VG, $925.00 B. *Courtesy of Past Tyme Pleasures.*

Shawnee Fire Insurance Company, sign, wood, litho, Tecumseh, Chief of the Shawnee, 21" x 15", VG, $395.00 C.

---

**Schoor-Kolkschneider Brewing Co's S & K Select,** sign, paper, German tavern, 19" x 14", EX ..........................................$350.00 C

**Schroeder's Honey Top Whiskey,** sign, metal, self-framing, "I'm In a Perdickermunt," 23" x 33", EX....................................$1,500.00 C

**Schroeder,** calendar, horseshoeing, blacksmithing, and general repairing, young girl in bonnet, 14½" x 20", EX...............................$450.00 C

**Schulteiss Beer,** sign, porcelain, German spelling of "bier," 24" x 47½", VG ..........................................................................$95.00 B

**Schuster's Root Beer,** tray, metal, boy and girl sharing a table, "Drink...It's Healthful," 13" x 13", EX ................................$450.00 D

**Schwen's Ice Cream,** sign, celluloid, company logo, "Delicious Malted Milk," 9" dia., NM.........................................................$300.00 B

**Scissors Cut Plug,** container, metal, vertical pocket tin, scissors on front, EX..................................................................$3,000.00 B

**Scott's Emulsion,** trolley sign, cardboard, boy and girl playing marbles, "Wise Parents Hand Down The Health Secret," 1920s, 24" x 11", VG...........................................................................$195.00 D

**Scotten Dillon Company, Detroit, Mich., Ojibwa Tobacco,** store bin, tin, litho, originally had 48 five-cent packages, 8½" x 11¼", G..........................................................................$325.00 B

**Scudder's Brownie Brand Confection Butter Maple Flavor,** container, Brownie characters, 1½-lb., VG......................................$155.00 C

**Scull's Coffee,** store bin, tin, great stenciling and litho, 21½" H, VG ..........................................................................$795.00 C

**Sea Foam Baking Powder,** sign, paper, company name, women swimming from a boat, 12" x 20", VG..............................$275.00 D

**Sea Gull Baking Powder,** tin, paper, litho, sea gull in flight, unopened, 2⅛" x 3¼", EX................................................$275.00 B

Shaws Malt Whiskey, sign, tin, litho, servant waiting on woman and child in foreground, 16" x 22", VG, $750.00 B.

Shell, sign, die cut, metal, one-sided, scantily clad girl, rare item, probably foreign, 6½" x 15½", EX, $1,300.00 C.

Sherrill-Russell Lumber Co., paperweight, glass, 1920 – 30s, 4" x 2½", EX, $75.00 C.
*Courtesy of B.J. Summers.*

Sherwin-Williams Paints, sign, metal, painted, "Cover the Earth," EX, $300.00 C.

Silk Hosiery, sign, mirror, acid-etched, figural hanging, 13" H, G, $625.00 B. *Courtesy of Richard Opfer Auctioneering, Inc.*

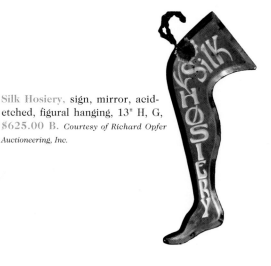

Seagram's Queen's & King's Plate Winners, sign, paper, 1905, 49½" x 35", G ........................................................$250.00 C

Seagram's Seven Crown, clock, metal housing with pressed form front, horses on front, 16" x 14½", VG........................$110.00 C

Seal of Kentucky Mustard, tin, paper, cardboard, litho, seal of Kentucky on front, Covington, Ky., 1½-oz., NM ....................$223.00 B

Seal of North Carolina Tobacco, box, wood, paper label, date on revenue stamp, 1883, EX ................................................$300.00 D

Seal of North Carolina, sign, paper, litho, six black men and a dog, 21¼" x 24¼", VG.......................................................$1,500.00 D

Seal of North Carolina, sign, paper, litho, woman lying on a day bed and a bird on a swing over the bed, inset of product in upper right corner, 12" x 7½", NM.............................................$255.00 C

Sealed Power Piston Ring Sets, calendar, paper, two boys boxing while being watched by a dog, 16" x 34", VG.......................$65.00 D

Sealed Power Piston Rings, ashtray, metal chromed and Bakelite bowl, 5" x 6", VG...............................................................$100.00 B

Sealed Power Piston Rings, sign, double-sided, light-up, dealer, 34" x 14" x 6", VG...................................................................$275.00 C

Sealed Power Piston Rings, sign, plastic, light up, logo on both sides, VG...................................................................$185.00 B

Sealed Power Piston Rings, thermometer, metal, scale type reading, "Franchised Dealer Expert Engine Service," 8" x 39", VG ...$195.00 D

Sealtest Dairy Products, clock, plastic, light-up, square, 15¼" sq., G ...............................................................................$1,115.00 C

Sealtest Ice Cream, menu board, tin, product name over nine message panels, 9¾" x 25⅝", G ...............................................$100.00 B

Sealtest Ice Cream, sign, cardboard, strawberry sundae, 19" x 20", VG ...................................................................................$55.00 D

Sealtest Ice Cream, sign, tin, embossed, self-framing, "Sealtest Ice Cream," 30" x 14", G .........................................................$195.00 C

Sealtest, menu board, metal frame with cardboard inserts for flavors and prices, 10" x 22", EX ...............................................$95.00 C

Silver Birch Chewing Gum, store counter display box with unopened packages of gum, 6¼" x 5½" x 4¼", EX, $1,500.00 B. *Courtesy of Wm Morford Investment Grade Collectibles.*

Silver Cup Chewing Tobacco, thermometer, metal, scale type reading, 38½" tall, VG, $225.00 C.

Silver Flash, gas globe, one-piece glass body, 15" x 6" x 16¼", VG, $3,500.00 B. *Courtesy of Collectors Auction Services.*

Sinclair Coal Co., thermometer, "Parade of the Finest," strong graphics, 8¼" x 38⅝", VG, $425.00 C.

Sinclair Opaline Motor Oil, sign, porcelain, double-sided, logo Dino, 1940s, 24" dia., EX, $1,100.00 B.

Sealy Mattress, display, cardboard, four-piece, die cut, litho, easel backs, life-size characters, man with cotton basket on his shoulder, a couple of black children, and scene of slaves picking cotton in field, VG ..................................................................$650.00 C

Search Light, match box holder, instruction on front, original box, NM ..................................................................$150.00 B

Sears Rivera Coffee, pail with small lid, 7¼" x 10½", EX ..$295.00 C

Sears Roebuck & Co Tea, pail, 5 lb., EX.........................$150.00 D

Sears Roebuck & Co., catalog, "Our Catalog List," 1909, 50 pages, VG.........................................................$50.00 D

Sears, Roebuck & Co., catalog, paper, farm equipment, 1938, 102 pages, VG .........................................................$65.00 D

Sears, Roebuck & Co, catalog, paper, Fall / Winter, 1912, 1458 pages, VG .........................................................$225.00 D

Sears, Roebuck & Co., catalog, paper, #112, hardbound, 1902, 1200 pages, EX.........................................................$250.00 C

Sears, Roebuck & Co., tape measure, cloth, "The world's Largest Store...," VG ................................................................$100.00 B

Sears, Roebuck and Co. Chicago, tip tray, metal, factory scene and Lady Justice, 6", EX.........................................................$75.00 B

Sears, Roebuck and Co., Sun-Kist, tobacco canister, tin, litho, 4¼" x 5", EX .........................................................$135.00 C

Seiberling Air-Cooled Tires, sign, porcelain, double-sided, 30" x 17½", VG ................................................................$375.00 B

Seiberling Tires, sign, cardboard, bust of a lady, " Mothers Too Perfer...," 26" x 43", EX .........................................................$165.00 C

Seipp's Extra Plae Beer, tray, metal, girl in pigtails at party in the moon light, 1911, EX .........................................................$200.00 D

Selmer Band Instruments, clock, light-up, band member in various poses for hour positions, 16" dia., EX ...............................$750.00 B

Seminola Cigar, sign, celluloid, embossed, Indian bust, 9" x 6", NM ..................................................................$135.00 C

Sir Walter Raleigh Smoking Tobacco, sign, porcelain, vertical pocket tin pictured, 1930s, 36" x 12", VG, $1,300.00 B.

Skinner's Satins, sign, tin, litho, self-framing, Indian in full headress, 16" x 19½", NM, $3,375.00 B.

Slade's Spices and Baking Powder, sign, paper, litho, small girl with flowers, 20" x 25¾", G, $475.00 B. *Courtesy of Richard Opfer Auctioneering, Inc.*

Smile, sign, tin, easel back, tripod, Smile man serving at counter, 1920s, 27" x 41", G, $1,000.00 B. *Courtesy of Muddy River Trading Co./Gary Metz.*

---

**Seminole Coffee,** can, metal, paper label, square, smaller top screw lid, Indian in profile, 3 lb., EX..............................................$110.00 B

**Seminole Coffee,** can, metal, slip lid, Indian, 1 lb., VG .$475.00 B

**Senate Beer,** door plate, metal, "We Recommend...Buy It Here," 11" tall, VG .....................................................................................$85.00 D

**Seneca Red Top Socks,** box, cardboard, Indian in center of arrowhead, kids ice skating, 5" x 14" x 2", NM ...........................$65.00 C

**Senn & Ackerman Brewing Co.,** pocket mirror, Elk Carnival, elk head in center, "Elks Carnival... Oct-1899," 2" dia., 1899, EX ......$150.00 C

**Senora Cubana,** sign, metal, embossed, die cut, Perecoy & Moore's Cigars, lady in fur jacket, 7¼" x 13", EX ............................$135.00 C

**Senour's Floor Paint,** sign, porcelain, "Water Proof / Heel Proof," 32" x 4", EX ...............................................................................$275.00 B

**Sensation Smoking Tobacco,** lunch box, metal, double handles, VG .......................................................................................................$25.00 C

**Sensible Tobacco,** sign, metal, "Wise Men Smoke...," 20" x 9", VG ...................................................................................................$200.00 D

**Serv-us Brand Coffee,** tin, litho, screw-on lid, steaming cup of product, 1-lb., EX ...................................................................................$95.00 C

**Serv-Us-Coffee,** can, metal, screw lid, 1 lb., VG .................$75.00 C

**Seven Up,** clock, glass, wood, and metal light-up, "You Like It. . . It Likes You," 16" x 16" x 4", EX ..........................................$135.00 C

**Seven Up,** clock, light-up, 7up with bubbles in center, 15" x 15", VG ...................................................................................................$145.00 C

**Seven Up,** clock, plastic face and wood frame, square, light-up, "You Like It...It Likes You," 15" x 15", G ..........................$95.00 C

**Seven Up,** door push, porcelain, "Fresh Up...Seven Up," 31" x 3", VG.................................................................................................$135.00 B

**Seven Up,** lamp, one-quart bottle base and Seven Up shade, from the San Diego, Calif. bottling company, 15" x 24", 1950s, VG ...$190.00 B

**Seven Up,** rack sign, tin, "You Like It...It Likes You," metal wire slots for placing bags, 38½" x 17½", EX.....................$275.00 C

**Seven Up,** sign, die cut, embossed, bottle, 13" x 44½", 1962, EX.................................................................................................$350.00 C

Smiley Sand & Gravel Co., playing cards, plastic, game birds on the back of the cards by noted naturalist artist Richard E. Bishop, double set in original container, one set is still sealed, EX, $75.00 C.

Smith Lumber Co., paperweight, glass, advertising strip in center with customer information, 1900s, 3" dia., EX, $145.00 C. *Courtesy of B.J. Summers.*

Snow King Baking Powder, countertop display, die cut, Santa Claus in sleigh being pulled by reindeer, 29" x 17", EX, $750.00 B. *Courtesy of Buffalo Bay Auction Co.*

Snow King Baking Powder, sign, cardboard, die cut, Santa in sled and reindeer, 1900s, 36" x 20", EX, $625.00 C.

Southern Bell Telephone and Telegraph Co./American Telephone & Telegraph Co., globe, milk glass, at one time these hung at Bell business offices, getting to be a hard item to find, blue lettering and bell on white, NM, $1,100.00 C. *Courtesy of B.J. Summers.*

Seven Up, sign, metal, 6 pack in center, "Fresh Up With...," 1950s, 60" x 36", NM.................................$700.00 C

Seven Up, sign, metal, "First Against thirst," 23" x 15", VG ..$95.00 D

Seven Up, sign, metal, "Fresh Up / 7-Up / Likes You," 26" x 35", VG ...............................................................$400.00 D

Seven Up, sign, metal, bottle shape with Bubble Girl on label, EX ....................................................................$975.00 C

Seven Up, sign, metal, double-sided, flange, "Likes You," 12½" x 10", 1946, EX ...................................................$275.00 C

Seven Up, sign, metal, rolled edges, oval with bubbles, "You Like It...It Likes You," 1947, 30" x 40", VG .............................$295.00 C

Seven Up, sign, tin, embossed, 13¾" x 18", 1947, VG.......$175.00 C

Seven Up, sign, tin, embossed, "Fresh Up," NOS, made by Stout Sign Co., 6¾" x 13¼", 1960, NM.........................................$125.00 C

Seven Up, sign, tin, embossed, a mesh wire frame, 28" x 50", VG................................................................$150.00 B

Seven Up, sign, tin, embossed, bottle neck, "Fresh Up with," 27" x 19", NM....................................................................$370.00 B

Seven Up, sign, tin, embossed, octagon, "it likes you," 14" x 13¾", G.....................................................................$225.00 C

Seven Up, sign, tin, vintage, "anti-acid...Lithiated Lemon Soda," 9" x 20", 20s, G ....................................................$325.00 C

Seven Up, thermometer, metal and glass, dial type reading, 7Up bubbles logo in center of face, 12" dia., EX.......................$210.00 B

Seven Up, thermometer, porcelain, bottle, "The fresh Up Family Drink," 15" tall, EX..........................................$150.00 B

Seven Up, thermometer, porcelain, VG............................$135.00 C

Seven Up, thermometer, tin, "Fresh Up," NOS, 6" x 15", NM..$225.00 C

Seven-Up, sign, curb side, policeman, "Slow School Zone," 34" x 61½", EX ..............................................................$1,500.00 C

Sexton Sanatary Ajax, garbage can, metal, salesman sample, 4" tall, EX................................................................$300.00 D

Southwestern Bell Telephone Co., sign, porcelain, double-sided, flange, 11" x 11⅞", 1950s, EX, $275.00 B. *Courtesy of B.J. Summers.*

Sparkeeta UP Soda, sign, cardboard, framed, "California's flavorite," pretty red-haired woman with bottle of product, 25¾" x 31½", NM, $325.00 C. *Courtesy of Autopia Advertising Auctions.*

Spear Head Plug Chew Tobacco, sign, tin, heavy relief and embossing, 28" x 10", EX, $500.00 B. *Courtesy of Muddy River Trading Co./Gary Metz.*

Springfield Breweries Co., calendar, paper, pretty lady with a large hat, all months show at once at bottom, printers proof, 1911, 23" x 31", VG, $2,000.00 B.

Squeeze, sign, "Drink...that distinctive carbonated beverage," young cartoon figures on bench in front of a full moon, 28" x 10", EX, $235.00 B. *Courtesy of Past Tyme Pleasures.*

---

Shaker and New Tariff Ranges, trade card, Lt. Greenley with Eskimos at North Pole, 10" x 6", NM ............................$130.00 B

Shaler Rislone The Oil Alloy, thermometer, metal, painted, vertical scale, product can to left of scale, 9½" x 25", EX ................$95.00 C

Shamrock Coffee, tin, litho, pry-lid, cloverleaf in back of steaming coffee cup, 4" x 5", EX ......................................................$75.00 D

Shamrock Trail Master Regular, pump sign, porcelain, single-sided shamrock, 10½" x 10½", VG ...........................$240.00 B

Shamrock, gas globe, plastic and glass, name on shamrock, 14" dia., EX..................................................................$550.00 C

Shamrock, gas globe, plastic and glass, shamrock and company name, 16" x 12", EX..........................................................$775.00 C

Sharp's Kreemy Toffee, container, metal, square, girl on front enjoying product, 5" x 4" x 7", EX .....................................$75.00 B

Sharpleigh Hardware Co., sign, tin over cardboard, "Hope Inspires...Work Wins...Success Rewards," St. Louis, U.S.A., 9¼" x 6¼", EX................................................................$50.00 C

Sharples, match holder, "The Pet of the Dairy," mother and daughter, great graphics, 2" x 7", EX......................................$195.00 C

Sharples, match holder, metal, "The Pet of the Dairy," NM...$775.00 B

Sharples, match safe, tin, litho, woman operating the product, 2" x 6¾", EX.....................................................................$285.00 B

Sharples, sign, metal, double-sided, die cut, man filling the separator while it's being cranked by a young girl, 19" x 27", VG........$650.00 B

Sharples, sign, tin, embossed, tubular cream separator, 10" x 14", EX...............................................................................$315.00 B

Shasta Coffee, can, metal, key wind lid, 1 lb., EX ............$340.00 B

Shasta Sparkling Beverages, sign, metal, mountain scenery, "Water-Mixes-Flavors, It Hasta To Be Shasta," 24" x 12", VG..........$180.00 D

Shasta Sparkling Beverages, sign, tin, snow-covered mountains, 23½" x 11½", NM .....................................................$180.00 B

Shave Master Electric Shaver, countertop display unit for Sunbeam shavers, 10" x 10" x 16", EX .............................................$215.00 B

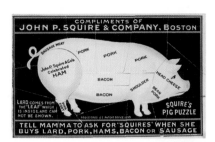

Squeeze, sign, porcelain, "Drink...that distinctive," 1940s, 28" x 10", EX, $500.00 B.

Squire & Company Boston, puzzle, cardboard, various cuts of meat from a pig, "...Squire's Pig Puzzle," 1899, 11" x 7", EX, $250.00 C.

Squire's Hams, sign, tin, embossed, self-framing, sitting pig in center of sign, "John P. Squire & Company, Boston,", 1906, 20" x 24", EX, $300.00 B. *Courtesy of Muddy River Trading Co./Gary Metz.*

Squirrel Brand Peanut Butter, pail, squirrel in center window, EX, $700.00 B.

Squirt, clock, light-up, large size boy and product bottle, 15" dia., 1946, NM, $600.00 C.

---

**Shave Master Electric Shaver,** countertop display unit for Sunbeam shavers, 10" x 10" x 16", G .................................................$105.00 D

**Shaw & Truesdell Scratch & Chick Foods,** sign, cardboard, farmyard scene, 21" x 31", F.................................................$310.00 C

**Shaw Piano,** sign, die cut, easel back, young girl with her dogs, 6¼" x 8¼", 1892, EX.................................................$45.00 B

**Sheboygan Natural Mineral Water,** sign, tin, litho, "Better Than Imported," Indian being served by black waiters, 1910, 10" x 14", EX.................................................$660.00 B

**Shell Air Meter,** sign, double-sided, die cut, clam, 11¾" x 11⅛", VG .................................................$950.00 C

**Shell Diesoline,** gas glaobe, glass, logo shape and debossed lettering, 18" x 17", EX .................................................$950.00 C

**Shell Fly Control,** sign, metal, black & red lettering, "Protected By Shell Fly Control Program," 18" x 15", VG .....................$100.00 B

**Shell Gasoline & Motor Oil,** calendar, pretty woman, titled Roxana, from Lockport, Illinois, with full monthly pad, 10¼" x 17", 1929, EX.................................................$135.00 C

**Shell Gasoline, Motor Oil,** thermometer, porcelain, clam shell logo at top and bottom of scale, 1910s, 27" tall, EX.................$3,800.00 B

**Shell Gasoline,** sign, porcelain, paddle-type in shape of shell clam, 15" x 12", EX .................................................$700.00 B

**Shell Gasoline,** thermometer, porcelain, scale-type, promoting both gasoline and motor oil, 7¼" x 27", VG............$1,800.00 B

**Shell Golden Oil,** watch fob, metal, shell logo, 1½" dia., EX..$225.00 C

**Shell Kerosene / Range Oil,** sign, porcelain, red lettering and logos, double-sided, 15" x 20", EX.................................................$2,300.00 C

**Shell Motor Oil,** sign, porcelain, die cut, double-sided, clam shell in center, in likeness of oil can, 15¾" x 20", G.................$600.00 B

Squirt, tray, tin, litho, serving, "Squirt, The Drink with the Happy Taste," 11½" x 14½", G, $275.00 B.

Squirt Soda, sign, tin, flange, "Drink...It's In The Public Eye," 1942, 18" x 14", VG, $400.00 B.

Stacey's, stemmed wine glass and swizzle stick, once a popular restaurant and lounge it's been closed for years, 1950 – 60s, 8½" tall, NM, $35.00 C.
*Courtesy of B.J. Summers.*

Staley's Vitality Dog Foods, sign, tin, self-framing, embossed, 19⅛" x 27⅛", VG, $175.00 C.

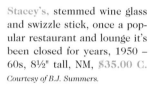

Standard Heating Oils, sign, porcelain, die cut, 24" x 15", EX, $275.00 C.
*Courtesy of Autopia Advertising Auctions.*

Standard Oil, sign, tin, die cut, double-sided, flange, "Credit Cards Good Here," NOS, first Standard Oil card sign, 23¾" x 25½", 1932, EX, $600.00 B.
*Courtesy of Autopia Advertising Auctions.*

---

**Shell Motor Oil**, sign, porcelain, oil being poured from can, Shell logo and red lettering, 41" x 40", NM ....................$2,000.00 C

**Shell Oil Company**, sign, porcelain, one-sided, "Private Road," 14⅞" x 11", VG ...........................................................$750.00 B

**Shell Oil**, toy truck, metal, Chevy style, foreign, 13" long, EX..$200.00 C

**Shell Premium Gasoline**, pump sign, porcelain, die cut, classic clam shell shape, 12" x 12¼", NM .....................................$975.00 B

**Shell Spirits / Oils**, sign, porcelain, double-sided, flange mount, die cut, "Stop & Fill Up Here With Shell," 24" x 18", EX ........$875.00 C

**Shell Station**, sign, porcelain, architectural shape of trademark clam shell, 23" x 24" x 7½", EX .........................................$800.00 C

**Shell Transmission Oil**, can, metal, grip handle and pour spout, shell lettering in red, 1 gal., EX........................................$225.00 C

**Shell**, badge, metal, in shape of company logo with red inlaid cloisonne Shell name, 2" x 2", EX ...........................................$450.00 B

**Shell**, clock, light-up, double-bubble, Pam Clock Co., New Rochelle, NY, great clam shell sign in center of clock face, hard-to-find this variation, 15½" sq., EX.......................................................$650.00 C

**Shell**, flag, cloth, early company logo in center, mfg. by Emerson Mfg., S.F., Cal., NOS, 70" x 47", 1920s, NM .........$350.00 B

**Shell**, gas globe, glass, red lettering on clam shell, one piece, 20" dia., EX.................................................................$850.00 C

**Shell**, gas globe, milk glass, one-piece, clam-shaped globe, 18½" h, VG.....................................................................$575.00 C

**Shell**, poster, paper, litho, "Share-the-Road Club," 39¼" x 56", EX .........................................................................$175.00 C

Stag Tobacco, humidor, tin, large stag on front and hunt scene on side, 6½" high, VG, $160.00 B.

Standard Oil, lighter, metal, premium give away by the distributor E.M. Bailey, Paducah, KY, 1½" x 2½" x ½", VG, $25.00 C. *Courtesy of B.J. Summers.*

Stanley Garage Door Holders, sign, tin, litho, vintage garage door, "Hold Your Garage Doors Open," 34" x 26¼", 1910s, EX, $1,000.00 C. *Courtesy of Autopia Advertising Auctions.*

Star Stamps, sign, tin, embossed, litho, "...Redeemed at Sears," 31" x 12", EX, $55.00 B.

Star Tobacco, sign, porcelain, "Sold Here," 24" wide, VG, $275.00 B.

---

Shell, radiator cover, cardboard, double-sided, 18" x 13½", VG ............................................................................$55.00 C

Shell, service station letter set, porcelain, one-sided, 15" H, VG ........................................................................$195.00 B

Shell, sign, cardboard, die cut, "Starts Quickly," Shell logo, 21" x 13", EX............................................................$85.00 C

Shell, sign, metal, one-sided, "Protected by...fly control program," clam shell logo, 18" x 15", G...........................$160.00 B

Shell, sign, neon and porcelain, shape of a clam shell logo, 48" x 48", EX ......................................................$1,500.00 C

Shell, sign, paper, "Super Shell," caracature waiting on trolley car, "Saves On Stop & Go Driving," 57" x 33", EX..................$225.00 C

Shell, sign, porcelain, shape of arrow, "From The Pump, Shell," 36" x 12", EX ....................................................$2,200.00 C

Shell, X-100 pump spinner, in original box, promoting motor oil, NOS, 14½" x 8" x 17", EX..................................$275.00 B

Shenango China / Inca Ware, ashtray, ceramic, salesman sample, Dixie Restaurant Equipment Co., 5" dia., EX .....................$50.00 D

Sherbrooke Pure Milk Co., sign, tin, double-sided, ice cream cone, 20" x 28", VG........................................................$80.00 B

Sheridan Sugar Co., pocket mirror, celluloid, factory, 2¾" x 1¾", EX..................................................................$95.00 C

Sherwin-Williams Auto Enamels, display, metal, man on top of car advertising sample colors below, 12" x 16", EX ...............$225.00 D

Sherwin-Williams Paints & Varnishes, sign, metal, flange, double-sided, "Sold Here," 22" x 16", EX......................................$250.00 C

Sherwin-Williams Paints and Varnishes, sign, porcelain, "Sold Here," "Covers The Earth" logo at left, top mounting holes, 22" x 16", NM.......$325.00 C

Stark Trees, sign, oil cloth, bear, "Stark Trees Bear" on his side, 15" wide, VG, $95.00 B.

St. Bruno Tobacco, sign, cardboard, 3-D, die cut, stand-up, from the Imperial Tobacco Co. of Great Britian, blacks packing tobacco leaves, 20" x 14½", 1915s, EX, $850.00 B. *Courtesy of Buffalo Bay Auction Co.*

Steamro Red Hots, sign, porcelain, 17¼" x 2¼", VG, $205.00 C.

Sterling Beer, sign, tin, banner with bottle image, chain hung, 1940s, EX, $325.00 B.

Sterling, thermometer, porcelain and brass, rare item, 9½" x 12¼", EX, $1,000.00 B.

---

**Sherwin-Williams Paints,** sign, porcelain, double-sided, flange, "Cover the Earth" logo, 33" x 48", NM .............................$900.00 C

**Sherwin-Williams Paints,** sign, porcelain, paint covering the world, 48" x 36", VG.............................................$275.00 C

**Sherwin-Williams Paints-Varnishes-Enamels,** sign, porcelain, double-sided, hanging, with bracket, 12" x 8", NM .........................$600.00 C

**Sherwin-Williams Paints-Varnishes-Enamels,** sign, porcelain, double-sided, hanging, with bracket, 12" x 8", VG .........................$275.00 C

**Sherwin-Williams,** sign, porcelain, single-sided, die cut, product pouring over the world, 35½" x 63", VG .........................$975.00 C

**Sherwood's Confectionery and Grocery,** calendar, Indians hunting buffalo, 7" x 9½", 1925, NM.................................$100.00 B

**Shick Shaver,** mirror, glass, painted, "No Blades / No Lather...," 7" x 10", EX ...........................................................$75.00 D

**Shinola Shoe Polish,** shoe horn, metal, supplies, 4" long, EX..$15.00 D

**Shipmate Cigarettes,** pocket mirror, two sailors on front, 2" dia., VG ...........................................................$185.00 B

**Showanda Cigar,** tin, paper label, round, Indian on front, 25-ct, EX.............................................................$185.00 B

**Shredded Wheat,** sign, paper, litho, framed, box of product and bowl of cereal, 16" x 10½", VG ...................................$60.00 B

**Shryack Rolled Oats,** container, from Missouri, 3-lb., VG ..$55.00 C

**Sidney Dillon Cigar,** sign, tin, litho, self-framing, horse, 22¼" x 17", EX..............................................................$450.00 B

**Sierra Ice Cream,** tray, metal, oval, deep sides, mountain logo, 16" x 13", EX.............................................................$250.00 C

**Sierra Ice Cream,** tray, metal, serving, 16¼" x 12¾", NM .$235.00 B

**Signal Gasoline,** pump sign, porcelain, trademark signal light in center, 11⅞" dia., VG............................................$400.00 C

St. Joseph Asprin, clock, glass and metal, light up, double bubble with difficult to locate 3-d center asprin, 15" dia., EX, $220.00 B.

Studebaker Authorized Sales & Service, sign, porcelain, double-sided, 48" dia., 1940s, EX, $725.00 B. *Courtesy of Muddy River Trading Co./Gary Metz.*

Success Manure Spreader, tip tray, metal, litho, horse drawn manure wagon at work, by Kemp & Burpee Mfg. Co., Syracuse, NY, 4¾" x 3¼", EX, $155.00 B.

Sunbeam Blue Ribbon, door push, metal, die cut, shape of a loaf of bread, 19" high, EX, $270.00 B.

Sunbeam Bread, door push, bread loaf cut-out in center of door bar, used on screen doors before air conditioning to protect screens, 1950s, 30" x 15", EX, $300.00 C.

**Signal Gasoline,** pump sign, porcelain, yellow name around traffic signal, 12" dia., EX .............................................$650.00 C

**Signal Lubrication Chek-Chart System,** sign, porcelain, double-sided, top-hung, 30" x 24", EX.....................................$400.00 B

**Signal Products,** sign, waxed cardboard, traffic light logo on yellow background, 21" x 13", EX................................$145.00 C

**Silencer,** gas globe, low profile metal body with two glass lenses, "Stops Knocks," "Made by Burford Oil Company," 15" dia., VG ....$1,300.00 B

**Silent Chief Gasoline,** sign, porcelain, Viking warrior, 40" dia., EX................................................................$15,000.00 C

**Silent Chief Motor Oil,** can, metal, Indian Chief, 1 qt., EX ..$800.00 B

**Silk Hosiery,** sign, mirror, acid-etched figural, 13" H, VG.$825.00 C

**Silver Birch Chewing Gum,** store counter display box with unopened packages of gum, 6¼" x 5½" x 4¼", VG.$1,000.00 C

**Silver Blend Brand Coffee,** can, metal, pry lid, 3 lb., VG......$365.00 D

**Silver Dust Flour,** thermometer, porcelain, scale type reading, product name at top and bottom, 4" x 16", EX .................$300.00 B

**Silver Flash,** gas globe, one-piece glass body, 15" x 6" x 16¼", F .........................................................................$1,625.00 C

**Silver Moon Brand Coffee,** can, metal, paper label, lady sitting on a cresent moon, slip lid, from Oliver-Finnie Co., Memphis, Tenn, 1 lb., EX.....................................................................$550.00 C

**Silver Spring Brewery Ltd.,** sign, paper, litho, fireman with a glass of the product, 16¼" dia., VG..............................$70.00 B

**Silver Star Condom,** tin, litho, streaking star, Silver Star Rubber Co., New York, NY USA, 2¼" x 1⅝" x ¼", G......................$825.00 B

**Silvercup Bread,** sign, metal, loaf of wrapped bread, "The World's Finest Bread," 18" x 12", EX .............................$110.00 D

Sunbeam Bread, sign, tin, self-framing, young girl eating a slice of bread, 19" x 55", EX, $800.00 C.

Sunbeam Bread, screen door, wooden, with metal embossed door, push bar, and pull handle, "with a Bonus," 34" x 82", NM, $450.00 C.

Sun Crest Beverages, clock, convex front glass, light-up, Swihart, 15" x 18", NM, $325.00 D.

Sun Crest, clock, metal and glass, light-up, bottle in center, Telechron, 15¼" dia., EX, $395.00 C.

Sun Crest, thermometer, metal, "Drink, refreshes you best," bottle to right of scale, 6" x 16½", blue, orange, and white, F, $115.00 C.

Silverwoods Deluxe Ice Cream, sign, tin, double-sided, "Dairy Products Advertising, Weston, Ontario," 23¼" x 35", VG .$80.00 B

Simmons Beautyrest Mattress, display, cardboard, die cut, lady on a cut away version of the mattress, 1950s, 46" x 15", EX ....$75.00 D

Simon's Roosevelt Havana Cigars, tin, rounded corner, litho with FDR's picture in cameo, 5" x 3½" x 1½", EX ......................$95.00 C

Simonds Circular Saws, thermometer, tin over cardboard, 7" x 19", EX ..................................................................................$135.00 C

Simoniz, display, cardboard, "Gives Lasting Beauty and Saves Finish, too!," metal can in center with man and woman polishing table and car, EX.....................................................................$135.00 D

Simplex, sign, tin, one-sided, embossed, 20" x 9", VG.......$275.00 C

Simpson Spring Beverages, bottle topper, cardboard, 18 Delicious Beverages, EX ........................................................................$45.00 C

Sinbad Coffee, can, metal, paper label, 1 lb., EX................$85.00 B

Sinclair Dino Gasoline, globe, plastic body and two glass lenses, trademark Dino dinosaur, 13½" dia., EX ..........................$475.00 C

Sinclair Dino Supreme, gas globe, plastic and glass, Dino on lens, 13½" dia., EX.....................................................................$375.00 C

Sinclair Gasoline, calendar, pretty woman with jump rope, by artist Earl Moran, 16" x 33½", 1946, NM ...................................$165.00 C

Sinclair Gasoline, gas globe, glass, one piece, black logo on white globe, 16" dia., EX ...........................................................$775.00 C

Sinclair H-C Gasoline, clock, metal, glass and neon spinner, 21" dia., EX..................................................................................$1,800.00 C

Sinclair H-C Gasoline, gas globe, glass and plastic, red, white, and black company logo, 14" dia., EX....................................$525.00 C

Sinclair H-C Gasoline, sign, porcelain, white, green, and red company lettering, 42" dia., EX .............................................$700.00 C

Sun Crest, sign, cardboard, die cut, woman at grocery with a 6 pack of the product, 32" tall, F, $85.00 B.

Sun Crest, thermometer, glass and metal, VG, $190.00 B.

Sun Drop, sign, metal, self-framing, scarce, "Have you had your lemonade today, made with pure lemon juice, sold only in bottles," 40" x 22¼", orange, blue, and white, G, $325.00 D. *Courtesy of Patrick's Collectibles.*

Sunkist Orange Juice, sign, litho, "I'll tell you a secret...Every day," girl with a glass, by Forbes, 1920s, 28" x 42", EX, $600.00 B. *Courtesy of Muddy River Trading Co./Gary Metz.*

Sunlight Soap, sign, die cut, litho, from Lever Bros., 8½" x 10¾", 1900s, EX, $400.00 B. *Courtesy of Buffalo Bay Auction Co.*

Sinclair H-C Products, chalkboard, metal, owner's courtesy panel, 12" x 24", EX .....................$175.00 C

Sinclair Oil, can, tin, litho, hand-soldered, early race car, "Opaline Motor Oil... Sinclair Refining Company...Chicago," 10½" x 8" x 3", EX.....................$395.00 C

Sinclair Opaline Motor Oil, sign, porcelain, "Authorized Dealer, Seals Power At Every Degree Of Wear," 48" x 20", EX ...$1,000.00 C

Sinclair Opaline Motor Oil, sign, porcelain, single-sided, 15" x 60", VG .....................$325.00 C

Sinclair Pennsylvania Motor Oil, sign, porcelain, trademark Dino image, 11" dia., EX .....................$350.00 C

Sinclair Power-X Gasoline, gas globe, glass and plastic, name and logo, VG.....................$375.00 C

Sinclair Power-X Super Fuel, bank, metal, in shape of gas pump, EX .....................$45.00 C

Sinclair Power-X, gas globe, glass and plastic, "Over 100 % Octane," 13½", EX.....................$275.00 C

Sinclair Shamrock Lubricant, can, metal, round, with cone lid, 3 lb., EX.....................$400.00 C

Sinclair, bank, metal, figure of a dinosaur, 9" x 6", EX...........$250.00 D

Sinclair, clock, metal & glass, illuminated with Dino, 1950s, EX .....................$500.00 D

Sinclair, Marx, toy tanker truck, 18½" long, red & white on green, EX .....................$675.00 C

Sinclair, pennant gas globe, narrow hull body with two glass lenses, 13½" dia., EX.....................$900.00 B

Sinclair, pump sign, porcelain, Dino, 7" x 5", EX.............$375.00 C

Singer Mfg. Co., calendar, heavily embossed, "Sewing Machine Makers for the World," young girl, 1898, 9" x 12", EX ....$53.00 B

Sun-Maid Raisins, sign, cardboard, trolley car, pictures of product boxes, "...Make a good pudding," 1920 – 30s, 21" x 11", G, $95.00 C.

Sun-Maid Raisins, sign, cardboard, trolley car, package and girl with a nickel for a package, 1920 – 30s, 23" x 13", EX, $135.00 C.

Sunny Side Grocery, truck, metal, repainted with reworked advertising for the business, "A & E Longo, Sunny Side Grocery, Winchester, VA.," EX, $8,200.00 B.

Sunoco Motor Oil, banner, cloth, 60" x 36", VG, $350.00 C.

Sunoco, Sun-Heat Furnace Oil, blotter, Disney theme with Mickey Mouse asleep in chair, 6" x 3¼", 1939, EX, $225.00 C. *Courtesy of Autopia Advertising Auctions.*

---

Singer Sewing Machines, calendar, metal and paper, "For Every Stitching Situation" with large trademark letter S, VG .....$375.00 D

Singer Sewing Machines, calendar, paper, heavy embossing, 1898, 9" x 12", EX ............................................................$65.00 D

Singer Sewing Machines, sign, porcelain, flange, double-sided, early s logo, 1920s, 12" x 19", VG ..............................$875.00 D

Sir Walter Raleigh Cigarettes, change receiver, metal and wood, cardboard cigarette box under glass, VG ..........................$115.00 C

Sir Walter Raleigh Smoking Tobacco, pocket tin, vertical, VG .$65.00 D

Sir Walter Raleigh Smoking Tobacco, sign, porcelain, pocket tin, 1920s, 36" x 12", VG .......................................$715.00 C

Sir Walter Raleigh Smoking Tobacco, sign, tin, "Smells Grands, Packs Right, Smokes Sweet, Can't Bite," 17" x 26", EX .....$100.00 B

Sir Walter Raleigh Smoking Tobacco, tin, Christmas motif, 1 lb., EX ............................................................$70.00 B

Sir Walter Raleigh, Union Made, sign, paper, smoking tobacco for pipe and cigarettes, 19¾" x 24", VG ........................$35.00 C

Skelly Fortified Gasoline, gas globe, glass and plastic, diamond logo, EX ............................................................$525.00 C

Skelly Gasoline, calendar, Earl Moran flag girl, 16" x 32½", 1946, EX...............................................................$145.00 C

Skelly Premium, gas globe, glass and plastic, diamond logo and three stars, 13½" dia., VG ...............................................$450.00 C

Skelly Supreme, clock, metal and glass, lettering diagonal on clock face, 16" x 16", VG .........................................$225.00 C

Skelly, fan, cardboard, trifold, Skelly service station, VG .$225.00 C

Skelly-Hood, snow dome, plastic and glass, for Skelly and Hood tires, billboard inside dome, 4" x 3" x 3", EX.................$130.00 B

Ski, sign, tin, one-sided, "drink," bottle water skiing, 31¾" x 11¾", G.............................................................$160.00 B

Sunset Corn Flakes, Distributed by Montgomery Ward & Co., cereal box, very scarce item due to limited production, EX, $135.00 B. *Courtesy of Buffalo Bay Auction Co.*

Superior Dairy Ice Cream, menu board, wood and metal, sliding menu strips, 86" wide, VG, $150.00 B.

Sutherland Medicine Co. Dr. Bell's Anti-Septic Salve, tin, trademark bell on top cover, 1910s, 2½" dia., NM, $35.00 C. *Courtesy of B.J. Summers.*

Sweet Cuba Fine Cut Tobacco, canister, metal, 8" x 8" x 10", G, $125.00 C.

Sweet Heart Soap, display, composition and paper, arms and legs move on baby, sign lights up, 32" long, VG, $475.00 C.

Sweet-Orr Union Made Shirts, box, cardboard, front with figures pulling on product shirt, 19" x 11" x 2½", VG, $175.00 C.

---

**Ski-Hi,** cigar tin, paper label, plane flying over city scene, 5¼" x 5", EX.................................................$3,000.00 B

**Skiles Electric Bread,** spinner, celluloid, in shape of hand with finger pointing to "Who Pays," "Electric Bread," 2½" x 1¼", NM.....$65.00 C

**Sky-View,** taxi roof sign, metal and glass, embossed lettering, art deco style, 19" long, EX.....................................$625.00 B

**Skylark Ethyl Gasoline,** globe, narrow glass body with glass lenses, 13½" dia., G.....................................$850.00 C

**Slade's Spices and Baking Powder,** sign, paper, litho, small girl with flowers, 20" x 25¾", EX.....................................$575.00 D

**Sleepy Eye Flour and Cereal Products,** sign, tin, litho, embossed, Old Sleepy Eye, rare and hard-to-find, 19" x 27½", VG...............$760.00 B

**Sleepy Eye Flour,** sign, metal, Indian in center, "...and cereal products," 19" x 27", VG.....................................$9,000.00 B

**Sleepy Eye flour,** sign, metal, Indian portrait, "Sleepy Eye The Meritorious Flour," 20" x 25", VG .....................................$2,500.00 B

**Sleepy Eye Flour,** sign, metal, Indian portrait, "That Sleepy Eye Flour," 13" x 19", EX.....................................$2,500.00 B

**Sleepy Eye Flour,** sign, tin on cardboard, beveled edge, by New York Metal Sign Works Co., Old Sleepy Eye in center cameo, VG.....................................$2,300.00 B

**Sleepy Eye Milling Co.,** barrel label, paper, "Strong Bakers," 16" dia., VG.....................................$450.00 B

**Sleepy Eye Milling Co.**, cook book, paper, 95 pages, EX ....$40.00 D

**Sleepyeye Beckstrand Imp. Co.**, license attachment, tin, die cut, 9¾" x 3", EX..............$100.00 B

**Slicker Pipe & Tool Company**, calendar, oil and gas well supplies with great litho at top of tear sheets of fishing scene, 1927, EX .......$55.00 C

**Slinky**, display, cardboard, "More Fun Than A Circus," boy with product, 1950s, 17" x 17" x 8", EX ....................$750.00 B

**Smile Orange Drink**, sign, paper, die cut, holding a Smile sign with Smile figures, 22" x 28¾", NM ................................$150.00 B

**Smile**, sign, metal, double-sided, flange, caracture orange man, "Drink Smile," 10" x 12", VG ..........................$425.00 B

**Smile**, sign, metal, orange man with bowtie, "Drink...Refresh With A Smile," 19" x 27", NM..............$900.00 B

**Smile**, sign, paper, orange man with a smile, 22" x 29", VG..$150.00 B

**Smile**, sign, tin, easel back tripod, Smile man serving at counter, 1920s, 27" x 41", EX....................$1,800.00 C

**Smilin' Sam**, peanut vendor, cast aluminum, from General Merchandise Co., in the shape of a man's head, 10" x 11" x 13½", 1931, VG ....................$2,050.00 B

**Smith & Rand Orange Sporting Powder**, sign, paper, two hunters pheasant hunting 21" x 22", 22" x 29", EX....................$2,800.00 B

**Smith Bros. Black Cough Drops**, banner, cloth, brothers, 27" x 14", EX ....................$95.00 B

**Smith Bros. Chewing Gum and Cough Drops**, blotter, Smith Bros. and product packages, 9½" x 4", EX....................$50.00 B

**Smith Bros. Cough Drop**, sign, paperboard, both brothers asking the public to be kind and not cough in public by buying their product, 24" x 16", EX ....................$98.00 B

**Smith Brothers Cough Drops**, blotter, cardboard, Smith Brothers, "For That Cough," 12" x 7", EX....................$22.00 D

**Smith Brothers Cough Drops**, trolley sign, cardboard, two cartoon kids, "And It's Just As Silly To Ever Be Without...," 28" x 18", VG ....................$180.00 B

**Smith Brothers**, blotter, their chewing gum, with both men on front, hard-to-find item, 9½" x 4", 1915s, EX ....................$95.00 D

**Smith Coal**, sign, porcelain, caracature lump of coal with shovel, "Smith Coal" at bottom, double-sided, 24" x 36", EX........$300.00 D

**Smith's Fine Bread**, sign, cardboard, train and sky with product banner over top, 17" x 13", EX....................$150.00 B

**Smith's Ice Cream**, sign, metal, one-sided, "It's Pleasingly Different," NOS, 31½" x 19½", NM....................$275.00 B

**Smith-Wolf Oil Co.**, sign, metal, die cut, embossed arrow, 19½" x 4¾", NM....................$135.00 C

**Smiths' Overalls**, sign, 7" x 2½", 1930s, NM ....................$225.00 B

**Smoke "BIJOU" Cigars**, stone litho, young girl with ocean scene in background, 15½" x 20", 1900s, EX....................$450.00 B

**Smoke Briar Pipe tobacco**, sign, cardboard, Victorian lady in yellow dress, 8" x 10", EX....................$95.00 C

**Smoke Hignett's Mixture**, sign, tin, litho, embossed, vintage touring car out for a drive in the country, 19½" x 13½", VG .$500.00 B

**Smoker's Dream**, sign, cardboard, "Big John Grandulated 54 Orphan Boy," product images on front, 14" x 19", VG ......$145.00 C

**Smoker's Dream**, sign, cardboard, Big John, Granulated 54, and Orphan Boy tobacco, with all three products, 13½" x 19", NM..............$107.00 B

**Smoker's Fun Shop**, display, cardboard, trifold "10¢ Each, 3 For 25¢," 21" x 14", EX....................$100.00 C

**Smokettes**, cigar box, southern plantation, EX ...........$60.00 C

**Smooth Sailin'**, candy box, two-part, sailboats on both sides, Hollywood Brands, Centralia, Ill., 10" x 8" x 2", NM ..................$35.00 C

**SMP Graniteware**, sign, cardboard, 1930s kitchen with lady at work using the product, 1930s, 22" x 28", NM ....................$650.00 B

**Snag Proof Boots**, calendar, "L" girl in cameo surrounded by brownies with products, Lambertville Rubber Co., 1910s, 8" x 12", EX....................$116.00 B

**Snapshot Black Sporting Powder**, tin, litho, geese on front, 3½" x 4¼" x 1", NM....................$95.00 C

**Snider's Catsup**, sign, metal, embossed, large catsup bottle and tomato on vine, 11" x 17", EX....................$300.00 B

**Snider's Catsup**, sign, tin, embossed, die cut, product bottle, 11" x 17", 1930s, NM....................$475.00 B

**Sno-King Peanuts**, candy bar store box, caramel nougat, snow scenes on front, 10" x 7¾" x 2", EX....................$45.00 C

**Snow Bird Cigar**, thermometer, wood, EX ......................$250.00 B

**Snow Crest**, crate label, paper, Washington Pears, mountains and orchards scenery, 1919, EX ..............................$35.00 C

**Snow King Baking Powder**, countertop display, die cut, Santa Claus in sleigh being pulled by reindeer, 29" x 17", VG.....$600.00 C

**Snow King Baking Powder**, sign, cardboard, die cut, Santa and the reindeer, 28" x 17", EX....................$250.00 B

**Snowdrift Perfect Shortening**, sign, porcelain, single-sided, container on center, 26" sq., G ..............................$250.00 C

**SOC Super**, gas globe, plastic body with glass lenses, 13½" dia., VG ..............................$425.00 C

**Social Tips**, cigar box label, inside of men's social club, EX.$135.00 B

**Society Marshmallows,** tin, slip lid, round, 4" dia., EX...........$150.00 C

**Socony Air-Craft Oils, Standard Oil of New York,** sign, porcelain, vintage airplane, very sought-after item, 30" x 20", EX .$1,050.00 B

**Socony Aircraft Oil No. 2 Heavy Medium,** sign, porcelain, two-sided lubster, 8" x 12", G.....................$130.00 C

**Socony Fuel Oil,** sign, cardboard, home delivery oil truck in snow, "Was Your Home Cold Last Winter?" 20" x 27", EX.............$295.00 C

**Socony Gasoline & Polarine Oil & Greases,** shoe brush, wood, 2" x 7", EX......................$35.00 C

**Socony Motor Gasoline,** gas globe, milk glass, one piece, embossing, 16½" dia., EX..........................$895.00 C

**Socony Motor Oil,** pump sign, porcelain, shield and product lettering, 13" x 15", EX.......................$195.00 C

**Socony Motor Oil,** pump sign, porcelain, single-sided, 13½" x 15", F .........................$110.00 B

**Socony Motor Oil,** sign, porcelain, product lettering around shield, 15" dia., EX........................$350.00 C

**Socony Motor Oils,** paperweight, mirror & celluloid, roadway and product sign, 3½" dia., EX........................$195.00 C

**Socony Polarine Oil,** watch fob, trademark polar bear, 1⅜" x 1⅝", VG ........................$75.00 C

**Socony-Vacumm Suggestion System,** suggestion box, wood, red pegasus on front, EX.......................$135.00 B

**Socony-Vacumm,** badge, metal, Pegasus in center of 5 point star, 1939, 2", EX ......................$450.00 B

**Socony-Vacumm,** sign, porcelain, "...Credit Cards Honored Here," 23" x 14", EX .......................$135.00 C

**Softex Shampoo,** countertop display, wooden box that folds out for three-level display and product container, 10" T, EX..........$55.00 C

**Sohio,** bank, glass cube, embossed, 5" x 5", VG.............$65.00 C

**Sol Coleman's Ko-Ko Tulu Chewing Gum,** trade card, cardboard, girl and doll, NM ........................$125.00 B

**Solace Tobacco,** box, cardboard, gold emblem on top, originally help 6 dozen packs, 1870s, 10" x 8" x 5", EX........................$65.00 C

**Solace Tobacco,** sign, paper, young girl on ladder, 12½" x 29", 1884, EX ........................$2,000.00 D

**Solene No-Nox Gasoline,** gas globe, wide body glass with double lenses, 13½" dia., G.......................$800.00 B

**Solitaire Coffee,** can, metal, key wind lid, boy on a horse, 4 lb., EX.......................$50.00 D

**Solo,** sign, tin, litho, painted, "Drink...High in Quality, 6 fruity flavors," 15" x 30", G.......................$75.00 C

**Sooner Select Oats,** container, oxen wagon and horseback rider, Lawton, OK, 1-lb., VG .....................$305.00 B

**Sorority Steel Cut Coffee,** can, metal, paper label, pry lid, 1 lb., EX.......................$400.00 B

**South Bend Watches,** dealer sign, metal, "...Sold By...," pocket watch image, 19" x 13", EX .......................$190.00 B

**South Bend Watches,** sign, tin, litho, "Sold By W.F. Sellers & Co.," 19" x 13", EX .......................$192.00 B

**South West Cigars,** box label, paper, "The Celebrated," 1889, EX .......................$80.00 B

**Southern Bell Telephone and Telegraph Co./American Telephone & Telegraph Co.,** globe, milk glass, at one time these hung at Bell business offices, getting to be a hard item to find, blue lettering and bell on white, VG.......................$525.00 C

**Southern Brand Pure White Lead Paint,** sign, metal, double-sided, flange, Dutch boy sitting on ledge with brush, 14¼" x 21", EX .$875.00 C

**Southern California Telephone Co.,** badge, cloisonne, bell shape, 2" dia., EX .......................$85.00 C

**Southern Railroad Tickets,** sign, glass, reverse gold lettering against black background, 28" x 5", EX.......................$75.00 C

**Southern Rose Hair Dressing,** calendar, fishing couple at top and bottle of product on each side of bottom tear sheet, 17" x 35", 1950, EX .......................$110.00 B

**Southwestern Associated Telephone Company,** sign, porcelain, double-sided, "toll line" pole in center, 30" dia., VG .........$425.00 B

**Southwestern Bell Telephone Co.,** sign, porcelain, double-sided, flange, 11" x 11⅞", 1950s, G.......................$180.00 B

**Sozodont Tooth Powder,** tin, litho, vintage era man brushing his teeth, with original box, 1¾" x 3⅞", 1900s, EX.................$475.00 B

**Spalding,** sign, porcelain over metal, double-sided, flange, "athletic goods...for sale here," 19½" x 19", EX.......................$1,600.00 B

**Sparkeeta UP Soda,** sign, cardboard, framed, "California's flavorite," pretty red-haired woman with bottle of product, 25¾" x 31½", VG .......................$200.00 C

**Sparkle Soda,** bottle topper, cardboard, elf and 5¢ price information, EX .......................$45.00 C

**Sparrow Chocolates,** serving tray, metal, young girl standing in a chair to climb onto a table after the product, 6½" x 8", EX .$350.00 C

**Sparrows Chocolate,** tip tray, metal, little girl climbing onto table for candy, 6¼" x 8⅛", G .......................$70.00 D

**Sparrows Chocolate,** tip tray, tin, litho, young girl in a chair reaching for the candy, 6½" x 8", VG ........................................$130.00 B

**Spartan Ethyl,** gas globe, high profile metal body with two glass lenses, 15" dia., VG ........................................$425.00 C

**Spartan Ethyl,** gas globe, metal and glass, company and Ethyl logo, 16" dia., EX ........................................$400.00 C

**Spear Head Chewing Tobacco,** sign, porcelain, red arrow, "Hits the Spot," 1920s, EX ........................................$250.00 C

**Spear Head Plug Chew Tobacco,** sign, tin, heavy relief and embossing, 28" x 10", VG ........................................$250.00 C

**Spear Head Tobacco,** sign, paper, Indian holding a spear, "Chew...Save The Tags," 22" x 16", EX ........................................$175.00 C

**Spearhead Plug Tobacco,** sign, tin, embossed, double-sided, hanging, diamond-shaped, 6" sq., EX ........................................$225.00 C

**Spearior Saws,** sign, tin, litho, wood-handled hand saw, 27" x 9", VG ........................................$210.00 B

**Spearmint Toothpaste, W.W. Wrigley,** sign, heavy cardboard, 24" x 18", G ........................................$55.00 C

**Spears Inspected Approved Station & Rest Rooms,** sign, porcelain, double-sided, 30" dia., VG ........................................$275.00 C

**Special Combination Coffee,** tin, litho, Sears Roebuck & Co., Chicago, Illinois, wire bail handle, 10-lb., black on green background, EX ........................................$80.00 B

**Special Train,** cigar box label, paper, train, VG ........................................$220.00 B

**Spectacles,** sign, reverse painting on glass, 20" x 8", NM ...$550.00 C

**Speedboat Mixture Tobacco,** tin, 1930s-style boat, 5¾" x 3¼", EX ........................................$275.00 C

**Speedboat Mixture Tobacco,** tin, 1930s-style boat, 5¾" x 3¼", G ........................................$225.00 C

**Speedwell Motor Oil,** sign, porcelain, double-sided, flange, young black boy being chased by a tiger, 23½" x 16", VG........$1,900.00 B

**Speigel,** catalog, paper, general furniture and home goods, 1928, 130 pages, EX ........................................$65.00 C

**Spiffy,** sign, metal, painted, flange, "A Swell Cola Drink," 12½" x 10", EX ........................................$150.00 C

**Spiffy,** sign, metal, painted, flange, "A Swell Cola Drink," 12½" x 10", F ........................................$75.00 C

**Sporting Beauty,** cigar box label, highly embellished portrait, 1896, EX ........................................$125.00 C

**Sportsman Tobacco,** tin, horizontal, horses on all sides, VG ..$25.00 D

**Spur,** sign, tin, embossed, "Drink Canada Dry... Ice Cold, It's A Finer Cola," 13½" x 30", G ........................................$75.00 B

**Squadron Leader Tobacco,** tin, litho, bi-plane on cover, NM...$120.00 B

**Square Deal Coffee,** tin, litho, hands shaking in agreement, 4" x 6", G ........................................$375.00 B

**Square Deal Rubber Shoes,** sign, metal, double-sided, flange, "...Sold Here," 18" x 9", EX ........................................$225.00 C

**Squeeze Orange Drink,** sign, tin, litho, embossed, "That distinctive," boy and girl looking at the moon, 27" x 19½", VG....$275.00 C

**Squeeze Soda,** sign, cardboard, "Had Your Squeeze Today?," 15" x 20", NM ........................................$325.00 C

**Squeeze Soda,** sign, cardboard, die cut, boy and grandfather fishing, "Between Bites Drink...," 20" tall, NM ........................................$475.00 C

**Squeeze Soda,** sign, cardboard, die cut, girl at the beach, stand up design, "Drink...Delightful and Cooling," 20" x 15", NM ....$300.00 C

**Squeeze Soda,** sign, metal, kids on beach, "Drink...All Flavors," 28" x 10", EX ........................................$250.00 C

**Squeeze Soda,** sign, metal, kids on beach, key hole symbol, 28" x 20", EX ........................................$375.00 C

**Squeeze,** sign, cardboard, easel back, bathing girl with large brim hat, 15" x 20", VG ........................................$275.00 B

**Squeeze,** sign, cardboard, easel back, sandlot baseball, 15" x 20", EX ........................................$425.00 B

**Squeeze,** sign, tin, litho, embossed, couple on a bench, "Drink...all flavors," 28½" x 10", VG ........................................$180.00 B

**Squirrel Brand Peanut Butter,** pail, metal, VG ..................$40.00 D

**Squirrel Brand Peanut Butter,** tin, litho, pry-lid, squirrel on front, 3-lb., EX........................................$225.00 B

**Squirrel Brand Salted Peanuts,** countertop display, cardboard, die cut, 12" x 11", EX ........................................$130.00 B

**Squirrel Brand,** sign, cardboard, die cut, cut-out of squirrel on top of sign, 11" x 12", EX ........................................$380.00 B

**Squirt,** calendar, paper, four different girls, all months complete, 1948, 16" x 22", EX ........................................$125.00 C

**Squirt,** clock, light-up, "Switch to..." Squirt Boy and product bottle, 15" dia., EX ........................................$375.00 C

**Squirt,** clock, metal, bottle and fruits image, 16" x 16", VG...$300.00 D

**Squirt,** delivery truck, tin, litho, friction movement, " in Reader's Digest," 8" L, EX........................................$175.00 B

**Squirt,** display figure, chalkware, bottle with Squirt Boy, 1947, 8" x 13", EX ............................................................$700.00 C

**Squirt,** glass, Squirt Boy, 4¼", 1948, EX ...........................$70.00 B

**Squirt,** menu board, tin, embossed, 19½" x 27½", 1950s, EX .**$225.00 C**

**Squirt,** sign, metal, "Just Call Me Squirt," 1940s, 50" x 50", EX ..**$300.00 C**

**Squirt,** sign, metal, double-sided, flange, "Switch To Squirt, Never An After Thirst," 18" x 13", EX ........................................$215.00 C

**Squirt,** sign, metal, painted, "Switch to," Squirt boy, 27¼" x 9¼", EX............................................................................$180.00 B

**Squirt,** sign, metal, red banded bottom, bottle on yellow background, "...Never An After Thirst," 28" x 10", EX .............$150.00 C

**Squirt,** sign, metal, self-framing, bottle and Squirt boy, "Drink...," 18" x 53", NM...............................................$650.00 C

**Squirt,** sign, paper, 6 pack, "Yes! We Have Squirt," 1950s, 16" x 8", EX ........................................................................$75.00 C

**Squirt,** sign, tin, double-sided, flange, "It's Tart Sweet," 18⅜" x 14", 1941, NM .....................................................$225.00 C

**Squirt,** thermometer, metal, painted, "enjoy...never an after thirst," Squirt to right of vertical scale, EX.........................$75.00 C

**Squirt,** thermometer, tin, embossed, bottle at right of scale, 5¾" x 13½", NM .....................................................................$350.00 B

**St. Bruno Flake,** sign, cardboard, stand-up, slaves in fields, by the Imperial Tobacco Company, 22½" x 18½", VG.............$1,275.00 D

**St. Bruno Tobacco,** sign, cardboard, 3-D, die cut, stand-up, from the Imperial Tobacco Co. of Great Britian, blacks packing tobacco leaves, 20" x 14½", 1915s, NM ......................................$1,000.00 C

**St. Joseph Aspirin,** clock, metal body with glass face, electric, light-up, 15" dia., EX .........................................................$395.00 D

**Stag Tobacco,** tin, litho, large buck and men on horseback, 4½" x 4" x 4", EX .........................................................................$95.00 C

**Stag Trousers,** sign, metal over cardboard, "We Are Authorized To Guarentee...," stag head over message, 13" x 19", EX..........$125.00 D

**Standard Ale,** sign, cardboard, delivery truck, Standard Brewing Co., Inc., Rochester, N. Y., 16" x 12½", EX.....................$100.00 C

**Standard Ale,** sign, cardboard, delivery truck, Standard Brewing Co., Inc., Rochester, N. Y., 16" x 12½", VG......................$75.00 C

**Standard Brewing Co.,** sign, metal, print entitled "The Execution of 38 Sioux Indians...," 26" x 18", EX................................$2,200.00 B

**Standard Brewing Co.,** sign, tin, litho, self-framing, grisly execution of 38 Sioux Indians while soldiers sit on the porch enjoying their beer, 26" x 18", VG...................................................$2,800.00 B

**Standard Brewing Co.,** tray, metal, "The Execution of 38 Sioux Indians At Mankato...," F ...............................................$300.00 C

**Standard Gasoline Polarine Motor Oil,** sign, porcelain, double-sided, 30" dia., G ...............................................................$325.00 B

**Standard Gasoline,** sign, cardboard, "Unsurpassed," Mickey Mouse on skis, 17" x 14", EX ......................................$525.00 C

**Standard Heating Oils,** sign, porcelain, die cut, 24" x 15", VG.**$195.00 C**

**Standard Mixed Paint of America,** tip tray, metal, "Goes Farthest...Locks Best...Wears Longest," product can in center of tray, 4⅛" dia., EX ...........................................................$55.00 C

**Standard Oil Co.,** gas globe, glass, crown shape with gold on white, 16" dia., VG .......................................................$425.00 C

**Standard Oil Co.,** gas globe, glass, crown shape, solid white, 16" dia., VG ...........................................................$425.00 C

**Standard Oil Co.,** gas globe, glass, flame shaped, red and white, although I've seen these items on pumps, they are also on top of the company's oval sign, 10" tall, VG.................................$425.00 C

**Standard Oil Co.,** gas globe, glass, red on white, 16" dia., VG ..**$450.00 C**

**Standard Oil Co.,** gas globe, metal and glass, Standard over blue flame, round, VG ...............................................$725.00 C

**Standard Oil Co.,** license plate attachment, metal, "Research Test Car," winger die cut crown on top of attachment, 5" x 9", EX................................................................................$250.00 C

**Standard Oil Co., Superla Cream Separator Oil,** can, metal, litho, cows and cream separator, 5" x 9½", VG ...........................$70.00 A

**Standard Oil Company of N.Y.,** sign, porcelain, "Polarine oil and greases for motors," 12" x 22", G ....................................$275.00 C

**Standard Oil Products,** sign, porcelain, 30" x 20", white on blue, VG ...............................................................$255.00 C

**Standard Oil,** mailbox, metal, for letters to Santa Claus, "letters mailed here will be postmarked with the famous Santa Claus, Ind., postmark," 12½" x 17" x 7¾", VG.......................$230.00 B

**Standard Oil,** sign, tin, die cut, double-sided, flange, "Credit Cards Good Here," first Standard Oil card sign, 23¾" x 25½", 1932, VG ................................................................$235.00 D

**Standard Sewing Machine,** sign, stone litho, paper, small child with cats, 12" x 22", VG ...............................................$255.00 B

**Standard Varnish Works,** sign, metal, self-framing, man behind the products, "The Man Who Knows...," 1909, 17" x 11", EX..**$275.00 C**

**Standard Woolen Co.,** watch fob, celluloid, "...Suits and Overcoats, Made To Measure...," 2" dia., EX.........................................$35.00 C

**Standby Tomato Juice,** sign, porcelain, button with product can in center, 35½" dia., VG............................................$275.00 B

**Stanley Garage Door Holders,** sign, tin, litho, vintage garage door, "Hold Your Garage Doors Open," 34" x 26¼", 1910s, VG......$625.00 C

**Star Brand Shoes,** sign, tin, embossed, young black boy shining shoes, produced by the Grimm Metal Sign Corp., St. Louis, "Yes sah !...Star Brand Shoes are better...sold at the best stores," 23" x 18", EX............................................$500.00 B

**Star Brand Shoes,** store wall mirror, "Are Better," 15½" x 21½", EX............................................$175.00 C

**Star Cup Coffee,** can, tin, litho, key-wound lid, king drinking a cup of coffee, 1-lb., EX............................................$190.00 B

**Star Naphtha Washing Powder,** sign, metal, embossed, "..½¢ A Package," 20" x 4", NM............................................$385.00 B

**Star Razor,** tin, complete with original safety razor and blades, litho on all sides, 2¼" x 1¼" x 1½", EX............................................$135.00 B

**Star Soap,** sign, porcelain, bar of soap, "Extra Large...Extra Good," 20" x 26", EX............................................$295.00 D

**Star Soap,** sign, porcelain, one-sided, "Extra Large, Extra Good," 20" x 28", VG............................................$425.00 C

**Star Tobacco,** sign, porcelain, "Star Tobacco Sold Here," 24" x 12", G............................................$135.00 C

**Star Tobacco,** sign, porcelain, single-sided, star over tobacco plug, 24" x 12", VG............................................$295.00 C

**Star Tobacco,** sign, porcelain, tobacco plugs, "Star Tobacco Sold Here," 26" x 13", EX............................................$400.00 B

**State Automobile Mutual Insurance Company,** sign, porcelain, one-sided, colorful castle over message, 27½" x 60", EX ...$305.00 B

**State Fair Rolled Oats,** container, slip-lid, Sedalia, Mo., fair building on front, 1-lb., 4-oz., EX............................................$130.00 B

**State House Coffee,** can, cardboard with paper label, Indian, slip lid, 1 lb., EX............................................$350.00 B

**State House Coffee,** container, paper on cardboard, Indian bust on back and State House on front, from Waterloo IA, all on bright yellow background, 1-lb., EX............................................$460.00 B

**Stay Cool Oil,** oil can, tin, "Keeps The Motor Cool," product label on front and back, 1-gal., EX............................................$35.00 C

**Steamer City of Erie,** tip tray, metal, rectangular, "Record 22¾ miles per hour...Daily Between Cleveland & Buffalo," ship at sea, 6⅝" L, EX............................................$250.00 B

**Steamro Red Hots,** sign, porcelain, hot dogs, for use on hot dog vendor cart, 19" x 3¾", EX............................................$225.00 C

**Stegmaier Brewing Co.,** match holder, tin, litho, 5" H, G.$110.00 B

**Stegmaier Brewing Co.,** tip tray, metal, round, Wilkes Barre, Pa., hand holding 4 bottles of product, 4⅛" dia., EX ...............$150.00 B

**Stegmaier Malt Extract,** match holder, metal, four bottles, EX.$125.00 C

**Stegmaier's,** sign, tin, litho, "We Serve...Gold Metal Beer," cone-top can and short neck bottle of product, EX............................................$72.00 B

**Stegner Lager Beer,** sign, glass, neon framing, 13½" x 6", EX...$230.00 B

**Stephens Inks,** thermometer, porcelain over wood, "for all temperatures," 12" x 61", VG............................................$350.00 B

**Stephenson Union Suits,** thermometer, porcelain, man holding the product, "Stephenson Union Suits for all seasons," made by Beech Enamel of Coshocton, Ohio, 8" x 39", 1915, EX...$275.00 C

**Sterling Beer,** figural bell, metal, "Mellow," rings when her hands are squeezed together, 4¾" x 14¾", VG............................................$135.00 C

**Sterling Beer,** mirror, Sterling logo on back, 14" x 10", EX ...$95.00 C

**Sterling Beer,** sign, tin on cardboard, beveled edge, food tray with glass of product, 19" x 13¾", EX............................................$399.00 B

**Sterling Beer,** sign, tin, litho on cardboard, from an original painting "A Night at the Circus," Evansville, Ind. brewery, 20½" x 27", 1938, VG............................................$325.00 B

**Sterling Cinnamon Gum,** package, 3" x ¾" x ½", EX............$65.00 B

**Sterling Gasoline,** pump sign, porcelain, single-sided, the ethyl sign in center, "A Quaker State Product," 11½" x 10", EX........$550.00 B

**Sterling Motor Oil,** can, metal, company logo in center, corner lid and spout, 1 gal., EX............................................$125.00 C

**Sterling Motor Oil,** sign, metal, double-sided, "tombstone," 26½" x 29", 1930s, G............................................$160.00 B

**Sterling Motor Oil,** sign, tin, embossed, 27½" x 13¾", EX..$725.00 C

**Sterling Spark Plugs,** display, tin, litho, product, 11¼" x 14" x 5¾", VG............................................$1,150.00 B

**Sterling Tobacco,** counter canister, small twist lid, 8¼" x 7", EX............................................$155.00 C

**Stetson Hats,** gift box, cardboard, New England type neighborhood scene, felt hat, EX............................................$75.00 C

**Stetson Hats,** sign, wood and celluloid, two hats on rack and window view of horse and cowboy, 17" x 14", EX............................................$400.00 C

**Stevens Firearms,** premium sewing kit, crossed rifles on front, 1" x 2¾", 1900s, EX............................................$150.00 B

**Stewart Clipping Machine,** sign, metal over cardboard, men at work with the machine clipping a horse, "Clips Horses, Mules and Cows...," 1900s, 18" x 15", EX............................................$825.00 B

**Stickney & Poor's, Mustards, Spices, and Extracts,** sign, paper, litho, framed and matted, 19½" x 24½", VG .....................$165.00 C

**Stoddard's Harness Soap,** sign, paper, livery stable scene, 18" x 12", EX .......................................................................$325.00 D

**Stoeckers,** sign, tin, painted, embossed, "It's got the pep...Old-fashioned lemon soda," lemon leaf in center of message, G .........$55.00 C

**Stollwerck Chocolat and Cocoa,** tip tray, metal, painted, 5⅛" dia., VG.................................................................................$65.00 C

**Stone's Peanut Butter,** pail, tin, wire bail handle, pry-lid, Duluth, MN, 5-lb., EX ........................................................................$85.00 C

**Stone's Regular,** gas globe, plastic body with glass lenses, 13½" dia., EX.....................................................................................$425.00 C

**Stonewall Jackson Tobacco,** crate label, paper, Jackson and "Fine 22 Twist," 1880s, 12" x 12", EX .........................................$250.00 C

**Storz Bitter Free Beer,** thermometer, dial-type, 12½" dia., EX ..$95.00 C

**Stowman Brother Oysters,** tin, Maurice River, N.J., 6¾" x 7¼", EX ...........................................................................................$95.00 C

**Straight,** sign, cardboard, die cut, "Smoke Inside...Cheroots, Baron & Co. Cigar Manufacturers, Baltimore, Md.," young woman framed by anchor, 1900, 10" x 14", NM.........................................$230.00 B

**Stratford Regency,** store display, cardboard, three-dimensional "The Dependable Pen," original pen, 1945, G ...................$33.00 D

**Stride Rite,** sign, metal body with glass face, light-up, 20" x 9", EX...............................................................................................$145.00 C

**Stromberg Carburetors,** sign, porcelain, "...Authorized Sales & Service," 36" dia., EX .........................................................$2,530.00 B

**Strong Heart Coffee,** can, tin, paper label, round, colorful Indian, 5¼" x 4¼", EX.....................................................................$300.00 B

**Strong Heart Coffee,** tin, litho, Indian in oval cameo on front and back, Charles Hewitt & Sons Co., 1-lb., EX .......................$550.00 C

**Strong Heart Coffee,** tin, litho, screw-on lid, Indian in center on front, 1-lb., EX.................................................................$467.00 B

**Stud Smoking Tobacco,** countertop display box, cardboard, product packages, 9½" x 5½" x 4", EX.........................................$75.00 C

**Studebaker Authorized Sales & Service,** sign, porcelain, double-sided, dealer, 48" dia., 1940s, NM...................................$1,000.00 C

**Studebaker Batteries,** clock, metal body with glass front, light-up, logo at top center with message at lower center, 15¼" sq., EX ......$450.00 C

**Studebaker Erskine Service,** sign, porcelain, two company logos and emblem name, 48" x 32", EX....................................$1,400.00 C

**Studebaker,** gas globe, glass, wheel logo on globe, 14" dia., EX ...$550.00 C

**Studebaker,** jigsaw puzzle, cardboard, various products and services, and two men on wagon, 6" x 7", EX .........................$300.00 C

**Studebaker,** sign, porcelain, "...Authorized Sales & Service," double-sided, 48" dia., EX .........................................................$775.00 C

**Studebaker,** sign, porcelain, "Service Station" script "Studebaker," double-sided, 30" x 14", VG...............................................$895.00 C

**Studebaker,** sign, porcelain, "Service," double-sided, large wheel logo, 20" x 24", EX..............................................................$1,500.00 C

**Studebaker,** sign, tin, single-sided, "The Sun Always Shines on the Studebaker," product wagon, 29½" x 24", F.....................$300.00 B

**Studebaker,** wallhanging, silk, "1954, World's Finest Performing V-8," 40" x 27½", EX..............................................................$375.00 C

**Stull Seeds,** sign, metal, ears of corn and man in center, 20" x 20", VG ...........................................................................................$95.00 D

**Sultana Coffee,** fan, cardboard, die cut, pet with bonnet-style hat holding a cup of product, from Great Atlantic and Pacific Tea Company, advertising on back of fan, 6¼" x 13", 1892, EX...............$95.00 C

**Sultana Peanut Butter,** pail, "Atlanta and Pacific Tea Company...New York, NY...Distributors," 1-lb., VG .......................................$55.00 C

**Summer Girl Coffee,** tin, litho, key-wound lid, 1-lb., EX ......$55.00 C

**Summer-Time Long Cut Tobacco,** tin, metal, pry lid, paper label pretty women in breeze, EX...............................................$150.00 C

**Summer-Time Tobacco,** container, paper, litho, pry-lid, NM ..$140.00 B

**Summit Shirt,** pennant, young man in the process of putting on French cuffs, 25" L, EX .........................................................$99.00 B

**Sun Crest Beverages,** clock, convex front glass, light-up, Swihart, 15" x 18", VG.................................................................$195.00 D

**Sun Crest,** calendar, paper, full pad, 1949, EX.................$155.00 C

**Sun Crest,** calendar, paper, full pads, 1942, VG.................$95.00 C

**Sun Crest,** clock, electric, light-up, Telechron, with bottle in center in green spotlight, 1940s, VG .....................................$350.00 B

**Sun Crest,** clock, metal and glass, sunrise logo on face, "Drink Sun Crest Beverages," 13" x 16", VG.....................................$225.00 C

**Sun Crest,** poster, cardboard, "Tingle-ated," 22" x 17", G ..$30.00 C

**Sun Crest,** sign, metal, "Get Tingle-ated and Drink..." on bottle cap design, 1950s, 36" dia., EX.................................................$195.00 D

**Sun Crest,** sign, metal, bottle on ground, 7" x 21", VG .........$135.00 D

**Sun Crest,** sign, metal, self-framing, "Just The Right Amount Of Sparkle," 41" x 23", VG.................................................$345.00 C

**Sun Crest,** sign, tin, self-framed, embossed, painted, 41" x 23", EX ..................................................................$325.00 B

**Sun Crest,** thermometer, metal, "Drink," "refreshes you best," bottle to right of scale, 6" x 16½", blue, orange, and white, G........$135.00 D

**Sun Crest,** thermometer, metal, die cut, bottle shape, 17" tall, VG ..................................................................$235.00 C

**Sun Crest,** thermometer, metal, die cut, bottle, vertical scale at bottom of bottle, EX ..........................................$75.00 C

**Sun Crest,** thermometer, metal, self-framing, scale type reading, bottle in water, 16" tall, VG...................................$145.00 C

**Sun Cured Crushed Tobacco,** vertical pocket tin, sun face smiling down on a tobacco barrel , EX ......................$1,760.00 B

**Sun Drop Cola,** sign, metal, bottle cap sign, EX...............$325.00 C

**Sun Drop Lemonade,** sign, cardboard, string hanger with die cut smiling lady, "The Perfect Mixer 5¢," 16" x 16", EX ............$45.00 C

**Sun Drop,** sign, metal, self-framing, "Have you had your lemonade today, made with pure lemon juice, sold only in bottles," scarce, 40" x 22¼", orange, blue, and white, EX........................$450.00 D

**Sun Flower Brand Steel Cut Coffee,** tin, litho, pry-type lid, large sunflower on front, 1-lb., 5¼" x 3¾", EX........................$1,100.00 B

**Sun Insurance Office Agency,** sign, porcelain, sun in upper right corner, 20" x 11", EX ....................................................$325.00 B

**Sun Spot Orange Drink,** sign, tin, store, "Drink America's favorite," 26" x 8", G .........................................................$125.00 C

**Sun Spot,** sign, metal, "Drink Sun Spot, Bottled Sunshine," 10" x 12", EX ....................................................................$55.00 D

**Sun Spot,** sign, metal, round, painted, flange, "Drink bottled sunshine," EX ..............................................................$185.00 C

**Sun Spot,** sign, tin, embossed, "Drink America's Favorite...made with real orange juice," 1940s, 11½" x 14½", EX.................$70.00 B

**Sun Spot,** sign, tin, litho, embossed, tilted bottle in upper left corner, 11½" x 14½", 1940s, NM...........................................$135.00 D

**Sun-drop Cola,** sign, tin, single-sided, self-framing, embossed, 28" x 12", VG..................................................................$165.00 C

**Sun-drop Gold-en Girl Cola,** sign, tin, die cut, bottle, 16" x 60", EX..................................................................$550.00 C

**Sun-drop,** thermometer, dial-type, 12¼" dia., VG...................$65.00 C

**Sun-Rise Beverages,** sign, metal, smiling sun face, "Discover Refreshing Pure Sun-Rise Beverages," 20" x 28", EX........$145.00 C

**Sunbeam Bread,** door push bar, metal, in shape of a loaf of bread, 20" x 9", EX ....................................................................$275.00 C

**Sunbeam Bread,** door push, bread loaf cut-out in center of door bar, used on screen doors before air conditioning to protect screens, 1950s, 30" x 15", G.......................................................$175.00 C

**Sunbeam Bread,** money clip, metal and plastic, Sunbeam Bread girl in plastic center, 1¾" x 1⅜", EX ......................................$125.00 C

**Sunbeam bread,** sign, cardboard, die cut, Miss Sunbeam holding a loaf of bread and an umbrella, 11" x 26", VG....................$595.00 C

**Sunbeam Bread,** sign, metal, die cut, loaf of bread, "Enriched Bread," 1957, 60" x 28", EX .........................................$1,500.00 B

**Sunbeam Bread,** sign, tin, self-framing, young girl eating a slice of bread, 19" x 55", VG ..............................................$375.00 C

**Sunbeam Bread,** store employee tie with charm type emblem at bottom Miss Sunbeam, NM ...........................................$135.00 C

**Sunbeam Bread,** thermometer, metal and glass, dial-type, trademark Miss Sunbeam in center, 12" dia., 1957, G..........................$375.00 B

**Sunbeam Rolls,** sign, metal, Miss Sunbeam, "Come In!, We Serve, The Best, Made With Sunbeam Rolls," 18" x 54", EX ...................$950.00 B

**Sunbeam,** door push, die cut likeness of loaf of bread, Sunbeam girl, "White Stroehmann," EX....................................................$165.00 D

**Sundown Coffee,** tin, paper label, Egyptian pyramid desert scene, from Wm. Scotten Coffee Co., St. Louis, MO, 1-lb., EX ..........$95.00 D

**Sunkist Orange Juice,** sign, "I'll tell you a secret...Every day," girl with a glass, litho by Forbes, 1920s, 28" x 42", VG............$225.00 C

**Sunkist,** sign, cardboard, die cut, in shape of elves around a lemon, 1950s, 11" x 17", VG .........................................................$35.00 C

**Sunlight Soap,** sign, litho, die cut, from Lever Bros., 8½" x 10¾", 1900s, VG..................................................................$225.00 C

**Sunny Brook & Willow Creek Distillery Co.,** sign, paper, factory, young girls visiting factory, and nude nymphs in stream, 33" x 26", EX..................................................................$2,400.00 B

**Sunny Brook Kentucky Whiskey,** display bottle, glass, painted label, EX..................................................................$40.00 D

**Sunny Brook Pure Rye & Sour Mash Whiskey,** sign, metal, "Age & Purity, None Better Under The Sun," 45" x 25", EX .......$1,800.00 B

**Sunny Brook Pure Rye Bourbon,** match holder, tin, litho, whiskey bottle, good, graphics, 5"H, EX.......................................$155.00 C

**Sunny Brook Pure Rye,** match holder, tin, litho, rye bottle, 5" H, VG ..................................................................$125.00 C

**Sunny Brook,** backbar display, paper-mache, lettered base with sea captain, 9" x 13", VG .........................................................$85.00 C

**Sunny Brook,** clock, metal body with glass front, light-up, "Time to come over on the Sunny Brook," 17½" x 10¼" x 3¼", EX.$130.00 B

**Sunny Brook,** match holder, tin, litho, bottle in center, souvenir of 1904 World's Fair, 3⅜" x 4⅞", 1904, EX .....................$400.00 B

**Sunoco & Disney,** blotter, "there's only one" with Mickey and Minnie, 7¼" x 4", NM.................................................$150.00 C

**Sunoco Sun Heat Furnace Oil,** blotter, Disney theme with Mickey Mouse asleep in chair, 6" x 3¼", 1939, VG ....................$175.00 C

**Sunoco,** blotter, Donald Duck in car being pushed by a billy goat, "A quick start," VG ...........................................$135.00 B

**Sunoco,** bottle rack, wire, for old oil bottles, holds 8 painted label bottles, 18" x 14" x 9", EX .....................................$435.00 C

**Sunray Cigar,** sign, paper, "pleasing to all, mild and fragrant," 15" x 8½", EX.................................................$165.00 C

**Sunray Natural Power Oils,** sign, porcelain, one-sided, 25" x 25", VG...................................................$850.00 B

**Sunset Brand Wheat Flakes,** box, cardboard, sunset on front of box, by Montgomery Ward, & Co., 8 oz., EX.....................$450.00 B

**Sunset Corn Flakes,** cereal box, distributed by Montgomery Ward & Co., very scarce item due to limited production, VG .........$120.00 C

**Sunset Trail Cigars,** tin, strong colors, cowboys on horseback, 6⅛" x 4⅛", EX.................................................$475.00 B

**Sunshine Andy Gump Biscuits,** sign, paper, die cut, window for Loose-Wiles Biscuit Co., 11" x 12", EX............................$350.00 B

**Sunshine Biscuit, Inc,** building plate, brass, self-framing, 21" x 21", VG ...................................................$475.00 B

**Sunshine Biscuits,** calendar, paper, Sunshine Girl by Earl Christy, 1922, 8" x 18", EX ............................................$65.00 D

**Sunshine Biscuits,** store bin, metal, glass top, EX ..............$65.00 C

**Sunshine Biscuits,** truck, battery operated, Metalcraft Corp. St. Louis, Made in U.S.A., with Goodrich Silvertown tires, 12" L, G.....$260.00 C

**Sunshine Cigarettes,** sign, metal, open pack, "Twenty for 15¢," 14" x 18", EX.................................................$150.00 C

**Sunshine Cigarettes,** sign, tin, painted, cigarette package, "Twenty for 15¢," 14" x 18", F ..........................................$175.00 B

**Sunshine Peanut Butter,** pail, tin, litho, wire handles, 1-lb., EX..$91.00 B

**Sunshine Premium Beer,** sign with clock, metal and glass, reverse painting on glass, 12" x 9", EX...........................................$295.00 C

**Super Kant-Nock Gasoline,** globe, wide hull body with two lenses, 13½", VG ...................................................$525.00 C

**Super-Shell,** poster, paper, "Saves on Stop and Go Driving," car and trolley, 57½" x 33", VG...............................$50.00 C

**Super-Shell,** poster, paper, litho, 57½" x 33⅜", EX.............$95.00 C

**Super-x,** bone, papier-maché, "Steel oil ring...Dry As A Bone" on front, rare piece, 24" long, EX...................................$225.00 C

**Superior Flower Seeds,** sign, paper, framed, large bouquet of flowers, 15¾" x 27½", VG...............................................$100.00 B

**Superior Northwestern Mixed Paint,** poster, canvas, German shepherd with paint can, 1920s, 48" x 36", VG........................$110.00 C

**Superior Peanut Butter,** pail, metal, circus scenes, 12 oz., EX..$600.00 B

**Superior Spark Plug Co.,** sign, metal, large spark plug and man, 7" x 18", VG...................................................$195.00 C

**Surburg's Tobacco,** tin, dome top, "High grade smoking tobacco," 7" x 4¼" x 5¼", VG...................................................$255.00 C

**Sure Shot Chewing Tobacco,** store bin, metal, Indian with bow and arrow, 15" x 10" x 5", EX...............................................$900.00 C

**Sure Shot Chewing Tobacco,** store tin, rectangular, "It Touches The Spot," Indian, bow and arrow, metal lid, NM .............$650.00 C

**Sure Shot,** countertop tobacco tin, graphics and message around container sides, 15" x 6½" x 10¼", G...............................$475.00 B

**Sutherland & McMillian Co. Columbia Spice,** tin, litho, 2-oz., VG...................................................$275.00 B

**Swansdown Coffee,** can, metal, snap lid, 3 lb., EX............$245.00 B

**Swansdown Coffee,** tin, swan in center cameo, 4¼" x 6¼", EX..$125.00 C

**Sweet Burley Light Tobacco,** tin, round, counter use, 8" x 10", EX ...$135.00 C

**Sweet Caporal Cigarettes,** fan, die cut, 6¾" x 9", EX.............$40.00 C

**Sweet Caporal Cigarettes,** sign, paper, toga-clad woman, 14" x 23", 1900s, NM...............................................$395.00 B

**Sweet Cuba,** counter bin, "Sweet Cuba Tobacco" on front, 11" x 8¼", G...................................................$255.00 C

**Sweet Cuba,** counter bin, slant front, "The Kind that Suits," from Spaulding & Merrick, Chicago, 8" x 8" x 9½", EX .............$275.00 C

**Sweet Mist Chewing Tobacco,** store bin, metal, square, smaller lid on top, EX ...................................................$350.00 C

**Sweet Mist Chewing Tobacco,** tin, paper litho label, 8" x 10" x 6½", VG ...................................................$30.00 B

**Sweet Mist Tobacco,** can, tin, litho, three children playing in a water fountain, 8½" dia. x 11½", VG...............................$135.00 B

**Sweet Mist Tobacco,** store bin, cardboard, from Scotten Dillon, Detroit, 8" x 6¼" x 11", EX...............................................$155.00 C

**Sweet Orr & Co.,** sign, tin, litho, tug-o-war using the product for a rope, 26" x 19½", VG...............................................$900.00 B

**Sweet Orr Union Made Pants Overalls, Shirts,** sign, porcelain, 27" x 9", EX...................................................$470.00 B

**Sweet Rose,** cigar cutter, cast iron, countertop, lighter with light, 7" x 10¼" x 12", EX ...........................................................$475.00 C

**Sweet Violet Cigars,** sign, paper, boy smoking a cigar, "An Expert Judge," 1900, 10" x 11", EX............................$100.00 C

**Sweet-Orr Pants, Shirts, Overalls,** sign, porcelain, union made label in center of message, 24" x 10", EX.................$225.00 C

**Sweet-Orr Trousers Union Made,** sign, porcelain, double-sided, flange, 18" x 8", EX ...........................................$350.00 B

**Sweet-Orr,** sign, porcelain, rare, round, "Clothes To Work In," the usual tug-o-war in the center, 17¾" dia., VG.......................$700.00 C

**Sweet-Orr,** sign, tin, embossed, "Wear Sweet, Orr & Co.'s union made Overalls and Pants," 10" x 7¼", EX..........................$60.00 B

**Sweetheart Pure Peanut Butter,** pail, tin, litho, wire handles, slip-lid, 9¼" x 10½", EX .........................................$82.00 B

**Sweetheart Sugar Cones,** tin, litho, ice cream cones on front, 12½" x 15½", VG ...................................................$245.00 B

**Swell Blend Coffee,** tin, steam ship on front, key-wound lid, 1-lb., EX ...............................................................$90.00 B

**Swell Magic Colors Bubble Gum,** store display, cardboard, original bubble gum cigarette packages, priced per package, 1960s, EX .......$10.00 D

**Swift & Co.,** watch fob, cloisonne, company logo, 1906, EX..$120.00 B

**Swift's Arrow,** sign, cardboard, die cut, double-sided arrow with product box in center, "Borax American's Best," EX......$75.00 B

**Swift's Ice Cream,** clock, metal body, light-up, message at top of clock face, EX.................................................$235.00 C

**Swift's Peanut Butter,** tin litho, "Swift's Premium Quality," 10½" x 10⅛", VG .........................................................$30.00 B

**Swift's Pride Soap,** sign, stone litho on cardboard, winged delivery boy delivering a box of soap, 9¼" x 13½", 1900s, EX ........$375.00 C

**Swift's Pride,** Soap and Washing Powder, cardboard fan with wood handle, woman with wash basket, 1910s, 9½" dia., EX .....$165.00 B

**Swift's Syphilitic Specific,** stringer hanger, cardboard, cut to look like cast iron caldron with bail handle, 1870-90, EX...........$95.00 C

**Swing's Coffee,** display, metal and composition, automated black man serving coffee, 29" x 18" x 16", EX ........................$2,300.00 B

**Syke's,** comfort powder, tin litho of pair of small girls, 4½", EX..................................................................$275.00 C

**Sylcraft**...Undergarments of Quality, box, cardboard, pretty woman on box top, 11¼" x 11½" x 1½", EX ...................................$30.00 D

**Sylvania Halo Light,** sign, neon, window, 20" x 19", EX ...$250.00 D

**Sylvania Radio Service,** thermometer, metal, painted, scale type with tube at bottom of thermometer, 8¼" x 38½", G ........$165.00 C

**Symphonie Powder,** sign, paper, framed, litho of pretty girl with a can of the product, 14½" x 20½", EX ...................................$60.00 B

Tacoma Beer, tray, metal, tin, round, two cats, "Best, East or West," 13" dia., VG, $165.00 C.

Taxi Crimp Cut Tobacco, vertical pocket tin, early taxi with two men waiting on street in formal attire, NM, $4,900.00 B. *Courtesy of Buffalo Bay Auction Co.*

Taylor Co. Cigars, sign, reverse glass, foil-framed, "Tobacco & Sporting Goods," NM, $575.00 B. *Courtesy of Buffalo Bay Auction Co.*

Taylor-Wilson Chevrolet, ruler, plastic and metal, message on one side only, 1950 – 60s, 2" x 2", EX, $10.00 C. *Courtesy of B.J. Summers.*

The Thompson Store, brush, wood and fiber, "Where You Expect Good Value and Find It," 7" x 1½" x 1½", EX, $65.00 C. *Courtesy of B.J. Summers.*

---

T T Bitters, match holder, tin, litho, wall-hung, Stulz Bros., Kansas City, Mo., Sole Owners, 3⅜" x 4⅞", EX...................................$425.00 B

T.C. Evans Agency Boston, book mark, tin, litho, promoting the company, EX.................................................$135.00 C

Ta-che, crate label, paper, California Orange, Indian profile, 11" x 10", EX .................................................................$35.00 D

Table King Coffee, tin, pry lid, "Makes A Good Meal Better," VG...........................................................................$85.00 D

Tacoma Brewing Co., note holder, celluloid, "For Your Beverage Wants Call...Main 2835," EX.................................$65.00 C

Tacoma Cigars, sign, paper, Indian princess, 12" x 20", EX..$650.00 B

Taft Oil Burners, sign, porcelain enamel, heavy, "authorized dealer for cook stoves...for room heaters," 22" x 13¾", EX ..........$350.00 B

Taka-Kola, tip tray, metal, "Every Hour...Take No Other," woman over clock face on tray center, 4¼" dia., EX ...................$325.00 B

Talbot's Ant Powder, store display shelf, tin, 14½" x 10½", EX $75.00 D

Tansill's Punch, cigar box, wooden, elf on inside lid and partial tax stamp on box, 50-count, 1901, G.............................. $65.00 C

Target Cigarette Tobacco, banner, canvas, man and a large package of the product, 118" x 43", EX........................................... $175.00 C

Tarr Beer, label, paper, with revenue tax stamp, 1933-36, 12 oz., VG .......................................................................$20.00 D

Tavern Beer, can, metal, cone top, vintage coach, EX...$120.00 B

Taxi Crimp Cut Tobacco, vertical pocket tin, early taxi with two men waiting on street in formal attire, F ..........................$425.00 D

Taylor Co. Cigars, sign, reverse glass, foil-framed, "Tobacco & Sporting Goods," VG.......................................................$425.00 C

Taystee Bread, sign, paper, "Enjoy...Famous for its freshness...today and everyday," chef holding bread, 1950s, 12" x 18", EX.............................................................................$40.00 B

Third Liberty Loan, poster, paper, litho, 21" x 28", VG, $275.00 B.

Thompson, Wilson & Co., Distillers, coin purse, leather, snap closure, front, "Compliments of...Paducah, KY," 1900 – 10s, 4½" x 2½", EX, $75.00 C. *Courtesy of B.J. Summers.*

Thompson, Wilson & Co., sign, paper, Roanoke Rye label, in original frame, 1900s, 14" x 19", EX, $475.00 C. *Courtesy of B.J. Summers.*

Three Rivers Whiskey, backbar bottle, glass, enamel lettering, a H. Weil & Sons label, 1900 – 10s, 1 qt, NM, $75.00 C. *Courtesy of B.J. Summers.*

Tip-Top Bread, sign, tin, loaf of bread on top of lettering, 30" wide, VG, $30.00 B.

---

**TE Tigre Tobacco,** store bin, metal, elephant and tiger, 9" x 5" x 5", EX.................................................................$145.00 C

**Teaberry Gum,** tin, litho, great graphics on all sides and on both the inside and outside of the lid, good strong colors, 6¾" L, EX .$225.00 B

**Tech Beer,** sign, metal, self-framing, painted, "Too good to forget," Pittsburgh Brewing Co., Pittsburgh, Pa., hunting scene, 26½" x 18½", VG .............................................................$135.00 C

**Tech Beer,** sign, metal, self-framing, painted, "Too good to forget," Pittsburgh Brewing Co., Pittsburgh, Pa., hunting scene, 26½" x 18½", G ..............................................................$125.00 D

**Tech Beer,** tip tray, metal, product bottle in center, "None Better" Pittsburgh Brewing Co., 6⅝", EX ....................................$95.00 C

**Ted Toddy Pictures Co.,** poster, paper, litho, "She's too Mean For Me," 26" x 39", VG.....................................................$100.00 C

**Teddie Peanuts,** tin, litho, large peanut, John W. Leavitt Co., Boston, Mass., 10-lb., 8¼" x 9⅝", EX ...............................$300.00 B

**Teddy Bears Brand Lemons,** sign, paper, two bears with lemons, 12" x 18", EX .......................................................$500.00 D

**Teddy Brand Peanuts,** tin, Jumbo Whole Salted Peanuts label on both sides, red, 1-lb., EX ...............................................$75.00 B

**Teddy Cigarettes,** pocket tin, Roosevelt's image, 50 ct., VG .$85.00 D

**Teem,** sign, metal, lemon logo, "An Ice Clear Lemon-Lime Drink," 1960s, 27" x 19", VG ......................................................$55.00 D

**Teem,** thermometer, metal, scale-type, bottle beside the scale, 12" x 27¾", VG ........................................................$135.00 C

**Telephone,** sign, metal frame and plastic message, light-up, for pay station booths, 19½" x 5¾", EX.......................................$175.00 B

**Telephone,** sign, metal frame and plastic message, light-up, for pay station booths, 19½" x 5¾", VG .........................................$165.00 C

**Telephone,** sign, porcelain, double-sided, "American Telephone and Telegraph Co and Associated Companies," Bell System logo in center, 20" x 20", EX ..............................................................$395.00 C

**Telephone,** sign, porcelain, double-sided, "The Pacific Telephone and Telegraph Co....American Telephone and Telegraph Co.," Bell System logo in center, 12" x 11", VG ...............................$225.00 B

Tobacco Girl, container, tin, litho, pretty young woman with a tobacco leaf, 6¼" x 4½" x 5½", VG, $1,500.00 B. *Courtesy of Collectors Auction Services.*

Touch Down Smoking Tobacco, sign, cardboard, die cut, counter, "Fragrant and Mellow with Age," with men at goal line, 9½" x 6", EX, $407.00 B. *Courtesy of Buffalo Bay Auction Co.*

Trasks Ointment, sign, cardboard, die cut, Magnetic Ointment for hemorrhoids and chafing, little boy and girl on front, 6¾" x 9", NM, $150.00 C. *Courtesy of Buffalo Bay Auction Co.*

Tree Brand Shoes, Battreall Shoe Co., sign, metal, flange, double-sided, NM, $1,000.00 D. *Courtesy of Riverview Antique Mall.*

---

Telephone, sign, porcelain, double-sided, flange, Bell System logo in center, 16¼" x 14", VG ....................................$225.00 C

Telephone, sign, porcelain, flange, "Public Telephone," early telephone in center, 18" x 18", EX............................ $225.00 C

Telephone, sign, porcelain, flange, "Public Telephone," very early cradle phone in center, 16" x 16", EX ...............................$575.00 C

Telephone, sign, porcelain, single-sided, hand pointing to phone, foreign, 31½" x 7⅞", VG....................................$235.00 B

Tellings Ice Cream, sign, cardboard, die cut, young child eating ice cream, 14" dia., VG.............................................$225.00 D

Tennessee Brewing Co., sign, metal, painted, "51 Extra Aged Splits 10¢," 20¼" x 28¼", EX............................................ $125.00 D

Terre Haute Brewing Co., Inc., tin, litho, for Champagne Velvet Beer, man fishing in stream, Terre Haute, Indiana, 19½" x 14½", VG ................................................................$160.00 B

Terre Haute Brewing Co., sign, pressed board, CV Beer, 16½" x 10½", EX ...........................................................$110.00 B

Terriff Talcum Powder, container, tin, litho, man, Portland, Mich, 2⅝" x 5¾", EX......................................................... $925.00 B

Tetley's Tea, sample container, tin, litho, elephant on lid, 2¼" x 1¾" x ¾", EX .........................................................$125.00 C

Texaco Diesel Chief Diesel Fuel, pump sign, porcelain, single-sided, "Made in U.S.A./3-11-61," 12" x 18", VG ........ $150.00 C

Texaco Fire Chief Gasoline, sign, porcelain, 18" x 12", EX....$275.00 C

Texaco Fire Chief, hat, celluloid, promotional, reflective front shield, 5" x 11", EX .............................................................$75.00 C

Texaco Fire Chief, hat, fireman's, plastic, large white shield on front with product message, 8" tall, white on red, EX ........$95.00 D

Texaco Fire Chief, pump sign, porcelain, one-sided, trademark fire hat, 12" x 18", VG .............................................................$115.00 C

Texaco Motor Oil, sign, metal, double-sided, painted, flange, "Easy Pour Can...Two Quarts," oil being poured from a vintage two-quart can, 17½" x 27⅜", G ................................$2,500.00 B

Texaco Tractor Lubricants, display, paper, shows correct products to use, VG.............................................................$85.00 D

Texaco, gas globe, narrow glass body with two glass globes, red star with green T, 13½" dia., VG ..............................................$525.00 C

Triangle Collars, display, metal with wood graining, for counter top display, 24" tall, VG, $325.00 B.

Triple 16 Cola, sign, tin, embossed, product bottle, NOS, 11½" x 31½", EX, $150.00 B.

Tubular Cream Separators, match holder, "The Pet of the Dairy," great woman with child at separator, 6¾" H, EX, $375.00 B. *Courtesy of Richard Opfer Auctioneering, Inc.*

Tucker Tire Co., knife, celluloid and metal, built in bottle opener and corkscrew, single blade, 3" long closed, VG, $25.00 C. *Courtesy of B.J. Summers.*

Turkish Trophies Cigarettes, sign, paper, litho, pretty girl with Turkish background scene, 20" x 30", G, $175.00 C.

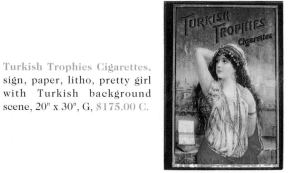

---

**Texaco**, pinback badge, metal, service station attendant's, Texaco Scotties, 3¼" x 3¼", EX .......................................$525.00 B

**Texaco**, restroom key tags, NOS, 3½" x 5½", EX .................$45.00 B

**Texaco**, restroom key tags, NOS, 3½" x 5½", NM .......................$50.00 C

**Texaco**, sign, porcelain, one-sided, "keyhole," "G.T. Fowle...consignee," 21" x 16", VG.......................................$250.00 B

**Texaco**, sign, porcelain, single-sided, dealer, "Gasoline...Motor Oil," 41½" dia., G........................................$155.00 C

**Texaco**, sleeve patch, cloth, star in circle at bottom of patch, lettering in black, 2¼" x 2", G .......................................$10.00 C

**Texaco**, thermometer, metal body, glass front, dial-type, dealer info around outside face, 12" dia., EX .......................................$325.00 D

**Texaco**, toy tanker, plastic, "Exclusive Texaco dealer offer," motorized, original cardboard box, 5" x 26½", EX.....................$200.00 C

**Texaco**, watch fob, metal, embossed, Texaco star, 1¼" x 1⅜", EX .......................................$240.00 B

**Texas Neon Adv Co.**, sign, porcelain, black lettering on inverted triangle, 7", VG.......................................$75.00 C

**Texcomo Coffee**, tin, press lid, "This Symbol Stands For Purity" with swastika symbol, before Hitler the swastika was considered a good luck sign, 6" x 8", EX .......................................$165.00 D

**Thermo Alcohol Anti-Freeze**, can, metal, Publicker Commerical Alcohol Co., handle and pour spout, 1 gal., VG .................$45.00 C

**Thermo Anti-Freeze**, can, snowman wearing a scarf, 6½" x 7¾", 1945, VG .......................................$75.00 C

**Thermo Denatured Alcohol**, thermometer, tin, "Protect Your Radiator With...," 16" x 72", G .......................................$350.00 C

**Thistle Brand Pure Lard**, pail, metal, name and logo, 6" x 5½" dia., VG .......................................$55.00 C

**Thomas A. Edison**, spark plug in original cardboard box, Edison-Splitdorf Corporation, G .......................................$30.00 D

**Thomas J. Lipton**, tea tin, litho, slaves, factory, and cattle, 8½" x 5½" x 6", VG .......................................$175.00 D

**Thomas J. Webb Coffee,** tin, key wind lid. "The Winning Cup," 1 lb., EX..............................................................$50.00 D

**Thomas Moore Whiskey,** tray, metal, pretty nude girl on a red blanket in a woodland scene, "Take A Little Moore...," 10" dia., EX...$675.00 C

**Thompson's Malted Milk,** canister, porcelain, lettering and shield, 9½" tall x 7" dia., EX ...........................................$500.00 D

**Thos. J. Scalon,** calendar top, tin over cardboard, litho, young girl, bar supplies and hotel china, 13¼" x 19¼", 1906, VG .........$225.00 B

**Three Feathers Choice Granulated Plug Cut,** pocket tin, vertical, VG ...................................................$275.00 C

**Three Knights,** condom tin, litho, three knights on horseback, Goodyear Rubber Co., NY, 2⅛" x 1⅝", EX .................$150.00 B

**Three RRR's Motor Oil,** can, metal, horse head in center, Russell Oil Company, 1 qt., EX ......................................$425.00 C

**3V Cola,** sign, metal, 29" dia., G .........................................$95.00 C

**Thrift Regular Gas,** globe, three-piece glass gill body with glass lens 13½" dia., VG ...............................................$600.00 C

**Thumper Sun Cured Tobacco,** pouch, cloth, VG ..............$10.00 D

**Thurber Coffee,** can, tin, litho, early company headquarters, 1-lb., 1880s, EX.............................................................$165.00 D

**Tidewater Associated Credit Cards Welcome,** sign, metal, double-sided, hanging, 20" x 14", EX ...................................$225.00 C

**Tidex Motor Oil,** can, metal, screw top, "Full Bodied Motor Oil," 2 gal., EX ..................................................................$95.00 C

**Tidex,** gas globe, low profile metal body with two glass lenses, 16½" dia., VG ...............................................................$450.00 C

**Tiger Bright Sweet Chewing Tobacco,** pocket tin, from P. Lorillard & Co., EX..........................................................$185.00 C

**Tiger Chewing Tobacco,** container, tin, tiger in center of lid in spotlight, 6" x 4" x 2½", EX..........................................$45.00 D

**Tillman Quality Coffee,** tin, key wind lid, unopened, 1 lb., EX.$90.00 D

**Time Super Gasoline,** pump sign, porcelain, "Super Gasoline," 9" x 14", EX ......................................................................$375.00 C

**Times Square Smoking Mixture,** pocket tin, slip lid, "...Mellowed In Wood," EX..............................................................$350.00 D

**Times Square Smoking Mixture,** pocket tin, vertical, Times Square, slip lid, 3" x 4½", EX.............................................$275.00 D

**Times Square,** Smoking Tobacco, pocket tin, sky line at night, flip-lid, EX ........................................................$2,255.00 D

**Timur Coffee,** container, tin, litho, pry-lid, Arabian-type rider on horseback, 1-lb., NM.........................................$1,210.00 B

**Tintex,** display cabinet, metal, woman using product, "Tints & Dyes Anything Any Color," 23" x 22" x 7", VG.........................$145.00 D

**Tintex,** sig, tin, painted, "tints as you rinse," woman tinting clothes, 21¼" x 23", VG...........................................................$75.00 C

**Tintex,** sign, tin, painted, "tints as you rinse," woman tinting clothes, 21¼" x 23", G.............................................$55.00 C

**Tip-Top Sweet Smoke and Chew Tobacco,** pail, paper label, 1926 tobacco stamp on lid, G .....................................$95.00 D

**Tivioli Brewing Co.,** tip tray, metal, bottle in center, Detroit, 4⅛" dia., EX..................................................................$95.00 C

**Tobacco Girl,** container, tin, litho, pretty young woman with a tobacco leaf, 6¼" x 4½" x 5½", F ............................$375.00 D

**Tobins' Cork Town Pipe Tobacco,** sign, rare piece, EX..............$600.00 B

**Toddy Pictures Company,** poster, paper, litho, "Return of Mandy's Husband" starring Mantan Morehead and F.E. Miller, 26½" x 40½", G .............................................................................$135.00 D

**Tokheim Gasoline Pumps Authorized Service,** sign, porcelain, one-sided, NOS, 19½" x 13", EX.....................................$450.00 C

**Tokheim Gasoline Pumps,** sign, porcelain, "...Authorized Service," 19½" x 13", EX...............................................$395.00 C

**Tokio Cigarettes,** sign, cardboard, stamped wood frame, man in turban enjoying a cigarette, good strong colors, 25" x 33", VG..........$210.00 B

**Toledo Scales,** sign, porcelain, 17½" x 11", EX.................$145.00 B

**Tom Keene Cigars,** sign, cardboard, easel back, store display of product container, NM ......................................$98.00 B

**Tom's Toasted Peanuts 5¢,** store jar, glass, lettering painted on front, EX............................................................$75.00 D

**Tom's Toasted Peanuts,** store jar, Tom's lid, EX............$75.00 D

**Tom's Toasted Peanuts,** thermometer, metal, VG.............$45.00 D

**Tom's Toasted Peanuts,** thermometer, tin, bag of the product on front, 6" x 16", NM ................................................$95.00 C

**Tom's,** sign, metal, embossed lettering, "Time Out For Tom's," products, 20" x 28", EX ....................................$500.00 B

**Tomahawk Scrap Tobacco,** sign, tin, litho, embossed, original oak frame, 9¼" x 12", EX ..............................................$500.00 B

**Tonka Smoking Mixture,** pocket tin, metal, soldiers by tent, rounded corners, McAlpin Tobacco Co., EX ..............................$225.00 D

**Top Notch Soda,** sign, cardboard, display area for list of products under area, 7" x 14", VG .......................................$55.00 C

**Topaz Roasted Coffee,** container, tin, paper label, knight on horseback, free sample container, 1⅞" x 2⅝", EX.....................$65.00 D

**Topsy City Dairy,** clock, electric, black child on face, promoting chocolate milk, 14¼" sq., EX ..............................$275.00 B

**Torrey's Original Old Mt. Vernon Ale,** tip tray, metal, product bottle in tray center, 3⅝" dia., EX.............................$85.00 C

**Totem Tobacco,** pocket tin, oval, good strong coloring, EX .$1,150.00 B

**Totem Tobacco,** pocket tin, totem pole and Indian smoking pipe, EX.........................................................................$1,200.00 B

**Touch Down Smoking Tobacco,** counter sign, cardboard, die cut, "Fragrant and Mellow with Age," men at goal line, 9½" x 6", VG .....$315.00 C

**Tower Gasoline,** globe, wide glass body with lenses, tower on face, 13½" dia., VG ................................................................$825.00 C

**Tower Root Beer,** sign, tin, embossed, bottle, "Like Mother Used To Make," 8¾" x 19½", EX....................................$100.00 B

**Towle's Blacksmith Syrup,** tin, litho, blacksmith scene on front, 5" x 4¾" x 2⅞", EX.....................................................$195.00 C

**Towle's Log Cabin Syrup,** pull toy, tin, litho, in shape of log cabin, 5¾" x 4¾" x 3¾", EX ...................................................$195.00 C

**Towle's Log Cabin Syrup,** tin, cabin shaped, people sitting on bench waiting to see Dr RU Well, EX.................................$350.00 D

**Townsend Cream Top Milk,** bill hook, celluloid, 2' x 2¾", Ex.$85.00 D

**Tracto Motor Oil,** sign, metal, embossed, painted, 35" x 11", NM.........................................................................$115.00 C

**Train Master Cigars,** pocket tin, vertical, train ticket, EX ..$85.00 C

**Trasks Ointment,** sign, cardboard, die cut, Magnetic Ointment for hemorrhoids and chafing, little boy and girl on front, 6¾" x 9", VG .........................................................................$95.00 D

**Traveler Leading Cigar,** canister, tin, round, "The National Smoke," VG..........................................................................$25.00 D

**Travelers Express Money Orders,** clock, light-up, 26" x 12" x 4¼", G................................................................................$35.00 C

**Treasure Island Honey,** tin, pry lid, boy and girl digging in sand for treasure, 5" x 4" dia., VG........................................$35.00 D

**Tree Brand Shoes,** sign, metal, flange, double-sided, Battreall Shoe Co., EX..........................................................................$850.00 D

**Trico Wiper Blades,** sign, tin, double-sided, flange, "replace your...once a year," 18" x 19¾", VG ...............................$195.00 C

**Tricora Corset,** sign, yard-long, 12" x 28", EX....................$575.00 C

**Triple 16 Cola,** sign, tin, embossed, tilted bottle under "It's Bigger, It's Better, 16 ounces," 11½" x 31½", G ...................$55.00 D

**Triple A Artesian Water,** sign, porcelain, logo and company name, 30" x 24", VG.................................................................$145.00 C

**Triple AAA Root Beer,** decal, girl with product, 5¢ root beer, 8" x 6½", EX ............................................................$15.00 C

**Triple AAA Root Beer,** sign, metal, self-framing, company logo and "Just Say...," 28" x 19", EX.......................................$175.00 C

**Triple AAA Root Beer,** sign, tin, single-sided, self-framing, bottle, 28" x 19½", VG..................................................$135.00 C

**Triple EXFamily,** sign, cardboard, basket of bread being carried by pretty girl, "The Standard Flour," 16" x 23", VG .................$375.00 B

**Triton 76 Premium Motor Oil,** sign, porcelain, tilted can "Only Two Changes A Year," double-sided, 30" dia., EX ...........$895.00 C

**Triumph Cycle Bath,** can, metal, a motorcycle in a man's claw footed bath tub, 1 pt., EX ....................................................$95.00 C

**Trojan T Gasoline,** sign, porcelain, 28" x 22", G .....................$215.00 C

**Trojan T Gasoline,** sign, porcelain, 28" x 22", VG.............$450.00 D

**Trojan-Enz Condom,** container, tin, litho, Roman helmeted man in center, 2⅛" x 1⅝" x ¼", EX..........................$300.00 B

**Trolley Chewing Tobacco,** store bin, metal, gold lettering and gold checkered border, scarce item, VG ...........................$1,150.00 B

**Trop-Artic Auto Oil,** can, metal, artic and tropical conditions featured, 5 gal., EX.................................................................$895.00 C

**Tropic Cigar,** can, tin liberty, "Othello" on front, 6¼" x 4" x 5½", VG .........................................................................$85.00 C

**Trout-Line Tobacco,** vertical tin, man netting a trout in a stream, EX.........................................................................$650.00 B

**Tru Ade,** sign, porcelain, double-sided, "Drink a better beverage, Not Carbonated," 1951, 20" x 14", EX ......................$250.00 C

**Tru Ade,** thermometer, litho, stenciled, bottle, 6" x 15", EX..$195.00 C

**Tru-Ade,** door push, metal, "Drink...Naturally Delicious Orange," 31" x 2½", orange on yellow, EX ......................................$135.00 C

**Tru-Ade,** sign, metal, double-sided, flange, wavy hand and bottle, "Drink A Better Beverage," 1951, 20" x 14", VG .................$250.00 D

**Tru-Test Pocketknives,** display case, wood and glass, three shelves and logo, back openeing, EX ...............................................$65.00 B

**True Fruit Soda,** sign, cardboard, "delicious," grapes and berries, 1905, 9" x 16", VG ......................................................$65.00 B

**True Fruit Soda,** sign, cardboard, grapes and berries, 1905, 9" x 16", EX.........................................................................$90.00 B

**Tube Rose,** sign, tin, painted, "It's mild and suits your taste," Scotch Snuff can at right of message, 27⅝" x 17½", EX ...............$115.00 D

**Tubular Cream Separators,** match holder, "The Pet of the Dairy," woman with child at separator, 6¾" H, G ...........................$195.00 C

**Tubular Cream Separators,** sign, tin, litho, separators, 28" x 5", EX ........................................................$245.00 B

**Tuckett's Old Squire,** pocket tin, vertical, litho, old squire in cameo, 3⅛" x 4½" x .785", EX ...........................$700.00 B

**Tuckett's Orinoco Tobacco,** tin, litho, Canadian, old man enjoying his pipe, 4¼" x 3¾", G.....................................$110.00 B

**Tucketts Orinco Cut Fine Smoking Tobacco,** container, tin, fishing scene, from Hamilton Canada, 3½" x 2¾" x 1⅝", EX.........$155.00 C

**Tudor Coffee,** container, tin, paper, litho, mansion on mountain, 1-lb., EX........................................................$95.00 D

**Tudor Tea Coffee, Cocoa,** watch fob, celluloid, vintage factory, 1¾" x 2", EX..............................................................$400.00 B

**Tums,** Baby Snooks toy, die cut, message on the back for both Tums and the NBC Radio Show of Fanny Brice, 16" T, 1950s, EX ........................................................$65.00 D

**Tums,** clock, reverse glass face, metal body, wood frame, light-up, 16¼" x 16¼", EX .............................................$155.00 C

**Tums,** fan, cardboard, pretty girl, "For Health & Beauty...," 6" x 11", EX........................................................$50.00 D

**Tums,** sign, cardboard, die cut, easel back, "Bring on your hot mince pie–all foods agree with me now, I use Tums for my Tummy," 9¼" x 15¼", EX ............................................$75.00 C

**Tums,** thermometer, metal, painted, vertical scale, "for the tummy...for acid indigestion, heartburn," messages at top and bottom of scale, 4" x 9", NM .....................................$95.00 D

**Tung Sol Electron Tubes,** clock, light-up, "Radio...Television ...Service," Telechron electric clock, 15" dia., VG .....................$175.00 C

**Turf Cigarettes,** sign, porcelain, "Quality Wins," Pegasus at top, 20" x 30", NM..............................................$225.00 C

**Turkey Brand Coffee,** watch fob, metal, product name, EX ........$95.00 D

**Turkish Dyes,** cabinet, wood and paper, moon & star logo, 17" x 27½" x 9", EX ...............................................$325.00 C

**Turnbull's Standard Scotch Whisky,** sign, tin, embossed, painted, "Offices-51 High Street, HAWICK," note spelling of whisky, 24½" x 18", G ............................................$135.00 D

**Turnbull's Standard Scotch Whisky,** sign, tin, embossed, painted, bottle in center, "Offices-51 High Street, HAWICK," note spelling of whisky, 24½" x 18", VG...............................$175.00 C

**Tuxedo Tobacco,** tin, "Specially Prepared For Pipe Or...," man in tuxedo, VG ........................................$140.00 B

**Tuxedo,** humidor, glass, paper label, wire-snap closure lid, 7" H, EX ..........................................................$175.00 C

**TWA,** ashtray, metal, airplane on arm over ashtray, 10" x 6", VG ..........................................................$195.00 D

**Twang Vitamin Root Beer,** sign, tin, embossed, "Save Caps for Premiums," 14¼" dia., G .........................................$65.00 C

**Twang Vitamin Root Beer,** sign, tin, embossed, bottle, tap, 14¼" dia., EX .......................................................$120.00 B

**Twenty Grand Double Edge,** display, cardboard, horse shoe shaped design for razor blade packages, 9" x 12", EX .....................$75.00 D

**Twin Cola,** sign, cardboard, "ice cold...a new thirst chaser," 9" x 11½", EX .......................................................$40.00 D

**Twin Oaks Mixture,** box, metal, casket shape with embossed product name on front, EX.....................................$145.00 D

**Twin Oaks Mixture,** pocket tin, flip lid, vertical message and lettering, EX........................................................$75.00 D

**Twin Ports Coffee,** container, paper label, screw-top, ocean vessel on front, 1-lb., EX ...............................................$135.00 C

**Twin Ports Steel Cut Coffee,** tin, ships circled around company name, "Where Sail Meets Rail," 1 lb., EX.........................$230.00 B

**Two Homers Cigars,** sign, paper label, clock hands to indicate time store owner would return to the store, 2 cigars 5¢, 12" sq., EX ..........$65.00 D

**Tydol Flying A,** banner, cloth, Flying A giant putting wings on older model car, 79" x 34", EX ......................................$155.00 C

**Tydol Flying A,** pump sign, porcelain, one-sided, 9¾" dia., G ..$300.00 C

**Tydol,** gas globe, low profile metal body with two glass lenses, 16½" dia., G ..........................................................$450.00 C

**Tydol,** license plate attachment, tin, die cut, embossed, "Running Man," 4½" x 6⅝", G ...........................................$135.00 C

**Tyee Tackle,** calendar, paper, young woman in a fishing scene, 12" x 16½", 1928, EX...................................$550.00 B

UMC Cartridges, sign, tin, die cut, painted, flange, bull head, G, $695.00 D. *Courtesy of Riverview Antique Mall.*

UMC Co., calendar, mother dog and pups, 14" x 28¼", 1894, EX, $4,550.00 B. *Courtesy of Past Tyme Pleasures.*

UMC Union Metallic Cartridge Co., calendar, Teddy Roosevelt and the 1st U.S. Cavalry "Rough Riders," top and bottom metal bands, 13½" x 28", 1899, EX, $425.00 C. *Courtesy of Past Tyme Pleasures.*

Uncle Sam Stock Medicine Co., Quincy, Ill., U.S.A., calendar, heavy paper, patriotic images of Statue of Liberty and naval ships returning home, great item, 1919, 15" x 20", NM, $225.00 B. *Courtesy of Buffalo Bay Auction Co.*

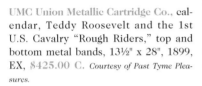

Union 76, Certified Service, toy truck, original box, steerable wheels, original decals, NOS, 24½" x 9½" x 9½", EX, $225.00 C. *Courtesy of Rare Bird Antique Mall/Jon & Joan Wright.*

United Motors Service, sign, porcelain, oval, early auto in center, 60" x 36", 1930s, EX, $1,500.00 B. *Courtesy of Muddy River Trading Co./Gary Metz.*

U and I Lemonade, sign, cardboard, single-sided, 22" x 19", VG ..$15.00 D

U.S. Army, sign, enamel, double-sided, "I Want You," designed to fit in metal sidewalk frame, 25" x 38", VG ......................$325.00 C

U.S. Cartridge Co., calendar, paper, large grizzly bear carrying a box of cartridges while a hunter hides in a tree, 14" x 26", 1922, EX................................................................................$325.00 C

U.S. Marine, lunch pail, tin, litho, "Smoke or Chew," service man on front, EX....................................................................$209.00 B

U.S. Quality Enameled Ware, sign, curved glass, light-up, store, enamel steam pot likeness in center, 7" x 13½", VG............$425.00 C

U.S. School Garden, poster, cardboard, young boy with large basket full of vegetables, "Raised 'em myself in my...," framed, EX..$200.00 C

Ubero Coffee Co., tip tray, tin, litho, coffee container in center, 4¼", VG .........................................................................$170.00 B

UMC "Club" Brass Shells, box, two-piece, 12 ga., 4¼" x 4¼" x 2¼", EX ............................................................................$80.00 B

UMC Cartridges, sign, tin, die cut, painted, flange, bull head, EX ...................................................................................$995.00 C

UMC Co., calendar, mother dog and pups , 14" x 28¼", 1894, G ................................................................................ $1,500.00 C

UMC Shot, poster, a covey of quail in flight, 15" x 29¼", 1908, EX ...................................................................................$175.00 C

UMC Smokless Powder Shot Shells, sign, paper, pups bedded down in an old hunting jacket, 1904, 16" x 25", EX................$1,050.00 B

United States Fur Company, poster, paperboard, black boys trying to run an animal out of a hollow log, only to discover it's a skunk, United States Fur Co., St. Louis Mo., "Ship us your Furs," 15" x 20½", 1920s, EX, $350.00 B. *Courtesy of Buffalo Bay Auction Co.*

U.S. Army, I Want You, sign, double-sided, designed to fit in metal sidewalk frame, 25" x 38", EX, $425.00 C. *Courtesy of B.J. Summers.*

U.S. Quality Enameled Ware, sign, curved glass, light-up, store, enamel steam pot likeness in center, 7" x 13½", EX, $550.00 B. *Courtesy of Muddy River Trading Co./Gary Metz.*

Utica Club, tray, metal, serving size, factory scene in center, 12" dia., VG, $45.00 B.

UT, lighter, metal, premium from Usher Transport, reverse reads "Our Only Product Is Service," made by Barlow, 1¼" x 2¼" x ⅜", EX, $25.00 C. *Courtesy of B.J. Summers.*

---

UMC Steel Lined Shells, sign, paper, three shells, "The Only American Steel Lined Shell, Buy Here," 17" x 24", EX..................$650.00 B

UMC Union Metallic Cartridge Co., calendar, Teddy Roosevelt and the 1st U.S. Cavalry "Rough Riders," top and bottom metal bands, 13½" x 28", 1899, VG .......................................................$250.00 C

UMC-Remington, poster, cowboy getting ready to go hunting, by Phillip R. Goodwin, 17" x 24½", 1910, EX .........................$325.00 C

UMWA, miner's hat, salesman sample, wood display, complete with helmet light, 15" x 17½", G ..............................................$110.00 D

Uncle Daniel Fine Cut Tobacco, product pack, paper, 1 oz., EX .....................................................................$145.00 D

Uncle Green, cigar tin, Liberty can with slip lid, EX.........$135.00 C

Uncle John's Syrup, display, cardboard, cut out, Uncle John pouring syrup onto a plate of pancakes held by a small child, 5 pieces, 24" x 40", EX ..........................................................$695.00 D

Uncle John's Syrup, display, paper, five-piece, store window, original envelope, measurement of Uncle John is 40" x 24", NM ......$600.00 B

Uncle John's Syrup, display, window, Uncle John pouring syrup on hot cakes being held by young boy, 45" x 50", NM ............$875.00 C

Uncle Sam Bubble Gum, trade card, cardboard, 1941, EX.$35.00 D

Uncle Sam Shoe Polish, container, tin, Uncle Sam on front and small boy polishing Uncle Sam's shoes on back side, 3½", EX...........$50.00 C

Uncle Sam Smoking Tobacco, pocket tin, vertical lettering, EX ..................................................................$1,980.00 B

Uncle Sam Stock Medicine Co. Quincy, Ill., U.S.A., calendar, heavy paper, patriotic images of Statue of Liberty and naval ships returning home, great item, 1919, 15" x 20", VG.............$155.00 D

Uncle Sam, cigar box, label, paper, Uncle Sam dropping cigars on the world, 9" x 6", VG.........................................................$45.00 D

Uncle Tom's Cabin, poster, cardboard, litho, black man dancing with a child, 21" x 28", 1890s, EX.....................................$275.00 B

Uncle Tom's Cabin, poster, exaggerated black man's head, "Jes Yo Come Along an' laff at Uncle Tom's Cabin," 41" x 89½", VG..$750.00 B

**Uncle Tom's Cabin,** poster, paper, litho, black man in front of cabin with young girl, Wm. M. Donaldson & Co. Pub's Cincinnati, Oh, 33½" x 27⅜", G ............................................$175.00 B

**Uncle Tom's Cabin,** poster, paper, litho, framed, "Topsy's Recreation" with Topsy in center, 45½" x 83", EX ........................$700.00 B

**Uncle Tom's Cabin,** printers proof, stone litho, by Donaldson & Co., Cincinnati, old black man seated next to a dog with a young white girl standing next to him, 33¼" x 27½", 1883, NM ............$350.00 B

**Uncle Tom's Chewing Gum,** display box, cardboard with paper label, with man in portrait beside product lettering, 9" x 4" x 2", EX ..$300.00 B

**Uncle Wiggily,** pail, early litho from the Mueller Keller Candy Co., St. Joseph, MO, Lang Campbell comic strip characters, 1923, EX ............................................ $475.00 B

**Uneeda Bakers,** display, cardboard, standup, boy in yellow slicker holding a glass front biscuit box, 51" high, EX..................$825.00 D

**Uneeda Bakers,** sign, cardboard, "Uneeda Bakers Premium Is The Prize Soda Cracker," in shape of blue ribbon, 19" x 37", EX .$45.00 D

**Uneeda Biscuit,** letter opener, tin, litho, trademark, boy in yellow slicker on handle, 1¾" x 8¾", G ............................................$55.00 C

**Uneeda Biscuit,** sign, cardboard, string-hung, "Don't Forget," kid in slicker, never used, 21" x 16½", EX ..........................................$275.00 B

**Uneeda Biscuit,** sign, paper, litho, wood frame, according to the info this was to be displayed only in November, 21½" x 12½", VG...................................................................$95.00 C

**Uneeda Biscuit,** sign, paperboard, trolley, product bound up on top of books, EX ............................................$60.00 B

**Unguentine,** display, cardboard, litho, sunburned woman applying the product, 22½" x 35", EX ............................................$100.00 B

**Union 76 Certified Service Truck,** toy truck, original box, steerable wheels, original decals, NOS, 24½" x 9½" x 9½", VG.........$165.00 C

**Union 76,** padlock, brass, with trademark, 3" tall, EX .....$125.00 C

**Union 76 Regular Gasoline,** pump sign, porcelain, one-sided, 9" x 11¾", VG ............................................$115.00 C

**Union 76,** salt & pepper set, hard-to-find, 2¾" tall, EX.....$200.00 C

**Union 76,** sign, porcelain, VG..........................................$375.00 C

**Union Club Whiskey,** sign, paper, steamboat race between the Robert E. Lee and the Natchez, wood frame, June 30, 1870, 28" x 20", EX............................................$500.00 B

**Union Diesel, Diesel Fuel,** pump sign, porcelain, one-sided, 11½" dia., G ............................................$160.00 B

**Union Farmer's Gin,** thermometer, vertical scale, "phone 32, Portageville, Mo.," country scene with silhouettes in foreground, 10¼" x 8¼", EX............................................$45.00 C

**Union Farmer's Gin,** thermometer, vertical scale, "phone 32, Portageville, Mo.," country scene with silhouettes in foreground, 10¼" x 8¼", VG ............................................$35.00 C

**Union Gasoline "Carigas,"** running board storage can, 1-gal., F ............................................$100.00 C

**Union Leader Cut Plug Tobacco,** sign, paper, Uncle Sam reading the Naval Review, "The National Smoke & Chew," 27" x 30", EX ............................................**$2,600.00 B**

**Union Leader Redi Cut Tobacco,** humidor, metal, trademark eagle image, EX ............................................$235.00 B

**Union Leader Redi Cut Tobacco,** tin, Uncle Sam smoking pipe on label, P. Lorillard Company, G..........................................$25.00 C

**Union Leader Smoking Tobacco,** paperweight, EX............$85.00 C

**Union Leader Smoking Tobacco,** paperweight, NM .............$165.00 D

**Union Leader Smoking Tobacco,** sign, metal, trademark eagle, 11" x 13", VG ............................................$200.00 D

**Union Leader Smoking Tobacco,** sign, tin, litho, with eagle logo in center, 10½" x 15", EX ............................................$225.00 C

**Union Leader,** container, tin, litho, milkcan-style, "smoke and chew...Cut Plug," hard-to-find, 4¾" x 9¼", EX.........................$350.00 B

**Union League Extra Fine Habana,** cigar box label, baseball graphics, EX ............................................$385.00 B

**Union Made Overalls,** sign, porcelain, one-sided, curved, 16" x 14", EX............................................$360.00 B

**Union Metallic Cartridge Co.,** box, paper over cardboard, litho, two-piece, duck in flight, 4" x 4⅛" x 25", VG ......................$55.00 C

**Union Metallic Cartridge Co.,** sign, paper, soldiers firing cannon, 22" x 26", EX ............................................$245.00 D

**Union Mills Flour,** sign, paper, baby laying in wicker basket, 21" x 17", EX ............................................$300.00 D

**Union Oil Motorite,** sign, porcelain, die cut, shield, flange, 19½" x 19¾", EX............................................$425.00 C

**Union Oil Motorite,** sign, porcelain, die cut, shield, flange, 19½" x 19¾", VG............................................$355.00 D

**Union Petroleum Co.,** pocket mirror, metal and glass, "Mineral Lard Oil, Never Sold To Dealers, None Genuine Without This Brand," 4" dia., EX ............................................$110.00 B

**Union Shop,** sign, celluloid, window, Bakery and Confectionery Workers, 12" x 7", EX............................................$55.00 D

**Union Star Brand Coffee,** can, metal, slip lid, paper label, "High Grade Blend," 1 lb.., EX ............................................$700.00 B

Union Workman 10¢ Scrap, sign, cardboard, man holding a pack of the product over one eye, "Here's Looking At You, Chew!," 1920s, 14" x 23", EX ..............................................................$210.00 D

United Airlines, bank, vinyl, in shape of Hawaii native, 9" tall, EX ...........................................................................$150.00 B

United American Ship Lines, sign, ship, 20½" x 26½", EX..$250.00 B

United Fashion Shows, banner, cardboard, string hanger, man & woman 1914 show, 13" x 14", EX .....................................$125.00 D

United Motors Service, sign, porcelain, car in center of oval orange background, double-sided, 36" x 21", EX ...........................$875.00 C

United Motors Service, sign, porcelain, oval, early auto in center, 60" x 36", 1930s, VG.......................................$1,000.00 C

United Motors Service, thermometer, wood, curved top, "Specialized Electrical Service," 4" x 15", VG.................................$75.00 C

United Motors, thermometer, wood, "Authorized Service," trademark at top, glass scale, 4" x 15", G..............................$120.00 B

United States 5¢ Cigar, cigar box, 250-count with stars and stripes on front and inside cover, NM...........................$150.00 B

United States Army Reserve, sign, porcelain over metal, double-sided, Minuteman in center, 36" x 36", EX .....................................$195.00 C

United States Brewing, sign, tin, litho, self-framed, men in boat and decal of bottles on frame portion, 19½" x 15½", EX ..........$475.00 C

United States Fur Company, poster, paper, litho, youngsters chasing a skunk out of a log, "An Unwelcome Surprise," 18½" x 24¾", G..............................................................................$200.00 B

United States Fur Company, poster, paperboard, black boys trying to run an animal out of a hollow log, only to discover it's a skunk, United States Fur Co., St. Louis Mo., "Ship us your Furs," 15" x 20½", 1920s, VG .............................................$275.00 C

United States Rubbers, calendar, trifold panels show young lady, girl with dog, and a miner wearing their rubber footwear, American Litho Co., NY, 1900s, EX............................................$145.00 C

United States Tire, sign, cardboard, in shape of tire, types of tires, 6¾" x 12", VG ....................................................$210.00 B

United States Tires, ashtray, metal and glass, embossing on metal, in shape of early tire on spoked rim, 1920..............................6" dia., VG ............................................................................$385.00 C

United Telephone Service Long Distance, sign, porcelain, double-sided, flange, 16" x 16", NM...................................................... $250.00 B

United Van Lines W. Jeff Hammond Moving & Storage, clock, metal body and glass face, light-up, EX.............................$175.00 C

United, unleaded globe, plastic body with two glass lenses, 13½" dia., VG ...............................................................$325.00 C

Universal Home Wares, clock, glass face and cover on a pressed cardboard body, light-up, "electrical appliances," EX .$125.00 D

Universal Olive Oil, tin, cherubs on label, 1-gal., EX ...$105.00 C

Universal Stoves and Ranges, match holder, good strong litho on tin, 5" H, EX................................................................$240.00 B

Universal Stoves, salesman sample, porcelain and cast iron, complete with case, 18" x 16" x 7", NM...............................$7,000.00 B

Universal Stoves, tip tray, metal, litho, with globe, 4¼" dia., EX............................................................................$115.00 C

Universal, container, tin, litho, Uncle Sam, slip-lid, 1-lb., EX .$163.00 B

University Coffee, can, metal, key wind lid, steaming cup of coffee, 1 lb.., EX...........................................................$235.00 D

Upper Peninsula Brewing Co., sign, wood, 5 older gentlemen talking at table, 25" x 16", VG.................................................$900.00 C

Upson Processed Board, sign, porcelain, single-sided, 40" x 20", F.............................................................................$50.00 B

Urbana Wine Co. Gold Seal Champagne, tip tray, metal, product bottle in tray center, 6⅝", EX............................................$90.00 C

US Ammiunition, sign, metal, military scene, framed, 1908, 28" x 23", EX ......................................................$1,600.00 B

US Marine Cut Plug Tobacco, lunch pail, metal, bail handle and clasp closure, VG.........................................................$575.00 C

US Marine Cut Plug Tobacco, tin, slip lid, message only, round, EX..........................................................................$600.00 B

US Marine Tobacco, roly poly, tin, Singing Waiter, EX .$5,750.00 B

US Shot Shells, sign, cardboard, fold out, die cut, "A Load For Every Purpose, A Shell For Every Purse," 60" x 40", EX....$850.00 B

US Tires, clock, wood, man's head with US on cap, 1914, 18" dia., NM .........................................................................$2,500.00 B

US Typewriter ribbon Mfg. Co., tin, slip lid, star design, EX...$45.00 B

USS Products, sign, metal, double-sided, flange, "Sold Here," 17" x 15", EX...........................................................$425.00 B

Van Camp's Concentrated Soups, display, cardboard, die cut, VG, $225.00 C.

Veedol, sign, tin, litho, single-sided, die cut, girl on skates, 5½" x 14¼", G, $350.00 C.

Velvet Smoking Tobacco, sign, porcelain, "...Sold Here," 39" wide, VG, $170.00 B.

Vermont Mutual Fire Insurance, sign, tin litho, self-framing, offices and buggy traffic in front, 20½" x 24", EX, $900.00 B.

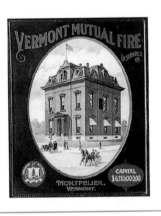

**V.D. Morgan Van Services & Storage,** calendar, paper, vintage moving van, 1950, 16⅜" x 24¼", VG....................$30.00 C

**Vacumm Mobiloils & Greases Gasoline,** sign, porcelain, 70" x 18", EX..........................$700.00 B

**Vacumm Oil,** match safe, metal and celluloid, 2" x 1", EX $200.00 C

**Vacuum Harness Oil,** sign, paper, litho, trotter on front, 1890s, EX..........................$195.00 C

**Vacuum Oil Company Gargoyle Mobiloil "E,"** oil can, metal, paper label, 1-gal., EX..........................$50.00 C

**Vadco Talcum Powder,** can label, paper, city buildings, 1923, EX..........................$35.00 D

**Vafiadis Cigarettes,** sign, metal, beveled edges, Cairo Hotel in upper corner, 13" x 9", EX..........................$125.00 C

**Valentine & Co.,** thermometer, celluloid, vertical, "why drive a shabby car...refinish with Valentine's Colors...," 5½" x 20", NM..........................$145.00 C

**Valentine's Valspar Varnish Paint,** thermometer, porcelain on wood back, product being brushed on wall, 1915, 12" x 50", EX...$725.00 C

**Valiant Authorized Service,** sign, porcelain, double-sided, 40⅜" dia., VG ..........................$400.00 B

**Valiant Authorized Service,** sign, porcelain, double-sided, 42" dia., EX..........................$375.00 C

**Valina Brand Coffee,** pail, metal, bail handle, rabbit and factory scene, 1890s, 4 lb., EX..........................$725.00 C

**Value Brand Coffee,** can, metal, key wind lid, lettering only on can, 1 lb., EX..........................$65.00 D

**Valvoline Oil Company,** pocket mirror, celluloid, in shape of oil barrel, 2¾" x 1¾", EX..........................$155.00 C

**Valvoline Racing Oil,** sign, tin, double-sided, 30" dia., EX ..$235.00 B

**Valvoline,** clock, neon, "motor oil...ask for," 18" x 18", VG..$650.00 D

**Valvoline,** thermometer, metal and glass, dial type, "Ask For The World's Finest," made by Pam, 12" dia., EX ....................$345.00 C

**Vam,** sign, metal, "Try New Vam For Healthy Handsome Hair...," barber's pole, 27" x 9", VG..........................$75.00 D

**Van Dam Cigars,** sign, tin, litho, embossed, trademark Van Dam, "Java Wrapped," 27¾" x 13½", EX..........................$160.00 B

**Van De Kamp's Bakeries,** poster, cardboard, sporting and camping scenes, 42" x 11", NM..........................$75.00 C

Vernor's Ginger Ale, sign, cardboard and metal, "...Please Pay When Served", 1930 – 40s, 12" x 11", EX, $300.00 B.

Vicks, door push, porcelain, Va-tro-nol, and VapoRub, 3¾" x 7¾", EX, $175.00 C. *Courtesy of Muddy River Trading Co./Gary Metz.*

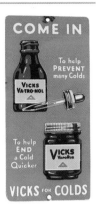

Victory Brand Pure Lard, can, metal, round wire handles, 25lb., G, $40.00 B.

Vulcan Plow Co., match strike, tin, litho, die cut, rare item, 2¾" x 7¾", VG, $625.00 C.

---

**Van Dyck Cigar,** sign, cardboard, hanger, Van Dyck, 8" x 12", EX ...................................................................$65.00 D

**Van Dyck Havana Cigars,** sign, tin, litho, die cut, in shape of artist palette, artwork of Van Dyck in center of sign, 13½" x 9½", EX.$675.00 B

**Van Heusen Collar,** sign, tin on cardboard, 13" x 6", EX..$70.00 D

**Van Houten's Cocoa,** sign, cardboard, original oak frame, woman in hat, frame etched Van Houten's Cocoa, 24¼" x 30¼", G.....$75.00 D

**Van Houten's Cocoa,** sign, cardboard, print in original oak frame, "Van Houten's Cocoa" etched into frame, woman in straw hat, 24¼" x 30¼", EX...............................................................$95.00 D

**Vanderbilt Premium Tread,** clock, round, light-up, logo in center of face, 1958, 14½" dia., EX....................................................$135.00 C

**Vanity Fair Tobacco Cigarettes,** sign, paper, two frogs, 9" x 11", VG................................................................................$75.00 B

**Vantage,** thermometer, metal, painted, three-sided, dial-type with message at top and scale at bottom, "Buy a pack today," white on blue background, EX ..........................................................$95.00 C

**Vaseline Cold Cream,** tin, sample, "...For The Skin and Complection," Chesbrough Manufacturing Co, EX...........................$35.00 D

**Vaseline Mentholated,** trolley sign, cardboard, nurse and the product box, 21" x 11", EX ....................................................$185.00 C

**Vaseline,** store display, tin, litho, counter, storage space inside and product display on front, 6¼" x 7¼" x 15¾", EX ..............$625.00 C

**Veedol Motor Oils,** sign, porcelain, double-sided, tombstone style, "100% Pennsylvania At Its Best," 22" x 28", NM ................$425.00 C

**Veedol,** banner, cloth, bird on clothesline lower right, "it's time to change to warm weather...," 58" x 36", EX .........................$155.00 C

**Velvet Brand Coffee,** pail, metal, bail handle, 5 lb., VG....$350.00 D

**Velvet Ice Cream,** banner, painted on canvas, "High In Food Value," 48" x 12", EX.............................................................$75.00C

**Velvet Ice Cream,** clock, light-up, clock under message panel, which is reverse painted glass, G .............................$235.00 C

**Velvet Pipe & Cigarette Tobacco,** sign, cardboard, open pocket tin, 8" x 14", EX .....................................................................$45.00 D

**Velvet Pipe Tobacco,** sign, porcelain, product package at left of message, "Aged In Wood," 39" x 12", EX .........................$195.00 D

**Velvet Tobacco,** watch fob, cloisonne, in shape of pocket tin, 1" x 2", EX...................................................................................$155.00 C

**Velvet... the Best Milk & Ice Cream,** clock, light-up, with message panel to right of clock face, EX .........................................$145.00 C

**Venables Chew Tobacco,** cutter, Pat.1875 with 1" & 2" measurements, EX ........ **$115.00 D**

**Vermont Mutual Fire Insurance Co.,** sign, tin, indented oval center that has headquarters building, 20¼" x 24¼", EX ...... **$950.0 C**

**Vernor's Ginger Ale,** dispenser, metal and porcelain, pressure gauge on top that reads "Look It's Cold," 31" tall, EX .... **$2,200.00 B**

**Vernor's Ginger Ale,** sign, cardboard, wood frame, "deliciously different!," woman with bottle, 21" x 11¾", EX .......... **$275.00 C**

**Vernor's Ginger Ale,** sign, cardboard, wood frame, "deliciously different!," woman with bottle, 21" x 11¾", VG ........ **$175.00 C**

**Vernor's Ginger Ale,** sign, chrome topper, from fountain dispenser, "Ice Cold," EX ........ **$85.00 C**

**Vernor's Ginger Ale,** sign, tin, self-framing, embossed, elf rolling a barrel of the product, 54¼" x 18⅜", 1940s, EX ........ **$410.00 B**

**Vernor's Ginger Ale,** thermometer, metal and glass, dial type reading "Drink...In Any Weather," 12" dia., EX ........ **$275.00 C**

**Vernor's,** menu board, tin, self-framing, 19" x 25", VG ....... **$95.00 C**

**Vernor's,** sign, porcelain,"Drink...DeliciouslyDifferent, 17" x 11", EX ........ **$275.00 C**

**Vess,** clock, metal, light-up, "Drink," 18" dia., EX ............ **$145.00 D**

**Veteran Brand Coffee,** tin, litho, old soldier, 1-lb., EX ........ **$135.00 C**

**Veteran Coffee,** can, metal, screw lid, lettering only, 1 lb., EX.. **$85.00 C**

**Veteran Coffee,** container, tin, key-wound, 1-lb., EX .......... **$65.00 B**

**Veteran Salt,** container, cardboard, paper label, unopened, 2-lb., EX ........ **$35.00 C**

**Vic's Special Beer,** sign, stamped celluloid over tin, Northern Brewing Co., Superior, WI, 5¼" x 11½", VG ........ **$55.00 C**

**Vic's Special Beer,** sign, tin over cardboard, from the Northern Brewing Co., Superior, Wis., 11⅜" x 5⅜", EX ........ **$75.00 C**

**Viceroy Open,** sign, plastic, package to right of message, 15¾" x 9", G ........ **$20.00 D**

**Vicks,** door push, porcelain, Va-tro-nol, and VapoRub, 3¾" x 7¾", VG ........ **$135.00 C**

**Victor Duck Decoys,** store piece, papier-maché, hand painted, 6" x 6" x 4½", EX ........ **$575.00 B**

**Victor Gaskets, Oilseals, Packings,** sign, metal over cardboard, products, 26" x 12", EX ........ **$325.00 C**

**Viola,** dispenser, ceramic, shaped like an urn, 17" tall, VG.. **$1,400.00 B**

**Virgin Queen Smoking Tobacco & Cigarettes,** sign, paper, bust of Queen, 18" x 22", EX ........ **$225.00 D**

**Virginia Dare Korker,** bottle topper, cardboard, "Drink...," VG. **$40.00 C**

**Virginia Dare Wine,** serving tray, metal, "The Drink of Sociability," grapevines and bottle of the product in center, 12" dia., EX ...... **$150.00 B**

**Virginia Dare Wine,** serving tray, Paul & Virginia in center, "American Wines," 12" dia., EX ........ **$195.00 B**

**Virginity Smoking Tobacco,** box, tin, litho, hinged lid, woman on lid, 7" x 4½" x 3⅞", EX ........ **$400.00 B**

**Viriginai Brewing Co.,** drinking glass with gold rim and etched name, "Southern Progress," 3½" tall, EX ........ **$175.00 B**

**Visa,** sign, porcelain, double-sided, smoking cigarette under product message, foreign, 27½" x 19", VG ........ **$550.00 D**

**Visible Gasoline,** gas globe, round ball-shaped, etched lettering, 13½" dia., VG ........ **$550.00 D**

**Vision Baking Powder,** container, paper label, cherubs, 3" x 7", EX ........ **$80.00 B**

**Vision Baking Powder,** container, paper label, young children playing, 3" x 7", VG ........ **$175.00 B**

**Voight Brewery,** match safe, metal, striker on back, both ends open, EX ........ **$125.00 C**

**Voigt Cream Flakes,** cereal box, cardboard, woman and cow on front, EX ........ **$215.00 B**

**Voltaic Compound,** calendar, die cut, promoting cure rheumatism and neuralgia, 5¾" x 10", 1892, EX ........ **$155.00 C**

**Volunteer,** cigar box label, paper, soldier, 4½" x 4½", EX.. **$50.00 D**

**Vuelta Seal Cigar,** sign, metal, double-sided, by Chas. Shonk, 17½" x 13½", EX ........ **$195.00 0 B**

**Vuelta Seal Cigar,** sign, metal, double-sided, by Chas. Shonk, 17½" x 13½", VG ........ **$145.00 C**

**Vulcanized,** sign, tin flange, double-sided, "We Repair Tubes," 17½" x 13½", EX ........ **$375.00 C**

Walgreen's, coffee cup, china, painted company name, Syracuse China, 3" x 3¼" dia., EX, $10.00 C. *Courtesy of B.J. Summers.*

Walk-Over Shoes, sign, steel, double-sided, flange, 13½" x 19½", EX, $600.00 B. *Courtesy of Richard Opfer Auctioneering, Inc.*

Wallace & Gregory Bros. pitcher, stoneware, front stencil, "...Elko County Pure Apple Juice Vinegar, Paducah, KY," handle on back side of pitcher, 1900s, 6" x 4¼" dia., EX, $115.00 C. *Courtesy of B.J. Summers.*

Wallace & Gregory Vinegar, pitcher, stoneware, incised front reads "Compliments of Wallace & Gregory Pure Vinegar Paducah Ky," handle on back side, made by J.A. Bauer Pottery, 1890 – 1900s, 6" tall x 4" dia., VG, $95.00 C. *Courtesy of B.J. Summers.*

War Bonds, poster, paper, 1944, 20" x 27", VG, $55.00 B.

Ward's Orange-Crush Dispenser, in shape of large orange with top pump, 14" T, EX, $1,150.00 B. *Courtesy of Buffalo Bay Auction Co.*

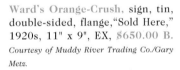

Ward's Orange-Crush, sign, tin, double-sided, flange, "Sold Here," 1920s, 11" x 9", EX, $650.00 B. *Courtesy of Muddy River Trading Co./Gary Metz.*

W Baker & Co.'s Breakfast Cocoa, tin, sample size, slip lid, "Absolutely Pure...Costs Less Than One cent...," 1½" x 1¾" dia., EX..................$165.00 D

W T Grant Stores, doll, vinyl, Bucky Bradford holding lollipop, 9½" tall, EX..................$95.00 C

W. Schneider Wholesale Wine & Liquor Co., jug, crock, 1- gal., brown over cream, EX..................$125.00 C

W.J. Guy Implement Dealer, sign, tin, embossed, farm implements in row between message lines, 28" x 10", EX........$275.00 B

Wabasso Fine Cottons, display figure, papier-mache, white rabbit with product name in raised gold, EX..................$275.00 B

Wadham's Gas, sign, tin, wood frame, 18" x 83½", F...$275.00 C

Wadham's Tempered Motor Oil, sign, tin, oil bottle in spotlight at top, 18" x 83½", F..................$325.00 C

Wagner Lager Beer, label, paper, Wagner Brewing Co., with Revenue stamp, 1930s, 12 oz., VG..................$25.00 D

Wagner Lockheed Hydraulic Brake Parts & Fluid, sign, tin, double-sided, flange, 12½" x 9¾", EX..................$175.00 B

Wagner's Ice Cream, sign, metal, ice cream products, "Eat...It's Good," 1920s, 19½" x 13½", EX..................$135.00 C

Wagner's Ice Cream, sign, tin, different ice cream products on a wooden serving tray, 1920s, 19½" x 13½", G................$250.00 B

Wagon Wheel, pocket tin, sample, wagon wheel and wagon train, 3" x 4½" x ⅞", EX..................$335.00 C

Wak-em-up Coffee, can, tin, litho, Indian in full headdress, 7½" x 8¾", EX..................$450.00 B

Wake Up Cut Plug Tobacco, tin, paper label, slip lid, rooster on front, EX..................$700.00 B

Wake-Em-Up Coffee, pail, metal, bail handle, slip lid, Indian, 9½" x 9" dia., EX..................$335.00 D

Walburn Ethyl Gasoline, globe, high profile metal body with glass lens, 15½" dia., VG..................$525.00 C

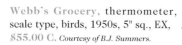

**Warren's Paints,** sign, porcelain, double-sided, 24" x 26", VG, $275.00 C.

**Weather-Bird Shoes,** sign, neon and porcelain, in the shape of a rooster weather vane, 17" x 25½", EX, $1,700.00 D.

**Webb's Grocery,** thermometer, scale type, birds, 1950s, 5" sq., EX, $55.00 C. *Courtesy of B.J. Summers.*

**Weille & Son,** brush, wood and fiber, "B. Weille & Son, Mens & Boys & Childrens Complete Outfitters, 409-413 Broadway, Paducah, KY," someone carved MAG on this one, 6⅞" x 2⅛" x 1½", EX, $55.00 C. *Courtesy of B.J. Summers.*

**Wells, Richardson & Co.,** sign, chromo-litho paper on canvas backing with embossed frame, lactated foods for infants and invalids, good rare piece, 25½" x 34¾", G, $500.00 B.

**Western District Warehouse Co.,** ad, paper, framed under glass, wintery scene with church and moon, snow on ground, 1890 – 1900s, 19" x 15", VG, $275.00 C. *Courtesy of B.J. Summers.*

**Walgreen Co. Peanuts,** container, metal, front reads "Freshly Roasted Salted Peanuts... Walgreen Co. Chicago," 1 lb., VG ......... $45.00 C

**Walk Over Cigars,** box label, paper, man walking through a banner with sports equipment, NM ................................................. $295.00 D

**Walk-Over Shoes,** sign, steel, double-sided, flange, 13½" x 19½", VG ......................................................................................... $450.00 C

**Walk-Over Shoes,** sign, tin, litho, single-sided, promoting Wm. Archdeacon Co., Grafton, W. Va., 23½" x 11¾", VG ......... $175.00 C

**Walker Products,** bill hook, metal and celluloid, "Ask For ...," three product cans, EX ................................................................. $35.00 D

**Walker's Talc,** can, tin, litho, woman on front, 1¾" x 4", EX ....... $325.00 B

**Walkers Grape Juice,** bowl, enameled, grape clusters, 19" x 7", VG ......................................................................................... $300.00 B

**Walkover Shoes,** display figure, plaster, old gentleman on base, 12" tall, EX ..................................................................................... $25.00 D

**Walla-Walla Peppermint Chewing Gum,** box, cardboard, 4" x 6" x 1", VG ......................................................................................... $50.00 D

**Walter A. Wood Hoosick Falls, NY, USA,** calendar, cardboard, mowing and reaping machines with horse-drawn reaper, 7½" x 8¾", NM ......................................................................................... $140.00 B

**Walter A. Wood Implements,** calendar, cardboard, 1892, double-sided, young girls in front of rake, implements on reverse, 1892, 6" x 7", NM ................................................................................... $125.00 C

**Walter A. Wood Mowing & Reaping Machine Co.,** trade card, cardboard, farm scene fold out, "For Sale By Enoch Bridges," 1880s, EX ................................................................................... $85.00 D

**Walter Baker & Co Breakfast Cocoa,** sign, metal, girl standing with a tray, "Pure, Delicious, Nutritious, Costs Less Than One Cent A Cup," 14" x 19", EX ............................................................................ $1,045.00 B

**Walter Baker & Co Limited,** tin, girl in apron, 1⅜" x 1⅜" x 1", EX .............................................................................................. $125.00 D

**Walter's Beer,** sign, porcelain, double-sided, iron frame, from Eau Claire, Wis., 60" x 37", NM ................................................. $425.00 B

**Walter's Pilsner Beer,** clock, reverse painted glass, light-up, "Time for," brown bear in center spotlight, 15" dia., NM ............ $293.00 B

Western Field, Leaded Waterproof Paper Shot Shells, box, cardboard, two-piece, grouse on label, 4⅛" x 4⅛" x 25", EX, $225.00 C.

Western Union, sign, porcelain, double-sided, flange, 24" x 12", VG, $225.00 B.

Western Union Telegraph and Cable, call box, porcelain, difficult to locate in good shape, 6" tall, EX, $110.00 B.

West Hair Nets, store display, countertop cabinet, West Hair Net and Electric Hair Curlers, 12¾" x 11¼" x 20", 1920s, EX, $2,500.00 C.

West Kentucky Coal Co., knife, celluloid and metal, two blades, "...The Company with the Coal and the Service, Paducah, KY," reverse side has Tradewater Coal logos, 2¼" long closed, VG, $15.00 C. *Courtesy of B.J. Summers.*

Wetherill's Floor & Deck Enamel, sign, wood, 35" wide, VG, $40.00 B.

---

Waltham & Warfield Pianos & Players, whetstone, rock and celluloid, "High-Grade...HD Strauch, Alexandria, SD," EX .........$18.00 D

Wampole's Antiseptic Solution, bottle, glass, paper label with cork top, sample size, EX ......................................................$55.00 D

Wampum Coffee, tin, bare-breasted maiden, from Duluth MN, 5½" x 9¼", EX.............................................................$225.00 C

Wan-Eta Cocoa, container, tin, paper label that bears the an Indian maiden, 4⅛" x 2½" x 1½", EX ....................................$65.00 C

War Chief Motor Oil, can, metal, screw on top, "100% Pure & Paraffine Base," 2 gal., EX ....................................$45.00 C

War Eagle Cigars, tin, slip lid, "2 for 5¢," EX ..................$175.00 D

War Eagle cigars, tin, slip lid, eagle, EX...........................$135.00 D

Ward's Lemon-Crush, dispenser, ceramic, in the shape of a lemon, metal pump at top, 13" tall, 1920s, EX.......$1,530.00 B

Ward's Lemon-Crush, dispenser, china, metal pump in shape of lemon, embossed lettering, 9" x 12¾", VG ..................$875.00 C

Ward's Lemon-Crush, dispenser, china, metal pump, in shape of lemon, embossed lettering, 9" x 12¾", EX .....................$1,500.00 B

Ward's Lime-Crush, sign, cardboard, "Deliciously Different," silhouette figure drinking the product, 24" x 14½", 1920s, EX ...$250.00 C

Ward's Orange Juice, dispenser with metal pump, ceramic, in shape of orange, 8" dia., x 13½", VG..............$1,550.00 B

Ward's Orange Juice, sign, tin, painted, "Drink," bottle to left of message, 28" x 20", EX ....................................................$125.00 C

Ward's Orange-Crush Dispenser, in shape of large orange with top pump, 14" , VG................................................................$975.00 C

Ward's Orange-Crush, sign, tin, double-sided, flange, "Sold Here," 1920s, 11" x 9", VG ..........................................................$475.00 C

Ward's Vitovim Bread, thermometer, metal, scale type reading, smiling baby, 1915, 21" tall, EX ........................................$300.00 C

Wareco Ethyl, gas globe, plastic and glass, service man in front of product name, 15½" x 10½", EX....................................$1,600.00 C

Wareco, sign, neon, waving service station attendant, 20" x 20", EX.................................................................................$250.00 C

Warner's Log Cabin Sarsaparilla, sign, metal, log cabin, "...Greatest Blood Purifier," 28" x 42", EX............................................$600.00 B

Whistle, bottle holder, cast iron, wall-mounted, hand holding the hourglass bottle, 10" x 3" x 2½", EX, $775.00 D. *Courtesy of Wm. Morford Investment Grade Collectibles.*

Whistle, clock, by Pam, elf pushing a bottle of the product 14½" dia., VG, $650.00 B.

Whistle, coatrack, wood, elves on top of coathook, 35½" x 8", EX, $275.00 B. *Courtesy of Autopia Advertisinig Auctions.*

Whistle, clock, pressed board, electric, die cut, "Golden Orange...Refreshment Time," 24" x 23", VG, $1,055.00 B. *Courtesy of Collectors Auction Services.*

Whistle, sign, cardboard, die cut, of woman with Whistle bottle, straw, 15¾" x 22¾", NM, $185.00 B. *Courtesy of Autopia Advertising Auctions.*

Whistle, sign, metal, embossed lettering and image, 54" x 18", VG, $170.00 B.

Whistle, sign, tin, one-sided, self-framing, embossed, "Sparkling Orange Goodness," 56" x 32", G, $250.00 C.

---

**Washburn's Ice Cream,** watch fob, cloisonne enamel, EX...**$170.00 B**

**Waterman Plumbing,** sign, porcelain, pointing hand in direction of business, 16" x 8", EX.........................**$250.00 C**

**Waterman's Ideal Fountain Pen,** countertop display case, wood and glass, lettering on front glass, 18" x 17" x 9½", VG ...........**$700.00 B**

**Waterman's Ideal Fountain Pen,** display, wood and glass, for counter top use, lettering on front, 16" x 17½", EX...........**$575.00 D**

**Waterman's Ideal Fountain Pen,** thermometer, metal, in shape of fountain pen, scale type reading, 1920s, 3¼" x 19½", NM....**$975.00 B**

**Watertite Paints & Enamels,** sign, metal, painted, embossed, 24" x 12", EX ...........................**$175.00 C**

**Watertite Paints & Enamels,** sign, metal, painted, embossed, 24" x 12", VG.............................**$145.00 D**

**Watkins Baking Powder,** tin, paper label, unopened, 4 oz, EX ..**$35.00 D**

**Watkins Egyptian,** talc, tin, litho, sphinx on front and pyramid on back, EX .........................................**$185.00 B**

**Waverly Kerosene, Lighting Heating Cooking,** sign, porcelain, pennant and Shell logo, 22" x 12", EX ...........................**$300.00 D**

**Waverly Oils & Gasoline,** sign, porcelain, barrel with name on ends, 16" x 10", NM .........................................**$2,500.00 C**

**Waverly Pure Rye,** ad, painted plaster, a three-man band, 25½" x 32", VG.........................................**$1,500.00 D**

**Waverly Pure Rye,** sign, Sample & Co., 84 Front St., NY, three black musicians in a stone archway, 25½" x 32½" x 1¾", 1900s, EX.........................................**$1,750.00 C**

**Wayne Dairy Ice Cream,** sign, porcelain, double-sided, hanging, 20" x 15", EX.........................................**$400.00 B**

**Wayne Feed,** thermometer, tin, die cut, chicken on feed sack, "a better fed for every need," 3½" x 6¼", EX .........................**$315.00 B**

White House Coffee, sign, tin, die cut, litho, double-sided, flange, hand holding a container of coffee, "None better at any price," 13½" x 8¾", NM, $4,800.00 B. *Courtesy of Buffalo Bay Auction Co.*

White Rock Beer, sign, tin, litho, wood frame, girl holding wheat with bottle of White Rock, The Akron Brewing Co., Akron, Ohio, 33" x 24¾", VG, $560.00 B. *Courtesy of Collectors Auction Services.*

White Rock, door push, tin, litho, product bottle, 1940s, 4" x 14", EX, $250.00 B.

White Rock, sign, tin, litho, "The Leading Mineral Water," 10" x 4", VG, $25.00 B.

White Rose Motor Gasoline, sign, tin, single-sided, two roses, 14¼" x 10¼", NOS, EX, $810.00 B.

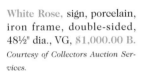

White Rose, sign, porcelain, iron frame, double-sided, 48½" dia., VG, $1,000.00 B. *Courtesy of Collectors Auction Services.*

Wielands Beer, serving tray, pretty lady reading, from San Francisco, CA, 1909, 10½" x 13¼", VG, $175.00 C.

---

**Wayne Gas Pumps,** poster, paper, pumps and other parts, 22" x 32¾", NM.............................................................$120.00 C

**Waynesboro Motor Club,** sign, porcelain, "AAA, Spring Water," 9¾" x 12", red, blue & black, G.........................................$200.00 C

**Wear U Well,** sign, porcelain, flange, 25" x 17", VG .$275.00 B

**Weather-Bird Shoes,** sign, neon and porcelain, in the shape of a rooster weather vane, 17" x 25½", VG.........................$1,000.00 C

**Weather-Bird Shoes,** sign, porcelain and neon, rooster on a weathervane, 17" x 25½", EX...................................................$1,700.00 B

**Web Foot,** cigar box, wooden, Indian maiden, 10-ct, 1920s, VG.$80.00 B

**Webster Cigars,** postcard, cardboard, Daniel Webster at Dartmouth College, EX .......................................................$45.00 C

**Webster Cigars,** sign, reverse glass, Noah Webster in center, 11½" x 15½", VG .......................................................$275.00 C

**Webster Grocery Co.,** container, cardboard, for Marvel Oats with mountain scene, 3-lb., 7-oz., EX .....................................$120.00 B

**Webster's Seeds,** counter box, wood, dovetailed corners, great graphics on inside paper label, 8¾" x 6" x 3", VG ..............$135.00 C

**Wedding Bouquet Cigar,** sign, tin, litho, embossed, early Puritan wedding scene, 27½" x 19½", EX .....................................$475.00 B

**Wedding Breakfast Coffee,** tin, Behring-Stahl Coffee Co., St. Louis, Mo., wedding party, 1-lb., EX...............................................$35.00 D

**Weddles,** tea tin, vintage automobiles on front and rear, 5" x 3" x 3¼", VG .......................................................$250.00 B

**Wee Willy Beer,** sign, glass, window, 14" x 6", EX....................$100.00 D

**Weed Chains,** sign, tin over wood, litho, hanging, tire chain over tire, 17¼" x 23¼", EX...................................................$1,400.00 B

**Weideman Boy Brand Coffee,** can, tin, litho, key-wound, trademark Weideman Coffee, 1-lb., 5" x 4", EX .................................$190.00 B

**Welch Juniors Grape Juice,** sign, tin, embossed, 1930s, 19½" x 13½", G........................................................$400.00 B

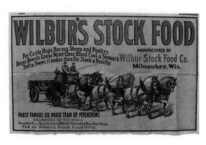

Wilbur's Seed Meal, box, wood with paper litho label, 20" x 22" x 36", VG, $7,000.00 B. *Courtesy of Collectors Auction Services.*

Wilbur's Stock Food, banner, cloth, 6 horse team pulling the product, 60" x 36", G, $525.00 B.

Wildroot Cream Oil, sign, cardboard, easel back, die cut, Fearless Fosdick, "Get Wildroot Cream Oil, Charlie!," 30" x 30¼", 1954, EX, $275.00 C. *Courtesy of Autopia Advertising Auctions.*

Winchester Arms & Ammunition, sign, metal, die cut, double-sided, hanging arm, probably a fantasy item, 41¼" x 6½", EX, $450.00 B. *Courtesy of Buffalo Bay Auction Co.*

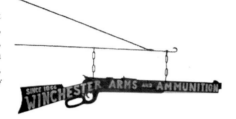

Winchester, calendar, paper, hunting scene in snow and desert with top and bottom metal strips, 14¼" x 27", 1899, EX, $1,500.00 B. *Courtesy of Past Tyme Pleasures.*

Winchester, calendar, paper on cardboard, litho, cold snowy hunting scene, partial monthly sheets, 1899, 16" x 19", G, $175.00 C.

Winchester Guns and Ammunition, sign, cardboard, four piece die cut store display, easel back, overall width 86½" x 42" high, VG, $720.00 B.

---

**Welch Juniors,** sign, tin over cardboard, easel back, "Drink A Bunch Of Grapes," 9" x 6", G .............................................$450.00 B

**Welch Juniors,** sign, tin, horizontal, painted, "Drink a bunch of grapes," product to left of message, 40" x 18", VG .......$375.00 C

**Welch Juniors,** sign, tin, unusual large size, 40" x 18", 1931s, EX .................................................................................$600.00 B

**Welch Juniors,** sign, tin, unusual large size, 40" x 18", 1931s, F ..$95.00 C

**Welch Motor Oil,** sign, metal, one-sided, painted, 24" x 9", VG ..$45.00 C

**Welch's,** sign, celluloid over tin, "The National Drink," made by Whitehead and Hoag, 10" x 10", EX ...................................$625.00 B

**Welcome Cigarettes,** sign, cardboard, die cut, patriotic woman with broom and dust pan, 1883, 16" x 11", EX.........................$275.00 D

**Wellington London Mixture,** container, tin, litho, 4⅜" x 3⅞", EX .................................................................................$325.00 B

**Wells Fargo,** key chain, metal, stage coach, 1950s, EX.$15.00 D

**Wells Richardson Lactated Food for Infants and Invalids,** container, tin, litho, slip-lid, 1879, NM .........................................$95.00 C

**Wells, Richardson & Co.,** sign, chromo-litho paper on canvas backing, embossed frame, lactated foods for infants and invalids, good rare piece, EX................................................................$950.00 C

**Welsbach Assures Dependable Lighting Service,** tip tray, metal, woman in chair with small girl in floor, 4⅛", EX ..............$220.00 B

**West Beach,** hair net display, metal, early car and pretty lady, 1918, EX ......................................................................$275.00 D

**West End Brewing Co. Utica, New York,** tray, tin, litho, Lady Liberty standing in center between beer keg and eagle, 13" dia., G ..........................................................................$163.00 B

**West End Brewing Co.,** tray, metal, Lady Liberty, 13" dia., EX..$325.00 C

**West Hair Nets,** store display, countertop cabinet, West Hair Net and Electric Hair Curlers, 12¾" x 11¼" x 20", 1920s, G .$750.00 C

Winchester New Rival Paper Shot Shells, box, paper, 8⅛" x 8⅛" x 2¾", F, $50.00 B.

Winchester, pinback, celluloid, by Whitehead & Hoag, 1896, 1" x ⅝", EX, $135.00 B.

Winchester Silvertip Bullet, sign, cardboard, double-sided, litho, 21" x 12¾", VG, $110.00 C.

Winchester, window display, target practice scene, 48" tall, VG, $500.00 C.

Winston, thermometer, metal, embossed, painted, "tastes good...like a cigarette should!," vertical scale at top right and product package lower left, no warning label, 6" x 13½", EX, $65.00 C. *Courtesy of B.J. Summers.*

The Wolf Co., sign, paper, litho, wood frame, promoting their Flouring Mill Machinery, Chambersburg, PA, 17¾" x 25¼", VG, $400.00 B. *Collectors Auction Services.*

Wonder Bread, Howdy Doody, display, heavy paper, die cut, stand-up, 5½" x 13", EX, $150.00 C.

---

**West Virginia Pilsner Beer,** poster, cardboard, woman and glass of beer, 14" x 22", EX ...........................................$175.00 C

**West Virginia Pilsner Beer,** poster, cardboard, woman and glass of beer, 14" x 22", VG ...........................................$125.00 C

**Westclox Pocket Ben,** sign, cardboard, school boy looking at his watch, 9½" x 13", EX...........................................$75.00 D

**Western Ammunition,** calendar top, paper, hunting dogs, 1932, 15" x 22", EX...........................................$195.00 B

**Western Ammunition,** sign, paper, "The Unexpected," 17" x 23", EX...........................................$675.00 C

**Western Ammunition,** sign, paper, hunter after ducks, "Super-X" loads, 20" x 35", EX ...........................................$925.00 B

**Western Auto Associate Store, Home Owner,** sign, tin, die cut, embossed arrow 33" x 9", EX...........................................$225.00 B

**Western Auto Associate Store,** sign, metal, die cut, arrow, 33" x 9", EX...........................................$185.00 C

**Western Auto,** clock, light-up, 12" dia., G ...........................................$200.00 B

**Western Cartridges with Lubaloy Bullets,** sign, store countertop, 7¾" x 8", EX ...........................................$65.00 D

**Western Cartridges,** sign, cardboard, men target shooting and a box of cartridges, 11" x 4", EX...........................................$200.00 C

**Western Club Whiskey,** bottle stand, pot metal, backbar use, 4" tall, EX...........................................$45.00 C

**Western Field Shotgun Shells,** box, cardboard, one-piece, quail on front of box, 25-count, VG ...........................................$165.00 C

**Western Ledger,** marker, tin, litho, on front Western Assurance Co., 3" x 12¼", EX...........................................$225.00 D

**Western Motor Association,** sign, porcelain, double-sided, "Approved Motor Court," 29" x 27½", G ...........................................$135.00 C

**Western New Chief,** sign, paper, ducks flying over water, "Power Behind the Blind," 13" x 17", EX ...........................................$900.00 B

**Western Shells,** sign, paper, ducks landing close to decoy, 16½" x 32", EX...........................................$750.00 B

Wonder Enriched Bread, sign, tin, embossed, "Helps Build Strong Bodies 8 Ways," product loaf, 30" x 18", VG, $130.00 C.

Wonder Orange, sign, tin, embossed, "Drink," spotlight on oranges at left of message, 1930s, 19½" x 13½", G, $225.00 B. *Courtesy of Muddy River Trading Co./Gary Metz.*

Woodlawn Mills Shoe Lace Service Station, metal, litho, in the shape of a service station, EX, $3,200.00 B. *Courtesy of Collectors Auction Services.*

Woolsey Cawlux, thermometer, tin, marine finish, 8" x 28", VG, $325.00 C.

Worcester Elastic Stocking & Truss Co., pocket mirror, celluloid, partially clad woman, EX, $400.00 B. *Courtesy of Wm. Morford Investment Grade Collectibles.*

W P A D Pierce Lackey, lighter, metal, radio tower on side sending out radio waves, never used, 1950s, 1½" x 2¼" x ¼", NM, $45.00 C. *Courtesy of B.J. Summers.*

---

**Western Super X & Xpert Ammunition,** sign, cardboard, die cut, "Shoot," geese in flight and product boxes, 10" x 9¼", 1927, EX .............................................................$80.00 B

**Western Super X .22 Long Rifle,** brochure, fold-out, product box on front, 6½" x 3½", EX .....................................................$55.00 D

**Western Super X Shotgun Shells,** box, G ..........................$20.00 D

**Western Super X Shotgun Shells,** box, two-piece, 4" x 4" x 2½", VG.................................................................................$30.00 B

**Western Super X,** poster, cardboard, hanging, cartridges arranged in shape of X, 21" x 13", EX .........................$230.00 B

**Western Super-X Shells,** sign, cardboard, stand up, counter, box of product and name, 11" x 21", EX .....................................$370.00 B

**Western Union Telegrams** sign, porcelain, flange, "may be telephoned from here," 22" x 12", G..........................................$225.00 D

**Western Union Telegrams,** sign, porcelain flange, "may be telephoned from here," sign, 22" x 12", VG..............................$255.00 D

**Western Union Telegraph and Cable Office,** sign, porcelain, double-sided, flange, 24" x 12¼", VG .....................................$200.00 B

**Western Union Telegraph** sign, porcelain, side-mounting tab, "here," 25" x 16¾", white and yellow on dark blue, EX....................$155.00 C

**Western Union Telegraph,** sign, porcelain, double-sided, flange, "Telegraph Here...Western Union," 25" x 17", EX..............$175.00 B

**Western Union,** bell page, product name on front, 3½" x 5¾", EX ...........................................................................$135.00 B

**Western Union,** sign, porcelain, business name only, 30" x 17", EX...............................................................................$175.00 D

**Western Union,** sign, porcelain, double-sided, flange, "Telegraph Here," 25" x 17", NM........................................................$220.00 B

**Western Union,** sign, porcelain, double-sided, flange, "Telephone Telegrams From Here," candlestick phone, 20" x 18", EX.$350.00 C

**Western Union,** sign, porcelain, flange, early "candlestick" phone in center, 18" x 19½", G............................................$575.00 C

**Western Union,** sign, porcelain, flanged, "Telephone your telegrams from here," candlestick phone at lower left of message, 18" x 19½", EX .............................................................$195.00 C

WPAD radio, thermometer, plastic and metal, dial type reading scale, on front shows its affiliation CBS and the AM & FM band frequencies, 1940 – 50s, 6½" x 7", VG, $55.00 C. *Courtesy of B.J. Summers.*

Wrigley Chewing Gum, counter display, cardboard, die cut, Wrigley man and young girl, promoting 1¢ P-K Gum, 12" x 8", EX, $425.00 C. *Courtesy of Buffalo Bay Auction Co.*

Wrigley's Doublemint, General Store, sign, porcelain, double-sided, 30" x 9", F, $2,400.00 B. *Courtesy of Wm. Morford Investment Grade Collectibles.*

Wurlitzer, sign, bubbling display, limited edition, great presentation piece, 1990, EX, $550.00 C. *Courtesy of Muddy River Trading Co./Gary Metz.*

Wyandotte Detergent, sign, tin, litho, self-framing, J.B. Ford Company, Indian in full headdress hunting bow drawn, 28" x 39", NM, $4,500.00 B. *Courtesy of Past Tyme Pleasures.*

Wyatt Bell & Co, cigarette case, metal, when ship's wheel is turned the center raises and brings up the cigarettes so they can be easily picked up, 1950s, 5½" tall x 4" at base, EX, $75.00 C. *Courtesy of B.J. Summers.*

---

**Western Union,** sign, porcelain, messenger, bicycle-mounted, 13" x 2¾", NM ..................................................$225.00 C

**Western Union,** telegraph key, porcelain, great blue and white colors, 3½" x 6" x 3", EX .........................................$95.00 C

**Western Winchester,** poster, paper, litho, men in cabin getting ready for duck hunting, G...................................$50.00 C

**Western Winchester,** poster, paper, litho, men in camp deer in background, G..........................................................$55.00 C

**Western Winchester,** poster, paper, litho, men in camp deer in background, VG.........................................................$95.00 B

**Western X,** brochure, four-page, fold-out, 3½" x 6¼", EX ...$65.00 D

**Western Xpert Shells,** sign, cardboard, standup of hunter, 1929, 7" x 18", EX.............................................................$95.00 C

**Western Xpert Super Target Load,** shell box, shotgun, F.....$9.00 D

**Western Xpert,** shell box, cardboard, shotgun, bird dog in field, 4" x 4" x 3", VG.............................................................$95.00 C

**Westfield Steam Laundry,** pinback, celluloid over metal, "Compliments of Westfield Steam Laundry Westfield, Mass.," 1¾" dia., VG.......................................................................$25.00 C

**Westinghouse Mazda Automobile Lamps,** display, metal, storage countertop cabinet, 24" t, EX.........................................$125.00 B

**Westinghouse Mazda Lamps for Automobiles,** store cabinet, metal, logo on end, 1929, black on orange, EX..............$295.00 D

**Westinghouse Mazda Lamps,** sign, paper, girl book illuminated by lamp, 41½" x 29", EX........................................................$65.00 C

**Westinghouse Radio,** clock, pressed cardboard body glass front and face cover, light-up, 15" dia., G ................................$135.00 C

**Westinghouse,** license plate attachment, porcelain, 10" x 5", EX ........................................................................$30.00 C

**Westinghouse,** salt and pepper shakers, plastic, in shape of a front load washer and dryer, dispensing holes at top, given to customers as premium items to help advertise their products, 50s, 2" x 2½" x 3¼", NM ......................................**$25.00 C**

**Westland Ice Cream,** clock, light-up, Covington, Ky., brand, 26" x 8¼", VG ..................................................**$200.00 C**

**Wet Weather Goods,** sign, cardboard, duck, "...Satisfaction For...," 18" x 11", EX ......................................**$295.00 C**

**Wetherill's Atlas Paints,** clock, metal, glass and neon, octagon, 18" x 18", EX ....................................**$450.00 C**

**Weyman's Cutty Pipe Chewing & Smoking Tobacco,** store bin, metal, for counter use, lettering and graphics in green, 13½" x 10" x 9", EX ....................................**$450.00 C**

**Weyman's Cutty-Pipe Chewing and Smoking Tobacco,** display bin, store, 9" x 10" x 13½", G ....................................**$400.00 B**

**Wheaties,** cereal bowl, milk glass, silhouettes of athletes, 2" x 5" dia., EX ....................................**$75.00 D**

**Whip,** pocket, tin, litho, horse and rider, 4½" x 3" x ¾", EX .**$12,350.00 B**

**Whippet & Willys-Knight Genuine Parts,** sign, porcelain, "Authorized Service," double-sided, 35½" x 24", EX ....................**$295.00 C**

**Whippet,** sign, tin, embossed, "Dollar for Dollar Value...Product of Willys-Overland Company," 22½" x 12", G....................**$225.00 B**

**Whis Motor Oil,** bank, metal, in shape of can, 2½" dia., EX..**$195.00 D**

**Whis Neatsfoot Compound,** can, metal, screw lid, bold product name lettering, 3½" dia.,. x 6½", EX ..................**$65.00 D**

**Whist Club Mixture,** tin, row of playing cards and product name, EX....................................**$875.00 C**

**Whistle Soda,** sign, cardboard, bottle, NOS, 9" x 31", NM.**$150.00 C**

**Whistle Soda,** sign, cardboard, vertical, 1948, 2¾" x 23", NM ..**$120.00 B**

**Whistle,** ad, paper, framed, die cut, from H. Gramse and Bro. Litho, Balto., Md., 23" x 7", VG....................................**$75.00 B**

**Whistle,** ad, paper, NOS, with boy and product bottle, 1950s, VG...................................................**$20.00 C**

**Whistle,** bottle holder, cast iron, wall-mounted figural hand holding the hourglass bottle, 10" x 3" x 2½", G..................**$350.00 D**

**Whistle,** bottle, applied color label, elves and logos on both sides Whistle cap, 12-oz., NM ....................................**$90.00 B**

**Whistle,** bottle, cardboard, die cut, "Litho In U.S.A.," 8" x 30½", EX....................................**$100.00 C**

**Whistle,** bottle, cardboard, die cut, Whistle Brownie at top of bottle, 2¾" x 11½", VG ....................................**$95.00 C**

**Whistle,** clock, pressed board, electric, die cut, "Golden Orange...Refreshment Time," 24" x 23", EX ..............**$1,200.00 C**

**Whistle,** clock, wood and masonite, "Golden Orange Refreshment Time," EX....................................**$575.00 C**

**Whistle,** clock, wood and masonite, die cut, painted, elf on one side of the clock and a bottle of the product on the other side, 23¾" x 23¾", NM....................................**$825.00 B**

**Whistle,** coatrack, wood, elves on top of coathook, 35½" x 8", G ....................................**$135.00 D**

**Whistle,** decal, unused, in shape of bottle cap, "Thirsty? Just...Refreshing Fruit Flavor," NM ..................**$15.00 C**

**Whistle,** display, cardboard, die cut, double-sided, elf pushing a cart that holds a 7-oz. bottle of Whistle, 7" x 7⅞", EX ............**$335.00 C**

**Whistle,** display, cardboard, die cut, litho, countertop, "Golden Orange Refreshment," Brownies pouring from Whistle bottle, NOS, 17" x 15", EX ....................................**$250.00 B**

**Whistle,** headband, paper, die cut, in shape of Indian headdress, 23½" x 5½", NM....................................**$100.00 D**

**Whistle,** menu board, metal, "Thirsty? Just Whistle," elves in the corner, 20" x 27", EX....................................**$275.00 C**

**Whistle,** sign, cardboard, boy long straw and bottle of Whistle, 14" x 11", VG....................................**$35.00 C**

**Whistle,** sign, cardboard, die cut, bottle, 1936, EX ...................**$140.00 C**

**Whistle,** sign, cardboard, die cut, easel back, elves marching and pushing a bottle of Whistle, 13⅜" x 11¾", NM....................**$400.00 B**

**Whistle,** sign, cardboard, die cut, girl between two large bottles of Whistle, 26" x 34", EX ....................................**$375.00 C**

**Whistle,** sign, cardboard, die cut, litho, "Thirsty? Just Whistle," Brownie at each end, 17⅜" x 4¾", VG..............**$95.00 C**

**Whistle,** sign, cardboard, die cut, store, small elf next to product bottle, 1951, EX....................................**$82.00 B**

**Whistle,** sign, cardboard, die cut, store, small elf next to product bottle, 1951, G ....................................**$65.00 C**

**Whistle,** sign, cardboard, die cut, woman with Whistle bottle with straw, 15¾" x 22¾", VG ....................................**$125.00 C**

**Whistle,** sign, metal, "Thirsty...Just Whistle," 1939, 24" x 12", EX ....................................**$525.00 C**

**Whistle,** sign, metal, bottle in hand, "Thirsty?," 30" x 10", EX.**$700.00 C**

**Whistle,** sign, metal, in the shape of an arrow, product in block letters, 27" long, EX....................................**$195.00 C**

**Whistle,** sign, orange, in new frame, 4¼" x 24", EX.**$170.00 B**

**Whistle,** sign, paper, framed, die cut, from H. Gramse and Bro. Litho, Balto., Md., 23" x 7", VG ....................................**$75.00 B**

**Whistle,** sign, paper, NOS, boy and product bottle, 1950s, NM.**$30.00 C**

**Whistle,** sign, porcelain, "Drink Certified Pure," scarce "certified pure" slogan, 20" x 7", NM......................................................................$700.00 B

**Whistle,** sign, tin, embossed, "On Ice," bottle in hand, 8¾" x 6", NM......................................................................$725.00 B

**Whistle,** sign, tin, embossed, "Thirsty Just...Certified Pure," bottle in center, 20" x 14", VG......................................................................$200.00 D

**Whistle,** sign, tin, embossed, "Thirsty...just Whistle," 12½" x 3", 1939, VG......................................................................$80.00 B

**Whistle,** sign, tin, embossed, "Thirsty? Just Whistle...morning-noon-night," 27½" x 12½", 1939, VG......................................................................$140.00 B

**Whistle,** sign, tin, embossed, musical notes and image of bottle, 30" x 12", NM......................................................................$210.00 B

**Whistle,** sign, tin, farm scene and Brownie hauling a large bottle of Whistle on a hand cart, 26" x 30", G......................................................................$300.00 B

**Whistle,** sign, tin, litho, arrow, NOS, 27" x 7", NM......................................................................$175.00 C

**Whistle,** sign, tin, litho, embossed, bottle in hand, "thirsty?...just Demand the Genuine Whistle," 27¾" x 9½", EX......................................................................$975.00 B

**Whistle,** soda glass, "Thirsty ? Just Whistle," 4" dia., VG......................................................................$20.00 D

**Whistle,** thermometer, plaster, scale type reading, elf and bottle, "Thirsty ? Just Whistle," 12" x 13", EX......................................................................$525.00 C

**Whistle,** thermometer, tin, painted, two elves holding a bottle of the product, 9" x 20", EX......................................................................$850.00 B

**White Ash,** Liberty can, "Genuine Sumatra Wrapped," 50-count, EX......................................................................$55.00 C

**White Bear Coffee,** container, paper on cardboard, polar bear on ice, 4½" x 3" x 6", VG......................................................................$275.00 B

**White Castle,** bridge score pad, paper, White Castle store on front cover of pad, 1950s, EX......................................................................$20.00 C

**White Horse Spice,** container, cardboard paper label, Indian on horseback, EX......................................................................$75.00 C

**White House Coffee,** match holder, tin litho, "The Very Highest Quality," White House, 5" H, EX......................................................................$450.00 C

**White House Coffee,** match holder, tin, litho, "The Very Highest Quality," White House, 5" H, G......................................................................$375.00 B

**White House Coffee,** sign, tin, litho, die cut, double-sided, flange, hand holding a container of coffee, "None better at any price," 13½" x 8¾", EX......................................................................$2,500.00 C

**White House Coffee,** tin, White House image product name above, key wind lid, 1 lb., EX......................................................................$50.00 C

**White House Ginger Ale,** tip tray, metal, bottle of product in center, "Standard Bottling & Extract Co., Boston," 4¼" dia., EX......................................................................$135.00 C

**White King Soap,** sign, tin, "tacker" type, box of the product pouring the granulated powder, NOS, 9⅞" x 13⅞", NM......................................................................$175.00 C

**White King Washing Machine Soap,** sign, metal, pouring box, "It Takes So Little & It Goes So Far" at bottom, 1920 – 30s, 10" x 14", EX......................................................................$275.00 C

**White King,** clock, tin, litho, additional reverse on glass, light-up face showing king in center, "Washes Everything," 1927, 24" x 17" x 6", EX......................................................................$1,275.00 B

**White Label 5¢ Cigars,** sign, tin, embossed, box of product, 13¾" x 10", EX......................................................................$198.00 B

**White Label Coffee,** tin, litho, hot cup of coffee on front label, 1-lb., EX......................................................................$125.00 C

**White Lilac Coffee,** can, tin, litho, Consolidated Tea Co., Inc., New York, rectangular, lilacs in bloom on front, 4¼" x 6" x 2⅞", EX......................................................................$450.00 B

**White Lion Cigar,** tin, lion's head on front and top, 6¼" x 5½" x 4⅛", EX......................................................................$135.00 C

**White Mountain Refrigerator,** sign, cardboard, embossed, "The Chest With The Chill In It," 10" x 18½", EX......................................................................$95.00 C

**White Owl Cigar,** lighter, trademark owl on side, 1½" x ½", EX......................................................................$130.00 B

**White Owl Squires,** tin, metal, product logo in diamond-shaped outline on front, yellow background, EX......................................................................$20.00 D

**White Rock Beer,** sign, tin, litho, wood frame, girl holding wheat, bottle of White Rock, The Akron Brewing Co., Akron, Ohio, 33" x 24¾", G......................................................................$325.00 C

**White Rock Lithia Water,** sign, tin, litho, self-framing, embossed, fairy at water on rock, 16½" x 19¾", EX......................................................................$875.00 C

**White Rock Sparkling Beverages,** sign, metal, die cut, fairy on rock, 18" x 13", VG......................................................................$500.00 B

**White Rock Sparkling Beverages,** sign, tin, double-sided, flange, fairy nymph looking at water, 18" x 13¾", EX......................................................................$475.00 C

**White Rock Water,** pastel on canvas, Psyche kneeling on rock studying her reflection in the water, the original oil was completed for the 1893 Columbian Exposition and adopted for use as White Rock logo in 1894, 42" x 62", 1910s, EX......................................................................$4,500.00 D

**White Rock,** sign, metal, topless nymph at water's edge, 13½" dia., VG......................................................................$295.00 C

**White Rock,** sign, paper, pretty woman in red pool cue and large bottle of the product, 15" x 21", EX......................................................................$395.00 C

**White Rock,** tip tray, fairy looking at its reflection in water from rock, 4¼" dia., VG......................................................................$180.00 B

**White Rock,** tip tray, metal, "The World's Best Table Water," fairy image on rock looking over water, 4¼" dia., EX ...............$300.00 B

**White Rock,** tip tray, rectangular, "The World's Best Table Water," fairy on rock over water, 6" tall, EX ....................$130.00 B

**White Rock,** tip tray, rectangular, "The World's Best Table Water," fairy on rock over water, 6", G .....................................$65.00 C

**White Rock,** tip tray, tin, litho, Atlantic City beach scene, Kaufman & Strauss Lithographers, 4⅜" dia., EX ...............................$375.00 B

**White Rock,** tray, metal, decorative border, tiger and pretty lady in profile, EX.....................................................................$75.00 C

**White Rolls Cigarettes,** watch fob, metal and porcelain, Ware-Kramer Tobacco Co., EX.....................................................$125.00 C

**White Rose Bock Beer,** label, revenue stamp, Dallas Brewery Inc., 12 oz., 1930s,EX.......................................................$55.00 C

**White Rose Flour,** sign, wooden, painted, self-framing, "Bakes Better Bread," 74" x 26",V G ...................................$365.00 C

**White Rose Flour,** sign, wooden, wood, frame, "White Rose Flour bakes better bread," 74" x 26", VG..................................$595.00 D

**White Rose Gasoline, Motor Oil,** sign, porcelain, one-sided, white rose in center, 72" x 17", G...................................$3,200.00 C

**White Rose Gasoline,** sign, tin, one-sided, self-framing, embossed, "Use The Best...To Get The Best," trademark Enarco boy holding sign, 40" x 26½", VG.......................................$400.00 D

**White Rose Motor Gasoline,** sign, tin, litho, rose, 13¾" x 9¾", EX.............................................................................$525.00 C

**White Rose No Knock,** gasoline globe, one-piece, trademark boy holding black board, EX.................................................$3,000.00 C

**White Rose,** bank, tin litho, "Quick Starting," Enarco kid board, 3½" x 2⅛", EX...............................................................$300.00 C

**White Sewing Machine,** puzzle, paper over heavy cardboard, litho by W.J. Morgan & Co., Cleveland, 1910, EX ....................$325.00 C

**White Sewing Machine,** sign, paper, mother at machine, 20" x 28½", EX.............................................................................$175.00 C

**White Slave Cigars,** box label, paper, oval containing slave girl, VG .........................................................................$235.00 C

**White Squadron Spice,** store bin slant front, litho, ships and other patriotic items, 7" x 9" x 10", EX.......................................$223.00 B

**White Star,** sign, cardboard, pretty girl flower and wearing a large hat, Andrew Lohr Bottling Co, located in Cairo, Ill, logo on back, 1890s, 11" x 11", EX.............................................$425.00 C

**White Swan Coffee,** tin, litho, swan on front, White Swan Spices & Cereals, Toronto, 1-lb., EX .......................$235.00 C

**White Top Champagne,** tip tray, metal, bottle on tray center, 4⅛" dia., EX.....................................................................$65.00 D

**White's Golden Tonic for Horses,** sign, paper, litho, horse in center, 21½" x 28", VG.........................................................$50.00 B

**Whitehead & Hoag,** calendar, pinbacks and badges, young woman at top, 1911, EX.................................................... $95.00 C

**Whitman's Chocolates,** sign, paper, girl on bench product, 13" x 10", EX.........................................................................$195.00 D

**Whitman's Chocolates,** sign, porcelain, "Agency Whitman's Chocolates and Confections since 1842," 39½" x 13½", VG........$245.00 B

**Whiz Bang,** display box, cardboard, rim fire cartridges, .22 shell on front, 10" x 5" x 4½", NM..................................$75.00 C

**Whiz Leaf Spring Lubricant,** display, cardboard, Whiz kids using the product, EX...................................................$675.00 C

**Whiz Nickel Polish,** can, metal, early sedan all shined up by the product, pour top screw lid, 1 qt., EX ..........................$75.00 C

**Whiz Oil,** can, metal early car inside fancy scroll design, by the R.M Hollingshead Co., screw lid, 5 gal., EX...........................$450.00 C

**Whiz Patch Outfit,** store display, metal, extra-heavy, man repairing tire on older model car, NM .........................$425.00 C

**Whiz Service Center,** display case, metal, car being worked on by baby in diapers and crown, 24" x 20" x 40", EX...............$375.00 C

**Whiz Stop Leak Radiator Compound,** display box, full, fold up lid, elves helping stranded motorist in early touring car, 14" x 6", EX..........................................................................$1,300.00 C

**Whiz Tar Remover,** can, metal, screw lid, old car being cleaned by the Whiz kids, 1 pt., EX......................................................$50.00 C

**Whiz White Rubber,** sign, tin, coating for tires, woman in vintage car, 12" x 17", EX...............................................................$525.00 C

**Whiz,** sign, cardboard, string hanger, cut in shape of bottle, "The Certified Drink," 1940s, 5" x 10", EX...........................$55.00 C

**Wickenburg, Arizona,** license plate attachment, metal, die cut, in shape of ten-gallon hat, NOS, 6" x 5⅜", NM .............$150.00 C

**Wiedemann Brewing Co.,** match safe pocket, plated brass, embossing on both sides, 1½" x 3", EX.......................................$225.00 C

**Wiedemann Fine Beer,** sign, plastic, 3-D, trumpeter swan flying over wetlands, 16" x 18", G................................................$45.00 C

**Wiedemann Fine Beer,** sign, plastic, 3-D, trumpeter swan flying over wetlands, 16" x 18", VG...........................................$65.00 C

**Wiedemann's Fine Beers,** sign, metal, product name and two product bottles, matted and framed, 1910s, EX.......................$625.00 C

**Wieland, John, Extra Pale Beer,** figurine, chalkware, San Jose, Calif., 3" x 9", G ............................................................$95.00 C

**Wigwam Brand Coffee,** tin, litho, pry-lid, Indian silhouette on front, 1-lb., EX ............................................................$75.00 B

**Wigwam Sugar Corn,** container, tin, hand soldering, Indian bow drawn in front of teepee, EX .........................................$350.00 B

**Wigwam,** spice container, cardboard, paper label, EX ........$75.00 C

**Wilbur's Cocoa,** container, small lid, paper label, cherub-like figure stirring a cup of the product, 2½" x 3⅛", VG .....................$95.00 C

**Wilbur's Cocoa,** glove hook, celluloid button, 2½", EX .......$75.00 C

**Wilbur's Seed Meal,** box, wood paper litho label, 20" x 22" x 36", F ............................................................$895.00 C

**Wild Woodbine Cigarettes,** sign, porcelain, one-sided, foreign, 48¼" x 17¾", VG ............................................................$375.00 B

**Wildroot Barber Shop,** sign, metal, embossed, self-framing, barber pole, 39½" x 13½", NM .........................................$150.00 B

**Wildroot Barber Shop,** sign, tin, single-sided, self-framing, 39½" x 13½", VG ............................................................$140.00 B

**Wildroot Cream Oil,** sign, cardboard, easel back, die cut, Fearless Fosdick, "Get Wildroot Cream Oil Charlie!," 30" x 30¼", 1954, VG ............................................................$225.00 C

**Wildroot,** sign, metal, embossed, painted, "Ask For," barber pole at right of message, 28" x 10", G ....................................$95.00 D

**Wildroot,** sign, tin, "Ask For...," barber pole 40" x 14", EX .........$75.00 D

**Wildroot,** sign, metal, embossed, painted, "ask for," barber pole at right of message, 28" x 10", VG ....................................$110.00 C

**Wildwood,** license plate attachment, tin, painted, "By The Sea N.J.World's Safest Beach," 6" x 6¼", EX .........................$135.00 C

**Will's Cigarettes,** sign, framed, 13" x 24", VG .....................$175.00 C

**Will's Cigarettes,** sign, framed, showing different planes and cars, "WD & Howills," 13" x 24" ............................................$55.00 D

**Will's Gold Flake Cigarettes,** backbar mirror, two-piece, heavy, "Smoke," hand-painted lettering, 70" x 26", G .....................$750.00 C

**Willard Batteries,** clock, light-up, center spotlight bearing message, 15" dia., VG ............................................................$250.00 C

**Willard Batteries,** sign, tin, one-sided, embossed, 39½" x 12", VG ............................................................$140.00 B

**Willard Batteries,** thermometer, dial-type, "check here," 16" dia., VG ............................................................$135.00 C

**Willard Battery Cables,** display rack, wood and metal, battery image above the product name, 17" x 12", EX .....................$75.00 C

**Williams Bread,** door push, porcelain and wrought iron, G .......$230.00 B

**Williams Bread,** door push, porcelain, "It's" Fresh lettering on an arrow Williams Bread at end of arrow, mounted by wrought iron brackets, VG ............................................................$265.00 C

**Williams Bread,** sign, tin, loaf of the product, 26" x 16", NM..$175.00 C

**Willow Spring Brewing Co.,** tray, metal, girl feeding horse, "In Kentucky," 13" dia., EX ............................................................$85.00 C

**Willys-Overland Company,** sign, porcelain, "Dollar for Dollar Whippet Product of," 36" x 24", cream on red, G ..........$375.00 D

**Willys-Overland Company,** sign, tin, embossed, for Whippet, 22½" x 12", G ............................................................$250.00 D

**Wilson's Certified Smoked Ham,** sign, cardboard, die cut, easel back, Uncle Sam slicing product, 29½" x 40", EX..............$180.00 B

**Wilson's Peanut Butter,** tin, litho, old woman in the shoe, 1-lb., EX ............................................................$375.00 C

**Winchester After Shave Talc,** container, tin, litho, hunter and his dog on front, NM ............................................................$250.00 B

**Winchester Arms & Ammunition,** sign, metal, die cut, double-sided, hanging arm, probably a fantasy item, 41¼" x 6½", VG......$225.00 C

**Winchester Cartridge Shop,** poster, paper, World War Two motivational "reveille for workers...taps for Japs," 14" x 22", EX.$250.00 C

**Winchester Cartridges & Guns,** calendar, paper, partial monthly pad, hunters holding horses, 1913, 13½" x 21½", EX...$2,200.00 C

**Winchester Double A Trap Loads,** shell box, shotgun, F ...$15.00 D

**Winchester Factory Loaded Shotgun Shells,** sign, cardboard, puppies gun, "Do You Shoot? We Have A New Stock Of...," 13" x 9", EX ............................................................$925.00 C

**Winchester Gun Advisor Center,** sign, tin, litho, shield-shaped on wood, 1950s, 20" x 20", NM ............................................$100.00 B

**Winchester Guns & Ammunition,** display, cardboard, die cut hunter and dog at fence, "A Good Harvest," two pieces, 1934, 42" wide, EX ............................................................$2,200.00 C

**Winchester Leader Waterproofed Paper Shot Shells,** shell box, two-piece, Winchester Repeating Arms Co., DuPont label on side, EX ............................................................$240.00 B

**Winchester New Gun Oil,** tin, bull's-eye on front, 1968, EX.$50.00 C

**Winchester New Rival Shells,** sign, cardboard, box of the product, 16½" x 10", EX ............................................................$95.00 C

**Winchester New Rival Shells,** sign, cardboard, box of the product, 16½" x 10", VG ............................................................$75.00 C

**Winchester Nublack Loaded Black Powder Shells,** box, 10-gal., two-piece, wild fowl in flight, 25- count, EX .....................$165.00 B

Winchester Paper Shot Shells, two-piece box, 32-gal., empty, 3" x 3" x 2½", EX...............................................................$150.00 B

Winchester Ranger Mark 5, shotgun shell box, F..........................$9.00 D

Winchester Ranger Super Target Load, shotgun shell box, G.$18.00 B

Winchester Ranger Super Trap Load, shell box, vintage shooter on front, 4¼" x 4¼" x 2½", EX.........................................$55.00 D

Winchester Ranger, shotgun shell box, F ...........................$10.00 B

Winchester Ranger, shotgun shell box, two-piece, geese in flight, 12-ga., 4" x 4" x 2½", G..................................................$55.00 B

Winchester Repeater Oval, shell box, 16-gauge, 4" x 4' x 2½", EX ..............................................................................$145.00 B

Winchester Roller Skate Rolls, box, cardboard, 11 wheels inside, VG ...............................................................................$65.00 C

Winchester Salesman, shot shell, sample box, window displays, 3" x 4¼" x 1", EX.........................................................$185.00 D

Winchester Shells, poster, wooden frame, "Shoot them and avoid trouble," 27" x 18¾", 1900s, EX........................$300.00 B

Winchester Shotgun Shells, sign, cardboard, string hanger, "Ask For...Sold Here," 9" x 12½", EX ...................................$1,400.00 C

Winchester Sporting Rifles & Ammunition, sign, cardboard, die cut, hunter shooting at deer, product name above hunter, 19" x 27½", EX ..........................................................$375.00 C

Winchester Staynless Cartridges, sign, paper, litho, various sizes of cartridges, 13" x 21½", EX...........................................$120.00 B

Winchester Super Speed Silver Tip Cartridges, decal, vinyl mounted on glass, product and a large bear pictured, 9" x 7½", EX....$125.00 C

Winchester Tires, sign, metal, embossed lettering, "...Customer Satisfaction Guarenteed," 54" x 18", EX .................................$165.00 C

Winchester W Shot Gun Shells, sign, cardboard, die cut, grouse perched on a fence, "Ask For...," 9" x 13", EX................$1,000.00 C

Winchester Western Silvertip CF sign, cardboard, cartridges, easel back, store, countertop, NOS, 24" x 20", NM......$100.00 C

Winchester Western, thermometer, "sporting ammunition sold here," shape of shotgun shell, 12" x 32", F...........................$55.00 D

Winchester Western, thermometer, "sporting ammunition sold here," shape of shotgun shell, 12" x 32", VG.....................$135.00 C

Winchester, calendar, bird hunter behind a couple of bird dogs in a fall hunting scene, 15¼" x 30¼", 1914, VG .................$480.00 B

Winchester, calendar, eagle and mountain goat, 15¼" x 30¼", 1915, EX............................................................................$1,050.00 B

Winchester, calendar, paper, full monthly tear sheets, hunting dogs at top, matted and framed, 1907, 13½" x 14½", EX ..........$675.00 D

Winchester, calendar, paper, hunting scene in snow and desert top and bottom metal strips, 14¼" x 27", 1899, EX...$1,500.00 B

Winchester, poster, "Big Game Rifles and Ammunition," early hunter on a mountaintop, complete metal bands on top and bottom, 15½" x 26¼", EX ....................................................$325.00 C

Winchester, sign, cardboard, countertop, die cut, easel back, vintage dressed man gun in front of product, 10" x 22", EX...$175.00 D

Winchester, sign, paperboard, litho, by H.R. Poore original oak frame, pair of dogs, 35" x 25½", 1907, EX ......................$425.00 C

Winchester, sign, porcelain, double-sided, flange, Winchester gun various sizes of shells and factory, 18" x 13½", EX.........$1,650.00 B

Winchester, stand-up, cardboard, die cut, C.G. Spenser, champion shot for Winchester, 10" x 22", EX.......................................$155.00 C

Winchester, stand-up, cardboard, die cut, grizzly bear, "from the grizzly to the squirrel," 13" x 22", EX ...............................$195.00 C

Winchester, window display, 4-panel fold display, front side displays Winchester products, back side shows Winchester logo of Junior Rifle Corp., 20¼" x 48" each panel, G....................$250.00 C

Winchester, window display, cardboard, different tools being used by various craftsmen, hard to fine item for Winchester tools, 48" wide, EX ..............................................................................$475.00 C

Wincroft Ranges and Stoves, trade card, Uncle Sam weather indicator, 3½" x 6", EX ............................................................ $45.00 C

Windsor Supreme, figural head pitcher, EX .........................$25.00 D

Wineberre Beverage sign, tin litho, embossed, "Sold Here," 17½" x 12", EX ...............................................................................$65.00 B

Wing's Baby Powder Talc, container, tin, litho, baby in center, from Frederick Ingram & Co., 1¾" x 4", EX.........................$95.00 C

Wingold Flour, cut-out, cardboard, give-away in uncut condition, delivery truck and train, by Bay State Milling Co., 12½" x 10¼", NM .................................................................................$65.00 B

Wings Cigarettes, sign, paper, lighted cigarette, 14" x 20", VG.$8.00 C

Wings Motor Oil, sign, porcelain, geese in flight, rounded top, 27" x 35", EX .........................................................................$1,100.00 C

Wings Regular Gasoline, pump sign, porcelain, single-sided, flying geese, 7" x 6", VG .........................................................$1,700.00 B

Winner Cut Plug Smoke & Chew, lunch pail, metal, wire bail handle, racing scene on front, 8" x 5" x 4", EX.........................$275.00 C

Winner Cut Plug Tobacco, pail, racing scene on front, "J Wright Co., The American Tobacco Co., Richmond, Va.," 4" T, VG.......$135.00 B

Winston, thermometer, metal, dial-type, painted product packages on both sides of dial, "the taste is tops...pack or box," EX .$40.00 D

**Winston,** thermometer, metal, embossed, painted, vertical scale at top right and product package lower left, no warning label, "tastes good...like a cigarette should!," 6" x 13½", VG .....................$45.00 D

**Wisconsin Engines,** sign, metal, embossed, painted, 30" x 24", G .................................................................................$235.00 D

**Wisconsin Engines,** sign, metal, embossed, painted, dealer, 30" x 24", VG ...........................................................$255.00 C

**Wise Potato Chips,** sign, cardboard, die cut, owl perched on limb, product name on owl, 32" high, EX ......................$55.00 D

**Wise Potato Chips,** thermometer, wooden, painted, from Berwick, PA, 2⅞" x 8⅜", EX ........................................$95.00 D

**Wishbone Coffee,** tin, wishbone on front, 7½" x 7½", EX .........$75.00 C

**Wishing Well Orange,** door push, porcelain, "We Sell Wishing Well Orange," 4" x 32½", VG .................................$195.00 D

**Wiss Scissors,** display, metal, "Genuine Wiss...Stay Sharpe," 36" high, EX ...........................................................$525.00 C

**Wisteria Talcum,** tin, sample size, two Japanese women, EX .$195.00 C

**Wix Oil Filters and Filterfils,** sign, reverse glass, light-up, 16" x 8" x 6", EX ...........................................................$225.00 C

**Wm Deering & Co. Grass Cutting Machinery,** sign, paper, people watching a horse drawn machine in action, 29" x 22", EX .$3,500.00 D

**Wolf's Head 100% Pennsylvania Motor Oil,** sign, metal, wolf head below product name, 23" x 30", EX.....................$95.00 C

**Wolf's Head Motor Oil,** curb sign, metal, painted, "We sell," logo in lower right, original cast base, raised letters, 59" dia., red, white, and green, EX .............................................$400.00 B

**Wonder Bread Howdy Doody,** sign, heavy paper, die cut, Hoody holding a loaf of Wonder Bread, NOS, 6" x 13", NM ..........$275.00 B

**Wonder Bread,** door push, metal, embossed, painted, "We Suggest...it's fresh," 27½" x 2¾", VG ......................$150.00 B

**Wonder Bread,** sign, metal, die cut, loaf of the product, "It's slo baked," 12" x 9", 1950s, EX...........................$235.00 C

**Wonder Orange,** sign, metal, "Always On Ice From Grove To You," group of oranges and ice, 1930s, 20" x 14", EX.................$295.00 D

**Wonder Orange,** sign, tin, embossed, "drink," spotlight on oranges at left of message, 1930s, 19½" x 13½", EX ..$350.00 C

**Wondercade Illusion Spectacular,** poster, paper, various acts to be performed, 22" x 28", NM ............................$40.00 D

**Wood's Mowers Walter A. Wood Mowing and Reaping Machine,** sign, cardboard, mowers and reapers in use, 1895, 27" x 19", G.................................................................$350.00 B

**Woodbury's Facial Soap,** box, cardboard, product name and inset of John Woodbury, EX ...................................$65.00 C

**Woodlawn Mills Shoe Lace Service Station,** service station, metal, VG .................................................................$2,000.00 C

**Woods Lollacapop Mosquito Antidote,** container, tin, mosquito on lid, 3¼" x 1¾" x ¾", EX .................................................$100.00 B

**Woodward Candy Co.,** tip tray, metal, man and woman in early dress product, 6¾" L, EX...........................................$190.00 B

**Wool Soap,** thermometer, metal, dial type reading arched above "Tiolet & Bath," 6" dia., VG .............................................$225.00 C

**Worcester Elastic Stocking & Truss Co.,** pocket mirror, celluloid, partially clad woman, G ...................................$200.00 C

**Worker Cut Plug,** lunch box, metal, wire bail handle, overall look of alligator skin, EX................................................$125.00 D

**Workman's Friend,** pocket mirror, celluloid, "For Removing Obstructions from Eyes and Other Uses Where Close Examinations is Required," 2½" dia., VG .........................................$65.00 D

**Wright and Taylor Old Charter Distillery,** serving tray, tin, litho, factory scene, 12" dia., VG .............................$330.00 B

**Wrigley Chewing Gum,** counter display, cardboard, die cut, Wrigley man and young girl, promoting 1¢ P-K Gum, 12" x 8", VG .................................................................$210.00 C

**Wrigley's Doublemint Gum,** matchbook, cardboard, front strike, "Enjoy...Healthful-Delicious," VG .........................$8.00 B

**Wrigley's Doublemint,** sign, porcelain, double-sided, general store, 30" x 9", EX ...................................................$3,900.00 C

**Wrigley's Doublemint,** trolley sign, cardboard, Santa Claus, "Take Your Choice Of Flavor," 21" x 11", EX............................$150.00 C

**Wrigley's Soap,** tip tray, metal, cat sitting on product bars, 3⅝" dia., EX ....................................................................$170.00 B

**Wrigley's Spearmint & Doublemint Gum,** sign, porcelain, "Ice Cream," 1912, 30" x 9", EX...........................................$1,400.00 C

**Wrigley's Spearmint Gum,** license plate reflector, celluloid, oval, reverse pack of gum, 6" x 4", EX ......................................$155.00 C

**Wrigley's Spearmint Gum,** sign, cardboard, "Pure Wholesome, Inexpensive," 21" x 11", EX...................................$55.00 C

**Wrigley's Spearmint Gum,** trolley car sign, cardboard, cartoon Dave Squeegee Famous Window Washer talking to a lady about the product, 21" x 11", EX......................................$75.00 C

**Wrigley's Spearmint Pepsin Gum,** sign, cardboard, die cut, girl holding oversized product packs, 1920s, 10" x 14", EX.....$475.00 C

**Wrigley's Spearmint,** poster, cardboard, single-sided, "Taste the Juice of Real Mint Leaves," 21" x 11", G .........................$135.00 C

**Wrigley's,** ad, paper, fan offer four different images to choose from, 8½" x 15", EX .................................................$135.00 C

**Wrigley's,** ad, paper, ice saving refrigerator assortments message context, 10" x 7", EX ..........................................$30.00 C

**Wrigley's,** ad, paper, offer of American Flag, 8" x 5", EX.....$35.00 D

**Wrigley's,** ad, paper, safety razor offer, 8" x 5", EX ............$35.00 C

**Wrigley's,** counter gum display, cardboard, held 20 of the 5-stick packages, the Wrigley arrow and pretty girl, 12½" x 9" x 6¾", NM..$375.00 C

**Wrigley's,** sign, cardboard, litho, the famous gum and its unique packaging, "In Bond," 22¼" x 12¼", VG..............................$45.00 B

**Wrigley's,** sign, cardboard, smiling lady behind cash register, 21" x 29", EX ........................................................................$495.00 C

**Wrigley's,** sign, metal, three different products to choose from, 12" x 10", EX.......................................................................$95.00 C

**Wrigley's,** trolley sign, cardboard, displays of gum, "Help Yourself...Good For You," 1927, 22" x 12", EX .........................$350.00 C

**Wrigley's,** trolley sign, cardboard, young girl receiving gum from older lady over the counter, "Mite Makes Rite," 20" x 11", EX ........................................................................$135.00 C

**Wrought Iron Range,** sign, paper, wood frame, 22½" x 16½", EX ..........................................................................$475.00 D

**Wunder Beer,** sign, cardboard, product name and "Full Alcoholic Strength," 1920s, 9" x 6", VG.............................................$65.00 D

**Wurlitzer,** sign, bubbling, display, limited edition, great presentation piece, 1990, VG ........................................................$300.00 C

**Wurlitzer,** sign, wood and glass, bubbling letters, "Musical Fun For Everyone," 1990, 19" x 6", EX .........................................$475.00 D

**Wyandotte Detergent,** sign, tin, litho, self-framing, from J.B. Ford Company, Indian in full headdress, hunting bow drawn, 28" x 39", VG .....................................................$2,100.00 C

X

"X" Liquid, sign, tin, embossed "Repairs Leaky Radiators," "X man" image at vintage auto area for current gas price at top, 19¼" x 27⅛", EX, $475.00 B. *Courtesy of Autopia Advertising Auctions.*

X Powder, countertop display unit of "X boy" packages of product, "Repairs Leaky Radiators," 10¾" x 15", VG, $165.00 B. *Courtesy of Collectors Auction Services.*

Yale Flashlight, display, metal, counter top, "...Use Only Mono Cells," 20" tall, VG, $275.00 B.

Yara Tobacco, sign, cardboard, trifold of class room, boy at blackboard and one being spanked, 30" x 20", EX, $475.00 C.

Yeast Foam, poster, paper, young girl at table in front of a stack of buckwheat cakes, 10" x 15", NM, $145.00 D.

Yopp Seed Co., knife, celluloid and metal, "mellon" knife for plugging watermellons for ripeness, this business is no longer in operation, 5½" long closed, VG, $35.00 C. *Courtesy of B.J. Summers.*

---

**Yacht Club Drip Grind Coffee**, tin, litho, key-wound lid, from Chicago, Ill., 1-lb., EX .............................................$135.00 C

**Yacht Club Smoking Tobacco**, pocket tin, vertical, bust on front, EX...............................................................$305.00 C

**Yacht Club Straight Bourbon Whiskey**, match book, front strike, 20 strike, NM .....................................................$5.00 D

**Yacht Cut Plug**, pocket tin, flat, sailing ships and product name, EX....................................................................$250.00 C

**Yale Coffee**, tin, Yale on flying pennant, slip lid, sample, EX.$145.00 C

**Yale Shirts**, display, cloth oxford shirt in celluloid easel, EX.$145.00 D

**Yankee Boy Cut Plug**, pocket tin, blond headed boy at bat, NM.$675.00 C

**Yankee Doodle Root Beer**, chalkboard, product name and Yankee, 19" x 27", EX ......................................................$135.00 D

**Yankee Razor Blade**, container, metal, patriotic theme on cover, from Reichard & Scheuber Mfg Co., NY, 2¼" x 1" x ¼", EX ............................................................$75.00 B

**Ybala's Spring Beverages**, sign, tin, embossed, product bottle, NOS, 9" x 20", NM...............................................$115.00 C

**Yeast Foam**, sign, paper, litho, framed, young girl pancakes, 11½" x 16¼", VG.....................................................$50.00 D

**Yeast Foam**, sign, paper, young girl at table pancakes, "Makes Delicious Buckwheat Cakes," 10" x 15", EX............................$135.00 D

**Yeast Foam**, wall dispenser, tin, litho, "Eat yeast foam" on side rail, 2¾" x 27", EX ..............................................$115.00 D

**Yello-Bole Pipes**, countertop display, cardboard & fabric wrapped unit, pretty girl and a honeycomb, easel back, 30" x 33", NM ......................................................$275.00 C

**Yello-Bole Pipes**, display rack, smiling woman sign on rotating display rack, EX.................................................$155.00 C

**Yello-Bole Pipes**, display stand, metal, plastic, and cardboard, featuring woman in green evening dress holding a sample pipe, 1950s, VG.......................................................$85.00 C

**Yello-Bole Pipes**, display stand, metal, plastic, and cardboard, woman in green evening dress holding a sample pipe, 1950s, EX .........................................................$155.00 C

**Yellow Bonnet Coffee**, tin, key wind lid, girl in bonnet, 1 lb., EX.......................................................................$185.00 D

**Yellow Bonnet Coffee**, tin, wound lid, woman in bonnet on front, Springfield, MO, 1-lb., EX .............................$125.00 C

**Yellow Cab 5¢ Cigar**, sign, tin, litho, embossed, "Takes The Right of Way," policeman at intersection old yellow cab, 1920s, 19⅞" x 6¾", EX.................................................................$1,000.00 B

**Yellow Cab**, cigar box, "Takes The Right Of Way," early cab, EX .............................................................$65.00 C

**Yellow Cab**, cigar box, man hailing cab, "takes the right of way," 1918, VG .............................................$80.00 C

**Yellow Cab**, thermometer, wood, painted, scale type, "Call A Yellow," 4" x 15", VG................................$275.00 C

**Yellow Kid**, pocket match holder, leather, Bartholomay's Brewing Co., logo on back and Yellow Kid on front, "match me if ye can," 2¼" x 5¼", EX ........................$495.00 C

**Yellow Kid**, poster, paper, promoting the syndicated comic strip series from the *New York Sunday Journal* newspaper, 20" x 15", EX .............................................$1,195.00 C

**Yellow Kid**, poster, paper, promoting the syndicated comic strip series from the *New York Sunday Journal* newspaper, 20" x 15", VG .............................................$125.00 C

**Yellow Strand Rope**, watch fob, porcelain, spool of rope, EX ..$75.00 C

**Yocum Brothers Cigars**, tin, brothers on the front label, 50-count, 6¼" x 4¼" x 5¼", EX ..................................$115.00 C

**Yosemite Beer**, sign, paper, Enterprise Brewing Co., pretty girl wearing a feathered shawl, 1898, 15" x 19", VG ...............$875.00 C

**Youth's Companion**, calendar, fold-out, 21" x 12", EX......$170.00 B

**Yuengling's Beer, Porter, and Ale**, tip tray, metal, eagle wooden keg, 4¼" dia., EX.................................$75.00 B

**Yuengling's Beer**, sign, metal, beer being poured from bottle to glass, 27" x 19", EX...............................$250.00 D

**Yuengling's Bottled Beer**, tip tray, tin, litho, young lady in bonnet, 4¼" dia., EX.................................$90.00 B

**Yukon Pernament Anti-Freeze**, can, metal, dogs pulling an Eskimo sled, 1 gal., EX.................................$105.00 C

**Yum Yum Tobacco**, pail, tin, "Manufactured by the American Tobacco Successors to Aug. Beck & Co. Factory No. 26, First District of Illinois," 6½" H, VG ...............................$85.00 B

# Z

Zambora Cigar, clock, Chicago World's Fair, although in the likeness of clock this wasn't ever meant to be a timepiece, and only had one hand, from J.P. Hier, Syracuse, NY, 1893, EX, $845.00 B. *Courtesy of Buffalo Bay Auction Co.*

Zenith, thermometer, tin, scale-type, embossed, "Long Distance Radio," 17" x 71", VG, $500.00 C.

Zephyr Gasoline, globe, wide body two glass lenses, 13½" dia., VG, $425.00 C.

Zinc Insulated Fences, jigsaw puzzle, EX, $300.00 C.

*Zipp's Cherri-O,* syrup dispenser, 1920s, EX, $325.00 D. *Courtesy of Buffalo Bay Auction Co.*

Zipp's Root Beer, dispenser, ceramic, metal pump at top, Robin Hood style person serving tray between two mugs, 1910s, 14" tall, EX, $2,575.00 B.

**Zanol Cocoa,** tin, cocoa leaves and company logo, ½ lb., EX .$45.00 C

**Zanzibar Carbon,** tin, paper label on front, depicting African village scene, 10½" x 6" x 8¼", VG.................$225.00 C

**Zeigler Coal,** sign, metal, product name, VG.................$75.00 C

**Zemo Clean Antiseptic Liquid,** sign, paper, "For Itching Skin...," 19" x 12", EX.................$115.00 D

**Zeno Gum,** tin, young man reaching for package of product, 9½" x 4½" x 2½", EX.................$55.00 B

**Zeno,** display, wood and glass, countertop, three-shelf unit, 10" x 8" x 17", EX.................$475.00 B

**Zephyr Gasoline,** gas globe, plastic and glass, "High Octane," 15½" x 12", EX.................$350.00 C

**Zephyr,** sign, metal, two-sided, 59½" x 37¾", VG.................$200.00 B

**Zepplin Motor Oil,** can, metal, ocean scene zeppelin in sky, 2 gal., EX.................$165.00 C

**Zero Flo,** sign, tin, paraffin base motor oil, painted, "Pours at 35° below," 28" x 20", white, orange & black, EX.................$155.00 C

**Zerolene,** sign, porcelain, "Standard Oil For Motor Cars," 24" dia., EX.................$875.00 C

**Zett's,** sign, paper, Bavarian street scene, 1920s, EX.................$155.00 C

**Ziegler's Beer,** sign, metal, beveled edges, "Drink...Beaver Dam Wisconsin," 11" x 8", EX.................$135.00 C

**Zig-Zag Cigarette Papers,** dispenser, metal, bottom opening for paper packages, EX.................$65.00 C

**Zig-Zag Cigarette Papers,** dispenser, paper, hands pulling papers at top of container, 6" T, EX.................$75.00 C

**Zingo Sweets,** tin, slip lid, round, vintage #2 race car, 12" x 10" dia., EX.................$215.00 C

**Zipp's Cherri-o,** syrup dispenser, 1920s, EX.................$1,500.00 B

**Zipp's Cherri-o,** syrup dispenser, metal and glass, 1920s, 13" x 18", F.................$1,400.00 C

**Zipp's Root Beer,** mug, glass, handle, black logo, 6" x 3½" dia., EX.................$175.00 C

**Zippo Lighters,** display case, revolving lighters, EX.................$175.00 C

**Zira Cigarettes,** sign, cardboard, for their satin wonder in each package, 16" x 13", VG.................$40.00 B

**Zira Cigarettes,** sign, metal, embossed, "Winning On Merit & 5¢," 12" x 24", EX.................$75.00 C

**Zwcol Wax,** license plate attachment, metal, "Drive Safe, Zeco Wax Your Car," EX.................$45.00 C

363

# PAST TYME PLEASURES

## Purveyors of Fine Antiques & Collectibles Presents Annual
## Spring and Fall Antique Advertising Auctions

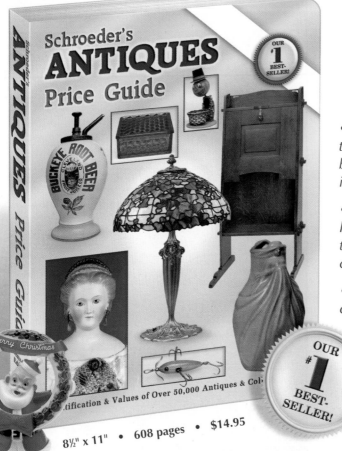

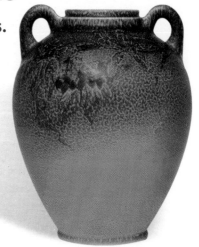